M000238275

¡NO PASARÁN!

ANTIFASCIST DISPATCHES FROM A WORLD IN CRISIS

Edited by Shane Burley

Foreword by Talia Lavin

Afterword by David Renton

With Editorial Support by
Paul Messersmith-Glavin and the
Institute for Anarchist Studies

Advance praise for *¡No Pasarán!*

"Academics and pundits have made careers out of debating the definition of fascism. We are deluged with books, each bearing its own definitions, prognoses, caveats, and warnings, only to be bumped off the bestseller list by the next self-proclaimed fascism expert. *¡No Pasarán!* is not that book. These writer-activists understand fascism to be a many-headed hydra that defies typologies and strongman tropes and can only be apprehended in the dialectic of resistance. Antifascism is not an exercise in abstract thinking but an active, collective struggle for a new world. This book will get dog-eared and dirty, but not by gathering dust."—Robin D. G. Kelley, author of *Freedom Dreams: The Black Radical Imagination*

"This diverse collection of writings by activists, journalists, and scholars is held together by one theme: understanding and defeating the fascist danger we face today. Our grave moment demands thinking that is both historically informed and attuned to new conditions, both critical and visionary, both militant and creative. *¡No Pasarán!* brilliantly achieves all of this."—Joe Lowndes, co-author of *Producers, Parasites, Patriots: Race and the New Right-Wing Politics of Precarity*

"Looking across history and around the world, *¡No Pasarán!* is a must-read for today's antifascists. These voices call us to embrace solidarity and self-defense and never abandon the fight for a better world as we confront the looming threat of far-right authoritarianism. This compendium of stories and analyses from the frontlines of antifascism will help us meet the daunting demands of our era with clarity, bravery, and camaraderie in the struggle."—Dan Berger, co-editor of *Remaking Radicalism: A Grassroots Documentary Reader of the United States, 1973–2001*

"Shane Burley's multifaceted compendium of writings on antifascist resistance and the far right considerably advances the breadth of resources available to researchers and activists. Drawing on many of the leading voices at the cutting edge of antifascist theory and scholarship, *¡No Pasarán!* skewers the popular one-dimensional interpretation of antifascism to reveal how our struggle must challenge all forms of oppression if we are to ever truly build a world free from fascism."—Mark Bray, author of *Antifa: The Anti-Fascist Handbook*

"This is one of my favorite kinds of book, an indispensable resource for creating a world where it would be useless. Equal parts handbook, history, and theory, it is both an excellent overview of militant struggles against fascism and a powerful weapon for the fights to come."—Vicky Osterweil, author of *In Defense of Looting*

"We can only really understand antifascism through the voices of those most committed to the cause. Above the hubbub of distortion, exaggeration, and half-truths, antifascist voices need to ring loud and clear. In *¡No pasarán!: Antifascist Dispatches from a World of Crisis*, these voices are unmistakeable. Drawing from rich stores of real-life experience, this forthright book wrestles with what it means for radical antifascists to resist the scourge of fascism and create a fascist-free future."—Nigel Copsey, author of *Anti-Fascism in Britain*

"*¡No pasarán!: Antifascist Dispatches from a World in Crisis* is a much-needed collection of essays from some of the most notable antifascists writing today. Focusing on how we got here as it pertains to fascism and white supremacy, along with what we can do about it, from a diverse cross-section of people who are directly doing the work, this book is a vital read for activists, journalists, and academics alike. These are political stories, and they are deeply personal stories, humanizing 'antifa' while detailing, with plenty of citations, why they—*we*—are absolutely necessary. Most importantly, these essays don't just highlight the social problems; they empower the reader to step up with their local community to solve them."—Kitty Stryker, editor of *Ask: Building Consent Culture*

¡No pasarán!: Antifascist Dispatches from a World in Crisis
Edited by Shane Burley, ©2022
All essays © 2022 by their respective authors
This edition © 2022 AK Press (Chico and Edinburgh) and the Institute for Anarchist
Studies

ISBN: 978-1-84935-482-0
E-ISBN: 978-1-84935-483-7
Library of Congress Control Number: 2022935894

Institute for Anarchist Studies
PO Box 90454
Portland, OR 97290
https://anarchiststudies.org
info@anarchiststudies.org

AK Press
370 Ryan Ave. #100
Chico, CA 95973
www.akpress.org
akpress@akpress.org

AK Press
33 Tower St.
Edinburgh EH6 7BN
Scotland
www.akuk.com
akuk@akpress.org

AK Press would be delighted to provide you with our latest distribution catalog, which
features books, pamphlets, zines, and stylish apparel published and/or distributed by
AK Press. Alternatively, visit our websites for the complete catalog, latest news, and
secure ordering.

Cover design by John Yates | stealworks.com
Printed in the United States

CONTENTS

FOREWORD: On the Uses and Manifestations of Antifascism 1
    Talia Lavin

INTRODUCTION: What is Antifascism? 5
    Shane Burley

I. FROM THE GROUND: INSIDE ANTIFASCIST ORGANIZING

Three Way Fight Politics and the US Far Right 20
    Matthew N. Lyons

Building Communities for a Fascist-Free Future 42
    Shane Burley

"We Can Do More Together": How Fighting Sports Build Confidence in
European Antifascist Networks 54
    Hilary A. Moore

The Black Antifascist Tradition: A Primer 63
    Jeanelle K. Hope

The Campus Antifascist Network 88
    Maximilian Alvarez

Antifascism Is Not a Crime: An Interview with David Campbell 97
    Kim Kelly

Lessons from a Lifetime of Antiracist and Antifascist Struggle:
A Memoir and Analysis 106
    Michael Novick

It Takes a Network to Defeat a Network: (Anti)Fascism and the
Future of Complex Warfare. 141
    Emmi Bevensee and Frank Miroslav

Subcultural Antifascism: Confronting the Far Right in Heathenry
and Heavy Metal 167
    Ryan Smith

II. GLOBAL SOLIDARITY: FIGHTING THE INTERNATIONAL FAR RIGHT

Why Does the US Far Right Love Bashar al-Assad? 192
    Leila al-Shami and Shon Meckfessel

The Other Aryan Supremacy: Fighting Hindu Fascism in the
South Asian Diaspora 210
    Maia Ramnath

How Far-Right Fantasies About Refugees Became Mainstream in Greece. 258
    Patrick Strickland

Global Neoliberalism, Fascism, and Resistance. 270
    Geo Maher

III. INTERLUDE

Some Names Have Been Changed. . . . .
    Daryle Lamont Jenkins

IV. OFFENSIVE IDENTITIES: INTERSECTIONAL EXPERIENCES OF RESISTANCE

Antifascism through the Lens of Transgender Identity 282
    Emily Gorcenski

Five Hundred Years of Fascism 312
    Mike Bento

Antiracist Skinheads and the Birth of Anti-Racist Action:
An Interview with Mic Crenshaw 331
    Shane Burley

Gringos and Fascism. 346
    Mirna Wabi-Sabi

Antisemitism and the Origins of Totalitarianism. 357
    Benjamin S. Case

"Kops and Klan Go Hand in Hand": An Interview with Kelly Hayes 377
    Shane Burley

V. RETHINKING THE WORLD OF RESISTANCE

A Partial Typology of Empathy for Enemies: Collaborationist to Strategic 388
    Joan Braune

The Meme Alibi 413
    Margaret Rex

Make Journalism Antifa Again. 435
    Abner Häuge

Nazis Don't Get Nice Things 442
    Margaret Killjoy

Surreal Antifascism, 1921–45 448
    Alexander Reid Ross

AFTERWORD: Perspectives for Antifascists 477
    David Renton

Notes. 481

Index 539

On the Uses and Manifestations of Antifascism

Talia Lavin

What is antifascism? What does it look like? And how does it manifest in the real world?

The simplest explanation is also the truest: antifascism exists in relation to fascism as antimatter does to matter—its opposite, and, hopefully, its equal. As fascism rises and spreads, so does the need for antifascism, and the people inspired to fight back. "Fascism," as broadly defined amongst an international, highly diffuse, and individuated network, is not subject to the slippery-slope arguments so often put out by currish and mealy-mouthed commentators: it is defined quite narrowly, as the words and actions of those who espouse a politics of genocide, who seek to destroy and harm members of marginalized groups, who openly or covertly align themselves with past and present fascistic movements, and who agitate for or commit acts of violence against the minorities they despise.

So much, so simple. The second component, however, and perhaps what makes the concept of antifascism so baffling and inimical to a media sphere that aligns itself most readily with institutions and with the state, is that antifascists are *nonstate actors*, individuals and collectives acting from no authority but their own desire for a better world. For historical inspiration, antifascists turn to those individuals who, in the 1930s, battled Hitler's rising Brownshirts on the street under the banner of *Antifascistische Aktion*, and the tens of thousands of volunteer fighters from all over the world who joined together in the fight against the would-be military dictator Francisco Franco during the Spanish Civil War. It's from the latter conflict that an antifascist slogan, used all around the world, arose, Dolores Ibarrurri's war cry: "¡No pasarán!" They shall not pass! This is the antifascist position: arrayed in defense against an encroaching force of destruction and violence, sacrificing their effort and their bodies to protect all they hold dear.

This is why, when a unitary, threatening, and sinister image of antifascists filters into public consciousness, I feel an urge to countermand it with my own knowledge of the beautiful, brave, complex, often female and queer-led, collectives with which people reach out to one another, grasp hands, and turn to face the threat, stronger because they are one another's company.

It's hard, however, to put a face on antifascism, cuddly or otherwise. For protection against the brutality of the fascists they oppose, and in order to avoid concentrating power in any given individual, antifa is largely anonymous and decentralized. Like everything else about antifascism, this is a defensive position. Antifascists are in a three-way fight, since they are nonstate actors whose commitment to protecting marginalized communities often puts them in opposition to the brutal and racist systems of law enforcement. Antifascists seek to protect themselves and their communities against fascists; but far from the fear mongering that gets so much purchase in the broader world, antifascism is a movement of reaction, which operates in opposition to extant and encroaching fascism. Antifascism is a movement of protection and is not a thoroughgoing political philosophy. It is rather a set of tactics and a commitment to that protective stance.

One of the things I love about antifascism—and the reason I feel comfortable defining myself as an antifascist, though it is not a sole political valence in and of itself—is the multiplicity of means and uses that go into the term. There are many methodologies and roles for antifascists; although this is elided by ungenerous and alarmist press coverage, street violence—countering fascist marches by physically interposing oneself between fascists and the public—is just a small nexus of antifascist activity, one part of a broad spectrum of activities that constitute antifascist struggle.

Methods to thwart fascism are at least as variegated as the ways to spread it, if not more so. Antifascism can utilize the full spectrum of human creativity: there are those who create antifascist art to undermine the spread of genocidal propaganda, and music that invigorates and inspires. There are those who provide food, clothing, safety gear, childcare, and water to street operatives; those who work bravely as street medics, bandaging wounds, and flushing tear gas from weeping eyes; and there is a whole range of activities, in the Internet age, that occur from behind the keyboard. These include infiltration and surveillance of fascist groups and relaying gleaned intelligence to others in order to anticipate fascists' movements. There is the intentional sowing of internal discord to thwart fascist operations. There is the digital detective work of unmasking the identities of those who seek to harm and threaten minorities from beneath the veil of anonymity, pairing ugly words and threats to real names and faces. There is the work of writing and education, whether journalistic or in the form of community resources to keep people aware of the state of fascist movements. There are those who call for boycotts of venues who host fascist conferences or events, in the effort to disrupt logistics, and to provide disincentives to take fascists' money. There are those who target the advertising and monetization of fascist blogs, shops, and video channels, or seek to deplatform fascist ideologues from social-media perches that enable them to recruit.

None of these activities are less or more antifascist; each is necessary, each is complementary, each is part of the broad, sprawling, individuated effort of building a dike against the rising tide of violent cruelty that threatens to sweep away our world. I am proud to be an antifascist, proud to stand shoulder to shoulder with the many people who contributed to this book, proud to be a part of a movement that stands without aid except one another to dismantle the fearsome and violent forces that would gladly sweep away all that is precious and good, all that is vulnerable and necessary, in the service of a cruel and violent image of the world.

What Is Antifascism?

Shane Burley

As I was filing into the Patriot Prayer rally in Portland, Oregon, the attendees started closing ranks and preparing to march, and I got nervous. The June 3rd, 2018, rally was simply the most recent in what had become a staccato series of appearances as far-right leader Joey Gibson and his Proud Boys hangers-on would repeatedly come to Portland to hold rallies laced with transphobic, anti-immigrant, conspiracy-minded speakers. The event was billed as a place to speak their minds, to confront the "intolerant left" of a city like Portland, but the fact that most attendees came suited in body armor, donning helmets and brandishing weapons, chiseled away at the veneer that this was about protecting free speech. These rallies had begun in Portland, Oregon in 2016 as Donald Trump's election neared. After a past far-right demonstration attendee stabbed multiple people on a Portland train in 2017 amid a racist rant, Gibson decided to hold yet another unpopular rally in Terry Schrunk Plaza, a park dead center in Portland's busy corporate district. Gibson's hundreds of attendees were met by antifascists on all sides with overlapping contingents, including the diverse coalition called Portland United Against Hate to the west, trade union activists and socialists to the east, and a militant bloc led by Rose City Antifa in the adjoining park directly to their north.

Rose City Antifa has a long history since its 2007 founding and was the first US-based organization to use the "antifa" label. They emerged out of a longer history of Portland's antifascist movement, including the earlier Anti-Racist Action (ARA) and a series of antiracist skinhead crews, the best known of which were the Baldies and Skinheads Against Racial Prejudice (SHARP). These earlier groups grew as neo-Nazi gangs patrolled the streets of working-class cities, dominating some of the most public areas in the city such as Pioneer Courthouse Square, just a few blocks from where Patriot Prayer was insisting on gathering. In the 1980s, Nazis had infiltrated popular bars and music venues, and ARA and various antiracist and "traditional" skinhead gangs pushed them out, refusing to shy away from direct confrontation when necessary.[1] These were young kids, often getting involved in cities around the country just because they saw the threat of neo-Nazi skinhead groups such as the White Knights and those associated with White Aryan Resistance (WAR).[2] In Portland, this became glaringly obvious when a gang affiliated with WAR called Eastside White Pride murdered Ethiopian student Mulugeta Seraw in 1988, leading to high-profile trials of WAR leader Tom Metzger and bringing the street battles out into the open. Rose City Antifa took up that tradition of street defense and chose a more explicitly activist orientation: they would get organized and use deep research and structured campaigns to push neo-Nazi groups such as the Hammerskins and Volksfront out of their community.[3] The ARA Network evolved into the Torch Network that linked together a growing number of antifascist groups including New York Antifa, Philly Antifa, Atlanta Antifascists, and Chicago Southside ARA. Over the years, these antifascist groups grew as the far right did, often challenging attempts by racists, antisemites, or nationalists to join parts of the left that were more vulnerable to manipulation.

But nothing compared with the explosion of antifascism as Trump came on the scene and the alt-right emerged as the largest white nationalist movement in decades. Hundreds of groups formed, with greater and lesser success, and Rose City Antifa was an example of how a well-organized, explicitly "militant antifascist" group could take on the far right.

On June 3rd, organizers with Rose City Antifa and other antifascist groups had amassed just around the corner from Gibson's rally, supported by hundreds of community members who, although often unaffiliated with any organization, wanted to support the effort: no one wanted the Proud Boys to have the run of the streets. Gibson led his crowd and his associate Haley Adams, a woman slight in appearance until her commanding voice grabbed your attention, called for the march to begin. She secured her own helmet, emblazoned with a sticker that said, "It's Ok to Be White."

Patriot Prayer started to move and Gibson, at the front, led them down a couple of blocks and, taking a sharp left, directly into the antifascists. A few seconds passed as a few far-right activists lingered up front, many with pipes and bats in hand, before they charged and began a full-frontal assault on demonstrators. Activists, most completely unarmed, were gang beaten, pulled to the ground where their heads were pummeled by a combination of boots and repurposed police batons. I had followed Gibson and now rushed into the crowd, seeing my friend Alexander Reid Ross trying to pull someone off the ground as he was being beaten nearly unconscious by a group of men adorned in paintball gear. Police eventually arrived, as a half dozen people lay on the ground, some of whom had to be rushed to the hospital with lasting injuries such as a skull fracture. I could still see their blood staining the concrete when I returned days later.

This was scary, and Portland was particularly egregious in this regard, but it wasn't unique. These were the scenes that were happening around the country, and they continued. After the protests responding to the 2020 police killing of George Floyd, Portland stood out as people kept up nightly actions for over a hundred days.[4] On August 22nd, a far-right mob arrived on the steps of the Multnomah County Justice Center, the courthouse that had been the target of much of these police abolition protests, where a line of armed men, holding shields, proceeded to carry out an unimpeded attack on journalists and demonstrators. Police stayed several blocks away, instructing people over the loudspeaker to "police themselves" and reminding us that everyone has a right to an opinion.[5] Later that night, the police used flash-bang grenades, teargas, and batons on a nonviolent abolitionist protest at a precinct across town.

Incurring this kind of violence had largely become par for the course. Between May 25th and July 7th, 2020 alone, there were 66 vigilante attacks on protesters, and there were 104 car-ramming attacks that year as well.[6] Police were engaging in violence against protesters at record levels, often motivated by the same conspiracy theories as far-right vigilantes. The year became incredibly deadly as assailants fired guns and threw homemade explosives at primarily nonviolent protesters who were doing things like blocking roads and crowding precincts to raise the profile of racist police killings.[7]

Over the Trump years, Portland was matched by other cities, such as Berkeley, where giant crowds set fire to the University of California Berkeley's campus rather than let far-right provocateur Milo Yiannopoulos speak, or in Boston, Massachusetts, where, just days after the violent "Unite the Right" rally in Charlottesville, Virginia, a failed Proud Boy rally was met by 40,000 counterdemonstrators.[8] Every attempt at a far-right rally—in California, Illinois, Georgia, and Texas—was met by antifascists, sometimes organized by ideologically driven militant antifascist groups, sometimes by liberal coteries of church committees and nonprofits, and other times by a mass of unaffiliated residents, tired of living in fear. All these were correctly captured under the banner of "antifascism," despite being incredibly distinct from one another, with their own unique approaches, tactics (even when they were more implicit than explicit), and demographics.

I'm writing this on the first anniversary of the January 6th "Capitol insurrection," where we were reminded just how volatile the far right can be, and what it means for them to have state support from elected leaders.

7

A largely unaffiliated mass, motivated by trenchant conspiracy theories, stormed what many assumed was one of the most heavily fortified buildings in the country, threatening to murder officials and leaving several people dead. This was a turning point for much of the country in the same way that "Unite the Right" was in August 2017, and the public is refusing to let it stand. Hundreds of people, both inside and outside of the US, are participating in the investigations into what happened, with group names like the "Deepstate Dogs" or the "Sedition Hunters." They are combing through videos and social media profiles, hoping to locate perpetrators and aid the Federal Bureau of Investigation (FBI) in bringing about successful prosecutions. These volunteers, certainly motivated by their own antifascist inclinations, are aiding law enforcement's alleged attempts to crush what is a broad, far-right movement. Does that make them antifascist? Or is there more to it than that?

To counter the bizarre smear campaign and conspiracy mongering around the term "antifa," many people have focused on restoring the legitimacy of the term by pointing out that it simply means antifascist: if you're against fascism, you are antifa. But it's more complicated than that. The term "antifa" means a particular style of militant antifascist organizing: closed organizations with well-trained members that combine deep research, doxing, pressure campaigns, and direct physical confrontation when necessary. You are not suddenly a member of some close-knit antifa group simply by virtue of attending a protest or voicing your discontent, and certainly not by acting as an unpaid agent of federal law enforcement.[9]

It certainly makes sense that there's an effort to restore the good name of antifa because it has been tarnished by spurious allegations throughout the Trump years. Legislation has been introduced to label antifa a "domestic terrorist group" despite no such legal category existing.[10] "Demasking" bills were introduced, or given new enforcement, in states around the country under the same model as was used to break up the criminal conspiracy of the Ku Klux Klan in earlier generations.[11] Complex conspiracy theories flourished about antifa's role in catastrophes, such as allegedly setting 2020's devastating Pacific Northwest forest fires, which became so trenchant that right-wing militias interfered with life-saving mutual aid work for fear that it was all an antifa plot.[12] Antifa was hiding around every corner, driven by their crystalizing hatred of American values, malevolence incarnate. Antifa became the go-to word for anything vaguely liberal, anything politically contentious. Environmental, labor, and antipolice protests were all quickly labeled antifa, despite having their own ideological and organizational histories. The people attending these demonstrations probably also hate fascism but, by collapsing those terms, the right-wing agitators who are driving this narrative revealed that their purpose was really to cause panic rather than describe reality.[13] Antifascists were grafted onto every piece of fear mongering and assigned to any despised personage, all in an effort to dehumanize activists, making it easier to justify violence against them despite antifascist violence being statistical noise when compared with the brutal legacy of white nationalism.[14]

Even when bad-faith actors aren't determining jargon, antifascism can be difficult to define. This comes, in part, from how we define fascism. For the Black Panther Party and many groups in what is sometimes called the "Black antifascist tradition," definitions of fascism include the police and state actors engaged in repression of social movements.[15] This would, reflexively, make antipolice organizing a necessary center of antifascism. Many Indigenous groups have extended this a step further by indicting colonialism itself, either as an earlier example of fascism, or with fascism being the logical continuation of the colonialist project.

I use what is often called a "New Consensus" definition of fascism as being a revolutionary ideology that seeks to use mythic narratives to build a society of hierarchical stratification and essentialized identity, codified through a cult of violence and actualized through populist mass participation.[16] It's not enough to say that fascism comes from above because, as I could see at the Patriot Prayer rally and we could all see from the easily available YouTube livestreams from the Capitol insurrection, there are also everyday people engaging with far-right movements as a way of protecting their privilege. It is also important to note that, although there is certainly overlap and fuzzy boundaries, the term "fascism" does not apply to all the far right, yet antifascism often takes on an expanded list of opponents based on their fascist potential or their ability to maintain some of the most egregious aims, effects, or consequences of fascism. This means that, although certainly relative, a definition of fascism must necessarily exist on its own with its own parameters, perspectives, and internal dialogue.[17]

Scholar of antifascism, Nigel Copsey, notes that it is not enough to define fascism and use it to define antifascism in its reverse. "The definition of fascism must rest solely with the antifascist, regardless of whether or not they assess/define fascism correctly," says Copsey.[18] He suggests that there has to be an "antifascist minimum," a base level by which all those labeled as antifascists repudiate fascism in all its forms. I will take this a step further and say that antifascism, at least when it comes to contemporary forms, is activism and organizing taken by people outside of the state and law enforcement. This means independent groups that take action to confront the far right not by relying on institutional power but by taking power into their own hands. The tactics, then, are widely diverse, but the "minimum" would define out police, for example, as a useful foil to fascist growth. Devin Zane Shaw outlines the difference between militant antifascism and liberal antifascism, wherein liberal antifascism "funnels resistance toward institutionalized forms of political representation."[19] Antifascism cannot be sustained ideologically by channeling it into the political machine of democratic governments, even if people can engage in antifascist organizing on the one hand and liberal electoralism on the other.[20] It is certainly true that a slate of arrests or a well-placed lawsuit can hinder, sometimes even obliterate, fascist organizations, but antifascism is bigger than this. Instead, it sees something fundamentally flawed in the state approach to fascism, at least in as much as it believes that independent action of some type is ultimately necessary. Watching Twitch streams for the FBI isn't going to be enough.

Because of this dynamic, when we say antifascism, we are saying more than opposition to fascism. Antifascism itself has a series of implicit ideological assumptions that change as it encounters other ideologies, influences, and personalities. Antifascism has a critical view of the world gleaned from the complicated role that fascism plays: we can now rethink our entire political vision from the knowledge that fascism is a possible outcome. Nationalism, state power, subcultures, social movements, religious life, and so many more areas can have antifascist interventions, a new perspective with which to challenge our assumptions. Antifascism can, and often is, unpopular: it must take on challenges where it sees potential far-right growth, even when that is not agreed upon by the larger public or a subculture. An example of this is the tension between antifascists and anti-imperialist groups, which often clash around support for despotic and racist regimes in the Global South under the guise of fighting US imperialism, or which adopt antisemitic conspiracy theories under the guise of subverting the banking class.[21] Antifascism proposes that our analysis may not be nuanced enough, that it must be challenged from a more intersectional place that looks at all forms of oppression, and that, if we don't, we could face disaster.

Antifascism has seen through real-world experience that the structures of the police have more often than not been turned on the left and marginalized communities rather than the far right. Inherent distrust of law enforcement is a core feature of this "essential type." Antifascism also assumes that extraordinary action is to be taken, that debate is not enough, because the threat of fascism is so great. This is what antifascist scholar David Renton locates as the core of the antifascist equation: the more clear the threat of violence, such as from groups like the Proud

Boys, or more blatant white supremacist groups, such as with the alt-right, the more clear it is that antifascist interventions are necessary.[22]

This dynamic means that antifascism is a controversial break with the faith in the state necessary for liberal democracy, which assumes the government and its agencies are a necessary preservative force for human rights (or at least a necessary evil). At the height of the panic over who and what antifa is, ostensibly liberal writer Peter Beinart wrote a piece for *The Atlantic* that criticized antifa for being as bad as the fascists because both are violating the boundaries of liberal democracy.[23] Conversely, this could be read as a "state of exception," some actors taking unaccountable action to stop forces that they believe the current system is simply unable to adequately neutralize. "By acting to protect vulnerable people and spaces and employing force, militant antifascists simultaneously usurp the role of law enforcement as protectors of safety and social order as well as challenge the legitimacy of the state's claim to a monopoly on that role and the use of force," says criminologist Stanislav Vysotsky, who analyzed the role that militant antifascist groups have in maintaining an antiracist community standard outside of the state's approach to laws, incarceration, and criminalization.[24]

It might be more appropriate to say that antifascism itself holds a few assumptions that its ethics and strategies are bound to; namely, that liberal democracy has cultivated this fascist problem and therefore is unable (or unwilling) to eradicate it. Antifascism has not always agreed on what fascism is and where it forms, but there is a general understanding that unchecked hierarchies and the legacies of colonialism, white supremacy, and other systems of oppression can move from a space of structural inequality to an increasingly lethal form of insurrectionary violence. This process is fueled by very real contradictions in the system itself: falling real wages, ecological and public health catastrophes, the conflicted role of identity, and the inability to adequately solve some of society's most pressing issues through existing channels. Antifascism both fills this gap and offers a glimpse of something more: a direct action–oriented social movement that refuses to play by the rules of a society that has repeatedly failed to live up to its promise of freedom and equality.

Within this, there is still the question of what can be considered antifascism, and the possibilities are only expanding. As we saw mutual aid groups form to support communities during the pandemic, many who were abandoned by state agencies, there was a repositioning for how this kind of support work was seen by social movements.[25] The ability of a mass movement or political project to reproduce itself depends on the ability of people to have their most basic needs met. You can't expect people to spend hours in consensus-driven meetings if they are working three jobs just to pay for their child's health insurance. Mutual aid is what sustained a lot of the action in the 2020 Black Lives Matter protests. In Portland, there were microgroups that took on different components of a support infrastructure: a group that gave rides to people to the protest, a group that delivered food to people on the demonstration line, one that raised bail funds, and another that picked people up from jail when they were bailed out. In other places that support infrastructure expanded so much that it became a microsociety itself, such as the Capitol Hill Autonomous Zone (renamed the Capitol Hill Organized Protest) that expanded the demonstration space into one founded on mutual aid as the principle of its autonomy.[26] These protests could be sustained over such a long time because there were people actively sustaining them, and that's the same with movements against the far right. "Antifascism exists in opposition to the weaponization of belonging by identity-driven, right-wing forces that feed on individualism, erase history, and fuel our complicity with atrocity," says Kelly Hayes, an antifascist abolitionist organizer and writer based in Chicago, Illinois. "That means part of our work is creating space for belonging in a time of collapse. Because if we don't, fascist forces will. We need to nurture empathy in a fearful world. We need to do the work of cultivating shared realities amid a great social fracturing into subrealities and unrealities."[27]

This mutual aid work is part of where the lines between different movements can effectively blur and do so in positive ways. The framework for mutual aid groups created in 2020 to meet the pandemic threat then was shifted to support the protests, then went on to help with natural disasters, then was ready to support unhoused communities during antihomeless "sweeps" and support eviction defenders as moratoriums concluded. The mutual aid that supports antifascists can easily support other types of struggle, binding together different social movements.[28] Likewise, antifascists offer their own type of service to these groups: they challenge creeping far-right ideas and activists, those trying to manipulate movements through "entryist" tactics, which are attempts by fascists to enter left-wing movements and corrupt or recruit from them. Antifascists also assist those needing safety and defense when threatened by reactionaries, which means that defending marginalized communities is of the highest concern. There is necessary cross-pollination; we are not alone in this fight. This fluidity can help antifascism be seen as one of many necessary and interweaving social movements.

The "great antifa scare" was followed by state repression, leaving many antifascist political prisoners in need of "jail support" and long-term help with re-entering society. "Supporting the people who courageously put themselves in the line of danger to confront hate is an essential part of being an antifascist," says William Tull, an administrator with the Antifa International collective that coordinates the International Antifascist Defense Fund. "Real solidarity happens when antifascists know they can rely on us all to back them up when they run into trouble. Fighting hate is never a crime. Anti-fascism is always self-defense."[29] The fund raises money year-round and distributes it to antifascist political prisoners and those facing medical expenses or loss of income due to antifascist activism.

As the distorted view of antifa activism overwhelmed media discussions, we started seeing intense repression against activists. People such as David Campbell were incarcerated for what they argue were acts of self-defense. Alexander Dial, in Portland, Oregon had to rely on the help of the International Antifascist Defense Fund and others as they fought a potentially long prison sentence for disarming a member of the American Guard when they were attacking antifascist demonstrators with a clawhammer.[30] "The Left is seeking progress and that means changing institutions in ways that [help the most] people. And if you're running these institutions that [are] capitalizing on marginalized populations, you are going to fight back [against those reforms] with all the powers of the system," says Dial.[31] The perception that antifascists were engaged in some type of criminal enterprise gave license to prosecute them even for virtual activities. Daniel Baker was given 44 months in prison for posting about self-defense on social media.[32] A group of San Diego activists were charged with criminal conspiracy based on the idea that they must have been in collusion because they interacted with the same social media content, showing a disconnect of the prosecution both on how social media works and the basic elements of community organizing.[33]

Many of the antifascism tactics discussed in this book necessarily rely on people outside of antifascist organizations. Rose City Antifa members often explain the difference between the inside and the outside of their organization, trying hard to make that distinction clear to onlookers so as to protect the surrounding community from the kind of vulnerabilities that organizers inside of antifascist groups face. Movements require organizers, as well as activists, or those who participate in less committed ways but who make mass strategies possible. What binds these people together is opposition to fascism and the "no platform" idea that space, resources, and even a voice should be stripped from the far right, and that this should be done through the horizontal participation of everyday people rather than solely relying on law enforcement. How this happens should not be prescribed ahead of time because it is context dependent; sometimes an art show works, other times a celebratory counterdemonstration, and sometimes a black bloc that physically blockades a space and tells the fascists "*¡No pasarán!*" (They Shall Not Pass!) makes sense.

Building a diverse and growing antifascist movement requires keeping tabs on the far right, which organizers such as Eric K. Ward remind us are a "social movement like any other."[34] Much of the past several years was spent explaining that all white nationalists are not the caricature of the Southern Klansman, toothless and inhabiting some elitist fantasy that urban liberals have of poor rural Americans. People like Richard Spencer, well-coiffed and educated, wearing a tailored suit and talking about "human biological diversity," are also white nationalists. But this should only be a starting point, and we must have an even larger picture of what the far right is, including when it pretends to be a part of the left. Many of the chapters in this volume have an international perspective on this issue and look at how the frenetic nature of fascist movements can make them seem invisible: fascists appropriate leftist tactics and language, they talk about "national liberation" and claim to be antiwar, and they sometimes even try to recruit in what feels like the least likely spaces of the radical left.

Antifascists are also going to have to adapt to new conditions and build a cultural plurality necessary to build an opposition with teeth. We need antifascist journalism that takes its operative principles from the disruption of far-right movements, just as we are going to need spiritual, subcultural, and art spaces to engage people on all levels.[35] Without acknowledging who our communities are and the different backgrounds we come from, organizers are unable to build a social movement that connects to our uniqueness or sees us as meaningful constituents of it. This also means a revival of antifascist history, viewing contemporary movements as an important part of this larger continuity rather than simply celebrating the heroics of Cable Street while forgetting the utility of open-source research and digital pressure tactics.[36]

"[T]o build stronger foundations of trust and commitment that are capable of sustaining larger network structures, we need to commit more deeply to those groupings of which we are already a part—our friends and social connections, our religious institutions or physical pursuits or hobbies, our neighborhoods," says Lara Messersmith-Glavin, a founding member of the Portland-based antifascist group Pop Mob, which used music and carnivalesque events to draw people into really large antifascist actions capable of taking on Patriot Prayer, the Proud Boys, and the alt-right. "We need to bring antifascist (antiracist, anticolonial, intersectional feminist, queer-liberatory, body-positive, antiableist) consciousness to our daily lives and practices with full mindfulness and commit to the long work of transforming those spaces we already inhabit into actively anti-fascist spaces, as well."[37]

Pop Mob is one example of this mixed method of building coalitions after witnessing events such as the 2018 Patriot Prayer–led attack on anti-fascists. Their goal was to get hundreds if not thousands of people to join antifascist actions in an effort to overwhelm far-right demonstrations that were happening monthly. They worked alongside militant antifascist groups on the one hand and liberal nonprofits and civic organizations on the other, acting as a bridge between the two and respecting the strategic value of each.[38] Communities around the world are experimenting with how to cultivate their own unique synthesis in an effort to adapt to rapidly accelerating change, meet people where they are at, and hopefully build free-standing movements that feel pertinent to the lives of the people in their orbit.

Part of this approach is to acknowledge our reality as inherently complex and part of huge, interlocking systems of oppression and inequality, finding a way for different organizations to weave together so that they can complement each other's approach. In Georgia, the Atlanta Justice Alliance formed to build up the Black Lives Matter (BLM) demonstrations in the wake of the killing of George Floyd. They have shifted gears to work largely on mutual aid, particularly on setting up food distributions and supporting houseless encampments, but that framework gave them an edge when far-right protesters were threatening to come to the state capitol. Typically, there are large tent encampments there, so the Atlanta Justice Alliance set about pressuring the city to keep open warming stations so they could help move the houseless communities away from the state capitol, where armed vigilantes would patrol, and to these expanded centers and hotels. "We kept people out of harm's way," says Raven, an organizer with the Alliance. "You've got to let other organizations and people in the community know what your goals are so that they know that you are aligning with their lines of thought and what their end goals are, even if they are not exactly the same. . . . You've got to create community in our community."[39]

The alt-right has hit serious interference, the larger Make America Great Again (MAGA) movement is reeling from the January 6th indictments and Trump's electoral loss, and there has been some retreat, but they aren't gone. To assume that small changes, such as Democratic Party victories, are a meaningful foil to far-right advancement is to misread the overall trajectory of their movement.

We are living through a break in the neoliberal consensus of recent decades and a collapse of the political center; although the larger societal shift will be uneven (and capital will try to force stability when it's profitable), it is unlikely to return to normal. Instead, we are re-entering the historical process, which is one of struggle with a vision toward something much bigger. Between January 2020 and July 2021, the Bridging Divides Initiative at Princeton University, which tracks far-right groups and violence, saw over 953 incidents from armed or paramilitary groups, 94% of which targeted BLM events. A full 14% of these involved shots being fired. A significant factor in this growth was myths about antifa or election-related conspiracy theories.[40] These theories became so extreme that they inspired situations such as law enforcement chasing phantom buses around Northern California, consumed by the idea that they carried a threatening antifa mob, or providing cover to right-wing politicians who believed it was actually antifa dressed in cosplay who stormed the Capitol rather than their own base of supporters.[41]

A 2021 study from the University of Chicago showed that around 21 million people thought it might be necessary to use violence to "restore" a Trump presidency, and over half of those believe in the antisemitic QAnon conspiracy theory, which suggests that a cabal of satanic pedophiles in the Democratic Party are harvesting the blood of children. A full 63% of these Trump faithfuls believe in some version of the "Great Replacement" theory that posits that whites are being demographically disenfranchised and replaced, potentially through "white genocide" or "mass immigration."[42] "In the last two years, we have seen mass terrorist attacks driven by white supremacy in the US and around the world. They have been inspired in particular by the ideas of the Great Replacement, which argues that white people are being genocided in their home countries and replaced by non-white immigrants," says Heidi L. Beirich, in her 2021 congressional testimony on "accelerationism," the far-right approach of using mass violence to destabilize society, which she says is growing on a massive scale.[43] An example of this kind of violence was the December 28th, 2021, shooting in Denver, Colorado, where a man radicalized in the fringe world of "manosphere" figures took a gun into several tattoo parlors and murdered four people.[44] From January 1st to May 8th, 2020, the far right committed 90% of terror attacks, according to the Center for Strategic and International Studies.[45]

The "End of History" that Francis Fukuyama heralded with the fall of the Union of Soviet Socialist Republics was a brief detour in the actual turmoil that marks the ongoing battle of the masses against those at the tip of the pyramid of wealth and power. Fascism is a possible pathway for that anger to take, and this new world of explosive crisis and change makes fascism an increasing possibility for how rage may be both expressed and cultivated by those in power. Antifascism is the option we have to both protect ourselves and channel discontent into the kinds of social movements that want to change the root of the suffering—inequality and structural violence—and create an alternative based on faith in human flourishing.

The tragedy of the early passing of anarchist anthropologist David Graeber was a shock and a surprise, particularly because we were living through a series of both crises and resiliencies that seemed plucked from his imagination. The first book by Graeber I ever read was *Fragments of an Anarchist Anthropology*, a tract that pulls together observations about Indigenous societies and their relationship to the political ideas of anarchism. Part of his fieldwork focuses on areas of Madagascar where the state had largely retreated, leaving remote regions to their own affairs. Graeber noted that, even in the absence of a state, which he defines as the codified monopoly on the use of violence, societies still needed social consensus.

"Those unwilling to establish an apparatus of violence for enforcing decisions necessarily have to develop an apparatus for creating and maintaining social consensus," wrote Graeber. "[As] an apparent result, the internal war ends up projected outwards into endless night battles and forms of spectral violence."[46] This "spectral violence" could take the form of mythic tales that promised violence from a supernatural realm. These mythic tales established social control by replicating the state's enforcement mechanisms, even if it just existed in the minds of the community. This has often been presented as a kind of "road untaken," a misstep in the creation of advancing civilization. But as Graeber and his coauthor David Wengrow say in Graeber's final contribution to this discussion, *The Dawn of Everything*, our society, and its institutions, do involve choice. "[We] could have been living under radically different conceptions of what human society is actually about," write Graeber and Wengrow. "It means that mass enslavement, genocide, prison camps, even patriarchy or regimes of wage labour never had to happen. But on the other hand it also suggests that, even now, the possibilities for human intervention are far greater than we're inclined to think."[47]

The threat of fascism is the threat that social change will go fundamentally wrong, putting us in a worse situation than where we began. There is no mistaking the despotic collapse we are witnessing in slow motion, from the fragmenting of the global economy to accelerating ecological devastation. Our society was not an inevitability, it could have been different, and so can our future. How it plays out depends on our intervention. Antifascism can act as an antibiotic against the worst inclinations and possibilities, which want to further reify social stratification and cruelty as a shortsighted way out for a privileged few. But we can choose something different entirely.

In thinking of how we want to respond, we also have the option of replicating models of state repression and mass incarceration, hoping that we will be able to wield those weapons against our enemies. Alternatively, we can let our responses to this threat reflect the world we hope to build. The state is the codification of explicit violence, but the consequences offered by custom, social accountability, solidarity, or even malevolent spirits are "spectral." "Antifascism is—besides merely being against fascism—the idea that we are indeed individuals with individual thought and ideas who have no desire to impose that will on others," says antifascist organizer Daryle Lamont Jenkins.[48]

Antifascists are coming together to defend communities without establishing the same structures, like hierarchical and violent law enforcement, that they likewise criticize. The alternative is to rely on each other and our ability to create consequences and accountability, without wielding systematized oppression. That community accountability is its own kind of "spectral violence," and it's one that hopes to provide a window into what safety could look like away from the auspices of courts and militaries and tribunals and firing squads.

Although the antifascist movement is regularly indicted for its supposed reliance on violence, the kind of fleeting conflicts engaged in by some militant antifascists pales in comparison to both what the fascists hope to dispense in the future, or how the police and perhaps military will act to "maintain order." Instead, the approach of antifascists is to confront violence, both structurally and ideologically, in an effort to unseat its very foundations. This idea holds antifascists accountable by forcing them to live up to ideals and refusing to sacrifice the ethics of a revolutionary society for the simple pleasure of defeating one's enemy.

I.

FROM THE GROUND:
INSIDE ANTIFASCIST ORGANIZING

Three Way Fight Politics and the US Far Right

Matthew N. Lyons

Discussions of far-right politics in the US often fall into one of two traps.[1] One pitfall is to see the far right as an extremist threat to democracy, a fundamentally un-American set of beliefs and practices that goes against the principles this country was founded on. Many liberals and some conservatives take this approach, expressed in the idea that we combat "hate" by affirming American democratic values. The problem is, the US is not and never has been a democracy. It's a country founded on slavery, genocide, and settler-colonial conquest, which has always had a shifting mix of pluralistic openness and political repression. Today, it is a deeply unequal society in which a tiny capitalist elite holds most economic and political power and multiple systems of dominance/subordination shape most human relations. Far-right politics grows out of that oppressive order and works to intensify it in many different ways. Glossing over these connections masks—and thus helps perpetuate—entrenched systems of power and institutionalized violence.

Another pitfall is to treat the far right as essentially a vehicle for protecting capitalist rule, a version of politics that's more explicit and more brutal than the procapitalist mainstream, but basically an extension of it. Many leftists and some liberals take this approach, which draws on a long tradition of radical antifascism.[2] It's a better starting point than declaring "hate is un-American," because far rightists have too many ties with mainstream America to be ignored, and white supremacist vigilantes have long helped the elites by attacking organized labor and communities of color. But today, US far rightists believe that the economic and political elites have betrayed them. They believe the elites are using multiculturalism, mass immigration, and globalization to weaken and destroy white Christian America. This is a substantive conflict that can't be reduced to rhetoric or hypocrisy.

In contrast to both of these approaches, what is called "three way fight" politics argues that fascism—and the far right more broadly—is best understood as an autonomous force counterposed to both the left and the capitalist state. The struggle for human liberation isn't just a struggle against a system of power and oppression and its supporters, but also a struggle against far-right forces that have a contradictory relationship with the established order: they're connected to it but also in conflict with it. Although far rightists may collaborate with capitalist and mainstream political forces, they seek to wrest political power away from the established elite, and they promote supremacist visions that clash with capitalist interests in real ways. This means that militant opposition to the status quo can come from the right as well as the left. Just because someone hates the rich and wants to overthrow the government, don't assume they're progressive.

The three way fight approach reflects ideas within radical antifascism going back to the 1930s or earlier, but it took shape in its current form in the early 2000s with publications such as *My Enemy's Enemy: Essays on Globalization, Fascism and the Struggle against Capitalism* (2001) and *Confronting Fascism: Discussion Documents for a Militant Movement* (2002). The *Three Way Fight* website was founded in 2004 by a group of antifascists, both anarchists and Marxists, to promote discussion and analysis of how antifascism relates to radical liberatory change.[3] As the website's "About" page notes:

> Our blog confronts complexities in the dynamics between [leftists, the established capitalist order, and an insurgent or even revolutionary right] that are often glossed over. We point out, for example, that repression isn't necessarily fascist—anti-fascism itself can be a tool of ruling-class repression (as was the case during World War II, when anti-fascism was used to justify strike-breaking and the mass imprisonment of Japanese Americans, among other measures). And we warn against far right efforts to build alliances with leftists as well as fascistic tendencies within the left (as when leftists promote conspiracy theories rooted in anti-Jewish scapegoating).[4]

Three way fight politics also highlights complexities in how the state repressive apparatus relates to armed right-wing groups. There is a long history of right-wing vigilantes helping the government suppress dissent and keep oppressed communities under control, and white supremacist ties with—and infiltration of—local police forces remain common in towns and cities across the US.[5] But the familiar antifascist chant, "The cops and the Klan go hand in hand," hides as much as it reveals, particularly at the national level. Federal security forces in the US are subject to a range of internal biases and external pressures, but they exist, fundamentally, to defend ruling-class power. In broad terms, paramilitary rightists serve that purpose when they defend the existing order, and clash with that purpose when they seek to overthrow it.

To show how a three way fight approach works and why it's useful, in this chapter I will apply it to analyzing the US far right's three big upsurges of the past half century: the neo-Nazi upsurge of the 1980s, the Patriot/militia movement explosion of the 1990s, and the rise of the alt-right in the 2010s. In each of these historical moments, in different ways, far rightists promoted oppression and inequality, but also militant opposition to the established order. We need to understand these contradictory politics if we want to develop good strategies for combating them.

Although my work is grounded in antifascism, in tracing the dynamics of political movements here, I will rely mainly on the concept of "far right" rather than "fascist." The term "fascism" is used in so many different ways and has accumulated so much emotional baggage that it can become a distraction, whereas using a less-controversial term makes it easier to stay focused on the substance of the argument. In the context of the US today, I define the far right to mean political forces that: 1) regard human inequality as natural, desirable, or inevitable; and 2) reject the legitimacy of the established political system. This definition cuts across standard ideological divisions. Among white supremacists, Christian rightists, Patriot movement activists, and other rightist currents, some factions are system loyal in that they want to work within the existing political framework, whereas other factions are far right or oppositional in that they believe the existing political framework makes achieving their goals impossible.

Which of these forces are fascist depends on how you use the term. To me, fascists are a subset of the far right: all far-right currents have, at the least, fascistic tendencies, but not all merit the fascist label. For example, a totalitarian drive to impose a single ideological vision on society as a whole is, I believe, a key feature of fascist politics, and not all far rightists have that totalitarian drive. Historically, fascists' ideological vision has usually centered on nationhood or race, but I would argue that it can also center on something else, such as religion. And although Donald Trump has aided and echoed far rightists, as discussed later, and is a serious danger in his own right, I don't think that his brand of racist authoritarianism should be called fascist.[6]

Far-right politics embodies a kind of double-edged ideology. On the one side, far-right groups offer people a way to defend the relative social privileges and power that they enjoy over oppressed groups such as people of color, women, lesbian-gay-bisexual-transgender (LGBT) people, and immigrants, and speak to fears that traditional privileges have been lost or are under threat. But the far right also speaks to people's sense of being disempowered and downtrodden by groups above them, by denouncing groups that they identify with elite power, such as the federal government, liberal intellectuals, global corporations, or Jewish bankers.

Far-right politics, as I've defined it here, has been exceptional in US history. In most periods, rightists have found ample room to promote human inequality within the established political systems, and have seen no need to challenge that system's legitimacy. The two main exceptions before the 1970s were: 1) the years after the Civil War, when the original Ku Klux Klan (KKK, or simply "Klan") and similar groups spearheaded a successful drive to overthrow the Radical Reconstruction governments across the former Confederacy and re-establish political white supremacy; and 2) the period 1933–41, when an array of pro-Nazi groups denounced Franklin D. Roosevelt's New Deal as part of a Jewish-Communist conspiracy and advocated some form of fascist or quasifascist state, until their movement collapsed with the US entry into World War II.[7] By contrast, the KKK of the 1950s and early 1960s was a system-loyal movement in that it used vigilante terrorism to defend the established system of Jim Crow segregation and whites-only political rule.

1980s Neo-Nazi Upsurge

The social and political upheavals of the 1960s, spearheaded by the Black liberation movement, spurred the re-emergence of far-right politics in the US. As the US government, under pressure from below, moved to dismantle formal, legal white supremacy and carry out a range of other liberal reforms, growing numbers of white supremacists began to regard the US political framework as incompatible with their racial goals. They also began to regard Jews—who for decades had been one of many targets of Klan bigotry—as a central, crucial enemy. As Eric K. Ward explains:

> The successes of the civil rights movement created a terrible problem for White supremacist ideology. White supremacism—inscribed de jure by the Jim Crow regime and upheld de facto outside the South— had been the law of the land, and a Black-led social movement had toppled the political regime that supported it. How could a race of infe- riors have unseated this power structure through organizing alone? . . . Some secret cabal, some mythological power, must be manipulating the social order behind the scenes. This diabolical evil must control

television, banking, entertainment, education, and even Washington, D.C. It must be brainwashing White people, rendering them racially unconscious.[8]

In this context, many veterans of the KKK and related groups began to look sympathetically at Nazism, which they had previously regarded with suspicion as foreign and unpatriotic. In the late 1970s and early 1980s, several distinct white supremacist currents began to coalesce around a new synthesis of Klan and Nazi ideology. Former Nazi student activist David Duke paved the way by forming a new Knights of the KKK in 1974. Although Duke disavowed violence and broke with Klan tradition by accepting women and Catholics as members, he also increased the Klan's emphasis on the "Jewish problem" and criticized segregationism as a "system of weakness and degeneration," advocating instead the creation of an all-white nation-state.[9] In the early 1980s, several prominent Klan leaders, including several of Duke's former lieutenants, moved from KKK organizations to Nazi-oriented ones. Some Klan groups remained wary of the shift, but the most successful ones tended to be those that embraced neo-Nazism or worked with overt neo-Nazis.[10] (Another group that helped shape the new movement was Posse Comitatus, a white supremacist and antisemitic network that rejected the legitimacy of government above the county level.[11])

Ken Lawrence of the Sojourner Truth Organization and the National Anti-Klan Network highlighted the change in a 1982 speech. In the 1960s, Lawrence noted, the Klan had been "essentially a backward-looking movement attempting to preserve what was most reactionary and most peculiar of the institutions of the segregated white South. It was under that banner . . . that it went out and did its beatings, bombings, lynchings, mutilations, and castrations." But by the early 1980s, the resurgent Klan had embraced a fascist political vision and strategy:

> [T]he role of racism and the role of anti-Semitism and the role of scape-goating in general is quite different ideologically for a fascist movement from that of a right-wing conservative movement or a traditional Klan-type movement. That is, it is *not* to put people in their place. It is *not* to make a sub-class out of them and to exploit, or super-exploit, their labor. It is *genocidal*. It is *exterminationist*.[12]

The key text embodying this new vision was *The Turner Diaries*, published in 1978 by William L. Pierce, a novel about a neo-Nazi revolution to overthrow the US government and exterminate Jews, people of color, and white "race traitors." In its account of an armed struggle whose targets included the Federal Bureau of Investigation (FBI) and the US military, Pierce's novel marked a dramatic shift for many white supremacists. *The Turner Diaries* drew a sharp line between revolutionaries and conservatives, who its narrator dismissed as "the world's greatest cowards."[13] Soon, many white supremacist groups were selling the novel at a bulk discount.

Spearheaded by neo-Nazis, the new movement—which repudiated loyalty to the US in favor of an all-white nation, although it had not yet embraced the term "white nationalism"—developed a variety of political styles and strategic approaches. Like Adolf Hitler and Benito Mussolini, some neo-Nazi activists used electoral campaigns to spread their message. In 1984, antisemitic publisher Willis Carto founded the Populist Party, which brought together activists from a range of older white supremacist groups and remained active until the mid-1990s. The party denounced the Federal Reserve System, monopoly finance capitalism, and world government, as well as immigration, gun control, and homosexuality. Its 1988 presidential candidate was Duke, who had resigned as head of the Knights of the KKK in 1980 to form the National Association for the Advancement of White People. In 1989, Duke won a seat in the Louisiana state legislature as a Republican. He then ran strong campaigns for US senator in 1990 and Louisiana governor in 1991, both times losing but securing a majority of white votes. Although some neo-Nazi electoral candidates were open about their politics, both Carto and Duke were cryptofascists, who masked their true ideology behind benign-sounding euphemisms such as "conservative" or "populist."[14]

In contrast to these initiatives, Tom Metzger's White Aryan Resistance (WAR), founded in 1983, developed a militant, street-fighting presence. Through its affiliate, the Aryan Youth Movement, WAR was one of the first neo-Nazi groups to welcome and promote skinheads, who, with their shaved heads, tattoos, suspenders, and combat boots, became a prominent fixture of the far right. Skinhead youth culture started in Britain in the late 1960s and later spread to other countries. Some skinheads were and are antiracist and antifascist, but others have embraced neo-Nazi ideology and symbols. WAR and some other neo-Nazi skinhead groups, notably American Front, promoted Third Position fascism, an ideology that originated in Italy in the 1970s and stood for rejection of both communism and capitalism. WAR proclaimed itself an anticapitalist, white, working-class movement; denounced US military intervention in Central America and the Middle East; embraced environmentalism; celebrated Third World anti-imperialist struggles; and sponsored an Aryan Women's League that advocated white power and women's power.[15] This highlighted a tendency by many far rightists to incorporate elements of leftist politics in distorted form as part of their militant opposition to the status quo.

The third major current of neo-Nazism, distinct from both WAR's street-fighting orientation and Carto's electoralism, was what Leonard Zeskind has called the movement's "vanguardist" wing—those who believed that the white race's future depended on a committed minority acting in secret to destroy Jewish power.[16] For instance, Pierce aimed to build his National Alliance into a revolutionary cadre by recruiting from "an elite minority carefully sifted out of the overall White population."[17] Robert Miles and Louis Beam, both former KKK grand dragons (state leaders), promoted the concept of the Fifth Era Klan, which, like the original Reconstruction-era Klan, would take up arms in a guerrilla war against the US government. Through their *Inter-Klan Newsletter & Survival Alert*, Beam and Miles promoted a decentralized strategy to protect the underground movement from being infiltrated and crushed. Miles wrote of organizing "a WEB, instead of a chain" of command, and Beam wrote an influential article advocating a program of "Leaderless Resistance," in which cells or even individuals would operate independently, making them less vulnerable to repression.[18] Both Beam and Miles became "ambassadors-at-large" of the Idaho-based neo-Nazi group Aryan Nations, which promoted a racist version of Christianity called "Christian Identity" and became a major force within the movement during this period.

In 1983, National Alliance member Robert Jay Mathews founded an underground organization known as The Order (after the fictitious revolutionary leadership group in *The Turner Diaries*), also known as the Aryan Resistance Movement or Silent Brotherhood. Like Aryan Nations and many other white nationalists in this period, The Order advocated formation of an independent all-white nation in the Pacific Northwest. The group issued a "declaration of war" against what it called the "Zionist Occupation Government" in Washington, DC, and conducted a series of robberies, killings, bombings, and other illegal actions during the roughly two years that it operated. The Order was influenced by both Pierce's elitism and Beam and Miles's call for immediate action, and recruited members from a range of white nationalist groups. The Order brought an organized section of the US right into armed conflict with the state for the first time in over one hundred years. Yet it was only the most dramatic group within an extensive underground paramilitary network that extended from Idaho to Missouri and from Arizona to North Carolina.[19]

Federal security forces played a complicated, shifting role in relation to the emerging neo-Nazi movement. In the 1960s, FBI agents consistently refused to protect civil rights workers and other African Americans

26

against white supremacist terror, and shielded at least one paid informant from prosecution for his involvement in Klan murders. At the same time, the FBI used a variety of covert tactics to disrupt and weaken Klan groups—not to end racist violence, but to rein in a heavily armed network that was operating outside government control. This effort contributed to a dramatic drop in Klan membership, but it also alienated many white supremacists, who felt betrayed by the FBI they had once revered. This helped open the door to more militantly oppositional versions of white supremacist politics.[20]

During the 1970s, federal agencies actively supported right-wing vigilantism in several instances. In 1971–72, the FBI sponsored a San Diego–based network called the Secret Army Organization, which operated in 11 states and targeted antiwar leftists with spying, vandalism, mail theft, assassination plots, shootings, and bombings.[21] Between 1969 and 1972, the US Army's Military Intelligence Corps and the Chicago Police Department jointly operated the Legion of Justice, with several hundred members in the Midwest, which burglarized, bugged, vandalized, and assaulted socialist and antiwar groups.[22] In 1979, an undercover agent of the federal Bureau of Alcohol, Tobacco, and Firearms (renamed the Bureau of Alcohol, Tobacco, Firearms, and Explosives after September 11th) helped plan the operation that led to the Greensboro massacre, in which a coalition of Nazi and Klan groups killed five people and injured 10 at an anti-Klan rally in North Carolina.[23] Despite the federal support, this event was pivotal in softening distrust between Klan and Nazi groups, and encouraged many white supremacists to turn toward revolution.

In the 1980s, the federal apparatus responded aggressively to the new armed revolutionary network. Terrorizing Black people and gunning down leftist demonstrators was one thing; robbing banks and armored cars, counterfeiting money, threatening judges, and killing police was something else entirely. From 1984 to 1985, federal agents killed The Order's leader, Mathews, in a shootout and rounded up about two dozen other members, who received sentences ranging up to 252 years for racketeering, conspiracy, and violating the civil rights of Alan Berg (a Jewish talk show host they had murdered in Denver). Over the following three years, the FBI and other agencies conducted "Operation Clean Sweep," which extended the crackdown to at least six other armed white nationalist groups. Defendants received sentences up to 39 years for armed robbery, illegal weapons possession, counterfeiting, conspiring to blow up buildings, and various other crimes. But the biggest federal prosecution effort—the 1988 Fort Smith trial of Miles, Beam, and 12 other white nationalists on seditious conspiracy and other charges—ended in acquittals.[24]

The federal response to the neo-Nazi underground in the 1980s high-lighted several points. First, it showed that the US government has the capacity to undertake a systematic crackdown against fascists and white nationalists—even under a conservative Republican president. (From 1986 to 1988, the Ronald Reagan administration also cracked down on the Lyndon LaRouche fascist network, which had previously enjoyed extraordinary access to administration officials, and sent LaRouche and many of his associates to prison for mail fraud and conspiracy.[25]) Second, federal agencies often have trouble grasping the paramilitary right's political and organizational character. As Zeskind argues, the Fort Smith prosecution failed partly because the FBI "conceptualized the Aryan underground as a pyramid" and did not understand its decentralized, web-like structure.[26] Third, a federal crackdown against the far right raises serious concerns for leftists because it bolsters the same repressive apparatus used against liberatory movements. For example, the seditious conspiracy charge used at Fort Smith has mainly been used against leftists, such as Puerto Rican independence activists in the 1950s and 1980s. These points belie claims that combating the US far right is a matter of "defending democracy"—and claims that the far right and the state are really on the same side.

The 1980s crackdown significantly weakened neo-Nazi paramilitarism and turned many activists away from an underground guerrilla warfare strategy. Yet The Order helped pave the way for several later paramilitary groups and initiatives, such as the Aryan Republican Army and Aryan People's Republic in the 1990s, and the 1995 bombing of the Oklahoma City Federal Building, carried out by neo-Nazi Timothy McVeigh and others, which killed 168 people.[27] The imprisoned Order members were celebrated as political prisoners or prisoners of war, similar to the way imprisoned members of left-wing guerrilla groups have been celebrated on the left. Neo-Nazis still commemorate December 8th, the day Order founder Mathews died in a standoff with the FBI, as Martyr's Day, and Order prisoner David Lane's "14 words"—"We must secure the existence of our people and a future for white children"—has become a rallying cry for fascists around the world. In broad terms, the 1980s neo-Nazi underground helped define a new era of far-right militant opposition to the state.

Neo-Nazism in the 1980s also influenced other rightists. For example, Duke's electoral activism directly inspired hardline conservative Patrick Buchanan to run for president, as discussed later, using many of the same themes.[28] Beam's call for "Leaderless Resistance" was taken up by the Army of God, a shadowy Christian rightist group that claimed responsibility for many violent attacks against abortion providers from the 1980s onward.[29] And within a few years, neo-Nazis were among those helping shape the much larger Patriot movement.

1990s Patriot Movement

The second far-right upsurge of recent decades took place in the 1990s, with the sudden explosive growth of the Patriot movement around fears that the globalist elite was plotting to disarm the American people, overthrow the Constitution, and impose a dictatorship. Tens of thousands of people joined hundreds of armed "citizen militias" to defend against an expected crackdown, with many times that number participating in the broader movement. Patriot activists formed dozens of so-called common law courts that claimed legal authority in place of the existing judicial system, and many put forward bogus legal doctrines such as claims that only the original US Constitution and Bill of Rights were valid and all later amendments were not. Many Patriot groups promoted dramatic and often wildly implausible conspiracy theories, whose scapegoats ranged from the United Nations or the Federal Reserve System to abortion providers or environmental groups. The Patriot movement didn't declare war on the US government, but it did foster an entire subculture that regarded the established federal government apparatus as evil and illegitimate, and built a network of private armed units and pseudojudicial bodies claiming to exercise government functions. The movement surged rapidly in 1994–96, then declined just as rapidly for the next several years (largely because of backlash following the 1995 Oklahoma City bombing) before rebounding after Barack Obama's election as president in 2008.

The Patriot movement's rise reflected a number of factors. Capitalist globalization (including the movement of industry from the US to the Global South and of workers from the Global South to the US) revived old rightist fears of world government and the sinister cosmopolitan elite. The collapse of the Soviet bloc and end of the Cold War in 1989–91 weakened the anticommunist unity that had long held the conservative movement together. Old debates began to re-emerge, and more rightists began to voice opposition to sections of the US political and economic elite. Self-described "paleoconservatives" (or paleocons; defining themselves in opposition to the "neoconservatives," who wielded a lot of influence in the Reagan and George H. W. Bush administrations) criticized US interventionism, global alliances, and Washington's close alliance with Israel, often in terms with anti-Jewish undertones. Paleocons also promoted economic protectionism and criticized mass immigration, especially from non-European countries.[30] In 1992, the paleocon Buchanan ran against incumbent George W. Bush in the Republican presidential primaries, declaring, "He is a globalist and we are nationalists. . . . He would put America's wealth and power at the service of some vague New World Order; we will put America first."[31] In this statement, Buchanan identified George W. Bush with collectivist world government and himself with the America First Committee, which had opposed US entry into World War II and had included both anti-interventionist conservatives and Nazi sympathizers. In turn, Trump's more recent use of the "America First" slogan echoed Buchanan.

Paleoconservatism celebrated European Christian traditions, disparaged multiculturalism, and overlapped with growing right-wing interest in antielite conspiracy theories. Some of these theories were rooted in antisemitism, identifying elite power with the workings of a sinister Jewish cabal, whereas others defined the evil elite in nonethnic terms, such as Freemasons or secular humanists. Sometimes, these two types of theories appeared together, such as in the 1991 conspiracist best seller *The New World Order* by prominent Christian right leader Pat Robertson.[32]

In more immediate terms, the Patriot movement's rise was sparked by two brutal displays of federal power: the 1992 siege and arrest of white nationalists Randy Weaver and Kevin Harris at Ruby Ridge, Idaho (in which Weaver's wife and teenage son were killed, as was a US marshal) and the 1993 federal assaults on the Waco, Texas, compound of the Branch Davidian religious cult, in which 82 cult members (including 22 children) and four federal agents died. Both the Weaver home and Branch Davidian compound were targeted because of illegal firearms charges, and both raids involved massive displays of deadly force by heavily armed federal agents. To many right-wing activists, these events signaled the rise of a police state intent on disarming the populace. This narrative was reinforced over the following year and a half, when the federal government enacted a national background check system for gun purchasers and an assault weapons ban.[33]

From the beginning, both journalists and scholars were divided about the Patriot movement's political character. Some saw it as a direct continuation and outgrowth of the 1980s white nationalist movement, whereas others saw the two as essentially separate phenomena. A few leftists even saw the militias as potential allies.[34]

The reality is that the Patriot movement formed as a political hybrid—a meeting place at which many different right-wing ideological currents converged and interacted. Debates about whether the Patriot movement was fascist or nonfascist missed the point: it was the first forum since the

America First anti-intervention movement of 1940–41 in which fascists and nonfascists worked in coalition on a mass scale.

As many critics have pointed out, the Patriot movement was influenced by the earlier white nationalist group Posse Comitatus, which rejected federal government authority and pioneered in forming militias and common law courts in the 1980s. Some Patriot groups borrowed Posse Comitatus's antisemitic conspiracy theories about the banking system and its bogus legal theory that the Fourteenth Amendment to the Constitution established a different class of citizenship for Black people from that held by whites.[35]

However, many other rightist currents also shaped Patriot movement ideology. For example, in the 1980s, calls for armed local militias to resist federal tyranny came not only from white nationalists but also from Christian Reconstructionists, a hardline theocratic branch of the Christian right. Starting in the 1970s, gun-rights activists promoted an insurrectionary interpretation of the Second Amendment—the idea that the Founding Fathers saw an armed populace as a vital counterweight to deter government from amassing too much power. Mormon ultraconservatives blended hostility to most federal government activities, antielite conspiracy theories, and a belief that the US Constitution was divinely inspired. The so-called wise use movement, based in western states, opposed federal environmental laws and regulations, glorified individual property rights, and warned against the sinister elite.[36]

Racial politics was a point of conflict within the Patriot movement. Some militia leaders (e.g., John Trochmann and Tom Stetson) were veterans of the white nationalist movement, whereas others (e.g., Samuel Sherwood, Jon Roland, and Norm Olsen) had no such ties. Some Patriot groups promoted blatant racism, whereas others barred white supremacists from joining or even confronted them directly. J. J. Johnson (who cofounded the Ohio Unorganized Militia) was himself African American and called the militias "the Civil Rights Movement of the '90s." As a rule, opposition to explicit racism within the Patriot movement embodied the mainstream ideology of "color blindness," which claims to treat everyone as individuals. Although this belief system masks—and thus implicitly reinforces—the ongoing reality of systemic racial oppression in society, it is a far cry from *The Turner Diaries*.[37]

Patriot movement debates about race were interwoven with disagreements about organization, strategy, and the nature of elite power. Historian Robert H. Churchill has argued that the militia movement included two distinct ideological poles. In broad terms, "constitutionalist" groups declared membership was open to all regardless of race or religion, regarded federal tyranny as a result of power's inherent tendency to corrupt, and advocated open, public organization of militias as the most effective deterrent. By contrast, militias with a "millennial" approach welcomed or at least tolerated white supremacists, viewed the conflict with the federal government in apocalyptic terms, advocated a secret, closed organizational structure, and in some cases favored pre-emptive violence against the sinister elite. These two ideological wings initially worked together and to some extent overlapped, but over time they increasingly diverged and came into conflict.[38]

This analysis is useful for understanding Patriot movement strategy. Some Patriot groups—probably oriented toward the movement's "millennial" wing—apparently planned (and occasionally carried out) bombings, arson, or other attacks, primarily against federal targets such as the Internal Revenue Service or the FBI. However, the movement's role in the period's most deadly and notorious antigovernment attack—the 1995 bombing of the Oklahoma City Federal Building—is tenuous. Timothy McVeigh, who planted and detonated the truck bomb, was a KKK member who promoted the neo-Nazi novel *The Turner Diaries*. He and the two other men convicted for the bombing apparently hoped to mobilize militia activists but appear to have been at most marginally involved in actual Patriot movement activities.[39]

The Patriot movement's most characteristic and distinctive strategic approach, which cut across its internal ideological divisions, was a strategy of "dual power": simultaneously withholding loyalty from established state institutions and prefiguring the system that activists hope to create. Both militia groups and common law courts represented counter-institutions—movement-based alternatives to official state entities that claimed the right and authority to exercise state functions, grounded their activities in a counter-ideology, and began to band together through movement-based institutional networks.[40] This is a revolutionary strategy that US leftists, both Marxist and anarchist, have often advocated but rarely implemented on a comparable scale.[41] Dual power was less dramatic and less dangerous than armed confrontation, but it challenged the state's legitimacy in ways that at least appeared to be more concrete and practical than words alone. More recent incarnations of the Patriot movement have continued the dual power strategy, such as by offering or providing state-like services to local communities.

Federal government responses to the Patriot movement took various forms. At first, federal agencies—wary of another Ruby Ridge or Waco incident—did little to clamp down on the movement. (Zeskind and others have pointed out that a predominantly Black or brown movement

32

spouting antigovernment rhetoric and conducting large-scale paramilitary training would have been treated very differently.) But after the Oklahoma City bombing (for which Patriot militias were widely but inaccurately blamed), the FBI pursued a wide-ranging crackdown. Dozens of movement activists were arrested for various plots to attack federal buildings and other targets. This campaign contributed to the movement's collapse in the late 1990s.[42]

Federal agencies also used infiltration techniques against the Patriot movement. Between 1991 and 1993, using a classic counterinsurgency tactic, FBI agents operated a phony neo-Nazi organization called the Veterans Aryan Movement to spy on the Patriot movement that was just beginning to coalesce at that time. This operation, code-named PATCON (for "Patriot Conspiracy") was supposed to investigate specific potential crimes, but almost none of the information gathered was used in prosecutions, and at one point PATCON operatives even withheld information from Army investigators about a theft of military equipment to protect their own operation. In 1995, the FBI recruited South Dakota–based militia leader John Parsons, who ran a communications center for some nine hundred Patriot groups nationwide, as a paid informant. The arrangement was revealed in 1996 court testimony and brought angry denunciations from several militia leaders.[43]

During this same period, the Bill Clinton administration also used the Oklahoma City bombing to help win passage of the 1996 Antiterrorism and Effective Death Penalty Act, which loosened restrictions on the wiretapping and other surveillance of alleged "terrorists," expanded the use of secret evidence to deport noncitizens, and, in the words of legal journalist Lincoln Caplan, "gutted the federal writ of habeas corpus, which a federal court can use to order the release of someone wrongly imprisoned." The law made the death penalty more "effective" by making it much more difficult for death row inmates to appeal their sentences, even though a notoriously high proportion of death sentences have been shown to have serious flaws.[44]

2010s Alt-Right

The alt-right, short for "alternative right," represents the third major upsurge of modern far-right politics in the US. The alt-right coalesced as an intellectual current around 2010 and first gained prominence in 2015 as a loosely organized right-wing movement that emphasized internet activism, was hostile to both liberal multiculturalism and mainstream conservatism, and presented itself as new, hip, and irreverent. Alt-right ideology combined white nationalism, misogyny, antisemitism, and authoritarianism in various forms and took on political styles ranging from intellectual argument to violent invective. White nationalism has constituted the movement's center of gravity, but some alt-rightists have been more focused on reasserting male dominance or other forms of elitism rather than race. Most alt-rightists rallied behind Trump's 2016 presidential bid, yet as a rule alt-rightists have regarded the existing political system as hopeless and have called for replacing the US with one or more racially defined homelands.[45]

The term "alternative right" was introduced by Richard Spencer and Paul Gottfried in 2008 and initially was a catchall encompassing paleoconservatives, libertarians, white nationalists, and other rightists at odds with the conservative establishment.[46] *AlternativeRight.com*, an online magazine that Spencer founded and edited from 2010 to 2012, became a popular intellectual forum for a range of dissident rightist views.[47] Gradually, the label alt-right became more closely tied to white nationalism and the goal of creating a white ethnostate, as a number of other white nationalist publications became associated with the term and as Spencer focused more sharply on white nationalism after becoming head of the National Policy Institute in 2011. Even those alt-rightists who did not put race at the center of their politics, such as Jack Donovan, rejected the legitimacy of the US political system.

Initially, the alt-right had virtually no direct ties with neo-Nazi or KKK traditions, but largely represented a more genteel, suit-and-tie variety of white nationalism, associated with pseudointellectual publications such as *American Renaissance* and *The Occidental Quarterly*. The alt-right drew heavily on paleoconservatism's hostility to both immigration and the "War on Terror," and especially those paleocons such as Sam Francis who began to talk openly about race.[48] Alt-rightists blended these influences with ideas drawn from the European New Right (ENR). Having started in France in the late 1960s, the ENR is an initiative among far-right intellectuals in several countries to rework fascist ideology, largely by borrowing elements of liberal and leftist discourse to mask their fundamental rejection of the principle of human equality. ENR members champion "biocultural diversity" against the homogenization supposedly brought by liberalism and globalization. They have argued that true antiracism requires separating racial and ethnic groups to protect their unique cultures, and that true feminism defends natural gender differences instead of supposedly forcing women to "divest themselves of their femininity."[49] In the US, organs such as *AlternativeRight.com* and *Counter-Currents Publishing* (also founded in 2010) took up ENR themes, but with a much blunter emphasis on race and the supposed threat posed by Jews and people of color.[50]

Several other political currents overlapped with the alt-right and contributed to its distinctive ideology: right-wing anarchists (including national-anarchists and Keith Preston's *Attack the System* website), who want to dismantle the centralized state but uphold nonstate systems of hierarchy and oppression; the male tribalism of Donovan, who advocates a social and political order based on small, close-knit "gangs" of male warriors; and the neoreactionary movement (also known as the Dark Enlightenment), an offshoot of libertarianism that rejects popular sovereignty and advocates small-scale authoritarian enclaves such as seasteads.[51]

Like other far rightists, members of the alt-right have endorsed some views usually considered liberal or leftist. Defying laissez-faire conservatives, many alt-rightists have supported single-payer health insurance as a way to help working-class whites, and some have advocated a kind of racist environmentalism.[52]

Starting in 2015, the alt-right broadened out from a small intellectual circle as a much wider array of online activists embraced the term. Many of these newer alt-rightists were based in discussion websites such as Reddit, 4chan, and 8chan, and they brought an aggressive mix of naked bigotry, vilification of opponents, and mocking irony and humor. Some of them, such as Andrew Anglin of *The Daily Stormer*, brought neo-Nazi–based politics into the movement.[53] Many newer alt-rightists also came from the "manosphere," an online antifeminist subculture of men who falsely claim that men in US society are oppressed by feminism or by women in general. Some manospherians advocate a traditional patriarchal family, whereas others have celebrated a predatory sexuality outside of marriage or have advocated (and in a few cases carried out) the mass killing of women. Under this influence, the alt-right increasingly embraced an intensely misogynistic ideology, portraying women as irrational, vindictive creatures who need and want men to rule over them and who should be stripped of any political role—a perspective that made the alt-right significantly more hostile to women than many older neo-Nazi groups.[54]

All the far-right movements discussed in this chapter have brought together different ideological currents, but the alt-right has been uncommonly successful in combining hardline rejection of the established order with a big tent ideological framework. Despite their shared politics, alt-rightists do not speak with one voice. For example, whereas some alt-rightists declare that abortion is inherently immoral and should be banned, others have argued that it is useful as a tool of eugenics, by limiting reproduction by communities of color and weeding out "defective" white babies.[55] Whereas many alt-rightists consider homosexuality in any form to be immoral and a threat to racial survival, sectors of the movement have welcomed some homosexual men while derogating gay culture. And although most alt-rightists have regarded Jews as dangerous outsiders who bear major responsibility for the decline of European civilization, they have disagreed about whether to work with them. Neo-Nazi–oriented alt-rightists reject any association with Jews and regard them as the embodiment of pure evil. Other alt-rightists, however, have advocated a tactical alliance with right-wing Jews against Muslims and immigrants of color, and have argued that migration to Israel will help prevent Jews from subverting Western societies. A few alt-rightists and their organizations, notably Jared Taylor's *American Renaissance*, have welcomed like-minded Jews to movement publications and events.[56]

Although the alt-right's mix of ideological themes and positions is distinctive, a lot of what has set it apart from earlier far-right movements has been its approach to organization, tactics, and political strategy. First, the alt-right was the first incarnation of the US far right to operate mainly online and to gather people not with physical demonstrations or mailing lists but with social media campaigns and internet discussion sites. Second, alt-rightists made skillful use of online tactics to attack opponents, which played a significant role in boosting Trump's presidential campaign. They circulated memes that were often based on mockery and ridicule, and they launched coordinated harassment campaigns, involving floods of vicious abuse, rape, and death threats, and doxing (public releases of personal information). Alt-right harassment campaigns were directly based on techniques developed by the manosphere to silence and terrorize women.[57]

Third, the alt-right's relationship with Trump represented an important departure from previous far-right strategies. For several years, alt-rightists had argued about whether to work within existing political channels or reject them entirely. Many sidestepped this issue, following the ENR's lead, and focused on a "metapolitical" strategy of seeking to transform the broader culture—or, as many alt-rightists put it, "move the Overton window" of acceptable discourse.[58] But others proposed a more innovative approach of working within the system to weaken it by advocating changes that sound reasonable but require radical change—a right-wing version of the Trotskyist transitional demand strategy. For example, one author urged alt-rightists to use the language of multiculturalism to complain about "legitimate" cases of discrimination against whites or members of other dominant groups—not to seek reform, but to use "the contradictions and weaknesses of the System against itself."[59]

At root, alt-right support for Trump followed a related approach of using the system against itself. Although Trump did not call the established political order into question, he offered a lot for alt-rightists to cheer. Not only did he advocate the harshest anti-immigrant measures of any major party presidential candidate in generations, encourage his supporters to use violence against opponents, and brag about sexually assaulting women, but his "America First" program also challenged conventional conservatism in ways that echoed earlier right-wing populists. Like Buchanan in the 1990s, Trump rejected Washington's free trade consensus in favor of economic nationalism and protectionism, called for the US to pull back from its global military role and system of alliances, and denounced the globalist financial elite in terms that echoed antisemitic themes. Like George Wallace in 1968, who appealed to working-class whites by defending both racial segregation and expanded welfare state policies, Trump took "liberal" positions on some domestic issues, such as protecting Social Security and calling for universal access to health care.[60]

Alt-rightists began praising Trump in 2015, and by mid-2016 most of the movement was applauding him. But this support was qualified by the recognition that Trump was not one of them—as they often put it, he was a civic nationalist, not a white nationalist. Trump, they argued, was not going to dismantle the US political system or create a white ethnostate, but he was addressing issues such as immigration and foreign policy in ways that created openings for alt-rightists to push their own positions, and—just as important—he was ridiculing and vilifying the conservative establishment. Indeed, alt-rightists initially supported him not because they thought he could win the nomination, much less the presidency, but because they hoped he would destroy the Republican Party. A minority of alt-rightists, meanwhile, opposed Trump because they believed he was loyal to Israel, promoted illusory faith in the US political system, or would co-opt their movement into supporting the established elite.[61]

Alt-rightists used their online activist skills to help Trump's campaign, attacking his Republican rivals as traitors and sellouts to liberalism, and Democratic nominee Hillary Clinton as an aggressive militarist who would #DraftOurDaughters in the name of feminism. In return, the Trump campaign gave the alt-right greater visibility, influence, and sense of purpose. No previous US far-right movement had ever achieved this kind of mutually beneficial symbiosis with a major political figure.[62]

Paralleling and to some extent facilitating the alt-right's symbiotic relationship with Trump, the movement began to find other tentative allies. As the alt-right grew and attracted attention, some system-loyal conservatives—who became known as the "alt-light"—took on the role of apologists or supporters for the alt-right, helping spread a lot of its message without embracing its full ideology or ethnostate goals. Many observers mistakenly equated alt-light figures such as Milo Yiannopoulos and Steve Bannon of the *Breitbart News Network* with the alt-right itself. Alt-rightists relied on the alt-light to help bring their ideas to a mass, mainstream audience (and in the case of Bannon and a few others such as Stephen Miller, to serve as go-betweens to Trump himself), but to varying degrees they also regarded alt-light figures with suspicion, as ideologically untrustworthy opportunists.[63]

Most alt-rightists were thrilled by Trump's upset victory over Hillary Clinton, but not because they believed that Trump shared their politics or would bring about the changes they wanted. Rather, they believed a Trump presidency would offer them "breathing room" to promote their ideology and win broader support. In turn, they saw themselves as the Trump coalition's political vanguard, taking hardline positions that pulled Trump further to the right while enabling him to look moderate by comparison.[64]

In the months following Trump's inauguration, alt-rightists made a push to strengthen their grassroots ties with other right-wing forces and expand their activism from the internet to physical rallies and street fighting. Alt-right groups began to focus on building actual organizations and holding public demonstrations, often in collaboration with alt-light and even Patriot movement groups, around themes such as Islamophobia and "free speech" (protecting political space against supposed repression by antifascists). Some of them also began to organize and train for physical violence and, with neo-Nazi skinhead groups and newer alt-light formations such as the Proud Boys, to engage in street fights with antifa.[65] These efforts culminated in the brutal August 2017 "Unite the Right" rally in Charlottesville, Virginia, at which one antifascist counterprotester was killed and the alt-right's white supremacist violence became national headlines.[66]

After "Unite the Right," the alt-right suffered a series of setbacks. Media companies forced several major alt-right websites to find new platforms or shut down entirely, infighting and personal conflicts weakened the movement and destroyed at least one major organization (the Traditionalist Worker Party), and antifascist resistance blocked their mobilizing drive. These setbacks also highlighted and reinforced the inherent differences separating the alt-right from system-loyal rightists.[67]

After the inauguration, alt-rightists also quickly became disillusioned with Trump himself. From the beginning, Trump's presidency rested on an unstable coalition of America First nationalists (who represented the politics he ran on) and conventional conservatives (who unlike Trump had a strong organizational base in the Republican Party and its affili-ates). As Trump attempted to steer between these positions, alt-rightists tended to see some of his actions (notably the crackdown on asylum seekers and undocumented immigrants) as positive but inadequate, and his concessions to establishment conservatism on many issues (from cut-ting corporate taxes and deregulating industry to staying in the North Atlantic Treaty Organization [NATO] and imposing sanctions on Russia) as disappointments or outright betrayals. As one alt-rightist put it: "We were promised isolation and got further Middle Eastern conflict, we were promised a protectionist economy and got watered down free trade, we were promised sealed borders and a wall and got hordes of feral Mestizos, and we were promised realpolitik and got slavish devotion to Israel." A key turning point came in April 2017, when Trump launched a missile strike against the Syrian military in response to a chemical weapons attack, in what most alt-rightists saw as a shocking capitulation to the foreign policy establishment. Some alt-rightists hoped that Trump's populist-nationalist tendencies could still win out, but others declared that he had been bought off or blackmailed by the Jewish elite, and urged alt-rightists to abandon electoral politics and prepare for many years of base building.[68]

Conclusion

In this chapter, I have discussed three major upsurges of far-right politics in the US over the past 40 years. These represent three related but distinct political movements, encompassing a range of ideologies and strategies, but all envision a deeply antiegalitarian society, and all reject the estab-lished political system as an obstacle to achieving their goals.

These movements can't be explained as expressions of "extremism" because all seek to bolster systems of inequality and oppression that are deeply rooted in US society, and all have interacted with mainstream forces that are loyal to the existing order. At the same time, these move-ments can't be explained as tools of the ruling class. All three movements have been deeply critical of the established political and economic elite and have rejected elite-defined goals and priorities in favor of their own supremacist agendas. Neo-Nazis and alt-rightists, in particular, have been sharply critical not only of liberal politicians but also conservative ones. Some neo-Nazis and Patriot activists have taken up arms against the state and have faced significant crackdowns as a result.

As I argued in the introduction to this chapter, the US far right embod-ies a double-edged politics, bolstering power and privilege over oppressed and marginalized groups, but also hitting back against the power of the economic and political elite. This double-edged politics has increasingly involved a contradictory response to the rise of neoliberalism, the set of economic policies and system of social control that has dominated US politics under both major parties since the late 1970s. Neoliberal policies include minimal regulation of business, reduction or privatization of social services, low taxes for businesses and the wealthy, free trade, and relatively unrestricted immigration. Neoliberalism emphasizes competition, market relations, and individual achievement, yet it also dramatically expands the state's repressive apparatus—including mass incarceration, mass surveillance, and the militarization of policing. Internationally, neoliberalism has supported an interventionist foreign policy designed to protect and expand opportunities for investment, trade, and profit making.[69]

The term "neoliberal fascism" has gained currency in recent years to describe the rightist upsurge. Although the term has been used in different ways, it often expresses the idea that neoliberal and fascist agendas have converged in one ideology, and that capitalists and far rightists are all pulling in the same direction. As Henry Giroux puts it, "neoliberalism and fascism conjoin and advance in a comfortable and mutually compatible movement that connects the worst excesses of capitalism with authoritarian 'strongman' ideals."[70]

The reality is much more conflicted. Far rightists have certainly supported some neoliberal policies. For example, neo-Nazis and other white nationalists have endorsed the rollback of social programs identified with people of color, Christian theocrats have often applauded the privatization of public services, and Patriot activists have called for dismantling environmental regulations and have embraced the ethos of individual property rights as a cornerstone of freedom. But far-right politics has also developed largely in reaction against neoliberalism. Non-European immigration and multinational free trade agreements are cornerstones of the neoliberal system and prime targets of far-right rage. Far rightists have also denounced the US economy's trend toward runaway financial speculation (an organic consequence of the deregulatory policies of the past three decades), persistent military interventionism overseas, and even—when it targets white people—militarization of the police.[71]

In broader terms, the far right's rise is rooted in capitalism's ongoing process of revolutionizing economic, social, and political relations. Historically, capitalism reinforced or created many boundaries, divisions, and social hierarchies to help enforce order and extract labor from subordinate groups. But in recent decades, many of these old social structures have been reconfigured or replaced through large-scale economic changes—such as industry moving to the Global South and millions of emigrant workers moving from the Global South into the US. Far-right politics expresses, in concentrated form, the fear and anger of groups whose historical privileges have eroded or seem to be under threat. Far rightists don't typically call the capitalist system into question, but they offer alternative visions for who should be in charge of class society and how it should be organized.[72]

US far rightists have little chance, at least in the short term, of seizing power and bringing about the kind of society they envision. But their impact extends far beyond that. Far rightists carry out harassment and physical attacks against targeted groups, and they encourage other people to do the same. They also influence other political forces across the political spectrum, from shaming conservatives for being "soft" on immigration to repackaging antisemitic conspiracy theories to reach a leftist audience. From Duke to Spencer, far rightists have repeatedly created more space for system-loyal forces to intensify their own bigotry, scapegoating, and violence, both by offering an example for system-loyal groups to learn from and by providing an "extreme" example that helps more "moderate" versions look legitimate by comparison. This dynamic alone didn't lead us into the nightmare of a Trump presidency, but it played an important supporting role.

Far rightists' conflict with the established order raises other dangers. Some far rightists aim to "take the game away from the left," as Metzger urged neo-Nazis to do in the 1980s—to supplant liberatory politics as the only real oppositional force, the go-to place for people to channel their rebellious hatred of the elite. At the same time, far-right "extremism" can provide a scapegoat that helps legitimize the status quo and justify the growth of state repression. Prosecuting neo-Nazis for seditious conspiracy or exploiting the Oklahoma City bombing to weaken habeas corpus are examples of this, but the dynamic is much older. In 1940, fear of Nazism contributed to passage of the Smith Act, which made it a crime to advocate the violent overthrow of the US government, and the Communist Party cheered when the law was used to prosecute fascist sympathizers during World War II. A few years later, scores of Communists were sent to prison under the same law.[73]

These dynamics make no sense unless we recognize that differences between rightist currents matter, that capitalists may choose liberal antifascist strategies as well as right-wing authoritarian ones, and that—as three way fight antifascists have argued for two decades—the enemy of our enemy is not necessarily our friend.

Building Communities for a Fascist-Free Future

Shane Burley

{*A version of this piece was previously published by* ROAR.[1] *Aside from some minor changes, it's a reprint and all quotes are from interviews with the author.*}

On August 17th, 2019, a coalition of antifascist and progressive groups in Portland, Oregon organized a rally to protest a Proud Boy event planned in the city.[2] The rally had a carnivalesque atmosphere created by Pop Mob—an antifascist group of Portlanders that seeks to "resist the alt-right with whimsy and creativity"[3]—and brought on a diverse range of organizations, from labor and religious groups and civil rights groups such as the National Association for the Advancement of Colored People to more militant organizations such as Rose City Antifa.

During the protest, the latter, along with autonomous black bloc organizers, acted as a buffer between the crowds at the carnival and the hundreds of Proud Boys amassing at the other side of the waterfront park both groups were occupying. This created a collaborative environment in which militant antifascists joined forces with a coalition of civic groups and successfully worked in concert to confront a common enemy; the crowds were safer because of the militants, and the militants had a sharper edge because of the hundreds of people standing at their backs. This type of coalition means that each group can bring their own unique strategy, tactics, and identity, and can find that, by maintaining their own distinct piece of the larger whole, the entire project becomes stronger.

Over the past several years of far-right confrontations, we have seen coalitions and collaborations—and at times also an overlap in membership—between a wide range of left-wing and community groups—including progressive religious groups, BLM organizations, migrant support groups, and traditional radical left groups—and more militant antifascist groups, and they have been able to turn out large numbers of people by working together. The public itself has grown accustomed to taking action in the streets from their participation in mass movements such as BLM, Occupy Wall Street, and even more liberal and conflicted events, such as the 2017 Women's March. This means that antifascist groups have a trained base for organizing in the communities they are a part of, a base that can adapt more quickly to coordinated actions such as rapidly assembled demonstrations to counter far-right mobilizations.

Antifascism draws its tactics from what works to stop the opposition. In doing so, there is a special relationship between antifascist organizations and their allies in society. A member of a militant antifascist organization often has a certain role in a confrontation: they plan the event, take on extra risk, and communicate with a mass of supporters. But the supporters are equally important because, without mass participation, it is hard to force a fascist rally from its intended space. This is the model that has worked in cities around the US and elsewhere around the world.

We are now hitting a period when antifascism has to remain ever present, not just to force back the encroaching far right, but to protect left-wing social movements, which are in a constant threat of state violence, redirection, and infiltration. Although there are peaks and declines in white nationalism and other far-right movements, the basic conditions have changed: the center has dropped out and the fringes are defining the added spectrum to global politics. Within this, the edges of fascist politics will increasingly be a piece of how many people manage the accelerating crises we are living through, and that brings in the pressing concern of violence with it. Fascist violence is not just incidental, it is a primary feature of these radical political ideas, which is a straight line to violence inside these moments and an ancillary feature of their influence on social consciousness. This puts the left under constant threat, particularly when organizing publicly in any way that challenges structural forces of inequality, which means the protected element is not only ideal, but required simply to function and reproduce itself. So the real questions are how to create a permanent bond between antifascism and the rest of the left, and how to integrate antifascist ideas into every type of social and civic organization that we use to build up the complicated network that makes up our communities.

Identifying the next steps requires a critical look at what was won and lost over recent years and hearing from those on the ground about what needs to change to eliminate fascism as a potential outcome to our current uncertainty.

Antifascism Must Keep Pace

Some conventional left thinking in the US blames the rise of the far right on Donald Trump, but this misses both the international context and how social movements work. There has been a return to nationalism and populism on the world stage—the rise of the far right cannot be relegated to the foot soldiers of just one strongman or political party. The far right in the US is not controlled by a single organization. Instead, at most of the countless far-right rallies that were organized in the run-up to the 2020 presidential elections, it was actually unaligned individuals who made up the majority of the crowds.

When Trump failed to get re-elected, there was no reason to believe that this trend would be reversed and, in fact, it may only be getting more severe.[4] A dependable framework exists with far-right movements: after a period of growth, their decline can be even more deadly.[5] Recent years have seen several mass radicalization events for the American right as conspiracy theories unseated consensus reality, from "rigged" elections to "demonic" vaccines.[6] Among the US far right, conspiracism is a central motivator, a break with reality that redirects working-class angst away from its proper targets—the rich—and back onto marginalized peoples, whether they are immigrants, Jews, or other racialized minorities.

There is no reason to believe we have seen the last of the far right: their violence is the new plateau and the crisis that birthed them continues. The consequences of the COVID-19 pandemic are continuing as new variants spread around the world. Economic instability is only fragmenting further, and the accelerating disaster of climate collapse is manifest as droughts are met by hurricanes are met by forest fires. The conditions for the far right to grow and flourish are there, with or without Trump. Therefore, antifascists must keep pace, stay vigilant, and act as the immune system for a new generation of social movements trying to fight back against a failing system.

An Idea, a Critique, and an Approach

Antifascism is unlike other social movements because, although radical in orientation, it only goes after the extraordinary. We can define antifascism as any organized action to resist the far right that does not rely on legal or state interventions, and instead uses community-based strategies—ranging from black bloc tactics to confront white nationalist marches all the way to street carnivals to disrupt far-right student groups on campus and music festivals to stop a venue from hosting a fascist speaker. The ultimate goal is to break the chain of the far right's functioning, and the tactics that support that strategy vary depending on the context.

"Antifascism needs to move in a base-building direction, prepared to build community-based dual power institutions as the settler-colonial capitalist state becomes increasingly incapable of meeting human needs or responding to cascading environmental crises," says Michael Novick—an organizer who has spent decades in social movements, from the Weather Underground Organization to the John Brown Anti-Klan Committee (JBAKC) and Anti-Racist Action. "We must build working and oppressed/colonized peoples' capacity to survive and overcome, so as to allay the fears that fascists seek to exploit to build their base and seek power."

Antifascism is, as the name assumes, a repudiation of fascism, but it also cannot be reduced to that. Antifascism is an idea, a critique, and an approach to conflicting issues all its own: it exists beyond just a response to a perfectly defined fascism. Instead, it actively confronts a variety of far-right movements that, themselves, move in and out of an ideologically consistent fascism. Some movements, such as the so-called alt-right, are taken on because their white nationalism is clearly articulated and therefore threatening. At the same time, antifascists take on the Proud Boys, not because they speak with a unified voice about their fascist ideals—when cornered, most of them reproduce unremarkable Republican talking points—but because their violence makes them an obvious target for antifascist community self-defense.

David Renton, an established antifascist historian with decades of experience as an organizer in the UK, admits that the lines are not always fully defined in terms of naming anything as fascist.[7] The "fascist" you are confronting in the streets "might be far right and moving toward fascism, or far right and moving away from fascism, and there are some quite gray topics and situations," he explains.

This current period of American far-right revival has been particularly extreme, and lasting. Despite losing their proxy totem in a Trump presidency, there is little reason to think that the shift toward far-right ideas and social movements will decline anytime soon. Fascist movements hijack the angst of privileged sectors of the working class and turn that fear into a rage directed at marginalized communities rather than those in power. The fuel for the growth of fascism, such as inequality and alienation, is structural—and is not going away soon.

Whereas the embedded white supremacy of empire and colonialism is painfully ordinary, fascism should be understood as extraordinary: they have common foundations but the tactics to confront them are sometimes different. How a community confronts police violence is not necessarily the way it would deal with the threat of white supremacist groups—unless their membership overlaps.[8] This means that collaboration between social movements is the marker of success in opposing fascism in all its manifestations, one that allows each organization or project to maintain its strategic focus on the immediate issues (e.g., the growth of the far right) while helping one another as part of the larger goals (e.g., dismantling racial capitalism).

Anyone Can Be an Antifascist

Antifascists have a lot to overcome. The right has always needed an effective enemy to rally against, usually beyond reason, logic, and reality. Immigrants, communists, Muslims, and, now, antifa have been effective measures of fear to goad their supporters into allegiance, or even violence. The image created of antifa in the US right-wing media, such as Fox News or Breitbart News Network, is largely of those media's own manufacture,[9] but it has created a significant barrier within some parts of the public, particularly blue collar, rust belt, and rural communities.

During the panicked responses to some of the crises of 2020, conspiracy theories drove violent responses from rural communities across the country as people thought antifa activists were responsible for everything from spreading COVID-19 to starting forest fires. In the rural counties around Oregon, where the fires ravaged as much as 12% of the area, militia groups set up "checkpoints" to stop what they believed were antifascists setting the fires. This potentially delayed rescue workers and people getting out of harm's way.[10]

This is the kind of delusion that has consequences for everyone in that it both neutralizes mutual aid efforts and transposes the frenzied fear that the fires inspired onto the public image of antifascism, which then loses even more potential support. Moreover, these are the same working-class communities that are prone in times of crisis to serious manipulation when they are not offered an alternative from the left.

"There's certainly a robust media ecosystem in place to work against us when trying to achieve those goals—sensationalizing events and editing footage to craft a narrative that doesn't match reality," explains an organizer with Rose City Antifa who asked to remain anonymous. "I think some of the ways we address this as a group is to be extremely detailed in our documentation, and as accurate as possible, as well as being as accessible as possible with those things."

That means there must be a process of recapture: taking back the paper image of antifascism and replacing it with nuanced reality. To do this, we have to be clear about what fascism is, and who is and is not a fascist or a threat to progressive politics and movements, while maintaining a high standard of accuracy and clarity in countering the far right. That dependability is essential to maintaining the argument that antifascist actions are warranted, that the opponents are, in fact, a threat to the community, and that antifascism is a key part of keeping our communities safe.[11]

Part of the reason why many working-class communities are alienated from the left is skepticism about the left's ability to make real changes in these communities. This is especially true when it comes to the supposed benefits or effectiveness of participating in mass actions, such as protests and street rallies.

There is a difference between the kind of agency that radical politics implies and the distanced hopefulness of electoralism. With the lack of civic organizations in most communities, few people are convinced of the idea that their participation in a project of social change can actually matter in a direct way. So, the goals and purposes of mass actions as well as their efficacy must be publicly communicated.

"We need to educate people, we need as shared a definition and conceptualization of what fascism is as possible, and we need to expand the cultural space for what antifascism is," says Kat Endgame of Pop Mob, which helped popularize the "everyday antifascist" concept as a way of telling people that anyone could be an active antifascist in their own unique way. This was meant to drop the barriers people might have felt to participating by thinking that only the most militant of confrontations was useful. "[We must] serve people. Have a functional purpose and try to achieve it as beautifully as possible. If the messages you are putting out into the world aren't resonating, it's not because the audience is somehow broken, rather that the message itself is unclear or not useful to the audience," she says.

One of the challenges in communicating the goals and purposes of radical movements to the public is that internally tactics are often confused with ideology and intensity with strategy. This can create a singular vision focused on only one way of organizing. The work that Portland's Pop Mob and others are doing in promoting a different image of antifascism is important for this reason, but also because we have to remain internally critical when some tactics are not carrying as much weight as they once did.

Consider, for example, the tactic of the black bloc. Abner Häuge, who runs the antifascist media project Left Coast Right Watch, is skeptical about the usefulness of the tactic when confronting fascists in public.[12] "I've seen a purity politics and fetishization of the tactic that I don't think is useful in the long run," Häuge explains. "I think people have to acknowledge that surveillance technology has surpassed what bloc tactics were initially useful for and other tactics are needed to augment them. Instead, what I'm seeing is people in bloc leaning into them more and focusing as much on policing the very few kinds of surveillance they can police (i.e., reporters and people openly livestreaming) and less on actually using their numbers and bodies to combat fascists in the street."

Whereas a number of antifascist groups allow some type of media access, seeing it as a way to spread the message, other autonomous organizers see media, even including left media, as putting them at legal risk when carrying out antifascist actions—a point that has proven true multiple times.[13] But this blanket prohibition on media ends up creating singular public perceptions, often controlled by the right's media figures who do not have the same restrictions. The question here is less whether the media puts the black bloc at risk, but whether tactics that necessitate an absence of observation are always the correct choice.

"I think, in order to win, antifascism needs to permeate daily life. Look at how well fascists and other right-wing conspiracy theorists have disrupted and inserted themselves into daily life by prolonging the [COVID-19] pandemic," says Häuge, referring to the politicization of public health measures such as mask and vaccine mandates. "I think antifascism needs sophisticated counters to not just the right-wing disinformation but the liberal passivity and needs to focus on platforming itself as much [as] or more than deplatforming fascists."

That liberal passivity—the idea that passive progressive politics could effectively improve the world through electoralism—was culled somewhat in the Trump years because he was seen by many center-leftists as "exceptional." But rather than simply writing liberals off, it is useful to help create a space in which they can be a part of larger movements that help radicalize them further on these underlying issues. That brings the other strategic elements together: public education, a variety of events, and the inclusion of a range of different groups so that the distance between the radical left and the center-left can be bridged. This should not be seen as allowing liberal objections to erode radical strategies, but as finding a way of reaching out to wider swathes of the population to move them along into organizing under the notion that our strength is in our numbers.

Building an Infrastructure of Care

In practice, antifascism is about opposition, but its success depends on much more than singular responses to fascism. Instead, an antifascist project that is part of a larger vision does so in collaboration with every piece of social life entangled in struggle: the legacies of colonialism, housing and workplace justice, the struggle against police violence, and the way fascism distorts our impulsive desires for liberation.

Fascism is a false solution to a real problem, the idea that you can build interconnection by reifying racial, gender, or other kinds of privilege into a hardened force of violent exclusion. According to Novick, antifascist organizing should be based on what we are *for*, not what we *oppose*: "Antifascism must see itself and function as a component of an overarching proliberation, prosolidarity movement for revolutionary social, political, and economic transformation—a proactive, rather than reactive, and affirmative, rather than negative, movement."

This also means getting to the core of why many people do not participate in antifascist actions: because they simply do not have capacity for it. To enable the masses to participate in antagonistic forms of organizing, they have to be able to meet basic needs, not just barely survive. Mutual aid plays a key role in this; it is what makes it possible for us to survive accelerating crises while simultaneously planting the seeds of a new kind of social relationship that antifascist groups can rely on to support activists.

Over the course of the months-long protests against police violence and the far right in Portland in 2020, mutual aid groups, many of which formed to provide needed support for the COVID-19 pandemic, became active in the struggle. Skilled street medics cared for the injured, others brought food and water, gave rides, bailed people out of jail, or any of a number of other activities that allowed the mass actions to function and to continue for as long as they did.

Engaging in mutual aid reminds us of what it feels like to extend protection and care, suggests Kelly Hayes, an abolitionist organizer in Chicago: "Mutual aid offers us an opportunity to reconnect at the most basic human level with our potential costrugglers in a fight against fascism. Community care creates new bonds of solidarity and reminds us that we must care for and protect each other."

"That is how we fight the normalization of mass death, by defying individualism and crossing the ideological fissures between us to extend care and build things together," Hayes adds. "We cannot win without caring for one another, and they cannot win without stripping away our empathy and will to protect and care for one another."

A structure of permanent care is critical for all types of organizing because it is what is necessary to allow communities and societies to flourish in general. You cannot expect someone who is working three jobs to pay for basic necessities to spend their time attending multiple consensus-driven meetings—let alone commit to the type of personal investments a lot of radical projects require. Even at the most individualized level, mutual aid work is necessary to build up the infrastructure for mass actions: providing protest-related medical care, food and water, rides if necessary, court support, and everything else. But it also adds another element: that of a fundamental alternative to the failing supply chain of resources we depend on, which is built on extractive industries, hyperexploitative workplaces, and unsustainable production and shipping methods. Instead, mutual aid is an infrastructure of caring, and so depending on it has the dual purpose of survival in the current moment and rethinking society in the long term.

"It's possible to do really good community organizing and create a scene in which the fascists are challenged, and to be prepared to be able to go head-to-head with them," says Jon Marley, a long-time organizer who worked with the JBAKC in the 1980s on projects that bridged the surrounding communities and their fight against the far right. "I'm not just talking about physically, but politically as well. Both on a larger public consciousness level, but also on a local neighborhood level . . . to create a community that takes care of each other," Marley continues. For Marley, this meant doing solidarity work with political prisoners, such as incarcerated Black liberation revolutionary Geronimo Pratt, as well as events that connected with the larger community, such as the Run Against Racism marathons that helped raise the profile of antiracist campaigns while engaging the community in a fun athletic event.

This requires coalition building to be intentional and to have a reciprocal relationship between groups whose prime function is antifascist community defense and other groups that support those aims yet are primarily active in other terrains. "It also requires reaching out to and developing relationships with organizations and groups that might not list antifascist organizing in their objectives—faith groups, labor groups, et cetera," says the organizer from Rose City Antifa. The organizer continues, "It's also important to be as welcoming as possible to people when holding events."

In Portland, part of Pop Mob's innovation was creating a community space that had value not just as a defensive measure against the far right, but as a community-building mechanism itself. Pop Mob organized a local carnival event through a mix of speakers, costumes, and music, something inspired by the Anti-Nazi League events to counter the National Front in Britain in the 1970s. The event brought people together in a joyous spirit, which in turn helped build more solid bonds among the community to make antifascism stronger in the future. This essentially means creating lower barriers to participation and allowing for different types of involvement.

Other possible ways to achieve this is through the organization of music and film festivals, educational talks, and food drives that are focused on "base building"—building a presence in communities that might otherwise be infiltrated by the right. "It's a slower kind of activism but no less important," adds Renton.

This approach is critical to creating long-term capacity because, without having a broader appeal and the ability to communicate on a mass scale, antifascist organizations cannot reach the level of popular participation to actually be effective when the time comes.

Darlye Lamont Jenkins of the One People's Project agrees: "We've got to start producing things that are beneficial to the community besides just the bulwark against [the far right]. . . . [W]e have to be able to do more community-based events like food drives and things like that. We got to be a part of the communities that we care about and that we are fighting in."

This ties in with mutual aid, as none of these projects—from organizing cultural events to building coalitions across different groups—operate in isolation and they rely on one another to build the bigger movement in the struggle for our collective liberation. Antifascism, in both its militant and "everyday" forms, is a single part of this struggle, one among many. When each of those parts begins to work in concert, you have the beginnings of a foundation for a totally new society, one that offers benefits—resources, defense infrastructure, collective pressure, and more—and a starting point for a revolutionary shift.

This is crucial if we want our communities to be able to confront the growing inequalities of the pandemic and to make these intersectional struggles, including antifascism, relevant to their lived experiences. Without that, it will be merely ideological posturing without weight or consequence.

Building a World Where Fascism is a Thing of the Past

Just as the right has been radicalized over the past decade, so has everyone else. The mass actions of 2020 in particular normalized protest activity, including militant demonstrations and occupations, for a huge mass of

Millennials and Gen-Zers, meaning that the surrounding community of activist supporters is more capable, adaptable, and accessible than before.

"The main thing the movement needs is a sense of unity and a commitment to mass organizing," says a member of Corvallis Antifa in Oregon, who asked to remain anonymous. "Many [antifascist groups] are forsaking mass mobilization and building holistic networks of community defense in favor of small-scale militant actions. Our enemies are coalescing and creating broad coalitions. We need to do the same with groups from across the left."

The antidote to fascism in all its manifestations is community building, centering a wide range of voices and viewing that plurality as a strength. This can—and should—bring in entire organizational federations and fields themselves, including emerging left powerhouses such as the Democratic Socialists of America or established radical strongholds such as the Industrial Workers of the World. But it should not be limited to them, and instead antifascists have to reach beyond the pool of radical leftists for new recruits to the struggle while using the left flank of supporting organizations to help radicalize the mass of new participants. The far right is mutating and changing, so centering only a specific set of tactics undermines the effectiveness of our collective struggle. This brings antifascism back into the larger field of transformative politics, one that looks beyond community defense at the socioeconomic conditions that birth fascism in the first place. This means that antifascism must expand, fill up cultural and political spaces, and become a common-sense approach to problems that will continue to be a threat as long as the shaky foundations of our society continue to crumble. The challenge for antifascist groups and organizers is to grow to a capacity that is capable of acting as a constant buffer for marginalized communities and the organized left fighting for a new world. Without it, there is no visible pathway to success, but only endless potential miseries.

"[Fascism] now is not the same as it was in the Nineties, but a lot of antifascists are still behaving as if it is. Lots of people are looking for boneheads to have street fights with, but a large part of the far right have moved on from that," says Jean-Pierre, a Belgian antifascist who is also a part of the Antifa International collective and the Leuven Anarchistische Groep. "[We] should try to make antifascism cool again, make it appeal to broader groups, start antifascist sports groups, subcultures," Jean-Pierre continues. Their experience comes from outside of the US, but the reality they describe is applicable here as much as there: mass organizing depends on building relationships, not just relying on a professionalized radical core.

The past should play an informative role in strategy, but not hinder it. The proof of tactics is in their effect and not in the ability of activists to re-live earlier victories. By getting the entire community involved, there are new possibilities, not only for how to defend against the onslaught, but also for how to build the kind of bonds necessary for the type of world where fascism is a thing of the past.

"We Can Do More Together": How Fighting Sports Build Confidence in European Antifascist Networks

Hilary A. Moore

"What's happening?" I asked. Worry twisted my stomach. This was my first Mixed Martial Arts (MMA) tournament. Fists raised in front of us. Fists raised behind us. My friend's face said *something* was off.

Moments before, we'd made jokes. The nerdy kind. The kind two radicals donning a new passion for fighting sports would find funny. *Over/ under that guy's a fascist?* Short fade, strong part, stone face. A projection, surely. An ethically questionable caricature. We let it go. *But, that guy? Definitely!* *"I'll give you 100 euros."* The jumbo screen boomed. Following a full card, finally, the title fight.

Fighter one entered the cage. *You have to be kidding me.* Our momentary self second-guessing dissolved. He fit the description as though he'd stepped off the page. His intensity was palpable, his gaze trained on some indistinct point.

Fighter two entered, running circles around the cage, waving to the crowd like a child. Goofy, happy even. We shoveled cold fries into our mouths and noted Goofy's shorts. Red on one leg, black on the other—the proverbial team colors. Antifascist? Coincidence? We laughed. It was starting to feel like *Karate Kid* or *Rocky*, "good versus soulless evil" carved out in stark contrast. First and foremost a business, these tournaments had recently forbidden displays of radical politics. So we laughed, leaning into the cartoonishness.

Our laughter quickly turned untenable. Stone Face split Goofy's eyebrow open. Blood splattered the floor. The referees paused for clean-up. Then, a relative silence broke before chants of, *"Ost, Ost, OstDeutschland!"* filled the space.[1] Their force grew with repetition. I looked to my friend, Vincent, of Afro-German descent, scanning his face for some read on what was unfolding. It told me all I needed to know. Two words, sequenced with a particular rhythm; a sometimes-ambiguous declaration of regional pride. But not when blasted from the throats of neo-Nazis. Those joining

54

the chant in our immediate proximity were steadily outnumbering those who hadn't. "Let's go," Vincent said, "*Now*."

We left our fries, squeezing past the chanters' knees. Stair after stair, we climbed out of the arena, pausing just before the exit. I turned to look back at the scene below, to find Vincent tapping feverishly into his phone as he summited behind me, backlit by the bright lights over the cage, white stage smoke billowing in the glare. In it, the show carried on. Fists pumped. The screen counted two minutes down. By the final seconds, Vincent had found Stone Face's name and picture in an antifascist report on neo-Nazi activity in Dresden. The clock ran out. The fascist fighter won.

That night rattled me. How did it happen? What were the implications? Clearly, somewhere in my periphery, far-right networks had found footing in fighting sports. A footing with material consequences. One that would likely cast new light on the very movements I'd already done so much work documenting.[2] Shaking off the emotional hangover, I began putting out feelers within my own networks in Berlin's Brazilian Jiu-Jitsu scene, chasing down threads that would trace from Germany to Poland, to Russia and Ukraine, to Greece and Italy—and back. Somewhat unexpectedly, I found *promise*, not just peril.

All signs of the far right's grip in European fighting sports point back to the name White Rex, a Russian neo-Nazi clothing brand and a major trendsetter. Starting in 2008, White Rex popularized their brand with unabashed references to Nazism by organizing far-right fighting tournaments. First in Russia, then in Kiev, Ukraine, and later in Rome, Italy, where the clothing company partnered with Italy's fascist movement, CasaPound. Tournaments drew hundreds and later thousands of white supremacists and white nationalists. Fighters united from across Europe through a volatile cocktail of lifestyle sport and contempt for refugees. Stylized social media campaigns lent an edge and legitimacy, attracting greater numbers of young people to martial arts—specifically through White Rex.

Proliferation led to affiliates and other far-right tournaments in Germany (Kampf der Nibelungen), Greece (ProPatria Fest), Poland (First to Fight), and Italy (Tana delle Tigri).[3] But European borders do little to contain White Rex's reach. In fact, the Rise Above Movement (RAM), a Southern California–based white nationalist fighting organization, joined the mix. RAM came under extensive investigation after posting beatings online and their wide swath of white nationalist ties were outed. So much so that ProPublica then tracked RAM's tour through Central and Eastern Europe. There, RAM members competed in prominent far-right fighting tournaments and met with White Rex founder, Dennis Nikitin.[4] Just a few months after Europe, these same combat-ready RAM members traveled to Charlottesville, Virginia. Their bloody participation in the deadly "Unite the Right" rally would become known internationally. Three RAM members would later plead guilty to "conspiracy to riot."[5]

White Rex was born during a time that local antifascists in Moscow, Russia colloquially refer to as the "street wars against Nazis." These battles hit a head in 2008, when a prominent antifascist activist named Fedor Filatov was murdered, and his death rocked the antifascist community. For a while, the loss stifled the movement's ability to respond to fascists, as Moscow's neo-Nazi scene doubled down in MMA. "An antifascist tournament was just a matter of time," according to "D," one the organizers of Don't Give Up, Russia's first antifascist fighting tournament. Don't Give Up was one part memorial. "We gathered our friends from different cities and countries to honor his memory together." And one part was preparation. "Since we confront very aggressive groups, the ability to defend yourself is very important," said D. Keeping people safe is a collective effort in Moscow.

At first, Don't Give Up was a small tournament. This was in part due to the learning curve of event planning. Mostly, though, it was down to immense pressure—political repression from state authorities, harassment and sometimes torture from police, and a prevalence of combat-ready neo-Nazis. Because participants in Don't Give Up were mainly activists of the antifascist movement involved in direct action on the streets, security was a major issue. It was a success if they could simply pull it off.

Don't Give Up struck a chord. What began as an event between a few friends turned into a networking apparatus for antifascist activists across countries. Soon, tournaments were organized in other post-Soviet cities where neo-Nazi attacks were on the rise, such as Kiev and Minsk, Belarus. At its peak, tournaments were organized simultaneously in cities across Eastern Europe. Winners then gathered to compete in a final tournament.

It didn't take long for other antifascist networks in Central and Eastern Europe to catch on. "If they can do it in Russia, then for sure we can do it in Poland," said Kamil, a coach and professional fighter at Freedom Fighters Gym, a self-organized training facility and martial arts league in Poznań, Poland. This seemed like a viable option given Poland's own recent experience with increasing infiltration in MMA, evidenced by a robust structure of far-right tournaments, sponsors, clubs, and organizations throughout the country. Groups such as Blood and Honor, National Rebirth of Poland, and All-Polish Youth, among others, are all active in mainstream MMA circles.[6]

Inspired by antifascist organizing in Moscow, Freedom Fighters Gym took a decidedly different approach—they chose to be highly visible. Posters are mounted throughout the city. The weekly class schedule and address are available on Facebook. Yoga and kettlebell training are held on Mondays, Thursdays, and Fridays. Crossfit and Muay Thai are held three times a week, with additional classes for beginners. And everything is free. This free membership comes with an invitation to become part of the community. Kamil described the reasoning behind this: "We are not a professional gym oriented toward fighting. If someone wants to fight, of course they can. We have our own league," he said. But, for Freedom Fighters Gym, fighting is not primary. "The most important thing," he emphasized, "is just to have a good time, to care about yourself, to be part of the project here. We encourage people. I believe then they also get closer to our ideas and the struggles we are in." The gym is nestled within Poland's oldest squat, Rozbrat, located in the heart of Poznań.

Rozbrat puts significant effort into reaching sectors of everyday life in Poznań. Organizing in a tenants' rights association and an anarchist workers' union, they reach new people via theater companies, factories, schools, and even hospitals. When coronavirus disease 2019 (COVID-19) hit, for example, Freedom Fighters Gym replaced punching bags with sewing machines. "We started an initiative with other groups to sew masks since hospitals did not have basic equipment," Kamil explained. Their masks reached health care workers, hospice workers, and people without homes when the Polish government was still busy denying the effects of the virus, a tactic Kamil says was lifted from the Donald Trump administration.

The vision driving this massive community effort is simple: self-organization. "We want to show how self-organization works. It builds community and it can be an answer to many of the problems we have now in society," Kamil said. Members at Freedom Fighters Gym often train at other gyms, taking this ethic with them. "We won't meet people in our city just staying at the squat," said Kamil. He added, "It also helps us to see if something dangerous is emerging in the sports scene." This is hardly an abstract preoccupation. In 2016, Poland's biggest far-right fighting tournament called First to Fight organized its second event in Poznań, bringing hundreds of right-wing fighters to the city.[7]

Among the problems Kamil referred to is the country's radical right-wing populist party, Law and Justice (PiS [Prawo i Sprawiedliwość]). With an absolute governing majority since 2015, PiS has rapidly shifted the political terrain further right while adopting the rhetoric of fascist groups.[8] Defense is their leading argument—defense of the nation from western Brussels, defense of Polish culture from impending migration, and defense of Catholic family values. These ideas, Kamil said, among others, make political life in Poland a "really a good field for right wing tendencies to flourish."

Most recently, the same scapegoat logic that got PiS into office was repurposed and redeployed from its well-worn xenophobic terrain, taking aim at the lesbian-gay-bisexual-transgender-queer-intersex-plus (LGBTQI+) community.[9] In May 2019, a documentary about child abuse in the Catholic church threatened the sanctity of the institution.[10] Tight alliances with the majority of Polish bishops saw the PiS lash out, shifting blame from the church hierarchy to an imagined LGBTQI+ influence.[11] Jaroslaw Kaczynski, leader and cofounder of PiS, spoke about "LGBT-ideology" in the party's 2019 re-election campaign: "We need to fight this. We need to defend the Polish family. We need to defend it furiously because it's a threat to civilization, not just for Poland but for the entire Europe, for the entire civilization that is based on Christianity."[12]

This sentiment spread like wildfire. It led nearly one hundred municipalities to adopt "LGBT-free zone" resolutions in which local commissions pledged to deny support for LGBTQI+-related events.[13] Funding for six of those towns was then blocked by the European Commission for rights abuses.[14] As tensions escalate, so has the rise in right-wing protests of equality marches, attended by some of the far-right combat-ready activists. Well-known fighter and would-be politician Marcin "Różal" Różalski, a six-time amateur Polish champion and European runner-up in kickboxing, joined the far-right ultranationalist youth club All-Polish Youth to protest the local equality march in the central city of Płock.[15] Journalists and "hate-watch" groups documented the rise of harassment in cities across the country: from throwing rocks and glass bottles, to lighting off fireworks, to passing out anonymous pamphlets on the "LGBT disease" and burning rainbow flags at Pride marches, to outright physical attacks.[16]

"In Poland, if you do something to support the LGBTQI+ community, this is already political," explained Lukas, a nonviolence educator and coach at RKS Gwiazda Gym (Moving Sport Club–Star) in Warsaw. "Our gym is for nonnormative people," she said, "but of course anyone can come as long as they respect our rules and the space." RKS Gwiazda Gym is located in Warsaw, arguably the most LGBTQI+ friendly of cities in the country. But Lukas admitted that, because the gym began around the same time that PiS came into absolute power, he was worried the club might be forced to shut down.

Run as a collective, RKS Gwiazda Gym is the only gym in Warsaw holding martial arts and self-defense classes for the rainbow community. People can join seasonal camps and movie screenings, as well as organize events such as fundraisers for people attacked at Pride parades; again, all free of charge. Costs stay low because that's a priority for members—and members make the decisions. This also means rotating training responsibilities and raising funds for equipment internally. "The most important thing is that people feel safe together," Lukas insisted. "You can be whoever you want to be and train however you want to train. That is the most precious thing in these trainings—that people don't have to pretend to be something they are not. So, payment is not so important."

The project started as a response to the problems often found in traditional gyms. "Many clubs are super normative about what a 'real' man means," Lukas argued. "Even if they don't say it, the culture of the gym says, 'Hey, this club is for real men.' They don't problematize it." He then talked about the obsession with being a "real man," and how a "self-made" man is central to most far-right ideology. She connected this to the onslaught of homophobic violence, "LGBT-free zone" legislation, struggles over restroom access, and the volatility of doctor's visits. Most gyms, he argued, are a mere continuation of traditional gender roles and toxic masculinity. "I've offered antidiscrimination workshops, so gyms can learn how to make the space more welcoming. But they don't do it. That would admit they have a problem." This kind of reluctance in mainstream gyms to directly address social issues is common. When pushed, some argue that fighting sports ought to be politically neutral. However, neutrality is increasingly difficult to maintain, given the stranglehold of far-right infiltration in Poland and across Europe.[17]

In contrast, self-confidence is the endgame of RKS Gwiazda Gym. "This is not a fighting gym. Self-defense *classes* don't actually keep you safe in a fight," Lukas explained, referring to the high level of long-term training needed to effectively fight back in the streets. So why do RKS Gwiazda Gym members train self-defense, even though none of them are street fighters? "It is a feeling," Lukas described, "It helps people shape their body in a different way. It can give people the self-confidence to react, even just to say 'no,' or to be assertive, or to run away." This matters a great deal in Poland. According to Lukas, "It is very important to feel strong in your body, even if you cannot say who you really are, but you can feel proud of it." Embodied self-confidence, and access to the kind of space to practice it, is its own kind of fight.

Fighting against outdated gender systems is a familiar cause for feminist martial arts gyms. Sidekick is one such example, based in Leipzig,

Germany. Born in 2016, Sidekick began rather small. But in short order, more people came to classes than their initial space could hold. Their draw is that they're the only gym in Leipzig specifically organized by and for people who identify as female, lesbian, intersex, nonbinary, or trans (FLINT). They offer beginner, intermediate, and advanced Muay Thai training, as well as strength and conditioning and yoga classes.

Sidekick is part of FLINT gym network, hosting training camps, offering advice about how to run feminist collective gyms, and providing connections throughout Germany, France, Austria, and Switzerland. "It's important to have another side [to] the sport," explained Imke, a founder and trainer at Sidekick. She stressed the importance of FLINT self-defense martial arts classes that are explicitly antiracist. Fred, a trainer at Roter Stern Jena (Red Star), a feminist martial arts gym in Jena, Germany, talked about the spike in popularity of women's self-defense classes in 2015, when more than a million people seeking asylum and refuge entered the European Union. "It was because of a racist idea," she said. Self-defense became code for defending white women from "strange male persons"—culturally understood as foreign or Black men—in Germany.

The racist origins of women's self-defense training is not particular to Germany. In fact, the US women's self-defense movement grew largely out of "racialized and gendered concerns about the future of the Anglo race and indeed the future of the nation," wrote Wendy L. Rouse, author of *Her Own Hero: The Origins of the Women's Self-defense Movement*. She described how middle- and owning-class white women were simultaneously combatting "feminine fragility" while reinforcing racist sentiments of "yellow peril," or anti-Japanese beliefs that put over 100,000 people with Japanese backgrounds into internment camps on the West Coast during World War II.

Back in Germany, the result was a doubling of gun sales, ammunition, and irritant gas in response to changing migration patterns in 2015. The far-right group Alternative for Germany (AfD) and the anti-Islam movement Patriotic Europeans Against the Islamicisation of the Occident (PEGIDA [Patriotische Europäer gegen die Islamisierung des Abendlandes]) posted rumors of increased rates of rape, assault, theft, and break-ins, blaming refugees on social media.[18] Even though women in Germany experience higher rates of sexual violence from their spouses or partners, rumors vilifying refugees had a social purchase.[19] The result was an increased number of German citizens arming themselves. Attendance at self-defense courses in major cities doubled and "the right-wing populists ha[d] made the new need to defend themselves their cause."[20]

Thus, some feminist gyms in Germany, such as Sidekick and Roter Stern Jena, are explicit about the ideas behind their training, and even offer workshops on antiracism and empowerment. Imke stressed the need for a "low limit for people joining the gym." The intention is to strike a balance between a clarity in politics and an accessible, welcoming space. Imke underscored the ambiguities that come with self-defense. "It's very important to make sure that people understand that you're not *that* kind of self-defense, that you have an antiracist standpoint," she said. Self-defense, then, becomes a means by which people either fight to enforce the status quo or to *survive* it.

Like Freedom Fighters Gym and RKS Gwiazda Gym in Poland, Sidekick and Roter Stern Jena in Germany see their self-organized antifascist gyms as a powerful case study in building self-confidence and community. Imke admitted that coming together and having a good time with likeable people is a big motivation for members. Going for drinks or hanging out after a training is part of that. It can generate self-confidence to be in public spaces in a more empowered way. It also brings new people together, based on shared antifascist values. "When I travel to another city, I know where I can go for training and find other people that I will feel at ease with," she explained. "It builds a network. You have a shared practice."

———

These conversations laid bare what I saw that night in the arena: fighting sports are a powerful vector for translating abstract beliefs into practice. There's a reason MMA is the fastest growing sport in history and why World Wrestling Entertainment enjoyed its long run. That a vast portion of society participates in fighting sports, from multiple vantages, is all the more reason to take seriously the impact of far-right engagement. This is particularly important as federal authorities, such as the Verfassungsschutz, Germany's version of the Federal Bureau of Investigation, peddles "both sides" arguments, equating antifascist fighting sports with fascist fighting networks.[21]

Fighting sports intensify the potency of beliefs already in circulation. The act of fighting is just as intoxicating as the cause someone fights for. It can be a means by which people who experience the privilege of an old world order fight tooth and nail to bend the present back, like White Rex calling on "Europeans to embrace the warrior spirit of their ancestors, and fight back against the modern world." Or it can become the means through which people practice the future possibility of a more just world.

As Kamil from Freedom Fighters Gym in Poznań put it: "We want to have people that will take a stand against the system. We want to help them become physically strong, to feel ready and confident. We hope they rely on their comrades and their teammates. So, we can trust that we know our own limits but also know what we can do together. When I think I have hit my limit, I want someone who can support me and help me continue. They can say, 'That is your limit, but we can do more together.'"

The Black Antifascist Tradition: A Primer

Jeanelle K. Hope

In July 1937, just before World War II and amid the rise of fascism in Europe, Langston Hughes delivered a riveting speech on the experience of the Negro in America, calling on his home country and the international audience he addressed—the International Writers Congress—to recognize the native fascism of the US. Hughes charged, "We [the American Negro] are the people who have long known in actual practice the meaning of the word Fascism—for the American attitude towards us has always been one of economic and social discrimination. . . . Yes, we Negroes in America do not have to be told what Fascism is in action. We know."[1] Much of written history on fascism has been limited to the immediate years following World War I through the fall of the Third Reich; thus, fascism is often interpreted as a historic politic and moment endemic to Europe, mostly impacting Jews and other European ethnic minorities. Contrary to this dominant historiography, fascism has and continues to manifest across space and time.

We are currently witnessing the global ascendance of a new wave of fascism with the US's President Donald Trump leading the authoritarian charge. Brazil's President Jair Bolsonaro, India's Prime Minister Narendra Modi, the Philippines's President Rodrigo Duterte, China's President Xi Jinping, and Britain's Prime Minister Boris Johnson have all embraced various facets of fascism—from authoritarianism, sentiments and actions that are systematically aiding genocide and ethnic cleansing, anti-immigrant rhetoric, to flagrant antidemocratic policies. The emergence of these leaders has thrust fascism back into the mainstream with disproportionate attention on the opposition—antifascist movements, in particular the vilification of "antifa" by right-wing political pundits and the Trump administration.[2]

As fascist regimes are met with resistance during this unprecedented historical moment marked by a pandemic (coronavirus disease 2019 [COVID-19]), the second wave of the #blacklivesmatter movement, plummeting global economic markets and historic unemployment rates, and global sociopolitical unrest, many at the grassroots are organizing and strategizing how to resist on all fronts. This chapter emerged as a response to a narrative put forth by many Black Americans on social media, and liberal Black political pundits, who view antifa or antifascism as not being part of Black liberation efforts, but a "distraction" and, moreover, a reduction of the politic and movement to white-led anarchism. But Black people have always had the boot of fascism on our collective necks.[3] Artists such as Hughes and Paul Robeson and early Black intellectuals such as W. E. B. Du Bois and Ida B. Wells understood the role fascism played in enslaving, repressing, and killing Black people during the turn of the 20th century. Furthermore, they worked to connect those struggles to what was occurring across the Global South and in Europe.

Black scholars have long turned to Cedric Robinson's seminal text, *Black Marxism*, to locate the origins of the Black radical tradition. Over the years, Robinson's work has been extrapolated by a host of scholars, such as Gaye Theresa Johnson, George Lipsitz, and Robin D. G. Kelley, to name a few. Their work has examined how Black people continue to resist and exist in the face of racial capitalism and build on the Black radical tradition.[4] But seldom have these works explicitly explored the role of antifascism in animating the Black radical imagination, nor have they truly engaged antifascism as a politic of Black internationalism.

This chapter reaches back in Black history and looks forward to current movements to examine Black intellectuals, organizations, and activist legacies of engaging antifascism as a framework and politic of strategic organizing from the 1940s to the present. Building on the work of Robyn Spencer and Dave Featherstone, throughout this chapter I use "Black antifascism" to describe the ideology and political position Black Americans have and continue to take in opposition to fascism, which has primarily manifested in forms of direct actions, anarchy, abolition, antagonistic struggle, and international campaigns against genocide. Black antifascism offers a more expansive understanding of fascism by centering the Black experience and locating its origins in European colonialism and imperialism, and later manifesting in the form of slavery, antiabolitionist riots, the rise of the Ku Klux Klan and white citizens' councils, the bombing of Black Wall Street and the Tulsa massacre, and urban genocide, among other historical moments. As Aimé Césaire captured in *Discourse on Colonialism*, fascism, as espoused by Benito Mussolini and Adolf Hitler, was nothing new—it was no more than European colonialism practiced on its own people instead of Africans and other people of the Global South.[5] Thus, tracing fascism back to its Black and colonial origins is crucial to being able to understand fascism's foundations, evolution across space and time, and enduring legacy.

Furthermore, this analysis and reclamation of Black antifascist history is also situated within the growing field of Black internationalism. Whereas this work largely centers on Black antifascism as articulated by Black people located in the US, Black antifascism as an ideology grows out of international struggles for Black freedom and liberation. There is no Black antifascism without transnational solidarities and the influence of thinkers such as Claudia Jones. Moreover, many of the Black antifascists mentioned throughout this work, such as Hughes, leveraged international audiences and connected the fascism Black Americans experienced to fascist struggles happening across Europe and the Global South. Thus, Black antifascism is inherently internationalist in nature, and many of the figures who we champion as Black internationalists, such as Du Bois, Jones, Malcolm X, and George Jackson, to name a few, were also antifascists. This work lays clear the intersection between Black antifascism and Black internationalism. Additionally, it helps disrupt the current trend in Black internationalist scholarship that often centers solely on the narrative of a single individual. In this chapter, I examine Black antifascism as a collective politic that has evolved over time through the work of various organizations and activists.

I start this chapter by first defining Black antifascism and succinctly tracing its early history from slavery to the 1930s. I then locate Black antifascism in four spaces: 1) international campaigns against Black and urban genocide in the US; 2) theorizing and political writings; 3) Black anarchy and calls for abolition and antagonistic struggles; and 4) grassroots organizing and community programming. This chapter is expansive, beginning in the immediate post–World War II period and moving across the post–civil rights era up to #BlackLivesMatter, but is in no way comprehensive or definitive. Starting with William L. Patterson, Robeson, and Du Bois's report turned 1951 United Nations (UN) petition—"We Charge Genocide"—on the American government's role in facilitating the genocide of Black people via lynchings and white terror, state-sanctioned violence, and systemic racism, I argue that Black antifascism has often focused on challenging the genocidal agenda of fascism by attempting to leverage the support of international governing bodies and by rightfully naming the systematic death of Black people due to various forms of racism as genocide. Beyond the work of Patterson and his cohorts, I also examine the many afterlives of the We Charge Genocide campaign, including its re-emergence in the M4BL organizations, Black Youth Project 100 (BYP100), and the Chicago-based organization We Charge Genocide.

Shifting to the Black Power era, I delve into how the Black Panther Party (BPP) engaged antifascism as a framework, and how this manifests in Huey P. Newton's theory of intercommunalism. I also turn to the BPP's 1969 United Front Against Fascism (UFAF) conference, which spawned a new organizing network that prioritized building solidarity through an antifascist politic—National Committees to Combat Fascism (NCCFs). Moving into the 1970s, I look at how Black antifascism evolved into Black anarchism and "antagonistic struggle" under the Black Liberation Army (BLA) and Street Transvestite Action Revolutionaries (STAR). Finally, this chapter begins to examine how current activists and organizations in the era of #BlackLivesMatter have engaged antifascism through the lens of abolition to combat the harrowing policies of Trump and systemic racism up to the present.

Although not comprehensive, this work begins to rightfully reclaim various Black historical moments and to present organizing as part and parcel of the Black antifascist tradition. This chapter reminds us that Black people have always been among the *vanguard* of antifascists.

The Intersections: Early Black AntiFascism (1930–50) and Black Internationalism

Because antifascism is a reactive response to fascism, to fully understand the politic and strategy of direct action, even as it relates to Black people, a quick reading of early European fascism is necessary. By far, no one has written as extensively on fascism as the Marxist theorist and revolutionary Leon Trotsky. In a 1931 letter, Trotsky distilled that:

The fascist movement in Italy was a spontaneous movement of large masses, with new leaders from the rank and file. It is a plebian movement in origin, directed and financed by big capitalist powers. It issued forth from the petty bourgeoisie, the slum proletariat, and even to a certain extent from the proletarian masses; Mussolini, a former socialist, is a "self-made" man arising from this movement.[6]

Trotsky argued that the emergence of fascism in Italy during the 1920s marked this transitional phenomenon whereby Italy, and soon other parts of Europe, moved away from and/or completely outlawed Marxism, communism, and other political parties and frameworks that advocated for a more egalitarian society. This stark shift was a direct response to the frustrations of the working class, in particular their failure to "complete what the Russian revolution had initiated."[7] With the masses in Italy on the brink of hunger and growing weary of their poor economic conditions, many grew dissatisfied with the reformist tendencies of the Italian communist and socialist parties, thus clearing the way for something new.

As Trotsky notes, fascism appealed to those across the class spectrum, but was largely financed by "big capitalist powers." He argued that fascism was tied to the "crisis of monopoly capitalism"; thus, fascism was never truly invested in creating class equality, but sought to leverage the petty bourgeoisie—both their support and "human capital"—to elevate the political rule and co-opt the entire state apparatus including the military, press, and universities.[8] In addition to widespread class appeal and capitalist undergirding, as fascism emerged in Germany, racial superiority—and later ethnic cleansing—became a key feature. The other danger of fascism was its extreme conservatism that stood in contradiction to Italy's and Germany's earlier notions of a social democracy. This allowed for the swift rise of authoritarian dictators and what Mussolini named as totalitarianism. This idea was best captured in his slogan, "All within the state, none outside the state, none against the state."[9] According to Keith Crawford, this outlook deemed that "all aspects of any individual's life were subordinated to the authority of the state."[10] To summarize European fascism: Italians and Germans had effectively signed up for a police state governed by a dictator (and their regime) that unilaterally controlled all institutions and aspects of society for the benefit of the capitalist elite and in the spirit of proving a racial/ethnic superiority that was rooted in white supremacy. To top it off, fascism spread like wildfire across Europe, acting as a form of native imperialism.

The preceding condensed history of fascism is certainly essential, but it is just one genealogical thread. As Bill Mullen and Christopher Vials offer, fascism in the US "has been both undertheorized and overimagined."[11] Although there arguably is no US fascist dictator equivalent to Hitler or Mussolini (Trump's presidency certainly was a contender), American fascism has long thrived under the stewardship of white supremacist leaders, settler-colonialists, and, in contemporary history, under the leadership of right-wing, conservative, and neoliberal politicians. American fascism is the propagation of a dual system of rights whereby whiteness has been afforded access to property, protection under governing documents, liberties, and freedom. Conversely, being a person of color, in particular a Black or Indigenous/Native person, one is often guaranteed a life of misery and social and economic oppression. Fascism in the US first manifested in the form of settler-colonialism, genocide, enslavement, and racial terror. These actions, as well as the creation of a two-tiered system of rights, are often (and rightfully) described as racism and white supremacy. However, when we step back and tease out the political authority that undergirds these systems—often a form of totalitarianism explicitly employed against Black people—it becomes quite evident that the state actively aiding (both historically and currently) in the repression, disenfranchisement, and murder of Black people in the name of white supremacy and capitalism is indeed a form of fascism. State-sanctioned anti-Blackness *is* fascism. It is this history and collective experience that enabled Hughes to brazenly claim that the American Negro does not need to be told what the meaning of fascism is, as fascism is engrained within the Black experience.

Beyond its manifestations in the US, fascism has been embedded within colonization and imperialism. For hundreds of years, European colonials were able to develop an authoritarian political rule across Africa, Asia, and Latin America that deemed the continents' Indigenous people inherently inferior and enslaveable. This early authoritarianism was stewarded by military and administrative forces sent by the British, French, Spanish, and Dutch empires. In some cases, European monarchs, such as Belgium's King Leopold II, directly led and oversaw heinous authoritarian practices and genocide for the sake of cash crop extraction, the advancement of modern capitalism, and European greed.[12] As historians, we seldom describe European colonizers and their political rule as fascists and fascism even though fascism clearly grew from practices, political rule, and ideologies first introduced in European colonies. Failing to draw these connections more concretely and not reading across archives only helps facilitate what Lisa Lowe describes as a historical disconnection in the interest of creating a redeeming liberal narrative.[13] Indeed, Europe's proverbial chickens came home to roost when fascism spread across the continent at the turn of the 20th century.

For Black people, there is little delineation between colonialism and fascism. This belief is echoed in Césaire's work, and by the Black internationalist Claudia Jones. Jones saw racism, colonialism, imperialism, and fascism as interconnected ideologies, politics, and practices that grew out of and informed one another. Jones claimed:

Imperialism is the root cause of racialism. It is the ideology which upholds colonial rule and exploitation. It preaches the "superiority" of the white race whose "destiny" it is to rule over those with coloured skins, and to treat them with contempt. It is the ideology which breeds Fascism.[14]

As a Marxist-feminist, Jones proclaimed during the 1940s and 1950s that Black women "needed to be mobilized for full participation in struggles against imperialism and fascism."[15] Jones and her communist contemporaries rightfully connected Ethiopians' struggle against Mussolini's fascism in the Second Italo-Ethiopian War to the infamous Scottsboro Boys case, and how McCarthyism was being used to silence Black American artists, thinkers, and activists.[16] These incidents and others were all part of fascism's continuum that long disproportionately impacted those across the African diaspora.

Paul Robeson, one of Jones's contemporaries, was also very vocal on how fascism curtailed Black liberation. During a House Committee on Un-American Activities (HUAC) hearing in July 1956, Robeson sought to defend his communist and antifascist stance, which had led to the stripping of his passport a year earlier.[17] Throughout the hearing, Robeson detailed his travels, noting how he witnessed the gripping effects of fascism in Europe and across the Global South. He articulated that his communist stance was born out of antifascism. Robeson charged that those appointed to HUAC were acting as "fascist-minded people."[18] He argued that he was the subject of these committees because of his opposition to fascism, and in turn grilled the committee on the US's role in enslaving and oppressing Black people. Robeson lived and died as an unapologetic Black antifascist internationalist.[19]

Prior to Robeson's hearing with HUAC, he traveled and spoke around the US, particularly in the South, inspiring other Black organizations and activists to also take up the charge of antifascism. In 1942, he attended the Southern Negro Youth Congress (SNYC) conference at Tuskegee University; he attended another SNYC conference in 1946.[20] Formed in 1936, SNYC was founded by high school and college youth who attended the National Negro Congress (NNC) hosted in Chicago, Illinois in 1936.[21] Although predating typical civil rights–era periodization, SNYC "protested fascism, war preparations, retrenchment in education and discriminatory hiring practice," and served as the first Black Southern-based organization to take up the issue of civil rights during the Great Depression.[22] Esther Cooper Jackson, a SNYC founder, described the organization as a movement aimed at fighting "for the end of the terror, assumed guilt, and economic depression facing Blacks across the country in the 1930s and 1940s."[23] The organization was based in Birmingham, Alabama, but spurred much of its activism out of South Carolina with the support of board member Modjeska Simkins.[24] At the outset, SNYC maintained deep ties to the Communist Party. The organization, which existed for nearly 12 years, primarily worked to organize Black folks in rural communities; successfully started a Negro Community Theatre in

Richmond, Virginia; lobbied and petitioned the war department and Fair Employment Practices Commission to address hiring discrimination, especially within defense industries; and vehemently challenged the New Deal's Agricultural Adjustment Act, which forced many Black farmers and sharecroppers off land during the Great Depression.

James Jackson (married to Esther Cooper Jackson), a key leader within SNYC, first started as an organizer with the Communist Party in 1931 and brought an internationalist and antifascist politic to the organization from his experience with the party.[25] During a voting event, Osceola McKaine, a SNYC organizer, declared, "whatever we do here in Alabama will affect the actions of the oppressed in South Carolina, in South Africa, in India and in Manchuria," thus linking the struggle of Black Americans to those across the Global South. Although Black activists largely supported the organization, its loose connection to the Communist Party drew concern and ire from the National Association for the Advancement of Colored People (NAACP).

The SNYC's antifascist, communist, and internationalist commitments and ties were further crystallized during the organization's seventh annual conference hosted in Columbia, South Carolina, in October 1946. The conference was attended by three thousand people, including Robeson, Du Bois, Simkins, Sallye Davis (Angela Davis's mother), Black and white delegates, and participants who represented labor organizations, veterans, teachers, international speakers, and attendees from the Soviet Anti-Fascist Youth Committee and All India Student Congress, among a host of others.[26] During the three-day conference, participants attended various workshops and teach-ins, as well as heard from a series of distinguished keynote speakers. Dr. Clark Foreman, president of the Southern Conference for Human Welfare, had worked to advance civil rights and integration-oriented policies within the Franklin D. Roosevelt administration, and was invited to the conference to deliver one of the many keynotes. Foreman lambasted his white Southern brethren, proclaiming, "[T]he rising tide of fascism in the South must be turned back before it has the chance to engulf the whole nation. Unfortunately, slavery has not disappeared from the South. Not only the Negroes, but the whites as well are enslaved."[27] He closed his remarks by calling for interracial solidarity to advance civil rights. Foreman was not alone in his sentiments on the rise of fascism in the South. Robeson also spoke at the conference on the topic, issuing an indictment of the American government: "[W]e must understand that in other parts of the world today our government has, up to this point, decided to throw its weight on the side of the remnants of fascism against the emerging democracies of the world."[28]

Beyond Foreman's and Clark's antifascist remarks, Du Bois delivered the closing address, calling on Southern Negroes to recognize that they were not alone. He first conveyed that their struggle was not an isolated one, but that the emancipation of the American Negro was tied to the "Negroes in the West Indies, to other colored races, and to the white slaves of modern capitalist monopoly."[29] Du Bois affirmed that this was indeed an international struggle that would require solidarity and unity around the eradication of both racism and capitalism. Toward the end of Du Bois's speech, he began to gesture toward his latest campaign—challenging the hypocrisy of the UN. His critique of the body began with a rebuke of Jan Smuts, South African military leader and original drafter of the UN charter. Du Bois found great consternation that Smuts, an architect of South African segregation that laid the foundation for future apartheid regimes, would have any role in determining what should be deemed human rights or crimes against humanity on a global stage. Like a true internationalist, Du Bois connected the struggle of South Africa to the American South, offering that segregationists, such as Smuts and then–US Secretary of State James Byrnes, "must in the long run yield to the forward march of civilization or die."[30]

Robeson's, Du Bois's, and Foreman's antifascist, internationalist, and prointegrationist words reverberated across the country as newspapers in South Carolina, most notably the local Black newspaper, *The Lighthouse and Informer*, published their speeches.[31] Conversely, the *Columbia Record*, *The New York Times*, *Beaufort Gazette*, and others portrayed the event as a Russian-sympathizer/procommunist event, further stoking McCarthyite and early Cold War rhetoric and divisions instead of grappling with the conference's condemnation of global racial politics and the rise of fascism.

From the outset, the Black experience in the US has been governed by fascistic values and racial terror. Thus, antifascism in many ways has been a natural response for Black people, whether it be through slavery abolitionist work, guerrilla warfare, on plantations, or through the work of groups such as the SNYC. Moreover, the work of Jones, Du Bois, and Robeson have not only helped us name the enduring legacy of white supremacy and racial terror as fascism, but have also linked the struggles of the American South to those across the Global South and to broader discussions on the rise of fascism in Europe. They saw and named these parallels and refused to allow the US to see itself outside the guise of fascism.

As Jewish people were met with near extermination in Germany, the UN was founded to help foster "international peace" and to sternly condemn the genocidal actions of Hitler and other fascist leaders in Europe. Simultaneously, Black antifascists were preparing their own case to charge genocide against the US government. This next iteration of the Black antifascist tradition focused on researching and creating reports and petitions that would be taken to the UN to detail how the US was indeed guilty of many human rights crimes. These activists and intellectuals firmly believed that the US should be charged with the crime of genocide.

We Charge Genocide: From William Patterson to BYP100

In November 2014, Jason Ware (founding member of BYP100), Mariame Kaba, and activists with the Chicago-based We Charge Genocide traveled to the UN Committee Against Torture hearing in Geneva, Switzerland to present a report on the disproportionate killing and torture of Black people by the Chicago Police Department.[32] Like generations of activists and intellectuals before them, this UN delegation named centuries of state-sanctioned anti-Black violence as genocide. This strategy of appealing to the UN and campaigning "We Charge Genocide" was first championed by William Patterson in 1951 when he presented a petition to the international body that sought to charge the US government with genocide.

The UN was formed in 1945 as a response to World War II, with the body's original commitments being to fight the Axis powers (i.e., Germany, Italy, and Japan) and foster world peace.[33] The body was able to emerge as many rejected the heinous and inhumane actions of European fascism. As Patterson and other Black leaders watched the UN react to "the Hitler crimes," they believed that they, too, had a case to make against the inhumane treatment occurring in the "black ghettos of American cities."[34] As previously mentioned, genocide and ethnic cleansing are intrinsic features of fascism. Given the long history of slavery, lynching, police brutality, and anti-Black state violence, Patterson, Du Bois, Malcolm X, the BPP, We Charge Genocide (the organization), and BYP100 have and continue to take up the We Charge Genocide campaign and appeal to the UN.

To step back a bit, Patterson and BYP100's work would not be possible without the groundbreaking work of Ida B. Well's antilynching crusade of the 1890s. As a Black woman investigative journalist, Wells was among the first to research, report, and speak out on the epidemic of lynchings happening across the nation, specifically in the South, following Reconstruction. Wells reported on lynchings for several Black newspapers and released a number of pamphlets that also included her research. "Lynch Law in Georgia" and "Southern Horrors: Lynch Law in All Its Phases" were among these works. Wells certainly predates the formal use of fascism as a term; however, she vividly described white violence and systemic racism as what can best be summed up as fascism. She captured how white citizens appealed to business and local leaders to justify and sanction the lynching of Black men, even detailing the "malicious" role of the Southern white press in these appeals and in perpetuating the intrinsic belief in Black criminality.[35] Wells surmised, "the South resented giving the Afro-American his freedom, the ballot box and the Civil Rights Law. The raids of the Ku-Klux and White Liners to subvert reconstruction government, the Hamburg and Ellerton, S.C., the Copiah County, Miss., and the Lafayette Parish, La., massacres were excused as the natural resentment of intelligence against government by ignorance."[36] In the final sentences of the pamphlet, Wells calls on Black Southerners to boycott, leave, and use the press to offer counternarratives. Decades after Wells's antilynching campaign, her strategy of investigating and documenting lynchings would be adopted by various organizations, intellectuals, and activists to argue the case of genocide.

During the 1940s, a number of organizations, including the NAACP and NNC, began to organize around appealing to the recently formed UN as a form of protest. The goals of the then-nascent campaign were to "internationalize the question of United States racism" by sending a delegation to the UN that would distribute a report and petition that sought to condemn the actions of the US, and to ask the UN to help end racial discrimination and anti-Black state-sanctioned violence.[37] As Charles Martin notes, the petition specifically called on the UN to "conduct studies documenting political, economic, and social discrimination against African Americans and make recommendations on how to end such human rights abuses."[38]

The report and petition were a collaborative effort that also led to political splintering. In 1946, Du Bois, who was still affiliated with the NAACP at the time, found the NNC report and draft petition to not be rigorous or compelling enough of a study to present to the international body. Being a trained sociologist, Du Bois helped redraft the work, transforming the document into a 100-plus page study—including an introductory essay and five in-depth research-based essays—that vividly detailed the experience of the American Negro, racial oppression, and state-sanctioned violence by delving into specific laws and practices.[39] In 1947, Du Bois unsuccessfully lobbied Eleanor Roosevelt and other members of the American UN delegation for support. The report was widely written off as embarrassing, "tattling," and political fodder for communist propogandists.[40] By 1948, the petition and report lost major traction. This came during a time when Du Bois increasingly disagreed with the more centrist direction Walter White sought to take the NAACP—one that was less concerned about internationalism, seemingly acquiesced to the US government to maintain a nonprofit status, and attempted to take a neutral or anticommunist stance even though many Black radicals of the period were either communists or written off as communists to dismiss their claims on racial inequality.

In December 1948, the UN facilitated the Genocide Convention, which helped define the crime of genocide and marked a major step toward the development of international human rights law.[41] Whereas many global leaders agreed that something needed to be done to prevent repeating the atrocities that happened during World War II, some US leaders, in particular Southern segregationists, feared the convention would scrutinize and internationalize domestic relations—an interpreted threat to American sovereignty and self-government.[42] In sum, the Southern racists were afraid that their "dirty laundry"—Jim Crow laws, lynchings, and racial terror—would be exposed and regulated by the international community. The convention was ratified in January 1951 with the US as one of the ratifying parties. This opened the door for the next phase of Black activism that continued to push the UN to condemn the US government's treatment of Black people. This time, they fully leveraged the language of the convention and charged the US with genocide.

At the forefront of this campaign was Patterson. Patterson had long been a fixture within Black and internationalist political circles with ties to the Communist Party, American Negro Labor Congress, International Labor Defense, the NNC, and later the BPP. As Gerald Horne outlines in his biography of Patterson, the lawyer, communist, and activist was determined and his commitment to revolution ran deep.[43] Throughout his life, he traveled to and was radicalized in Moscow, Cuba, Hamburg, Paris, the San Francisco Bay Area, and Chicago. He organized in solidarity with and worked alongside Robeson, Du Bois, Robinson, Newton, Angela Davis, among a host of others. Patterson started off as a lawyer and soon left his firm "devoting his life to the Communist party and its idea of a step-by-step drive to socialist revolution, paved all the way by one democratic advance after another."[44] His "road to revolution" started when he made his first trip to Moscow in 1927, and, during the immediate years after, he worked on what would be his first major organizing project—the Scottsboro Boys trial.[45]

In 1946, Patterson founded the Civil Rights Congress (CRC), a merger of older labor and civil rights organizations including International

Labor Defense, the National Federation for Constitutional Liberties, and the NNC.[46] The organization provided legal aid and resources to African Americans who were unjustly sentenced to capital punishment or ludicrous sentences and charges. Most notably, Patterson and the CRC helped defend victims such as Rosa Lee Ingram, William McGee, and the Martinsville Seven.[47] The organization focused on these cases as they sought to prevent a growing phenomenon of "legal lynchings," or state-sanctioned anti-Black violence. Moreover, the CRC sought to directly challenge nefarious court proceedings that were eerily similar to the Scottsboro Boys case from a decade earlier. Patterson and the CRC even appealed to the newly formed UN on behalf of their clients for support.[48] Because of their international appeals and communist ties, the organization's actions were deemed subversive and flagged by the Harry Truman administration. However, this did not deter the CRC or Patterson, as they "doubled down" on their engagement with the UN in the 1950s.

Patterson intently followed the politics and outcome of the Genocide Convention. From a legal standpoint, he recognized that the Genocide Convention and defining of international human rights law gave the organization necessary grounding to elevate the mission of their legal work. On December 16th, 1951, Patterson and delegates from the CRC traveled to Paris to present a report and petition charging the US with genocide on the grounds of systemic racism and state-sanctioned anti-Black violence. The 200-plus page report-turned-book built on the work of Du Bois, Robeson, the NNC, and the NAACP. However, the NAACP chose not to support Patterson and the CRC's crusade because they believed the allegations of genocide were unfounded.[49] But the NAACP was not alone; many contested whether genocide accurately captured the depiction of the Black experience. This is something that many continue to debate today.

In the opening statement of the report, Patterson, the CRC, and the petition signees helped frame and define genocide within a US context:

> Thus, the foundation of this genocide of which we complain is economic. It is genocide for profit. The intricate superstructure of "law and order" and extra-legal terror enforces an oppression that guarantees profit. This was true of that genocide, perhaps the most bloody ever perpetuated for which two hundred and fifty years enforced chattel slavery upon the American negro. Then as now it has increased in bloodiness with the militancy of the Negro people as they struggled to achieve democracy for themselves.[50]

Their framing of genocide was based on racial capitalism, in that Black bodies were killed and exploited during enslavement and the present for the sake of profit. The report included hundreds of accounts in a chapter entitled "The Evidence," which was broken down into three sections: 1) killing members of the group; 2) causing serious bodily and mental harm to the members of the group; and 3) a smaller subsection on special cases of soldiers being brutalized. The accounts ranged from the story of J. C. Farmer, a Black veteran who was shot and attacked within one hundred feet of his mother by a mob of over 20 white men, to an 11-year-old boy, Albert Peterson, who was "burned so badly [by the son of a white police officer] that the flesh hung from his body."[51] Neither the victims nor their families ever received justice.

Furthermore, the report detailed the harrowing effects of systemic racism, as it included data from the US Census of Manufacturers on wage inequality between Black and white workers. Disenfranchisement and voter terror, as well as "racist laws," were two other significant sections of the report. The report explicitly identified the similarities between "Hitler's Nuremberg Laws against the Jews and white supremacist laws in the United States against the Negroes."[52] In closing, the report called on the General Assembly of the UN to draft a resolution and declare that the US had been guilty of genocide, condemn the US's actions, and work to ensure the prevention of further genocide. The "We Charge Genocide" petition provided a preponderance of evidence to the UN to rightfully sanction the US; however, politics within and outside the governing body prevented the document from being seriously considered. Many non-aligned countries expressed interest in the petition but feared upsetting the US and losing economic aid. In addition to the NAACP refusing to support Patterson, a Black UN delegate alternate, Dr. Channing Tobias, challenged Patterson's use of "genocide" and wrote him off as "disloyal."[53] Given the politics of the Cold War and Red Scare era, much of the petition and Patterson as a figure were written off as propaganda and anti-American. The report was later published as a book and widely circulated across Europe and countries of the Global South.

Patterson and the CRC's work with the "We Charge Genocide" petition helped complicate discussions on genocide and challenged the US's racial politics on the global stage. Although the UN failed to take up the petition in any substantive way, the pioneering work helped spur years of antifascist activism and a growing body of research on Black urban genocide. By the 1960s, Malcolm X and other civil rights and Black Power leaders began to use genocide and other language from the petition to describe the Black experience, and to bolster their political platforms. Moreover, Patterson's and the CRC's legacies live on through the current work of BYP100 and the Chicago-based We Charge Genocide grassroots organization.

Black Panther Antifascism

As the specter of fascism faded in Europe, many youth activists in the US during the late 1960s who had coalesced around the Third World Liberation Front, Black Power, Asian American, Native American, and Chicano movements soon recognized that their radicalism and direct actions would be met with brute police violence, government surveillance, and unjust political incarceration that rivaled the earlier civil rights movement. The BPP was at the forefront of this new wave of activism. By 1969, the organization had endured numerous militarized raids and shootouts at BPP offices and party members' homes, most notably the killing of Fred Hampton in his Chicago home, the Los Angeles Police Department's (LAPD) 1969 attack on a BPP office, and the Sacramento Police Department's 1969 raid of a BPP office on Father's Day in the city's historically Black neighborhood of Oak Park.[54] Although the BPP had repeatedly experienced state repression, the heightened militarized response of local and federal law enforcement helped shift the BPP's understanding of what was at play. Emory Douglas, the BPP's minister of culture, often drew illustrations of pigs to represent police officers during the early issues of *The Black Panther*, and chants such as "off the pig!" were popularized at rallies. But 1969 marked a shift in BPP rhetoric—they began to unashamedly use the word "fascist" to describe police (or "pigs"), the US government, and American capitalism broadly. For example, in a 1969 issue of *The Black Panther*, prominent BPP member "Bigman" authored an article entitled, "Fascist California Grape Growers Use Mass Media to Combat a Living Wage."[55] In a 1970 issue of the paper, "slumlords" and police in Winston-Salem, North Carolina were described as fascists.[56] In that same issue, the BPP levied that it was "becoming increasingly clear that pigs [were] waging a war of constitutionalized fascism against the people of America in general and Black people in particular."[57] Thus, by 1969, the BPP was indeed an antifascist organization and viewed American fascism as the primary threat to Black people.

Over the last 20 years, there's been a proliferation of work on the BPP, many works exploring the organization's gender politics, delving into specific programs the BPP piloted, and providing autobiographical accounts.[58] Broadly, the BPP's politics have been described as Black nationalist, Marxist, Maoist, and revolutionary internationalist. What has often gone unexamined is the BPP's shift toward antifascism.[59] This shift was spurred by the BPP's increasingly violent interactions with law enforcement, their interest in coalition building with other radical organizations of the era, and the influence of international movements that also identified fascism as a barrier to Third World liberation. The BPP's engagement with antifascism was crystallized when the organization hosted the United Front Against Fascism conference on July 18th–21st, 1969 in Oakland, California.

Borrowing the name of Georgi Dimitroff's report presented at the Seventh World Congress of the Communist International in 1935, the UFAF conference brought together over five thousand people who the BPP described as the "New Left"—a range of radical leftist organizations from the 1960s, including Students for a Democratic Society (SDS), the Young Lords Party, the Brown Berets, the Red Guard Party, the Asian American Political Alliance, Los Siete de la Raza, Black Student Union members, student organizers from the Third World Liberation Front, the Young Patriots, and a host of other organizations.[60] Held at the Oakland Auditorium and "Bobby Hutton Park," this event marked a turning point for the BPP. Cofounder of the BPP, Bobby Seale, shared:

> This conference is not called just to save the Black Panther Party. It's called so that we can save the people, and save the people's organizations. Because if the pig power structure is allowed to get away with what they are trying to do to the Black Panther Party, they'll be allowed to do the same to any organization, any union, any church, any group of people who are using their basic democratic rights as a weapon against oppression.[61]

The conference program included a series of keynote speakers, debates, and workshops on issues such as Marxist theory, gender politics, political prisoners, health, and student activism.[62] Some of the event's key speakers were the BPP members Seale and Roberta Alexander, Asian American Political Alliance founder Penny Nakatsu, field secretary of the Young Patriots William "Preacherman" Fesperman, member of Los Siete de la Raza Oscar Rios, and SDS member Jeff Jones.[63]

Although the primary goal of the convening was to work to "develop a united front against fascism in America" and establish "community control of police on a national scale," 1969 had also marked a major shift in the BPP's gender politics, and discussion on the issue certainly came to a head during the event.[64] Earlier that year, Eldridge Cleaver, a leader within the BPP, had apologized for his chauvinistic and misogynist rhetoric that was popularized in various speeches, his slogan "pussy power," and his book *Soul on Ice*. However, women BPP members, as well as Chicana and

Asian-American women from other organizations, used the conference space to vehemently challenge and lambast various organizations for refusing to recognize the vital role of women, dismissing their claims of sexual abuse and harassment, and failing to elevate women to positions of leadership. During the women's panel, Alexander powerfully proclaimed, "[B]lack women are oppressed because they are black, and then on top of that, black women are oppressed by black men. And that's got to go. Not only has it got to go, but it is going"; she was met with rousing applause.[65] Alexander's remarks were followed by Nakatsu, who tied the issue of male chauvinism to fascism, noting how women, specifically Asian and Asian-American women, have died and been subjected to violence while challenging fascism, which historically has been informed by militarism and masculinist rhetoric.[66] The women's panel argued that fascism could not be dismantled without seriously addressing male chauvinism and misogyny and understanding how these logics were interconnected. In short, one could not be antifascist while being a misogynist.

In addition to addressing gender politics, another major outcome of the conference was the creation of the National Committees to Combat Fascism. This new organizational structure aimed to be a multiracial network that both coalesced around the BPP's platform and organized for community control of the police. With few non-Black members within the BPP, the NCCFs offered an opportunity for whites and non-Black people of color to engage the organization. Gayle, a former NCCF Berkeley member, described the space and dynamics in an oral history interview:

> We were unique in that our group of the National Committee to Combat Fascism in Berkeley [California] was the only white group. And there was also a moratorium for a while on new Panther chapters because the Party was growing so fast that it was really hard to keep control of who was doing what all over the country. For a while, instead of having new chapters formed, they formed National Committees to Combat Fascism. . . . We had our own community center, ran our own programs. . . . We actually chose to take leadership from the BPP. We functioned as a chapter. Because we were in the Bay Area close to central headquarters, we attended political education classes with the Party. We went to distribution on Wednesday nights, worked on getting the newspaper out. We walked the picket lines, you know, anything, any activity where multiple chapters came together, we participated.[67]

Although there were dozens of NCCFs across the nation, the NCCF that Gayle was a part of was one of the most successful and in essence

functioned as an all-white BPP chapter. In 1970, the Berkeley NCCF organized a campaign for community control of the police in Berkeley that
was later placed on the city ballot.[68] Beyond the campaign, the Berkeley
NCCF's community center offered a number of intercommunal programs,
including a free childcare program, first aid medical classes, a poison
control program, and free plumbing and maintenance services. The NCCF
later went on to help bolster Seale's 1973 campaign for mayor of Oakland.[69]

Beyond the UFAF conference and NCCFs, antifascism as an ideology
helped propel the organization's internationalism. As Sean L. Malloy and
Judy Tzu-Chun outline in their respective works, *Out of Oakland: Black
Panther Party Internationalism During the Cold War* and *Radicals on the Road:
Internationalism, Orientalism and Feminism During the Vietnam Era*, the BPP
was deeply invested in international struggles, developed Party chapters
abroad, and traveled across the Third World extensively to embattled
countries during the Cold War to gain a better grasp on resistance efforts
and to further imagine the organization as one that was Black internationalist in nature and transcended national barriers. Similar to how they
characterized the repression the BPP faced at home in the US, they often
characterized imperialist regimes that sought to destabilize countries
across the Global South, including Vietnam, Guinea-Bissau, Cuba, and
others, as fascistic.

Soon after the UFAF conference, the BPP founder Newton introduced
the theory of intercommunalism to help encapsulate the BPP's antifascist position. Newton's theory described the structure of the world as "a
dispersed collection of communities," not nations, where key institutions
were governed by and used to support a small group of people—often the
elite—for the sake of empire building.[70] Newton argued in 1970 that the
world was in a state of reactionary intercommunalism (i.e., imperialism)
that benefited the elite. He called for the BPP and other radical Third World
organizations to help shift the world toward a culture of revolutionary
intercommunalism, whereby the masses would control key institutions,
thus dramatically changing the material conditions of those who had been
marginalized. He surmised that revolutionary intercommunalism had the
ability to "nurture those things that would allow the people to resolve the
contradictions in a way that would not cause the mutual slaughter of all of
us."[71] In sum, Newton's theory of revolutionary intercommunalism built
on communist ideals and moved beyond it by imagining a world without
borders and governmental authority. With this new theorizing undergirding the BPP's antifascist position, by 1970 the NCCFs were renamed
Intercommunal Committees to Combat Fascism (ICCFs). The rejection
of "nation" and "nation-state" were integral to Newton's and the BPP's

coalescing around internationalism and understanding that antifascism had to be a global, intercommunal project.

Overall, the NCCFs/ICCFs were an underdeveloped network that struggled to meet many of its goals. This was in part due to the fact that, post-1969, the BPP began to implode and hit a sharp decline because most former leaders were dead, incarcerated, or in exile. By 1972, aside from a few autonomous chapters, the BPP had consolidated its work around Oakland and focused primarily on maintaining intercommunal programs such as the Black Panther school and Intercommunal Youth Institute.

The BPP's UFAF conference and creation of the NCCFs/ ICCFs represented another iteration in the long tradition of Black antifascism. The organization used its newspaper to argue that the police, US government, and American capitalism composed a fascist apparatus that aided in the repression of the BPP and people of color broadly. Moreover, Newton's theorizing of intercommunalism helped further internationalize the BPP's understanding of antifascism and arguably gestured toward the next phase of Black antifascism—anarchy—as Newton believed that from revolutionary intercommunalism the world would transform to a system of "pure communism and anarchy."[72]

From Black Antifascism to Black Anarchy and Antagonism

As the 1970s emerged and the BPP waned, Black antifascism once again evolved. Black activists began adopting more antagonistic and offensive strategies that directly challenged the state through both violent and non-violent means. Black antifascists in this period coupled the BPP's notion of self-determination with anarchism. They created autonomous housing and new survival programs that no longer relied upon hierarchical organizational structures. And they brought forth a new kind of creative activism that sought to imagine life beyond the state and government authority. Although they maintained antifascist politics, Black activists from this era began identifying as antagonists and anarchists.

Although often conflated, anarchy and antifascism are quite different ideologically, albeit inextricably linked. Antifascism is a reactive response to fascism, and those who organize in the name of antifascism are committed to dismantling fascist regimes with the goal of creating a more democratic, equitable, and just political system, whether that be a communist state, democracy, socialist nation, et cetera. Additionally, all antifascists do not maintain a singular political viewpoint. Thus, a number of political perspectives could be represented in an antifascist movement or coalition, including communists, socialists, anarchists, liberals, centrists, et cetera. They are solely united around dismantling fascism. Conversely, anarchists are vehemently opposed to the establishment and state. They are antagonists who believe in the abolition of government, institutions, and authority. Although anarchy is often solely viewed as chaos and aggression against the state, anarchism is also a framework that is used to critique hierarchies and reimagine a world without systems of domination. Where anarchy and antifascism intersect is around their interest in seeing the demise of fascist governments; however, their views of a collective future may differ. Although the BPP was certainly antifascist, aside from Newton, they largely maintained the belief that either some form of communism, socialism, or Black nationalism would best facilitate Black liberation. For Black anarchist and antagonist groups of the 1970s, such as the BLA, MOVE, and STAR, any kind of authority, whether it be Black led or white led, was problematic.[73]

As Dana Williams argues, the decline of the Black Power era was in part driven by major political splintering and factionalization within the BPP. There were three major factions: the Oakland Black Panthers (they were much more invested in local electoral politics), various autonomously run chapters across the nation, and former members who went on to create the BLA.[74] The collective was formed following the expulsion of BPP leader Eldridge Cleaver by Huey P. Newton. Cleaver, unlike Newton, maintained that violence and armed self-defense were necessary to achieve Black liberation. The BLA departed from the BPP's political ideology of Marxism-Leninism and Maoism and adopted a much more insurgent and anarchist position. From 1970–81, BLA members coordinated a number of strategic attacks and bombings on government and private property, ambushed several police officers, and facilitated various prison breaks and an aircraft hijacking.[75] Although the decentralized organization had members and networks across the nation, some of their most notorious members and incidents were based in New York and New Jersey. The BLA's most infamous act of antagonism was the 1973 killing of a New Jersey state trooper that led to Assata Shakur, a prominent BLA member, being sentenced to life in prison. Six years later, she escaped from prison with the help of Mutulu Shakur and other BLA members.[76]

Although the government classified their actions as acts of domestic terrorism, the BLA maintained that Black people needed an army to defend themselves. Other BLA members, such as Ashanti Alston, have deemed their actions as necessary anarchy to challenge fascistic institutions. Alston, who remains one of the most vocal Black anarchists of the era, started off as one of the founding members of the Plainfield, New

Jersey BPP chapter. After witnessing several BPP members die at the hands of state-sanctioned violence or be charged with unsubstantiated crimes, Alston and his Plainfield comrades sought to stand off against the state. Early into Alston's tenure with the BPP, he expressed growing weary of the organization's preoccupation with political education and ideology, lamenting, "[W]e don't have to wait to have no developed ideology, don't have to wait to have all the answers; we figure it out as we go. Because our situation is bad. We don't have the luxury of sitting back and doing all sorts of fanciful ideological positions: we'll figure it out as we go."[77] Because of their radicalism, Alston and other members of the more anarchist-leaning BPP chapters in New Jersey and New York were targeted by law enforcement and linked to various police shootings, most notably the 1971 Panther 21 trial.[78] Three years later, Alston, now a member of the BLA, was arrested on burglary charges and sentenced to 11 years in prison.[79]

Although the BLA is no longer active, Alston continues to give talks and writes about Black anarchism. In a recent interview, he spoke extensively about how his politics and evolution as an anarchist have been influenced by Black feminists, intersectionality, identity politics, and queer theory.[80] He recalled receiving a queer theory book from a comrade that helped shift his understanding on how capitalism and fascism were also impacting other marginalized groups:

> And so in reading it, I'm also challenging myself in terms of my perspective, 'cause queer theory is telling me something about identity, different lifestyles, and what historical forces have done, and that capitalism does, more than just exploit a class. It ruins people for all kinds of different reasons. So now my vision of the world changes more. It becomes more inclusive, a lot more lifestyles, than I had, maybe in the '60s.[81]

Alston understood the various ways fascism was also ruining the lives of queer and trans people, and why it was integral to also be in struggle with other marginalized people. Moreover, he began to make connections to how queer folks also engaged facets of anarchy in their own organizing.

In the same tri-state region, Alston's time with the BLA ran parallel with the emergence of the gay liberation movement and the Stonewall uprising in New York City. Furthermore, much of the state-sanctioned violence and repression that the BPP and BLA were confronted with was used to terrorize queer and trans people. Black queer theorist, Cathy Cohen, has long argued that queer politics and theory entail unsettling, constantly redefining, and subverting notions of sexual expression and sexual categories.[82] Queer politics directly challenge and antagonize "the multiple practices and vehicles of power" that render queer people invisible by putting forth a new set of "anti-normative characteristics and non-stable behavior."[83] For many Black and Latinx queer and trans people straddling the margins of race, gender, sexuality, and class, liberation also included challenging fascism and state-sanctioned violence head-on, often while leveraging anarchist, or what they described as "antagonistic," strategies.

After years of being terrorized by New York Police Department officers from the Public Morals Division, lesbian-gay-bisexual-transgender (LGBT) community members, led by Marsha P. Johnson and Sylvia Rivera, came together in the summer of 1969 to revolt against the frequent police raids that were conducted at the Stonewall Inn—an LGBT bar and haven in Greenwich Village. For nearly a week, LGBT community members threw bricks and other projectiles at the police and demanded that law enforcement cease conducting unlawful and discriminatory raids on LGBT establishments. Following the uprising, some LGBT activists continued to organize around gay liberation in a manner that sought to directly challenge law enforcement and American fascism; one of these groups was STAR, Street Transvestite Action Revolutionaries.

After witnessing how transgender women were being marginalized and ridiculed within the white-cis–dominated gay liberation movement and subjected to state-sanctioned violence and harassment regularly by law enforcement, a group of predominately Black and Latinx transgender women—Johnson, Rivera, and Bubbles Rose Marie—founded STAR in 1970. At the outset, the organization sought to provide immediate support for homeless LGBT youth, primarily other trans people of color.[84] The first STAR house was an abandoned trailer truck that was later recovered by its owner. They later moved to a partially burned building in the Lower East Side, where the collective lived, working together to cobble together funds for rent, food, and other necessities.[85] Although organizations prior had created communal housing, STAR's vision of providing housing for trans people of color and simultaneously using the space to organize demonstrations that were inherently antagonistic was very much revolutionary for the time.

Johnson, a Black transwoman, helped craft the organization's political platform, stating, "[W]e believe in picking up the gun, starting a revolution if necessary. Our main goal is to see gay people liberated and free and have equal rights like other people in America."[86] Unlike the white LGBT organizations of the time, STAR was not afraid to be antagonists and they refused to settle for parades and what felt like mainstream LGBT inclusion; instead, they sought "gay power." Consequently, STAR members were vilified within gay activist circles. In a 1971 issue of *The Village Voice*, STAR was described as:

> A sub-culture unaccepted within the subculture of transvestism and looked down at in horror by many of the women and men in the homosexual liberation movement. Sylvia and Marsha and Bambi and Andorra with their third world looks and their larger-than-life presences and their cut-the-crap tongues do not "fit" at a GAA [Gay Activist Alliance] meeting.[87]

Even as transwomen who helped spark the gay liberation movement, they were unwelcomed within the more prominent LGBT spaces because of their race and class position, or, as *The Village Voice* put it, their "third world looks."

STAR described themselves as "antagonists" and staged various demonstrations, including a sit-in at a New York University residence building, during their nearly four-year existence. STAR maintained a political ideology and strategy that provided the type of intercommunal programming, similar to the BPP, that allowed them to reimagine and create a world that housed, fed, and cared for those on the margins of the margins. Although short lived, STAR certainly left a legacy that foregrounded antagonism within queer and trans organizing that a new generation of Black transwomen and nonbinary activists have built upon in the era of #BlackLivesMatter.

Black Antifascism and Abolition in the Era of #BlackLivesMatter and Trump

Into the 1980s and 1990s, the type of radical activism that helped define US urban cities in the 1960s and 1970s was certainly less visible in some regards; however, the ideology of Black antifascism continued to evolve. As major struggles against mass incarceration, harsh sentencing laws such as California's three strikes law and the 1994 Violent Crime Control and Law Enforcement Act, and the privatization of prisons mounted, so did calls for prison abolition. Prior to her pivotal work, *Are Prisons Obsolete?*, Angela Davis—who had deep roots in the Black Power movement, Communist Party, 1970s prison abolition work alongside George Jackson, and antifascist organizing—founded Critical Resistance, a national prison abolition organization, in 1997 alongside Black geographer Ruth Wilson Gilmore and environmental activist Rose Braz. The organization's mission of dismantling prisons drew on the legacy of the abolition of slavery. They identified the prison-industrial complex as a system designed to "contain, control, and kill those people representing the greatest threats to state power."[88] It was in this moment that Black antifascism had come full circle, as the language and framework of abolition helped characterize one of the first major movements mounted against a fascist system—slavery—and was once again being used to organize a new movement. Critical Resistance helped reintroduce abolition into the Black antifascist lexicon and as a framework for contemporary Black activists.

Over the last two decades, abolition as a framework and organizing principle has gained considerable traction. After being sentenced to serve 41 months in prison in 2012 for second-degree manslaughter over an act of self-defense against a known white supremacist, CeCe McDonald, a Black transwoman activist, committed her postincarcerated life to prison abolition. She firmly believes[89]:

> We can't hold onto these powerful institutions that oppress people and expect that they will go away just because we reform them. Of course, change is good, but in instances of systematic oppression, like prisons, there is no way for it to be reformed. . . . [W]e'd have to abolish all those powerful institutions that allow that energy to navigate through our lives.[90]

As a grassroots organizer and educator, McDonald works to develop abolitionist curricula for educators to integrate into the classroom and for political education. Her work as an abolitionist not only builds on the legacy of STAR, but also speaks to how a younger generation of activists are engaging elements of Black antifascism and anarchy. McDonald's case, which gained national attention, unfolded alongside the emergence of #BlackLivesMatter. She was incarcerated the same year Trayvon Martin was killed by George Zimmerman, and her release happened just months before Michael Brown's death ignited an uprising in Ferguson.[91] During both of these early moments of the then-nascent movement, activists within the network of #BlackLivesMatter and the M4BL coalition began calling for increased community oversight of police and the complete abolition of the police.

More recently, calls for abolition have only intensified given the deaths of George Floyd, Breonna Taylor, and Ahmaud Arbery. Moreover, abolition has also gained traction as an internationalist politic, as police abolition movements modeled after current US Black activism have emerged in the UK and Canada, not to mention the ongoing abolish

Immigration and Customs Enforcement movement that is challenging the very notion of borders in the US. Although the mainstream media and even some Black neoliberals and conservatives are often characterizing abolition as a new demand, the long tradition of Black antifascism tells us otherwise. As Avery Gordon captures so succinctly, "[A]bolition involves critique, refusal, and rejection of that which you want to abolish, but it also involves being or becoming unavailable to servitude."[92] This assertion means that we have to actively reject the very systems that have been enshrined in our social lives and that help compose our material realities. It requires creating an "indifference" to systems of power that can be leveraged to imagine something wholly anew.[93] Whereas creating this indifference and committing to rejecting the status quo are certainly necessary individual acts, it is just as important for them to be collective ones.

In a moment when people are being used as political fodder and deemed disposable by various fascist regimes across the globe, while simultaneously confronting a ravaging pandemic and callous acts of state-sanctioned violence, not to mention the growing confluence of social movements from Occupy Wall Street, Standing Rock, immigrant rights, to #BlackLivesMatter, and so many others, we may be at a political moment when abolition and other elements of Black antifascism are fully engaged on the global stage. Indeed, there is much that the Black antifascist tradition provides us for this political moment, and it is important, now more than ever, that we embrace, engage, and evolve within this tradition.

The Campus Antifascist Network

Maximilian Alvarez

{*Maximilian Alvarez was one of the early organizers of the Campus Antifascist Network (CAN), a confederation of local organizations based on college campuses and aimed at coordinating with staff, faculty, and students to resist attempts by the far right to gain a platform. College campuses had become a primary area where the alt-right and other right-wing grifters were attempting to use disingenuous claims of "free speech" to manipulate universities to give them a stage and a microphone. Several antifascist groups popped up at schools around the country, and the CAN was an incredibly notable effort to build a model that was easily replicable. In the following interview, Alvarez interviews two other founders, David Palumbo-Liu, faculty member at Stanford University, and Bill Mullen, formerly of Purdue University, about the formation of CAN and what this model provides to the larger antifascist movement.* —Shane Burley}*

Maximilian Alvarez: I would love to start out the interview talking about your own histories with antifascist politics (and what "antifascist politics" has meant to you over the course of your lives). Was antifascism always an explicit focus or defining characteristic of your politics? Or was it more of a "no-brainer" that followed from your other political commitments? (And has your relationship to/perspective on antifascism changed over the years based on the historical contexts you were living in, the people you were living around, the battles you were fighting, etc.?)

Bill Mullen: I've been on the socialist left most of my adult life, so I know that socialists and communists have historically been the best fighters against fascism. I've always been involved in antiracist work that is obviously a building block for fighting fascism. At Purdue, we organized something called the Purdue Antiracist Coalition against the growing white backlash in the early 2000s against everything from [Barack] Obama to the protests against police violence. [Donald] Trump's campaign in 2015 and election in 2016 were game changers for me. His open "dog whistling" to white nationalists and white supremacists and classically fascist appeal to white resentment seemed like an immediate threat. It was clear that immigrants, people of color, the poor, the working class, had fresh targets on their back. The last thing is that I've worked at US universities since the 1990s. I knew the far right was always trying to organize there— this goes back to the Young Republicans in the 1990s that had begun to mobilize around white nationalist themes. I'd had skirmishes with them already too.

The other important piece of my politics, especially since 2009 when I signed the US petition for Boycott, Divestment, Sanctions (BDS) against Israeli universities, has been around Palestinian liberation. It has been pretty clear that the far right and many Zionist politicians and organizations often collaborate. Deep Islamophobia and support for eth-nonationalism characterize both. Fighting for Palestinian freedom has always been implicit for me in fighting against the global far right.

All these events in combination led me to want to work with others to organize against fascism on campuses once Trump was elected. The timing seemed right too because, since Travyon Martin's shooting in 2012 and the rise of BLM [Black Lives Matter], so many students, faculty, and others were way more alert to the role of the police and the state in advancing dangerous right-wing authoritarian politics. As I see it, when we formed the Campus Antifascist Network in 2016, we were trying to advance and defend an already-burgeoning antiracist movement.

David Palumbo-Liu: I grew up in the SF [San Francisco] Bay Area [California], attended San Francisco State in the late 1960s and then [University of California] Berkeley. In the political discourse—especially from the Black Panthers and fringe groups such as the Symbionese Liberation Army—"fascism" was sometimes even more present than "racism" because so much activism was around police and state violence. I saw troops on the streets of Berkeley and I was charged by mounted cops at SF State. But it really wasn't until my work with BDS and the struggles over Palestinian rights that I started getting a more formal understanding of the term. Like the word "apartheid," "fascism" was attached to Zionism, and it took (and still takes) a great deal of clarity and self-confidence to debate those who feel these words do not apply to the Zionist state. And certainly, during the Trump campaign, we saw nearly every facet of fascism daily.

Maximilian Alvarez: Let's talk about the CAN origin story. What were the circumstances that led to the creation of CAN, and how were you two involved? And (obvious question, sorry!) what compelled you to get involved in the first place? Given everything else you were already doing, professionally and politically, why not leave it to someone else?

Was there anything about your particular positions as venerable tenured professors that played into your decision? I ask because it was obviously hard for us to get a lot of tenured professors involved in any capacity with CAN, but it was also quite difficult to get them to appreciate the tactical value of their positions and to *use* their status/protections/connections/et cetera for the cause. That has obviously never been the case with you two.

Bill Mullen: My thinking began to change when I took part in a giant march at Purdue after the killing of Trayvon Martin. Black students organized a march of about four hundred people—the biggest demonstration I had ever seen at any campus I'd been on. Students also began to openly confront a racist administration over unequal conditions on campus for students of color. I also participated in an Occupy Purdue chapter in 2011 that began to make clear more and more people were understanding the state and capitalism as a threat to their lives. The "We are the 99%" slogan was not just a slogan against the rich but an understanding that "we are many/they are few," as we say on the socialist left. That is, that elites in power will do anything to smash and undermine the power of the vulnerable. This is an understanding that lends itself to understanding the threat of fascism.

To be honest, in my 30 years of teaching, it has always been students—not faculty—who've led grassroots resistance work—whether it's to get a Black Studies program off the ground, or to reduce student fees. When we put together a call for a CAN chapter on campus, almost everyone who showed up was a student. It's not that faculty don't feel and understand oppression and want to organize against it, it's more that students live closer to an experience of dispossession—they are often poor, or don't have health insurance, or experience racism or sexism acutely on campus. They are therefore the "advanced section" of the political class on campus and the ones most inclined to organize.

David Palumbo-Liu: I think Bill would agree with me on this—we two had been working on US Campaign for the Academic and Cultural Boycott of Israel (USACBI) for so long and so intently, that we were really in tune with the ways the academy, and right-wing academics and their enablers in representative politics and conservative think tanks (here and abroad), can come down hard on any kind of dissent, especially organized dissent. Milo Yiannopoulos and Charlie Kirk, and before them people like Peter Thiel and Dinesh D'Souza, were already getting buy-in from the Koch brothers and others.

So I remember talking with Bill about the linkages, and pretty early on we thought it would be good to start having conversations. Charlottesville

[Virginia] convinced us to jumpstart CAN. I think we got a draft of a mission statement and a website up pretty quickly after. A lot of the impetus for starting much earlier than we had intended was the need for self-defense for antifascists on campus, especially students.

Maximillian Alvarez: Can we talk about the kinds of actions CAN focused on and why? How would you describe the purpose and goals of the kind of organizing CAN did?

As educators ourselves, for instance, we knew that education was one critical tool we were committed to using, but CAN's activities weren't just limited to teach-ins and informational protests.

Bill Mullen: There were four kinds of activities we focused on at the start.

The first, as you say, was education. We created a Campus Antifascist Network syllabus and encouraged people to form groups on campus to study the history and rise of fascism.[1] This seemed important given that the US has not had an "open" history of fascism, but also to remind people that there always have been antifascist movements in the US—from the socialist movement of the 1930s, to the Black Panther Party in the 1960s.[2]

The second was a call to organize individual campus chapters of CAN [see the Appendix. –Ed.]. This was to give people a chance to identify and protest against local conditions, to put down intersectional political roots on campus, to organize a united-front coalition "from below." We ended up with 16 campus chapters in the US, UK, and Canada.

The third was a focus on challenging right-wing and far-right speakers and groups when they tried to speak on campus [see the Appendix. –Ed.]. Remember that in 2016 and 2017, Richard Spencer and his like were desperately trying to recruit college students to the new far right by speaking on campus. They were successful in some cases in speaking, like at the University of Florida. We felt it was important to challenge that messaging. It was also important to challenge the far right's use of "free speech" to deliver fascist messages on campus.

Lastly, we wrote articles for the public sphere about the emergence of CAN and the campaign by the far right to infiltrate college campuses.[3] We knew it was important to try and build a national and international movement since the far right was organizing everywhere in the world—in the UK, for example, Tommy Robinson was building a far right and using college speaking events to do so.

Maximilian Alvarez: This is something I myself have written a lot about and have talked through over the years with both of you, but I think it's a really important question to consider, especially as higher education is experiencing a major crisis as a result of COVID-19 [coronavirus disease 2019] and the economic crash.

The first word of "CAN" is obviously "Campus," signaling that this is an organization/network that takes up the antifascist cause in the world of higher education. But I think it was always a question we and others wrestled with: Were we just antifascists who happened to be living/working/organizing on campuses, or were we antifascists who were committed to fighting the fascist creep as it manifested within the world of higher education?

I know this is not a totally "either/or" question, but I think meditating on this will be a nice setup for the remaining questions, which will ask about how and why neoliberalized higher [education] has made itself uniquely vulnerable to fascist offenses while also becoming a subject of unique fixation for fascistic operators and far-right politicians. How did you two navigate this question yourselves?

Bill Mullen: That's a really great question. I think the answer is both. The university *is* a social institution composed of many of the same social relationships that constitute the broader capitalist society. Especially on large public university campuses like the one I worked at for many years, working-class people, women, LGBTQ [lesbian-gay-bisexual-transgender-queer] people, BIPOC [Black, Indigenous, and people of color] people experience the same forms of social oppression and discrimination and class subjugation that they do off campus. What we call "neoliberalism" in higher education is really just the same thing people in all parts of capitalist society have experienced in recent years—austerity, precarity, attacks on public goods. So it should not surprise us that the far right immediately understood the university as one of its "bases."

In fact, the far right, like American Vanguard and Proud Boys, explicitly attempted to appeal to "white resentment" against things like "multicultural education" (or what is called in the private sector, "corporate diversity") to recruit.

Another way of putting this is that CAN always assumed that the university was a *workplace*. That students and faculty inhabit college campuses in literally the same way they inhabit their workspaces and homes. Keeping a campus "safe" from fascism is the same as keeping fascists out of factories, hospitals, unions.

At Purdue, we had white supremacist groups dropping flyers on a regular basis onto the campus grounds. This is meant to terrorize people where they live and work. Sweeping them off campus is really an organized social action, like a strike, to make sure ordinary people control the conditions of their lives and keep them free of violence, physical and otherwise.

David Palumbo-Liu: Campuses are perceived as a threat, and the threat of "radicals on campus" deployed by the right to get media attention.

They are also used opportunistically by alt-right grifters, and by campus Republican groups. Each and every right-wing group (e.g., TPUSA [Turning Point USA]) is connected to the conservative machinery outside of campus. So, financially and politically, doing antifascist work on campus automatically means you are fighting fascism off campus.

Ninety percent of the students who are doing antifascist, antiracist, anti-Zionist work on campus are also working for workers' rights, including graduate student rights as well as service worker rights.

Finally, again in the Bay Area, there is so much (but not enough) interconnectivity between labor organizing, DSA [Democratic Socialists of America], housing rights, and other groups, and this means academics like myself speak at those events and those folks are invited to campus.

I would simply add something I think we are all thinking about: Things are going to get much more dangerous as Trump goes out of office and off the mediascape. The things Shane Burley talks about are going to grow—that is, internet organizing and actions by fascist groups. I fear they are going to start getting very tech savvy, and we need to be able to monitor them and expose them. They will keep morphing and infiltrating. And students/young people are really important in fighting on this front—old guys like Bill and me are way behind the times. And, of course, we cannot imagine the FBI will be only looking for fascists.

Appendix

Here are two essential documents from the CAN created by the founders to help in building up the network and allowing groups to establish their own local chapters. Because these were autonomously forming groups, it was important for them to build the local chapters themselves, adapting to their own local conditions and creating an alliance based on CAN's principles.

The two documents included herein are guides for how to build a local CAN chapter, respond to an attempt by a far-right speaker to visit campus, and determine what it would take to build up an organized response.

Building a CAN Chapter at Your Campus

1. Create a call-out and announce the formation of a campus antifascist group or club. Call the group CAN (Campus Antifascist Network). This is to ensure uniformity across campuses and assure that no branch is

isolated. Reach out to all potential groups on campus who are most vulnerable to fascists—Black student unions, LGBTQ, Sanctuary Campus groups, Indigenous groups, Latinx student groups, feminists, Muslim groups, as well as academic units, such as Ethnic Studies, that may feel vulnerable. Also reach out to community groups, including a variety of trade unions across professions.

2. Publicize the call-out widely. Print posters with the CAN graphic from the website, clearly marking date/time/venue of the meeting. Make sure you put up these posters all around campus and in nearby cafés, public libraries, et cetera. Bring to the meeting the CAN mission statement, CAN's solidarity statement with Charlottesville, and the CAN [Antifascism] syllabus. Use these to tell the history of the group and its rapid growth: from 40 to 300 academics and more than 1,500 members on the Facebook page. Show people the CAN website and Facebook page. Ask people to join CAN and show them how to do it.

3. Assess local conditions for building an antifascist group. Are there any existing antifascist formations to collaborate with? Are there community groups you should be working with? Assess the local presence of fascists/neo-Nazis/white supremacists on campus or in your community. Study them and keep track of any attempted local actions. You may want to develop a rapid response team to react to fascist incidents and meetings or attacks on individuals.

4. Schedule a teach-in, workshop, or reading group on fascism to educate your members. The CAN syllabus has many good readings and can be found at: www.campusantifascistnetwork.com/resources.

5. Check to see whether anyone on your faculty is already a CAN member; if so, invite them to be part of the teach-in. If not, approach faculty who might be sympathetic to an antifascist teach-in and request they lead one.

6. Be public in your organizing work but organize independently of the university administration. You may not want to become an official student group if that curbs your ability to organize.

a. Schedule a separate meeting to discuss security and self-defense. Use the "What to Do When a Fascist Comes to Your Campus" document as a guideline for discussion. Assess which tactics/strategies are most likely to work given local conditions if fascists come to campus. Discuss the most secure ways to communicate within the branch.

b. If right-wing activism is already dominant on your campus and you fear disruption, take the following steps:

i. Make plans with other antifascists before the first meeting to determine how you will handle a confrontation.

ii. Ask a sympathetic faculty member or members to the first meeting. Fascists are less likely to act out if faculty are visibly present. Understand that tenured faculty often have more *freedom and leverage*. If you'd need to approach a faculty member who has not approached you first, take this into consideration.

c. Send information about your club/group to the CAN Network for posting at the website: cannetwork.fighttheh8@gmail.com.

What to Do When a Fascist Comes to Your Campus

1. *As soon as you hear they are coming, organize a public meeting.*

a. Find a location and issue a leaflet advertising this meeting and distribute and post them broadly across campus and in important community locations (progressive bookstores/coffee shops, etc.).

2. *Before the meeting reach out to key organizations and individuals to attend the meeting and ask them to join an antifascist coalition against the fascists who plan to come:*

a. On campus, contact sympathetic faculty organizations (faculty union; faculty governance bodies; organizations of progressive, queer, Jewish, Muslim, and faculty of color) and student organizations that would be targeted by the fascists (students of color, Jewish, Arab, Muslim, immigrant, progressive, prolabor, LGBTQ students).

b. Off campus, contact sympathetic labor unions; immigrant, LGBTQ, Jewish, Muslim, and people of color organizations; and progressive churches, mosques and synagogues.

3. *At the organizing meeting, work to build a consensus—or, at the minimum, a majority of people at the meeting around the following points:*

a. The need for a demonstration to confront the fascists. Fascists are not engaged in "speech"—they are not coming to campus to convince people of their reactionary ideas but to intimidate and terrorize.

b. Inform the university of your intention to *demonstrate* against the fascists while recognizing the need to organize independently of the university police and administration. If the university bans the fascists, they will use the precedent to ban our activities as well.

c. Issue a leaflet for the demonstration, as early as possible, specifying the *date* and *venue*, that will be broadly distributed and posted on campus and in the community—with a special emphasis on members of the coalition mobilizing their organizations and constituencies. *List* all the organizations involved in organizing the demonstration—this will ensure that those organizations mobilize their members.

d. Begin the process of training trusted members of the coalition to organize self-defense against the fascists—we cannot rely on the campus or local police to protect us against the fascists' violence.

e. *Elect a demonstration steering committee* to handle issues of speakers at the rally, security, self-defense, and whether to attempt to shut down the fascist meeting. We need to have consensus that such an action will only be undertaken if we clearly outnumber the fascists and are likely to disperse them. We do not want to engage in a confrontation that we might lose—that would only embolden the fascists.

4. *On the day of the demonstration:*

a. Make sure that the coalition steering committee and activists trained in self-defense and marshalling arrive *at least one hour* before the time of the demonstration. They should "scout out" the area, determine where to station marshals and self-defense groups, and determine possible routes to either disrupt the fascist meetings or effectively retreat in case of attack.

b. Begin speeches when the crowd is of sufficient size—the program should *last less than 30 minutes*, followed by massive chanting and possible disruption.

c. Remember: *As organizers of the demonstration, you have the responsibility of not only getting out the maximum numbers, but ensuring their safety, whether in an effort to disrupt the fascist action or not.*

d. At the end of the rally, the organizers and marshals need to organize demonstrators to leave the action in groups to avoid being isolated and attacked by the fascists.

Antifascism Is Not a Crime:
An Interview with David Campbell

Kim Kelly

The night of the fight, David Campbell had just wanted a cup of coffee, and maybe a little whiskey to warm up. He was leaving a protest when an altercation broke out between the group of fellow antifascists we were walking with and a gaggle of drunken Trump supporters leaving a white nationalist gathering in Manhattan. The ensuing fracas was a blur, but ended with David in handcuffs—and in agonizing pain after a gang of violent New York Police Department officers brutally broke his leg in several places.

He was hit with a jaw-dropping array of absurd charges, dragged through a long legal nightmare, and ultimately sentenced to a year in prison. The legal system and its agents hammered away at him, drawing out the proceedings for years and trying to paint him as some kind of antifa bogeyman while the then-president howled about "anteefa" from his bully pulpit and fascist pundits fanned the flames. The men who'd started the altercation that night faced zero consequences for their actions, but Campbell—a mild-mannered part-time funeral director and French translator with a beaming smile and penchant for bad puns— became a political prisoner.

It's my firm belief that he was imprisoned for his politics, and for his unapologetic public stance as an antifascist. What would've been written off as a glorified bar fight had the parties involved been drunk football fans or belligerent tourists instead became a prison sentence, undertaken during a deadly plague, within one of the most notorious jail complexes in the US.

During his time inside, he did his best to stay connected to friends and comrades, read copiously, and made friends with the other people trapped there with him; during the early days of the pandemic, he helped organize a strike to protest the lack of basic hygiene and safety, and won concessions that benefited his entire dorm. When he finally came home, he was greeted by a loving community that had been counting down the days along with him. That Campbell survived the ordeal is a blessing, and that he came out of it stronger and even more committed to the cause is incredibly admirable.

When I spoke to Campbell for this interview, the memory of his "welcome home" party had already begun to fade and we were both excited for him to begin the next chapter of his life in a new country. As I write these words now (December 2021), it's been even longer; he's since settled into a new routine far away from the US and its horrors, and we're planning a reunion for when he's briefly back Stateside for the holidays. The difference between what his life was like inside and what it's like now beggars belief, and is a rare happy ending. Far too many other people in his position spend much longer stints behind the walls; some political prisoners have their youths stolen from them, or lose their entire lives to the criminal injustice system. Antifascism is not a crime, and until the day we free them all, this is Campbell's story.

Kim Kelly: OK, David Campbell, how long have you been a free man?

David Campbell: I've been a free man for 10 months.

KK: Looking at where you were 10 months ago, and looking at where you are now, how are you feeling?

DC: I feel great. I felt great 10 months ago, but I also felt very overwhelmed by things. I didn't go away for that long, enough—you know, 12 months, a year, is long enough to develop new habits and get disacquainted.

When I came out, there was a lot that was kind of weird for me at first. That feeling of being overwhelmed was kind of secondary to the joy of being out. And now I feel—I don't feel discombobulated anymore. I still feel joyful to be out.

KK: Do you miss those heady early days when you were a newly freed, antifascist political prisoner? I know you got a lot of drinks out of that.

DC: I did get a lot of drinks out of that. I also got a lot of food. I got an apple pie that was delicious. That was also kind of overwhelming because it was an avalanche of people that wanted to see me.

But I can't really say I miss it. I would rather have this balance that I'm at now, this balance that I think I have now, where it's like—you know, it's less of an act of like everyone's running around trying to see David and more of like, you know, that's a thing that happens.

KK: No plexiglass, no shitty tattooed guards chasing us out.

DC: Yeah, dude. Yeah, that's huge.

KK: Antifascists from around the world reached out and sent you books and sent you letters. Could you talk a little bit about what it was like in terms of the community support that you received from people you didn't even know, just because of who you were and why you were in there?

DC: It was absolutely incredible. And it was something I didn't see coming. I knew my defense committee had my back and my friends, but people who just knew about my case and were there for me had my back as well.

I was watching people giving a shit about my case take shape in little dribs and drabs from inside like through phone calls and letters and stuff. I called people on the second day. And they were like, oh, you know, this group Montréal Antifasciste wants to translate your sentencing statement into French and publish it on their website.

Some of those people wrote to me for the entirety of my bid, and I'm still in touch with some of them after my release. Yeah, it's still something that really is moving for me to talk about personally. Like it's very fucking cool.

And I think everyone wants to be supported through a hard time. Everybody wants, on some level, to feel like they deserve to be the center of attention for at least a short period of time. So that's an element of it.

What moves me about that is that it's an expression of solidarity, that people are volunteering their time and energy and money because they care about me as an individual even if they don't know me because of the stance that I took, a stance they agree with, as part of a movement that I believe in, a movement they believe in. It trickles down to supporting an individual, but it's really about keeping the movement going and making it stronger.

KK: How does it sit with you, the difference between the outpouring of love and support you got from the antifascist world and from other people who don't like Nazis, and the way that you were painted in the press and the right-wing attacks that you underwent? Even though the entire case is a right-wing attack.

DC: That's a good way to frame it. I never thought about that. The original report of the officer—he has an interest in covering his own ass. But it is a right-wing attack.

He's got an ulterior motive, which is to justify his use of force and him choosing me to arrest. He is dragging me through the mud and playing into this caricature of antifa or antifascist activists as dangerous, unhinged, out of touch with reality leftists, which is completely ridiculous.

Those attacks were part and parcel of my case. That's why I ended up going to jail because the whole thing was to make an example out of this guy, who's already been presented to the public as a really "bad guy."

And then seeing the support and response to that from antifascists, it was just something I had hoped was gonna come through. I wasn't super involved in any anarchist activist or antifascist activist worlds before. I never intended to get arrested. And I had been urging people not to fight the fascists that night if they came out looking for a fight. But it happened.

KK: Could you talk a little bit just about what that was like, how people on the inside reacted when they heard about why you were there?

DC: Yeah. I mean, I kept it quiet from corrections officers (COs) for obvious reasons. You don't expect COs, who are essentially wannabe cops stuck in a box, to be very sympathetic to leftist activists. You would imagine they would be kind of [Donald] Trumpy. And I knew that the dynamics of Trumpyness among COs were a little different at Rikers before I went there. That's one of the reasons I decided to go there.

First, it's important to understand that, when I say I decided to go to Rikers, I mean that my lawyers said we can push for this amount of time to be served at Rikers instead of upstate in the state prison system. I resisted all that very strongly until it became very clear that I had to take a deal that included jail time.

When I say I decided to go to Rikers, I mean my lawyers came to me and said, "We convinced the DA [district attorney] to allow you to serve your time at Rikers." And that's kind of a concession for the DA because it's local, and there's no parole tail. So serving time at Rikers, most people don't have probation or parole when they get out. If you serve your time upstate in the prison system, you have parole for at least as long as you were in.

Rikers is closer, so people can visit you more frequently. Another factor that was directly brought up in discussions with the DA by my lawyers is that I could be at risk of violence from COs or Trumpy inmate gangs upstate in the prison system. Rikers is safer.

I had a lot of support from antifascists before I went in, so they put me in touch with other people who'd done time for political reasons. I talked to a few friends of mine I knew who'd done time for just whatever reasons.

At Rikers, most of the guards, most of the COs, are Black and brown people. A lot of them are immigrants themselves. A lot of them are first generation. They show up, and that's the job they take to build a better life for themselves or whatever. I'm not getting into whether that's justifiable or not. Personally, I don't think it is.

But these are human beings. Trumpism is so deeply tied to white nationalism—it's built around a core of white nationalism—so a lot of people of color know that it doesn't pass the "smell test." While they may do the job for the money, they aren't foaming-at-the-mouth Trump supporters. There were a lot of mixed conversations; sometimes people recognized me and asked if I was antifa, some of the COs who were people of color made sympathetic comments.

Most of the inmates are not Trumpy there. Many were broadly supportive, particularly among communities of color, who may not have a deep political consciousness but knew they opposed racism. But it's not a political discussion most of the time.

Most people were like, "Oh my god, that's awesome!" I could pretty solidly rely on getting a good reaction and a goodwill boost in whatever housing unit I was in. After a few months, after I kind of had a feel for what things were like in there, I could pretty much bank on it. Like if a dude asked what I was in for, and I told him straight up, which you always do—you can't not answer that because that's mad suspicious.

KK: Especially the nerdy white guy, right?

DC: I could pretty much bank on that. After I felt like I had sort of the lay of the land to some degree—I mean, that's kind of dangerous. You don't wanna feel like you know it all in there. And I certainly don't claim that I do now, even after 12 months, the 12 months that I did. But after I felt I had a handle on it, I could pretty much bank on getting a good reaction out of people, at worst an ambivalent reaction.

KK: So given the generally positive or ambivalent, or at least not actively hostile, reaction that you tended to get in there when you did mention your politics, how did you practice antifascism while you were in this context? Because we talk a lot about everyday antifascism looks like, and it looks very different when you're on one side of those bars than when you're on the other—what did that look like for you?

DC: It is different just because it's a different world, and there are different rules, and it's an environment of enforced scarcity. There's this sense that they're always trying to come in and literally put their fingers in your stuff, to control your life. And so there's this sort of us-versus-them mentality that's sort of common. The worst thing you can be called is a snitch.

That sort of strain came out very strong when coronavirus disease 2019 (COVID-19) hit, and we did our strike. That there's us. There's the prisoners. And then there's the COs. And, at the end of the day, most guys felt that it was OK to have a rapport with COs, get along, appreciate them as human beings, but in the end we are on different teams. So that was the basis for our solidarity: we're on the same team, and the guards are the enemy. It's simple, but it works.

KK: Seems like an inherent solidarity there, given that there is already an us-and-them dynamic. You've said that a lot of the folks you talked to didn't really have a very developed political consciousness when you met them; did you make any inroads with other folks there in talking about politics?

DC: I'm not really a preachy kind of person. If people ask me questions, on the other hand, I'll generally do my best to answer them honestly. There were people who asked what my politics were about. Why you would go out there and fuck up Nazis? I say, listen, everyone has a right to an opinion, but if you go out and start organizing in support of white supremacy, we have a problem.

I offer the basic antifascist talking points: you can dress up racist ideas that ultimately lead down to genocide in a lot of paperwork and suits, but at the end of the day, it's just violence.

So those sorts of talking points, just talking with people about that, and they would respond to that pretty well. A political prisoner I met before I went in said he read Assata Shakur's biography publicly as a declaration of his politics and to help meet people, which I thought was a good idea.

It was a great book. It had been on my list to read for a while. Everything in jail is public. You don't have any privacy. Everything is visible and something that people are gonna absorb and register and talk about maybe. If you're reading a book about a Black Panther, and you're a skinny white boy, people are like, yo, what's up with that dude? So that's a topic of—that's a conversation starter with a lot of people.

KK: Did that happen?

DC: I read that book, and people talked. Some guy who was only in for two weeks, because I was in short-term jail, came up to me at a meal and said that Assata was running from the police after the turnpike incident and then she went and hid out at his uncle's house in Queens.

People would ask about the book and then we get into kind of deeper political discussions on that. People would send me zines and stuff, and I would just leave them out. Sometimes the dorm was packed to the fucking gills, and there were no empty beds. But if there was an empty bed, people would generally set it up as a library bed.

There was one guy, Italian Joe. He was a crack addict and a part-time plumber who just wanted to know what's up with anarchism and anti-capitalism, antifascism. He started asking for more and more literature. And I got some people to send stuff in to pass to him. Within a couple months, he started declaring himself an illegalist anarchist communist. They searched his bunk during the [George] Floyd rebellion. And he had all these zines, like *A World Without Police*.

KK: I'm interested in how either the ideas that you exchanged with other people or just your experience itself changed your politics. One thing I will tell you, from being your friend and from talking to you when you're in there and now talking to you after, is that I think that you've become a little more pragmatic and more accepting in the ways that you see people and language. One of the things we talked about a lot was like how there's so much homophobia and misogyny and transphobia flowing in there, but you can't go up and fight every guy who drops an "f-bomb" or says something derogatory about a woman because that's just the cultural situation you're in. So you had to kind of accept like, OK, these guys are gonna be my neighbors. And some of them are gonna be my friends. And they're gonna say stuff that wouldn't be acceptable at a meeting or in the spaces I'm usually a part of. How would you describe your own political evolution during this process?

DC: I had some experience working with a lot of working-class dudes, maybe a little rough around the edges, outside before I was locked up. But to live 24/7 with dudes who, you know, are expressing very freely misogyny, homophobia.

I've never been a person who's as big on language, or what some people would call identity politics, as some of my comrades. So it was a little easier for me not to chase dead ends.

There was a dude who stood up for a trans person's pronouns and the right to be addressed as they wanted to be addressed while using language that would be considered extremely offensive to most people I know who care about trans rights and things like that. It wasn't because they were trying to be a dick about trans folks, but because they didn't have the language for it.

That is a beautiful thing, it's a first step, and the next step is to talk about the language itself.

So that, other stuff politically, I mean, now, in terms of action, I limit myself a lot. Because I can't get in trouble again. I stay away from things that have really any risk. But it gave me a lot to think over in terms of how the prison-industrial complex works, why it continues to exist when it clearly doesn't actually work in the way it claims to. I didn't have any information about day-to-day life, but I could assume it was gonna be shitty and pretty absurd. And, you know, it was. But those things, those understandings, preincarceration, they are just not—they're fundamentally not the same as living through it and experiencing it. That informs my feelings about my politics a lot. It did—it gave me a lot of data to work with. I never liked cops, but I really hate them now.

KK: Well, I think a lot of people we know hate cops. But it's interesting to talk to you about that because it shows such a failure of the system. You are specifically the exact kind of person who's supposed to benefit from them, a nice, middle-class, educated, white guy.

DC: They're protecting me, yeah.

KK: And yet they broke your leg, and they threw you in a cage. And now you've come out of it being even more against them than you were before. And if they can't win you over, then what hope is there that they would have to be able to make inroads with someone who's had a much harder road?

DC: It's important to acknowledge that the way I was treated, the law under which I was prosecuted and convicted, all that stuff has been tested on Black and brown people, mostly young men, for decades.

I do think that maybe I've become more pragmatic in some ways. The thing about—the COs too, and I—this is maybe territory I shouldn't stray too far into because, again, I don't want people to think that I'm giving COs, let alone cops, like some sort of off here. Because I'm not. But I do think that, even if someone—if you consider someone to be your enemy or your opponent or your oppressor, there's also a lot of value in being able to sympathize with them and see what factors drive them.

KK: A "know your enemy" kind of situation?

DC: Know your enemy, but also what are their wants and needs? Why are they doing this in the first place? Most COs are not there because they wanna watch people have fucking cage matches to the death every day. It's just the mundaneness of it that strikes you most is that these people are just bureaucrats.

There were a lot of COs that I brought up standard abolition talking points with, like, wouldn't you take the same job and benefits to go work at a community center? And they were like, "Absolutely, right away." Strategically, if you can anticipate their needs and offer them something different, something that might be fulfilling for them in a better way.

KK: What you're describing is a power dynamic where even a benevolent oppressor is still an oppressor.

DC: De-radicalizing people by appealing to their humanity is super effective. A lot of militant antifascists who say, "What are we gonna do? Like sit down, invite the Nazis over for dinner one by one?" And it's like, yeah, I mean, that sounds pretty silly. And it won't work with a lot of people. I think in combination with the opportunity to get punched in the face while going out in the street, that tactic works pretty well.

I've had friends, normie friends, ask me, what can they do to offer movement support, besides supporting me? Well, you can spread the word about my case. You can share it on social media or just talk about it with people in conversation that you think might be receptive to it or people that—you know, even people you don't think will be very receptive to it. And you can do the same thing with "the movement," with "antifascism."

But you can normalize it by saying, "I am a middle manager for Capital One, and I support antifascism. And I have a friend who is locked up for it right now." And that's all. You don't have to necessarily put yourself at risk, but offer public support right where you are at.

KK: What kind of things did you learn that you could offer to another political, antifascist prisoner? What wisdom would you impart to someone who was facing incarceration?

DC: It's different based on what you are in for, if you are a political prisoner. So you are asking what can I do to help myself get through this in one piece? And that is reaching out. Appeal to people who are willing to give you support based on your political beliefs.

I have been very candid with people who showed up for me. I was not an "antifa superstar," who was in the center of all organizing. But once it happened, I had to be like: This is who I am, and I identify as an anti-fascist political prisoner. And if you have a political case, there are entire networks that fall into place for you. They will also want you to inform on other people to get a shorter sentence, and I knew I couldn't live with myself even if I got a shorter sentence if I did something like that. It's a conscious thing. They will give you time anyway. So if I went in and snitched in whatever capacity, people would find out. People always find out. That stuff has a way of coming out.

So if that gets out—and it will—that you sat and talked with the DA or the cops, you lose all the movement support. You go through whatever time, even if it's shortened, without any support. And if other guys inside find out that you're a snitch, dude, it's gonna be hard.

They told me they weren't gonna offer me anything less than four years unless I would go talk to them. And I sat on that for a year, and they slowly started to come down on the sentence they were offering and ultimately gave me 18 months. But I made my peace with doing four years. At the end of the day, that was the right decision.

Lessons from a Lifetime of Antiracist and Antifascist Struggle: A Memoir and Analysis

Michael Novick

It's critical to understand that the roots of what is called fascism run very deep in the history of US settler-colonial society. I say this as someone who has been doing antiracist and antifascist work, particularly among people of European descent in the US, unceasingly since the 1960s.[1] I want to discuss some of the lessons I have learned in a lifetime of struggle and study, and then apply those lessons to an analysis of what fascism is and how to fight it.

To get to why these lessons apply to the question of fighting fascism in the 21st century, it's fundamental to understand that because of the settler-colonial basis of the US state and society, founded on enslavement, land theft, and genocide, what came later to be called fascism has always been an essential part of the political basis and functioning of the US. Jingoistic racial nationalism, slave labor, police-state repression, hyper-masculinism and misogyny, genocide, ethnic cleansing, and glorification of war have been part and parcel of how the US has been built and ruled from its inception.

Three Lessons from the Late 1960s

1. Struggles That Do Not Center Challenging Institutionalized and Internalized Racism Are a House of Cards

I have an Orthodox Jewish immigrant, working-class background. My father came to the US from Poland as a teenager in the early 1930s. Most of his family in Bialystok was later wiped out in Adolf Hitler's genocide of European Jewry, particularly in the crushing of a ghetto rebellion in his hometown. He became a US citizen by serving in the Army late in World

War II. My parents met on a picket line when my mother was fired for joining District 65, a left-led Congress of Industrial Organizations (CIO) union on the Lower East Side in New York City (NYC). After I graduated from yeshiva high school, I attended Brooklyn College, which was then a tuition-free four-year public college. From 1964 to 1968, I got involved with student rights and free speech struggles, antiwar and antidraft activities, and joined Students for a Democratic Society (SDS). The college had been led for decades by a right-wing ideologue, Harry Gideonse, who had purged several generations of leftist students and faculty. In an era that was known for what Herbert Marcuse, a leftist philosopher, termed "repressive tolerance," the experience of Brooklyn College made it clear that any effective resistance was met with as much repression, and as little tolerance, as deemed necessary.

Toward the end of my junior year, we won a campaign to restore campus-wide student voting for student body president (which had been eliminated when student body officers had opposed the Korean War). I ran for and was elected student body president. That year, disclosures came to light of the involvement of the Central Intelligence Agency (CIA) in numerous organizations, including the American Federation of Labor–CIO's international office, and CIA subsidies of various journalists and public intellectuals to run stories or publish material supportive of the agency's clandestine efforts. I attended the National Student Association congress in Maryland where previous leaders of the association were called to account for their involvement with the CIA, and SDS ran a counter-convention.

In my senior year, we self-published a student evaluation of the teacher's handbook that the college administration tried to pull the plug on, and started draft counseling programs through the student council as opposition to the Vietnam War and the draft grew. We sat in when they tried to shut the school library for the night school students because of budget issues and won an instantaneous special appropriation from the state legislature to keep it open. We held a massive student strike to protest the expulsion and arrest of several SDS members who tried to leaflet a recruitment table set up by the Navy.

At the urging of the small campus Black Student Union (BSU) and Puerto Rican Student Union (PRSU), we then turned our attention to the fact that only a dozen Puerto Rican students and about 25 Black students were enrolled out of 10,000 students. We began to demand a special admissions program for two thousand Black and Puerto Rican high school graduates that coming fall and an ongoing open admissions program thereafter. In response, almost all the student support we had amassed in the other struggles evaporated. Lower-middle–class and working-class students, mostly Jewish and Irish Catholic, protested that such a move would lower the academic standards, and thus the value of their degree, or that their younger brothers and sisters would be displaced.

This was an abject lesson that unless you are consciously organizing and educating about the realities and impact of racism from the jump, and struggling about how racism is internalized and institutionalized, any other organizing you do, or base you may build, will not be principled or sustained.

The struggle was eventually won, and none of the feared consequences materialized.

2. Antiracist Struggles for Self-determination Will Both Radicalize and Polarize White People

The white campus left had been divided among SDS (both Progressive Labor Party [PLP] and Revolutionary Youth Movement factions), Youth Against War and Fascism (close to Workers World Party), the W. E. B. Du Bois Club (close to the Communist Party), and the Student Union. After discussions with the BSU and PRSU, we decided we should take the initiative and stage a disruption around the demand that they and other Black and Puerto Rican students had raised around the City University system. We all united and, along with other unaffiliated radicals, carried out a sit-in in the registrar's office,

This struggle was able to unite forces in the left that usually refused to work together. But simultaneously, radical right-wing reactionaries launched a counterprotest, trying to attack the sit-in. These included the Young Americans for Freedom, an anticommunist group started by William F. Buckley, and the Jewish Defense League (which, at the time, was composed of Jewish street toughs and ex-Marines, and was more stridently anti-Black than anti-Arab). They physically removed from campus a contingent of Columbia SDS students who had come to support us.

Such a polarization is inevitable because of the grip white settler-colonialism has on the consciousness and practice of even many working- and lower-middle-class people in the US, and their reaction may be violent. We didn't cast the struggle at the time as explicitly antifascist (although we threw the term "fascism" around), but both the use of physical violence by thuggish reactionaries and the history of repression at the college to purge left influences can be seen in retrospect as reflecting fascist elements of US political culture, designed to defend racial segregation and oppression.

3. The Level of Repression in Any Multiracial, International Struggle Will Generally Be Heaviest against Black People, Indigenous People, and People of Color

About 45 students involved in the sit-in were suspended, arrested, and, in my case and that of a few other graduating seniors involved, expelled. But eventually some of the charges were dropped, sentences were light or suspended, and the expelled students were readmitted on suspension and able to graduate the following year. But as the struggle in the city over community control of the (NYC public) schools heated up, along with the struggle for open admissions to the taxpayer-funded City University of New York and its campuses, the New York Police Department and Brooklyn district attorney's office staged massive raids and leveled totally trumped-up felony charges against leaders of the BSU and PRSU.

The charges were like a Brooklyn version of the bizarre felony conspiracy case going on at the time against the Panther 21—claims that the students had plotted to blow up the Brooklyn Botanic Garden and other claims that would have been laughable if they weren't serious crimes carrying long sentences. Thankfully, in those times, the spirit of resistance to state repression was high and generalized, and, just like the lengthier and better-known case against the Panther 21, the fabricated charges against the Black and Puerto Rican Brooklyn College students ultimately dissolved in dismissals or acquittals.[2]

Three Lessons from the Mid-to-Late 1970s

1. White Supremacy Will Corrode and Disorient the Left without Conscious Struggle and Vigilance

As the high tide of radical struggle in the US during the "long Sixties" began to recede, many in the white left began to make individual accommodations and compromises, landing, like flotsam after a storm, in jobs at nonprofits and other professional bureaucracies or economist "bread-and-butter" labor union positions. Even the smaller groups that professed to maintain revolutionary commitments began to trim their sails to the prevailing winds. In 1975, as part of the June 28th Union, a mostly white gay men's socialist, feminist, anti-imperialist collective from the Bay Area, California, I attended the Hard Times Conference in Chicago, Illinois called by Prairie Fire Organizing Committee (PFOC).

PFOC had started by reprinting the book produced by the Weather Underground Organization (WUO) of the same name.[3] At the conference, we in the June 28th Union swiftly joined with criticisms being lobbed at the organizers by Black, Puerto Rican, Chicano, Native American, and Asian-American participants. It became clear that PFOC, and by extension the WUO, had abandoned a revolutionary anti-imperialist perspective. They had begun to ignore the leadership and self-determination of the anticolonial, antioppression struggles of Black, Indigenous, and people of color (BIPOC) communities and nations inside the US. Eventually, it came out that the WUO, behind the scenes, was angling to surface from the underground and declare themselves the leadership of a "new communist party."[4]

The Hard Times Conference struggle led to splits and the dissolution of the WUO. PFOC on the West Coast, which I eventually joined, recommitted itself to solidarity with national liberation struggles inside and outside the US, and to a focus on women's leadership within the organization.

2. Self-Determination Means That Anticolonial and Other Liberation Movements Set the Terms and Timetable of Their Struggles

Among the various forms of internationalist solidarity taken up in the PFOC milieu was the issue of Puerto Rican independence. I joined the Puerto Rico Solidarity Committee (PRSC), a national formation in the US that supported the *independentista* (independence) movement. But struggles quickly emerged over the question of the strategy and tactics of various elements within the independence movement in Puerto Rico and within the Puerto Rican communities in the US. Armed struggle formations had emerged, attacking US military and other installations in Puerto Rico and symbols or perpetrators of US colonial domination in the US itself or expropriating funds, as was done by Los Macheteros.

Some solidarity activists, who were comfortable with calling for the release of the five Puerto Rican Nationalists who had committed similar armed actions in the 1950s, were not prepared to defend or support such an approach to decolonization at that time. This ignored the reality of the intense repression carried out by the US against public sectors of the Puerto Rican independence movement, including massive intelligence and snitch files on individuals. Entrapment operations and infiltration of proindependence organizations, including assassinations, were carried out by every repressive and counterinsurgency agency in the US, from the Federal Bureau of Investigation (FBI) to Naval Intelligence. Solidarity activists seeking to limit the Puerto Rican struggle to electoral activity reflected illusions about the nature of the US state itself, and about the space for electoral struggle to somehow reform or even overturn colonialism.

I was part of a sector that split from the PRSC and started the New Movement in Solidarity with Puerto Rican Independence, in response to leadership from the Movimiento de Liberación Nacional (MLN) in the US and La Liga Socialista Puertorriqueña, public organizations that supported the right to struggle for independence by any means necessary. We offered public support to the clandestine armed organizations, such as the Fuerzas Armadas de Liberación Nacional (FALN) and Los Macheteros.

A review of the earlier history of US solidarity-based efforts with Puerto Rico reinforced this understanding. During the 1950s, the Puerto Rican Nationalist Party under Don Pedro Albizu Campos launched a proindependence insurrection and attacked Harry Truman in Blair House for using aerial bombardment and massive repression, and later attacked Congress over repressive legislation against the Puerto Rican labor and independence movements. But the Communist Party of the United States of America (CPUSA) concluded that the US-imposed "Commonwealth"[5] had "resolved" the colonial contradiction of Puerto Rico. Every Puerto Rican cadre in the CPUSA immediately left the organization in response.

The lesson for solidarity work in my day was clear—the role of US leftists was not to dictate to anticolonial forces, but to work to expose and undermine colonialism and support for colonialism within the US, and to defend the anticolonial struggle of Puerto Ricans. We translated and published communiqués from the clandestine organizations explaining their actions.

3. Character Counts

My engagement with the MLN, then a joint Puerto Rican and Chicano/Mexicano organization, when many others of my generation in the white left were settling into academia, nonprofits, or the corporate world, sustained my commitment to revolutionary politics.

The MLN had strong relationships with revolutionary-minded sister organizations in Puerto Rico. They came together partly in response to federal grand juries investigating the FALN. The Feds subpoenaed people from New York, Illinois, Colorado, New Mexico, California, and elsewhere involved in grassroots projects that had received some funding from the United Methodist Church because Carlos Alberto Torres, whom the Feds had concluded was involved with the FALN, was associated with the Methodist network of "Latino" groups. Those who received the grand jury subpoenas were given a "transactional immunity" that stripped them of Fifth Amendment protections and threatened them with jail for contempt of court. But they still refused to collaborate or testify. Many were incarcerated for this principled defiance of the grand jury.

One, Ricardo Romero, who had been a leader on the Crusade for Justice and of the Poor People's March and encampment in Washington, DC after the death of Martin Luther King, Jr., was locked up for three years when he was served with a new subpoena immediately upon completing his first sentence for contempt of court for refusing to testify. This emphasis on the ability to stand on principle even at a cost was vital. It clearly inspired widespread community support and admiration that helped build political support and draw in allies from faith-based, labor, and other groups for the struggle to free political prisoners. Far from being quixotic, such actions helped define a stance of noncollaboration and uncompromising opposition to imperialism that cohered and strengthened a mass base of support. It also served to expose the state's fundamental disregard for alleged constitutional rights, such as the Fifth Amendment, or the right to silence. The principled resistance and noncollaboration rendered the coercion and repression futile.

A Lesson from the Mid-to-Late 1980s: Never Let the Nazis Have the Street

The Greensboro massacre in 1979 exposed the beginnings of what later came to be known as the Nazification of the Ku Klux Klan (KKK, or simply "Klan"). A United Racist Front of Klansmen and neo-Nazis in North Carolina killed several members and associates of the Communist Workers Party. These racists and fascists were acquitted in both state and federal courts. There had been federal and police informants in their midst who played roles in arming and uniting them. This process advanced through the 1980s with a wink and a nod from the Feds during the Ronald Reagan administration.

Reagan had announced his presidential campaign on a "states' rights" platform in Philadelphia, Mississippi (site of the murders of civil rights workers James Chaney, Michael Schwerner, and Andrew Goodman), and later paid his respects at the Nazi Schutzstaffel cemetery in Bitburg during a state visit to Germany. There was a neoliberal attack on labor, and the retreat of much of the Black liberation movement due to the impact of the Counter Intelligence Program (COINTELPRO).

Much of the left turned toward reformism and electoral politics, such as Jesse Jackson's Democratic Party primary runs for the presidency, retreating from concepts of dismantling the empire or overturning capitalism and white supremacy. Into the vacuum this created stepped neofascist forces, inculcating a new generation of mostly disaffected white youth. They created a violence-prone racist "bonehead"[6] subculture that sought to dominate punk, skinhead, and other music and social scenes. I was part of a reconstituted John Brown Anti-Klan Committee (JBAKC), which we brought together as a direct-action anti-Klan organization with an express commitment to solidarity with Black liberation out of pre-existing anti-Klan groups associated with PFOC, the May 19th Communist Organization, and others.

The JBAKC sought to offer a revolutionary, internationalist alternative to both the fascists' appeal to youth and the liberal opponents of the KKK. Liberal strategy oscillated between efforts to "ban the Klan" through legislative and police action and to urge communities to stay away and ignore KKK rallies. Counterposed to either of those approaches, the JBAKC advocated confrontation and counterorganizing, whether in the prisons or on the streets. We aimed both to foil neo-Nazi efforts at domination by intimidation, and to arm young people with a revolutionary antiracist and antifascist perspective that criticized the system and the liberal elite, rather than defending it.

The JBAKC chapter in Los Angeles dealt with an alliance of Tom Metzger's White Aryan Resistance, the local KKK and Nazi Party, and a crew from the Idaho-based Aryan Nations, including its top leader, Richard Butler. They held a triple cross-burning in the San Fernando Valley; several of the cross-burners became members of the white supremacist underground called The Order or the Silent Brotherhood (Bruder Schweigen), from whom the "14 words" slogan and the "14/88" numerology still popular with neo-Nazis derived.

The JBAKC, and later the more spontaneous and mass-based Anti-Racist Action (ARA)—which was a multitendency network that included at various points anarchists, anti-imperialists, some Trotskyists, and many unaffiliated antiracists—had great success in countering the Nazi bonehead scene that emerged among fans of fascist bands such as Skrewdriver. JBAKC and ARA worked with groups such as Skinheads Against Racial Prejudice (SHARP), Skins and Punks Against Racism (SPAR), and Red & Anarchist Skin Heads (RASH). Through mechanisms such as Rock Against

Racism (RAR) shows, tabling at the Warped Tour and the OzzFest, and, in Los Angeles, the punk-based Human Earth & Animal Liberation (HEAL) conferences, ARA chapters worked to block and scuttle Nazi attempts to dominate scenes in Minneapolis, Minnesota, Portland, Oregon, Columbus, Ohio, Chicago, Philadelphia, Pennsylvania, and elsewhere.

After JBAKC people left LA, I continued doing opposition research on local neo-Nazis and launched People Against Racist Terror (PART; later Anti-Racist Action Los Angeles/People Against Racist Terror [ARA-LA/ PART]) in 1987 when I learned of a planned LA appearance of convicted Birmingham, Alabama church bomber J. B. Stoner in Glendale, California. Over one thousand people turned out for the protest we called, eventually termed an illegal assembly and dispersed by Glendale police after a few Nazi boneheads who showed up to attend Stoner's talk got the worst of a confrontation. At its height, the ARA Network had over one hundred chapters around the country, large conferences, regional gatherings, national network travelers who could help start and vouch for new chapters, a legal defense war chest, and multiple publications and zines. These included *Turning the Tide: Journal of Inter-communal Solidarity*, which I started producing in LA in 1988 in organizing around a long-delayed trial for Metzger and other local Klan and Nazi types for the 1983 triple cross-burning.

At the height of the ARA Network, the publication *Turning the Tide* had 10,000 or more copies of every issue being distributed around the country, along with 30,000 or more copies of the *ARA News* zine out of Columbus. That militant opposition to the Klan and Nazis, willingness to engage in community self-defense, and a radical antiestablishment stance against all forms of racism, sexism, and oppression made ARA a principal vehicle for radicalizing young people, particularly (but not exclusively) white youth, in the later Reagan years, through the George H. W. Bush administration, and into the Bill Clinton era.

Lessons from the 1990s

1. Antiracism Is the Firmest Ground for Antimilitarism

In 1991 in LA, PART struggled to get the local coalition against the first "Gulf War" (the George H. W. Bush war on Iraq over its invasion of Kuwait) to take up the "the war at home" in response to the police beating of Rodney King. There were Black GI war resisters at the Westwood antiwar protests, and some people of color groups in the antiwar coalition. But the peace movement in LA by and large did not show up for the protests called for by the Black community outside Parker Center (LAPD headquarters, which was named for a notoriously racist former chief). Peace activists did not see the connection between the war in Iraq and the "war at home" against Black people, and thus did not take up the demand for fundamental changes in policing and the firing of then-Chief of Police Darryl Gates.

Gates had claimed that more Black people were killed by police choke holds because they had different throats. He had swept homeless people and migrant street vendors into jails and border patrol deportation proceedings in preparation for the LA Olympics in 1984. Enjoying lifetime tenure like other LA police chiefs before him, and possessing intelligence dossiers on many political figures in the city, Gates used his power to increase police funding, militarization, and "occupying army" techniques in Black and brown communities. (The comparison is to J. Edgar Hoover's blackmail of establishment political figures to render the FBI immune to oversight.)

The failure of the white left broadly beyond the peace movement to join in solidarity with the Black-led struggle was a factor in the frustration of the Black community, and again reflected illusions about the nature of so-called democracy in the US. The acquittal of the cops who beat Rodney King led to the 1992 rebellion (which was multiracial, especially in South LA). The earlier failure to bring the peace movement into solidarity and unity with the Black community struggle also led to the rapid deflation and dispersal of the peace movement as the first Iraq invasion came to a swift conclusion.

ARA nationally learned and applied some lessons from this experience under the Clinton administration. Columbus ARA seeded the audience with people prepared to speak out disruptively when Madeleine Albright, Clinton's secretary of state, came to Ohio State University to beat the drums for Clinton's intention to involve the North Atlantic Treaty Organization (NATO) in the war in the Republic of Kosovo. The protesters planted around the venue peppered Albright with challenges about the continued sanctions and no-fly zone in Iraq (an act of war) and her statement that the deaths of children that resulted were an acceptable price to pay.

2. Liberal Reformism Is Part of the Problem and Increases the Repressive Power of the State

After the 1992 LA uprising, the time was ripe for radical demands and changes regarding racist policing. Michael Zinzun was a former Black

Panther and head of LA's Coalition Against Police Abuse, which tracked officers involved in racist violence, alerting people in other communities when such cops switched departments. He launched an initiative effort to amend the LA city charter and create an elected board with subpoena power and the ability to fire cops, to exert community control over the police, along with a special local prosecutor to handle cases of police abuse of power, brutality, and other criminality. But the American Civil Liberties Union and Southern Christian Leadership Conference decided instead to back the Christopher Commission, an elite body appointed by Mayor Tom Bradley (a Black ex-cop) and Gates to probe the Rodney King beating and LAPD operations and to propose reforms. The abandonment of Zinzun's proposal by civil libertarians and the Black establishment doomed it to failure. The Christopher Commission proposals did little or nothing to change the LAPD, except to put a five-year term limit on the police chief.

In the 1990s, ARA-LA/PART helped build the "Crack the CIA Coalition," a multiracial, international coalition influenced by disclosures that linked CIA support for the Nicaraguan Contras with CIA protection of drug dealers shipping drugs and guns into South LA. This in turn helped spawn the crack cocaine epidemic and subsequent turf wars between the Crips and Bloods. The LAPD has always been tightly integrated into the national security state, particularly the CIA.

3. Antiracists Must Be Antisexist, Profeminist, and Committed to Accountability

The ARA Network was repeatedly hobbled and derailed in many localities by key weaknesses even as it grew rapidly across the country in the 1990s. Until the emergence of the antiglobalization movement, it seemed to be the "only game in town" for a lot of young (predominantly, but not exclusively, white) radicals not interested in campus politics and facing continued Nazi outrages and efforts to control youth scenes.

The source of many of ARA's failures to capitalize on this momentum was sometimes referred to as "manarchism": a combination of male chauvinism and individualism that resulted all too frequently in sexual exploitation and oppression of female members. Splits and drama occurred as people within or between chapters would often choose sides based on personal loyalties, street credibility, or reputation. A factor in this may have been that, because of the relatively low basis of unity and the need for security in dealing at the street level with fascists, many chapters were built as much on personal affinities and relationships as on conscious political organizing or study. Even though many women played leading roles in many chapters and in the network as a whole, there was an aspect of unexamined and uncorrected masculinism that repeatedly surfaced. This was despite protocols and training about listening to survivors, insisting on consent and equality in relationships, or readings exposing and opposing male chauvinism and supremacy.

Chapters, including major ones in Columbus and Chicago, repeatedly fell apart over such incidents and failures to respond properly. This was paralleled by an inability to build sustained structures and organizational mechanisms for carrying out tasks and plans. There was a probable over-reliance on personal affinities and shared experiences in physical confrontations with neo-Nazis and Klansmen to cement the network together. This helped lead to its disintegration in the 2000s, when the flip side of bitterness over personal failings and disappointment in upholding commitments or exercising good "security culture" led to insurmountable problems between people and chapters.

Strengths and weaknesses are often dialectically interconnected. Weaknesses of spontaneity and a relatively simple basis of unity were easily exploited by the state. The willingness to throw down and face physical confrontations with fascist forces, and the reliance on personal trust relationships and vouching rather than abstract ideological agreement, allowed ARA to grow and spread rapidly as a cultural–political phenomenon. But they also impeded our ability to stabilize and build network capacity and that of individual members and chapters, or to learn and apply lessons from errors or failures. Another factor may have been that, because of security concerns in dealing with fascist groupings, ARA often held itself aloof from other elements of the left as it began to develop.

Lessons from the 2000s

1. Antiracists Need a Strong Antirepression Component and Deep Roots to Withstand State Attacks

ARA began to fade somewhat nationally as the antiglobalization movement came to life starting in 1999 and many other avenues for radical direct action activism became available to people. There were, however, a couple of key developments that ARA-LA/PART was involved in to try to bring a community organizing approach and anticolonial politics to the burgeoning antiglobalization struggle. In 2000, the Democratic National

Convention (DNC) was scheduled for LA and a large local movement coalition, augmented by national forces such as the Direct Action Network, began organizing and mobilizing for protests. ARA-LA/PART was involved in building a coalition-within-the-coalition, focused on a day of action against the criminal justice system. We had to withstand repeated efforts by the Revolutionary Communist Party and the PLP, both laying claim to being a Maoist vanguard, to hijack this coalition for either of their rival projects. Instead, we built a broad-based and community-centered coalition that put forward interrelated demands to end police abuse, end mass incarceration and the prison-industrial complex, free all political prisoners, and end the racist death penalty.

We had speakers from Leonard Peltier's Defense/Offense Committee, All of Us or None (a formerly incarcerated people's movement), and Death Penalty Focus, as well as major cultural figures. But more importantly, we drew out almost six thousand people, mostly local and mainly young people of color. We marched from Pershing Square to the LAPD headquarters and then back to the Staples Center, home of the DNC, where people refused to enter the "free speech" pens that were erected by authorities to limit our protest activity. Workers, tourists, and shoppers in downtown LA were treated to the jaw-dropping sight of armored personnel carriers with more cops than a person might typically see in a lifetime.

On the heels of this, we were involved in a statewide effort to unite antiauthoritarians and anti-imperialists in the antiglobalization movement around a program of community base building. The effort overcame some sectarian differences and put together a fairly successful conference dedicated to dialogue between antiauthoritarians and anti-imperialists. It was predicated on, and came close to achieving, a makeup that was at least 50% female and at least 50% people of color. One project that came out of this was a Cop Watch in Long Beach, California, as the whole purpose and focus was to try to sink deeper roots in communities and neighborhoods.

Cop Watch, which several ARA chapters had been involved in during the 1990s, is a direct action, antifascist, and antiracist initiative aimed at delegitimizing the police and transforming the culture of communities from one of fear, compliance, and obedience to one of vigilance, resistance, and community defense. But after months of organizing, this project was swept away with September 11th and the "War on Terror." The Long Beach cops harassed residents who came to the infoshop where Cop Watch was based, shined spotlights on and took photographs of people, threatened local homeless people and organizers if they associated with Cop Watch, and eventually beat, injured, and arrested a number of young Long Beach anarchists, including a couple of major felony arrests.

This organizing effort was not able to withstand the intense level of repression during the growth of the police state and of jingoistic, prowar sentiment after September 11th. ARA nationally and locally, however, with a longer history, was able to carry out some important work in this same period. Internationally, the ARA Network held its conference in Canada in October 2001, barely a month after September 11th, called for solidarity with Afghan women and people, and opposed US and Canadian military action in Afghanistan. Locally, ARA-LA/PART, which has a history of organizing actions on December 10th, Human Rights Day, on the anniversary of the Universal Declaration of Human Rights, was instrumental in putting together a coalition and action opposing the US invasion of Afghanistan. But, in general, not only the antiracist movement but the broader left suffered tremendous setbacks in this period that took almost a decade to recover from.

2. A New Generation Must Shape Its Own Struggles and Leadership without Erasing or Dismissing Elders' Lessons and Contributions

The left has been plagued and weakened by discontinuities in its development due to state repression, the impact of unexamined or uncorrected errors, and the demoralization and defeatism that comes with significant losses. New forces began to emerge in the mid to late 2000s that suffered from that same lack of continuity, mentorship, or torch-passing transitions that can take a struggle to the next level. In white antiracist activism, there was a transition away from either explicitly anticolonial solidarity and militant direct action antifascism and toward efforts to build a "white antiracist culture and community." This has some strengths but could be difficult to distinguish from academic or corporate efforts to examine "whiteness." It has taken the better part of a decade to morph that into formations such as Showing Up for Racial Justice (SURJ) and its LA affiliate, White People for Black Lives, which have embraced active solidarity, recognizing the leadership of the current generation of the Black freedom struggle and Indigenous people's movements. But the long lag time before self-examination, focus on "white privilege," and separation from militantly antiracist and anticapitalist politics took, and continues to take, a toll on the development and revolutionary mindedness of this movement.

At the same time, in LA, Oakland, California, and elsewhere, a new, militant, and professedly revolutionary tendency emerged, out of the gangs and in the prisons, trying to lay claim to the mantle and legacy of the Black Panther Party (BPP). ARA-LA/PART worked with one such formation, the Black Riders Liberation Party (BRLP), that styled itself "the new-generation Black Panther Party." But there were serious contradictions between the BRLP and actual surviving members of the BPP. This new generation expressed a lot of bitterness at what it perceived as failures, particularly a failure to sustain the struggle and pass the torch with a high level of resources, consciousness, and organization intact.

The BRLP was not wrapped up in the antisemitism and antiwhite rhetoric that characterized the New Black Panther Party, which owed more to reactionary elements in the Nation of Islam for its ideology than to the original BPP. But the BRLP's overemphasis on militarism as an antidote to reformism and disdain for any input or critique coming from Black elders were weaknesses that allowed the group to become excessively hierarchical. Any criticism of the top leader was seen as a counterrevolutionary attack on the organization, allegedly inspired by COINTELPRO operations—the FBI-led domestic counterinsurgency war against the original BPP, the American Indian Movement (AIM), Chicano/Mexicano groupings, and other leftists in the 1960s to 1970s.

Lessons from the 2010s

1. The Road to Hell Is Paved with Good Intentions

The realization developed that "Black faces in high places"—such as the presidency of Barack Obama—did not mean that the US was "postracial." In fact, the strength of racism and reaction was growing. During this period, the Occupy Wall Street movement arose to challenge economic inequality, and a revived mass Black struggle challenged and inspired others, including white people, to step up their resistance. Occupy LA was a mixed and contradictory bag, with libertarians, corporate Democrats, conspiracy theorists, and a lot of other elements contending with left and anticapitalist anarchist forces. The proximity of the encampment around Los Angeles City Hall to a large and increasingly well-organized and mostly Black Skid Row community of unhoused and ill-housed people had a radicalizing effect. I was involved in efforts to bring the BRLP into contact with the Occupy movement and into communication with the older generation of Black former political prisoners and political prisoner/prisoner of war supporters in the Jericho Movement. But, in both cases, the BRLP seemed intent primarily on attracting material support and aid.

New formations did develop, such as an Inter-Communal Solidarity Committee, with efforts to bring together radicals from Occupy with BLRP members in LA and Oakland. But serious contradictions emerged, specifically related to criticisms leveled at the top leader of the BRLP, his abusive behavior toward comrades and especially women, and other improprieties.

I only belatedly broke ties with and extricated myself from my relationship to the BRLP, but not before they led to sanctions against me and my separation from the Torch Network because of the mistrust my actions supporting the BRLP generated. We printed both the criticisms and the sanctions against the leader of the BRLP and myself, and my self-criticism, in *Turning the Tide*. It has taken years to make amends and overcome some of the damage I did to relationships, and this is not yet fully accomplished.

2. Prisoners Lead in Overcoming the Carceral State

The prisoner hunger strike that spread nationally from Pelican Bay State Prison in 2013 demonstrated the power of principled resistance and unity to overcome fascistic conditions of repression, racial divisions, and isolation. ARA-LA/PART and *Turning the Tide*, which was distributed free to thousands of prisoners over the years in California and nationally, played a role in helping spread the word both behind prison walls and in the outside world of "minimum security." Lessons from George Jackson and the prison movement of the 1970s were applied in practice to great effect, and showed that people could withstand torture and overcome isolation and solitary confinement.

Sadly, support for those elements behind bars and their struggle was very uneven in LA, centered mainly on family members of those incarcerated. In the same period as a series of protests outside the Ronald Reagan State Building called by supporters of the prison hunger strikers, for example, there was a major political repression case going on in LA against Carlos Montes, a former Brown Beret and long-time leader of Chicano struggles. He had been named as an unindicted coconspirator in a major FBI frame-up in Minnesota. In LA, he was brought up on weapons charges based on a decades-old conviction. Dozens from LA leftist groups turned out for his court appearances, but few if any then joined us in proceeding over to the State Building just a few blocks south for the solidarity actions around the hunger strike.

This reflects narrow and sectarian definitions of what constitutes "the left" and of who is a political prisoner. They failed to recognize the enduring power of the prisoners' example and solidarity, in their "Call to End Hostilities," which broke down barriers between Black, white, and *Norteño* and *Sureño* prisoners. That agreement to stop fighting each other and organize against the prison system's torture and rights violations sparked the hunger strikes that eventually involved 30,000 or more prisoners and spread nationwide. The lessons of the ability to organize and unify people under the totalitarian conditions that prevail inside "prisons within prisons" merit much greater attention by antifascists. Prisoners' struggles demand the solidarity of the labor movement in this country, and should be a priority focus of left labor organizers. Antifascists should also commit to solidarity with these prisoner struggles and learn from them. The capacity to withstand torture demonstrated initially by BPP political prisoners and then much more widely is of particular significance as the state and fascists turn toward more brutal methods.

3. Black Love Matters

The more uplifting lesson from the past half decade or so is that, as Ernesto "Che" Guevara said, a "true revolutionary is guided by great feelings of love." There are certainly a lot of criticisms of and divisions within Black Lives Matter (BLM) as a movement. But it has shown tenacity, demonstrating the transformative power of the abolitionist perspective. BLM has provided the unifying example, at least here in LA, of strong conscious solidarity with Chicano/Mexicano and Latinx families and movements, with Asians in struggle, and with Indigenous people. That impact has pushed many white people into both in-the-streets solidarity and into committed and ongoing antiracist organizing. It has been an important lesson about the power of love, the depth of cultural and spiritual expression as key aspects of liberatory struggle, and the strength that comes from the intersectional resistance that can overcome the divisions that racial-capitalist, heteronormative, patriarchal power structures seek to impose and have us internalize.

I still believe that self-critical examination of our weaknesses, errors, and failures is imperative to overcome them and build forward. But I also recognize more clearly the redemptive power of affirmation, of appreciation for our strengths and perseverance, of celebrating our victories and unities. In LA, BLM, allied with the Los Angeles Community Action Network on Skid Row and the Stop LAPD Spying Coalition and its uncompromising and radical critique and exposure of the essentially oppressive, white supremacist, exploitative, and repressive nature of policing, has impacted large sectors of the left and large numbers of white people, not least in White People for Black Lives.

Struggles have emerged within formations such as Democratic Socialists of America–LA, Ground Game LA, and many other groups that are seeking to embrace the Black radical tradition, deepen understanding about racial capitalism, and recognize the need to avoid the snares of reformism. I still work with other Black forces that are highly critical of BLM, and I am sure that struggle will play itself out, but I have come to believe that ideological struggle about the correct line only goes so far. These struggles sometimes lead to sterile dead ends of "either/or," and we need principled unity, positivity, and sometimes "both/and" approaches that can lead to open-ended transformations.

Lessons from the 2020s

We have to go all the way this time. The stakes are now too high, the consequences of another failed movement upsurge too great. More successful fascist organizing, and a willingness within the corporate political parties and system to countenance it, are rooted in a deepening crisis. Climate catastrophes are piling up—floods, droughts, fires, killer heat, rising seas. These are compounded by the coronavirus disease 2019 (COVID-19) pandemic and the prospects of further pandemics as disease vectors are impacted by climate change, corporate agriculture, and the invasion of wildlife terrain by human fields, feedlots, and farming.

I was sure that a revolution was imminent in the US itself 50 or so years ago, when imperialism looked like it was on the ropes. Now that I am in my seventies, I see the undeniable necessity of that revolution, everywhere and every day. There has been a clear embrace of fascism and war by the rulers of this society in the face of insurmountable and irreconcilable contradictions in their system and within their own ranks, let alone with the great majority of humanity.

If we are to triumph and prevent the calamities and atrocities this necrotic system will visit upon a suffering humanity and planet, we must extract the lessons from all those previous efforts, experiences, advances, setbacks, and failures so that we can get it right this time. Fascism, linked to global warfare, is the clear direction the rulers are heading, and the total surveillance society is already at hand.

But it is also true, as Bantu Stephen "Steve" Biko of the Black Consciousness Movement in South Africa expressed, that the greatest weapon in the hands of the oppressor is the minds of the oppressed. Key to building an effective revolutionary antifascist movement is breaking the identification with the oppressor, and the power of white supremacy and imperial privilege to shape people's consciousness. To do so, we must study the ebb and flow of the contradiction between the power of the state and the corporations and that of the resistant working people and anticolonial struggles. We must never accept the fascists' claims of invincibility and inevitability. And we must provide people with antidotes to fascists' attempts to appeal to them as the solution to the crises.

Lessons from History and Study

Fascism has had many definitions, but can best be understood as bringing the methods of rule common to colonialism to bear on reshaping the state and society in the metropole. This is a non-Eurocentric view, seeing the world from the perspective and experience of the peoples who have been victimized by and resisted colonialism. Colonizers used genocide; glamorized military strength; relied on slave labor; emphasized techniques of divide and conquer, ideological domination, and reshaping the cultures they encountered; and incorporated their own working and petty proprietor classes into imperial conquest.

Not that every fascist party or formation has developed in an imperial country or hearkens back to imperial or colonial ambitions, dreams, or realities. But the formation of a visceral, cross-class identification with a leader and a reactionary community, the martial and militarist reorganization of daily life, racial nationalism, masculinism, and similar features of most fascist ideologies, formations, and regimes, are all characteristics of colonial rule, along with slave labor and genocide.

The US is a settler-colonial society in which both state and class formation are intimately connected to land theft and to racial hierarchies and racialized exploitation. Here, such methods have been used from the start and are still being used against internally colonized and subjugated peoples. In the US, fascism is not a threatening prospect of the future but a reality of our history and current social, political, and economic arrangements.

You cannot defeat fascism with an appeal to alliance with liberalism or ruling capitalist parties. In fact, the idea that opposing fascism is meant to save the established order becomes part of the appeal that fascism uses to further recruit people fed up with the current system.

Identifying fascism, in the US context, exclusively with the political right and Republican Party is hopelessly naïve. There is both collusion and contention between elite and powerful proponents of sometimes disguised fascist "solutions," and lower-middle–class and even working-class elements cohering in openly fascist formations.

ARA consistently held that "fascism is built from above and below" and supported the need for both militant antifascism vis-à-vis the Nazi formations as well as antirepression efforts directed at the state, such as Cop Watch. The JBAKC was organized on a more clearly and consciously internationalist basis of solidarity, particularly with the Black freedom struggle and the New Afrikan liberation movement. ARA-LA/PART has always tried to incorporate both elements, with a focus on prison/police abolition work, concrete internationalist solidarity with struggles inside and outside the US, and support for political prisoners being key to its continuity.

There are, roughly speaking, three views of fascism out there: 1) how fascism presents itself; 2) how competing rulers and competing strategies and ideologies within imperialism present it; and 3) how working-class revolutionaries, anarchist or socialist, have traditionally seen it. I would posit, based on a lifetime of practice in antiracist, antifascist, and internationalist solidarity struggles, that all three views are incorrect and incomplete.

Fascism falsely presents itself as revolutionary, anticapitalist and anticommunist, nationalistic and militaristic, a vanguard that welds together a *volk* into a fighting machine. It proposes a new state and social order that purges weakness, sentimentality, and "alien" influences, particularly insofar as it defends "womanhood" or traditional masculinity.

Competing imperialist ideologies portray fascism as uniquely totalitarian, nationalistic, militaristic, racist, religiously rigid, and xenophobic, to which antigay and antiwoman have been added more recently. These proimperialist liberals would like to portray themselves (falsely) as a bulwark against fascism.

Communist and anarchist analyses have tended to portray fascism as reactionary and anti–working class but as using racial and religious scapegoating to manipulate workers into lining up behind an iconic "maximum leader." Sexual repression, including supposedly latent or repressed homoeroticism, is often emphasized.

All three views portray fascism as the master of propaganda and spectacle (and as noted, as nationalistic and militaristic).

What's wrong with these views? How can a more correct understanding guide antifascist practice?

Fascists, rival imperialists, and Euro/worker-centric communists and anarchists all have, for purposes of their own, reasons to disguise the true nature of fascism and to distinguish it categorically from other "less-evil" forms of class society and oppressive, exploitative rule.

Fascists want to present themselves as revolutionary anticapitalists (and may even believe they are) to cement a mass base and mass participation in their effort. Other rulers and imperial ideologies or strategies want to portray fascism as evil incarnate, the bogeyman in comparison to whom their exploitation, oppression, militarism, and repressive measures look benign or justified. They use fascism as a threat to dangle if resistance steps up—"Look how much worse things can be; we're the best deal you're going to get."

Euro/worker-centric socialists and anarchists are oblivious to the true nature of fascism—and of their own projects—because many believe their approach will run their advanced industrial societies better (i.e., deep down, they still accept the empire). In some cases, they are actually seeking an alliance with "their own" ruling class, with whom they believe they can make common cause against the fascists.

If all these views are incorrect, what is correct?

People understand that there is a fundamental connection between imperialism and fascism. As the US has become more blatantly imperialist, there is a common widespread fear that "fascism" is on the immediate horizon. The left used antifascist rhetoric against George W. Bush, the right used it against Obama, and even the "center" got into the act using it to describe Donald Trump.

But to really understand what is going on, we need to take a step back to get a clearer and more valid picture of the real context of empire and class society within which fascism operates.

The Imperial Roots of Fascism

The Western European nation-states where modern fascism came to or sought power are better understood as empire states. Great Britain, France, Spain, et cetera were each an empire in themselves, controlling dominated peoples and other language groups consolidated within a territory and an economic bioregion through the leadership of the capitalist owning class, called the "bourgeoisie." Leadership necessarily implies the independent participation of other classes and strata (higher *and* lower), whose efforts were cohered with and subsumed into the bourgeoisie's project. Germany and Italy—where fascism emerged most fully and (briefly) triumphantly—had both failed, under "normal" bourgeois rule, to consolidate such empire states completely or in a timely manner.

Each of these countries' fascists set themselves the task of accomplishing what their bourgeoisies had failed to do: propel Germany and Italy into full domestic empire state status and full international participation in carving up the rest of the globe. This motivated Germany's blitzkrieg and Italy's bombing of Libya and invasion of Ethiopia. For Germany, especially, this meant redrawing the map of Europe itself and building an extensive empire within the heart of Europe. This ultimately proved intolerable to the British (and the US), who thus eventually depicted Hitler's Germany in particular as beyond the limits of "acceptable" imperialist behavior. Because that land base extended into the zone of influence and ultimately the territory of the old Czarist empire of the Slavs, reconstituted as the Union of Soviet Socialist Republics, Hitler was inevitably thrown into conflict with the Soviets as well as the British empire. When the Soviet resistance proved capable of withstanding and countering the Nazi invasion, the US and Britain finally opened the "second front."

But Hitler's philosophy, ideology, and mechanisms of rule were rooted in imperialism, in lessons learned from US empire building and scientific "race relations," as well as that empire's industrialization, modernization, and integration of immigrant workers into an "Americanized" proletariat. Hitler studied, referenced, and emulated US reservations and geographic transfer of Indigenous people, the promotion of eugenics, the use of sterilization on racial minorities and people deemed genetically inferior, US white supremacist mass organizations, and the mass merchandising of KKK paraphernalia. Some of the cells that formed Hitler's National Socialist German Workers' Party (Nationalsozialistische Deutsche Arbeiterpartei; the Nazi Party) were actually composed of former German members of the US KKK who returned to Germany in the 1920s after the KKK collapsed.

Nazi views and practices also grew out of the German colonial experience in Africa, where they carried out a genocide of the Herero people of the Republic of Namibia (formerly known as German South West Africa). The Nazi Party distinguished itself from other right-wing parties and movements, however, in its willingness to develop armed power outside the alleged "monopoly" of the state and to carry forward independent action based on other class strata, regardless of bourgeois dictates. Nonetheless, even the Nazi Party, like Benito Mussolini's fascists, participated in and was legitimated by the bourgeois electoral system.

Fascism: Bringing Colonial Rule Home

Fascism can best be understood as bringing the methods of imperial rule in the colonies into the metropole. This is true regardless of whether the societies in which it was imposed or organized had a previous imperial history. It is no coincidence that Francisco Franco of Spain launched the Falangist campaign from a colonial garrison, or that later French fascist forces were based among the settler-colonists of Algeria.

In the colonies, genocide has been the rule, not the exception, of imperial practice. "Democracy" is only for a select few settlers; dictatorship and slave labor apply to the Indigenous and other colonized people. The corporate model of economic organization, later applied by the fascists to the state itself, developed in colonial enterprise. The first corporations were the colonizing corporations—the British East India Company, Hudson's Bay Company, Royal Africa Company, and others. They could bear the costs and risks of colonization because of shared and limited liability, and they exercised state power directly over the colonized territories and populations. The risks that were shared under crown authority to form joint stock companies were greater than could be borne even by the state itself. The model also worked to bribe and implicate large sectors of society in the trade of enslaved people and other extremely risky but highly profitable enterprises. Although the British crown enjoyed a monopoly on the "trade" of enslaved Africans, it did so through a corporate entity that allowed for joint ownership, although with most of the profits enriching the monarchs.

In the sense of "incorporating" a popular base into the state, the mass base of participation in colonial rule came via the settler population, which participated actively and often independently in land grabs and extermination without waiting for bourgeois legitimacy.

All this was translated to the metropole by Hitler. Except that, in this case, the mechanisms—dictatorship, slave labor, corporatization of the state and society, mass participation in militarism, looting and oppression sometimes independently of the bourgeoisie—were seen operating directly within the German population itself, including against its racially, religiously, and ethnically defined minorities, and against its European neighbors. Hitler was intolerable to Winston S. Churchill and Franklin D. Roosevelt, not because of philosophical differences, but because the state he created empowered Germany to remake the existing world economic order. Hitler's genocide of the Jews is defined as unique because it was carried out against Europeans, within Europe; but the Western capitalist powers did nothing to rescue or even admit Jewish refugees.

US capital played a strong role in building Hitler's war machine, perhaps hoping, as Britain did, that it could safely be directed against the Soviets. In any event, once the die was cast and global war became inevitable, the "democracies" showed no compunction in waging warfare on a mass scale against both German and Japanese civilians. Nor, once the war was won, did the US delay in swiftly incorporating the Nazi apparatus into the US military, space program, and national security state apparatus, especially the CIA.

Colonialism is not dead history. Although most (not all) direct external colonialism has been ended, colonialism persists in neocolonialism and in settler-colonial societies (e.g., the US, Israel, Canada, Australia, etc.). It is at play in the class contradictions in much of Latin America as well, where the ruling class and its allies are mostly the descendants of European colonizers, and a bulk of the oppressed and exploited working classes and peasantry are of Indigenous and African descent. Moreover, the imperial societies have been recolonizing the globe under doctrines of neoliberalism, direct corporate rule via forms such as the World Trade Organization, and, increasingly, the direct application of military might.

However, to say there is no difference between capitalist imperialism in general and fascism in particular is wrong. Fascism is a form of imperialism *in extremis*, moved to taking desperate measures in the name of survival (often, but not only, because of the strength of its conscious opposition). The degree to which fascism must emphasize its mass appeal and revolutionary face is a measure of the weakening of the grip of "normal" imperial and colonial thinking within the working classes of the colonizing powers.

It is important to understand that saying imperialism sometimes takes fascist form is not the same as attributing fascism (or racism) to a "ruling-class plot." All forms of imperialism have been cross-class projects in which working and other "subordinate" classes have participated independently and directly, not merely under the direction of the bourgeoisie or ruling class.

When there is not a revolutionary anticapitalist and anti-imperialist threat manifest in the ranks of working and oppressed people, fascism may still appear necessary or desirable to the rulers or other strata because of other threats or weaknesses of the bourgeoisie and its state.

What's more, fascist regimes are not necessarily going to ally with each other because of ideological affinities. Alliances will shift between and among "democracies" and "dictatorships," just as they did before, during, and after World War II. So, we may see US Christian fascists opposing Arab Muslim fascists or Hindu supremacist fascists, or US white nationalists making common cause with Zionists. This does not preclude fascist initiatives within their own society. Similarly, state- and bourgeois-based fascist elements may move against other fascist forces within their own society, particularly those that emphasize the antielitist face of fascism.

Fascism has also presented itself at times as a competing ideology for state building and economic advancement in colonized societies, in opposition to anarchist, communist, and other socially liberatory ideologies. Colonial and settler-colonial rulers may find such fascist uprisings unacceptably threatening to their interests. We can find fascist kernels in communities of color as well as within the white population. Although such fascisms have often been subordinate to larger imperial forces, to the extent they prove capable of or interested in independent action, the fascism of imperial powers may define them as an enemy.

What we must understand however, is that the US is a particular case because the US is a settler-colonial, as well as an imperial, society. It has always had elements of what later became known as fascism operating directly within its society and state against internally colonized and enslaved populations and in conquered and annexed territories. The mass participation and base for this has been the white settler population (although people of color have at times also been incorporated in a neocolonial or modified settler role).

George Jackson: "Fascism is Already Here"

This is what George Jackson—a leader of the revolutionary prison movement in the 1960s and 1970s, a field marshal in the BPP, and author of *Soledad Brother* and *Blood in My Eye*—meant when he said, "[F]ascism is already here."[7] It was not rhetorical hyperbole or meaningless substitution of "fascism" for capitalism, or something else we don't like. Instead, George Jackson saw the "Black colony" inside the US and especially how Black people within the prison system lived—and still live—under conditions of fascism.

But this is not true only in the prisons, nor does it apply only to white people. Privileges are widely used by prison authorities to control prisoners and gain their acquiescence and compliance. This gives us a perspective on the use of privilege within society at large. The "carrot" and the "stick" work together to divide and demobilize people. Black and *Raza* youth are channeled into prisons, into parasitic criminal organizations, or into the military or neocolonial regulation systems. This is a manifestation of fascist-style domination and incorporation of a threatening population. The fundamental basis of white privilege is that white working people are for the most part spared such fascist methods of rule so long as they remain loyal to the system that dominates others more completely.

So there are substantial mass strata, including among white workers, for whom fascism of the more modern, "European" form has appeal, as well as sectors of the bourgeoisie and of the bureaucratic governing class that are accustomed to, and predisposed toward, ruling in a fascist style, emphasizing authoritarianism. There are several distinct streams promoting fascism that have been increasingly converging in the Trump and post-Trump era.

In the face of growing and intersecting crises in the political, economic, and environmental spheres, fascism presents itself in a multifaceted way. There are five main forces competing, contending, and colluding in building a fascist response and "solution" to the problems of the empire. Antifascist forces committed to human liberation and planetary survival must simultaneously challenge the empire itself, develop solutions for the problems fueling the fascist response, and disrupt the fascist forces. To do so, we need to get a clearer picture of the fascist elements and the contradictions among them:

1. Self-proclaimed Nazis, although not necessarily the largest threat, are a place to start. This is the element with the most explicitly racist approach, based on open white supremacy. They incorporate traditional Nazi/fascist or Klan symbolism, and the traditional scapegoating of Jews. This faction has an opportunist tactical flexibility. It benefits from effective use of the media to magnify its forces and appeal. Nazis seize on every sign of racial friction. They appeal to younger whites, both male and female, with a sense of grievance about lost entitlements. They often present themselves as antiestablishment or even anticapitalist, yet usually seek protection from the cops. They use methods of physical intimidation, as most bullies do. But like all bullies, they are highly susceptible to organized physical resistance.

2. Clerical fascism is a second major component, also connected to an element of traditional fascism. It is based in religious fundamentalism and often incorporates well-established and well-funded religious organizations, whether churches or lay fraternal groups. They base their appeal on a sense of moral decay under the empire, but they are otherwise often more than happy to operate within mainstream political institutions. In the US, this is mostly Christian fascist groups, which focus on antiwoman and antigay organizing, opposing abortion and other reproductive rights, gay marriage, and similar issues. But in a global context, Jewish fundamentalism linked to a more secular, but still religiously justified, Zionism is an important element of this tendency; in the US, Christian and Jewish Zionists make common cause. In the colonized and semicolonized Muslim world, Muslim fascist fundamentalism plays a role more similar to that of Western Nazism, presenting itself as the voice of grievance, with an antiestablishment, "anti-imperialist" politics.

3.   Direct-action "patriots" have fed a resurgence of the worst components of the old militia movement. They're most interested not necessarily in replacing, but in supplementing, the power of the state. Although some elements engage in anticorporate or antipolitical rhetoric, most in this faction, like the Christian fascists, are generally content to seek entry into and work with mainstream political power. Thus, such vigilante projects work with state forces such as the border patrol, or even run for elective office. They sponsor propositions targeting immigrants, particularly Latinx communities, and work closely with Republican office-holders. Although sometimes professing not to be racist, they also provide a convenient conduit and nesting place for Nazi and white supremacist forces. For example, demonstrators at anti-immigrant protests and pro-Trump rallies in Orange County, California, showed up waving swastika and Confederate flags, and attacked counterprotesters with brass knuckles. Some then went on to the Charlottesville, Virginia "Unite the Right" rally. Anti-immigrant, anti-Mexican, anti-Muslim, and anti-Asian stereotyping and violence have been a growth area for a mass base for fascist solutions.

4.   An element within the military, law enforcement, and state security forces, operating independently of the official chain of command, is a fourth component of a fascist movement. This aspect has leaped to the forefront with the storming of the US Capitol and the role of the Oath Keepers and various active-duty cops and military who had a role in the insurrection. It's also manifest in the resistance by police associations to vaccine mandates. But the increasing use of mercenaries by the empire, as well as concerns within the ranks and the brass about the inadequacy of current domestic and international counterinsurgency efforts, is also resurrecting it. Continued setbacks in, and withdrawals from, Iraq, Afghanistan, and other fronts of the "endless wars" could increase this component dramatically, with a possible appeal among demobilized and disoriented veterans unable to find a productive niche in civilian life. The high-ranking military warnings that the Afghanistan withdrawal will restore a safe haven for "terrorists," as well as the corporate media attacks on Joe Biden for "cutting and running," are evidence that such tendencies are arising within the ruling class itself, as well as among disaffected veterans such as the Oath Keepers.

5.   Fascist elements within the state, the corporate parties, and the ruling economic and political elite are the fifth element because fascism is built from above as well as below. The Grand Old Party (GOP; i.e., the Republican Party) has been increasingly willing to seek one-party rule through voter suppression and claims of electoral fraud, raised to a fever

pitch by Trump. They provide red meat and marching orders to the clerical and vigilante fascists, and reward or protect fascist elements within the military and law enforcement. Multimillionaires and billionaires have funded protofascist organizing and various "alt-right" and "alt-light" transmission belts. This will grow as the disastrous consequences of empire, and the inability of the rulers to "deliver the goods" to anybody but an increasingly narrow stratum of the wealthy, erode popular support. The Democrats offer at best token alternatives to, if not outright reinforcement of, these approaches. This shows the systemic nature of the crisis and the limited options available to the rulers as the crisis deepens.

The turn to fascism implies a change in the composition, structure, powers, and rationale of the state, and in the forms of domination and exploitation of the metropolitan working classes. The types of oppression and exploitation that have been directed at the (internally) colonized population begin to make themselves felt against the settlers as well, even as they are being courted and propagandized to adopt a new and more intimate and totalitarian identification with the rulers and empire.

I think this continues to describe what is happening in the US today. A process is underway of fundamentally transforming the nature of the US state, not merely quantitatively in terms of repression, but qualitatively in terms of its fundamental modes of operation and social contract. This is happening simultaneously from the top down (orchestrated by the neo- and paleocons and a supportive faction of the bourgeoisie) and from the bottom up (by clerical fascist forces and neo-Confederates closely allied to the rulers).

Working-class white people and small businesspeople are being drawn into openly and expressly neo-Nazi and other armed and violence-prone formations. What we are seeing today is an integration of those groupings, facilitated by the Trumpist takeover of the GOP, which is being converted to an unapologetically fascist party.

But the Democratic Party, despite seeking to appeal to a different base, is simultaneously promoting corporatization, intensified state surveillance, public–private partnerships, and other elements of a kind of fascist state reconstitution. Antifascists can neither direct all our fire at the Republicans nor expect to find allies in the ranks of the Democratic Party apparatus. We need to find ways to disrupt the fascist base of the Republicans and drive wedges between the Democrats' base and their elite strategists and officeholders.

Overall, we must seriously prepare for situations of much more naked repression, perhaps akin to those that have pertained in the colonial and semicolonial areas—the dirty war in Argentina, the Augusto Pinochet regime in Chile, the death squads in Central America, the Israeli occupation forces in Palestine, et cetera. Such repression in the US may sometimes target open, self-proclaimed fascists. Because the rulers' goal is stabilization in crisis, threats to stability are unwelcome. But, in general, each repressive measure by the state and corporations, even if claiming to be targeted at the threat of right-wing or racist violence and misinformation, is likely to be used against leftists and liberation movements.

Economic and Ecological Crisis of the Empire and Industrialism

These statist, proimperial forces see quite clearly that the economic and environmental crises facing their system require a reincorporation of mass support on a different basis than simply the old imperial, white supremacist bribe. They foresee a period of increasing militarization of the entire society and a girding up to confront China and Russia in a new Cold War that could heat up quickly. Biden made it very clear that the US withdrawal from Afghanistan was necessary to enable the US military to focus more clearly and directly on China. Trump's trade war, generally sustained by the Biden administration, whose foreign policy and diplomatic initiatives are also expressly designed to counter China, could transform rapidly into a military showdown. The prospect of taking on that battle, in the context of a dwindling economic pie of which the billionaires are taking a larger share, necessitates both increased repression and inventive methods of obtaining consent, for which "fascism" is as good a code name as any.

The reason it's important to consider whether a fascist state is on the horizon in the US is not a matter of semantics, but of survival. Or perhaps more accurately, we need to understand exactly how the rulers and street-level fascists are transforming the nature of the state, and what initiatives toward fascism will be undertaken by the state itself.

What is vital is seeing how what is happening is rooted in preexisting cross-class alliances that must be smashed if we are to have a chance at turning the crisis into an opportunity for a liberatory transformation of this society. If people see antifascist struggle as a means to return to a mythical democratic, egalitarian past, we are indeed doomed.

In a certain sense, whether we call it fascism is immaterial. The question is, what room do we have to maneuver, what timetable do we have to operate on, what methods of organization and struggle are appropriate or likely to be successful in the current period? The timetable and nature of organizing, as well as the means of struggle appropriate and necessary to pursue, will be affected by the nature of the state and the extraparliamentary fascist forces we confront. So will the kind of alliances we can make and the type of organizations we build.

Withstanding Fascism and Brutality

Fascism, however we define it, has meant a particularly brutal and harsh form of governance within imperial metropoles, a more active pursuit of genocide, and a more totalitarian form of the domination of labor and other mass organizations.

Other forms of social and political organization are also capable of excesses, but fascism distinguishes itself by seeking to reconstitute the individual personality and the state in a "revolutionary" fashion. In the Third World, imperialism has long operated through dictatorial, militaristic puppet regimes that carried out bloody repression. It's arguable whether these can be called "fascist"—they are responding to pressures from above and outside their own societies, and often have a limited mass base within. But if we are facing anything close to that type of repression and death squad–type activity inside the US, we need to adjust our organizing dramatically, as the BPP tried to do in the 1970s.

The current political context in the US calls for a whole range of things connected to the idea of more clandestine struggle, although not exclusively illegal or armed action. We need to incorporate the same understanding that "from-below" fascist forces have long grasped: independent political action must make use of all forms of struggle, and all means of exerting countervailing power.

The abiding lesson of the history of fascism is that the alleged state monopoly on armed power is a polite fiction aimed at disarming the oppressed. Particularly in the US context, in which armed settlers operated independently of the state to capture land, suppress rebellions by enslaved people, and carry out other colonial functions, it is fatuous to believe that only the state acts as an armed agent. Class fractions, regional networks, and other social elements have always been armed and used arms to advance their interests in the US. Pacifism is exclusively a pathology of the left. We need to develop the capacity to defend ourselves and our communities.

Conscious internationalism (or intercommunalism) is essential. Leadership in antifascist struggle has always come from people of color, particularly Black and Indigenous people. The African Blood Brotherhood after World War I was involved in resisting the Klan and became a constituting force in US communism. The BPP formed the National Committee to Combat Fascism in the early 1970s to fight what was later exposed as COINTELPRO. The AIM in Minneapolis, Minnesota developed one of the first Cop Watch programs, similar to the efforts of the BPP under Huey P. Newton and Bobby Seale in Oakland. The joint Mexicano/Puerto Rican MLN had an antifascist analysis. The Red Nation today is a leading element of Indigenous-based, revolutionary class consciousness.[8] The centrality of anti-Blackness to almost all varieties of racism, fascism, and reaction means that antiracism and solidarity with the Black freedom struggle must be central to any definition or practice of antifascism.

Similarly, any legitimate form of antifascism must oppose capitalism, empire, and US militarism and intervention in Latin America, Africa, and Asia, as well as the continuing US land theft and oppression of Indigenous people, or US colonialism in Puerto Rico and elsewhere.

In the mainstream media, the transformation of journalism and entertainment into corporate/state propaganda is virtually complete. Court rulings have made it clear that freedom of speech and the press are essentially protected only for corporate interests. Alternatives are happening—developing our own media, pirate radio, webcasting, using Indymedia—but remember, the internet is closely monitored and subject to being choked off. Most social media are corporate dominated and integrated into the total surveillance society.

We need our own media. I have persisted in publishing *Turning the Tide* as a print newspaper (as well as online, also expanding to a separate ARA e-newsletter during the COVID-19 pandemic). We distribute thousands of copies over the course of a year to prisoners around the US, who are now grappling with the deadly consequences of the COVID-19 pandemic on top of the general repressive nature of prisons and the targeting of political and politicized prisoners.[9] The paper is also simultaneously a way to communicate to the larger movement the antifascist and antiracist initiatives and lessons coming from the prisoners.

We also need to cultivate relationships with commercial media that serve people of color. In NYC, Chicago, LA, Atlanta, et cetera, there are Black, Spanish-language, Asian, and other "minority"-oriented media outlets that still provide an outlet that is unavailable in general-audience print and broadcast media.

The pandemic has made it all the more important to focus energy on less-public forms of organizing than rallies and demonstrations, including mutual aid. We need to organize deeper and more sustained initiatives of our own away from public scrutiny, with us not only reacting to state and fascist provocations. We need to listen more, as a means not only of intelligence gathering on the enemy, but also of understanding what's on the minds of the people we want to work with and among. We need to develop community-based grassroots antiracist and antiempire work that has endurance, promotes sustainability and environmental restoration, and rewards people in the doing of it.

Antifascists can never abandon confrontation with Nazis, but public venues are going to be increasingly controlled and subject to massive repression. The current quiet of the antiwar movement in the face of ongoing war has to do partly with the hold of illusions about the Democrats. But it also reflects the inefficacy of street demonstrations in stopping war, and the effectiveness that militarized police had in disrupting anticorporate, antiglobalization street actions.

We need to think about methods of infiltration and subversion of state and fascist initiatives, as well as counterorganizing a base for antiracist culture and resistance among people who would otherwise be drawn to the Nazi positions. Cyberwarfare and hacking are certainly useful tools, both for disruption and for educational exposures. But we also need to present, or help people develop, efficacious alternatives to statist or fascist ideas.

Organizing Below the Radar

We need to build a legal/self-defense component into all our work, anticipating busts, frame-ups, and harassment. We need to build stronger outside networks of support, materially and otherwise, for people locked down. There needs to be thought about safe houses, cultivation of supporters who never do anything public to identify themselves with the antiracist and antifascist movement, secure means of covert communication, transportation, and dissemination of information. In other words, we need to adopt some methods of organization that are well suited to conditions of occupation or fascism.

To the extent we can get at all ahead of the curve on this, it will be a lot easier to do, and a lot likelier to survive the repression. We need to think about building redundancy into all the mechanisms we create in case we lose some.

Organizing and outreach into the prisons and the military are priorities. These spheres, along with workplace organizing, have always faced some of the characteristics of occupation or fascism that impede open organizing and require more secretive methods. They are vital areas in which to work. The degree of state repression applied in these arenas under normal "democracy" is a measure of their strategic importance. They are also central to eroding the power of the state and the elite, and to building our own countervailing power.

They are an important proving ground of our ability to organize under such conditions and of our capacity to craft a message and practice that engages the people we want to reach. This is also true for work with high school students, for many of the same reasons (especially given the penal character of a lot of public schools, and as the military increasingly penetrates the schools for recruitment).

One key to understanding fascism is to grasp, and counter, the appeal fascism makes to women based on traditional gender roles and binaries. The male-dominated left tends to discount the revolutionary potential of women, as well as trans, gender-fluid, and nonbinary people. We need a strategy to deal with the role of violence in the lives of women and children, and to counter the efforts of fascists to present themselves as the answer to women's problems. A fuller discussion and an attempt to develop practice based on a deeper understanding of those issues must take place in a sustained way. Leadership on this is coming from those people, and must be heeded. The embrace of the slogan "All Black Lives Matter," specifically referencing lesbian-gay-bisexual-transgender-queer (LGBTQ) Black people, by BLM is exemplary. Similarly, campaigns such as "No Justice, No Pride," opposing "pink-washing" by cops trying to insinuate themselves into commemorations of the Stonewall rebellion against police abuse, led by drag queens and trans people, point the way toward an intersectional opposition to the "woke" police state.

The state has moved on this in various ways. The use of Afghan women as justification for waging war on al-Qaeda, the Taliban, and other Muslim forces is one clear example. Another notable one is the creation by the Pentagon of a network of organizers out of "army wives," whose job it is to maintain morale and support for the war efforts among the families of the troops, which complements the recruitment of women by the military, the intelligence community, and law enforcement.

Faith-based groups, some of whom are hard-core pacifists, must be addressed in an antifascist strategy, just as "White Rose" Catholics formed one base of antifascist resistance in Hitler's Germany. Such groups also have a long history of civil resistance, sanctuary-type activities regarding unjust immigration policies, and otherwise breaking the law or doing secret work for reasons of conscience. I think we might be able to learn a great deal from them. Followers and associates of the antiwar priests known as the Berrigan brothers (Daniel and Phillip) carried out a 1970s burglary of the Media, Pennsylvania, FBI office. They exposed the existence of a widespread FBI snitch network. The files these religious pacifists stole exposed the suborning of civil servants, college registrars, postal workers, and others to spy on every Black college student in the US and other potential "subversives."

It was this break-in that eventually led to the revelation of the existence of COINTELPRO, a domestic warfare program against the BPP and other elements of the Black freedom struggle, and against the Puerto Rican, Chicano/Mexicano, American Indian, Asian/Pacific Islander, and other movements, including various communist, Trotskyist, and New Left groups. It would be nonsensical to imagine that such efforts at infiltration, disruption, and surveillance are not still taking place today.

We need to begin operating as if fascism is fully in place. This is not defeatism, because only by acting in this way will we be able to turn the dynamic around and use the crisis as a basis for a truly revolutionary transformation of society. We similarly need to start working with the understanding that it is too late to reverse global warming in the short term. We need to build community-based efforts to live under the harsh environmental conditions that will prevail over the next decades. Anything less is suicidal.

Over many decades, I have persevered in active, conscious solidarity with revolutionary-minded Black, Chican@/Mexican@, Puerto Rican, Asian, and Indigenous groups. I have been sustained in my commitments to antifascism and liberation by the lessons I have learned through open-hearted and open-minded participation.

I have accepted repeated invitations to the Tierra Amarilla Youth Leadership Training brigade, where young Chican@/Mexican@ campers discussed around nightly campfires the pains of colonization, lifted their own spirits with the prospects and experience of solidarity, and challenged me to do the same. I have gone repeatedly on the 50-500 Elders Committee Little Tokyo to Manzanar 250-mile spiritual prayer run, with Japanese, Japanese-American, and Indigenous runners, and learned abiding lessons on collective struggle and spiritual dedication. I have engaged with the Jericho Movement to free all political prisoners, reverse the attacks by COINTELPRO, and read the works of people free in their own minds and steadfast in their resistance despite 40 or more years of incarceration. I joined the 50th-anniversary Venceremos Brigade to do agricultural and solidarity work with Cuba, and saw firsthand how people with few resources can develop and be willing to fight to defend agro-ecological and health care systems superior to anything capitalism has developed in the US.

All antifascists of European descent, such as myself, must respond to that type of leadership by building a substantial base for revolution among significant numbers of white poor and working people. We have no more time for betrayals, or for learning from defeats. In other words, we need to take the current political, economic, and environmental crises as the breeding ground, not for fascism, but for an independent, revolutionary anti-imperialist offensive![10]

It Takes a Network to Defeat a Network: (Anti)Fascism and the Future of Complex Warfare

Emmi Bevensee and Frank Miroslav

As We Become More Deeply Interconnected, Our World Becomes More Complex

The last decade has seen a veritable sea change that disrupted common-sense assumptions about how politics is conducted. One of the most concerning developments is the shift by various strands of fascism to being more horizontal and to using distributed organizing mechanisms, all while attempting to preserve their reactionary, "traditionalist" core. In response to this, antifascism must continue to adapt to this shifting terrain and use the tools of complexity as leverage against the coercive simplicity of the fascist hydra. Whereas the fascists use complexity to promote their violent and overly simplistic worldview, antifascists can use complexity to cultivate richly diverse and evolving networks of resistance.

As Warfare Continues to Complexify, Fascism is Adapting and So Should Antifascism

We are already in the era when anyone can three-dimensional (3D) print[1] and mill anonymous rifles and use encrypted Peer-2-Peer (P2P)[2] technology to organize a swarm of nameless people to dox and then, ultimately, drone strike[3] a target's house.

Although the capacity for violence unleashed by emerging technologies is concerning, we have good reasons to think that antifascists (and antiauthoritarians more generally) are better suited for this type of conflict even if it nets some fascists momentary victories.

To understand why, let us briefly define a working definition of complexity. In this chapter, we are using it to refer to the number of possible actions a system can take at any given point in time, with more complex systems capable of more complex actions. A further point of nuance is that systems are made up of systems and that increased complexity at one level comes at the expense of complexity at another. To give an obvious example, the set of actions available to the cells in your body must be restricted so as to make your body functional.[4]

This sort of restriction might seem like an argument for hierarchy, but restricting complexity necessarily means restricting information flow. Hierarchical systems must limit the amount of information that comes up to them so as to not be overwhelmed. They are also difficult to rearrange in the face of change, especially if they are constructed in such a way to protect the interests of an elite.

This is of direct relevance to thinking about fascist and anarchist political aims. The fascist drive to return to simple communities and ways of life can be characterized as a desire to *minimize and constrain* social complexity. The anarchist desire for a liberated world, in contrast, ultimately means *increasing and sustaining* social complexity.

Of course, neither of these drives result in simple linear progress toward simplification or complexification. Increasing complexity is in many cases instrumentally rational for fascists to achieve particular ends. Likewise, there are instances when anarchists must limit the actions of others to achieve particular ends. Complexity is a byproduct of a freer world and should never be made into an end in and of itself.

Fascists see the increased capacity and complexity brought about by technological advances merely as an end toward achieving reactionary "traditionalism," and as such face a constant tension between the tools they use and their ultimate goals. Antifascists and antiauthoritarians, in contrast, see the enhanced capacity that comes with increasing complexity both as a means *and* as an end. There is considerably less dissonance between our desire for collaboration because creating more engaging systems of coordination is both a means and an end. We celebrate this collaborative process both for what it produces, the increased ability for us to build egalitarian social structures, and for our experience of the process itself.

Informational Shifts Erode Industrial Assumptions

To surmise technology in a few words is to do violence to the subject. Technology is an immensely complicated matter with considerable political, economic, and psychological factors (to name just a few) driving its usage and development.

Nevertheless, for the sake of brevity we must make simplified claims. Information technology has led to the democratization of considerable agency to individuals. Individuals or small groups or networks of individuals gain capacities that once required hundreds or thousands working in concert, to say nothing of capabilities that have never before existed. This is technological superempowerment.

The capabilities and flexibility of information technology has consequences for all of society, but those that are most relevant to our thesis are the ways it can erode the hegemony of legacy media and institutions by lowering the cost of creating and distributing information while making collaboration between individuals significantly easier.

These "one-two punches" of prior forms of informational hegemony eroding and the ease of collaboration played significant roles in protests such as the Arab Spring, Occupy Wall Street, Black Lives Matter; electoral successes of figures such as Donald Trump or Jair Bolsonaro; and the success of political movements such as Brexit.[5] The starkest example of the discontinuity between what has been enabled and the assumptions of industrial-era institutions can be seen in how semidecentralized, ragtag reactionary organizations such as the Taliban have held off and ultimately won against the most well-funded and equipped army in the world.[6]

To those plugged in to the internet, such advances in complex online warfare seem like ancient history because of how normal it all seems. But it's worth remembering how recent this shift is. For example, the 2016 paper, "Kek, Cucks, and God Emperor Trump: A Measurement Study of 4chan's Politically Incorrect Forum and Its Effects on the Web," which analyzed the outsize impact that the relatively nominal /pol/ channel on 4chan had on the broader alt-right and white supremacist ecosystem, as well as the 2016 US election.[7] When we talked with one of the authors, they said that they found it difficult to get the paper published because reviewers felt it was "too niche." Such assumptions seem ludicrous today when we have things like QAnon which, birthed from 4chan and 8chan, going from being a minor internet conspiracy to having a serious impact both on US and global politics more broadly, as seen with its part in global coronavirus disease 2019 (COVID-19) misinformation.[8]

Such dangerous antirationalism taking hold at this scale is concerning, but it's worth remembering that positive memes can also take hold. During this time, we have also seen networked struggles for human freedom, such as the worldwide increase of antigovernment protests from Chile to Kazakhstan to Belarus to the US.[9] Not every protest movement is necessarily always positive, but the fact it is occurring at such a scale is still a reason for optimism.

Barring an outright global collapse, it's a safe bet that such disruption will continue to be the norm. As antifascists and antiauthoritarians, we must both adjust to these trends and help direct them if we have any hope for success in this new terrain. Although there are good reasons to believe that antiauthoritarian value systems have some edge in this increasingly volatile political climate, such advantages will not automatically deliver us a better world. Technological superempowerment benefits both those seeking to do good and those seeking to do bad. We need to consciously integrate and leverage them to have any hope at bringing about a liberated future for all.

Decentralized Reaction

> *AWD [the Atomwaffen Division] requires more scrutiny because of its growing global reach, ability to plan and execute violence, and, much like the broader WSE [white supremacist extremist] movement, AWD's leaderless structure and ability to adapt, under new names and with different branding make it easy for AWD to deflect attention and regroup, all while using the same underlying tactics. AWD's chameleon-like capability can confuse and disincentivize authorities to track its members down, even as the group grows its international presence.*
>
> —The Soufan Center, "The Atomwaffen Division:
> The Evolution of the White Supremacist Threat"[10]

A 13-year-old child was exposed for leading an international white terror organization connected with a bomb plot placed anonymously through the internet.[11] A US citizen fled to Russia after seeking work with US intelligence agencies and serving in the US Special Forces.[12] From Russia, and with unknown connections to the Kremlin, he ran another white terror organization online that was associated with several murders and an attempt to start a protracted race war in the US.[13] Many of these organizations identify as engaging in "leaderless resistance."[14] Even when they maintain significant internal hierarchies, the prevalence of strong encryption and the internet, as well as emerging P2P decentralized technologies, has allowed a degree of stochastic, or even gamified, terror that does not rely on the typical command-and-control structure people assume is necessary for these types of attacks.

There are a number of reasons this kind of distributed white terror is becoming more popular; the most obvious of which is that it works. The Islamic State of Iraq and Syria (ISIS), the Atomwaffen Division, or a random internet troll in one country can create slick propaganda that inspires unpredictable mutations and attacks in other countries. There is a "propaganda of the deed" element at play: one mass shooter with a livestream and a manifesto can inspire a copycat killer with the same motives without either being plugged into formal fascist organizations. If this sounds sort of like insurrectionary anarchism—minus the concern for freedom, well-being, noncoercion, and empathy—that's because it kind of is. The same reasons that anarchism is a hard ideology to kill is now empowering the most hierarchical ideology in history: fascism. But how can this be true?

White nationalist organizations are often almost comically hierarchical with all the dweeby pomp of grand wizards seemingly plucked from a fantasyland. This is because fascism worships power and that power is executed through authoritarianism and explicit hierarchy. So Louis Beam's "Leaderless Resistance" doctrine—ultimately utilized by neo-Nazis such as White Aryan Resistance founder Tom Metzger for the creation of racist skinhead gangs, and now in different ways by the modern 8chan extreme alt-right—was quite a transformation. It emphasized that having a central figure, even in a clandestine organization, made it easier to just kill or imprison that individual and destroy the movement.

For example, the Southern Poverty Law Center (SPLC) repeatedly sued Ku Klux Klan organizations until they fell apart. Similarly, an incestuous trailer park brawl between the leaders of the Traditionalist Worker Party completely destroyed the organization from the top all the way down.[15]

Conversely, mechanisms of indirect coordination, through the environment, between agents or actions, called "stigmergy," stimulates the performance of a succeeding action by the same or a different agent. Stigmergic networks are good at routing around the damage in a network (e.g., an arrested member) and adopting other swarm tactics that leverage high levels of individual or group autonomy instead of relying on control hierarchies to manage things.[16] If an organization has no leaders, who can be killed or arrested to maim them? One can find leaderless resistance movements throughout history, but the proliferation of contemporary networked information technology has supercharged them in all spheres of life.[17] So now many organizations are maintaining their own internal hierarchies, but using this networked horizontal resistance to spread both propaganda and the will and skills to inflict violence or enact change.

To understand how this emerging conflict will likely play out, we need to grasp the fault lines and underlying motivations of the participants involved. The primary fault line can be found in one's response to increased complexity.

Complexity is underlying root issue that fascists are against, and this explains their disgust at globalization; at gender, racial, cultural, economic, and sexual diversity; and at many other things they find degenerate. It explains their antirationalist appeals to a made-up essentialism, their willful ignorance about the mutability of biology and culture, and the cross-cultural trade and communication that has defined our history.[18] Things were never as simple, homogeneous, or monolithic as they claim.

Such a narrative has resonance because complexity is admittedly uncomfortable and unsettling. Investigate any subject in detail and you'll find that many of the common-sense assumptions you were raised with are insufficient or wrong. This is uncomfortable because it means even our most cherished beliefs can be discredited. Some of this discomfort is sociological—for example, the schooling system most people are subjected to does a poor job at teaching people how to think critically and the demands of most people's modern work life further steal the time they could use to work through such problems. But even in an enlightened society that had gone beyond such problems, the cognitive effort of restructuring our models of the world would still be a demand on people. Reworking your mental models is just *hard*.

Such cognitive limitations do not mean that we should give up the struggle for a better world. It merely means that we should be strategic in how we go about doing it. We want to avoid both the top-down approach of building a better world by imposing it from above, as well as the anti-rationalism of reactionaries wherein any novelty is seen as threatening. The path forward is one in which we use an evolutionary approach that employs rationality and respects the inherent limitations imposed by complexity, as well as builds in mechanisms to correct mistakes, missteps, et cetera. With the primary point of contestation identified, we can now discuss how the conflict has been fought and how it is likely to play out in the future.

Fourth-Generation Warfare

Before we try to determine the future of conflict, we need to look to the recent past to see how decentralized forms of warfare arose and operated.

Probably the biggest change in how wars are fought came with the deployment of atomic weapons at the end of World War II. The sheer destructive potential of nuclear weapons has made state violence extremely costly and completely changed the assumptions about how conflict works. Before nuclear weapons, wars between industrial powers were primarily wars of attrition in which the combatants went head-to-head with their productive capacities. The destructive capacity of nuclear weapons made such an approach to conflict irrelevant because each side would be able to easily annihilate the productive capacity of opponents.

This shift was further complicated by technological progress in other areas and the emergence of an increasingly interconnected world. Durable, cheap, replicable, and easy-to-use weapons like the Kalashnikov AK-47 were vital in decolonization struggles that aimed not at destroying the army of the colonial state, but merely making the cost of occupation sufficiently prohibitive so that the colonial powers would withdraw. Such a strategy was further enabled by the rise of an interconnected world market (which created a more diverse way to be attacked) and an increasingly educated and wealthy populace in the colonizing country (who were intolerant of the casualties these conflicts caused).

These trends gave rise to what theorists call "Fourth-Generation Warfare," which is not fought between states, but rather between states and "nonstate actors." Instead of directly attacking the army of the enemy, you go after their weak points. The primary goal of Fourth-Generation Warfare is not the destruction of the enemy, but instead undermining their resolve so that they no longer feel comfortable pursuing their goals. One of the strengths that more decentralized forms of struggle have over the hierarchical entities they face is that they can leverage ambiguity and uncertainty to confound the bureaucratic decision-making processes of hierarchies.

The most influential theorist of this new form of combat was the US Air Force Colonel John Boyd. His concept of the observe, orient, decide, act (OODA) loop is probably the most famous model for how to make decisions under conditions of uncertainty and time pressure. Originally developed to describe the process of decision-making by fighter pilots engaged in combat, it was then generalized and has now become a staple of strategic thinking writ large.[19]

The steps in the OODA loop are pretty simple to understand. The *observe* step is where an actor takes in information from the outside world. The *orient* step is where the actor either constructs a new model of reality or modifies a previous one to better reflect the information received. The *decide* step is where the actor makes a decision about which course of action to take going forward. The *act* step is where the actor carries out the decision.

The central part of the OODA loop is the orient step. The process of orientation is what separates the OODA loop from trivial self-correcting feedback systems. Reorientation involves changing the actor's model of reality, the filters by which they receive information, the process by which they make decisions, and the approach they take when it comes time to act.

Such an approach is necessary when operating within any complex environment that cannot be fully modeled. You cannot understand a complex environment from first principles. As such, you need to adopt a trial-and-error approach wherein you construct and test models of reality to see how they fare.

Things become even more complex when you have adversarial actors facing off against each other. Combatants now not only have to keep up to date with the environment, but also keep up with each other. This is where things get really interesting. An actor who can grasp what's going on inside its opponent's OODA loop can "get inside" and disrupt them by acting in such a way that they find it difficult to respond to.

What many people take from this is that you should move through the OODA loop more quickly than your opponents. And although there is some value to be had in speed, what really matters is the orient step. Even if you can quickly observe, decide and act, if you can't escape from your poor model of the world, then your actions will be ineffectual because they don't accurately reflect reality.

Further complicating matters is each individual being able to run through their own OODA loop and share what they uncover with other people. This increases the iteration speed significantly by allowing individual actors to share information among themselves. Hence, successful approaches or useful insights can quickly be spread throughout the network.

This form of organizing poses significant challenges to hierarchical forms of organization because hierarchies justify themselves on the idea that those in charge know best. But in an environment in which things are constantly changing and enemies are actively trying to out-think you, bureaucratic approaches are less effective because they can't adapt to change and can be gamed by intelligent adversaries.

This approach to conflict has been tremendously successful. The most famous example is with the US remaining in decades-long corrosive quagmires in Iraq and Afghanistan that resulted in significant economic and "soft power" loss. There are many other examples of networked insurgents defeating much larger powers, such as the wave of global protests that took place over 2019–21. These could be described as "open-source protest," in which tactics and strategies that arose in one place quickly were adopted in another and in which there was no real figurehead.

Of course, the motivation of the people involved in these movements varied significantly. From ISIS to the alt-right, we have plenty of examples of reactionaries embracing these techniques to further reactionary ends. Many were reactionaries who employed more complex and adaptive forms of organizing and who did so with the ultimate aim of making the world more simple and rigid.

Given the limitations of states and hierarchical forms of organization more generally, when faced with such forms of organizing, we will have to employ networked forms of organization to fight back. The questions are, then, what does this form of conflict look like and how might we go about winning it?

Networks Versus Networks

Much of the literature on Fourth-Generation Warfare looks at it from the perspective of insurgents fighting against states or would-be states. This is for the obvious reason that most scholars who write on such topics have institutional allegiances to states. There are, of course plenty of examples of networks fighting networks—from movements such as GamerGate, to interforum troll wars, to fights between hackers. But, to our knowledge, no one has put together a theory on networks fighting networks.

But there are signs that things could drift in this direction. As early as 2002, military strategy analysts such as John Arquilla were already predicting the inevitable failures of the "War on Terror," stating that, "A hierarchy is a clumsy tool to use against a nimble network: It takes networks to fight networks, much as in previous wars it has taken tanks to fight tanks."[20] But just because such ideas are being considered by theorists does not mean they'll be implemented. For example, in 2016, US military command had still not taken the lesson, with retired general Stanley McChrystal stating:

> We have to learn more quickly because if each individual or each part of the network learns every one of the bitter lessons of fighting an insurgency or terrorism, it's just too slow. We can't afford to keep relearning the same lessons. The whole organization has to learn. You might think that we do learn, but as organizations—and even individual organizations are often siloed internally—it's hard to do that. When organizations are separate, and not really networked, it is almost impossible. All the information we needed to prevent the 9/11 attack existed within the U.S. government. We just couldn't connect the dots.[21]

Of course, although the US or any other state might benefit from moving toward a more decentralized form of organizing, there would be a small minority who would lose out. Individuals who benefit from the structure of the hierarchy—be they the people with authority, the people who advise them, the equipment manufacturers, et cetera—all benefit considerably and as such have a strong incentive to keep the status quo momentum rolling. Because there are strong incentives to keep the current structure, existing security states are likely to drift in a direction of imposing a more and more totalizing surveillance state.[22] The only alternative to this solution is adopting organizational forms that are equally adaptable to the threat we face.

The obvious reason hierarchical solutions are favored by those who benefit from the status quo is that networked forms of organization are not just a neat tactic or strategy in the here and now, they are likely to serve as the building blocks of an alternative form of social organization that could replace the nation-state in the long run. The forms of organization that we experiment with and refine today could very well end up serving as the basis of new forms of social organization that are adopted by the majority of people.

It is understandable why theorists looking at networked conflict don't want to consider the radical implications of their ideas. Even if they're for upending the status quo, it is a nonstarter to propose ideas that demand radical structuring of not just the institution of the military but the entire society underlying those institutions.

This does not mean states adopting more networked forms of organizing won't happen—there may be contexts in which external pressures are sufficient to overcome the concentrated interests and genuine reform happens. Or social pressure from below may result in more decentralization.

But this means, when it comes to internetwork conflict, the most important insights are probably going to come from those who *do it*. What follows is not an attempt to provide the definitive text on the subject, but rather to open a conversation. We are trying to sketch the basics of internetwork conflict, with full knowledge that we might very well be wrong on various issues.

Toward a Theory of InterNetwork Conflict (and the Edges Antifascists Have)

When you are a network fighting another network, trust is critical to success. Due to the speed at which conflicts occur, accurate information and integrity of systems are essential. Lack of trust means that both are brought into question. If you are working off poor information or your systems are compromised, you cannot make informed decisions. When you cannot make informed decisions, you lose all the value that would be gained by organizing as a network.

Each side of a conflict should adapt the innovations their opponents have made if it is possible to do so. The open nature of networks means there is a trade-off between popularizing a successful strategy and having opponents adopt it. This makes the open-source warfare described by John Robb more challenging. Any discovery you make can be used against you. Furthermore, even if you don't use it, you run the risk of your opponents uncovering it.

But this does not mean that the two sides will converge in terms of tactics, strategy, and infrastructure. Simple tactics that work will become universalized; more complex tactics or technologies that require resources, skills, relationships, and/or infrastructure will not.

It is in being able to execute and defend against complex tactics that we believe conflicts between networks to be decided. In a conflict between two opposing networks that are otherwise roughly equal in capacity, whichever network can effectively perform actions that the other cannot will be more likely to win. This is because the more flexible a network can be, the more it is capable of responding to actions by the other network and better at finding vulnerabilities in their opponents.

The psychological and moral status of the actors involved is key. Individuals need not be physically incapacitated to be removed from network conflict. They merely need to no longer believe in the struggle. The entire point of autonomous forms of organization is that you make a trade-off by allowing more autonomy because you rely on intrinsic internal motivation that comes from within to motivate individuals instead of extrinsic external motivators that come from outside. Intrinsic motivators can be enlightened ("By engaging in this struggle, I am helping bring about a better world") or basic ("I want to make sure the comrades in my unit survive," or "I want the people who invaded my country to fuck off"). This is not to say there is no material reward or forms of punishment, merely that the open nature of networked organization makes it harder for institutions to reliably reward individuals who assist in pushing forward a network's goals or punish those who mess up and hinder its success.

If our hypothesis about what ultimately decides how networked conflicts play out is correct, this is a relief because there is good reason to believe that committed antiauthoritarians will be able to build strategic capacities that authoritarians will struggle to contend with.

The simplest reason for this is the rigidity inherent to authoritarian ideologies. For an authoritarian order to be achieved, the agency of the people it rules over must be restricted. Forcing a complex system into an arbitrary configuration means reducing its resiliency and adaptability while requiring a significant amount of energy to keep more fluid parts locked into a more rigid formation.

Moreover, truly flourishing in a world in which iterative, networked approaches dominate requires personality traits that are uncommon with serious authoritarians. Humility and adaptability when you are operating in an uncertain environment are vital because any successful tactic is liable to be broken down and figured out eventually. Being overly wedded to any one approach is a recipe for disaster. Likewise, curiosity, empathy, and being open minded are vital when dealing with problems and building relationships in a complex domain. The interconnected nature of problems in this domain means that any solution is going to run into problems. Authoritarian ideologies that centralize decision-making to a small group run afoul when the leaders can no longer make informed decisions.

Of course, many authoritarians are happy to embrace less rigidity in pursuit of domination. One of the case studies Boyd himself uses is the Nazi Wermatcht, which pioneered a decentralized form of warfare with the Blitz that gave considerable autonomy to units in the field. But by the end of the war, such organizational forms were commonplace throughout the Allied armies and the Nazis had not made any further innovations. We see echoes of this contradictory approach with alt-right figureheads, such as Richard Spencer, who publicly portray themselves as champions of free speech, free inquiry, and debate, yet openly admit in private that they want a society in which they have control over what is acceptable speech.[23]

Such an instrumental approach to leveraging autonomy and decentralization can only work when your enemies refuse to adapt. Leveraging a fancy new tool to get one over on your enemies is one thing, but allowing it to totally transform you is something else entirely.

The sharp rise and fall of the alt-right is an excellent case study of these tensions. In 2016, the alt-right was primarily going up against the Democratic Party and the mainstream media. Such industrial-era organizations manage to survive by relying on considerable barriers to entry that they themselves reinforce so as to deny any meaningful competition.[24] The slow decision-making loop of such institutions and the distorted view of reality held by the people who make them up meant that the alt-right could easily swarm them and take them apart.

But after Trump's victory, the alt-right became increasingly disorientated. Some of this was that they were then fighting against more fluid opponents who were responsive and dynamic. But it was also that the movement lacked any coherent goal. Electing Trump was a goal that the broad swath of the right could get behind. However, once elected, the differences in what they wanted, combined with antifascist pressure, resulted in internal fracturing.[25] The result was the eruption of clear fault lines not just in tactics and strategy, but also level of commitment. Many supported the Trump campaign because it was fun, exciting, and novel. Once they discovered that actual political change is difficult and unrewarding, many jumped ship.

This brings us to the value of having clearly defined, coherent values.

When we say "values," we do not mean rigorously worked out ethical philosophies. Rather, we mean clarity about what a movement stands for and what its goals are and the degree to which those values reflect reality and are internally coherent.

Clarity in this domain is important because of the problem of updating your models of reality. When you change your model of reality, you must map the values and the goals you hold so that they make sense in this new model of reality.

Mapping values onto models is central to the orient step in Boyd's OODA loop, which is why a significant portion of his writing is concerned with the question of values. His reason for focusing on values is partially because he emphasizes how values that are lived are important for interpersonal trust between people, but also for allowing autonomous action. When the environment changes significantly or you become aware of a world-shattering revelation, your previous assumptions about how to reach goals you had may be totally invalidated, to say nothing about the coherence of the goals and values themselves.

Under hierarchical forms of management, only those with authority need concern themselves with such shifts. But with more decentralized forms of organizing that give more autonomy to individuals who were previously subordinated, this comes with the responsibility of making decisions for themselves.

The ability of individuals to reorientate will be limited by the values they hold. This doesn't mean that they won't be able to hold worldviews that are in conflict with values; cognition is a complicated process and nobody is 100% coherent. But it does act as a source of cognitive friction while preventing them from holding worldviews that are in obvious contradiction with their values.[26]

Fascists tend to justify their values through either might-makes-right nihilism or by appealing to essentialist assumptions about how the world should be. Both perspectives on the world drift in an antirationalist direction to avoid dealing with evidence that contradicts core assumptions, such as how power is decidedly not a universal currency that can get you anything you want.

Nor is it to deny that there is a biological basis to humans or that we have tendencies that encourage ugly ways of behaving. But fascist appeals to an essential state of being that we must abide by lest we be punished by god/nature falls apart when you do even the slightest inquiry into the sheer diversity of ways we've lived throughout history, to say nothing of the ways we might modify it in the future.

The context we operate within is not some static fact, nor is it out of our control. Our individual actions shape it and we can be more or less conscious about this process. As anthropologists such as Christopher Boehm have shown, actually existing stateless societies were not populated by naïve Rosseauian innocents who only lived in such a way because they had no knowledge of hierarchy, but rather were conscious and active about suppressing the emergence of dominance hierarchies.[27]

Basing your worldview and values on irrationalist grounds does not make someone incapable of reason. Plenty of reactionaries are well educated and logical. Throughout modernity, authoritarian regimes have shown that they are certainly capable of instrumental reasoning. Our claim is merely that fascists (and authoritarians more broadly) will find it difficult to explore reality beyond a limited "common sense" that they find comforting. This means that they will find it difficult to both theorize about possibilities beyond and will struggle to reorientate their models of reality to account for significant changes. This could lead to violence to create their simplified views, but it could also lead to cascading systemic failures.

Practical Knowledge: Stigmergic Organizing, Skills, and Decentralized Infrastructure

Over the last few decades, we've seen the emergence of world-changing technology that demands a new set of skills. We have outlined a brief overview of how to perform particular tasks, skills that are worth investing in, and emerging technologies that could create significant changes.

It should be noted that everything we list here is specific to a particular time and context. As the conflict evolves, as new technologies are developed, and as the broader environment changes, many of the particular details are liable to change with them. We therefore recommend that activists grasp or have people they trust who understand the fundamentals of science, technology, engineering, and mathematics fields, such as physics, chemistry, computer science, and engineering, while keeping up to date with developments in technology and theory. It should go without saying that you should try to create diverse sets of skills far beyond technology in the development of practical autonomy and organizing patterns that can be applied to a wide range of other forms of resistance.

Social Media

Antifascist networks can continue to develop decentralized strategies for gaming the centralized algorithms of platforms such as Twitter, Facebook, and YouTube in ways the far right is already doing. When it comes to applications, they operate differently from one another.

Secure platforms such as Signal or P2P technology such as Riot or Element (formerly Matrix) allow for small, closed groups to communicate and strategize. These approaches are high security because they are open source and are built on software that is difficult to shut down.

Next up are more medium-sized, low-privacy platforms such as Facebook groups or Twitter private message groups. These also operate on commercial platforms and are easy to infiltrate, but are useful for some strategies.

Finally, we have large-scale platforms such as Telegram channels, Twitter, TikTok, Instagram, and Facebook, which distribute content to an open channel comprising anyone in the public. As these are completely open, they can easily be surveilled by fascists or law enforcement. Despite this, such platforms can be useful for certain strategies. They can also be run by small teams who share login details between each other so as to increase content production and engagement.

These tiers of groups can be used to game algorithms and provide exposure for strategies and tactics such as (but not limited to) the following.

Retweet- or Facebook-Sharing Trains

This is pretty self-explanatory, but is just a way to artificially boost the content of trusted users or organizations whose content we want to spread. Make America Great Again (MAGA) Facebook groups are extremely skilled at this.

Strategic Use of Hashtags

Hashtag campaigns can be collectively developed or centrally administered to influence or introduce narratives.

Follow-Trains and Block-Lists

Groups such as these can be used to decentrally inflate follower counts of important accounts or interconnect existing online networks. They can also aid in the mass blocking of threatening accounts.

Support of Trusted Alternative Media Outlets

Utilize these strategies to combat media monopolies and force more mainstream media to publicly address the realities of radical organizers and people on the ground. This can also be useful for drowning out competitive fascist, conspiratorial, or disinformation alternative media outlets. Conspiratorial outlets utilize a tactic wherein a wide variety of blogs syndicate or minorly adjust and then republish each other's articles to create a sense of consensus and leverage a story into larger media outlets.[28] Although this is unethical for disinformation purposes, it is an avenue of struggle for legitimate alternative media and can be coupled with these social media strategies.

Alternative media is especially important given how poorly the mainstream media is doing at navigating the current informational landscape. A major reason is because of how transmission typically works. Prior to the internet, authoritarian governments relied on the centralized nature of information technology to retain control over the information people received. The decentralized nature of the internet has changed how this is done. Because communication is difficult to block, repressive governments, and others,[29] have adopted the "Firehose of Falsehood" model,[30] wherein they flood multiple channels with constant messages without regard for consistency or accuracy. The aim of such an approach is not to get the targets to believe anything, but rather to induce chaos and uncertainty that makes them unable to react effectively to anyone who'd look to take advantage of them.

A major reason the establishment media cannot deal with such a state of affairs is the sheer complexity of the world. The cozy, mutually beneficial relationship between the media elite and the elite in other spheres was serviceable when the average person did not have much in the way of media outside of them. The problem is both the institutional allegiances massive media companies have and the basic information-processing limits.

Because the problem is inherent to how things are organized, institutional change and reform is fundamentally limited. To truly see a shift in this area means effectively building up a new epistemic ecosystem of distributed agents that can effectively process, filter, and communicate. It may take us decades to get the majority of people on board with a big change of values. But we don't need the majority of people to adopt such an approach to see that changes are happening. Being more accurate means we can do more with less because we don't waste energy, resources, and time on useless projects. Media environments that are more inclusive and expansive can pick up on dynamics that go unnoticed. As such, even partial movement in this direction can yield returns that more than make up for the energy expended.

Dogpiling, Mass Reporting, and Brigading

Creating groups for social media channels to coordinate mass actions, such as blocking, reporting, or harassing (bad) people, is a useful tactic. These groups can help push back against attempts to brigade marginalized people by fascist groups, to attack fascist information warfare, or simply to more effectively promote radical counternarratives in the mainstream in a way that gives the appearance of a consensus. Further, just like right-wingers do, a large Telegram group or the like can be used to coordinate efforts to mass report or otherwise harass dangerous actors.

Open-Source Insurrection

The last decade has seen the emergence of a set of protest tactics that have spread from place to place very quickly. The result is that we increasingly have something like an open-source toolkit for insurrection. Street riot techniques and tactics have been spreading from Hong Kong to Portland, Oregon, just like protests have been spreading from Chile to San Francisco, California, as people around the world learn from each other's strategies and test them in ways that will inform others. These experiences can also be documented to share with others, such as in the famous zine, *Bodyhammer: Tactics and Self-Defense for the Modern Protester*, which breaks down the basics of things like shield walls and shield construction techniques in reproducible ways.[31]

Branding

Obviously, activists hate the concept and practice of branding (for many good reasons), but the basic principles of strategic messaging, catchy graphics/videos, and basic search-engine optimization are useful. The far right intuitively accepts this, as evidenced by heavily branded groups such as Patriot Front and Identity Evropa, whereas the left tends to throw the baby out with the bath water. Within this set of tactics are questions about how to communicate messages that groups such as the anarchist public relations project the Anarchist Agency are addressing,[32] whereas other effectively branded movement outlets such as It's Going

Down, Unicorn Riot, and CrimethInc. Ex-Workers' Collective show examples of how branding can be used effectively. Glossy and flashy media all the way from memes to well-edited videos get people excited to become involved. Clear messaging increases and directs this momentum.

Memes

Need we say more? No, but seriously. Memes are high-context packages of compressed information. Because of the compression, they are not good at nuance, but they are uniquely suited toward virality and thus spreading a highly simplified message as far as possible. This is decidedly the movement territory of internet-fluent radicalized Gen-Zers, although us ancients can participate effectively as well. Just take a complex idea, make it simple and funny. The right knew the power of trolling and harnessed it to help build the alt-right Trump phenomenon. What can we do?

Run Experiments

You can literally just run tests to see what kind of content you can share and what kind will get you suspended or "shadow banned" on social media so you know where the line is so you can create content that will be seen by the most people. See what posting times work best and get the best results. Pay attention to analytics such as impressions, which show you how many people are seeing or interacting with a post and who they are. Constantly share information about these experiments with others. Sex workers are among the most experienced in this form of renegade search engine optimization work because of their experience of resiliency amid online repression, so listen to them.

Open-Source Investigation

Open-source investigation (OS-Inv) is a set of tactics and tools designed to use publicly available information to validate critical details of an event.[33] OS-Inv is a more journalistic variant of the term "open-source intelligence" (OS-Int), which is primarily associated with police and intelligence agencies (both private and governmental). OS-Inv research is often associated with organizations such as *Bellingcat*, but has roots and robust networks of more activist-aligned researchers as well. Because OS-Inv generally relies on freely accessible information, two important things are possible. The first is that, if a researcher is transparent about their methods, they can be validated or questioned by anyone. The second is that it better facilitates the use of different scales of networked investigation by letting people come together to collaborate on investigations.

An example of this kind of networked research is the process through which both fascist and antifascist networks coordinate, often without knowing each other's real identities, to dox, or maliciously expose, the details of an enemy. In the case of antifascists, this is often done to bring public scrutiny on those engaging in white supremacist organizing whereas fascists primarily do it as a means of directing extrajudicial violence and mass harassment. Doxing is generally achieved through the combined use of various forms of open-source investigation, alongside careful scrutiny of the (often inaccurate) information maintained by online data brokers such as Spokeo or ThatsThem.

Like the other social media tactics, coordination in these networks generally occurs at different levels across a spectrum of trust, security, and publicness. So a very small group of trusted activist researchers will usually coordinate over an end-to-end encrypted medium such as Wire or Signal, then sometimes boost those efforts in slightly larger communities that are slightly less vetted. Then, finally, these efforts will be put forward on highly insecure and public platforms such as Twitter or Facebook, where the largest number of people (including various infiltrators) can interact with the work. Some OS-Inv tasks, such as geotagging a photograph, often require a large number of people looking at the problem while other tasks, such as doxing, require much more trust, security, and extreme care to verification.

Some of the key areas that OS-Inv is concerned with are:

Information verification: We live in a time when convincing misinformation can be produced and spread for very little. Verifying whether something happened helps us stay informed rather than deceived.

Investigation of individuals: Through the internet, you can find a lot of information on people.

Social networks: Mapping the social networks of people can be very useful.

Geo/cronolocation: There are techniques you can employ to identify the location and time an event took place.

Reverse image and video searching: Search engines such as Google Images now have the capacity to reverse image search, which can be useful for tracking where images have been posted throughout the internet. You can also use it to track videos, although that is less effective.

Metadata: Media and messages that have little in the way of information may still have value in the information attached to them such as location, time sent, and the sender/receiver of the message.

Archiving and recording information: Although websites such as the Internet Archive and Archive.today are good at recording much of the internet, a lot makes it through the cracks, especially when it comes to real-time events.[34] Recording or downloading livestreams, social media posts, et cetera can be invaluable when they are unlikely to be recorded. The question of how archives will be used in things like international war-crimes trials remains open.

Google dorking and advanced searches: You can use the advanced search functions of search engines such as Google to find valuable data or hard-to-find content.

Flight/vessel tracking: There are websites such as www.flightaware.com that allow you to track flights. Likewise, www.vesselfinder.com lets you find ships.

OS-Inv efforts aimed at tracking fascism can be supplemented with various open-source tracking tools such as the Social Media Analysis Toolkit (SMAT) and other online platforms.[35]

Artificial intelligence (AI) tools also have a role to play in open-source intelligence. Although many see AI as solely the domain of states and corporations, second-rate versions that are less effective but easier to build can still be powerful. This is because activists aren't looking to dominate others and maintain hierarchies, merely just remove the capacity for others to dominate others. As such, the tools only need to recognize a small fraction of society instead of everyone. An example of this in practice is a recent story of activists in multiple countries who have attempted to use facial recognition machine-learning algorithms to identify police who obscure their identities and badge numbers.[36] This was possible because of the small sample size of police officers and the fact that the average police officer is far more likely to be responsible for violence than the average person. Instead of trying to track an entire population of individuals who each have a very low chance of engaging in violence on any particular day, it is instead merely tying the face of someone who definitely committed violence to a small set of faces. This makes it a far more tractable problem simply because the margin of error is much lower.

All these OS-Inv and social media strategies can be done with little to no centralization. Minor forms of consensual centralization can exist in specific tactics such as the creation of a public Telegram channel, but still work best in relatively leaderless environments with very few bottlenecks to information flow and feedback loops. A wide variety of attack surfaces exist in organizing models such as this (e.g., coups by infiltrators or the spread of misleading information by a rival with a shared short-term goal). The more decentralized these structures are, the more uncontrollable they are, but also the harder it is to get very far in a coup scenario. A sufficiently patient enemy can build the trust needed to get admin rights on a Facebook group and then introduce a variety of tactics of disruption, but a sufficiently networked community can pretty quickly rebuild and perform damage control if a single person has limits on how much power they can actually accumulate.

Decentralized Infrastructure

One of the most important trends in the last few decades has been the emergence of technologies that offer the possibility of the significant decentralization of vital services, reversing the centralization enacted under the modern state.

A primary driver in this shift is the insufficiency of the existing infrastructure we inherited from the industrial era for contemporary challenges. Existing infrastructure is overstretched and because of this is vulnerable to disruption. Security experts have noted the vulnerability of US infrastructure in a variety of ways, such as the fact that much of what we all rely on to survive is extremely antiquated, centralized, and fragile.[37] Moreover, it can often be scanned through services such as Shodan,[38] which looks specifically at the "internet of things," including those often employed by infrastructures such as power grids.

Decentralized infrastructure is therefore not just preferable because it gives people more autonomy, but also because it provides a form of passive defense by reducing attack surfaces and preventing cascading failures. Decentralization also allows for more redundancy by letting people assess their risk profiles from where they are, instead of having it thrust upon them by some authority.

In the last decade, solar and wind went from requiring state subsidies to be competitive, to being the cheapest new form of energy without subsidies.[39] Then, 3D printing, although still not advanced enough to go head-to-head with highly optimized mass production on quality or price, is still serviceable enough to somewhat decentralize the process of firearm production.[40] Automated forms of small-scale agriculture now exist.[41]

We have examples of community-owned mesh networks that supply decentralized, resilient internet to people, some of which span thousands of kilometers.[42] All these technologies allow individual communities to be far less reliant on an increasingly fragile economic system, which, in turn, lets them better resist both capitalism and fascism as well as collapse scenarios.

There are also emerging decentralized infrastructure and production technologies that have yet to reach maturity but show promise. These include, but are not limited to:

- The open-source homebrew medicine project Four Thieves Vinegar.[43]

- Efficient solar-powered desalination technology.[44]

- Low-cost housing in the form of Wikihouse.[45]

- The Open Source Ecology project, which looks to create a set of blueprints for "civilization."[46]

- Clean protein in the form of cell- or plant-based meat, which requires significantly less inputs than animal agriculture.[47]

Now, of course, all these technologies can be used by fascists. Many fascists and reactionaries openly call for closed off, autarkic societies, and these developments could help make this a reality by reducing the cost of creating closed-off communities that are largely disconnected from the broader world.[48]

However, were we to develop technologies to such a point that they could deliver autarky, they would have a dramatic effect on broader society and would likely reduce the cost of living significantly. The political consequences of this cannot be downplayed. One of the strongest drivers of an overall increase in liberal attitudes among people in the second half of the 20th century was the general abundance brought about by the postwar economy. This likely led to the rise of what the social theorist Ronald Inglehart called "post-material values," such as individual autonomy, gender equality, and environmentalism, popular among the youth at the time.[49] If decentralized infrastructure becomes widespread enough and brings down the cost of living, it would likely foster further drift in such a direction. Dedicated fascist enclaves would be capable of resisting the trend, but the rest of society would presumably drift away from them in terms of values.

Peer-2-Peer Technologies

As increasing pressure is applied to the rapid growth of white supremacist organizing through the internet, white supremacists have begun to migrate to more resilient services, including P2P, which is a more horizontal infrastructure for the internet. They tend to use P2P technology for things like file storage, forums, communication, and funding.[50]

The primary risk of fascist usage of P2P technology is the organizing of hate-based violence, harassment, and the spread of fascist content. Many in the P2P community are attempting to perform risk mitigation, but this approach can only go so far. P2P technology offers incredible potential for antifascism and human collaboration more broadly, but also poses inherent challenges related to its ungovernability. Antifascists are also increasingly adapting to this landscape and utilizing it strategically to their own ends, especially as the state and corporations such as Facebook[51] increase repression. Platforms such as Secure-Scuttlebutt[51] and algorithms like TrustNet[52] that leverage more robust and feature-rich decentralized technology such as subjective moderation through networks of reputation[53] are important territories for the future of resistance in these spaces. Furthermore, autonomous internet technologies such as Libre Mesh[54] being currently deployed in Indigenous and Quilombo territories in Brazil suggest radical possibilities for our autonomy in the face of disruption or collapse.[55]

General Skills

If we are to adopt more flexible infrastructure and technology, then we need to have the skills and knowledge to operate it.

One of the biggest problems with the contemporary left is that, despite the obvious overwhelming importance of information technology to everyday life, there is very little in the way of concerted efforts to spread and popularize knowledge of information technology. Most young people have at least a surface-level familiarity with how information technology works, thanks to its ubiquity. But when it comes to the actual principles of how these technologies work, their understanding remains shallow.

Thankfully, we don't have to reinvent the wheel to address this issue. People have always been trying to do educational outreach for this sort of thing. Some of it is explicitly political; for example, the emergence of CryptoParty,[56] in which people put on open events in which they explain how to protect oneself digitally, online guides such as the Electronic Frontier Foundation's Surveillance Self-Defense guide, or, more recently, the Vitalist-styled Deep May technology autonomy project.[57] But much of this work is also apolitical, such as the massive proliferation of online learning services and material that we've seen in the last decade. This can and should be leveraged so that people have the skills and knowledge to understand and use the technologies we have described.

One of the most encouraging things about the contemporary left is how it has engaged with theory. Go online and you will see folks from radicals to reformist social democrats/left liberals who are familiar with a broad swath of positions and concerns, the diversity of which puts the mainstream media to shame. Although there is a lot of crud in day-to-day discourse, the fact that conversations happen at all is a good sign.

We don't want to downplay the difficulty of encouraging a shift in norms and values toward becoming more technically proficient and applying those skills—many online leftists are primarily engaged because being a leftist is a way to have an identity first and foremost. But because there are so many people out there, even convincing small percentages to shift their behavior can result in large numbers who are more proficient and actively involved.

Finally, these skills and general outlook serve a dual purpose when it comes to fighting capitalism. Contemporary capitalism is increasingly characterized by rentier behavior across the board, which means that the source of profits derives not from the exploitation of workers, but rather from various rents.[58] Profit in developed countries is derived not from centrally located factories, but rather from diffuse mechanisms of rent extraction.

This form of exploitation is more pervasive, which makes it both more insidious, but also fragile in ways that prior capitalist arrangements weren't. It requires the construction of a vast set of laws and regulations so as to maintain profitability and considerable enforcement mechanisms that can back it up. This means that inequities are maintained not by centralized factories that enable economies of scale, but a patchwork of laws and controls that are far more nebulous than prior forms. Such ambiguity and complexity favor more decentralized forms of organization over the mass movements of the 20th century.

Thus, the capabilities we develop to engage in networked antifascism serves networked anticapitalism, and *vice versa*. Skills, infrastructure, and insights used to fight one threat can be repurposed to fight the other.

Toward a Complex Internationalism

> *"[F]ailed" political movements—OWS* [Occupy Wall Street], *Idle No More, the Arab Spring—were not failures. . . . They were moments that radicalized . . . the activists who would take the streets next time. They provided real-world lessons on which tactics worked and where the weaknesses were. They were battles, not the war. The only thing more extraordinary than a social justice prevailing at all is for it to prevail on its first outing. . . . [T]his book doesn't try to predict or set out a program for getting from here to some better nation there. Rather, it posits what a better nation might look like, and some vectors to approach it. That's because . . . the first casualty of any battle is the plan of attack. No point in planning out a detailed route across territory that will shift dramatically the moment we set out. Better instead to know where we're heading and improvise along the way, letting coordination do the heavy lifting that was once carried by detailed (and brittle) advance plans.*
>
> —Cory Doctorow[59]

The world is scary. As things become more complex, they also move more quickly. New developments make every day a rollercoaster of victories and tragedies. Although this environment is inherently difficult, it also opens distinct possibilities to those who are willing to do the hard work, who learn how to swim with changing tides. Only networks can defeat networks, and it will be the networks that can adapt and anticipate change that will achieve persistent victories over their entangled opponents.

The last decade saw a global wave of networked activism on both the fascist right and the radical left that has impacted the world significantly. This is a likely precursor to what political struggle in the 21st century will look like.

Although the fascist right made many gains in this period, we also saw its weaknesses and limitations. Their strongest victories came from taking state power and opposing liberal regimes. While concerning, we must remember that such forms of organization are ill-suited to the dynamism of the 21st century.

In contrast the most explosive, adaptive, and courageous movements were the ones that were fighting for social justice. The mass antiauthoritarian protests in Hong Kong that began in 2019 exemplified the spread of complex tactics over the internet. But the seeds of that protest were planted by the 2014 Umbrella Revolution protests, which were themselves inspired by the Arab Spring. Although such movements have failed to build information-age institutions that can replace the nation-state, we must remember just how long it took liberalism to replace monarchism.

The revolutions that created liberal political forms that superseded monarchism required not just sacrifice from radicals and the mobilization of the masses, but also significant build-up in terms of developing counterpower, new norms, new ideas, and new technologies over the course of centuries. To move beyond the nation-state, we will require similar preconditions (that we are far more interconnected, educated, and technologically capable means that we can expect it to move a lot faster, however).

It is in the stigmergic organization we have seen across the globe that you can see glimmers of a genuinely bottom-up internationalism that goes beyond the wildest dreams of 19th-century radicals. Such sparks of a better world are the polar opposite of the endless patchwork of tyrant prisons desired by fascist identitarian politics. Our internationalism is built on the solidarity of love and the recognition that, in a complex, dynamic world, everyone has something to contribute. We are willing to build alliances that cross boundaries and interrogate fundamental dynamics instead of appealing to simplistic essentialism or groundless mysticism. Our strength lies not in seizing any outmoded institution, but instead in laying the foundations for technologies of collaboration that, if realized, will enable magnitudes more creativity and cooperation than anything prior.

The war is already here and the worst is likely yet to come. Rather than choosing simple sides, we can build a more ethical and networked left international. War crimes and enforced simplicity are the weapons of the fascist. Complexity, international solidarity, and adaptability are ours. When we fight, we aren't defending a decaying liberal order, but instead we are building the knowledge, skills, technologies, and relationships that are the foundation of a worthy successor society. We go to bury the worst of the old world while birthing the best of the new.

Subcultural Antifascism:
Confronting the Far Right in Heathenry and Heavy Metal

Ryan Smith

There is a rising worldwide clash between a renewed, internationally backed fascism and those fighting for a better future. Subcultural scenes are no exception, with many now locked in wars of ideas of varying intensity. In these cauldrons of turmoil, new ideas, tactics, and approaches are being tested by antifascists in less-than-ideal environments, with growing success. These spaces, which this chapter will refer to as "embattled communities," provide antifascists all over the world ideas, examples, and important lessons in resisting fascism.

This research focuses on two potent examples of such embattled subcultural communities: the world of heavy metal and Norse Paganism. Both communities have long, complicated histories with elements of the modern far right thanks in part to both being early targets for fascist entryism. They also share many of the same hallmarks as other subcultural communities in their relative lack of truly dominant institutions and the pervasive influence of subcultural capital. This combination of shared factors makes both ideal for better understanding how antifascists in subcultural communities can resist and eventually roll back fascists in their own spaces.

The best place to begin is with the concept of embattled community. These are communities, as defined by shared space or affinity, in which antifascist and fascist groups are engaged in active conflict. Such clashes can range from soft power struggles for support to hard power use of force and violence. Embattled communities all face their own degrees of confrontation in clashes that remain an extension of the larger struggle against the reactionary and fascist right. Embattled communities share some broad similarities with the environmental justice concept of frontline communities, although the direct sources of harm and pollution are very different.[1]

An embattled community is not facing the same challenges as those confronting fascist entryism. "Entryist" attempts are best seen in this framework as the first wave of broader fascist attempts to spread their influence into new spaces, with embattlement as one outcome. This condition is characterized by a state of continuous struggle and confrontation in which fascist groups participate openly in shared subcultural spaces, recruit, and can openly harass or attack perceived enemies. Entryism is characterized by fascists being forced by lack of support, strength of opposition, or a combination of the two to operate covertly. To put it bluntly, the problem facing embattled communities is the rats are already inside the walls.

A good example of both can be found in the actions of the alt-right in the San Francisco Bay Area, California, and Portland, Oregon, between the election of Donald Trump and the events of 2020. In the Bay Area, the last major alt-right rallies were in August 2017 following a string of tense, clashing demonstrations, recruitment attempts, and scattered reports of hate crimes.[2] Large-scale public mobilizations in conjunction with targeted direct action effectively repulsed entryist attempts whereas remaining alt-right groups operated largely underground. Portland, by contrast, has been facing a years-long struggle with fascist groups.[3] This conflict has seen overt actions occurring with regularity and tacit support from the police despite active, vigorous opposition by local antifascists and community groups.[4] Portland clearly qualifies as an embattled community in the antifascist struggle, especially in contrast to the Bay Area, which saw brief surges of fascist entryism that were quickly forced underground.

It is also possible for communities to be facing embattlement and entryism from different groups. A good example is Glasgow, Scotland, where several attempts by openly fascist and far-right groups to rally and operate in the city have been constantly frustrated by local radicals.[5] In stark contrast, the Orange Order, an unquestionably reactionary Protestant Unionist group with a history of anti-Irish bigotry among many similar attitudes, operates with such impunity they successfully defied a local council order banning a planned march due to fears they would riot.[6]

For an embattled community, the struggle with fascism is an ongoing effort and, for Norse Paganism and elements of the heavy metal scene, started with the fascists holding the upper hand. This means any antifascists doing work in such spaces, whether they are from that community or are from an existing antifascist group, are in it for the long haul. Whatever knowledge they have of the modern far right is usually shaped by these experiences and in some cases can be quite intimate. For antifascists who call them home, the struggle with the far right is a very real part of their lived experience.

What further distinguishes the heavy metal and Norse Pagan communities from what you see in antifascism in society at large is how their specific subcultural spaces operate. An important theory for understanding this is Antonio Gramsci's hegemony theory. According to Gramsci, society is defined, shaped, and influenced by key institutions whose job is to perpetuate the control of a smaller group of people over the general population, known as hegemony. Many supporting institutions, including but not limited to academia, religion, law enforcement, the nuclear family, and the state, maintain through actions and manufacturing the ideas used to justify the system.[7]

Subcultures are like the broader cultural hegemony in how both have specific institutions that produce the ideas, practices, and aesthetics while being influenced by the outside society. The main point of difference is how genuinely powerful these subcultural institutions are within subcultural spaces and what gives them power. For subcultures such as heavy metal and Norse Paganism, the main institutions are content creators and platforms, including authors, bands, religious organizations, record labels, publishers, vendors, web groups, festivals, and blogs. Their relationship to participants in these communities is very much like the core to consumer dynamic, a theory first formulated by researchers studying subcultural communities.

One good example of this dynamic is from a study of the power dynamics of skateboarding communities in which sociologist Tyler Dupont probed into how these informal hierarchies functioned. At the top of the skater pyramid, according to Dupont, were the most dedicated skateboarders, people who were highly knowledgeable about the sport or who filmed skaters doing runs, helping promote the visibility of specific skaters and the activity in general. The next down were the less-known members of the community who nonetheless were seen as active participants and were regular members of community spaces. At the bottom were those who were new to the sport, consumed products of the subculture, or were otherwise not seen as authentic by people who were more heavily invested in the scene.[8]

According to Dupont, the main form of power expressed in these communities was through the accumulation and use of subcultural capital. The heart of this was the constant work by skaters to assert their authenticity and dedication to their shared community. Being a skater, in these cases, was more than just about participating in the sport, as it was said to include a broader mindset of rebellion, creativity, and free expression. Skaters expressed these shared ideals through consuming subcultural products, participating in shared activities, and, most importantly, demonstrating skill in skating, knowledge of the scene, or filming skaters in action, thus producing content and spreading the ideas associated with that content.[9]

Dupont argued that subcultural capital within the skating communities he observed was far more malleable than is the case in broader society. He claims that loss of esteem and perceived failure to live up to the ideals of the subculture could damage a participant's standing. Long-time content creators, whether they are skaters, store owners, or producers of skater media, can fall from grace very quickly if they're seen as selling out or otherwise acting inauthentically. These content creators operate in an environment in which the consumers have far greater power to make or break them, yet also hold considerable influence when they enjoy broad support.

Much like these skating communities, the worlds of heavy metal and Norse Paganism are ones in which subcultural capital in all its forms reigns supreme. Most of the institutions draw their influence from how many people consume the content they create and promote. Their influence is good only as long as people in the relevant subcultural spaces spread their content. As long as this process stays in motion, the subcultural elite will continue to enjoy considerable influence and leeway in defining the subculture. The moment this stops is when such capital can dry up or, if the cause of the drop is due to some serious breach with the community, vanish surprisingly rapidly. This malleability presents antifascists with a different set of challenges and opportunities, as shown by the experiences of metalhead and Heathen antifascists.

Antifascism in Heavy Metal

The metal scene is no stranger to controversy or conflict. As a subculture rooted in the loud, brash style of their chosen music, metalheads can be quite passionate in expressing their opinions on anything. This environment has made metal a long-standing target for recruitment and subversion by the far right, but has also given birth to what music journalist Kim Kelly has dubbed "the new wave of antifascist black metal."[10] Some of the artists on the crest of this wave had a lot to say on the subject.

For nonbinary-identifying Richard "Lord Gaylord" Weeks, owner and operator of Blackened Death Records, becoming an antifascist was less intentional and more driven by the circumstances around them:

> I actually accidentally stumbled into antifascism in 2015. I've been a
> big fan of neofolk for years, but the flirtations and outright support

a host of the bands have for fascism was always a turn off. I eventually decided to start an "antifascist neofolk" band and people were so angry. [Laughs] At first, I had no idea how so many people could be angry at something as positive as being antifascist. I then learned about antifascism, antifa, anarchism, and all that good stuff. I unfortunately also learned that fascism was alive and somehow growing. As the years went on, fascism got louder, so my own artistic output also had to get louder. I eventually transformed from turning a blind eye to fascism, Nazism, and racism in the scene to outright hunting it down and helping to stamp it out.

In the case of Justin Pierrot of Stormland, his spiritual journey was a major factor in his support for antifascism:

My journey into Catholicism spurred a turn to the left, if you can believe it. As I became more interested in social justice and listening to/helping marginalized people thanks to my faith, it was only right to be antifascist. I'm still learning, but I do my best to share and to learn from others. I also try to keep an eye on the rest of the world in a way that many North American and Eurocentric antifascists don't. So I share information about [Narendra] Modi's increasingly violent Hindu nationalism in India, [Rodrigo] Duterte's Marcosian activities in the Philippines, et cetera, where I can too.

To Jon Crowbane of Petrichor, resisting the far right's rise was never a question but a clear necessity:

I've been quite active in resisting the rise of fascism in our politics and society in the last five or so years. Before that, I never really thought we'd have to specifically fight publicly endorsed, media-backed, hard-right conservatism like we are now. It never seemed to me that our nation would cheer for death camps, public executions, deportations, and suppression of political opponents. Part of that was probably not really acknowledging the true nadirs of public opinion (for example, you'll probably have found people banging the drum for the death penalty if you looked hard enough) and part of it is how radical the right has forced its supporters to become in order to align with right-wing dogma.

Antifascist work runs equally deep for the members of Dawn Ray'd:

We have been involved in antifascism for a lot of years, it is something we are passionate about, and believe an autonomous, militant approach using a diversity of tactics is required to defeat fascism and fascist street movements.

For all these artists, there is no question how long fascism has been involved in the world of heavy metal.

Lord Gaylord: The spread of fascism in metal is down to not just the fact counterculture draws in ne'er-do-wells, but also that, for a long time, many just accepted it as a small part of the scene. A lot of people have known about NSBM [National Socialist Black Metal] since its inception and, while that genre has had its ardent idiotic following, there are people who just outright ignore it like it doesn't affect them. But it affects all of us.

Justin Pierrot: I think the main causes behind the spread of fascism in metal are a combination of people looking for gimmicks to shock with and eventually becoming those gimmicks, and people looking to recruit disaffected, mostly white, male youth who are disconnected from their larger community.

Jon Crowbane: I think it's a conscious choice. Traditional "fascism" in the sense of the traditional Italian Fascism and Nazi German fascism would have actually seen the sort of music we play as being degenerate. They'd have written it off as mongrel culture and idolized some sort of imagined heritage of Greek art and Renaissance composers as their cultural ideals.

There also appears to be an oft-touted concept of "political correctness" which the right (including the far right) cling to as if it were a shield. Which is the idea that their views (which are unpleasant to much of the population given that many people are decent and can be kind and just want everyone to get along and have a chance) are somehow being suppressed by some sort of great conspiracy to hide their great ideas about how skin color or biological origin makes some people better than some other people. It speaks to an enormous lack of self-confidence that they have in their own personalities or talents that they must try to trade exclusively on the volume of melanin in their cells. The "political correctness" row has morphed in recent years into a "offense culture" row whereby people on the right believe that, before 1994, nobody was ever offended by anything and that now, in 2019, everyone should be offended all the time because that's what "free speech" is. This then feeds a sort of "edginess" culture of vice-signalers, desperate to offend by any means necessary, due to a complete lack of anything else of value to say.

Dawn Ray'd: I think there are a number of different strands. Bands like

Slayer have used *totenkopf* and flirted with Holocaust imagery as cheap shock tactics as a way to make themselves look dangerous, but are not actually fascists. This does normalize the use of fascist imagery, however, and blurs the lines of what is acceptable, meaning fascist agitators and conspirators were able to infiltrate these scenes relatively unchallenged. Fascism seeks to radicalize youth movements as a recruiting ground; it happens in lots of different cultural scenes. Ultimately, it has been a very intentional infiltration of an otherwise very positive music scene; fascist groups have moved in in very calculated ways, as there is nothing inherently fascist about heavy metal music.

Not only are there many different avenues fascists use to shore up their base in heavy metal, they also use the music and metal venues as recruitment tools.

Lord Gaylord: Hate groups use metal to recruit people by saying "you're not a part of society, but there's a place for you here with us." And once those tendrils are inside the minds of the disenfranchised, that's when fascism and hatred grow and fester like a disease. This is why we need to be super vigilant about allowing shit like NSBM inside the scene because, while heavy metal can make you feel strong and empowered, feeling strong and empowered by putting down and putting out others because of the color of their skin, the country they were born in, or their religion is actually evil. And it's not "a satanic dragon fighting the gladiator of heaven" silly heavy metal "evil," it's real evil. Racism and Nazism are real evil and have no place on this planet.

Justin Pierrot: I think there's a pipeline. It goes from "Hey, check out this band. Yeah, the lyrics are crazy, but the riffs!" into, "Check this out! Did you see this about (x) group? I know, but you have to keep an open mind!" into, "Yeah, (x) is awful! They're what's wrong with the world!' When you combine that with metal's oft-combative mindset, I think you can see fascists can recruit people. I almost fell victim to that as a teenager, honestly.

Jon Crowbane: Heavy metal is, and likely always will be, incredibly cool. Boring, old, cranky, uptight conservatism really struggles to attract young audiences because shitting on people because they're poor, Black, gay, or all three is very, very uncool. As a result of that, conservatism targets these niche audiences desperate to retain relevance in a world where the majority of the pain and suffering we all feel on a daily basis is due to the greed, malice, ignorance, or incompetence of rich old men.

There's multiple black metal shows across Europe and beyond where printed white supremacist material has been distributed among the crowd, forcing the audience to make a choice. Do they violently reject it from their scene, or do they move over and allow the neofascists in to become a part of it?

Dawn Ray'd: It has worked similarly to, but much slower than, image-board culture. Lightweight political imagery is floated, and when people are normalized to that, then more intense references are made, and so on until the Overton window of metal is pushed to the right. This makes more room for very extreme right-wing ideas and doesn't leave any cultural space for the left wing.

Black metal at the start was simply about satanism, fantasy, and war (see Venom, Bathory, Sarcophago, Darkthrone), but characters like Kristian Vikernes started to use far-right imagery and language, then bands like Graveland were more explicit, throwing Roman salutes in photographs, using swastikas, et cetera, but still mixing it with a layer of fantasy to muddy the waters somewhat. This then makes bands like Goatmoon and Absurd seem not out of place all of a sudden, and then you have people like Hendrick Mobus as prominent figures in a music scene whilst also being actively involved in far-right political groups and looking to recruit from a scene of angry white men. This then sees Golden Dawn member Giorgos Germenis of black metal band Naer Materon get elected to the Greek Parliament.

To these artists there is no question why it is absolutely necessary for them and other metal artists to speak out.

Lord Gaylord: Promoting antifascist, antiracist, anti-Nazi, pro-LGBTQ [lesbian-gay-bisexual-transgender-queer], proequality inside of counter-culture movements is very important. Counterculture movements like metal, neofolk, punk, et cetera are all underground and thus call out to those who have been pushed out of society. And, unfortunately, Nazis, fascists, racists, et cetera are also looking for "safe spaces" and latch onto these musical scenes. It's imperative we push the hate out of these movements or we risk having them taken over by those Nazis, fascists, and racists. Being a queer person in the heavy metal scene and still seeing words like "fag" bandied about recklessly is sad, aggravating, and downright anger inducing. Metal is for everyone and not just straight white dudes.

Justin Pierrot: I don't necessarily promote antifascist politics and views in the same way as a Dawn Ray'd, a Gaylord or a Neckbeard Deathcamp do. But I signal boost and share what I can because it's what I feel I can best do to contribute. I can't necessarily be out on the front lines, but I can spread information.

Jon Crowbane: That's who we are as people. It's difficult for me to say we specifically promote antifascist views in our music or lyrics because we don't, but we all live our lives in a way that resists the spread of fascism and we are all somewhere on the left politically, which of course tends to embrace collectivism and shun nationalism. As for how that impacts the art we do or the music we put out, we have never knowingly shared a platform with artists we believe to be promoting or endorsing far-right views. We actively would choose not to be a part of any of those platforms. We want to eliminate safe spaces for racists and misogynists and xenophobes and transphobia and all the other wanker beliefs.

Dawn Ray'd: Because it is the morally right thing to do, and we live in times that do not afford us the luxury of remaining silent or inactive. Some people maybe feel they can laugh at far-right groups, or that it is some abstract conflict that doesn't affect them. Other people see the very urgent nature of antifascism, and because of who they are, the areas they live in or their very identities, are not able to laugh about or ignore this struggle. Some people talk about the weather.

For these antifascist metalheads, there is no question of the need to take a stand. Fascists, for them, are both an enduring problem and an unwelcome interloper into something they love. This has inspired fierce opposition and as we will soon see similar how conditions for Norse Pagans sparked a parallel response.

Antifascism in Norse Paganism

Like heavy metal, Norse Paganism, also known as Heathenry, has had a long, messy history of fascist activity, organizing, and recruitment. For a long time, it was very normal for much of the Pagan community to assume all Norse or Scandinavian practice was a front for racism and bigotry. Even today, in spite of the work of dedicated antifascists and antiracist Norse Pagans, also known as Heathens, there is still a lot of work to be done in the face of very similar challenges to those confronting antifascist metalheads.

Sophia Fate-Changer, a Queer Latinx Heathen, is a highly active organizer in Heathen antifascism, founder of the Between the Veils Pagan event nonprofit, and was a founding member of Heathens United Against Racism (HUAR). HUAR was a group of inclusive Heathens who organized against the far right. In her words:

> Our organization has formed a global network of people fighting racism in their local areas. Collecting information about prominent groups and

individuals within Norse Paganism, and warning the wider community about such entities, so they can be avoided, and not given platforms for operating, or recruiting. We have also pushed the standard of what is considered normal, healthy Heathen practice to be inclusive.

Another member, Maia, started working with antifascists in the 1980s while attending ACT UP events, which were confronting the AIDS crisis. They now do antifascist research work as well as acting as a street medic.

For Mikaela, a 23-year-old mixed-race polytheist who describes herself as "a young woman of African, Native American, European and Asian descent," such work was often challenging and could be quite draining:

My experience with antiracism has been not only emotionally taxing but disorienting. Many communities in Heathenry prefer to not even discuss racism and that extends into certain communities with focuses on Germanic religion more than it does Celtic communities. I also unfortunately see people lean toward historically incorrect practices because reconstructionist spaces can be very vague about their stances at times. I used to be an admin for what's now a fragmented version of a community outreach group I'm not comfortable discussing right now.

In the case of Carl, another Heathen leftist, he keeps things online for safety concerns, something a lot of antifascists share because of the potential for retaliation from the far right. Kevin, an anarchocommunist Norse Heathen, has a different experience because they have had a lot of in-person organizing experience. "I have marshaled rallies, done event security, patrolled areas looking for propaganda to take down, done online research on dangerous individuals, and other things," says Kevin.

For Heathens, the roots of fascist spirituality run through both Norse Paganism and society at large:

Sophia Fate-Changer: Norse Paganism/polytheism is simply a microcosm of larger society, so the same problems we see on a larger scale in society are also a problem within our smaller community. Because racism exists, especially here in the US, and over the past few years has become, unfortunately, more normalized in our political climate, we see it magnify in our community as well. I also feel like there are folks misinterpreting and misappropriating our lore in order to justify their toxic beliefs.

Maia: At least in the US, Heathenry was started by racists and fascists. Almost all modern Heathenry is a revival of 18th- and 19th-century revivals, which were thoroughly permeated by the racist ideas of the time. It is far more unusual to find an actively antiracist group of Heathens than a racist one in the US.

Mikaela: I honestly wouldn't know in depth what causes bigots to gravitate towards European spirituality. Maybe it's because those people are already part of outcasted groups to begin with. They tend to occupy spaces where the demographic up until recently has been predominantly young white men. Places like gamer forums, local heavy metal scenes, occult shops and gatherings. On one hand, it's not hard to figure out how these men are being funneled into religious spaces but, on the other hand, it is very difficult to understand how our leadership lets this happen. I think the growth in bigotry comes from us being sent men who are already part of shamed, yet, elective demographics (choosing to isolate yourself from society). These young men already see themselves as disempowered victims by the time they pick up their first copies of *Culture of the Teutons* or *The Druids Primer*. They step in the door with disruption and establish power structures that they crave but have never had in mind. They don't enter our space and become racist, they already are racist, with a good addition of having been traumatized emotionally and unable to find a religion that matches their self-image. This problem didn't appear out of nowhere; these men are products of countercultures that are mostly encouraging of nonaccountability.

Carl: There were a host of intersecting factors that allowed fascist viewpoints to grow in Norse Paganism and Heathenry. The first of which is the obvious answer that any cosmology that dictates a glorious warrior afterlife is going to be much easier to adapt into a violent worldview than one that does not (i.e., Christianity). Odin wants warriors and leaders, no question, while it takes some fair twist and turns to torque Christianity into glorifying those same traits. Once that is established, one can easily begin to dismiss Christianity as "a Mediterranean cult," they can then argue it is not right for Europeans to belong to it, bringing in a toxic and nationalist worldview. So without much work, one has a warrior religion that reinforces a nationalist viewpoint—a perfect breeding ground for fascism, all without any serious examination or scholarly insight into what was actually believed or practiced pre-Conversion. Sprinkle in some traditional (Christian) gender-role doctrines and selective bits of text and older (often biased) scholarly works, and one has all the framework needed to keep fascist ideas firmly rooted in Norse Paganism and Heathenry. However, it behooves us to remember fascism is a virulent parasite attached to Heathenry, not its roots.

Kevin: A major factor is the availability of beginner-level learning material written by cryptofascists, sometimes even outright fascists, and people who otherwise hold reactionary views in common with fascists. A secondary contributing factor to this first point is that most of the scholarship on Norse and Germanic studies that is in the public domain is from an era when reactionary nationalistic romanticism was a component of the mainstream of Norse studies. I think it's also important to recognize the actual authoritarian and violent tendencies in some Norse literature and remember that it was produced in the context of actual tyrants trying to seize power—many antiauthoritarian Heathens have difficulty recognizing that Norse society consisted of internal class struggle just like our current society, and the literature reflects that. The fascists exploit it, while the rest of us sweep it under the rug.

Many of the methods used by fascists, surprisingly in spite of their considerable influence, focus much more on the subtle and exploiting people's vulnerabilities:

Sophia Fate-Changer: There are multiple approaches, and several partial phases that can happen in recruitment. I believe their strongest tool is subtlety. Appealing to vulnerable and/or naïve people. People that are at highest risk of recruitment are white prison inmates who are forced into white supremacist gangs for survival, many of whom are attracted to a brand of Norse-inspired spirituality called "Odinism." Fascist organizations in the US will send clergy to prisons and end up validating inmates' beliefs surrounding white supremacy.

Other groups that are at risk are white people who are looking for alternative forms of spirituality and are attracted to the idea of "going back to their roots." Often folks will be attracted to organizations without realizing they are exclusive, or not seeing the visions of these groups as inherently racist, because they have branded themselves instead as "folk" religions, who are for people whose ancestors were of northern European heritage.

Carl: In my experience, it's usually through a very insular mindset. They steadily argue against any "other" they can label (right now, the popular targets are Muslims and leftists) as "enemies at the gate, come to take what's rightfully yours." It preys on the isolationism and individualism and capitalist greed that is so deeply entrenched into the West nowadays. This has the added benefit of being able to ignore scholarly and historical findings about pre-Conversion worldviews because, quite frankly, it's a different world now. Usually recruitment consists of social media/YouTube/et cetera input that takes classic fascist ideology and couches it into Heathen worldviews. Ancestor worship becomes "Blood and Soil." *Innengard* and *utengard* became nationalism.[11] Sacral kingship becomes a slavish devotion not just to the leader of whatever group has recruited the individual, but secular government leaders as well, regardless of their own faith.

Kevin: I think that the most important thing here is the valorization of violence shared by fascists and much of Norse literature. The alt-right narrative that modern society has emasculated men who by nature are supposed to be violent and warlike can be easily supported by Norse literature (although I strongly suspect that an uninformed and stereotyped popular concept of "Vikings" is more influential in that regard than actual Norse literature). Without context and cohesive understanding—things that actually take time and work to acquire—isolated passages from the *Eddas* and sagas are valor-porn. This is related to a parallel factor which is the brutal misogyny and queerphobia of some Norse figures like Haraldr hárfagri [Harald Hard-Ruler] and Eiríkr blóðøx [Erik Bloodaxe], figures who should be hated by Heathens but largely aren't because Heathens don't bother to know their history.[12]

As an aside, this is something that radicals should be more willing to grapple with too. Nonviolent liberals dismiss this as "it was a different time" but the fact is that we *are* engaged in class warfare, and Norse literature is very clear about what to do about it: protect your people by any means necessary; give no *friðr* [peace] to any oppressor.

Fascists also leverage their gains in Norse Pagan spaces to recruit more people to their cause:

Maia: There are multiple entry points for fascists due to shared symbols and shared history. I think that this allows them to foster a sense of camaraderie and kinship. People naturally give more credence to the things that are said by members of their in-group. And I think that makes a lot of the initial barriers to recruitment much less of an issue.

Carl: I think a good deal of the recruitment comes not as a religion, but as a worldview. I know the words are deeply intertwined, but there is a subtle difference, I think. When one is often converted/recruited into Christianity, the focus is usually on "saving the soul"—the religious aspect, the metaphysical, which then in turn leads to "serving your fellow man." Fascists reverse that focus—do it all right and you'll end up in Valhalla, probably, but what's more important is the here and now (which, because Heathenry is a world-embracing Pagan worldview, makes an unfortunate sense). The here-and-now tribalist mindset of "protect what's yours" rings strongly for many of the disillusioned in the modern West. Once that in-group feeling is established, that is when the rest of the twisted cosmology comes into play, just to reinforce all the recruitment efforts that have come before. From there, it's just a short hop into ancestor worship as an inroad into "Blood and Soil" ideology. It is distressingly clever, the pathwork they've paved.

Kevin: Fascists and other reactionaries involved in Norse Paganism are extremely prolific with regard to producing entry-level educational material. Very often, Google queries that newcomers to Heathenry will tend to search, such as "Asatru calendar," pull up racist websites as the number one result. They provide an appearance of genuine information and learning to people who do not yet have the experience and knowledge to differentiate good from bad information. They also severely distort and misrepresent facts about history, taking advantage of the US's abysmal education system. For example, I've seen folkish people argue that keeping nonwhite people out of Heathenry is justifiable because non-Jews can't convert to Judaism—this is obviously wrong and easily disproven, but someone who is very uneducated about Judaism is at risk for believing it. They could then form beliefs about their own identity on the basis of this lie, beliefs which are harder to dismantle later on after further beliefs and experiences are formed that hinge on the original misunderstanding. So there is a whole constellation of misinformation that is presented to people as "heritage" that even many nonfolkish Heathens accept as reality while denying that it has modern relevance (when the fact is that the values of Norse society are not racist and are relevant in modern times).

Even though the heavy metal and Norse Pagan communities have different motivations and histories with fascism, both are facing aspects of the broader white nationalist movement and have experience with their preferred tactics in such subcultural spaces. These similarities in approach show the far right has found ways to adopt their political toolkit to environments with far more fluid institutions and less durable power structures. Yet, even as these communities are facing the latest mutation of the fascist virus, they have also found ways to effectively resist infection.

Responses to Fascism

As the experiences of metalhead and Norse Pagan antifascists shows, both communities are facing very similar problems with the far right. It should then come as no surprise, once you get past the differences between heavy metal and Norse Paganism, that many of the specific obstacles for the antifascist struggle are very similar. Even though these subcultures have very different power dynamics, the common refrains of apathy, indifference, and quiet complicity run through the heart of both communities' struggles, often paired with the inherent risks in antifascist work.

Lord Gaylord: The obstacles we face are centrists. We know right-wing bands are going to hate us. You will never see someone with both Satanic Warmaster and Neckbeard Deathcamp albums in their collection. But centrists are a different story. Those with shallower views on politics generally will be okay with shit like NSBM existing while saying RABM [red and anarchist black metal] bands are "just as bad." It's fucking aggravating because antifascism is a response to fascism and not the other way around, but centrist metal fans say they are both "just as bad." We need to break down these walls erected by "apolitical" assholes. Music is not apolitical, metal is not apolitical, *everything* is political, whether they like it or not.

Justin Pierrot: The stubborn tendency of many people to try and be "apolitical," which is in itself making a political choice. They stick their heads in the sand, and that ostrich tendency is tough to deal with. There's also the idea that any and all antifascist bands need to be promoted when, in reality, a band has to have something to it beyond antifascism and "crust" in its genre tag to reach people.

Dawn Ray'd: A lot of people rely on heavy metal as a way to escape, a way to engage with something that is not connected to the stress of the outside world. We all like to run away sometimes: books, films, or music. I understand why some people are hesitant to get drawn into this conflict. However, we either learn from the mistakes of the past and fight the fascists today, or fight them tomorrow when they are even stronger again. We have to show people that these are real-world issues, when a band throws a roman salute or *sieg heil*, it isn't some edgy gesture to make them seem controversial, it is a message sent out that threatens the lives of marginalized people. It is encouraging ideas that actually cost lives in the real world. For too long we have allowed them to exist and assumed the fascists in this scene are just an eccentric harmless oddity, but we can see now that that is not the case.

Sophia Fate-Changer: Because there are multiple approaches to antifascist action, it is sometimes difficult for different groups to come together to create one cohesive vision. I think it's important to have people with a variety of talents and methods to solve a problem, but not everyone will have the same end goal for an action. It is important for local antifascists to work together and organize, and have multiple backup plans and methods to escape a situation. Taking precautions like using secure networks for discussion, using an alias, becoming familiar with the area you're holding your action, and the area around it. Familiarizing yourself with the fascists that are in the area, or who are planning to come to the area—if they have a certain dress code, or known tactics to antagonize.

Maia: One of the biggest obstacles is the refusal of the average Heathen to see that there is a problem. If the problem is recognized, the obstacle becomes having to face the fact that their friends of many years are fascists and what to do about it. The likelihood that anyone has been in American Heathen circles for more than a couple of years and not met fascists approaches zero.

Carl: One of the biggest obstacles to antifascist action, quite frankly, is the momentum that the fascists have built. Antifascism in Heathenry, let's be honest, is starting the race in last place. Between [Heinrich] Himmler's occultism in Nazi Germany, [Carl] Jung's often mischaracterized essay "Wotan," and the racist origins of Odinism in North America, there is a lot of material and work that have already been put into molding a profascist Heathen worldview for decades, if not nearly a century by this point.

I moved past all of these problems by studying the sources, reading as many interpretations as I could get my hands on, and asking the question anyone who's been online for more than a day should be asking when they read anything, "Who wrote this, and why?"

Kevin: Organizing within Heathenry has been difficult. The biggest obstacle is that there are many people who might be sympathetic, but who I won't call on for help because I am not confident enough that they won't, for example, call the cops. There is a serious lack of actual radical analysis of racism and its relationship to capitalism and settler-colonialism, so people are unable to react in an effective way. A good example of how this manifests was at a ritual for trans empowerment. The liberal Heathens who attended the ritual hung up their banners as a show of support and solidarity with the trans community. Meanwhile, at the direction of the ritual organizers, my kinsman and I worked with local Wobblies to provide security. This was so the people who were there to celebrate their own histories and identities could do so safely and uninterrupted. This is often the case, so I sidestep them and organize with non-Heathen radicals instead.[13]

In the face of such challenges, these antifascists have applied proven methods in the broader struggle with their own unique adaptations. Some of what they propose is based on proven experience whereas other observations are drawn from places where antifascists can do better:

Lord Gaylord: For antifascism to really grow in the metal scene, we need to excise filth like NSBM, we need to conquer the stigma from centrists, and we need to make the music louder than the message. On paper, it sounds simple enough, but we are gonna have to keep on it. [Adolf] Hitler never went away on his own. [Benito] Mussolini never went away on his own. This isn't a difference of opinions, this isn't "just music," this is humanity. This is a war. This Earth has no room for racism, Nazism, or fascism. Neither does our music.

Sophia Fate-Changer: Creating an online presence to get the word out to thousands of our followers has proved to be a great way to get people involved. Encouraging people to meet locally and setting a standard that Heathenry can be inclusive has pushed a lot of Heathen groups worldwide to adopt inclusive mission statements and protocol to keep fascists out of their practices. Emphasizing that bigoted members of our community are the minority (although a very loud and visible minority, a problem many religions have) has brought a lot of people out of solitary practice, from my observations, and into inclusive communities; simply by existing, they end up being part of the solution to creating positive change.

Justin Pierrot: I think the best way to promote antifascism in metal is just getting out there and being personable. Don't limit yourself to exclusively antifascist metal spaces. Preaching to the converted only gets you so far. You have to get out there and win hearts and minds, and there are people who are already out there winning those hearts and minds that we can take cues from. But at the end of the day, to borrow a sentiment from Catholicism, go out and be in the world, even if you're not part of it.

Maia: I think what works for drawing attention to the issues is showing up making friends and constant feeding of information. For organizing with other antiracist, antifascist Heathens, unless you happen to be lucky, start your own group.

Jon Crowbane: We can't just tear it all down and burn it. We have to be inspirational. We all have to be the powerful light-in-the-darkness force that makes people want to be good to each other and to understand that society is about our responsibility to each other, about the contributions we all make (in art, wealth, culture) and about how we continue to make things better, not to make things worse for other people.

Dawn Ray'd: Speak out about it in a way you feel comfortable and suits your band. Try and say things onstage, in the liner notes of your record, and on social media. We have to normalize the challenge to the right wing and embolden resistance in every way we can think of. We have to try and take back control of online digital spaces from the Nazis, and we mustn't let them prey on another youth movement as they have done so many times before. Music is powerful; it is meant to be bold, strong, and brave. It is meant to be imaginative and creative, and passionate. Far-right imagery and ideas are the opposite of all those things; they are cheap (and at the expense of marginalized folks) and lazy and cruel.

Carl: In my limited experience, counterpunching propaganda is very useful in undermining any authority or respect profascist Heathens have acquired. Blog posts addressing legitimate arguments, memes pointing out the ridiculous positions they are forced to take, and ensuring moderates are fully aware of who is profascist (with evidence—Trump's "witch hunt" hogwash is very popular with the profascist crowd and evidence must be available before any accusations) are key to reducing the flow of profascist propaganda online.

Kevin: My geographical area has a long history of what in recent times has become known as "callout culture." In the years I've been here, there have been several important community-wide (meaning of a few hundred people) waves of severing ties with certain individuals because it was discovered that they had affiliations with folkish groups. This is comparable to Declaration 127, but we were doing it for years already by then.[14] That refusal to interact with racists has a cascading effect that leads to a relatively healthy and safe community. My kindred applied this on a smaller scale when we were invited to a coordinating committee of local pagans (of various traditions) who also invited a known racist. I attended one meeting to announce my unwillingness to participate in a group that had a racist member, explained my reasoning so that others in the group (most of whom were unfamiliar with folkish Heathenry) would have to make the same decision. This was successful and the racist has been removed from the group.

And despite the setbacks and challenges, most of these activists remain guardedly optimistic about their chances. They also make it clear this won't be a short, easy struggle:

Lord Gaylord: Ultra–left-wing bands are still in their infancy right now. You have bands like Iskra and Propaghandi who have been around for years, but the new wave still has a lot to do. We're still considered "flash in the pan" bands. We are sought out by people who are very specifically looking for antifascist bands. We have to keep our heads down and get on with it. The music needs to become louder than the message so the message can then shine through.

Sophia Fate-Changer: Yes. Organizations don't like to admit that the way they've done things for years has enabled racism and other bigotries to flourish. But we have managed to budge even the most stubborn of organizations to update their standards a little at a time. I think it's always been understood by the core players of Heathen antifa that we are here to create overdue, progressive change if we are going to survive as a popular and growing practice. We aren't here to make people comfortable, we are here to initiate difficult conversations. We are here to question you. We are here to shed light on dark places, and we will continue to do so.

Justin Pierrot: Bands like Terminal Nation, Svalbard, and Redbait are on the come-up, and older bands like Sacred Reich on the comeback, they're getting their message out there. I think they're also emboldening other artists whose music may not be explicitly antifascist to make more public statements. And the more these bands, that are high quality musically, engage in this, they take away space from sketchier bands in terms of press coverage. After all, why waste ink or bandwidth on the sketchy band when there's one just as good or better that's not full of walking bags of enema waste?

Maia: I think we've been successful in calling attention to the problem and I think that things like Declaration 127 are evidence of that. Because of some of the history of American Heathenry, there will always be racist, fascist Heathens. I think that we are doing a much better job of differentiating them from the rest of us and I hope that as people arrive that makes a difference in the directions they go.

Jon Crowbane: Many well-funded far-right talking heads are broke or too scared to operate now specifically because of the work of antifascists. The work of antifascists has forced companies like Facebook and YouTube to actually start enforcing their Terms of Service (ToS) when it comes to extremism. They've had the rules for years, and under scrutiny have pointed to how it violates their ToS, but only recently have they been forced to actually act and to start removing the conspiracy theorists, antisemites, Islamophobes, and other bigots from those platforms, in the same way they have always done if a woman's breast accidentally comes out.

The agitation, awareness, and public consciousness has been stimulated to such a point now where being aligned with extremism on the far right will be damaging to advertisers, and that's why things are finally happening. Fucking tragic, isn't it? Huge communities shunned, targeted, and oppressed, and power didn't give a shit. Pepsi can't move as many drinks, and heads start to roll? Fucking tragic.

We also have to acknowledge that the majority of the media operating in any of our countries simply is not there to represent us, and it's definitely not there to inform us. It's there to make money from showing us advertisements, and, perhaps most importantly, media is used to discipline, direct, and coerce the public toward different viewpoints. You certainly don't have to look very far to see very specific partisan agendas being pursued by different outlets that, far from representing the population, are actually attempting to condition it. Media that does this is (and should be) terrified that, since they fuel the hostile environment of fear, alienation, and suspicion that makes prejudice so insidious and successful, they are also a target for anyone who meaningfully wants to limit the reach of ultranationalism and neofascism.

Carl: Are the fascists still growing their ranks? Yes, but I would posit that it's a factor less than it would have been without antifascist efforts. There are always going to be individuals who gravitate to fascist ideology, and they need little to no prompting or help from the current propagandists, and I say that it is only those predisposed individuals that are now being recruited. Those on the fence, those who would have sought out Heathenry first, only to find fascism, are now finding communities that provide an alternative that didn't exist before, and that's why the efforts aren't specifically noticeable right now, because we're just seeing people join Heathenry, perhaps not antifascist Heathenry, but the point is they're still not joining the profascist Heathenry, and I count that as a win.

Dawn Ray'd: Black metal is a scene that for the most part tries to avoid politics of any kind. The majority of bands are not openly political, be it left or right wing, most bands sing about fantasy, war, depression, or nature; abstract, escapist things. It is music that is primarily engaged with for escapism, it soundtracks fantasy landscapes, references magic or Satanism, and is often not concerned with reality or normal life. However, we have come to a point where we can no longer be so inward looking, as already that escapism has been betrayed by the far right and so must be combated.

Before we released our record in 2017, there were no black metal bands being as vocally antifascist as we were; I think it is fair to say we were probably the first. There still aren't many actual black metal bands fighting this yet; bands like Underdark and Woe are explicit in opposing fascism.

Kevin: What I described about my geographically local community kicking out the folkish has been very successful, but further action has not. I think this is for the same reason I cited earlier, which is a lack of radical analysis. The most common tactics used in my local community to fight racism are pure spectacle with no actual change to social structures or change in the relationship between Heathens and non-Heathen marginalized peoples. Most Heathens want to be seen as a "legitimate" religion by the hegemonic powers such as the state, established churches, nongovernmental organizations, et cetera. That means they are more accountable to the cops than to the victims of police violence. To put it bluntly, the vast majority of Heathen "antifascist" organizing in my

community is actually advancing white supremacy rather than dismantling it, albeit in a liberal form rather than an openly fascist one.

Even though fascist forces enjoyed several advantages to complement
their long-term campaigns, antifascist metalheads and Norse Pagans have
achieved several notable victories. There is certainly room for improvement, as all these activists made clear, and this struggle won't be over
anytime soon. They also leave no question that any antifascist campaign
must do more than just stop fascists—they need to offer new, more just
alternatives for their communities. Yet there is a sense they are making
gains and changing conditions for the better.

Winning the Battle

Although antifascist metalheads and Heathens have developed many different responses, tactics, and methods for countering fascist campaigns,
their struggles are only just beginning. The road ahead for these and other
antifascists working in other, similar communities is long, but hopefully
the success and mistakes in heavy metal and Norse Paganism will help others find success. As much as both communities are still heavily embroiled
in struggle, they have nonetheless seen significant breakthroughs.

In the metal scene, the 2019 Black Flags Over Brooklyn music festi-
val organized by Kim Kelly heralded the arrival of antifascist black metal
as a genuine force to be reckoned with. This was followed by Bindrune
Records' 2020 Overgrow to Overthrow compilation released in the heart of
the George Floyd uprising. All profits were donated to Black Lives Matter
and the lineup included many Black Flags Over Brooklyn headliners.
Less visible but equally vital has been the continuing growth of antifascist metal digital spaces, such as the People's Black Metal Necroposting
and Red & Anarchist Black Metal, that show their enduring, expanding
appeal.[15]

In Heathenry, years of agitation have borne some early fruits. In
September 2016, a coalition of 180 Heathen organizations from 20 different countries released a joint statement known as Declaration 127, which
officially denounced the Asatru Folk Assembly (AFA), one of the largest Heathen-identifying organizations in the world, as racists. It further
stated members of the AFA were barred from the signatories' spaces and
events, effectively banning them from a clear majority of Heathen spaces.
Declaration 127 has become a point of solidarity and support for it has
become a common litmus test for determining whether an avowedly

inclusive group or leader is genuine in their commitment to inclusivity. Actively antiracist, antifascist, multitradition Pagan events such as the Gathering Paths events, organized by Between the Veils, further show momentum is only increasing for organized, antifascist spirituality.[16]

In closing are the final thoughts of these antifascists for every metal-head and Heathen doing the work or who want to do more:

Lord Gaylord: If you are sympathetic to our cause, tell your friends. Spread the music, share the music with everyone. Know antifascists who don't listen to metal? Share it with them—the music might not resonate with them, but the message will. Have a friend who listens to NSBM? Get them out of that dead-end scene. If they really won't drop the racist music, drop the friend. Don't be *milquetoast* with this stuff, don't turn a blind eye, tear it down. The moral is, don't sit back and relax. This is a warzone, get up, get out, and get to work.

Sophia Fate-Changer: If you are part of a community, or if you're building a community, make sure that your community standards are known. Have inclusive language, and be loud and proud about the fact that you don't want fascists to sit at your table or share your horn. Most importantly, make plans for if and when a fascist does come to your table—make an enforceable protocol to handle the situation so that you keep yourself and the rest of your community safe. It can be scary, so be prepared. Find other antifascist Norse Pagans. We are everywhere at this point.

Justin Pierrot: Be aware that there are many different approaches to antifascism and many different ways for people to get there. There is a place and time for violence, but that doesn't mean that a pacifist approach is always wrong either. Be pragmatic, be willing to listen to people, especially marginalized voices, and don't be afraid to look a bit deeper into new bands so you can listen to ones better attuned to your morals and ethics.

Maia: There are a handful of good antiracist, antifascist Pagan groups on the internet. HUAR is one such. Join some. It's a good opportunity to discuss and to get support from others who are like-minded. If you can't find any local groups to join in real life, find one other person and advertise that you will be at local coffee shop number three every Sunday evening from six to eight and do it. Sit there and educate yourselves; eventually, other people will show up if you keep posting that it's happening. Good luck!

Jon Crowbane: It doesn't have to be your *raison d'être*. You don't have to release an album with 12 tracks about kicking neo-Nazis in the head. You just have to be a decent person and acknowledge that you have a platform and that people are listening to you. You can either use that platform to resist harmful views, to passively acknowledge them, or to endorse them, but please be aware, the people who are listening are your fans. They (hopefully) buy your music and support what you do. If you really cared for them back, you'd want them to find peace and happiness and love, and no neofascist can ever find peace and happiness. The entire viewpoint is based on false premises of extinction and hatred. You'd be condemning them.

Also, please don't be afraid to own your opinions. You'll probably catch some flak for it, especially if you're careless enough to be online, opinionated, and female. But we will support you if you are doing the right thing.

Mikaela: Stay true to yourself and remember that your ancestors want to be remembered with dignity. You are responsible for yourself and you have an obligation to protect new polytheists from hatred.

Dawn Ray'd: Get involved! Take action both within music scenes but also outside of them. Learn from people who are more experienced and get good at security culture. Antifascism needs a lot of different people with a lot of different skills, it needs practical robust defense in the streets, it needs culture, it needs sports fans, it needs everybody, and everyone has something they can offer!

Carl: You're not going to convince fascists to stop, but putting out the alternatives and counterarguments are still necessary because of those seekers I mentioned previously. Speak up when something doesn't quite jive with pre-Conversion worldviews. Question authority (respectfully, but firmly) when it's demanded that you be silent. Sunlight really is the best disinfectant on fascist ideology, and the more they're called to the mat, the less room they have to stand.

———

As is shown by the struggles of Heathen and heavy metal antifascists, organized antifascist action by members of these subcultures gained significant successes thanks to their intimate understanding of their respective scenes and their willingness to confront the far right directly. These actions are buttressed by a consistent understanding that, if fascism finds any safe haven, it will work to transform that space into a platform for propagating the fascist cause. Even though the experiences of Heathen and heavy metal antifascists are heavily influenced by the particular conditions of their respective subcultures, they nonetheless clearly demonstrate the far right cannot be debated from power. They must be confronted with alternatives that have the strength to utterly displace them.

II.

GLOBAL SOLIDARITY:
FIGHTING THE INTERNATIONAL FAR RIGHT

Why Does the US Far Right Love Bashar al-Assad?

Leila Al-Shami and Shon Meckfessel

On August 12th, 2017, 20-year-old James Alex Fields, Jr. drove his car into a crowd in Charlottesville, Virginia, killing 32-year-old protester Heather Heyer, and injuring numerous others. Fields had long been public with his far-right views, and efforts by his alleged colleagues in the fascist group Vanguard America to disavow his allegiance were unconvincing. In seeking to understand Fields's motives, the many journalists and others who checked his Facebook account were greeted perhaps by an unexpected image of Syrian President Bashar al-Assad (hereafter, Assad), with the word "Undefeated." Why, they found themselves asking, would an American white nationalist celebrate a Muslim Arab leader, and what might this say about the movement it emerged from?

Fields is not the only far-right activist to display admiration for Assad. A number of other attendees of the "Unite the Right" rally expressed similar sympathies. One protester boasted a T-shirt emblazoned with the words, "Bashar's Barrel Delivery Co," in reference to the improvised bombs that have caused thousands of civilian deaths and turned whole Syrian cities into rubble. Another declared, "Support the Syrian Arab Army . . . fight against the globalists!" to which alt-right YouTuber Baked Alaska responded, "Assad did nothing wrong, right?"[1] Far-right figures expressing common cause with the Syrian dictator long predate this rally. As far back as 2005, Klansman-cum-state legislator David Duke visited Damascus, Syria, and, in a speech aired on Syrian state television, declared that "part of my country is occupied by Zionists, just as part of your country, the Golan Heights, is occupied by Zionists. The Zionists occupy most of the American media and now control much of the American government."[2] Assad's regime has only increased in popularity with the far right since.

The far right has been at the forefront of some of the "antiwar" protests on the occasions when Western states have carried out limited airstrikes on military assets of the Syrian regime (but not when phenomenally larger and more fatal airstrikes targeted nonregime areas). In April 2017, Donald Trump ordered a strike that hit an empty regime military base in response to chemical attacks on the town of Khan Sheikhoun days earlier. Richard Spencer joined in a #StandWithAssad Twitter campaign and led protests in front of the White House denouncing the strike.[3] On Twitter, he declared, "The #AltRight is against a war in Syria. Period. We want good relations with Bashar al-Assad, and we urge Trump to halt the rush to war."[4] White nationalist magazine *VDARE* responded: "The #AltRight is now totally independent of Trump, and this anti-West, pro-terrorist foreign policy. Organize, organize, organize."[5] Ann Coulter declared: "I don't care if it was Assad who used these chemical weapons. . . . I'm tired of regime change. I'm tired of war."[6] Tara McCarthy, host of *The Reality Calls Show*, stated: "The #AltRight is portrayed as bloodthirsty, ignorant and vicious yet every Alt Right person on Twitter right now is campaigning against war."[7]

Although not every individual on the far right holds such sympathies—one post on the far-right "Vibrant Diversity" channel offers, "Daily Reminder that Assad is not based he is a non white dune coon"[8]—far-right adoration of Assad is widespread. Some support mirrors more commonly held notions about Assad: that he is the only force effectively fighting the Islamic State of Iraq and Syria, that he is protecting Christians and other religious minorities, or that he is somehow holding the country and region together. Many others, however, demonstrate clearly fascist motives. Here we seek to analyze US fascist sympathy for Assad to better understand the mechanics of contemporary US fascist movements, their primary motivations, and their concerns.

What's to Like: Fascist Influence in the Roots of the Modern Syrian State

On March 3rd, 2018, Justin Burger, a "major" in Georgia in the now-defunct Traditionalist Worker Party, and "Rock," one of his comrades, had a conversation on the #tradworker Discord channel, subsequently leaked by Unicorn Riot. In the conversation, Burger takes offense at a meme showing a swastika among other symbols opposed to Assad.

JUSTIN BURGER: Assad is a Ba'athist, the closest still living incarnation to NATSOC [National Socialist]. . . . Cyprian Blamires[9] claims that "Ba'athism may have been a Middle Eastern variant of fascism." According to him, the Ba'ath movement shared several characteristics with the European fascist movements such as "the attempt to synthesize radical, illiberal nationalism and non-Marxist socialism, a romantic, mythopoetic, and elitist 'revolutionary' vision, the desire both to create a 'new man' and to restore past greatness, a centralised authoritarian party divided into 'Right Wing' and 'left-wing' factions and so forth; several close associates later admitted that [Michel] Aflaq had been directly inspired by certain fascist and Nazi theorists."

ROCK: Can we just admit that Assad is our guy

Hecc they even get sworn in by doing the Roman salute I believe.[10]

Burger's claim that the Ba'ath Party manifests a historical continuity with National Socialism contained a kernel of truth. The Syrian regime's authoritarianism and cult of personality around the president reflect in many ways the totalitarian regimes (both fascist and communist) of the 20th century, which, coupled with the Syrian regime's strong nationalist identity, holds appeal for many on the contemporary far right.

The Arab Socialist Ba'ath Party came to power in 1963 through a military coup. It was founded on an ideology incorporating elements of Arab nationalism and Arab socialism, both witnessing popular resurgence in the wave of decolonization. Its early ideologues—Michel Aflaq (a Christian), Salah Al-Din Al-Bitar (a Sunni Muslim), and Zaki Al-Arsuzi (an Alawite)—advocated a renaissance of Arab culture and values and the unification of the Arab countries into one Arab state led by a Ba'ath revolutionary vanguard. The 1973 Constitution declared the Ba'ath to be "the leading party in the society and the state," indicating a level of consolidation of state under the party reminiscent of Vladimir Lenin's or, equally, Benito Mussolini's models.[11]

From the outset, Ba'athist ideology sought to mythologize the "Arab Nation," a notion imbued with a romantic vision of past greatness that would both counter the humiliations wrought by French and British colonial rule and build a new nationalist identity. A fiercely secular movement that attracted the support of minority groups, the Ba'athists reworked religious symbolism in service to Arab nationalist goals. They paid tribute to the role of Islam in Arab society—especially its contributions to Arab culture, values, and thought. The slogan of the Ba'ath party—"One Nation, Bearing an Eternal Message"—has obvious religious connotations, particularly the play on the word "message" (*risala*), the term used for the message revealed to the Prophet Mohammed, and the word "nation" (*umma*), which is usually used to refer to the global Muslim community. Aflaq envisioned a sublimation of religion and society into the more modern form of nationalist identity: "Europe is as fearful of Islam today as she has been in the past. She knows that the strength of Islam, which in the past expressed that of the Arabs, has been reborn and has appeared in a new form: Arab nationalism."[12]

The Ba'ath Party advocated socialist economics but rejected the Marxist conception of class struggle. Aflaq believed that all classes among the Arabs were united in opposing capitalist domination by imperial powers, proposing that nations themselves, rather than social groups within and across nations, constituted the real subjects of struggle against domination. Coming to power, the Ba'ath pursued top-down socialist economic planning based on the Soviet model. It nationalized major industries, engaged in large infrastructure modernization that contributed to the nation-state–building enterprise, redistributed land away from the land-owning class, and improved rural conditions. These populist policies brought the party a measure of cross-sectarian peasant support. At the same time, leftists were purged from the Ba'ath Party early on, and later all leftist opposition would be either co-opted or crushed. Following the corporatist model, independent associations of workers, students, and producers were repressed and new parastatal organizations said to represent their interests emerged.[13]

Hafez al-Assad came to power in 1970 in an internal coup directed against the left-wing faction of the Ba'ath Party. Under his rule, Syria became a totalitarian police state based on the tripartite control of the Ba'ath Party, security apparatus, and military, yet power was centralized in the presidency. Hafez al-Assad reigned supreme as "the Eternal Leader" or "the Sanctified One." His portrait and statues decorated buildings and the main squares of cities and towns. Hafez al-Assad rose from modest origins to the state personified. From schools to national events, carefully choreographed spectacles of public worship were used to reinforce the cult of the president and enforce the conformity and submission of the populace, without ever needing to win over individuals' private thoughts or convictions.[14]

Dr. Rahaf Aldoughli argues that nationalism and the "cult of Baathism" formed part of the indoctrination of the Syrian citizen from an early age and went hand in hand with the normalization of militarism, enforcing both masculinity and physical power as key markers of identity and constructing the image of the heroic Arab man as the ideal citizen. School children faced compulsory conscription into two Ba'ath-affiliated organizations: the Ba'ath Vanguards Organization (during primary school) and the Revolutionary Youth Union (during secondary school). Aldoughli argues that these "two organizations mobilize children through enforced training and membership in paramilitary groups that perpetuate ideals of masculinist militarism, conceptualizing them as expressions of nationhood." During enforced mass marches, school children were taught to chant" "[W]ith blood and soul, we sacrifice ourselves for you, Hafez."[15] Today, the same slogan is chanted in support of his son.

In Hafez al-Assad's Syria, all political expression and opposition was severely repressed to the extent that the country became, in the words of leftist dissident Riad Al-Turk, "a kingdom of silence." The prison system, and the entire security apparatus, acted as the primary means of social control through both the perpetuation of fear and the delivery of punishment for acts of transgression. The brutalization of political opponents through the system of incarceration is powerfully portrayed in prison memoirs such as *The Shell* by Mustafa Khalifeh and accounts by the poet Faraj Bayrakdar and leftist dissident Yassin Al-Haj Saleh. For political prisoners, torture was a key feature of detention. In 2017, it emerged that the Syrian leadership had gained some of its interrogation and torture techniques from former Schutzstaffel commander Alios Brunner, a man described by Adolf Eichmann as the architect of the "Final Solution." The Nazi war criminal, given safe haven by the regime, died in Damascus, Syria in 2001.[16] Unmitigated brutality was used by the military to crush uprisings against the regime in 1963, 1964, 1965, 1967, 1980, and 1982, culminating in the massacre in Hama, Syria, where between 20,000 and 40,000 citizens were killed, and much of the ancient Old City was leveled by Hafez al-Assad's air force.[17]

When Assad inherited the dictatorship from his father in 2000, little changed except the cosmetics of discourse. The arbitrary detention, torture, and summary execution of dissidents continued and prisons were filled with leftists, communists, Kurdish opposition protesters, Muslim Brotherhood members, and human rights activists. The economic situation worsened due to the increasing neoliberalization of the economy, which continued to concentrate wealth in the crony-capitalist class of those loyal to, or related to, the president—a feature of his father's rule. For example, Assad's maternal cousin Rami Makhlouf was estimated to control some 60% of the economy through business ventures, including mobile phone monopolies, tourism, real estate, banking, and construction. Meanwhile, ordinary Syrians became increasingly impoverished as subsidies and welfare were dismantled and unemployment rates soared, particularly among youth. It was both political repression and this desperate socioeconomic situation that led to the uprising in 2011, arriving in the context of a transnational revolutionary wave sweeping the region.

Assad's response to the uprising was to wage what the United Nations (UN) has termed a state policy of "extermination" against those who demanded democracy and dignity.[18] Since 2011, Syrians have been bombed, gassed, raped, starved, tortured, and driven from their homes. Some 400,000 people had been killed, according to a 2016 UN estimate,[19] with many more at the time of this writing, given the scale of ongoing violence. Tens of thousands have been imprisoned, many suffering the most sadistic forms of torture practiced on an industrial scale. More than half the population no longer lives in their own homes, having fled barrel bombs, chemical massacres, and starvation sieges carried out by the regime with the assistance of its allies, Russia and Iran. Herein lies a key appeal for the international far right: an authoritarian strongman prepared to unleash violence on an unimaginable scale to crush dissent who avoids any accountability.

Making Thanatocracy Great Again

If there is one characteristic that distinguishes historical fascism from other political ideologies, it is the explicit embrace of mass violence as a means to achieve political goals, particularly the systematic implementation of mass murder of internal populations. Although both capitalist and state-communist regimes have repeatedly employed mass murder as a political tool, fascism has been unique in ideologically defining itself through its reliance on internal mass violence, even as an end in itself. As fascism scholar Robert Paxton explains, "The legitimation of violence against a demonized internal enemy brings us close to the heart of fascism. . . . It was the genius of fascism to wager that many an orderly bourgeois (or even bourgeoise) would take some vicarious satisfaction in a carefully selective violence, directed only against 'terrorists' and 'enemies of the people.'"[20] Whereas Joseph Stalin's followers long denied his mass murder campaigns, Adolf Hitler's followers have been more likely to embrace their history of mass violence as justified and emblematic of their beliefs.

The scale of violence in Syria is shocking, even by the dismal standards of our day: casualties number well over half a million. According to the Syrian Network for Human Rights (SNHR), 93% of civilians killed in the conflict have been killed by regime forces.[21] The large majority of these deaths have been due to the intensive, years-long shelling of cramped residential neighborhoods, hunger sieges, and targeting of medical and other survival infrastructure. However, a notable proportion has also been exterminated through the industrial-scale implementation of torture within Syria's extensive incarceration network. Although many supporters of Assad attempt to deny or minimize these crimes against humanity, it is precisely this cruelty that appeals to so much of the far right, and likely lies at the base of much of its support.

Syrian activist and sociologist Yasser Munif has described how the Assad regime has instrumentalized violence to the extent that it has actually innovated a new system of governance.[22] Munif builds on Achille Mbembe's notion of "necropolitics," which "operates by deploying its lethal power and making decisions about who can live and who must die."[23] However, in Munif's reading, necropolitics (which Mbembe was applying to the practices of postcolonial violence) focuses too much on diffuse, often nonstate violence to exploit and enslave, which he feels fails to encapsulate the Syrian situation. Munif introduces the category of "thanatocracy" as a subset of necropolitics, which emanates predominantly from a state/sovereign power seeking to *preserve* its position and which has more interest in the *extermination* of those who threaten the survival of the despotic order than *exploitation*. Assad's regime has, by this definition, been exemplary, and indeed its genocidal conduct in successfully preserving its position throughout the Syrian conflict has opened space globally for the politics of thanatocracy. In addition, the asymmetric nature of Assad's thanatocracy satisfies fascist fantasies of complete state power, as in its "absolute control over vertical power.... Their air forces can hit any target anywhere in Syria and cause immediate death."[24]

A further appeal for the international far right may be Assad's successful demonizing of his opponents as the "other," whether foreign agents or Islamist terrorists, to legitimize their liquidation in the eyes of his supporters. From the first days of the uprising, the regime attempted to portray a diverse, popular protest movement calling for democracy and social justice as a conspiracy against Syria, directed by outside countries and religious extremists who worked to undermine the stability of the country. In Duke's view, "Assad is a modern day hero standing up to demonic forces seeking to destroy his people and nation."[25] One post on the white supremacist site Stormfront affirms Assad's rhetoric that the uprising is simply a state-sponsored Islamic fundamentalist conspiracy, whatever its liberatory claims: "Al-Assad has done a good job keeping out the muslim [sic] extremists. The current uprising is orchestred [sic] by muslim [sic] extremism and disguised as a 'fight for freedom and democracy,' funded by Saudi Arabia scum."[26] Ironically, Assad himself is at least in part responsible for the rise of Islamist extremism used to dismiss his opponents, and not only due to the chaos and trauma he unleashed upon the country, which provided a fertile breeding ground for extremism to thrive. As the regime was rounding up thousands of prodemocracy protesters for probable death-by-torture, it released numerous Islamist extremists from detention, which went on to establish some of the most hardline militant groups that came to dominate the field of battle.[27] Assad hoped that the specter of Islamist extremism would both frighten Syrian minority communities into loyalty and silence the West's opposition to what the regime would now frame as part of the global "War on Terror." It is a strategy that has had considerable success.

As Al-Haj Saleh argues, the US-led global prioritization of the War on Terror and the "securitization of politics" became very useful for the Syrian regime in its counterrevolutionary war. He argues that this "priority given to terrorism isn't merely a function of the genuine security threat it poses, but also its usefulness in consolidating the prevailing system, and indeed uniting the ranks behind its leading elites in confronting a formless menace." It also serves to mobilize the public against the "terrorist enemy," which is equated both in Syria and globally with Islam. This "combined genocratic effect of the securitization of politics and the Islamization of terrorism makes [Western leaders] liable to cooperate with, or at least tolerate genocidal regimes that exclusively murder their Muslim subjects." State violence is seen as the antidote to Islamic terrorism, conferring legitimacy on the existing state and "paving the path for genocide" and, "by contrast, all resistance to tyranny or genocidal states is relegated to illegitimacy."[28] This legitimization of state violence against any dissent or resistance provides an ideal precedent for fascist politics, even in quite different contexts.

The deeply Islamophobic far right has certainly embraced the War on Terror narrative and its acceptance of mass violence against Muslims. That Assad himself is a Muslim (from the Alawi sect, an offshoot of Shia Islam) is only occasionally a cause for passing consternation. For example, "Flaxxer" on the Traditionalist Worker Discord channel explains that "Shias are typically less Muzzie. Assad is a Shia."[29] Others prefer to envisage Assad as a secular leader fighting Islamic extremists who pose a threat to the Christian (white) world. As the far-right Twitter user @iWillRedPillYou (account suspended at the time of this writing) claimed in an interview: "[W]ithout Assad Muslims would conquer and likely decimate those remaining Christians."[30] Like George Zimmerman, the Latino man who murdered Trayvon Martin on evidently racist grounds, Assad's own racial and religious affiliations matter less than his willingness to use racialized dehumanization as a justification for murder; this willingness works to qualify him as effectually white in the eyes of his Western fascist followers.

It can be argued that, in fascism, individuals seek to achieve "freedom" through complete identification with a state unfettered in its exercise of violence. The Syrian state, even before its repression of the Syrian Revolution, has been exemplary in this regard. One blogger by the name Jules Etjim explains the state-constituting role of transgression in the widespread use of torture in the 1970s and early 1980s. Not only were potential opponents terrified into submission; complicit subjects were invited into a sort of freedom-through-the-state by identifying with this transgression of "long established social boundaries":

> The "lesson" of torture was intended to be internalised by everyone including the torturer who was transformed into a willing instrument of the "torture state." The transition to exterminatory torture—in our terms, the transition to thanatocracy—was part of a genocidal continuum that disclosed the state had obtained "absolute freedom" to overstep human standards and boundaries without any normative or ethical limit other than the practical limit.[31]

Such "absolute freedom" of the state realized by transcending all normative and ethical limits presents an unparalleled fantasy fulfillment for those who identify their own desires with the exercise of state violence.

The purposeful, instrumental, systematic application of extreme violence is central to our cultural memory of fascism, and Nazism in particular, and this memory finds chilling rejuvenation in Assad's state. Munif relays the account of one former prisoner, who "explains that every prison is required to deliver, on a weekly basis, a specific number of corpses. If on a given week the Branch does not meet the required number of dead prisoners, then some individuals are selected to receive an air injection in their arterial lines and die quickly."[32] Although such cruel practices may seem arbitrary, the entire range of violence directly serves to solidify and reproduce the thanatocratic state. "The spectrum of violence starts with the fear of being arbitrarily arrested and subjugated to torture. It includes sieges and subsequent starvation. It involves the various ways Syrians are tortured and indiscriminately killed. In many of these cases, torture is not performed to gain information, but rather to actualize state power," says Munif.[33] Such systematicity is often very purposefully utilized to shape the social imaginary, making social alternatives unthinkable, such as, for example, in crushing areas where autonomous self-organization (through the establishment of local councils and independent civil society networks) was the strongest. According to Munif, "There is often a strong correlation between a neighborhood or village's ability to develop successful grassroots politics and the level of punishment it receives. The more inhabitants are able to produce autonomous politics, the more they are perceived as a threat to sovereign power, and as a result, are punished."[34]

As the Syrian regime has made use of such ruthless means to crush alternatives and retain its hold on power, it has also provided the US far right a promising precedent. Justifying its systemic mass violence by appropriating the American discourse of an ongoing War on Terror, the Assad regime has succeeded, for the most part, in deflecting serious criticism, and has shown that systematic practices of thanatocracy can be enacted in our day with relative impunity. It is no wonder that those aiming to institute such practices find his precedent inspiring.

Respectability Politics of the Far Right

Not all current proponents of far-right politics openly embrace genocidal violence. The alt-right as a movement has defined itself by embracing a veneer of respectability, especially by disavowing the swastika-sporting neo-Nazi crowd and the mass violence they openly advocate. Readers may recognize Spencer's talk of "peaceful ethnic cleansing" as an oxymoron and not be fooled by his hipster haircut and tailored suit. Yet if many people can still only recognize Nazis as boneheads[35] screaming *"Sieg Heil"* from their trembling *1488*-tattoo–laden necks, then this suggests that polite, groomed, articulate young men and women couldn't possibly harbor fascist beliefs.

Respectability politics within the US far right did not begin with Spencer and the alt-right. In 1989, Knights of the Ku Klux Klan (KKK, or simply "Klan") founder Duke won a seat in the Louisiana state legislature by leaving his swastikas and Klan robes in the dresser. Fresh out of prison for tax fraud, Duke convened a 2004 meeting around the "New Orleans Protocol," which a number of prominent far-right leaders signed on to, consisting of the following three points: "1) Zero tolerance for violence. 2) Honorable and ethical behavior in relations with other signatory groups. . . . 3) Maintaining a high tone in our arguments and public presentations."[36] By playing down the inevitable violent consequences of fascist politics, the far right presents a more presentable face to the broader public, which both denies fascist violence while normalizing the discourse that inspires it.

Assad presents a remarkably successful model for emulation for movements that seek to shift the "Overton window"[37] and reframe the politics of cruelty as a reasonable option within mainstream discourse. According to Al-Haj Saleh, Syrians fighting for liberation and survival are forced to fight simultaneously against two guises of fascism: "Against the Assadist necktie fascists and against the Islamist long-bearded fascists."[38] The tie-wearing variety have gained much more sympathy in the West because of their apparent containment of fascists of the bearded variety—even if the regime is actually responsible for much greater mass violence and destruction. Spencer, enthused by Assad's necktie presentability, notes that he was "educated in the West and offer[s] a civilized variant of Islam. . . . His wife is a very beautiful and sophisticated woman as well."[39] Spencer's mention of Assad's wife Asma al-Assad is telling: as a former financial services professional with a computer science degree, born and raised in London, England, she was once featured in *Vogue* magazine article entitled, "A Rose in the Desert." As Spencer notes, she presents a promising example for anyone hoping to make genocidal politics respectable.

Conspiracy Theories as Fascist Respectability

In tandem with seeking to make fascistic politics more presentable through the well-groomed image of its proponents, the propagation of conspiracy thinking can be understood as a means of introducing far-right elements into broader discourse. Because odd explanations are less likely to trigger objections in mixed company than open calls for dehumanization and violence, conspiracy theories can often function as useful ways to indirectly introduce elements of far-right thinking, without having to carry through with the implications. As Jason Stanley writes, "Conspiracy theories do not function like ordinary information; they are, after all, often so outlandish that they can hardly be expected to be literally believed. Their function is rather to raise general suspicion about the credibility and decency of their targets."[40]

The campaign of disinformation following the chemical weapons massacre in Khan Sheikhoun, Syria, in April 2017 provides an example of how conspiracy theories originating in Russian or Syrian state media or far-right sources can then be amplified to penetrate the mainstream and academia. Following the attack, pro-Assad media quickly tried to shift blame away from the regime, with *Al-Masdar News* claiming it was either staged by "terrorist forces [that] used gas on the kidnapped civilians from pro-government towns" or that the chemicals had been accidently released when a weapons factory was bombed by the regime.[41] The *Al-Masdar News* article was written by Paul Antonopoulous, formerly a leader at the Australian Hands Off Syria Coalition before being outed as a Nazi who posted vile racist comments on the white supremacist site Stormfront. The false-flag story was then picked up by alt-light[42] site Infowars.

In an article written for the site by Syrian-Australian Assad supporter Maram Susli ("Partisan Girl"), the site claims the humanitarian organization the White Helmets, which she describes as an "Al-Qaeda affiliated group funded by George Soros," was behind the attack. Susli herself has far-right sympathies, appearing on podcasts hosted by Duke and having been interviewed by Spencer and Lana Lokteff. Her claims were then given more credibility when echoed by a retired professor and weapons specialist from the Massachusetts Institute of Technology, Theodore Postol, who wrote a "scientific" report absolving the Syrian regime of any blame and denying that chemical agents were used.[43]

Postol is no stranger to absolving the regime of responsibility for chemical weapons attacks. As he disclosed on the "Anti-Neocon Report" podcast run by Holocaust denier Ryan Dawson, one of his sources is Susli, who he considers "a solid scientific source."[44] Postol's conspiracy was favorably echoed by figures ostensibly on the left, such as John Pilger, Noam Chomsky, and Seymour Hersh. Hersh has been given a platform to spread his repeated chemical weapons massacre denial by both the mainstream *London Review of Books* and alternative news outlet *Democracy Now!*[45] The conspiracies surrounding the Khan Sheikhoun massacre have been thoroughly debunked, including by local sources, independent open-source investigators at *Bellingcat*, and UN war crimes investigators, yet the claims have not been retracted.[46]

Conspiracy theories reached their peak in April 2018 when the US, UK, and France took limited military action, targeting regime military assets and chemical weapons facilities following a chemical weapons attack in Douma, Syria that killed at least 34 people, including children sheltering in basements from aerial bombardment when the attack occurred. Coulter called it a "faked attack" and Alex Jones claimed on Twitter that the "false flag chemical attack could start a wider war."[47] On Fox News, Tucker Carlson claimed that those saying Assad carried out a gas attack are "making it up" to justify a regime change war.[48] Mike "Enoch" Peinovich, a white nationalist leader and podcaster, blamed the Jewish people, calling the claims "(((neocon))) bullshit," using the parentheses that far-right activists use as a signifier for Jews.[49]

Many parroted the Kremlin's line suggesting it was a false-flag attack staged by rebels, or even Western countries. The Russian Embassy in the US put out a statement by the Foreign Ministry on Facebook rejecting reports of a chemical attack carried out by Syrian regime forces as "fake news" aimed "at justifying external military strikes." It suggested that the White Helmets were responsible for the false allegations.[50] The White Helmets, volunteer first responders who rescue victims of Russia's and Assad's scorched earth campaign from the rubble and are often the first on the scene to witness and record these states' crimes, have repeatedly been the target of conspiracy theories to discredit them. These conspiracy theories have been spread by the Russian state and far-right activists.[51] They have also been spread by those who identify as being on the left, such as the writers at *The Grayzone*.[52] Conspiracies concerning the White Helmets have reached millions of people on Twitter and dominated public debate.[53] According to Olivia Solon, writing for *The Guardian*, "By gaming the social media algorithms with a flood of content, boosted by bots, sock puppet accounts and a network of agitators, propagandists are able to create a 'manufactured consensus' that gives legitimacy to fringe views."[54] Antifascists certainly need to be aware of the ways in which far-right discourse can infiltrate the left and mainstream through conspiracy theories and actively seek to combat such attempts.

Fascists against US Imperialism

In February 2013 at a march in Sacramento, California in support of the Assad regime, one of the attendees, French far-right leader Serge Ayoub, was asked the reasons for his support. He replied: "Of course, it is our duty to support their cause! Syria is a nation, a homeland, a socialist country with national supremacy. They are fighting for secularism, and they are subject to an attack by imperialist America, globalization and its salafist servants and Qatari and Saudi mercenaries. The purpose is to destroy the state."[55] At first glance, Ayoub's analysis might seem uncharacteristic of fascist discourse and more typical of its political opposite. Aren't leftists usually the ones to protest against "an attack by imperialist America" on "a socialist country?"

It has never been true that objections to "Western imperialism" have been the prerogative of the radical left. Historically and up to the present, far-right opposition to "globalism" and the entanglements of empire has been foundational, often serving to separate the far right from establishment conservatives. It is important to remember that the largest profascist organization in US history,[56] the America First Committee, which counted nearly one million members, existed for the sole purpose of opposing US military intervention in World War II. As America First spokesman and famed aviator Charles Lindbergh made clear at the time, the far right can have its own reasons to oppose empire: "It is time to turn from our quarrels and to build our White ramparts again. This alliance with foreign races means nothing but death to us. It is our turn to guard our heritage from Mongol and Persian and Moor, before we become engulfed in a limitless foreign sea."[57] Lindbergh went on to blame Jewish ownership of media and control of government for the US interest in intervention.[58]

Mistakenly thinking that any opposition to foreign policy entanglements are somehow leftist leads to the view that any right-wing talk of "anti-imperialism" is only an insincere ploy meant to infiltrate left spaces and discourse. However, this reading does not tell the whole story. As much as the far right *does* sometimes poach from the far left to bolster its rhetoric and numbers, criticism of and opposition to imperialism *per se* has as a long—and authentic—history on the far right. As Matthew N. Lyons says in his book *Insurgent Supremacists: The U.S. Far Right's Challenge to State and Empire*:

> Far Right anti-imperialism doesn't fit old school leftist assumptions that opposition to empire is inherently liberatory or progressive, that Far Rightists always promote military expansionism, or that fascists are basically tools of the ruling class. These assumptions weren't true in the 1930s or the 1960s, and they're certainly not true now. As the 9-11 attacks in 2001 made clear, some of the most committed and important opponents of U.S. global power are on the Far Right.[59]

Fascists have long proffered strong criticism of imperialist military ventures *as* imperial ventures. Notably, by the time fascists came to power in Italy and Germany, neither country had had the chance to stake out their claims in colonial lands as had Spain, France, and England, for example; only recently had they even come to exist as states. As they tried to catch up with their own colonial projects, they were quick to claim their own colonialism as "anti-imperialist." Enrico Corradini, author of the fascist geopolitical approach that formed the basis of Mussolini's foreign policy, borrowed from left theories of class and adapted them to fascism's ultranationalism: "The class struggle, said Corradini, was real enough, but it pitted not workers against capitalists within the nation, but poor proletarian nations against rich plutocratic nations on the international plane."[60] The formulation is strikingly similar to Lenin's maxim that "under imperialism the division of nations into oppressing and oppressed ones is a fundamental, most important and inevitable fact."[61] However, whereas Lenin was clearly advocating for colonized and economically exploited lands to determine their own fates against the colonizing and exploitative habits of empires, and which itself never ultimately superseded class struggle, Corradini was arguing for the "right" of less-developed European nations to their own respective plunder of assumably non-European nations—particularly Italy's "right" to plunder Libya and Ethiopia—and that such national priorities supplanted internal social conflict. This interpretation of "class struggle" in nationalist and geopolitical terms, with all the ambiguities of this interpretation, became a foundational move for Ba'athism.

Within the Nazi Party of the 1930s, Gregor and Otto Strasser proposed to unite with the Union of Soviet Socialist Republics (USSR) against imperial Britain and France, and the party later worked with both Indian and Arab independence movements to undermine imperial British rule. After World War II, Johann von Leers, who had worked under Joseph Goebbels's Nazi Propaganda Ministry, moved to Egypt along with thousands of other Nazi Party members. In 1958, he wrote: "One thing is clear—more and more patriot Germans join the great Arab revolution against beastly imperialism. . . . Our place as an oppressed nation under the execrable Western colonialist Bonn government must be on the side of the Arab nationalist revolt against the West."[62] Within the US, Francis Parker Yockey determined that, under Cold War conditions, the US had become the primary opponent of the fascist movement, and advocated that fascists join with the USSR and Third World liberation movements as the most effective means of fighting American power. In Italy, members of the fascistic Third Position movement advocated the simultaneous fight against capitalism and communism, including calling for alliance with the far left. Third Positionists in the UK were supportive of Libya's dictator Muammar Gaddafi as well as the Islamic Republic of Iran and Louis Farrakhan's Nation of Islam.[63]

Most relevant to developing US fascist geopolitics is the more recent influence of the European New Right (ENR). ENR thinkers have appropriated poststructuralist theory to deconstruct liberal concepts, clearing the way for an intellectualized cryptofascist politics foundational for contemporary movements.[64] ENR thinkers have focused on delegitimizing human rights, sexual equality and fluidity, antiracism, and religious diversity as apparitions of Western cultural hegemony, and strongly advocate for policies opposed to such liberal ploys, such as Russia's vicious anti–lesbian-gay-bisexual-transgender-queer (LGBTQ) legislation. ENR's founder Alain De Benoist, for example, in his book *Beyond Human Rights: Defending Freedoms*, "deconstructs this idea [of 'natural rights'] and shows how the myth of a 'natural man' who possesses rights independent of his community is indefensible, and how this conception of rights has, in modern times, led to their use as a weapon by stronger nations to bludgeon those weaker states which do not conform to the Western liberal-democratic form of rights, as we have recently seen in action in the former Yugoslavia, Iraq and Libya."[65] ENR fellow traveler and Kremlin advisor Aleksandr Dugin similarly frames fascistic opposition to human and individual rights as a means of limiting Western hegemony. Dugin instead advocates for "Eurasianism" and a "multipolar" world, which, like Corradini's "proletarian nation" theory, advocates divvying up of global spoils into spheres of influence as "anti-imperialism." He calls for "clean, ideal fascism" with "a new hierarchy, a new aristocracy... based on natural, organic [and] clear principles—dignity, honor, courage, [and] heroism."[66] Notably, this "pluralism" admits only two options, with no possibility of self-determination: "There is no 'third position,' no possibility of that.... The same ugly truth hits the Ukrainian 'nationalist' and the Arab salafi fighter: They are Western proxies. It is hard to accept for them because nobody likes the idea to be the useful idiot of Washington."[67] For Dugin, a Russian-dominated counterpole is the only alternative to Western hegemony.

Depressingly, such campist thinking often finds its way, unmitigated, into the "anti-imperialist" radical left. In September 2019, Damascus hosted "The Third International Trade Union Forum for Solidarity with the Workers and People of Syria against the economic blockade, imperialist interventions and terrorism." More than 200 delegates from over 50 countries attended, including participants from the Arab Labour Organization, the Organization of African Trade Union Unity, a number of national trade union delegations (seemingly unaware that all independent trade unions are banned in Syria), as well as activists from US proregime, Syria-solidarity, and antiwar organizations and a number of fringe bloggers and Twitter personalities who describe themselves as "independent journalists."

In the Final Declaration of the Forum, the participants affirmed their support for Syria's "national struggle against policies and violations of imperialist, Zionist and reactionary forces"; saluted the "victories of the Syrian Arab Army and the allied and supporting forces over the armed terrorist gangs"; and extended "sincere greetings, respect and appreciation to the patron of the forum His Excellency, Mr. President Bashar Al-Assad . . . for all that Syria offers in support of issues of liberation, justice and peace in the world."[68]

As left radicals often focus on issues that distinguish them from liberals, far rightists often zoom in on their differences from the "cuckservative" establishment right, such as on interventionist foreign policy. The broader "what business of it is mine" discourse finds its alt-right form in one article by Charles Lyons awkwardly titled, "Bashar Al Assad Never Called Me Goyim," in which he observes, "After the failed wars and beginning to examine the racial issues back home ... [w]e began to see that this globalist foreign policy was not in the interest of White Americans. All these neoconservative wars overseas were to advance the geopolitical interests of Israel and Zionism."[69] Many fascists take Russia's backing of Assad as reason enough to support him.[70] Although Assad has made far more use of the Syrian Arab Army against Syria's own citizens and essentially left Israel unmolested—demonstrating at times a willingness even to relinquish the Golan Heights—the far right often praise Assad for formally being at war with Israel, which resonates with their historic antisemitism. As is clear when Spencer appeared on *Russia Today* in 2012 to bemoan the defeat of Gaddafi, and is reaffirmed by a number of commentators on the white nationalist website *Counter-Currents Publishing* on their love of Hugo Chávez, the authoritarianism of "strongmen" leaders is often reason enough for adoration and support, whatever their geopolitical affiliations.[71]

Hierarchy and Mass Murder as Tradition

One final aspect of the Assad regime's appeal to the far right can be read in the way the regime is repeatedly understood as somehow "traditional." One member of the Traditionalist Youth Network endorsed supporting Assad by describing the Syrian conflict as "the first truly winnable 'hot' engagement of the nascent Traditionalist Bloc of nations aligned against the Modernist Bloc in the world order."[72] What, one might ask, defines a "Traditionalist Bloc"? As Gregory Hood (the pseudonym of Kevin DeAnna) wrote for the fascist publication *Counter-Currents Publishing*:

> The Russian (and Syrian) alternative is not perfect.... It is not the kind of system we should seek to emulate. However, it is an exception, and it is tied to hierarchical social systems, a renewal of Tradition, and at least leaves open the possibility of a renewal of patriotism and white racial identity.... Syria ... stands for autonomy—a responsible governing class that identifies its well-being with that of continued survival of the state and the national population, not just some economic system or abstract creed.[73]

Where, one might ask, is Hood getting this association of "a renewal of Tradition"? As Stanley reminds us, fascism never fails to appeal to a mythic past, which is defined entirely by its uses for the political project of the present, bearing little or no relation to factual historical record.[74]

Central to this project, as Hood himself acknowledges, is the assertion of "hierarchical social systems," including a "renewal [of] white racial identity." However many social systems Syria has witnessed over the millennia, none of them has approached the Assad regime in violence or centralized hierarchy; indeed, a historical "tradition" of genocide has been more typical of Hood's own country than of Syria. Hood's assertion about Assad's purported traditionalism makes sense so long as "tradition" is taken *only* to mean hierarchy and justifications for mass violence, with no other measure of the historical past. And how, one might ask, could a dictator willing to murder 5% of his own population and displace half of it to stay in power be understood as identifying its well-being with the national population? The answer is, as Hood says, by taking the "continued survival of the [Assadist] State" as the exclusive measure of their "well-being." For Hood and fellow fascists, "the people" exist only insofar as they reflect the state, are only a population to the extent that they conform to an idealized "national population," and everyone else—even if they make up a majority of the country's population—have no claim to existence. In this sense, the Assad regime certainly presents an exemplary case for putting into practice the values of the far right.

The contemporary American far right is not usually associated in popular discourse with historical erudition, philosophical subtlety, social psychological foresight, or geopolitical sophistication. However, the assumption that openly racist, starkly inegalitarian, genocidal politics only issue from "ignorance" and "backwardness" has left many opponents to these movements unprepared to respond to them in their current depth and breadth. Attention to the motives and affiliations that these movements express, in particular among themselves in presumed private venues, but also strategically in more public ones, can provide a starting point for a useful study of contemporary far-right movements as they actually exist. The fact that observers are often surprised by far-right admiration and adoration of Assad can be taken as a sign of the importance of such cases. This should raise particular concern for antifascists, as some of the key mechanisms for far-right propagation have taken place through apparently left channels and rhetoric. Ultimately, the situation poses a double question: First, how might we better oppose fascist movements, given what such affiliation reveals about their workings? And, second, under the conditions of our era, what would an authentically antifascist approach to international and transnational political solidarity look like?

The Other Aryan Supremacy:
Fighting Hindu Fascism in the South Asian Diaspora

Maia Ramnath

Introduction

An antifascist situated in the South Asian diaspora in North America has to be doubly vigilant. You have to show up, along with your antifa comrades, when the Proud Boys or the Ku Klux Klan come to town. But you also have to show up for things your white left comrades may not have on their radar, like the World Hindu Congress (WHC) or a visit from Narendra Modi. There is little overlap in the crowds to be seen at each set of events, indicating who is most invested in each front of struggle. Yet the connections are powerful.

Hindutva is increasingly recognized as a form of fascism, part of the global phenomenon of surging far-right ethnonationalisms, although at the same it is a uniquely Indian formation rooted in a very specific history. Domestically, it dwells in the complex infrastructure of a "family" of organizations known as the Sangh Parivar, all various fronts and affiliates of its parent body the Rashtriya Swayamsevak Sangh (RSS), established in 1925. Its founders venerated the brahminical worldview and admired Adolf Hitler and Benito Mussolini.

In fact, the Nazi construct of the Aryan—with all its racial pseudo-genealogy, mystical primordiality, and glorious destiny—was rooted in German Indology and Orientalist scholarship that defined Nordic and Sanskritic/Vedic branches of the master race. Those who identified with the latter—the brahminical imaginary—eagerly concurred with that construct and its Aryan supremacist implications.

The Sangh "family" worked quietly on the margins for decades after independence, having been discredited by its distance from the freedom struggle and its culpability in the murder of Mahatma Gandhi, but all the while systematically building its base and counterpower to emerge as a rising force in the 1990s. Even more empowered since 2014, it now exercises significant clout in state power, social dominance, and cultural influence.

Internationally, it is asserting its presence in the South Asian diaspora, seeking to implement its agenda by exerting insidious economic and ideological influence upon American academic and political institutions. In doing so, the Sanghis opportunistically exploit the good intentions of white liberals and progressives eager to support multicultural diversity and immigrant communities of color, without realizing the nature of what they're endorsing.

It is crucial for antifascists in the West—including those of South Asian background—to understand the connections between these two particular manifestations of fascism to fight more effectively on all fronts of a global struggle. This in turn requires understanding the links between colonialism and fascism, as historically related expressions of racial supremacy with its disciplinary regimes of oppression and exploitation. And with fascist, colonialist, and white supremacist forces so aggressively reinforcing one other in the world, it is that much more urgent for the antifascist, anticolonialist, and antiracist forces to forge connections at multiple levels.

Hindutva in India

Defining Hindutva

Translated literally as "Hindu-ness," Hindutva signifies Hindu ethnonationalism or Hindu fascism. As such, it is a modern political ideology that parallels other European fascisms and far-right ethnonationalisms while drawing upon late 19th- and early 20th-century religious revivalism in colonial India. The anti-Hindutva organizing coalition Alliance for Justice and Accountability (AJA) describes it as "an ethnonationalist movement that uses religion to justify atrocities against Dalits and religious minorities and as a distraction from [an] economic agenda of concentrating land, money and power and resources (in upper caste hands)." Its tactics of "cultural and political warfare" include the "weaponization of Hinduism." Or, as RSS founder Vinayak Damodar Savarkar put it almost a century ago, the goal was to Hinduize politics and militarize Hinduism. It seeks to rewrite history; routinize violence; silence or intimidate anyone deemed inferior, impure, alien, critical, or dissenting; dominate the mind space;

and saturate the social fabric en route to controlling levers of state power in India while using the diaspora as a rich source of funding and international legitimacy.[1]

The mode of identitarian, majoritarian blood-and-soil ideology and Bharatiya culture embodied in the Hindu Rashtra is an explicit rejection of the type of civic or territorial nationalism promoted by the mainstream of the Indian independence movement and that was hegemonic during the first few decades of independence. Although never perfectly realized, the ideal of a social democratic secular republic representing a proudly pluralistic composite culture was at least proposed as an aspiration. By contrast, the Hindu Rashtra "rejects the notion of a composite and pluralist Indian identity historically developed as a complex synthesis of different cultures and faiths."[2] It demands an exclusively Hindu fundamentalist ethnostate with a culture and civilization reductively defined as coterminous with its own iteration of brahminist dogmatism, emphasizing purity, virility, militarism, caste hierarchy, and misogyny.

We can't look at the "Nehruvian" India uncritically either—namely the mainstream founding ideal of a secular, democratic-socialist republic with a multiethnic composite culture. In implementation, it fell far short of the anticolonial struggle's more radically emancipatory visions, or the founding paradigm as articulated in the constitution, critically revised and challenged by B. R. Ambedkar. These shortcomings—from the failure to adequately address caste oppression, minority exclusion, and socioeconomic inequity to the decades of corruption, elitism, scandal, dynastic politics, and ineffectual governance—created an opportunity for the rise of the far right since the 1980s. Yet when such an opening appears, something has to be poised to move into it. Where did it come from?

Vedic Aryan Brahminism: A Prehistory

Did India model its nationalism and fascism on Europe's? (Is that in itself a colonialist question?) Or is Hindutva something distinct, with internal origins? Both are true. Modern Hindutva is the result of a reciprocal recognition, a mutually constituted collaborative construct.

Colonial knowledge production generated bodies of comparative philological and philosophical scholarship through the translation of classical Sanskrit texts. Some of the revealed philosophical ideas were popularized in the West during the early to mid-19th century, inspiring American Transcendentalists and German Romanticists alike. And some of the revealed ideas (or the theories extrapolated from them when interpreted through certain lenses) also influenced or interacted with more sinister lines of thought emerging toward the later 19th century, such as German ethnonationalism, playing out into the mythology of the Aryan master race, along with the emerging pseudosciences of anthropometry and eugenics that British administrators applied toward a racial infrastructure of governmentality in South Asia, using "the ethnographic state" for purposes of colonial control.

In the 1780s, as the British East India Company began to consolidate its economic and then territorial control of the subcontinent, scholars such as Sir William Jones—linguist, high court judge in British India, and founder of the Asiatic Society in Calcutta, India—began translating Sanskrit texts. Aside from academic interest, these texts were also studied for the purpose of formalizing the organization of legal structures, in consultation with Brahmin interlocutors (the traditional guardians of Sanskrit scriptures); thus, the emphasis on purity and caste hierarchy in the normative social order they portrayed.[3]

Jones's research led to the seminal recognition of a relationship between the Eastern and Western classical languages—Sanskrit, Latin, and Greek—via a putative common ancestor. The word *"arya"* in the Sanskrit texts meant noble or honorable, and referred to those who worshiped the Vedic proto-Hindu gods; Jones applied it to those who spoke their language. There were three versions of this philological relationship and its evolutionary path (not *yet* projected onto the racial). Each is favored in different political contexts, although the first is most scientifically supportable:

The bidirectional Indo-European common root theory: a common root language originating in the Caucasus mountain region during the Neolithic era was the progenitor of both Eastern and Western branchings.

The unidirectional "Out of India" theory: Sanskrit is the oldest and the linear ancestor of the Western classical languages; the original Aryans came from the high Himalayas (or perhaps deeper into the subcontinent).

The unidirectional "Arctic Origin" theory (the reverse to the former): The root language was born in the north and the original Aryans came from the Arctic into India, there to degenerate, sadly, into darker-skinned shadows of their former selves.

This could also be considered a distortion of what is in the Indological context known as the "Aryan Invasion" theory, compatible with the Common Indo-European root theory: that the Vedic people entered the subcontinent via the Central Asian steppe and encountered there the ancestors of today's Adivasis and Dravidian peoples,[4] long after the mysterious rise and decline of the ancient Indus Valley civilization (whose cultural and biological DNA are present among the mix of all northern and southern demographics within the subcontinent).[5]

British Orientalism

The people of South Asia confused the British. Although colonial racial logic demanded that South Asians be designated collectively as inferior, what was to be made of the extreme heterogeneity and "kaleidoscopic diversity" of the subcontinent's cultures, languages, and ethnicities?[6] The Raj administrators' answer was to develop a two-tiered racialization whereby all colonized "natives" were considered inferior to the European colonizers—a binary differential line essential to maintaining the structure of empire—but at the same time with a steep hierarchical gradient *among* this colonized group. (Thanks for the handy concept, Brahmin interlocutors.)

A flexible race theory could then be used "to construct categories of caste, tribe, nation and communal/religious groups, to read race onto them, and to locate them within the hierarchical order of History,"[7] and, most importantly, to manage and discipline them for the security and efficient wealth accumulation of the empire. From the 1870s onward, the colonial taxonomy of racialized castes and tribes—diligently utilizing the new techniques of census taking, photography, and anthropometry (i.e., measuring people's heads with calipers)—presented people not as individuals but as specimens of biologically determined types. These were described in terms of quantifiable characteristics, which applied not only to physical but to mental and moral qualities. In this way, resistance and noncompliance were pathologized as proof of congenital savagery and backwardness, whereas loyalty and obedience were proof of being "civilized."

The Aryan Invasion theory supported the construct of "martial races," designating those slated for recruitment into the British overseas army, consistent with the construction of the Aryan as northern/Western, lighter skinned, and more masculine/virile than the southern/Eastern, darker-skinned, less trustworthy Dravidian groups and thus (in accordance with the theory of shared origin for the Vedic and Western peoples) more racially pure and less adulterated by intermixture with the prior southern inhabitants—an aversion to mixing portrayed as the source of degeneration or impurity. This modification to the Aryan race theories could then explain why the martial and higher caste people, although less inferior than others, were still inferior enough to be colonizable: their "contamination" by non-Aryans acquired in the tropical climate had caused their failure to progress civilizationally, like their European cousins.

Another significant racial construct was the notion of castes or tribes of hereditary criminals: the Criminal Tribes Act of 1871 instituted systems of surveillance, carceral control, and restrictions on spatial location and movement, plus sexual policing to restrict reproduction of criminal genes—all of which bear a family resemblance to later apartheid systems, fascist racial laws, and ghettoization.[8]

German Indology

Romanticist philosopher Friedrich Schlegel was intrigued by Jones's ancient Aryans, those hypothetical Nordic-Indic ancestors imagined as heroic Himalayan sages and warriors, from whose western journeys originated the European peoples, and from whose southern journeys emerged the Vedic people of India. Max Müller (a student of Friedrich Schelling, associated like Schlegel with Jena Romanticism as well as Indian philosophy) is considered the father of Indology: translator and scholar of comparative philology, religion, and philosophy, Sanskritic studies unfolding in tandem with German Romanticism. Born and educated in Germany, Müller spent much of his career in Britain (1850s to 1880s, spanning the transition from British East India Company to Crown rule), where his Sanskrit translations were published with the support and cooperation of the British East India Company.

Neither Schlegel nor Müller had intended racism or antisemitism by their Aryan studies (quite the contrary); that would come later. Yet by the late 19th century, the concept of the mythic Aryan ancestors proved greatly appealing to German nationalists who began to conflate linguistic etymology with racial genealogy, blending the terms Aryan, Nordic, and Indo-Germanic into an emblem of master-race supremacy.[9] Obsessed with locating the original Aryan homeland, their chauvinism led them to turn away from the Out of India theory to envision the ancient master beings as originating in the absolute north, not just from the north relative to the Indian subcontinent (i.e., not the Himalayas), but Scandinavia or even beyond: the North Pole, or a lost Atlantis.

Hindu Nationalism

One Indian nationalist who embraced this theory was Bal Gangadhar Tilak, a fiery mobilizer, Hindu revivalist, and Sanskrit scholar who wrote *The Arctic Home in the Vedas* (a location he deduced from astronomical/

calendrical calculations) in 1903.[10] Tilak also promoted the political mobilization of Hindu national/religious feeling through cow protection, festivals, and scriptures—with particular emphasis on the Bhagavad Gita, interpreted as a justification and call for militant action through the path of karma yoga: the path of political action (as opposed to the paths of devotional worship, contemplation/meditation, or philosophical study) as spiritual methodology. Although politically radical, he was deeply reactionary on matters of caste and gender: He was against colonial rule, but what was he for? By focusing on the Vedas, venerating the Brahmin, "Tilak sought to articulate an Aryan myth that would not only reawaken Indian pride in the glorious past but also confer legitimacy on the traditional institutions of Brahminism and caste society."[11]

Similarly, the goal of the Arya Samaj—a reformist organization founded in 1875—was a return to Vedic principle; internalizing Western criticisms of practices such as caste and idolatry led the Arya Samajists to "reform" caste by replacing the current *jati* system with an idealized, socially integral *varna* system in accordance with Vedic terminology of Brahmins, *kshatriyas*, *vaisyas*, *sudras*, and "untouchables." The Aryan Invasion theory included an account of the origins of this system in which, prior to their arrival, the Vedic people had been internally divided into warrior, priestly, and commoner classes, yet all were further differentiated from the laborers and outcastes who originated from the darker, conquered Dravidians. (Many caste abolitionists share this descriptive analysis while reversing the valorization.)

Christophe Jaffrelot, one of the foremost scholarly analysts of Hindu nationalism, calls this the "emulate and stigmatize" or "strategic emulation" tactic, by which the local elite in an era of "self-strengthening" and national consolidation aspired to the traits that had made their colonizers dominant. This meant seizing upon the martial vigor and virility denied to themselves, but attributing those traits to their own traditions: that is, "resisting an external threat by borrowing the traits which endowed its instigators with strength, always under the pretext of a return to the Vedic Golden Age,"[12] or "under the pretext of a reinterpretation of Hindu traditions," which then "enabled them to regain self-esteem, defend their threatened identity and demonstrate how the values of the dominant power could be adopted with advantage."[13] It's a rather twisted hall of colonial psychopathology mirrors: *We resent your domination. We have an inferiority complex. We have a superiority complex. We want to assert our feelings of wounded superiority in ways that will also earn your admiration, through traits that you yourself ascribed to us. We can take pride in the things that the people we want to be like, say they like about us.*

Arya Samajists changed their self-identification from Arya to Hindu in 1911, after forming the Hindu Sabha to unify Hindus as a counterbalance to growing Muslim solidarity, as well as to pressure the secular Congress, which they felt did not adequately protect Hindu interests. It was at the first Hindu Sabha conference in Punjab, India, in 1909 that Tilak's colleague Lala Lajpat Rai suggested an alternative to the Indian National Congress's (INC) usage of nation to mean "all the peoples who live under one common political system and form a State" in accordance with the political theories of Enlightenment liberalism. He preferred what he attributed to a German idea of nation that "did not necessarily signify a political nation or a State," but rather a people, "implying a community possessing a certain civilisation and culture. Using it in that sense, there can be no doubt that Hindus are a 'nation' in themselves."[14]

The Sabha shaped a number of prominent nationalist militants and radicals within the Swaraj (self-rule) movement of the early 20th century, of which Tilak was a leader. Tilak was a strong influence on future Hindu Mahasabha chief B. S. Moonje (1927-37) who in turn mentored founding RSS leader and Hitler fan K. B. Hedgewar.

So did India learn fascism from Europe? Or did Europe learn it from India? (Did the Aryans come from the Arctic or the Himalayas?) Nazism built upon Aryan supremacist racial theories derived from German Indologists' study of Vedic civilization. Hindu nationalism modeled its form and structure on German ethnonationalism, but with brahminist/proto-Hindutva ideological content, reappropriating a self-aggrandizing mythology approved by the very people whose political mobilizations they wanted to emulate. To use Tayyab Mahmud's words, they appropriated the "racialized discourse of nationhood," adopted aspects of the "colonial discourse of the Aryan race, and made Aryan racial identity an overarching theme of national renaissance and renewal."[15]

So, let's look at the next turn of the wheel.

Hindutva between the Wars (1925-48)

Savarkar

Savarkar was a militant veteran of the Swadeshi movement, both in India and abroad. His 1909 book on the 1857 mutiny remained popular among freedom fighters and patriots (and anathema to British authorities). He was influenced by Mazzinian nationalism, as were many during the Swadeshi period, but increasingly also by German ethnonationalism, especially the ideas of Johann Kasper Bluntschli. It was during his years of political imprisonment on the Andaman Islands penal colony and Ratnagiri jail (1911–24) that his Hindu nationalist ideology crystallized. He published the seminal book, *Hindutva: Who is a Hindu?*, in 1923.

From the start, Hindutva was defined against its "others," seen as threats, rivals, and powerful foreign forces, be they British or Islamic. Hindu-ness to Savarkar meant "common affinities, cultural, religious, historical, linguistic and racial, which through the process of countless centuries of association and assimilation moulded us into a homogenous and organic Nation and . . . . induced a will to lead a corporate and common National life. The Hindus . . . are an organic National Being."[16]

A Hindu was one "who inherits the blood of the great race whose first and discernible source could be traced from the Himalayan altitudes . . . and claims as his own . . . the Hindi civilization, as represented in a common history, common heroes, a common literature, common art, a common law and common jurisprudence." The Hindus were "not merely the citizens of the Indian state because they are united not only by the bonds of love they bear to a common motherland but also by the bonds of a common blood. They are not only a nation but a race-jati," meaning a brotherhood produced by a common blood: namely that of the "mighty race incorporated with and descended from the Vedic fathers."[17]

In other words, unlike the members of the civic republic envisioned by the INC, a territorial nationalism that could include within its social contract everyone living together in the same area, Hindus constituted a cohesive nation by virtue of blood, soil, and a culture defined tautologically as Hinduism itself. He claimed the Indian motherland, the *matri bhumi*, as not only their geographical but their spiritual home, unlike South Asian Muslims with a spiritual home in the Arabian peninsula. (By contrast, Pan-Islamist Indian nationalists among his contemporaries eloquently expressed the compatibility of their Muslimness and Indianness: for example, in Khilafat movement leader Muhammad Ali's famous Venn-like image of the "two overlapping circles of equal size" representing his community's identification with both India and the Islamic world.)

Despite the emphasis on blood, Savarkar's take on race was somewhat slippery. He did say there was only one human race and that anyone could in theory marry and assimilate into Hindu civilization (perhaps as a way to finesse the fact that the Vedic people had themselves initially mingled with the prior inhabitants of the subcontinent). However, that civilization was structured around an incontrovertible racial hierarchy: Brahmins, as the pure-Aryan elite descended from the Vedic heroes, remained above and apart, whereas others who might be incorporated would take only subordinate roles within the varna structure, presumably grateful for the chance to serve in lowlier functions as part of the integral whole.

The RSS

Maybe Hedgewar was to Savarkar as Vladimir Lenin was to Karl Marx: translator of ideology and theory into organizational action plan. Established in Nagpur, India in 1925 with Hedgewar as its head, the RSS was envisioned as a vehicle for building up Hindu culture and identity, strengthening national and moral character through physical training and service. The RSS leaders admired European fascism for its effective organization, discipline, strong leadership (they lionized Hitler and Mussolini), and the muscularity and militancy of its totalizing culture for inducing rapid national progress.

Moonje was particularly impressed by Mussolini's educational model, which he viewed upon a visit to Italy in 1931. He noted approvingly the recruitment of young children for indoctrination and training. He "loved the organized, disciplined quality, the sense of unity" that he saw in them, and hoped to adopt "Italy's approach to national regeneration and remilitarization to make them strong, not weak and peaceful."[18]

When Mussolini asked for his guest's opinion, Moonje said, "Your Excellency, I am much impressed. Every aspiring and growing nation needs such organisations. India needs them most for her military regeneration.... I was charmed to see boys and girls well dressed in their naval and military uniforms undergoing simple exercises of physical training and forms of drill." And so it was to be in the RSS. At the same time as they mirrored Mussolini's, these methods were also a continuation of an Indian tradition: the *akharas* (martial/spiritual training cells) that flourished among the Bengali and Maharashtrian revolutionists of the Swadeshi movement, but imparting an even further intensified religiosity. From the start, RSS *shakhas* trained in drill marching, calisthenics, sword and staff fighting, and priding themselves on martial readiness.

As for Hitler, Hedgewar's successor M. S. Golwalkar thought that his "Final Solution" idea for the Jews in Germany sounded like a great model to apply to Muslims in India. He approved of Germany's "race pride" and the actions taken in its name. "To keep up the purity of the Race and its culture, Germany shocked the world by ... purging the country of the semitic Races—the Jews. Race pride at its highest has been manifested here," said Golwalkar. "Germany has also shown how well nigh impossible it is for Races and cultures, having differences going to the root, to be assimilated into one united whole, a good lesson for us in Hindusthan to learn and profit by."[19]

Race was more central to Golwalkar's thinking than to Savarkar's, although still hazy in definition and tending more cultural or spiritual than biological. Even though the majority of Muslims in India were descended from converts generations before, and that the demography of South Asia is extremely intermixed across region and religion, Golwalkar portrayed Muslims as a foreign imposition upon the Hindu/Indian body. In his view, "There are only two courses open to foreign elements, either to merge themselves in the national race and adopt its culture, or to live at its mercy so long as the national race will allow them to do so and to quit the country at the sweet will of the national race. . . . That is the only logical and correct solution."[20] In other words, the two options for minorities are absorption/assimilation, or expulsion/elimination. But doesn't that sound like the definition of genocide?

Sangathan Structure

According to the *sangathan* (organizational) model, the RSS developed into a proliferating of shakhas, or branches, first in Maharashtra, its birthplace, then spreading northward throughout Uttar Pradesh (UP) and Punjab. In 1931, there were 60. By 1939, there were 500, with 40,000 *swayamsevaks* (active RSS members); a year later, 700, and membership had doubled. By 1948, they had swelled to 600,000 members concentrated mainly in the north and central regions[21]—what is known as the Hindi heartland, and the seat of the Vedic Aryavarta.

Each shakha was a grassroots rhizome: from joining what seemed liked wholesome, patriotic boy scout troops, offering a sense of camaraderie and the chance to feel part of an embracing community, members would be drawn deeper into meetings and ceremonies, led by ideological indoctrination to more openly bigoted rhetoric and more openly violent activities.

The *sarsanghchalak* was the supreme leader for life, with absolute authority: this was Hedgewar until his death in 1940, succeeded by Golwalkar. But the shakhas functioned largely on their own, following a shared set of rules without micromanaging from above. There were local, district, and provincial levels, mapped in zones according to pragmatic communication routes.

Swayamsevaks (or *kar sevaks*, activists) were the committed volunteers selected from among the participants in the shakha activities. Each took a pledge spoken before an image of Hanuman, dedicating himself for life to the service of the cause, country, religion, and Sangh "with all my physical, mental and monetary strength" (1929 version) or "heart and soul" (1938 version).[22]

Pracharaks were the full-time cadres who had undergone training as propagandists, teachers, organizers (Instructor Training Camps and Organizer Training Camps were launched in 1927). Pracharaks were viewed as models of virtue, dedication, austerity, and celibacy: that is, as ideal karma yogis.

With evident admiration, American scholar and sympathizer Walter Andersen, in an interview with Ajaz Ashraf, describes the new generation of pracharaks as highly idealistic, self-sacrificing exemplars of the RSS goal of "creating a new man." They tend to be "[a]lmost all . . . college educated. That fits into their scheme in which education is a very important element. It is, in a way, very Brahminical. Most are high caste, but not all." He denies that they evince hateful attitudes. Rather, Andersen claims that, unlike the rank-and-file foot soldiers, who might be more driven by prejudices (about Muslims, Christians, and communists) and grievances about the past, "In terms of personality, the younger of them have what you can call national idealism. Some have compared the RSS to a casteless Hindu monastic order. They give up on families, don't have assets, and the organisation supports them. They have to have idealism to commit their entire life [to the RSS]." Resisting the conventional pressure to marry and cultivate careers, "They have to be rebels not to do what their families want them to. . . . RSS pracharaks come across as missionaries who want to do good in the world. They are the messengers of dharma."

Although the predecessors of Hindutva had been prominent in the early 20th-century Swadeshi movement, the RSS did not play a major role in the interwar anticolonial liberation movement, which largely aligned itself with international antifascism. Their flavor of nationalism was diverging from the ideals and dreams voiced in the INC by people such as Jawaharlal Nehru, Abul Kalam Azad, and Ambedkar with his critical interventions toward greater equality and caste abolition. Not that this vision was perfect in concept or implementation; it can be amply faulted for its shortcomings, limitations, and failures of inclusion. Nevertheless, it was utterly anathema to the goals of Hindutva.[23] The Hindu Mahasabha was expelled from the INC in 1937 for its communalism; Savarkar was Mahasabha president from 1937 to 1942. Golwalkar wrote in his 1939 book, *We, Or, Our Nationhood Defined*, that Congress-style civic/territorial nationalism was wrong and German-style ethnonationalism was right. Congress prevailed in the 1940s. Fascism and empire suffered major defeats. But the wheel was not done turning.

Hindutva in the Postcolony (1948–2020)

The India and Pakistan to which the British Raj handed over power in 1947 weren't the countries the left wanted. A Nehruvian/Ambedkarite India was not the country that the right wanted either.

After former swayamsevak and Savarkarite Nathuram Godse assassinated Gandhi in January 1948, for being too conciliatory to the Muslim community and to Pakistan, the RSS was banned. The ban was provisionally lifted the following year on the condition that they write a constitution to make transparent their organizational structure and regulate their political participation. No matter; being relegated "only" to social and cultural functions, not seeking electoral/state power, was fine for Golwalkar's strategy.

The RSS didn't want to be a political party; better to serve as "dharmic counselor" to the state, an influential power behind the throne, as brahminical gurus to classical Hindu kings. According to this much longer and ultimately more dangerous game, the plan was not seizure of the state— at least not immediately—but seizure of society: total penetration and cultural saturation to render India, Hinduism, and the RSS interchangeable. This strategy is similar to what Alexandra Minna Stern identifies as the metapolitics approach of the US alt-right and European New Right, accumulating in the culture to shift minds "upstream" from state-level politics, whether as a preliminary step toward that, or as a goal in itself.[24] "Continuously expanding amongst the Hindu society we hope to reach a stage where the Sangh and the entire Hindu Society will be completely identical," said Golwalkar in late 1947, carrying on Hedgewar's dream. "This is bound to happen in the course of time for there is no escape."[25] Only then, after long ripening, would they move aggressively into the political and social mainstream. When opportunities opened up for them to make a move decades later, they were ready.

Family of Fronts

Maintaining its mystique behind the curtain, enjoying plausible deniability of involvement, the RSS launched an array of specialized front groups for key sectors of society, particularly those where the communist party had a presence. Often billed as "charities," the RSS could disperse influence through them while funneling money toward itself without ever raising funds in its own name. Each played a role in a complex division of labor, from running rural schools (Ekal Vidyalaya), to relief work and service (Sewa Vibhag), to party politics (Jana Sangh), to paramilitaries (Bajrang Dal). The women's branch, the Rashtrasevika Samiti, began in 1936. Later they added groups for students and workers.

The youth wing, with a bullish presence on university campuses, was the Akhil Bharatiya Vidyarthi Parishad (ABVP), founded in 1948 as a way to evade the ban. Like other student groups, the ABVP contests elections for student leadership while grooming future (RSS and Bharatiya Janata Party [BJP]) party leaders. According to the Coalition Against Genocide's RSS primer, "ABVP has a reputation for violence, vituperation and hooliganism, and is often used by the Sangh to disrupt progressive events on campuses, carry out moral policing and enforce a socially conservative agenda in universities."[26]

The Vishwa Hindu Parishad (VHP) was founded in 1964 as the ecclesiastical wing. Its stated goal was to consolidate the plethora of Hindu sects into a more unified body with internally consistent doctrine, a form novel for Hinduism—again, the "stigmatize and emulate" tactic. The formalized doctrine, of course, would align with the brahminical worldview.[27] S. S. Apte, the VHP's first general secretary, presented its purpose as follows: "It is . . . necessary in this age of competition and conflict to think of, and organize, the Hindu world to save itself from the evil eyes of all three" rival spiritual families: Christianity, Islam, and Communism. It engaged in missionary and proselytizing activity while promoting yoga, ayurveda, and vegetarianism, which have ballooned into mammoth industries. (Western progressive consumers who are into yoga, alternative medicine, and non-Western spiritualities might want to research their products' labels for Sanghi-linked enterprises.[28]) In practice, the VHP was a vehicle for demagoguery, inciting violence, and religious intolerance. The Central Intelligence Agency flagged it as a "militant religious outfit" in 2018.[29]

Even more overtly violent is the Bajrang Dal, established in 1984 as the VHP's paramilitary wing, which is to say its on-the-ground rabble-rousing muscle. It has been described as a harnessing of lumpen youth, or as a "fighting protection squad for the other organizations."[30] Attendees at its training camps learn to use firearms, tridents, and simple brute force "to beat those who do not respect Hinduism." Targets may include Muslims, Christians, and any intellectuals, journalists, or artists who criticize the Sangh.[31]

Despite their skepticism of politics in the era of Congress dominance, RSS leaders consented to the founding of the Bharatiya Jana Sangh (BJS) as a political party in 1951 once they were assured of their ability to control it. This was the beginning of a long internal debate, continued into the days of the BJP, on whether the clout to be gained through participating in parliamentary politics was worth the risk of compromising their agenda or diluting their ideological or ethnonational character; hence, whether to emphasize general issues of socioeconomic populism to widen their appeal or specifically identitarian concerns pitched to the base. Founder Syama Prasad Mookerjee wanted an "intercommunal, conservative, all-India party" allowing for a rapprochement of these ethnonationalist extremists with more mainstream Hindu traditionalists, and pushed back a bit against total RSS control. In 1954, Deendayal Upadhyaya as new BJS general secretary brought it more into conformity with Golwalkar's Sangh. Golwalkar wanted political parties to answer to the RSS, not the other way around.

At the time of the Emergency (India's two-year period of suspended civil liberties and authoritarian rule) in the 1970s, the BJS joined the Janata Party coalition, an unwieldy big tent held together only by antagonism to Indira Gandhi and the Congress-dominated political status quo of corruption, elitism, hypocrisy, and dynasticism. Although the content of their political ideas was wildly different, the BJS had already established working relationships with Jayaprakash "JP" Narayan's grassroots revolutionary movement, which provided a major component of the Janata Party. Historians such as Jaffrelot, Gyan Prakash, and others suggest that there were ideological convergences between the JP movement and the BJS; but, based on their descriptions, the points of commonality sound to me less ideological than structural, less about content than form—namely, shared emphasis on decentralization, bottom-up power, and valorization of the village and *panchayat*. But the ultimate values, ethos, aspirations, and ideals to be served through those vehicles were utterly different. At the time of its founding, the BJP played lip service to Narayan's *sarvodaya* and "Gandhian socialism"—of which Upadhyaya had selectively incorporated and adapted some aspects for his philosophy of Integral Humanism (akin to Golwalkar's Organicism), as the Jana Sangh's doctrine. According to Thomas Blom Hansen, this offered them a way to work in coalition and "ideologically hijack" the legitimacy conferred by those ideas. For their cultural nationalism. But the mask fell away by 1990 when they were "freed from [the] restraints" of coalition.[32] It looks to me as if the participants in the Janata Party who were questioned for their choice of bedfellows had entered into the alliance thinking they could influence or change the others, or at least assert their will over their partners to prevail in the government. All were wrong; thus, it broke apart.

It also strikes me here that the Sangh's antipathy toward everything to do with Nehru's version of nationalism encompassed not only the Nehruvian idea of India but also the Nehruvian theory of the state (as a top-down, highly centralized technocratic bureaucracy). In retrospect, their rejection was not absolute; their rejection was in the context of Nehru's paradigm. Nevertheless, this is also perhaps why the narrowly state-oriented view of politics underestimated them for a dangerously long time: that's not where they were operating, by design.

After the grab bag Janata Party, the BJS disbanded, to be succeeded in 1980 by the BJP. By this time, they were much less wary of taking part in politics, perhaps because they were much more confident in their ability to carry out their unadulterated agenda.[33] Today, RSS control of the ruling BJP is no secret. Thus, their aversion to seeking state power was tactical, strategically timebound. Their long-view methods had called for reversing the direction of takeover: Once they had won enough hearts and minds, there would be no need to force it from above; they would rise inevitably from below, at which point taking power would be organic and inevitable (like a ripe fruit falling into a lap, says Jaffrelot).[34] And if they were indeed biding their time until the moment when they felt confident in their transformation of society to take state power—and now they *have* taken state power—then we should be very afraid of this society.

After Ayodhya

Since the post–Cold War liberalization of the Indian economy plunged it into the sea of global capitalism after decades of insulation, the neoliberal capitalist and far-right ethnonationalist agendas have dovetailed at the elite level even while, at the popular level, the appeal of the latter is being stoked by the destabilizations wrought by the former. Soon after that shift, the Ram Janmabhoomi movement exploded in 1992, opening a new period of aggressive Sanghi ambition and a new round of sectarian violence and retribution.

In the northern city of Ayodhya, the VHP had launched efforts since the 1980s to reclaim the site of a 16th-century mosque built by the founder of the Mughal Empire. The RSS claimed it was the birthplace of Ram, mythical hero of the classical epic Ramayana and an avatar of Vishnu. Although the claim was archaeologically and historically unsupported, priests had snuck in to place an idol there in 1949, which they portrayed as a miraculous visitation on the site of the purported birth.

In 1992, VHP and BJP organized a nationwide *rath yatra* ("pilgrimage procession," or road-touring rally) ending in Ayodhya with a riot at the mosque site as Hindutva activists stormed the building and tore it down, launching a wave of violence in cities around the country. Following the Babri Masjid demolition, RSS and Bajrang Dal—whose core mission included furthering the building of the Ram temple—were banned again, briefly; again, the ban was revoked a year later. In the decades since, although the construction of a temple on the site was held up in court, devotees from throughout the country and the diaspora avidly donated money or inscribed bricks for the anticipated day. During all those years, too, the cycle of violence and revenge continued.

In 2002, a train en route to Godhra, India was set on fire. Fifty-eight Hindu pilgrims returning from Ayodhya died. Whether the cause of the fire was accidental, an act of conspiracy by Muslim groups, or an act of conspiracy by Sanghi Hindu groups—a false-flag action to provoke and legitimate violence, as has happened on other occasions—remains disputed. Regardless, the accusation that it was set by Muslims unleashed pogroms of "revenge" in the province of Gujarat. With the complicity of the provincial government—vigilantes obtained names and addresses of victims from voter rolls; under orders, police stood back and let them murder close to two thousand people; hundreds of women were raped in graphically brutal ways, with particular savagery against pregnant women and babies; Muslim homes, businesses, and places of worship were destroyed.[35] The VHP president praised the outcome as a successful experiment that might be copied throughout India. Shiv Sena chief Bal Thackeray approved too, calling Muslims a "cancer" in India that could only be cured through removal.[36]

The chief minister of Gujarat at the time of the massacres was Modi. From modest beginnings—later key to his appeal, persona, and personal mythology—he came up as an ABVP student leader and RSS pracharak. He had chanced into his recent appointment as unelected chief minister of Gujarat as a replacement for an ailing and unpopular predecessor. For years after these events, he faced international sanction as a human rights violator for his role in the massacre and was denied a visa to enter the US. That changed when he became prime minister in 2014 as head of the ruling BJP.

Modi's "Gujarat model" exemplifies the collusion between neoliberal and ethnonationalist strands. As he moved from the provincial to the national stage, his leadership was branded around his record of development and investment in his home province (largely an overhyped façade)—advertising shining prosperity, economic growth, and modern consumer abundance; in a word, capital accumulation. If you want that, he implied, just look the other way and ignore the ethnic cleansing and genocidal bigotry that are its price. In essence, he was calling for a devil's bargain amalgamating two strands of the right. As populist demagogue, Modi stokes a near-divine cult of personality, and, frighteningly, accurately represents a sizeable swath of the population.[37]

The frequency of lynchings and atrocities against Dalits and Muslims has leaped significantly since 2014. The rationale for violence often travels under the banner of cow protection—meaning that those involved in the important buffalo meat or leather industries, who are often Muslim or Dalit, may be brutally murdered and abused if seen to be dealing with a dead animal, or transporting or storing beef. The perpetrators of such deeds are confident not only of impunity, amnesty, and acquittal, but even the likelihood of praise and congratulation from politicians for their "brave" deeds on behalf of the Hindu nation.

Another lynchable offense is falling in love with someone from the wrong caste or religion, for the Sanghis are also on vigilant guard against the dreaded "love jihad": the evil propensity of wily Muslim men to seduce innocent Hindu maidens into conversion, marriage, and—here's the kicker—production of lots of Muslim babies. Despite their overwhelming numeric majority and socioeconomic dominance, demographic replacement is an existential anxiety for Hindu nationalists. Short of being killed or driven out ("*Pakistan ya qabristan*," to Pakistan or to the graveyard, is a common chant), those who have converted to Christianity or Islam, or whose ancestors did so many generations ago, might be urged toward *ghar wapsi*—homecoming, returning to the fold of Hinduism, the body of the nation—in whatever portion of the integral body they are to be allowed.

Modi is only one of a number of far-right politicians gaining influence and power. There's also Amit Shah, home minister and Modi's righthand man; RSS chief Mohan Bhagwat; and Yogi Adityanath, an extremist monk elected as chief minister of UP in 2017. Adityanath promotes cow protection and is a particular foe of love jihad. His personal militia, the Hindu Yuva Vahini, stands poised to engage in acts of violence, intimidation, and arson at his bidding. At a rally in 2008, he told followers, "[I]f Muslims take one Hindu girl, we'll take one hundred Muslim girls. If they don't behave, we will give it back a hundred times more with interest. If they kill one Hindu, we'll kill one hundred Muslims."[38] His supporters have called for exhuming Muslim women from their graves and raping the corpses. He hopes to install idols of Hindu deities in every mosque.[39]

Modi's re-election in 2019 was taken as a mandate to aggressively pursue an agenda dreamed of for decades, now without constraints. In August 2019, they moved to definitive takeover of Kashmir, a contested region fought over by India and Pakistan and largely under Indian military occupation since 1948 despite its popular movement seeking independence. Constitutional articles 370 and 35A were unilaterally revoked to erase the region's special autonomous status, instead enforcing direct federal control from Delhi and opening the door for the first time to land acquisition by nonresidents. In essence, this means replacing the prior Muslim-majority population with Hindu settlers, and replacing Kashmiriyat—the prior culture of the region, known for syncretism and communal harmony—with Hindutva conforming to the rest of India's ascendant nationalism.

In November 2019, permission to build the Ram temple in Ayodhya was finally granted.[40] Then came the implementation of a series of laws that, in combination, aimed to transform Indian citizenship into Hindu-exclusive status. The National Register of Citizens (NRC; test run in Assam for eventual national application) required people to document their family residency since prior to 1971 (the year the creation of Bangladesh generated a cross-border refugee wave in the region). This abruptly stripped two million people of legal citizenship and rendered them effectively stateless, even if their family had lived there for generations. The goal was to distinguish legal citizens from those designated as migrants, outsiders, or foreigners; the result was to redefine many citizens as foreigners.

Combined with the National Population Register's (NPR) population and citizenship database, this would create new categories of illegal "infiltrators" and place them in detention camps. The last piece of the puzzle, making a path to citizenship explicitly dependent upon religion, was the Citizenship Amendment Act (CAA), which decreed that refugees would be accepted from other countries in the South Asian region *except* Muslims, which would exclude some of the most serious refugee crises anywhere in the world—most visibly, the Rohingya from Myanmar.

Nationwide protests erupted in cities and universities all around the country in December 2019 and January 2020, spearheaded by Muslim communities and supported by a broad swath of society upholding solidarity. Demonstrations and occupations persisted and spread despite heavy state repression and state-sanctioned vigilantism, only to be derailed by the coronavirus disease 2019 lockdown starting in March. Hindu nationalists scapegoated Muslims for the spread of the virus.

Hindutva in America

The Diaspora

Extended Family of Fronts

A "roadmap" for the 21st century laid out in 2019 illustrates the importance the RSS places on the overseas Indian community. In the US, the Sangh maintains organizational counterparts to each of its Indian groups. The RSS analogue is the Hindu Swayamsevak Sangh (HSS), BJP has the Overseas Friends of the BJP (OFBJP), VHP has the Vishwa Hindu

Parishad of America (VHPA), and ABVP has the Hindu Students Council (HSC).

Their interlinked strategy works *politically*, to push their agendas through US policy, financing and lobbying politicians in Washington, DC; *culturally*, to gain international legitimacy for their image and narrative, with a big investment in academic penetration; and *economically*, to direct funding toward their activities in India and to promote corporate business and investment partnerships. They host briefings, cultural events, and youth camps, "educating" politicians and the public with their propaganda messaging. Expert spinmeisters, they make opportunistic use of the liberal language of multiculturalism, minority rights, human rights, and religious freedom to defend their own interests in the US while actually doing the opposite thing within India, namely committing violence and discrimination against minorities and attempting to define state citizenship in religious terms.

The global Sangh is present everywhere the diaspora reaches. It spread first to East Africa, with the first overseas HSS shakha forming on a ship to Kenya in 1947. There are now 720 shakhas in 32 countries.[41] The US hosts more shakhas outside India than anywhere except Nepal. Replicating the domestic RSS structure, the HSS is the parent body headed by a Sanghchalak. As in India, shakhas function autonomously in day-to-day practice while complying with global coordination. They run week-long ideological, physical, and organizational training camps, from which alumni who attend further trainings in India might potentially join a pool of new pracharaks who could be assigned anywhere in the world.[42] As in India, the Sangh distributes its educational and charitable service functions through dozens of groups that maintain nominal independence while providing convenient fronts through which to distribute ideological influence and route funding to the Sangh.

The VHPA was founded in the 1970s with chapters throughout the country. Its "primary function" is to do "support work for the Sangh in India among the professional Indian diaspora" through conferences and cultural events, and to fundraise via the various Sewa Vibhag entities. These are the polymorphous organizations throughout the country that make up the Hindutva movement's service wing, keeping their Sangh connections well masked. The US-based India Development and Relief Fund has funneled millions of dollars through Sewa International (coordinating Sewa Vibhag's overseas activities) to the RSS.[43]

The VHPA also helped launch the HSC as the global Sangh's student wing, active on college and university campuses throughout the US. While maintaining scrupulous distance from the Sangh (HSC declared itself

separate from the VHPA in 2005, likely to distance itself from global condemnation of the Gujarat carnage), the HSC promotes Hindutva ideology
"under the guise of liberal Hindu socio-religious thought," according to
the Coalition Against Genocide, to "mobilize the diasporic student population around the issues of an embattled Hindu identity and legitimize
the Sangh family of organizations as valid representatives of the Hindu
diasporic community."

HSC student leadership alumni have been central to the growth of
the Hindu America Foundation (HAF), founded in 2003 by Suhag Shukla
and Mihir Meghani, previously founding president of the HSC at the
University of Michigan, who had reached out to members of the VHPA's
governing council in 1998 with the goal of establishing a body through
which "[t]o address issues affecting . . . Hindus worldwide . . . [t]o begin
to establish a Hindu voice in the American and Canadian media . . . [t]o
present a Hindu . . . agenda to public officials of the US and Canada . . .
[t]o encourage HSC chapters to educate people about issues affecting
us."[44] From HSC to HAF, Meghani was ideally positioned to bridge the
generation gap from first- to second-generation immigrants: that is,
equipped to communicate to the American mainstream (as opposed to
speaking to and within an Indian extremist bubble).

Meanwhile, if there is a bad cop to HAF's good cop—because it is still
not feasible for Hindu nationalist vigilante squads to beat people in the
streets of Jackson Heights, Houston, or Jersey City—Bajrang Dal's international presence takes the form of a website called HinduUnity.org (based
in the US and Israel).[45] According to the Campaign to Stop Funding Hate,
it has previously been deplatformed by its web-hosting service "because
of the venom that it spews, and its frequent calls to violence against specific individuals and against Muslims in general." As a sample, the primer
cites a passage that appeared on the site under a "Hindu Force" pop-up
window: "Revenge on Islam must become the sole aim of the life of every
Hindu today. Islam has been shedding Hindu blood for several centuries.
This is something we should neither forget nor forgive. This sinister religion has been striking at Hinduism for just too long. It is time we resist
this satanic force and kick it back into the same pit it crawled out of."[46]

Just as the Sangh manipulates the sentiments of liberal multiculturalism in the US, it also preys on the sentiments of the immigrant experience,
using the second generation's desire for cultural connection and the first
generation's desire to instill traditional moral values in their American
children. Both generations may feel empowered by taking pride in their
heritage when othered and alienated by mainstream society.[47] As framed
by RSS propaganda, "[T]he primary purpose of the HSS is to protect the

children of Hindu parents from the 'vicious propaganda and corrupt conversion techniques of Christians and Muslims.'" In other words, not only to maintain their connections to India, but to maintain the purity of their Hindu identity.[48]

But to whom do such messages appeal? Hindutva has its base of overseas support in the most affluent segment of the South Asian diaspora—those most likely to align themselves politically with the elite, which in the US means claiming adjacency to white status, unlike those less-advantaged members of the diaspora who are more likely to align themselves in solidarity with other racialized immigrant and minority groups. So to better understand what's happening now—and to fight it—we need to look at how South Asians have fit into the histories of race, immigration, and racial justice in the US—both where they've been positioned and where they've tried to position themselves.

Immigration

The South Asian diaspora is not a monolith but a microcosm of the subcontinent's demographic and ideological divisions, refracted through both US and South Asian contexts. How each element fits into racial politics of the US corresponds to how it fits into ideas of Indian nationalism.

Desis (as South Asians are called collectively) in North America refer to Indians, Pakistanis, Bangladeshis, Kashmiris, Nepalis, Sri Lankans, Indo-Caribbeans (from Trinidad, Surinam, Guyana), Indo-Ugandans, and others with complex histories of migration through labor and indenture. Although there are over five million South Asians estimated in the US as of 2020, they were sparse before the turn of 20th century, when a modest flow of a few thousand mostly male laborers—working in lumber, agriculture, and railroads—plus a sprinkling of peddlers/traders and a few students and scholars (some of whom paid their way as workers too) established a presence mainly on the West Coast and in a few large cities. Like other Asians (and indeed anyone not from Northern and Western Europe), they were virtually barred from entry, let alone citizenship or land ownership, by restrictive immigration legislation in 1917 and 1924.

But after the 1965 Immigration and Nationality (Hart-Celler) Act abolished national origin quotas, this changed dramatically. Moreover, thanks to Cold War strategic calculations, the US sought to attract Third World immigrants who were highly trained professionals in certain fields such as science, medicine, and technology. An influx of doctors, engineers, and programmers from the subcontinent (preselected as such by types of visas given) helped give rise to the model minority myth effect. This first big postwar wave of South Asian immigrants, it's often pointed out, were thus the beneficiaries of both the Indian independence struggle and the American civil rights struggle, but without the experience of having had to fight for political freedom or racial justice.

This strata dominated the image of the South Asian community even as the number of working-class, low-income, and/or more marginalized immigrants from the subcontinent has ballooned since the 1980s. Desis are just as heavily represented (and stereotyped) among taxicab drivers, street vendors, domestic workers, and convenience store and gas station owners/clerks as they are among software engineers, doctors, and entrepreneurial motel franchise owners. They have shown themselves just as likely to differentiate themselves by class, caste, religion, and national origin as to affiliate with one another as South Asians.[49] Thus, the distancing of the "model minority" from undesirable minorities and "bad" immigrant groups occurs not only between South Asians and other Black and brown minority groups, but *within* the South Asian diaspora—between those most likely identified as Indian, Hindu, *savarna*, middle class, white collar, educated, affluent, and those who are most likely lower caste, working class, minority, Muslim, or Dalit.

And these differences are further reflected in their attitudes and attempts to self-position/self-identify relative to the US racial order. Those who are nonwhite but relatively privileged in the South Asian context may resent being racialized and denied the full inclusion to which they feel entitled. Their grievance isn't a principled objection to racism or xenophobia, but rather to mistaken identity, resentment at being misclassified as nonelite (alongside religious and caste minorities and working-class Desis). In other words, the complaint is, "We were miscategorized," not "These racist categories are wrong."

New immigrant groups can try to gain admittance into the charmed circle of whiteness but, to do that, they have to prove their eligibility through certain benchmarks of economic success, educational attainment, and cultural assimilation; one of the ways to demonstrate assimilation is to perform the requisite racism against designated groups and embrace the structures of white supremacy. Self-identified Hindu Americans (a term rising in popularity in contrast with Indian Americans or South Asian Americans) are seeking admission to a more advantageous positioning within the white supremacist structure via their identification with Aryan supremacy at the expense of other people, rather than positioning themselves in solidarity with other people against the white supremacist structure.

This was intensified even further after September 11th and the unleashed Islamophobia that heavily targeted South Asian Muslims (Pakistanis, Bangladeshis, and Indians): for some Indian savarna Hindus seeking inclusion/incorporation into the American mainstream, the strategy to distance themselves from these stigmatized groups was perfectly compatible with their existing principles.

Hindutva in US Electoral Politics

Founded in 1992, the OFBJP helps raise funds for the BJP and counteract critical narratives of the party through positive propaganda messaging. Playing a direct role in Indian domestic politics, they phone-banked heavily to get out the vote and some even traveled to India to mobilize voters for Modi's re-election in 2019. Since the 1990s (more pronounced after September 11th), Hindutva in the diaspora is also keen to insert itself into US politics, attempting to build ties between a US and an India whose domestic and international policies are increasingly dominated by their far-right elements. The same stratum of wealthy donors, entrepreneurs, and chief executive officers who fund the BJP also fund political candidates in the US to support the probusiness (and pro-Hindutva) Indian-US relations they want. Modi's supporters in the South Asian diaspora have also proven to be avid supporters of Donald Trump.

The nonpartisan Hindu American Political Action Committee (here's Meghani again, on the board) supports congress members who they think will promote their agenda. Primary among these is Tulsi Gabbard, the first Hindu member of Congress and a Hindutva darling. Gabbard is of white and Samoan ethnicity, representing Hawaii as a Democratic member of the House. She was raised in a fringe sect of Hinduism related to an offshoot of the International Society for Krishna Consciousness (commonly referred to by its acronym ISKCON or the Hare Krishnas) and considers herself a devotee of the Bhagavad Gita and a karma yogi. A military veteran, her record on US foreign policy is deeply Islamophobic. She maintains close personal and family ties to Hindutva luminaries who cherish her dedicated service to their cause. The VHPA's Gaurang Vaishnav endorses Gabbard as someone "who aligns with their way of thinking, who believes in the same values as them," and understands what they want, thanks to her Hindu faith.[50] But Gabbard is a unique exception, and in most cases Hindutva supports Republicans.

The Republican Hindu Coalition was established in 2015. Steve Bannon was named its honorary cochair in 2019. Shortly before the 2016 presidential election, they held a lavish fundraiser for Trump in New Jersey, framed as a cultural celebration (Bollywood-themed extravaganza) and human rights effort helping refugees (Kashmiri Pandits). Three years later, a massive event billed as "Howdy Modi!" was staged in Houston, Texas: promoted as celebration of a visit by India's prime minister, it doubled as a Trump re-election campaign rally.[51]

There, Trump embraced Modi and pledged his support to the Indian-American community (insofar as he understood it), saying, "We'll take care of our Indian American citizens before we take care of illegal immigrants that want to pour into our country."[52] Of course, pointed out Rashmee Kumar of *The Intercept*, this statement overlooked the many noncitizen and undocumented Indian residents in the US, or the growing number of Indian immigrants crossing the border from México. Those are more likely to be religious and caste minorities who may be severely persecuted at home. Due to his own ignorance, Trump took the Hindutva forces at their word for what India and Indian Americans signify: wealthy, upper-caste Hindus. Why wouldn't he? They made sense to him.

The Houston rally was widely received as Modi's endorsement of Trump, who took the visit as "an occasion to consolidate the Indian American voter" (or at least the Hindu-American voter), in their new turn toward the Republican Party. The mirror image of the "Howdy Modi!" event followed with "Namaste Trump," when the US president visited India in early 2020 in what Pallabi Munsi called "a thinly veiled attempt to woo the 4.5 million–strong and wealthy Indian American community—a third of them of Gujarati origin—to the president's cause in November."[53] (The visit coincided with, and remained sequestered from, the massive nationwide protests against the CAA/NRC/NPR.)

There were also Democrats on the stage in Houston who said they were there in support of a "bipartisan" Indian-US relationship, holding out for a vision of pluralist secular democracy. And Hindutva supporters do still donate to Democratic campaigns, hedging their bets, seeking influence wherever they can get it. Until recently, people of Indian origin tended to vote Democratic in US politics, even those who supported far-right politics in India. The apparent discrepancy lay in calculated self-interest. They viewed the Democratic Party as favorable to minorities and immigrants, and the Republican Party as antiminority and anti-immigrant. But Hindu Americans' own self-specification is revealing a contradiction.

They are troubled by the influence of the Democratic Party's Progressive Caucus, which they suspect of not really favoring *all* minority communities but "only those it views as victims of social injustice," *unlike* themselves. They proudly point out that "Hindu-Americans unlike other minorities are not victims of social injustice but are successful, high achieving."[54] Disgruntled, they note that the Democrats do not sufficiently favor "[m]inority communities with high levels of educational attainment and income," including

Hindu Americans, one of the most financially successful and educated religious groups in the US (note that they do not refer to ethnic groups—that would force their statistics to be combined with other segments of the South Asian diaspora, of which they are but one sliver)—a clear admission from "Hindu Americans" that they represent a privileged class that has tried to take advantage of minority status while distancing themselves from more-disenfranchised groups that they consider inferiors.

They also accuse the Progressive Caucus of viewing them "as being aligned with whites as privileged oppressors."[55] But this is quite correct, on their own terms; they have intentionally aligned themselves with whites as a privileged class, but with a positive instead of negative connotation. A century earlier, the handful of Indians seeking naturalization as American citizens routinely did so under the designation of "Caucasian," which was available to them under the racial categories of the time (as neither "Negro" nor "Mongoloid"). In a landmark 1923 immigration case, as racial restrictions on immigration were growing stricter, Bhagat Singh Thind attempted to argue his "Caucasian" race classification before the US Supreme Court based on "Aryan" ethnicity supported by anthropological evidence, despite his deceptively dark complexion. The court ruled against him based on contemporary common-sense understanding of the terms Aryan and Caucasian to specify white or European.

Today, "Hindu Americans" want to align themselves with not just whiteness but white supremacy, belying their disguise as brown immigrants. As reported by Krishna Kumar in *India Today*, these "hurt and disappointed" diasporic ethnonationalists were "rattled" by the "recent emergence of anti-Hindu and anti-India propaganda" from progressive Democrats who were "maligning" India or "meddling" in its affairs by their criticism of Modi's actions.[56] This included prominent progressive Democrats of Indian descent, such as Pramila Jayapal and Ro Khanna, targets of their bitterest vitriol as race traitors to Hindutva.[57]

Given the increasing "dissonance between the core values and interests of the aggrieved Hindu-Americans and the interests of the Democratic Party," they warn of a shift of allegiance, miffed at being taken for granted.[58] And whereas would-be progressive liberals had to be manipulated and taken advantage of through their support for diversity, multiculturalism, and well-intentioned friendliness to brown immigrant groups, when dealing with the right wing, there is no subterfuge needed. Their principles align much more neatly with the Trump-era Republican Party; they promote themselves as natural partners, chiming perfectly with a common agenda. The further right the Republican Party gets, the more affinity the diasporic Sanghis affirm with it.

They declare themselves "fiscally conservative and socially moderate" (which is to say, fiscally neoliberal-capitalist and socially far right). After all, this demographic migrated to the US "to escape socialism and vile social engineering policies that have been championed and promoted for over half a century" by the INC.[59] (One might compare anti-Castro Cubans, or pro-Shah Iranians, as affluent right-leaning immigrant-minority communities in the US). With that reference point in mind, they oppose high taxes, Medicare for All, and "excessive" government spending or economic intervention; they vehemently oppose Affirmative Action (as disadvantageous to themselves, fearing the loss of their own demographic overrepresentation in American universities).[60] Naturally, they also take a strident anti-Islam stance, aligning them with counterterrorism policies that, in practice, have defined terrorism as synonymous with Islam (although in terms of domestic terrorism, the frequency of white supremacist violence in the US and Hindu supremacist violence in India are statistically much higher).[61] They support Trump's border wall and border security initiatives (again proving they only ever favored rights and freedoms for "good" immigrants such as themselves).[62]

Beyond lobbying and funding, they have ventured toward fielding their own representatives directly. Exemplifying a self-described "new generation of Indian American and Hindu American leaders who do not become pawns in a globalist ideological agenda that undermines their own integrity as well as the national interests of their adoptive homeland"—note the "globalist versus nationalist" dog whistles—is former defense acquisitions contractor and Trump supporter Manga Anantatmula.[63] Politically activated through the struggle against Affirmative Action in US higher education,[64] in early 2020 she announced a run for the House of Representatives from the 11th Congressional district of Virginia (South Asian–heavy and Democratic-leaning Fairfax County). Her platform: "Making Americans Great Again" (explained as an acronym of her own name, Manga)—low taxes, helping small to medium businesses, affordable health care, and strengthening the US–India relationship (specifically Trump's US and Modi's India).[65] And, with these, Benjamin Netanyahu's Israel.

After all, the aspirational "gold standard" for Hindutva political mobilization in the US is right-wing Zionism.

Zionism and Hindutva

These two religious ethnonationalisms have always had much affinity in

India as well. Hindu nationalists are avid students of Israel's effectiveness as an aggressive, militaristic ethnostate that conflates religion and culture.

Savarkar and Golwalkar, even while modeling their ethnic management policies on Nazi antisemitism, were at the same time the Zionist movement's biggest supporters in India—"diametrically opposite" to the views of Gandhi and Nehru, who opposed both antisemitism and Zionism.[66] Supporters of a Hindu Rashtra (and some ideas of Pakistan) recognized and related to the Zionist demand for a state founded on religious identity, which they too wanted. At the time of the 1967 war, RSS favored the US and Israel, admiring especially "the success of Israeli arms," and "tried to bolster this stand by discovering affinities between Zionism and Vedic culture" and locating Judaic origins in the Vedas and Dharmashastras.[67]

Jaffrelot observes that, since 2014, India has moved emphatically toward an Israeli-style "ethnic democracy," meaning a "democratic" state with two-tiered citizenship whose *demos* consists of a particular majority "ethnicity" receiving preferential treatment while minorities defined as outside the *demos* must accept a subordinate status as second-class citizens.[68] Both Zionism and Hindutva have offered the rationalization that Muslims have plenty of other states they could go to, whereas Jews and Hindus, respectively, have only the one true spiritual soil—assuming that all states are to be defined as essentially ethnonationalist-religious entities!

Throughout the 1990s, India's defense and security relationship with Israel grew steadily under both Congress and BJP governments: Israel provided arms sales, counterterrorism consulting, and surveillance technology to India, its biggest client (India's previous major defense and security relationship had been with the Union of Soviet Socialist Republics, until its demise), while India launched spy satellites for Israel. After September 11th (set alongside India's 2001 Parliament bombing and the 2008 Mumbai attacks linked to Islamist guerrilla groups backed by Pakistani intelligence services), India was keen to position itself as part of a US-Israel-India axis of Islamophobia in the global "War on Terror."

Although Indian foreign policy had previously supported the Palestinian cause, it now shifted into an attitude of reciprocation in which India agreed that Palestine was Israel's domestic concern whereas Israel agreed that Kashmir was India's domestic concern. There, the BJP aspires to replicate the practices of Israeli settlement in the West Bank by establishing exclusively Hindu settlements, engineering demographic change through both force and law, and expanding the military, security apparatus, and surveillance capacity over all aspects of Kashmiri life. Palestinian scholar Abdulla Moaswes calls it a convergence of logic stressing "security, counterterrorism, and the threat of Islamic extremism" as they exchange information, operational experience, and tactics, including "arbitrary arrests, extrajudicial killings, enforced disappearances, curfews, collective punishment, administrative detention, torture, rape and sexual abuse, suppression of freedom of speech and assembly, house demolitions").[69] BJP government officials have bragged about matching Israel-grade tactics, applying its lessons for suppressing popular resistance in the Palestinian occupied territories. "Indeed, Israel's muscular brand of militarism seems to have become aspirational for India," observes historian Ipsita Chakravarty. "When the Indian Army reportedly launched 'surgical strikes' across the Line of Control in 2016, in response to a terrorist attack on an army camp in Kashmir's Uri town that was blamed on Pakistan, Modi compared it to the exploits of the Israeli Army," Chakravarty continues.[70] Sandeep Chakraborty, India's consul-general in New York, said of the goal of settlement building to bring the Hindu population back to Kashmir, "If the Israeli people can do it, we can also do it."[71]

Here's another domestic/diaspora cognate: As a Hindutva-dominated Indian government aspires to be Israel, Hindutva lobbyists aspire to be the America Israel Public Affairs Committee (AIPAC). Since the 1990s, but here too escalating drastically after September 11th, ambitious Indian-American businesspeople looked admiringly to the American Jewish Committee (AJC) and AIPAC as exemplars for their clout in Washington, DC. Under these groups' guidance, they formed the United States India Political Action Committee (USINPAC) to pursue their goals using similar tactics of lobbying and influence.[72] Indian, Israeli, and American interests were in alignment, they claimed, on account of their shared priority in confronting Islamic terrorism. Right-wing Hindu Americans were also eager students of the technique of making religion, national identity, and state policy synonymous, so that criticism of one could be framed as prejudice against the other. Just as AIPAC and other Zionist propagandists denounce criticism of Israeli state policies as antisemitism, a frequent HAF tactic is to denounce critiques of the Hindutva agenda (from members of Congress, scholars, or journalists) as religious discrimination against Hinduism.

Rama Lakshmi in *The Washington Post* writes that the Indian government has come to think of BJP-supporting demographics overseas as "a valuable portion of India's foreign policy, in much the same way the Jewish diaspora in the United States influences international policy and opinion on Israel."[73] This is made explicit in a quote from BJP general secretary Ram Madhav: "We are changing the contours of diplomacy and finding new ways of strengthening India's interests abroad. . . . That is the longterm [sic] goal behind this diaspora diplomacy. It is like the way the Jewish community looks out for Israel's interests in the United States" while simultaneously cultivating diasporic participation in domestic politics; in other words, using the overseas population as a motor for both domestic and international directions.

One does have to wonder what Hindutva's Zionist allies make of their Hitler fetish.

Hindutva in the Universe

And the Circle Turned Again: Savitri Devi

The ongoing reciprocal reinforcement of Hindutva and Nazism—and a bridge from the Indian to the international far right—is exemplified by the rather bizarre (and, to many, obscure) but pivotal figure of Savitri Devi. Although she was active in India during the 1940s, I introduce her here because her significance was far less to the history of the Indian domestic right wing than to the later political theology of Western fascism. A European woman of Greek-French origin who spent many years in India, she preached an Aryan-supremacist mysticism that extrapolated race theory into a cosmic faith.

Born Maximiliani Portas in 1905, she was initially mobilized by Greek nationalist feelings and resentment of Britain's imperial behavior after World War I. Her love of classical Greek aesthetics, philosophy, art, and architecture grew into an intense hatred of Judeo-Christian civilization and thence a vicious antisemitism. Building directly on the theories of the Indologists about the notion of an originary Indo-European Aryan race progenitor, she saw in India—at least in the brahminical Vedic version of it—what she thought was the world's only pure Aryan civilization to survive intact from the dawn of its glory days, thanks to the caste system, which she admired as "the Aryan archetype of racial laws intended to govern the segregation of different races and to maintain the pure blood of the . . . fair-complexioned Aryans."[74] She subscribed to the Aryan Invasion theory and its explanation for the varna system, the structure through which the Brahmins had preserved what their Nordic/Germanic cousins had lost but were fighting to restore. She arrived in India in 1932; in 1937, she began working with the Hindu Mission in Calcutta, and soon married a Nazi-sympathizing, Aryan-racist Brahmin named Asit Krishna Mukherji.

Devi embraced aspects of Hindu cosmology and philosophy, including the cyclical concept of time—a repeated passage of decline from a Golden Age to Dark Age, culminating in a cataclysm of destruction followed by rebirth and glorious restoration. Kali Yuga, Ragnarok, and the Greek age of iron sound much the same. (Still, for all their talk of infinite eternal cycles, Devi and others certainly seem to fixate on one effectively linear, historically bounded segment of modern time.) She also highlighted the concept of the avatar: the recurrent manifestation of Vishnu in incarnate form at key transitional points in the cycle, to play a role in dharmically rebalancing the universe. Previous major avatars were the deified heroes of the Indian epics, Rama and Krishna; the most recent, and to her the most glorious, was none other than Hitler, perfect man and chosen one, with a cosmic role to play in catalyzing the redemptive orgy of destruction out of which the Aryan race alone would emerge to start anew, purified and revivified.

By the late 1930s, Hindu nationalists were watching Germany "with a jubilant hope," said a Mahasabha spokesman: "Germany's solemn idea of the revival of Aryan culture, the glorification of the Swastika [an ancient Sanskritic sun symbol of life and health], her patronage of Vedic learning and the ardent championship of the tradition of Indo-Germanic civilization are welcomed by the religious and sensible Hindus of India . . . Germany's crusade . . . will bring all the Aryan nations of the world to their senses and awaken the Indian Hindus."[75]

As a traveling lecturer for the Mission, Devi interlaced Nazi propaganda with her Hindu preachings. Meanwhile, in Germany in 1937, Schutzstaffel (SS) Reichsführer Heinrich Himmler appointed Walther Wüst as head of the SS-run research institute, the Ahnenerbe (Ancestral Heritage Office), which would include a "Department of Indo-Germanic-Aryan linguistics and culture."[76] Wüst was yet another scholar of Sanskrit, ancient Indian literature and philosophy, anthropology, and comparative religion; like Devi, he discerned connections between European and Indian legend, was enamored of the Rigveda and saw it as "more than a Hindu holy book; he believed it was also an important document of the Nordic race,"[77] which in ancient times had traveled eastward and southward, bearing the marks of an ancient sun worship cult. Himmler was fascinated. He and Wüst saw India's Brahmin elite as the descendants of the Nordic master race who had diligently protected the purity of their blood over the centuries despite the general racial degeneration of intermarriage imposed by South Asia's debilitating climate. After the war, these two branches of believers in the Vedic-Nordic Nazi faith were united.

Mr. and Mrs. Mukherji had spent the war years in Calcutta doing clandestine support and light espionage for the Axis powers, while in their spare time studying Vedic traditions, yoga, and *Mein Kampf*, confident that there would be plenty of time afterward to visit the triumphant Reich. Too late, Devi traveled to Germany in 1948 and was devastated at its defeat and even more at having missed out on the glorious days of Hitler's ascendancy. Now she toured the ruined country, seeking out other covert true believers and distributing now-proscribed Nazi propaganda. For this, she was imprisoned, happily, alongside former camp commandants, SS veterans, and war criminals, thus retroactively solidifying her lifelong membership in this brethren of warriors for the cause. She was released through her husband's intervention in 1949.

Although she returned to India several more times and ultimately died there, she played no active role in the growth of postcolonial Hindutva. Rather, her activities and influence were in the Western arena, through her prolific writings extrapolating Aryan supremacist race theory beyond one historical moment into a universal millennarian amalgam of Vedic myth to the Nordic *völkisch*-heathen-occultist and antihumanist deep ecology strands of contemporary fascism. (She was a significant inspiration in the fascist esoterica of Julius Evola and Miguel Serrano.)

Meanwhile, Hindutva's fascination with Hitler is evergreen, along with the ideas that first inspired Devi when she encountered India. Thackeray opined in 1967 that India needed a Hitler today to whip it into shape, and in 1993 he repeated Golwarkar's transposition of Hitler's polemic into the South Asian context, replacing Germany's Jews with India's Muslims. Journalist Shrenik Rao describes various Hindu nationalist Facebook pages, whose vocabulary of tropes and images sound directly lifted from Devi's 1930s rhetoric, with slogans like *"Hari Om Heil Hitler"* and *"Aum, Heil Aryan, Heil Aryavart," "Jai Shree Ram, Heil Hitler,"* "Nazi the Great," and "Hitler was the supporter of Indian nationalists." They juxtapose images of Hitler and Vishnu (whose "ultimate" avatar many Sanghis too believe him to be, heralding the end of the Kali Yuga); they trumpet Aryan racial superiority and denounce racial (or caste) mixing, degenerating the "pure Aryan blood line"; they locate Nazi propaganda in the Bhagavad Gita and its "Kshatriya code." Rao reports that, to judge by the comment threads on such pages, there is increasing contact between Hindu Nazis of this kind and neo-Nazis around the world.[78]

Devi would be delighted.

Universals and Particulars

Although Hindutva's manifestation is specific to the Indian context, it is also consistent with a global phenomenon, showing certain commonalities with far-right groups everywhere.

For one thing, the factors that created an opening for the RSS/VHP to burst forth from margins to center after 1992 were similar to the preconditions for the rising appeal of right-wing identitarian ideologies in the West: economic precarity heightened by the effects of globalized neoliberal late capitalism, combined with domestic social shifts wherein marginalized and disenfranchised minorities (in India, largely Dalitbahujan and Muslim) were asserting greater demands for rights, representation, equity, and advancement, and actually starting to gain some traction. The group previously feeling secure on top of the pyramid of privilege (in India, largely savarna Hindu men) feels its exclusive advantage slipping as other people make claims on a share of what they themselves already had, and lash out to prevent others from getting access.

In the reactions to this sense of threatened supremacy, Hindu nationalist proclivities share clear affinities with what Stern describes in her study of the US alt-right. Their white nationalism strongly emphasizes not just the separation but the *hierarchy* of different racial stocks, based in the idea of the naturally elite and the naturally inferior, explicitly rejecting the principle that all are created equal. The resonance of this mentality with brahminism and the caste system is striking.

So too with the linkage of misogynistic hypermasculinity to this idea of natural hierarchy, essentializing not just race but gender characteristics as inborn, biological, immutable, and rigidly separate. In the brahminist imaginary, violent misogyny is celebrated and male dominance presumed, although women who proudly espouse "traditional" roles can sometimes be movement leaders. This is compounded by the particular postcolonial pathology fixated on the assertion of manhood and strength to counteract emasculation by colonial domination (or in the Western case by feminism, or so they say).

One difference, though, is in Hindutva's attitude to celibacy: whereas the phenomenon of the "incel" (involuntary celibate) in the misogynistic white right wing portrays denial of sexual fulfillment as a trauma, an injustice, and a justification for mass murder, the Hindu tradition makes celibacy into the badge of a strong spiritual warrior. Nevertheless, gruesome sexual violence performed upon the bodies of Muslim and Dalit women has been a recurring tactic of Hindutva assertion of power—in Kashmir, in Gujarat, in the villages of the Hindi heartland—even while the mirror image of this, the ideation of Muslim male sexuality (in both envy and anxiety), drives obsessive fears of violation, loss of purity, demographic submergence, replacement and dispossession, or racial and social degeneration.

Echoes of the Jim Crow South and the Make America Great Again (MAGA) brigade?

Different strands within the American (and postcolonial British) far right sometimes disagree about whether to emphasize antisemitism ("Jews are the worst") or white supremacy ("Blacks are the worst"). For Hindutva, a cognate might be emphasis on Muslims (as wily semite invaders) or on Dalits (as dark-complected subordinate workers)—although these are far from mutually exclusive; just different entry points based on different structural relationships (threat from outside, impurity from below). Hindu nationalists in the US readily embrace not only American Islamophobia but American anti-Blackness.

Another difference in brand, among Western fascists, is between those who favor unreconstructed Nazi iconography and those who prefer to polish a more stylish image of the right updated for the 21st century, more palatable to a wider audience.

Many Sanghis do still admire and emulate Nazism, and its opponents frequently link them to that iconography to make a point.[79] Rao reports anecdotally on seeing a contemporary pool parlor in Nagpur called "Hitler's Den," filled with Nazi kitsch; its swastikas were definitely the Nazi variety (standing on the corner), said Rao, not the ancient Sanskrit symbol (on the flat edge). *Mein Kampf* is commonly read as a bestselling pop business management strategy manual comparable to Niccolò Machiavelli or Sun Tzu. But is there also an Indian alt-right?

It may be less a subsequent replacement of one image with another than an enhancement of an existing division of labor, as was the case throughout the life of the postindependence RSS: so that there can be a hygienic separation (although both are valued) between thuggish ruffians and slickly telegenic spokespeople with an eye to overseas audiences as well as domestic mainstream appeal.

Profiling the new Indian Institute for Democratic Leadership (IIDL), journalist Vidhi Doshi describes a school for professionalizing political operatives trained in public speaking, debate, governance, social media, election campaigning, and political thinking. For example, Doshi sits in on a class in which students brainstorm talking points for debate on banning beef—a key issue and dog whistle for the Hindu right. The instructor advised that the message could be pitched more effectively in terms of health and environmental concerns than in terms of religion.[80]

These students' mindsets also illustrate something widely recognizable to me since the turn of the 21st century, which is that the same matrix—namely, disgust with the manifest failings of neoliberal global capitalism, elite corruption and hypocrisy, growing social inequity, and the alienation of consumer society—provides the stimulus for both left and right reactions. Economically destabilized by late-stage global capitalism, disillusioned by mainstream/centrist institutions, people seek alternatives of all sorts on all sides. Right-wing content aside, the school's model of professional politicos offers a marked alternative to an earlier model of powerful dynastic families and patronage networks cultivating *quid pro quo* vote banks. Any of us—especially if we are young, alienated, or disenfranchised, discontented seekers—may be susceptible to various propagandas or messages. The students Doshi describes are not (yet) right-wing ideologues; they appear to her as "bright, argumentative and charismatic," discontented with the status quo, suspicious of the mainstream media, and sharply critical of corruption and globalization. Why could such students, who "felt passionately about systemic change," not have gone down a leftward path—as several decades before, they might have done?

Identitarian politics have something to do with it. For better and for worse, the personal becomes political if a way to make sense of one's individual discontent or trauma is available through identification with a larger community—perhaps accessed (and amplified) online. In my observation, in the US, systemic alienation in young, straight, cis, white males may lead some to become alt-rightists or mass shooters whereas systemic alienation in young queer/trans/women of color may lead some to an awakening into radically antiracist, liberatory, decolonial solidarities. (Among second-generation Indian kids, this can mean either involvement in the HSS/HSC/HAF complex or in antiracist, liberatory, decolonial solidarities.)

Doshi observes that the IIDL students happen to be overwhelmingly male, and overwhelmingly savarna Hindu, mostly from the Hindi heartland. It's not official, it just happens to be that way. Plus, fees are pricey and facilities lush, so they also just happen to be mostly of a certain class status. Doshi notes that the demographics of the student body "roughly matched the BJP's core demographic."[81] The IIDL claims no official relationship with the BJP, nor are graduates officially required to affiliate to any particular party. But its parent organization was affiliated to the RSS and the office of its director, formerly RSS-linked Vinay Sahasrabuddhe, is in the BJP's Delhi headquarters. Course materials and lectures frame analyses in ways that tend implicitly toward conclusions in line with BJP politics, and Doshi compares the IIDL's versions of history and society to those of Bannon and Nigel Farage, in which the solution to contemporary ills lies in the revival of religious cultural traditions. The graduates "represent a generation of future leaders that seems disconnected with India's founding principles. To Sahasrabuddhe, they will be the country's saviors—or at the very least, the BJP's."[82]

Capturing the "Mind Space"

From the start, RSS strategy was built on capturing hearts and minds first, and gaining political power afterward. This has proven to be a canny path to political power. Hindutva has an outsize presence on social media platforms as well as a heavy influence on public discourse through popular culture and journalism. In India, some mainstream news media outlets function as virtual BJP mouthpieces, whereas independent journalists and public intellectuals who report critically on the doings of the BJP/RSS complex may face harassment or death threats—in a few cases, these threats have been carried out. In the US, dueling lobbyists carry out a war of influence on Capitol Hill (HAF versus Indian American Muslim Council or South Asian Americans Leading Together) while a war of memes unfolds in the Twittersphere and a war of narratives in universities. Notably, whereas the mindscape battleground inside India centers on the identity of the nation and its history, the mindscape battleground of the diaspora community here has to work through the tropes of an American social/cultural context.

In 2019, RSS chief Bhagwat announced the release of pracharak and ABVP organizing secretary Sunil Ambekar's new book, *The RSS: Roadmaps for the 21st Century*, laying out a detailed "vision for every sector in the country."[83] Three out of the plan's four major components were educational, aiming to "Indianize" (which is to say saffronize, or Hindu-ize) the education system and create alternate narratives—essentially, to rewrite history and use it to indoctrinate students at every level from primary to advanced.

The BJP-run state and its private-sector business allies fund *ashrams*, *gurukuls* (Sanskrit schools), and religious education projects. Through Ekal Vidyalaya, they run a network of schools in tribal areas, heavily targeted for recruitment and indoctrination of Adivasi communities. They have removed professionally respected scholars from leadership positions at prominent academic research institutions and universities (e.g., the Indian Council on Historical Research [ICHR], Indian Council on Social Science Research [ICSSR], Nehru Memorial Museum and Library, and Bombay Film Institute), and replaced them with their own puppets.

The roadmap calls for institutions such as the ICHR and ICSSR to highlight "Indian methodologies" and "give currency to the works of genuine historians" whose work is fact based to unmask "falsehood and misrepresentations." "Remedial action" should be taken against historiography based on "prejudices, distortions and manipulations." Given that this is more or less a direct inversion of what they are actually doing, one's head spins to hear this.

Altogether, these policies echo Himmler's 1930s Aryanist project to bring German academia into his purview and ultimately control teaching and research. "By placing SS officers in key academic positions, he planned to obtain control one day over everything taught in university classrooms," writes Heather Pringle. "In this way, the Nazi version of history, prehistory, literature, genetics and biology would replace authentic scholarship," Pringle continues.[84]

Postcolonial History

At times, the RSS Roadmap's agenda for history seems to echo postcolonial historiography—which takes a critical stance toward the hegemony of Western epistemological frameworks—but here twisted insidiously. "For far too long, invalid views, speculative distortions, unfounded opinions and colonial prejudices have occupied the history establishment in India."[85] This would certainly have been true had it been written a century ago. But the RSS is clearly referring to the last half century of postindependence historical scholarship, which has tended to be humanist, progressive, or left-leaning in politics; valorizing social histories from below or from the margins; and scrupulously rationalist and fact based in research. Written now, in the context of RSS actions to dominate the national mind space, it means replacing history with propagandistic legend and science with anti-intellectualism and superstition.

RSS pedagogy prioritizes the rewriting of textbooks throughout the primary education system. Textbooks issued by a BJP-controlled Rajasthan government circa 2018 (a prototype for a national curriculum now beginning to appear in other provinces too) craft a past that shifts the weight of attention toward events and actors they consider important to emphasize Hindu dominance and demonize Islam, as well as "subtler . . . updates," which, according to A. G. Noorani, "promote the BJP's political programme and ideology. They argue for the veracity of Vedic myths, glorify ancient and medieval Hindu rulers, recast the independence movement as a violent battle led largely by Hindu chauvinists, demand loyalty to the state, and praise the policies of . . . Narendra Modi."[86]

These efforts have been replicated in the diaspora too—here yet again manipulating the language of liberal multiculturalism calling for tolerant awareness of different religions and cultures. But they're not just advocating for India's inclusion in the curriculum; they're trying to take control of *how* India is represented to the West, claiming sole authority for a brahminist, Aryan supremacist narrative—as if those representations and narratives were not heavily contested *within* India and South Asian diasporic communities. "Taking advantage of the broad definition of American multiculturalism—namely, that each racial, ethnic, religious community gets equal access to the celebration of their identities, these [Sangh] organizations sought to whitewash particular histories of discrimination [carried out by caste Hindus] that they claimed interfered with their ability to take pride in their identities," explained Coalition Against Genocide.[87]

HAF, along with another HSS creation, the Hindu Education Foundation (HEF), were central players in the California middle school textbook controversy spanning from 2005 to 2017. They intervened in the publication of updated texts they deemed "anti-Hindu" by pushing a batch of edits to the California Board of Education. Objections included presentation of the Aryan Invasion theory (now out of favor among Hindu nationalists, for undermining their efforts to claim subcontinental indigeneity) and references to the caste system and caste oppression or ill treatment of women in traditional India—all thoroughly documented through established academic scholarship and challenged through a long history of South Asian social justice activism. They lobbied against the term "South Asian" (which many in the diaspora prefer as a more inclusive term for the region, reaching beyond any nationalist lens) in favor of India. All this would present Hinduism and India in a bad light, they argued, and amount therefore to discrimination against Hindu students, whose self-esteem would suffer traumatic blows. Nevertheless a coalition of scholars, activists, and community organizations led by minority religious and caste voices fought back successfully to counter their attempts "to insert new content that represented a Hindu nationalist and Brahmanical perspective."[88]

For public pedagogy, the plan also calls for new museums glorifying Hindutva's gallery of heroes, especially Shivaji, the 17th-century Maratha king and Mughal nemesis. Besides rewriting history, demolishing mosques, and physically attacking people, efforts are underway to erase all Muslim names from maps (e.g., the rich-historied Allahabad, renamed Prayagraj). After all, a core principle of Hindutva posits a "continuous thousand year old struggle of Hindus against Muslims as the structuring principle of Indian history" while presuming both Hinduism and Islam, ahistorically and incorrectly, to be homogenous monoliths.

But other historians, anthropologists, and social thinkers (e.g., Romila Thapar, Gail Omvedt, Wendy Doniger, Amartya Sen) use a different structuring principle, to make sense of the patterns of South Asian civilizational history as a dialectic of centripetal versus centrifugal politics; purifying orthodoxies versus proliferating heterodoxies; the authoritarian, patriarchal caste hierarchy of the brahminical worldview versus the powerful egalitarian (sometimes anticlerical, antiestablishment or antinomian) countercurrents that have challenged it—including Buddhism, Jainism, and Sikhism. In other words, the "brahminical imaginary" is no more essential, defining, old, or authentic than the philosophies and movements that have offered it sharp critiques and compelling alternatives over millennia.

In the Nehruvian era, too, history had been central to the public pedagogy of citizenship, forging a secular "national ethos."[89] This Nehruvian "idea of India" envisioned a South Asian civilization defined as a unique synthesis, incorporating elements from the ancient Indus Valley, southern/Dravidian, northern/Sanskritic, Islamicate (Persian, Turkic, Central Asian), and other ingredients added to the mix over many centuries; asserting that the complexity of the *masala* is precisely what had catalyzed its most notable flowerings and accomplishments. This was an aspirational narrative of mixing and syncretism, a culturally composite society whose high points were the reigns of Ashoka and Akbar holding together confederations of diverse populations within a tolerant, pluralistic framework.

Now, according to Robert Worth, pro-RSS culture minister Mahesh Sharma "has said he hopes to rewrite the conventional narrative about India as a multicultural tapestry, and to inculcate the belief that the ancient Hindu scriptures are historical facts, not legends."[90] To the Sangh, it is clear that the battle to control access to the past is essential to the ability to dominate the present and sway the future.

A major project of the VHPA and HSS was the WHC in September 2018, billed as a celebration of the 125th anniversary of Swami Vivekananda's popularization of Hinduism in the West at the Chicago World's Fair of 1893. But a statement from AJA said the WHC was "built to create a platform for mainstream Hindu fascism to take the global stage,"[91] or, the way Indian Vice President Venkiah Naidu put it to the gathering, to generate "Hindu unity and resurgence."[92] Bhagwat was a featured speaker; other speakers included prominent Hindutva ideologues known for their extreme views and aggressive interventions into academic and media spaces, such as Francois Gautier and Rajiv Malhotra, founder of the nonprofit Infinity Foundation, whose mission seems to amount to an attempted hostile takeover of professional academic scholarship in the guise of spurious "Indic Studies."

Other delegates encouraged Hindus to reproduce more, staving off the feared dwindling of their population under a supposed onslaught of Muslim births, to "protect their 'social and territorial integrity.'" This fear of demographic collapse was a recurring theme of the conference (as it is a recurring theme for white/Aryan supremacists in the US, accompanying the fascist obsession with purity of blood and racial health). Population control was stupid, some suggested (despite India's rapidly growing 1.3 billion-and-counting population, of which 80% are Hindu), and had left Hindus at a disadvantage for being the only ones to follow it. HAF Dharma Ambassador Dilip Amin displayed posters (later taken down from the VHP website) denigrating mixed marriages and opposing "love proselytization," or, as they would say more openly in India, love jihad. They were already discussing the CAA/NRC/NPR.[93]

Indigeneity

Media strategies were a big piece of the WHC programming—although Hindu nationalists have proven adept at packaging and promoting their own ideas, they are also devious in appropriating and distorting the languages of decolonization, indigeneity, and environmentalism. To compare again Stern's assessment of the American alt-right, they carry forth leading ideas of right-wing thought-leaders combined with "appropriation of concepts from the left."[94]

But if the Sanghis take up anticolonial or antioppression language, it's not because they oppose colonialism or oppression but because they object to being lumped with the colonized instead of the colonizers, where they feel they belong. They want to be seen as elite, not subaltern; strong, not weak; superior, not inferior. That's for someone else. This can be seen in the casteism, colorism, and anti-African attitudes prevalent within the Indian community. It can also be seen in the (neocolonial) drive to possess Kashmir not to mention reclaiming all of "Akhand Bharat," or undivided India, including not only the prepartition territories of Pakistan and Bangladesh but all the South Asian countries and their regional peripheries extended through Afghanistan, Myanmar, and Tibet.

This is why we can never equate nationalism with anticolonialism—particularly a nationalism of the Hindutva variety, which, as Thapar points out, based its own logic in colonial categories and historiography, and did not have a goal of decolonization but rather of establishing a religious ethnostate. Independent India's (and Pakistan's) colonial inheritance—that which the new states took over from the colonial state when it handed over power to them—included governmental, juridical, military, and police infrastructures; political identity categories as units of interest and representation; and territorial claims and boundaries.

The lines on the postcolonial map had for the most part been drawn by colonial activities, conquests, and interventions. In places where the inhabitants had only ambiguously or reluctantly been incorporated into the British Raj, once the Raj pulled out, they didn't necessarily want to be handed over to the new state built on those same boundaries either. Kashmir is a case in point, as is Assam, along with the other northeastern states. This is also why an anticolonial history of South Asia can't afford to be uncritical of the Nehruvian consensus either: Colonialism and empire in South Asia are not just about European versus Asian, but various centralizing states versus various regions and borderlands, ancient and modern.

And in fact the invasion that most bothered Hindutva—the one they framed as the cataclysmic moment of destruction, the beginning of the end of the imagined Golden Age—was not the arrival of the British East India Company in the 17th century, but of Muslim sultanates starting in the 11th century and lasting until the Mughal Empire was dismantled by the British in 1857. And Dalit and Dravidian movements might say the real colonial problem in South Asia began with the Vedic Aryan invasion of the second millennium BCE.

In this sense, the Vedic/Aryan steppe arrivals were neither more nor less foreign to the subcontinent than the Central Asian/Turkic/Persian arrivals who came along much the same pathway later on, once all these ingredients entered into the rich civilizational mix. But to stave off this acknowledgment, the Aryan origin theory swings back again so that Hindu nationalists may lay claim to the status of indigeneity in the subcontinent, legitimizing their resistance to foreign (Muslim) invaders. Malhotra and Gautier promote the Out of India theory of Aryan origins, which they also name the Indigenous Aryan theory—thereby staking their claim to the geographic territory while appropriating the language and moral high ground of Indigenous sovereignty claims elsewhere in the world. In fact, Hindutva has often tried to appropriate a variety of previously existing local spiritual and cultural practices. A major ambition of the Vanvasi Kalyan Kendra (and note that the term *vanvasi* connotes simply forest dwellers, as opposed to *adivasi*, which connotes *original* dwellers) is to proselytize among tribal communities, inculcating Hindutva ideology through education and development projects while calling them to return home (*ghar vapsi*) to the Hindu fold. In this way, Hindutva identifies itself with Adivasi populations while incorporating and in the process Sanskritizing Adivasi culture, traditions, holidays, and ritual practices.

Actually, the term "*völkisch*," not Indigenous, is a far more apt analogue for Hindutva's far-right ethnonationalism. Their claims to territorial exclusivity, expelling or exterminating those who don't fit into the vision ("*Pakistan ya qabristan*"), are equivalent to the blood-and-soil claims of white nationalists, not to interrelational, place-based, Indigenous (non-state) sovereignty claims. Like anti-immigrant rhetoric in the US, it is simultaneously an erasure of prior Indigenous inhabitants and an appropriation of the claim to sovereignty by right of prior inhabitancy.

As Noorani frames it, the modern Indian national ideal was actually expressing something quite different: *not* based on presumption of primordial origin or purity, but on a trope of in-gathering, absorption, inclusion, incorporation. He writes, "The great poet Raghupati Sahay alias Firaq Gorakhpuri summed up our ethos beautifully in a single couplet: 'Sar zamin-e-Hind par aqwame-e-alam ke Firaq / kafile aate rahe aur Hindustan banta gaya' [On the soil of Hindustan, O Firaq / Caravans from all over the world kept coming, / And so was Hindustan built]."[95] Azad spoke similarly to Congress in 1940: As a proud Muslim, he said, "I am [also] proud of being an Indian. . . . I am an essential element which has gone to build India, I can never surrender this claim. It was India's historic destiny that many human races and cultures and religions should flow to her, finding a home in her hospitable soil, and that many a caravan should find rest here. Even before the dawn of history, these caravans trekked into India and wave after wave of newcomers followed. This vast and fertile land gave welcome to all and took them to her bosom."[96]

As an alternative to xenophobic or nativist nationalism, this is an alluring vision, and a worthy social principle.[97] But it also illustrates how South Asian engagement with Indigenous issues can never coincide in a simple way with the history of its national liberation movement against British imperialism, including its left and antifascist aspects. Terms such as "Indigenous" or "autochthonous" could be used in a more granular way, for specific regions or groups, but not for the subcontinent-sized nation as a whole.

Today, the struggles of Adivasi peoples facing land expropriation, intensive resource extraction, and incursion into their lifeways are among the most powerful popular resistance movements in recent decades; the military and administrative domination they experienced under the British has continued and even intensified under the independent Indian state, in the name of development. Ultimately, even more benign nation-states are still nation-states. Instituting a new nation-state is not the same as decolonization, when it functions to hijack rather than dismantle colonial control structures and resource extraction methods.

Environmentalism

Despite its dedication to a neoliberal development agenda, Hindutva also piggybacks on environmental rhetoric to put a left-liberal green spin on religious traits such as vegetarianism—as if the brutal murders of Muslim buffalo traders or Dalit leatherworkers in the name of cow protection were acts of environmental protection and not of ethnonationalist bigotry. It is also true that many people seek to connect their spiritual values, ethics, and cosmologies to their concern for ecological sustainability, environmental justice, and social justice. Hindutva is an opportunistic colonizer of these impulses too.[98]

For example, Murali Balaji describes a conference at Yale in 2019 on Hindu Earth Ethics and Climate Action, with the goals of tying "the Hindu scriptural teachings on seeing the divinity in all beings to taking everyday action in fighting climate change and global warming" and placing environmental issues "at the heart of Hinduism."[99] In a 1968 speech, Golwalkar had lauded the sacredness of the land, soil, rivers, lakes, and mountains of Bharat alike as all the object of Hindu worship and pilgrimage.[100] But (aside from the rank hypocrisy of mouthing such sentiments while unleashing such aggressive deforestation, pollution, and extractive industry) this mode of "geopiety" was weaponized to disqualify anyone alleged to bear loyalty to an extraterritorial holy land (e.g., Mecca, Karbala, or Jerusalem) from the right to set foot on the sacred soil while extending the claims of exclusive sacredness to land occupied by other people.

Gopal Patel (one of the conference organizers, executive director of the UK-based Hindu climate action group Bhumi Project) said that the Dharmic faiths (namely Hinduism, Buddhism, and Jainism) have a different intrinsic approach to climate and environmental issues than the Abrahamic religions (Dharmic versus Abrahamic being another Malhotra preoccupation). Is this a decolonial point against Western hegemony? Or a coded dig at Christianity and Islam in the subcontinent? Cunning; it could be taken either way. The Dharmic view, claims Patel, is less anthropocentric and more biocentric: not just human life but "all life has rights." This sounds good on its own, and in other contexts may be applied in a genuinely decolonial manner. But to the brahminical worldview, not even all *human* life has rights: the CAA, NRC, and NPR are attempting to code that distinction into law. So did the Manusmriti, centuries ago. So are they saying that all life has rights *except* the lives of the wrong sort of humans?

HAF was a cosponsor of the conference, although its participants also included supporters of the Sunrise Movement and Green New Deal; surely not all the participants from different cultural, spiritual, and environmental organizations were sanghis, or even the dupes of sanghis. Yet where left and right converge on a topic of shared interest, we should pay attention.

Right-wing environmentalism is not new. There is a persistent strand of green fascist thinking—an antihumanism with genocidal ideation that overlaps with deep ecology, adding the Malthusian nuance that the only humans who are meant to survive amid the restored glory of earth, which they worship according to their (heathen or Vedic) traditions of earth-mother and sun-god, are the Aryan master race. (Devi was a conduit for this.)

Such a convergence can be exploited by the right as either an entry point or a mask. A student of progressive instincts, coming from a second-generation Indian background, may be earnestly seeking a way to act on the issues she cares about (climate change, anticolonialism) while reconnecting to her cultural identity, and reassured to see her own positioning as being on the right side of struggles for justice, not knowing that its rhetoric is being hypocritically deployed to protect Indian structures of oppression and privilege. Observes Balaji, "Some [participants] noted that they became climate change activists before making the connection with their religious identities." Exactly. For our hypothetical student, bait may be the correct way to see it. But there are other paths she could take.

Conclusion: How We Fight (against Fascism in the South Asian Diaspora)

Antifascists in the South Asian diaspora have a unique opportunity to illuminate the historical, ideological, and methodological links between colonialism and fascism. Anticolonial voices from Aimé Césaire or Mulk Raj Anand in the 1930s to J. Sakai or Enaemaehkiw Wakecanapaew Kesiqnaeh today, have pointed out that fascism in the 20th century only brought home to Europe and turned inward the logics, biopolitics, and necropolitics that Europeans had long been perfecting upon racialized "others" in the colonized world. To the colonized, the phenomenology of fascism that so shocked the north were all too familiar. German nationalists had closely studied the techniques of the British in India and US policies of Indigenous genocide on the Western frontier and racial segregation in the South. Both Germans and the British studied Vedic brahminism as a prototype for hierarchical racial systems.

Just as trends shifted in the prevalent theory of Aryan origins (from India to the West; from the far north to India; or from somewhere in the middle to both Europe and India), we might ask the same thing about Aryan*ism* (i.e., about the far-right politics of Aryan-supremacist ethnonationalism). In fact, it's a vicious cycle of mutual influence, a feedback loop enhanced with each turn of the screw. Whatever the trajectory of shared origins, it seems that the flows of Aryan supremacism are always reconverging.

They share an obsession with purity, a fetishization of violence, and the hope pinned on "military regeneration" to "restore lost manhood" (Moonje). In India, Aryanist racial theories developed first in service to colonial policies, then later in service to a national project and the attempted construction of an ethnostate. There are resonances between the ancient "graded hierarchy" (Ambedkar's term) of caste, the elaborate taxonomies applied by the colonial regime to classify and manage the people of India in late 19th century, and the racial grading/ranking system adopted by the SS in the 1930s.

Twenty-first century Hindutva ideology is a toxic brew that includes precolonial brahminism, internalized colonial-era Orientalist tropes, and pathologies of postcolonial nationalism, which distort anticolonial rhetoric. Similarly, Hansen identifies several sources of contemporary illiberal/authoritarian politics in India: that which was already part of the brahminical imaginary; that which elite segments adopted from the colonial state structures, policing, and legislation; and that which was built by postcolonial governments' security apparatus "in the name of protecting national unity and sovereignty."[101]

As South Asians and as Indians, *we* need to take responsibility for that, not shunting all blame for all ills to colonialism. (Perhaps this too is a perversely anticolonial act: to reclaim what they appropriated from us of both evil and good.) For example, it's important to recognize that the British and German scholars did not invent caste oppression. They found it in existing texts and practices that far pre-date European colonialism. What they did is collude with their select "native informants" in making those texts canonical and that worldview synonymous with the sole authoritative definition of Indic civilization.

But the brahminical imaginary was not the whole of Indic civilization. The tradition of contesting the brahminical worldview is as perennial as the brahminical tradition itself. There have always been political and philosophical challenges to it in texts and social practices that have equal claims to age and authenticity. So antifascists in South Asia and its diaspora also need to be caste abolitionists, as well as anticolonialists. And in the US, being a caste abolitionist must go along with opposing, not emulating, white supremacy.

Furthermore, it is important for anticolonialist South Asians—as history demands that we *do* have a strong awareness of anticolonialism—to keep in mind that recognizing colonialism and imperialism in South Asia today must include the actions of the Indian state as well as of the US, internally and internationally. Linking (anti)colonialism to (anti)fascism in the South Asian context means not equating everything Indian (or from the Third World or Global South) with anticolonialism, but recognizing colonial structures and racial supremacist logics wherever they appear, and whoever carries them out. Hindutva's potency highlights the dangers of using nationalism as a vehicle of anticolonial struggle; nationalism is a rival cousin in the family of colonialism and fascism, not an intersectionally emancipatory alternative.

The Sanghis represent only a small slice of the South Asian diaspora, albeit disproportionately outsized in terms of wealth, power, visibility, and influence exercised through funding and lobbying. Counterdemonstrations at any of their events represent a much deeper and broader spectrum of religious minorities, marginalized castes and communities, and ideological dissenters, whose political engagement manifests through involvement in grassroots intersectional feminist, antiracist, anti-imperialist social movements in multiracial coalitions. Groups such as New York's Desis Rising Up and Moving and Taxi Workers Alliance, and the Bay Area, California's Asians for Black Lives, are good examples of this kind of radical praxis and analysis.

Coalitions of progressive organizations such as the Dalit feminist-led Equality Labs, Stand With Kashmir, and South Asia Solidarity Initiative (building on earlier efforts by India Civil Watch, Forum of Inqilabi Leftists, and others) supported Dalit, Kashmiri, and Muslim community members marching in cities across the US in January 2020 on a national day of action intended to launch a "Stop Funding Genocide" campaign. Crowds stood outside Patel brothers in Indian enclaves of cities across the country holding posters in Bengali, Tamil, Hindi, English, and Assamese against CAA, NPR, and NRC.[102] Some have called for a Boycott, Divestment, Sanctions (BDS)–style boycott targeting diasporic businesses whose owners finance the Sanghi agenda or display Modi iconography in the dense Indian enclaves of New Jersey and New York City, to disrupt their funding flows and challenge their propaganda.[103] Activists in such groups do increasingly use the language of fascism in relation to Hindutva, although many others, especially within the subcontinent, object to this language as a Western concept inappropriate to apply (as a form of intellectual colonialism) to the internal specifics of an autonomous context. What I'm arguing for here is precisely to make that link, on the level of organizing in the diaspora, in which international connections, convergences, and parallels are clear to see.

Such efforts show that other solidarities are possible that are simultaneously antifascist and anticolonialist. For example, just as India under BJP leadership has emulated Israel, so on the other side have Kashmiris learned from Palestinians, viewing Palestine through the lens of empathetic solidarity since the 1960s even as the prevalent characteristics of those resistance movements have evolved in tandem. In the 1960s to 1970s, notes Moaswes, the Kashmiri liberation movement aligned itself with other anti-imperialist struggles of the time, such as those in Vietnam, Palestine, and apartheid South Africa, which tended to lean leftist and secular. From the 1980s onward (the US having deliberately armed and funded Islamist jihadi groups as proxies against the Soviet bloc during the Cold War while condoning or supporting the crushing of leftist groups in West, Central, and South Asian countries, and shoring up complicit authoritarian rulers), militant resistance groups became more religious in character, such as Hamas in Palestine and Hizb-ul-Mujaheddin or Lashkar-e-Taiba in Kashmir. The same geographic anti-imperial solidarities remained, but now framed in Islamic-world rather than Third Worldist terms. This increased even more markedly in the 1990s as the rise of Hindu nationalism intensified the communalist framing of the Indian state and conflict in South Asia. Moaswes predicts increasing interdependence between colonial processes in Kashmir and Palestine: "What Israel does in Palestine is likely to occur in Kashmir, and what India does in Kashmir is likely to occur in Palestine. In aiming to dismantle Israeli apartheid, it is essential to observe its global consequences . . . [which] will require a multilateral confrontation." [104]

So we challenge a fascist Indian regime for its colonialism, colorism, caste-ism, and xenophobia; and we fight the elements within our own ambiguously racialized diaspora who aspire to align with those who benefit from the structures of white supremacy, rather than with those who fight against these structures, who choose hierarchy over equality, and exceptionalism over principles of justice. AJA urges savarna Hindus in the diaspora to deepen their awareness of structural injustice, linking their functional understanding of their caste positioning in India to anti-Blackness and white supremacy in the US (instead of fixating on favorable representation for Hindus in academia, media, and the "yogaverse") while taking leadership from Dalitbahujan organizers. [105] Such a wake-up call would require a shift in the way Indian Americans position themselves relative to other racial and ethnic groups in the US, leading to greater solidarity among communities of color and abandonment of "model minority" aspirations to elite inclusion.

Antifascists of all backgrounds need to acknowledge the role that colonialism played in the development of Aryan racial theories through practical experiments in the laboratory of colonial India. We need to understand how modern racial theories were forged in the institutionalization of empire and then reapplied in Europe in the form of fascism.[106]

South Asian antifascists need to attack all components of this combustible combination. We need to carry on the *tradition* of fighting the brahminist imaginary inside the subcontinent, our own domestic fascism and racism; and, in diaspora, we need to link ourselves to other antifascist, antiracist, and anti-imperialist struggles, placing ourselves in solidarity with those who fight it and not those who perpetuate it. To weave that network of resistance, we need to understand historically the kinship between fascism and colonialism as logically consistent racialist systems.

Liza Featherstone observes, "Americans, even on the Left, tend to be clueless about foreign countries, but the rising far right thinks globally."[107] AJA spokespeople point out that ethnonationalist authoritarians in many countries are forging a global fascist network "whether it's Trump, [Jair] Bolsonaro, or Netanyahu," or, of course, Modi. Of course, the threat that is even more deeply concerning is not these individual strongmen but the magnitude of popular support for the racism, misogyny, violence, and bigotry they represent. The far-right forces of the world do not hesitate to recognize, embolden, and strengthen one another; so too should the forces opposing them recognize our resonances and relationships. If Western antifascists want to defeat fascism at the global level, they would do well to support their South Asian comrades against Hindutva—the other Aryan supremacy.

How Far-Right Fantasies about Refugees Became Mainstream in Greece

Patrick Strickland

{*Names marked with an asterisk (*) have been changed for safety concerns.*
—Patrick Strickland}

It was February 2020, and clusters of asylum seekers trudged along the grassy shoulder of the road. There was no sidewalk on either side, only a path worn bald by foot traffic. Women carried bags full of groceries as they walked together, men smoked cigarettes and fiddled with their phones, and a few children chased after one another. The closer we got to the refugee camp, the more olive trees climbed up from the earth. The trees hunched forward like dismembered scarecrows in the orchards unfurling on the outskirts of the village; their limbs had been severed as all winter long the camp residents had hacked branches off the trees for firewood. As we turned around the bend, a half-painted façade of a building appeared: an aluminum factory that was later turned into a waste processing plant. The plant eventually closed down and, in 2016, Greek authorities refashioned the site into the refugee camp known as Vial.

I was in the middle row, seated behind the driver's seat. Local humanitarian Antonis Vorrias manned the aging van, a Volkswagen Transporter with mud spattered across its flanks and a kayak fastened to its roof. Vorrias floored it, and we rattled past Greek *tavernas* and staggering stone farm homes, down the dizzying, four-mile path from his home in Chios Island's namesake town to Chalkio, a village home to a few hundred Greeks and nearly five thousand asylum seekers. Gray knots of clouds spangled the frigid February afternoon.

Next to me in the van's middle row sat a colleague, photographer Nick Paleologos, and on the bench behind us was Nadir Zitaway, a Palestinian refugee from Syria. Another humanitarian volunteer from Spain rode up front, switching the radio station every few moments. "Antonis," shouted a voice from the line of asylum seekers that had formed outside Vial. "How are you?"

"Hi," Vorrias said. "How are you?"

"Hello, my friend," said another.

"Hello, hello," Vorrias replied, waving out of the window with his left hand and navigating the van with his right.

The van quivered to a halt not far from the entry of Vial. Knots of gray clouds bobbed above, and a group of police officers stood posted in front of the camp. Ribbons of barbwire crowned the fence tracing the camp's perimeter. Containers-turned-residences were organized in tight columns beyond the chain links. Shanties and tents spilled across the olive groves surrounding the camp. The smell of burned wood and seared plastic filled the humid air.

As we slipped out of the van, a coterie of children—between five and eight years of age, I guessed—hurtled toward us, one so fast that they tumbled facedown onto the earth. His face was contorted in pain but, within a few moments, laughter drowned out his sobs. "Ali Baba," the children screamed, calling Vorrias by the nickname he earned from his apparent resemblance to the protagonist of "Ali Baba and the Forty Thieves," the folk tale in *One Thousand and One Nights*.

Fifty-two-year-old Vorrias's silver hair frames his face, dangling to his shoulders. When his twin brother accompanies him to Vial, the children shout, "Two Ali Babas!"

Vorrias started earning nicknames after the refugee crisis hit Greece nearly five years earlier. At the time, the refugees and migrants he met in the now-shuttered Dipethe and Souda camps called him "The Pirate"—a moniker that alluded to his appearance as much as his presence on the sea. Only a year before the crisis started sending waves of refugee boats to the Greek islands, he founded a volunteer humanitarian group that, among other activities, searched for and rescued people who'd gotten lost in caves on Chios. Once the boats started washing up on the island's pebble-studded shores in 2015, he would hop on a wave runner and push out into the crashing water, yank people from sinking dinghies, and shuttle them to dry land.

Vorrias made friends with the asylum seekers populating the camps on Chios, but on an island where voters skew right, his humanitarian activities didn't win him much favor among locals. When the European Union (EU) and Turkey reached a deal in March 2016, the Greek government banned asylum seekers from leaving the islands until their applications were processed. With new arrivals stuck in limbo on Chios, far-right attacks started to mount: threats were issued, firebombs thrown, tents burned, stones hurled, and refugees beaten. A small but vocal group of far-right attackers targeted refugees, humanitarians, solidarity activists, and reporters. One day in April 2016, someone stopped Antonis on the street. "You're on the list," the man told him, "and you'll get what's coming to you sometime soon."

That day in early February, Vorrias walked through Vial, chatting with asylum seekers. A small band of children tailed him, chanting, "Ali Baba! Ali Baba!"

A few hours away on Lesbos, the island housing more than 20,000 refugees in the Moria camp, violence swelled.[1] The week before I met Vorrias, riot police showered protesting refugees with tear gas and fired a staccato of flash-bang grenades. Afterward, seven far-right assailants were arrested for intimidating asylum seekers with sticks and other makeshift weapons. Sitting on his couch the next day, Vorrias explained that Chios had yet to see the same magnitude of violence the island endured in 2016. "Right now, things are calm here, but you never know if things are going to turn out how they were in 2016," he said, referring to the far-right unrest on the island nearly four years earlier.

Vorrias recently opened his home to a handful of asylum seekers, particularly vulnerable individuals struggling amid the chaos of Vial. Built for fewer than 1,400 people, the camp now held more than 4,700 residents—but more than half lived in hardscrabble structures and shotgun shacks springing up in the fields surrounding Vial.

Zena* was one of those living in Vorrias's apartment. At 29 years of age, she arrived on Chios in November 2019. Fresh from a Damascus, Syria hospital, where she had surgery that removed part of a cancerous tumor in her brain, she returned to her home in Qamishli, Syria in October and found it flattened. Her father told her that her two daughters, 1 and 6 years of age, perished under the Turkish airstrike that destroyed her home. Worse still, her husband had left her. She needed to escape the war and seek better medical treatment in Europe, her father insisted.

Zena grew up fantasizing of visiting Greece, but what she found on Chios didn't line up with her childhood daydreams. As she stood at the entrance of Vial and stared out at the sprawl of tents and shacks, her stomach plunged. Notoriously understaffed and undersupplied, the camp's medical team could not provide the medicine she required for her recovery. She would wait hours in line only to be given an ibuprofen or two. On her own in a tent, she spent her days weathering harassment. "I'm a woman alone," she told the camp administration. She wanted a space inside the camp, where she felt she'd be safer in a container than she would be in a tent in the surrounding field. She asked, "How am I supposed to protect myself?"

"Who told you to come here by yourself?" replied one worker, Zena recalled. The camp staff said they had no openings inside, and she stayed outside Vial for nearly two weeks. "One second in Vial," she says, "feels like a year."

She spent a few days contemplating suicide, but one day when she spotted a humanitarian team from the International Committee of the Red Cross, she felt a sudden urge to inquire about her daughters. After checking, an aid worker informed her that their names weren't on the list of the dead from the period when the airstrike slammed into her home. Her hope swelled. Maybe her children had survived, she thought.

It took a few days to track down her estranged husband but, through inquiring with friends and family, she eventually got her hands on his new phone number. When he picked up, she heard the children's voices in the background. It suddenly dawned on her: Her father, believing it the only way to convince her to leave the war-ravaged country, had lied to her.

Since learning that her children were still alive, Zena changed her mind. She wanted to return to Syria. Vorrias eventually took her in, despite knowing the risk in a community increasingly hostile toward asylum seekers. With the Greek government planning on building closed detention centers, her plan to return to Syria was complicated.[2] "Do you know any other way to go back?" she asked, a question to which I had no answer. She spent days sitting on the couch in Vorrias's living room, not far from the wood stove heater he kept burning all day and night. She wore a beanie to hide her surgical scar.

Before the month ended, locals on Chios and Lesbos revolted against the government's plans to build closed detention centers. Taking to the streets, they clashed with riot police, burned garbage bins, and attempted to block construction crews from reaching the sites earmarked for closed centers.[3] As far as locals saw it, closed detention centers meant the refugees would be become a permanent fixture on the island, although the government insisted to the contrary, and the mobs of locals taking to the streets no longer wanted asylum seekers nearby.

By mid-February 2020, local Greek officials on the Northern Aegean islands that had refugee populations were staging protests they hoped would put pressure on the government.[4]

When the "refugee crisis" first hit Greece in the summer of 2015, hundreds of thousands of people fleeing war and economic devastation passed through the country, most of them bound for Western Europe: Austria, Germany, Sweden, and elsewhere. In March 2016, the EU and Turkey struck up the migration pact that prompted countries across the Balkans to seal their borders.

Still reeling from an economic crisis that would not end until late 2018, Greece became a holding pen for refugees and migrants. Although arrivals slowed down, boats continued to arrive on Greek shores and people continued to traverse the country's land border with Turkey. The refugee camps filled up, the detention centers grew increasingly crowded, and discontent took root among local communities.

During elections in 2012, a fascist party called Golden Dawn clawed its way into parliament, riding a tidal wave of frustration over the country's economic crisis and shifting the blame to the refugees and migrants the party despised. All around the country, Golden Dawn members and like-minded far rightists hunted down and bloodied migrants and political opponents. In January 2013, two Golden Dawn supporters knifed to death Pakistani migrant worker Shahzad Luqman in downtown Athens, Greece. Nine months later, a party member stabbed and killed Pavlos Fyssas, an antifascist rapper, in the Keratsini borough of Piraeus. Between 2012 and 2018, the country saw 988 such attacks, according to the Athens-based Racist Violence Recording Network. Over the years, antifascists had battled Golden Dawn and other far rightists in the streets.[5] They'd rallied in defense of migrants and others in the far right's crosshairs. In some cases, they'd firebombed and otherwise destroyed Golden Dawn's offices.[6] They carved out spaces where Golden Dawn and other fascist militants couldn't safely go.[7]

When the left-wing Syriza party took over the government after soaring in legislative elections in January 2015, Golden Dawn saw its rank in the parliament climb as well. Even while facing charges of operating a criminal organization, Golden Dawn clenched the spot as the third-largest party in the Hellenic Parliament. Attacks on migrants and antifascists slumped for a period but never halted. With the trial against Golden Dawn attackers unconcluded and dragging on, far-right violence was back on the uptick after a few years.[8]

Local frustration with Syriza's refugee policies continued to swell and, in July 2019, the right-wing New Democracy party, itself a virulently anti-immigrant outfit, ousted its left-wing opponent, Syriza. In those same elections, voters booted Golden Dawn from the parliament, but more than half of the neo-Nazi group's former electorate instead cast their ballots for New Democracy, which vowed to ratchet up deportations by the thousands, floated the idea of building a border wall in the Aegean Sea, and started construction on closed detention centers, resisting backlash from locals who opposed the permanence signified by the new facilities. With detention centers filling up again, the right-wing government had successfully co-opted the antirefugee sentiment once peddled by Golden Dawn.

One Sunday afternoon, in late February 2020, I drove to Amygdaleza, a migrant detention center on the outskirts of the Greek capital. I parked in a muddy lot across the street and approached the entrance with a fellow reporter and Arash Hampay, an Iranian who became a refugee rights advocate after receiving asylum in Greece.

Seven miles from central Athens, Amygdaleza sits on a slope in Acharnes, a working-class suburb overlooked by the snow-capped peaks of Mount Parintha. In April 2012, at the height of Greece's crippling economic crisis, the government opened Amygdaleza as the country's first migrant detention center.[9] Locals initially protested the center, but at a time when factories in the area were laying off thousands, the government insisted that the facility would create jobs, buoy the local economy, and enable authorities to clamp down on crime and undocumented migration. Throughout the years that followed, hunger strikes, protests against the overcrowded living conditions, and suicide attempts were a constant reality inside the facility's walls. Rights groups, migrant advocates, and activists have consistently called for its closure.

We joined a queue of a few dozen people in front of the sprawling compound. A gust of wind swept past the entrance, carrying errant items of rubbish. A woman sat on a curb; on her lap was a crying child swaddled in blankets. A man shouted into the receiver of his phone, cursing in Arabic. Many of them held bags filled with clothes and canned foods. Most of the people waiting there were refugees and migrant workers themselves, hoping to visit less-fortunate loved ones inside. A few nervously puffed cigarettes. Everyone clutched their residency documents.

Behind the latched steel gate stood a Greek police officer, tall, slack faced, and in his early 40s. Posted atop a nearby watch tower, another police officer gripped a rifle and periodically peered down at the small crowd through sunglasses. Menacing coils of barbwire crowned the chain-link fences and cadaver-gray walls surrounding the detention center. Every 20 minutes or so, a police van—navy blue, rickety, and weather-worn—hauled up to the other side of the gate. A group of visitors spilled out of its rear door and the next batch of visitors piled in.

The police officer manning the gate took his time inspecting everyone's documents and passports before allowing them to enter for a visit.

In front of me, a Pakistani migrant worker in his mid-20s spoke neither Greek nor English, and he struggled to communicate with the officer. He handed over a sheaf of papers and the police officer shot him a shifty look. The top sheet appeared to be an email from the migration ministry: a document the migrant worker believed confirmed his legal status in the country. Original documents only, the police officer barked. The Pakistani man fumbled through his papers, tried to offer an explanation in clipped sentence, but the police officer grew impatient. "My friend, I am a policeman," he said. He shoved the papers back into the visitor's chest and dismissed him with a quick wave of his hand. "Go."

My turn came and I handed over my US passport. A puzzled expression spread across his face, but he waved me through when he found my entry stamp. He did not ask if I was a journalist, how I knew someone inside Amygdaleza, or why I was there. I slid onto the frigid steel bench in the back of the police van, joining a handful of men who entered before me, some chattering in Punjabi. When the van reached capacity—nine passengers, everyone's hands folded in their laps and knees touching one another's—the officer appeared at the backdoor. "Numbers?" he said, referring to the identification numbers of the detainees we were visiting. He jotted the numbers in his notepad, stared hard at the page for a moment, and then slammed the door with a thud. The engine grumbled and we set off. I peeked through little holes spangling the metal casing fastened to the back window: egg-white administrative buildings, cracked cement walls, and rolls of concertina wire whizzed past.

The van shivered over potholes and we bounced into each other. The drive braked to a stop, the backdoor swung open, and we all climbed out onto the gravel walkway. We formed a line outside a container, inside which we would visit the detainees. Beyond a chain-link fence, a trio of men cast glances our way. They listened to a radio blasting rap music. "They're crazy," a guard said. She was in her mid-20s and had a tight smile framed by tufts of brown hair that spilled from beneath her police cap.

"Yeah, well," said another guard, a man with a black balaclava pulled halfway up his face. "Arabs."

I couldn't tell what language the men were speaking, but I knew it was not Arabic. I assumed the police officer was using "Arabs" as a blanket term for everyone locked away in Amygdaleza. He rubbed the chill from his hands and turned to me. "Inside," he ordered.

In the container, two hard-faced guards barked commands as we entered. Visitors slid their bags across the chest-high inspection table and the guards, scowling, rifled through them. They sniffed inside packets of cigarettes, ostensibly looking for drugs—they found none. They did find objectionable items, however: certain liquids and oils, which they shoved back across the table. "Not allowed," they said.

Along with the other visitors, we sidled up in front of four small holes in a glass panel that separated us from the detainees. Hussein* appeared at the doorway opposite the panel. He waited until an officer motioned for him to approach the glass. He wore a tired gray sweatshirt with the hood pulled up on his head and a smattering of teenage acne flecked his cheeks. He was tall enough that he had to bend down to speak through the holes in the glass panel. He told us that, six days earlier, police officers stopped him in Exarchia, a neighborhood home to many refugees and migrants in Athens and known for the anarchist and antifascist groups that called it home. When he couldn't produce his residency documents, the police led him to a paddy wagon and carted him off to a nearby police station. He found himself in Amygdaleza later that night, sharing a container with five Afghans.

We asked how conditions were inside.

"Terrible," he said.

Cockroaches skittered across the floor and along the walls all day and night, he explained. Next to us, a visitor and a detainee spoke in Arabic, both of their faces near the glass. The visitor said the cops had inspected each individual cigarette the visitor brought for his friend. Together they laughed the sort of pitiful chuckle you let out when you pity someone for being dim.

Hussein went on telling us about life in Amygdaleza—"It is very bad," he said—but the roar of simultaneous conversations between visitors and detainees left us straining to hear his words through the small punctures in the glass. Every few moments, the guards yelled at someone about using their cell phones, which visitors are barred from using inside the facility. Down the row of visitors, one man lifted his cell phone up to the glass, maybe to show his friend on the other side a photograph. "That's it," a guard said. "Close your phone." He paused a moment and then his face glazed red. He threw his arms in a sudden fit, waving visitors out of the container. "It's over. Finished."

——

The next day, a disturbing video emerged on social media: A detainee reportedly setting ablaze his container to protest the squalid living conditions in Amygdaleza. I messaged Hussein on the encrypted chat app WhatsApp but received no reply. I called and texted with no luck. A week grumbled past. Whether his phone was dead, broken, or confiscated, I could not say. Whether he had been deported, shipped back to an island, or moved to another mainland facility, it was impossible to know with any certainty.

I contacted another detainee in Amygdaleza, a Syrian refugee called Noah. Along with his brother Muhammad, he fled Idlib under barrel bombs and airstrikes. The brothers were detained upon arrival on Kos Island in August 2019. Authorities eventually transferred them to Amygdaleza. After three months there, neither had a lawyer nor knew what to expect. They wore the same shirts and pants they wore when they arrived half a year earlier. "In Greece, there is no such thing as law," Noah told me via WhatsApp.

I asked about the cockroaches Hussein had mentioned, whether Noah's container had similar infestations.

"Yes," he said, matter-of-factly.

"Is it true the food arrives moldy?" I said, recalling a complaint I'd heard in several camps on the islands and the mainland.

"Not always . . . just sometimes," said Noah. "But the food is not good or healthy."

"It's undercooked?"

"Correct," he said. He waited a few moments to send another message, and then: "And the bathrooms are not clean."

"Are the toilets broken?" I asked. During the dozens of times I visited refugee camps in Greece throughout the last four and a half years, I had never seen a facility where at least some of the toilets hadn't fallen into disrepair.

"See for yourself." He sent me photographs of the bathrooms, layers of filth accumulated on the toilets and showers. He sent a short video clip, just 13 seconds, of him walking through the container in which he slept. He was one of 18 people in the container, he said, and the video revealed several bunk beds and a few mattresses on the floor. Blankets were strung up on clotheslines, marking off patches of personal space in the container.

The pressure of surviving in overcrowded spaces, the indignities the guards heaped upon the detainees each day, and the lack of clarity about their futures led a group of Syrians and Palestinians in Amygdaleza to plan a hunger strike for better living conditions. (If the hunger strike did happen, news of it never made it outside the detention center.) "They treat us like animals," he said.

But the hunger strike never came. On February 26th, Greek authorities recorded the country's first case of coronavirus disease 2019 (COVID-19), the coronavirus that went on to kill millions around the world.[10] After hearing the news of the virus, Noah told me that he worried the pandemic would eventually lash its way into the Greek refugee camps and detention centers. A few days later, he went dark. I called and texted, but as with Hussein, Noah's phone went straight to voicemail.

———

Several weeks passed before I heard back from Hussein and Noah. Greek authorities had transferred Hussein to a closed detention center inside the Moria camp on Lesbos Island, and Noah and his brother were shipped back to the refugee camp on Kos Island.

By late February 2020, more than 13,000 refugees and migrants had gathered on the Greek–Turkish border.[11] Hoping to pressure the EU into striking up a new migration pact, the Turkish government had ordered border guards to stand down and bused refugees and migrants from across the country to the frontier.[12] Antirefugee protests grew around Greece.[13] On the land border, armed vigilantes hunted for people who crossed into Greece irregularly while far-right assailants attacked asylum seekers, journalists, and humanitarians on several Greek islands.[14] Refugee social centers were burned down, press workers were mobbed and beaten, and nonprofit employees found their vehicles smashed up.[15] On Lesbos, some nonprofit groups packed up and abandoned the island. By early March, the situation was spiraling out of control and appeared poised only to worsen.

Two weeks into March, however, another threat emerged. As the COVID-19 pandemic fanned out across the country and around the world, the Greek government announced a partial shutdown that started on March 14th.[16] Gyms, restaurants, bars, and cafés shuttered, and authorities barred large gatherings, such as concerts and festivals. Over the weeks that followed, the lockdown was extended to include additional restrictions on travel and movement. The government also required everyone moving around in public to carry a passport or identification card, a rule that left undocumented people with few options. In the camps, refugees now faced new restrictions on movement, but the social distancing promoted by the Greek government and watchdogs was not an option.[17]

As the COVID-19 tally soared, human rights organizations, aid agencies, and advocacy groups called on the Greek government to remove asylum seekers from the packed camps and relocate them to safer and more sanitary facilities. Those calls went unanswered, and the Greek government instead placed tight restrictions on asylum seekers in the camps. Unable to travel to the Greek islands, I reached out to Mohsen, a 38-year-old Iranian marooned in the Moria camp. He told me that the camp had few doctors and scarce supplies, and that the food was unsanitary. "There are a lot of people in the [fields]," he said of the overcrowding.[18] "They don't have anything to keep them warm [or] clean, and there's no electricity,"

For years, antifascists and refugee solidarity activists had fought the far right around Greece, squaring off with the neo-Nazi Golden Dawn movement and battling antirefugee vigilantes in the streets of cities around the country.[19] But the far-right backlash in early 2020 had been widespread and intense, and New Democracy controlled the government and all its forces.

In late March, a United Nations High Commissioner for Refugees (UNHCR) spokesperson, Boris Cheshirkov, told me that it was only a matter of time before the corona virus hit the country's refugee population. "So far there have been no cases of the novel coronavirus among refugees and asylum seekers in Greece," he said. "But thousands of refugees and asylum seekers in Greece—including many who are older and vulnerable—are in locations where health services are overstretched," he continued.

At the time, more than 35,000 asylum seekers were living on five Aegean islands in camps designed to accommodate an estimated 4,500 people. "UNHCR has repeatedly alerted about the need to urgently improve living conditions [in the camps]," Cheshirkov added. "Hygiene and sanitation, and access to health services are priority areas, but the overcrowding has been a serious concern for months."

A week after I spoke with Cheshirkov, on March 31st, 2020, the Greek government confirmed the first COVID-19 case in one of the country's refugee camps. In Ritsona, a camp located an hour's drive north of Athens, a woman had tested positive. Within a few days, the number of confirmed cases in the camp climbed to 20.[20] Three weeks later, 150 residents in a refugee facility in Kranidi tested positive for COVID-19.[21] (How many refugees and migrants would eventually catch COVID-19 is impossible to know, but when vaccines finally became available, the government wasn't shy in revealing that residents of the crowded camps were not among their top priorities.[22])

All around Athens, on daily trips to the pharmacy or the grocery store that month, I would pass checkpoints manned by Greek police officers. The officers would check pedestrians' documents as they navigated the city and, more often than not, they would target migrants and refugees for stops. With the New Democracy government quietly working to implement migration policies that aligned with Europe's most virulently far-right movements, it was not hard to imagine a future in which migrants and other newcomers faced long-term limitations on movement.

Meanwhile, the government set its sights on squats in Athens and beyond, which had long been a staple of the antifascist and refugee solidarity movements in Greece.[23] Squats were cleared. Refugees were rounded up. Antifascists and anarchists fought back as best as they could, but the lockdown kept many inside and years of pressure had no doubt left them in a tough position.[24]

By early May 2020, the Greek government began reopening the country to everyone except those in the refugee camps.[25] The daily tally of new COVID-19 cases had slumped, and the reopening was slated to take place in phases. In the camps, however, Greek authorities were tightening the restrictions on asylum seekers. By the end of 2021, the government erected a handful of closed refugee centers—effectively jails—that would go in the place of the shuttered open camps.[26] The number of refugees and migrants reaching Greek shores plummeted.[27] Greek authorities ramped up pushbacks and violence aimed at preventing refugees from reaching the country in the first place.[28] Meanwhile, seizing the opportunity to exploit pandemic-related restrictions, the government used COVID-19 as a pretext to clamp down on protests—with tear gas and water cannons.[29]

The last time I heard from Noah, in spring 2020, he was still in a camp on Kos Island. He had little hope left. COVID-19 would likely continue ravaging the refugee community long after Greece's lockdown eventually ended, and I asked him how conditions were there. "It's very bad here," he said. "Very bad."

His response was short. There was little left to say.

Global Neoliberalism, Fascism, and Resistance

Geo Maher

{ *This chapter was originally written as my acceptance speech for the Dallas Smythe Award of the Union for Democratic Communications (UDC), November 2nd, 2019 at California State University, East Bay. It has since been presented, in slightly different forms, at Diablo Valley College and Bard College at Simon's Rock. Thanks to the UDC, all my interlocutors at these events, and the editor of this volume.* }

Our world is on fire, but not only in the most obvious of ways—from California to Australia and the Amazon. In fact, our world has been on fire for nearly a decade, but the past few months and years have really been something else. Puerto Rico, Ecuador, Haiti, West Papua, Hong Kong, Lebanon... and Chile. Chile. Chile. Nearly half a century ago, Chile was *the* laboratory for neoliberalism in a region that would soon become the same, but the experiment failed long ago, and today it seems as if Chileans—straitjacketed by a radically neoliberal legal and economic structure—have finally had enough and have taken to the streets uninterrupted for months, demanding radical change. As one sign held at the demonstrations put it: "the neoliberal model was born in Chile and will die in Chile." We can only hope.

What does neoliberalism have to do with fascism? Everything, as it turns out. As Karl Marx reminds us, people don't walk willingly into capitalism, much less the grueling, treacherous, soot-covered, and blood-soaked world of early British capitalism. Five hundred years ago, it took the enclosure of formerly common lands followed by the flogging, branding, ear-clipping, and imprisonment of the human by-product of this enclosure—the so-called rogues and vagabonds—it took what Marx collectively deemed "bloody legislation against the expropriated" to "convince" people to become workers and to subject themselves to wage-discipline in the dank, dangerous factories of the dawn of capitalism.[1] As Marx put it: Capitalism does not emerge naturally or gradually, but instead comes into the world "dripping from head to toe, from every pore, with blood and dirt."[2]

People didn't *want* or *choose* capitalism, and so it took brute force to impose what Marx sarcastically called the "'eternal natural laws' of the capitalist mode of production."[3] The fact that we see so many people today handing themselves over to capitalism voluntarily is not proof of the opposite (much less that capitalism reflects some mythical human nature). It simply means that the hegemonic mechanisms, put into place over time to convince people that capitalism is eternal and there is no alternative, have been largely effective. But the increasingly overwhelming *rejection* of capitalism and preference for socialism (or even communism) by young people also shows the limits of this effectiveness, the powerful countervailing tendency of what happens when hegemonic mechanisms are not enough to obscure the real functioning of the economy and society.

This hegemonic breakdown is on full display today in Chile, where the word "neoliberalism" is on the tip of every tongue, but everywhere synonymous with fascism. It was Augusto Pinochet who overthrew the elected socialist Salvador Allende in 1973 and who—in blood and fire—offered his country over to the neoliberal shock doctors known as the Chicago Boys. The formal end of the Pinochet dictatorship has concealed the very real persistence of fascist power and the continuities of Chile's fascist enclosures—in property, in education, in land tenure, and in water rights. This explains the apparent belatedness of the crisis on the streets today, in which the same Chile that helped begin this broad sweep of a half-century history *finally* rejoins it on the other end.

What happened in between? Neoliberalism was imposed across Latin America by force and by fraud, promising economic growth as a metaphorical rising tide that would lift all boats (the less-comical version of "trickle-down economics"). But, as David Harvey has argued, although neoliberalism claimed to be "a *utopian* project to realize a theoretical design for the reorganization of international capitalism," in reality it has always been what he calls "a *political* project to re-establish the conditions for capital accumulation and to restore the power of economic elites."[4] In other words, its "utopian rhetoric mask[ed] a successful project for the restoration of ruling-class power."[5] As long as wealth could be extracted, it really didn't matter how few boats the tide lifted. The result in Latin America was not growth but the opposite—what is called a "lost decade" in which the only thing that grew were the rolls of the impoverished, the unemployed, and the so-called marginals inhabiting the *barrios* and *favelas* swelling to surround the major cities.

But in the lost decade, not all was truly lost: Resistance was born in precisely those spaces abandoned by capital and the state, with Latin America becoming a new kind of laboratory for a new kind of world.[6] Where the neoliberal state withdrew, communities began to organize themselves collectively and often through directly democratic mechanisms. In Bolivia, when the state refused to provide water, for example, communities dug wells and created self-managed water systems; in Venezuela, armed collectives pushed out narcotraffickers and police as communities provided their own security, water, garbage pickup, and recreation activities for the youth. And when the state and private capital returned to stake their claim over these territories—notably with Bechtel Corporation's attempt to privatize Bolivian water in 2000—this evasive Gramscian war of position became a frontal war of maneuver. Explosive resistance and the repressive "whip of the counter-revolution" entered into a mutually reinforcing spiral that emboldened movements, brought down governments across the continent, and eventually propelled leftist leaders into state power.[7]

But, over time, against the accomplishments and encouraged by the limitations of what are called the "Pink Tide" governments,[8] a new wave of covert and overt fascism has emerged—through elections (in Colombia and Argentina) but also through soft and hard coups, some feigning constitutional legitimacy (in Paraguay and Brazil) and some hardly even bothering (notably, in Honduras and, more recently, Bolivia). Some, such as Brazil's Jair Bolsonaro—elected only after a soft coup and with his main contender Luiz Inácio Lula da Silva jailed on bogus charges—explicitly endorse the fascist model of dictatorships past. But more often, such explicit fascism has spread by more subterranean means, in new far-right networks expanding across the region whose sole task is the destruction by force of leftist alternatives in Venezuela, Bolivia, Colombia, and elsewhere. But if the historical pendulum seems to be pressing its full weight against us today, this rightward swing was not inevitable and is not invincible. It stands on the weakest of foundations, governing a crisis it cannot resolve, feet of clay more evidently weak and crumbling by the day, as the electoral defeat of right-winger Mauricio Macri in Argentina demonstrates.

Why all this talk of Latin America? Because these are the dynamics governing *our* world and, although we like to think that we are on the vanguard of historical dynamics, in many senses we are closer to the tail. This is because neoliberalism didn't really land in the global core until nearly a decade later, and always in a slightly mitigated form, with its most fascist elements more concealed. This fascism was always there, of course: Who could forget that, when Pinochet was detained in the UK on the orders of a Spanish judge, Margaret Thatcher celebrated his eventual release by sending the dictator a decorative silver plate symbolizing the defeat of the Spanish Armada? "I hope you will appreciate and enjoy the symbolism!" said one fascist to another. The irony is only doubled when we realize that Spain, like Chile, remains institutionally fascist to this very day; but, as is often the case, the irony is only apparent. Chile's so-called democratic transition is a near carbon copy of Spain's, which, instead of seeking actual justice, simply buried its fascism just under the surface (e.g., former dictator Francisco Franco's rotting corpse, which was only recently exhumed and moved from his fascist shrine at El Escorial).

It is only in the context of this broad historical *Sturm und Drang*, the hegemonic tug-of-war spread across the globe, that we can properly grasp the microdialectics of resurgent fascism and antifascist resistance in the present. This is because today's global fascist renaissance is a *direct* response to the failure of this neoliberal model, to the crisis it has wrought worldwide, to the collapse of the failed marriage between liberal democracy and the so-called capitalist end of history. This model could not deliver globally as it could not deliver decades earlier in Latin America—in part because it was never truly intended to because global neoliberalism was always more myth than model. The invisible hand was never invisible, the free market never free.

The liberal or neoliberal center is collapsing today, whether we are referring to the Clintonite neoliberalism of welfare reform, mass incarceration, and North American Free Trade Agreement (NAFTA), or to the equally spectacular disintegration of the European Union. In the vacuum created by the collapse of liberalism, the world polarizes dramatically, opening up the possibility of radical options on the right as on the left. Liberalism cannot respond to the crisis for reasons that are both economic and political. Economically, liberalism claims to stand for universal equality, but at the cost of the absolute detachment of the social (i.e., the economic realm) from the political, at least when it comes to popular demands for social equality. This equality may be a mile wide, but it's no more than an inch deep, limited to the formality of voting every four years, and so liberalism becomes, in Antonio Gramsci's terms, "saturated," unable to fulfill its promise.[9]

On the political level, liberalism refuses to defend itself and can only defend the rights of those who would see it destroyed. This chronically suicidal liberalism is once again trying to off itself today by defending the illiberal right and legitimizing the same Donald Trump it had once denounced as fascist. Again, Gramsci, for whom the separation of powers characteristic of liberal democracy is an attempt to "crystallize permanently a particular stage of development," resonates today vis-à-vis the electoral college and the US Senate as apparently insurmountable barriers to substantive change.[10] But in a polarized, populist context, many liberals can see only danger and cling desperately to institutions that have never served the people. If it's fascism we are up against, the US Supreme Court won't save us and the Federal Bureau of Investigation (FBI) sure as hell won't either. And when it comes to spectacular failure to grasp the inescapable nature of our moment, Hillary Clinton stands out: running a traditional and pragmatic campaign in a time of populist polarization. With Joe Biden, the Democratic Party has opted to watch the sequel.

By contrast, populisms on the right and left have sought to respond directly to the nature of the moment, but the two could not be more dissimilar. Confronted with the real crisis of late-stage neoliberal capitalism, right-wing populism offers cynical lies and scapegoats: what Mike Davis called "Trump's reindustrialization cargo cult"—blaming migrants and Muslims for the ills of capitalism while promising the magical return of jobs that never materialize.[11] But, in some ways, the fact that anyone actually believes that a billionaire cares about the poor is perhaps the truest testament to the profound *desire* among many for an alternative. Left-wing populism, by contrast, offers a different path out of the crisis: providing true explanations of economic interests and forces, naming and blaming real rather than imagined enemies, and mobilizing "the people" toward a more ambitious socialist and even communist project.

But when things fall apart, people build their populism with the materials at hand, which is why left-wing and radical populism tends to emerge in the Global South, where material conditions and histories of struggle allow the left to better control populist narratives, whereas the populisms of the Global North tend toward the right. This is true of the US and Western Europe's antimigrant panic, but also, crucially, the crisis-ridden frontlines of Eastern Europe, broken by post-Soviet shock therapy but provided no alternative to or protection from the ravages of global capital; as a consequence, the open resort to fascism is frighteningly mainstream. As should be clear by now, Trump isn't the cause of a global fascist resurgence that both precedes and exceeds him, but he did nevertheless have his finger on the global pulse, entering seamlessly into global fascist feedback loop as both an effect and as a powerful cause in his own right.

When it comes to the failures of liberalism, the creeping fascist threat, and so many other things, it gives me no great pleasure to say today that *we were right*. We were right that Trump might be able to harness and ride white resentment to an unexpected electoral victory in 2016, and that in a populist moment mainstream political polling is prone to spectacular failure because its assumptions don't hold. We were right that, despite stoking political panic about Trump's fascism, the Democratic Party would immediately normalize him as a legitimate leader—in Clinton's words, we should give him "a chance to govern." We were right when we insisted that the question was not so much Trump's own fascistic tendencies, but the emboldening of those fascist movements that saw his election as their time to shine and crawled out of the gutter and into the mainstream through what I call a "Trojan Horse strategy"—sanitizing their ideas to make them more palatable by downplaying overt references to Nazism and privileging the language of white victimhood over white supremacy.

We were right when, during the brief interregnum between Trump's election and inauguration, I came under a sustained attack from the full spectrum of the white supremacist right—an outrage campaign fed directly from sources such as the antisemitic and neo-Nazi *The Daily Stormer* and *Fox News*. We were right when we insisted that this was not an isolated case, but a systematic offensive carried out by a well-oiled machine. We were right when we said that there would be more cases, and there were many: Keeanga-Yamahtta Taylor, Tommy Curry, Johnny Eric Williams, and many, many more, mostly Black and people of color faculty but almost uniformly sharing an antiracist politics that was intolerable for the right. We were right when we argued that the fascist right and the mainstream right were connected by a clandestine conveyor belt consisting of sites such as Breitbart News Network and staffed by the likes of Milo Yiannopoulos and Steve Bannon—relationships later confirmed by a *BuzzFeed News* exposé.[12]

We were right, and here there is absolutely no reason for celebration, when we argued that the threat of alt-right neofascism was *real* and that the danger it posed was *existential*: tragically, mass shootings in Pittsburgh, Pennsylvania, Christchurch, New Zealand, and El Paso, Texas, have only proven just how right we were. It gives me no pleasure to have been right about such things. But it does give me some pleasure to emphasize that we were also right about other things; namely, how to fight back—and the imperative to fight white supremacy and fascism directly and head-on. We got together, forming the Campus Antifascist Network (CAN), disseminating information, and preparing for quicker and more effective responses to the inevitable repetition of the outrage script against leftist professors and students.[13] We fought battles of ideas and battles in the streets with tactics ranging from Nazi punching to infiltration, from doxing to deplatforming. And although some of us paid a disproportionate price, we won some crucial victories and, most importantly, we began to push back and stem the fascist tide on campus and beyond.

We were right about what I call the *dialectics* of Nazi punching. I'll spare you all the Georg Wilhelm Friedrich Hegel today, the role of conflict and oppositional struggle in setting into motion a spiraling process of developing and deepening self-consciousness—a direct antidote to liberal views on social change.[14] I'll simply say that, whereas many attempted to frame the glorious sucker-punching of white nationalist Richard Spencer as an isolated act devoid of social content, an unnecessarily provocative distraction from real politics, what really unfolded was exactly the opposite: a profound national debate from *The New York Times* to *Teen Vogue* in which many wondered aloud whether it's okay to punch Nazis (after all, many of our grandparents *killed* Nazis), but more importantly, whether fascism and white supremacy are simply ideas like any others to be tolerated and respectfully debated among polite society, essential commodities in the "marketplace of ideas." We said no, and we were right.

We were right that, despite the condescending scolding of a fake-woke left-liberalism, that there is in fact *no* trade-off and *no* contradiction between fighting the overt and in-your-face white supremacy of Identity Evropa, the Proud Boys, and Trump and fighting the long-term structures of white supremacy—policing, prisons, and the border—in which Democrats are equally complicit if not more so than their Republican counterparts. We were right when we insisted that keeping Nazis off the streets was not a distraction from the so-called real work, when we pointed out that *the same people* doing one were also consistently doing the other, and, most fundamentally, that crushing fascist organizing was key to preventing the white supremacist ideas from infiltrating the mainstream through the alt-right Trojan Horse, and that doing so helped open up radical new possibilities on the left as well. Spencer himself put things as clearly as possible when he admitted that "antifa is winning" and that street resistance had made public alt-right organizing nearly impossible, cutting off at the knees its mainstreaming strategy.

According to Natasha Lennard, whereas the liberal response—debating fascism to somehow prove it wrong—leads to a "deteriorating stalemate" that facilitates the expansion of fascist forces, "the antifa strategy aims to create material, felt consequences for neo-Nazi, white supremacist groups, and those who would organize with them."[15] As antifa tactics have proven effective and the very real fascist threat has been demonstrated by mass murder, many previously loud voices have gone strangely silent: those who had insisted that the fascist threat was exaggerated, that antifascists are glorified live action role players, those who echoed fabricated right-wing talking points about antifa violence, and who argued—most perversely—that resisting and shutting down fascism actually encourages its growth;

the many more who insisted that we should dialogue, debate, and defeat fascists on the battleground of ideas—a view that conspicuously neglects the fact that people don't embrace white supremacy because it makes logical sense, and that it's not about reason but about affect. All these voices have fallen silent as the direct relationship between expanding fascist networks and mass murder have become absolutely undeniable.[16]

But the simultaneity of effective public antifascist resistance and mass violence by fascists also points toward dangerous times ahead. Events such as those of Charlottesville, Virginia were key turning points that instead of "uniting the right" shattered their precarious unity. But as far-right organizations splinter and become disillusioned with Trump, they spin off as free radicals that can be even more dangerous (a repetition of what happened with far-right militia forces in the 1980s under Ronald Reagan, when a disillusioned far right slid from pro- to antisystemic, giving rise to the militia movement).[17] Thus, although we can and should claim victories when battles have been won, the war is far from over, and the coming months and years will be treacherous indeed. We have already seen this clearly enough in massacres in Christchurch and El Paso—both fueled by paranoid theories of white genocide and the so-called Great Replacement—with El Paso and the Pittsburgh synagogue shooting, in particular, showing how Trump's antimigrant panic has dovetailed seamlessly with global white victim narratives. Recent statements by and arrests involving groups such as the Atomwaffen Division and The Base make clear that the most extreme fascist fringes won't be throwing in the towel any time soon.[18]

Similarly, the battle for campuses is far from over, and here the nexus between neoliberalism and fascism is equally undeniable. It is not just any university that is being targeted by the right today, but the neoliberal university, public and private alike, the university that, starved of resources, is suddenly subject to outside forces like never before. Much has been made of the effective privatization of public education in the US (and here Chile is very much in the same boat), skyrocketing of once minimal tuition and fees, and the political control the ensuing debt exerts over an entire generation. Much has been made of the "adjunctification" of the university, which is not merely an economic question but a political one as well—that is, not simply the poverty wages but the administrative *power* that precarious academic labor makes possible (those adjuncts attacked by the right in recent years don't even need to be *fired*—their contracts are simply not renewed).

But the neoliberalization of the university goes much further than the restructuring of academic labor. It involves the simultaneous withdrawal of public funding and the injection of private funding from corporations, foundations, and individuals alike. The political implications have been severe: on the one hand, right-wing speech has been propped up by private money without even having to justify itself as academically legitimate. Think, for example, of the pseudoscientist Charles Murray's campus tours—fully funded by dark money to spew long-discredited eugenics theories under the guise of academic respectability. And this is not even to mention the many institutes for free market economics, hawkish foreign policy, or so-called American values that have been created on campuses with little to no oversight. The flip side of this, which I know very well, is what I will call the "donor veto." Just as private money has bought hiring lines and invited lectureships, it has simultaneously narrowed the spectrum of acceptable speech and action on campuses. The invisible underside of right-wing outrage campaigns against faculty is the withdrawal—threatened or actual—of millions of dollars from universities that refuse to adequately deal with problematic faculty members or unruly student organizations.

The far-right views campuses as both what we could call "soft targets" in terms of being prime recruiting grounds for disaffected, resentful white men with victimization complexes and of being the breeding grounds for everything they despise—all things Black, brown, queer, and communist—which makes college sound pretty amazing, honestly. But more fundamentally, universities are soft targets for the right because they remain hamstrung by perennial contradictions of so-called free speech and academic freedom. When we shut down the white supremacist right on campus, we are accused of violating principles of free speech, even though the First Amendment literally doesn't apply at private universities (when I was under attack by the right, I could claim no First Amendment defense). Free speech, arguably the most mythical of American myths, is amorphous to the point of utter incoherence and deployed with the utmost selectivity—whereas the right attacks us without regard, liberals insist that we must defend even legally unprotected racist speech to demonstrate adherence to a broader (read: imaginary) principle. And universities and colleges, with their admissions procedures, academic hiring criteria, and curriculum standards—not to mention their increasing resort to privately policed campus borders—would seem one of the strangest possible places to insist that free speech prevails. As we have insisted and must continue to insist: The question is not one of free speech but of access to a privileged *platform*, which is not guaranteed.

As a concept, academic freedom fares little better than free speech, deployed only marginally more often to defend faculty; on this point, we stumble hard on the question of *who* this principle is meant to apply to. Although developed to protect faculty, of course, even academic freedom has been leveraged by the right to defend invited speakers funded by right-wing dark money. And when academic freedom is actually mobilized to defend faculty members, they are most often on the right, as with the case of University of Pennsylvania law professor Amy Wax, who has made a series of increasingly unhinged racist and eugenicist statements *about her own* Black law students, leading those same students to question her ability to teach;[19] in other words, academic freedom for racist faculty to shut down legitimate concerns of the students whose educational rights are undermined by their racism.

Moving forward, we need to be sharper in our analyses and in our organizing both on campus and beyond. We need to understand free speech and academic freedom not as lofty principles but as *material phenomena* that exist only on a specific terrain and are deployed most often in defense of the powerful against the weak. Although this doesn't mean abandoning free speech and academic freedom, it does mean realizing that—as I often say—free speech and academic freedom are *shields*, but we need *swords* to move forward. We need to be clear that there can be no free speech for fascists and no platform for white supremacy. This doesn't mean demanding that that the state or the universities shut down speakers—we are more than happy to do so ourselves, precisely through those direct mobilizations that are only selectively recognized as "free speech." We should demand academic freedom for members of the academic community—but we should be clear that this is about freedom for *all* members equally, all protesters, all student organizers, and particularly those women and people of color notably excluded from academic freedom and threatened by the right. We should insist that there is no academic freedom or speech rights for rich donors, no speech for off-campus racists, no right to intervene in the community and put its members at risk. All this, of course, entails messy debates moving forward but, if we are going to defend academic spaces and communities from fascism and neoliberalism alike, there is simply no alternative.

In a recent article about the many dangers facing the long-belated Chilean Spring, Lili Loofbourow points to both the promise and the perils of inherently unstable signifiers. The presence in the streets of Santiago, Chile of protesters dressed as the Joker, for example, shows how such symbols can be stripped of their reactionary content and fused to mass movements. The same can be said of the pot-banging *cacerolazos* popular today, which have their origins with the anti-Allende right that mobilized economic crisis to install fascist dictatorship. But these processes can also move in reverse, and the point is less about the signifiers themselves than about what it is that they point to in the real world: the fact that moments of crisis such as the present can tip us either right or left. We stand, Loofbourow insists, perilously at the watershed separating the two: "When chaos comes, a lot of spectacles don't work the way you'd expect. . . . This could go wrong at any moment."[20]

Gramsci once wrote something to the effect that, "the old world is dying and the new world struggles to be born. Now is the time of monsters." Although the translation is not exact—the original refers to an "interregnum" marked by "morbid symptoms," not monsters—some mistranslations gain popularity and, in this case, go viral for a reason.[21] After all, there's no denying that such imagery is perfectly suited to the unmitigated monstrosity that was the year 2020, moreover providing a welcome reminder that we need not always be frightened of the monstrous, and that the new world is never born before we ourselves create it.

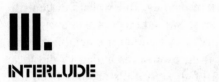

III.

INTERLUDE

Some Names Have Been Changed

Daryle Lamont Jenkins

Today, there isn't much of the New Brunswick, New Jersey left that I enjoyed when I was growing up back in the day. Thirty years of gentrification under the usual guise of "progress" wiped most of that away. They cleared out the projects for new luxury homes and entire neighborhoods have disappeared over the decades from extensions added to the local megahospital replacing them. Much of the city's history has been lost to the wrecking ball, including the clubs and venues where I was a regular, seeing local bands that either went on to fame, such as the Bouncing Souls, or who never did but were still a large part of what made the scene so nice. This was one of the worlds I lived in during the Nineties. I have hours of video footage of bands playing venues like the Court Tavern, the Roxy, the Melody, and Bowl-O-Drome, all shot for public access shows I was producing. But I also have videos from the other world I was in, the one of political activism.

I started getting involved in political advocacy as soon as I left the Air Force and much of that was the beginnings of what I do today, keeping an eye on right-wing hate-mongering that, at that time, was still going relatively unchallenged. My concern for how we were going through life at the time, with all the drama from the far right, prompted me to look to some more unconventional circles for solutions. That search was encouraged by the unconventional music circles I was a part of, and it always became damned interesting when those two worlds—music and activism—collided.

After about a decade or so living in Philadelphia, Pennsylvania, I moved back to New Brunswick, a town nicknamed "Hub City" because of how important a hub it was for colonial travelers and traders. I had missed my home. It was here that I started my organization One People's Project. I am not in the music scene as much these days, but my political world is thriving. And now you have a few neo-Nazis posting up stickers and flyers in town every now and again, which was something we didn't see in the Nineties. Back then, the far right was pretty much relegated to South Jersey. Should they venture too far north, they would get an immediate bullseye on their asses, and there have been many times when someone's steel-toed boot would find their target!

We didn't have a lot of locals involved in those types of politics, although I do remember dropping someone at a local bar because I heard they were tagging signs and buildings with swastikas. I ended up becoming a bouncer there a few weeks later. I guess they liked my work! (Curiously, the tagger eventually moved to New York City [NYC] and got a name for himself in the crust-homeless scene as "LES. Jewels"; when he died in 2013, I had to shake my head at all the tributes and murals that were done in his name.)

See, if I don't care about optics today, I definitely didn't consider them when I was a 20-something punk scenester. Optics are how the public sees you, and it is something that one who regularly engages with the public should be concerned with. Bad optics hurt reputations and one can have doors shut because of them. You see people engaged in political advocacy relying on optics to make themselves look good, or to make the other side look bad. The optics can be fabricated and promoted, or they can come out of something very real.

With the exception of the moments when we need to counter some of the lies about the work we are doing, bad optics never concerns antifa because we have other things that bother us: namely, disallowing bad people from doing bad things to innocent people. That was the same back in the scene before I even knew the word "antifa" existed. We brawled with Nazis back then, and we didn't wait for rallies to happen. It was simply a matter of refusing to give any quarter to Nazis or make any excuses for them. When you are talking about a punk scene in particular, you are talking about a place to go where you can come as you are, away from a mainstream culture that says you need to do this or that to get ahead. It is where you can say, "No, I do not!" and still flourish. For some reason, Nazis still think that some iconoclastic or radical cultural space should include them, and they are seeking to do even worse to us than the mainstream politicians and corporations would. That was intolerable, and it still is. So we would say "no" to them, and that's just the way it went. And there were some hellified brawls, especially if Nazis came to town! And it's like I said earlier, when my political world and musical world came together, it was really damned interesting and it made for one hell of a soundtrack!

The soundtrack for one particular and notorious throwdown would probably be Ska considering it was a Ska band's crew that I was a part of.

I am going to refrain from mentioning names because, even though this happened in January 1995, it's out of respect that I'll keep them private. After all, some geriatric bonehead might catch wind of this and—well, I suppose these days they would spam me and everyone else that was involved on social media with their ramblings about how we were terrorists and what not, but that's still a pain in the ass. Funny as hell, but a pain in the ass. Hell, the now-deceased lead singer of a band from the bonehead crew that was the focus of everyone's ire that night wrote a song about me a few years ago, so living rent free in their heads is a given at this point!

Anyway, it was January 1995, a few weeks after we all rang in the New Year. Nineteen ninety-five was the most eventful of my life up to that point because we had the Oklahoma City bombing, when an avowed white power advocate killed 168 people by blowing up the Oklahoma City Federal Building, which brought all the antifascist stuff I had been working on into play. I moved to Cleveland, Ohio, started making hard-left turns politically, and found myself going to my first Anti-Racist Action (ARA) conference.

ARA was an antifascist network that was the prominent enemy to everything neo-Nazi. Founded in 1989 in Minneapolis, Minnesota, it had chapters across the country and around the world, and its main focus was to rout neo-Nazis and white supremacists. Were they in prominence today the way they were then, we would be talking about "Anti-Racist Action" in the same way that we talk about "antifa." In other words, Fox News would be demonizing ARA as a threat.

Today, ARA has morphed into the Torch Network, a confederation of antifa groups, and they still have a lot of relevance. But ARA as an organization has been replaced by more localized groups around the globe. After this particular conference I went to, ARA became one of the most prominent antifascist organizations in the country and a name that stoked the ire of many a neo-Nazi for a good 20 years! I also started showing up around then at more right-wing events. Simply put, I needed to see the enemy up close and personal in its own element. This included a Black conservative conference in Washington, DC a week after the O. J. Simpson verdict that featured Patrick Buchanan, of all people, as the keynote.

At the beginning of 1995, I was writing op-ed pieces for a New Jersey newspaper and basically shifting a lot of things around in my life. But because it was January, what everyone was thinking about was the sweep of Congress the Republicans had for the first time in 40 years. The talk at the time was how the new House speaker Newt Gingrich was going to run roughshod over the civil rights that we fought for decades to achieve and maintain, and no one knew what to expect or how to fight back yet. This particular day, however, was time set aside to finally chill, get away from such concerns, and I did it at the Café Newz, a popular coffeehouse on Easton Avenue that we all frequented. That goal changed pretty quickly.

It was a Friday, and a day off from work, so I spent it in a television studio working on the latest episode of *Channel X*, an underground music show I was producing. Afterward, I headed over to the Café Newz, where I caught up with a lady friend. I was talking with her and seeing what she might be doing that evening, and we were having a good time, when some friends of ours came in. They were the sax players of the aforementioned Ska band; we exchanged the usual pleasantries, and then one got down to business. They weren't there to chill. They were there to sound an alarm.

"Yeah, there's some Nazis hanging out at the Court Tavern," one said, referring to a local club where his band regularly played. "We're going to get some people together and chase them out of town."

He didn't say this in a panic, or even angry. He just said it matter-of-factly because, when Nazis show up, it is a given that "chasing them out of town" is what one is supposed to do. My lady friend understood when I told her I had to go. The Court Tavern is probably a half mile from the Café Newz. There was a McDonald's there at the time inside a parking deck that has since been torn down. By the time we got there, we had a sizable crew, mostly coming from a house where a crew of traditional skinheads lived.[1] One of us was a former neo-Nazi who had a death warrant on his head after he renounced those beliefs and gave up names of Nazis to a local leftist group.

We were all pumped up, which was good for me because, even though it wasn't as cold as it had been, the thin bomber jacket I was wearing was not doing the trick. It was what I was wearing after my old one, which had "AFRICA" on the back of it, had disappeared, and I hadn't bought a new one yet.

We didn't know what we were going to do yet. We knew that we could not engage in anything inside the club, which would be akin to setting fire to your house. Two of us went in to confirm that the boneheads were actually inside. They were from a Nazi crew in Atlantic City, New Jersey, one of them a guitarist for a well-known neo-Nazi band called Aggravated Assault, and there were four of them. That was four too many. This was a crew that had a notorious reputation. They were one of the first neo-Nazi crews that called themselves "skinheads" in New Jersey and were known for assaults and even murders well into the 2010s, but it was incredibly rare that they would take a chance showing up in New Brunswick. They left the tavern, walking outside right where we had congregated.

I was looking at them for a few seconds, and then one of the Ska band's lead singers asked them if they were with the skinhead group Atlantic City Skinheads—which we already knew the answer to because the woman who was with them was wearing the crew's name on her hoodie and another bonehead in the group, the guitarist for Aggravated Assault, had the Nazi crew's patch on his flight jacket. They only went a few more steps before one of them got cracked across the head with a truck chain—beginning the throwdown.

We were all doing something. Fists were flying, boot parties[2] were being held, and there was virtually no way out. I say "virtually" because the woman the boneheads were with disappeared, leaving her three companions to their beatdown. I saw people I never thought I would ever see fight throwing down in the most uncharacteristic ways. Well, uncharacteristic as far as I knew up to that point. This particular Ska band would later develop a minor reputation for throwing down when someone pissed them off. And when we are talking about a Ska band, we mean big men in flashy suits beating the holy shit out of these Nazi characters.

The neo-Nazi guitarist was on the wrong end of my well-dressed friend's fists, and the fight was getting to be too much for him. At one point, the guitarist lost his shoe in the fight and my friend merely took it and used the heel of it to beat him some more. I almost started laughing until he pushed the guitarist into my arms and I got back into character and leveled a few blows of my own. The guitarist had had enough, apparently, because he tried like hell to get away. The only way he was able to leave was to wrestle out of his brand-new flight jacket and run down the block—with one shoe on. I was left there with his jacket in my hands.

His brand-new jacket.

That was just my size.

I removed his club's patch off the front, the small UK flag patch off the back, and wore it over my thin jacket, comfy as hell for the rest of the night!

The brawl was winding down at that point. My crew cornered one of the Nazis in the parking lot and he was shouting at them that he wasn't a Nazi, which we knew wasn't true due to the colors he was flying. The former neo-Nazi who was with us was shouting his head off at him, "Kill me now! Come kill me now!" while another was shouting, "Get on your knees! Get on your knees!"

Then came another shout. "Yo, 5-o! 5-o!" It was time to go. We simply ran back to Easton Avenue. As we passed the McDonald's, we saw a sister sitting at a table watching us—with her hand in her coat pocket, holding something heavy and concealed. It was definitely time to go!

It wasn't long before we all got together at a pizza joint near Café Newz to debrief the confrontation. I showed everyone the club patch that used to be on the jacket I was now wearing and everyone let out a cheer. It was our trophy for the evening! That was when my best friend Torrey came in—he was pissed that he missed the whole damned thing. Apparently, the boneheads ended up hiding out at the Italian restaurant across the street.

Again, we needed to make sure, so we sent one of our guys to check it out. When he walked in, he was told the restaurant was closed. When he asked about the four patrons sitting at the bar, he was again told they were closed. Our friend walked out and gave a Nazi salute then pointed behind him to indicate to us that, yeah, the night might not be over. He was wrong; it was over. The police showed up. It was just two officers and they went straight to us.

"Hey, what's going on?" one of us asked.

"Apparently everything that's going on concerns you!" one officer said.

Believe it or not, that was the end of it. The two officers simply went there to check things out, and they talked to us. We all went home after that. No arrests were made and we never saw the boneheads again in New Brunswick (although the guitarist has performed that song his lead singer wrote about me many years later). As far as the police were concerned, two different crews had beef, and as long as the beef didn't continue into the night, it was over. They couldn't care less if they were Nazis or if we were anti-Nazis, "trad skins," whatever. And I hadn't ever heard the word "antifa" yet, so the drama and controversies people now know around militant antifascism was nonexistent. I suppose for the cops that showed up, the less paperwork, the better.

It wasn't long before I bastardized the flight jacket. I started putting my own patches and pins on—some promoting bands, but mostly political ones like an inverted US flag symbolizing distress, a crossed-out swastika patch, and an ARA patch on back. I wore it for several years. I still have it somewhere, but I don't do patches like I used to. My father called me out on that, actually. We were driving somewhere and he said, "You know, if I was a boxer, I would say you were telegraphing your punches. I already know what you are going to throw before you throw it!" Now I am often more reserved with how I really feel unless you want to get into a conversation with me; I don't want people to think they know everything I'm about before talking with me. Being cooler, quieter, gives me access to spaces that telegraphing myself wouldn't allow for. The Nazi's patch I took off is now framed in my office.

While we are on the subject of "whatever happened to . . . ," that Ska band I was rolling with grew to become one of the more popular bands in the scene across the country, and it spawned a second band that became ever bigger. Torrey, my best friend since we were kids, went through a series of personal issues and ended up getting shot and killed while sleeping in Golden Gate Park in San Francisco, California, a few years later. The Court Tavern closed recently, but the building's still there. The Café Newz was demolished years ago and a fenced off vacant lot is all that remains. We all scattered across the country, and some of us are full-on antifa today.

New Brunswick isn't as rough and tumble as it used to be, but it is also gentrified now. It's quieter, at least to someone reminiscing about the 1990s. For me, that's okay, I guess. I miss the music I was around. I miss the people I used to roll with. Sadly, however, the fascist political ideas I used to fight have now become commonplace. The racists we were fighting in the streets back then are older now and many are in positions of power. What motivated the Nazis to show up hasn't disappeared, it has only grown.

Five years after all the fun and excitement on Church Street, there was a white supremacist attorney named Richard Barrett who had an organization called the Nationalist Movement that wanted to hold a rally in Morristown, New Jersey, some 45 minutes away from New Brunswick. New Jersey didn't have too many hate rallies at the time, but we were definitely concerned because, just six months before this was announced, there was a Ku Klux Klan rally in NYC, only the second one in its entire history. Barrett was a gloryhound who would inject himself into various situations and try to make them about himself. He was a pariah, even among his fellow hatemongers. Don Black, who runs the neo-Nazi website Stormfront, made it clear how much he despised Barrett and why: "He attacked every legitimate White Nationalist leader on his website with the most outrageous lies—David Duke (whom he claimed was responsible for having had [sic] imprisoned), William [L.] Pierce, Matt Hale (whom he also claimed responsibility for imprisoning), my family and me (even family members who are not publicly active), and many others," he wrote. "He was a piece of filth."[3]

Regardless of his status with the rest of the white power scene, we organized a coalition of groups and residents to oppose their rally with a Fourth of July rally of our own, which we called the "One People's Rally" to recognize how we were coming together as one people. Over 300 people came out to oppose the fewer than 10 who joined Barrett. There were scuffles with the police as well as arrests. There were also speeches and bands playing, all in a successful effort to drown out Barrett and his supporters. One of those bands was the Ska band that I was rolling with five years earlier.

After the rally, we decided to keep that coalition going, and "One People's Rally" became "One People's Coalition" and eventually One People's Project, the organization I lead today. Meanwhile, one of the people who stood with Barrett turned out to be someone who was adopted and raised Jewish and is currently a member of the same Nazi crew in Atlantic City we encountered. Drugs, arrests, and a slew of deaths has made that crew a shell of what they once were. Barrett returned the following year with another rally, but his turnout was even worse than the year before.

I don't brawl anymore. To be real, I didn't do a lot of it back then, but it was truly special when I did! I will still do what I have to do if the situation is unavoidable, but it's not the same as it was when I was 25 years younger. I molded One People's Project to use my vocation as my weapon of choice—journalism. And it has served me well, and I have been able to hasten the demise of several large hate groups with that weapon, shut down hate conferences such as the American Renaissance conferences of 2010 and 2011, and pioneer what folks now call "doxing." Frankly, even though I borrowed this methodology from antiabortion groups that were doing it to abortion providers at the time, I saw it as a form of reporting when I started doing it. Today, others are zeroing in on neofascists with the same tactic, and it has proven to be particularly effective.

And yes, when people want out of those hate circles, I am willing to talk with them and help them with that transition. It doesn't mean they will no longer have anything to atone for, but if they want off that battlefield, I like being there to lead them in the right direction. This has raised my profile significantly, with documentaries and movies featuring actors I admire playing me; and, yes, I enjoy the limelight! Why? Because I know I can use it to build on the work. It will always be about the work.

When the time comes that I can no longer be a part of this fight, the words I write and the work I have done will still be there for people to learn from and to model their strategies on. But everything I do today has its foundations in what I and others did back in the day. It is about fighting. Perhaps not always in ways I did back then, but those experiences gave me a solid foundation to work from.

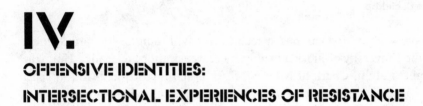

IV.

OFFENSIVE IDENTITIES:
INTERSECTIONAL EXPERIENCES OF RESISTANCE

Antifascism through the Lens of Transgender Identity

Emily Gorcenski

The Backdrop

In the lead-up to a campus speech by alt-right founder Richard Spencer at the University of Florida in 2017, mere weeks after the deadly "Unite the Right" rally in Charlottesville, Virginia, a neo-Nazi named Colton Fears was interviewed by a *HuffPost* journalist. "Basically, I'm just fed up with the fact that I'm cis-gendered, I'm a white male, and I lean right, towards the Republican side, and I get demonized if I don't accept certain things," Fears said.[1] Contemporary neo-Nazis and neofascists often attempt to frame themselves as victims instead of aggressors, often by recycling the social justice language of the progressive left. Fears, wearing the smart side-part that was *de rigeur* of the alt-right—along with a pin bearing a Nazi insignia—was no different in this regard. But it was his use of the term "cis-gendered" that caught my attention. Surrounded by a swarm of media, he was selling the idea that because he was white, because he was male—and coequally, because he was not transgender—he was the real victim, that his voice was being silenced, and that his opinions were being pushed out of mainstream discourse. Hours later, Fears would be arrested for being an accessory to attempted murder, a charge to which he pleaded guilty and was sentenced to five years in prison.

In the 2010s, lesbian-gay-bisexual-transgender-queer-plus (LGBTQ+) rights began to make significant advances within industrialized nations. From the legalization of same-sex marriage to stronger civil rights protections, queer rights appeared to be on the right track. In late 2015, US Attorney General Loretta Lynch announced that the Department of Justice would start interpreting Section 1557 of the Affordable Care Act to include antitransgender discrimination among its protections, an act that would have significant benefits in access to medical transition coverage.[2] Two years prior, Laverne Cox graced the cover of *Time* magazine alongside

292

the headline, "The Transgender Tipping Point."[3] Cisgender allies began carrying the banner of trans rights, and for a moment it looked like the movement for transgender equality was marching steadily forward. Alas, this progress was met with stiff resistance.

Facing the failures of neoconservatism's economically centered posture in the first decade of the 2000s, the American right needed a new energy. The failures of the Tea Party movement in the late-2000s showed that government spending and economic austerity were not enough to rally conservative America behind a single movement. The American right needed something younger, more original, to differentiate it from the stodgy and uninspiring neoconservative movement that had dominated the late 20th century. One such movement, the neoreactionaries (NRx) showed some early promise for them.[4] Heady and intellectual, NRx was a movement that thrived online, capturing the kind of Millennial and modern energy that the Tea Party failed to engage. The NRx movement carried modern conservatism into the social media era and, in doing so, introduced Millennials to conservative philosophy. But the movement, which mimicked the academic left with lengthy prose and complex and bespoke vocabularies, failed to engage mainstream politics outside of the digital bubbles. It had promise, but was too abstract.

As this happened, a fringe online drama was rapidly unraveling. GamerGate, however it began, rapidly became a proxy battle between Third Wave feminism and a patriarchal status quo. Emerging from social networks, GamerGate was a strictly online phenomenon, with most of the participants being Millennials tired of being alienated by and antagonized by cable news and op-ed columns. It was in this movement that the patterns and practices of what would be known as the "alt-right" movement would be solidified. GamerGate popularized the pejorative term "social justice warrior" ("SJW"), and many trans folks were targeted along with cisgender women by the GamerGate movement. Indeed, GamerGate was deeply antifeminist and deeply antitransgender, and from it the seeds of what would become the contemporary neofascist movement were sown. By the end of 2016, significant portions of the GamerGate movement evolved into the anti–political correctness (anti-PC) culture movement colloquially described today as the "alt-right."

A central characteristic of this movement was its palatability to mainstream culture. Although undoubtedly white supremacist, this new movement exploited mainstream biases and ignorance. Rather than shaving their heads and marching around with swastika tattoos, this movement was well dressed. Instead of writing 10,000-word, incomprehensible blog posts framing exhaustive visions of a white, monarchist ethnostate, as the NRx movement did, this new movement was simply spoken and optimized for the ephemeral, "share-first read-later" social media ecosystem. Some conservative organizations, thirsty for a paradigm shift after losing *Obergefell v. Hodges*, saw promise in these digital battles over feminism. Breitbart News Network writer Milo Yiannopoulos became a major figure in GamerGate[5]; before long, Yiannopoulos was using his platform to attack transgender individuals regularly.[6] Yiannopoulos, a boisterous gay man with a highbrow English accent, did not fit the mainstream vision of a white supremacist. By 2017, conventional media, perhaps perplexed by the outward appearance of figures such as Yiannopoulos and Spencer, wrote glowing profiles of emerging leaders in what would soon be revealed as a dangerous and violent white supremacist movement.

This new right-wing movement began to flex by breaching the sanctity of conventionally progressive spaces. Embarking on a speaking tour targeting typically liberal and progressive public universities, Yiannopoulos exploited free-speech principles to push inflammatory rhetoric. In late 2016, he used the deadname of a trans student while deliberately misgendering her and mocking her appearance.[7] Weeks later, his speech at University of California Berkeley was protested by antifascist demonstrators, the first of a series of events in 2017 known as the "Battle of Berkeley." Political rallies with violent neo-Nazis in attendance were becoming increasingly regular. By the time spring came in 2017, a culture war that started on social media had moved off the internet and onto the street, where real blood was being spilled.

The Reification of White Supremacy

If we are to accept this abridged, incomplete, and simplified history that frames trans antagonism as a central point of leverage for the growth of the modern extreme right, then we must also acknowledge that the contemporary neofascist movement is firmly entangled with antisemitism, Islamophobia, anti-Blackness, xenophobia, misogyny, homophobia, ableism, and many other forms of hate. There is no value in attempting to order these hatreds by which is worse, or which breeds more violence, to say nothing of intersectionality. But, in this chapter, we focus on the trans antagonism of the far right, and the role that trans people play in contemporary antifascism. The reader is asked to view this writing through an intersectional lens by assumption, both for the expansion of one's thinking as well as the convenience for the reading (and writing!) of what follows. Indeed, a discussion of the need for and relevance of comparative forms of analysis awaits, but before we can engage with the theory, it is necessary to further comprehend the present context.

There is little doubt by now that the alt-right is a fundamentally white supremacist movement and that many of the major figures in the GamerGate era collaborated with white supremacists. Emails leaked in October 2017 showed that Yiannopoulos himself worked closely with white supremacist and neo-Nazi figures during his tenure at Breitbart. It is accurate to state that white supremacy has existed for as long as the concept of whiteness has, and the fact that we have any substantial white supremacist element in our contemporary politics is not the result of some novelty. But it is also accurate to state that the white supremacist movement in the late 2010s looked much different than it did in the preceding decade. The alt-right has been much more successful at recruiting and movement building than its white supremacist forebears. Part of this is due to the way that the movement capitalized on identity politics, including trans identity. The difference is scope and focus. Whereas previous white supremacist movements would often recruit based on a grand future vision of, say, a white homeland, the alt-right focused on immediate issues that had mainstream support. The alt-right mastered "entryism"; that is, the radicalization of normal people. In their parlance, the alt-right sought to "redpill" the "normies." To accomplish this, it was necessary to build layers of abstraction between the issues brought forward by the alt-right and conventional white supremacy, counterintuitively making it *more* difficult for the average reader to connect the dots. This is no mistake: To explain how trans antagonism is a white supremacist concept requires a more complex journey through history, colonialism, and gender studies—topics with which the average cisgender person is not likely to regularly engage.

The alt-right accomplished its rapid growth by pressing many single issues in parallel. Abortion, immigration, and trans bathroom rights all became entry points to the same white supremacist movements. Throughout 2016, during the US presidential election campaigns, "meme wars" between the right and left duked it out in social media spaces. These campaigns saw the expansion and refinement of GamerGate tactics. A harassment campaign coordinated by Yiannopoulos targeted *Ghostbusters* actor Leslie Jones, a Black woman, eventually harassing her until she deleted her online presence. Then-candidate Donald Trump regularly shared alt-right memes, giving legitimacy to the growing movement. It's impossible to quantify how much a role these digital provocations played in the election of Trump. But it's clear that, in combination with the more standard conservative online commentary, these behaviors had a role in Hillary Clinton's "basket of deplorables" comment that the right wing quickly latched onto as a rallying cry and a source of pride. Following Trump's election, the alt-right won its biggest battle yet in an ever-expanding culture war.

Systematic racism cannot be overlooked in this discussion. By early 2017, the US had enacted a travel ban on inbound travelers from five Muslim-majority nations and began preparations for building a border wall.[8] After years of Black Lives Matter (BLM) protests against police brutality, at least five US states in early 2017 were considering bills limiting the liability of drivers who hit protesters in the street.[9] Enabled by social media platforms, the resurgent conservative movement was enjoying this string of success. Soon, trans identity became a proxy for progressive thought by the right, with conservatives memeing jokes about identifying as an "attack helicopter" and chiding people online with quips of, "Did you just assume my gender?" Before long, trans rights became the butt of nearly every conservative joke.

The alt-right didn't take its foot off the gas here, either. Leaked logs from neo-Nazi and alt-right chat rooms show that trans antagonism was a staple of far-right chatter. Transgender antifascist activists, myself included, found themselves targeted, both online and in physical space. On August 11th, as I livestreamed the infamous "Unite the Right" neo-Nazi tiki torch rally at the University of Virginia in Charlottesville, a neo-Nazi named Taylor Wilson screamed in my face, "What kind of freak are you, to cut off your part?" Throughout the weekend, I was the target of comments such as, "Science says there are only two genders!" and, "Is that a chick or a dude, ewww." In leaked chat rooms, another neo-Nazi posted a photograph of the bull bar on the front of his truck with the comment, "eats trannies," an obvious insinuation that he would gleefully run me down in the street.

If there is a thesis I am to communicate from this all-too-brief history of the alt-right, it is that transphobia is one of the more significant avenues with which neofascism connects to mainstream conservatism. In my studies of contemporary white supremacy, neofascism, and the alt-right, I have found the modern groups and organizations to be principally concerned with movement building. Within this framework, trans antagonism becomes an axis of hate that is more "legitimate" in mainstream views. Antitransgender sentiment does not require the kind of dog whistles that other forms of hate require. In fact, as I will soon discuss, trans antagonism enjoys a strong, mainstream foothold even among movements that otherwise consider themselves to be liberal or progressive. To address fascism and antifascism through a lens of transgender identity requires us to address how trans antagonism is a form of white supremacy that is both insipid and incipient; to address the hatred of trans people among fascist extremists requires us to address this same form of hatred in mainstream, quotidian life.

We must understand white supremacy as a consolidating, exclusionary force, designed not only to coalesce power in whiteness, but also through patriarchy, Christian supremacy, colonialism, and cisheteronormativity. Within this framework, I have identified nine main axes of hate through which contemporary white supremacy influences and recruits from mainstream politics: misogyny, homophobia, transphobia, ableism, xenophobia, Islamophobia, antisemitism, anti-Indigenousness, and anti-Blackness. These are the tendrils to which hardcore white supremacist groups reach out to ensnare people orbiting a space of generalized "anti-PC" sentiment. These axes will allow us to understand trans antagonism in a lens of fascism and white supremacy using comparative analysis without engaging in "oppression Olympics." Rather than viewing these axes—and their intersections—in terms of who has it worse, we can understand them by how white supremacists leverage them to shift conversations, concoct narratives, recruit, cross-pollinate with other forms of hate, and ultimately gain access to mainstream discourse. White supremacy is no longer a single ideology, but rather an accumulation point sitting at the intersection of many similar hate-based ideologies. Using this lens, I'll use contemporary and historical parallels in hopes to convey how trans identities and trans lives must be defended if fascism is to be eradicated.

Trans Antagonism in the Modern Conservative Discourse

Faced with a series of losses to progressive forces and a global recession caused by war and austerity policies, modern conservatives turned to more regressive forces to build power. In the course of just a few years, conservative rhetoric underwent a tone shift. Instead of warning its base that liberals were coming for their wallets, they sounded an alarm that liberals would soon be coming for their culture. Gay marriage enjoyed strong public support, and the decisions in *United States v. Windsor* and *Obergefell* were the first major progressive victories in a renewed culture war. Turning to its evangelical base, American—and international—right-wing movements soon shifted gears to a more favorable battleground: transgender rights.

Despite significant lobbying from transgender rights groups, major civil rights organizations back-burnered the trans movement in the fight for gay marriage. Trans equality was seen, even among progressive organizations, as a worthy but distant cause, and one that would potentially endanger the fight for marriage equality. The right took this opportunity to use trans people as a wedge issue among progressives and, in doing so, found willing allies in the neofascist movements.

From 2015 onward, rhetoric and legislative action increased against trans people. North Carolina passed House Bill 2 (HB2), a law restricting trans people's rights to use the bathroom of their gender in public buildings.[10] Several dozen similar bills were introduced throughout the US. At the end of 2016, during the lame-duck session, a federal judge in Texas enjoined a recent ruling regarding Section 1557 of the Affordable Care Act that would ensure equal rights to health care for trans people.[11] In mid-2017, the Trump administration began efforts to ban transgender people from serving in the military. Although most of these legal and legislative attempts failed, the message was clear: Conservatism was firing a broadside against progressivism, and trans people were the main target of the salvo.

The arguments proffered by conservatives were familiar: Trans people, they claimed, were a threat to vulnerable women in bathrooms, vulnerable girls in changing rooms, vulnerable families in public spaces. They argued that trans people have a mental illness and should be pitied, not given access to transition care. They argued that trans people have enormous medical costs for which the public ledger would be held to account.

These arguments were not limited to the American context. Under Viktor Orbán, the far-right Hungarian president, gender studies programs at Hungarian universities were abolished.[12] Romania soon followed suit,[13] although it was later overturned by the country's highest court.[14] Orbán used emergency powers granted to him during the coronavirus disease 2019 (COVID-19) pandemic to institute regressive legislation restricting trans rights: Legal names were only allowed to come from a list of acceptable male or female names. No unisex names were allowed, and one could only change their name to one on the list corresponding to one's birth certificate gender.[15]

In Poland, Andrzej Duda successfully campaigned for president on an explicitly anti–lesbian-gay-bisexual-transgender (LGBT) platform.[16] Under Putin, Russia outlawed LGBT activism.[17] In Recep Tayyip Erdoğan's Turkey, Pride parades have repeatedly found themselves under attack.[18] In Brazil, Jair Bolsonaro's victory came at the expense of intense anti-transgender sentiment.[19] Globally, trans antagonism was being used as a foothold to embolden and empower the far right, and it was effective in this role.

What may be surprising, however, is how little resistance the opposition proffered. Rather than addressing the far right face on, largely neoliberal parties instead ceded this ground. This may not be a purely strategic error. In fact, the unfortunate reality is that transphobia is tragically common within these neoliberal and progressive groups.

Nowhere is this clearer than in the UK. Trans people in the UK have faced a barrage of slander in the mainstream British press. Major celebrities—among them, *The IT Crowd* writer Graham Linehan and *Harry Potter* author J. K. Rowling—have used their immense public reach to question transgender rights, particularly the rights of trans children and the organizations that support them.[20,21]

As with bathroom bills proposed by conservative politicians, the arguments that figures such as Rowling and Linehan use are thinly veiled attempts to masquerade hate as legitimate concern. These arguments range from concern over the sanctity of women's safety in women's spaces, to the well-being of children in schools, to the rights of people who explore their gender and ultimately decide that they are cisgender after all. This feminist movement forms itself around a brand of biological essentialism: their central argument is that biology is fixed, that there are two genders, and that transgender people should not be afforded coequal rights to cisgender people of that same gender identity.

What may seem odd is that the movement is otherwise outwardly accepting of nonconforming behavior. A man is free to wear a dress, they'll say, but someone assigned male at birth should never be given access to women's spaces so as to protect (cisgender) women. This movement initially referred to itself as trans-exclusionary radical feminism (TERFism). Rebranding itself in recent years as "gender critical feminism," it may be difficult to immediately see the connections to fascism and white supremacy.[22] After all, your typical neo-Nazi is emphatically not accepting of a man in a dress or a transgender woman. The far right depends on this seeming contradiction. Because the far right perceives itself as being against the status quo, it is not uncommon for far-right movements to seek ideological cover by co-opting the legitimacy of centrist or progressive spaces positioning themselves similarly. For instance, the Boogaloo movement, which originated as a violent militia movement seeking to foment a race war to accelerate the decline of the political class in America, attempted to position themselves as allies to the BLM movements during the protests after George Floyd's murder in 2020.[23]

However, a more careful analysis of TERF discourse reveals how the movement is stitching itself to many of the other axes of white supremacy radicalization I mentioned earlier. If one reads TERF forums long enough, one will encounter many of the familiar arguments parroted by white supremacists. Transphobes will point out that many early trans researchers were Jewish, for instance.[24,25] There are frequent suggestions that trans people are mentally ill and require hospitalization; there are arguments that gender dysphoria is often comorbid with autism.[26] What makes these arguments so striking is that underneath many of them is a kernel of truth.

Effective propaganda is not entirely built on lies, but rather relies on a blend between truth, lies, and exaggeration to overwhelm the mark in an attempt to onboard them. The most effective conspiracy theories and "fake news" stories rely on these elements of truth to plant the seed of a thought and to inoculate it from doubt. It's true that many of the early gender and sexuality researchers were Jewish. It's true that trans people, often by virtue of the oppressive ways in which we are treated by society, experience depression, anxiety, post-traumatic stress disorder, and other mental health disorders disproportionately frequently. It's true that many trans people are indeed autistic as well.

These facts could be used to drive better care for and elevate public acceptance of trans people. Multiple studies have shown that trans people, when given access to proper medical, mental health, and legal services, have far lower rates of attempting suicide and better mental health and disposition.[27,28] But instead of using these facts to lobby for better trans support, the TERF movement uses arguments completely isomorphic, and sometimes identical, to those used by neo-Nazis and white supremacists who advocate violence against trans folks. There is little structural difference between the arguments, "I don't mind if a man wears a dress but he can't identify as a woman to use my bathroom" and, "I'm not racist, I just think that white people deserve to be in charge of their own ethnostate."

Indeed, the fact that the TERF movement is so strong in the UK means there is little coincidence that it often engages in forms of hate that are relatively mainstream. TERFs have frequently argued that Muslim rights should be restricted because of the ways they believe some Muslim women are oppressed. TERFs, many of whom identify as lesbians, are often openly hostile to bisexual women. And, ironically for a movement that frames itself as "gender critical," TERFs regularly police cisgender women's appearance both online and in physical spaces by accusing them of looking like men.

The fact that TERF arguments stray so far into antisemitism, homophobia, Islamophobia, and misogyny—four of the radicalization vectors presented earlier—is no mistake. At least one prominent TERF has accepted speaking invitations from the Heritage Foundation, a right-wing evangelical organization with deep political influence in the US and UK and an openly stated goal of restricting trans, queer, and women's reproductive rights.[29] A recently published book by Helen Joyce arguing against trans rights includes one of the all-time classical antisemitic tropes: that George Soros is secretly funding a transgender movement. The Anti-Defamation League states, "In far-right circles worldwide, Soros' philanthropy often is recast as fodder for outsized conspiracy theories, including claims that he masterminds specific global plots or manipulates particular events to further his goals. Many of those conspiracy theories employ longstanding antisemitic myths, particularly the notion that rich and powerful Jews work behind the scenes, plotting to control countries and manipulate global events."[30] Joyce's argument is as antisemitic as it is factually incorrect. In her book, *Trans: When Ideology Meets Reality*, she claims that Soros's Open Society Foundation (OSF) donated $100 million to the US-based Human Rights Campaign in 2010.[31] In fact, OSF gave that money to Human Rights *Watch*, a research nongovernmental organization (NGO) investigating human rights abuses worldwide.[32]

Joyce is not alone in her abuse of factual matters in an attempt to stoke fears of a shadowy Jewish cabal secretly running the world, as the trope is traceable at least as far back as *The Protocols of the Elders of Zion*. Such derivative works are common among white supremacy feeder movements. The far right sees the TERF movement as dual use: It can be leveraged to sway people to its reactionary causes, and it can use the feminist movement to sanitize its image for those with a less-educated or less-critical view of the dynamics of gender discourse in the 21st century.

To be clear, not every TERF becomes a neo-Nazi, and many openly despise and disavow the far right. The point is not to view these movements as strict subsets of one another, but rather to view them as gravity wells that will capture some percentage of participants and send them into an inwardly spiraling orbit toward white supremacy. The neo-Nazis don't need to recruit *all* the TERFs; rather, they just need some TERFs to willingly or unwillingly promote their messages of hate. TERFism is, in essence, a feeder ideology for a more virulent and hateful belief system.

This pattern hasn't escaped scrutiny. Judith Butler, longtime scholar of gender and author of *Gender Trouble*, published an op-ed in *The Guardian* that pulls no punches in comparing what they call the "antigender" movement to both contemporary and historical fascist movements, citing Umberto Eco's popular list of the 14 elements of fascism.[33] Calling for radical feminists to shed their ties to various reactionary movements, Butler's piece ends with call to antifascist solidarity that is both clear in its phrasing and ambiguous in its intent: Are they calling for antifascist solidarity against the exclusionary forms of radical feminism, or are they hopeful that a movement that has defined itself around exclusion could suddenly reject its fascist tendencies? If it is the latter, where is the historical precedent?

Connections to a Deeper History

Nevertheless, it's not unfair to consider TERFism as a direct form of white supremacy when one considers a more distant historical context. Trans people have always existed, and when we explore what gender means in a modern context, particularly in the white, Western, or industrial world, we do so in relation to a notion of gender largely enforced through European colonialism and imperialism with roots in the church. From the Roman emperor Elagabalus to the modern-day Kinnar in India, nonbinary and transgender identities have existed for thousands of years in cultures all around the world.

As European settlers began to colonize the globe, they enforced European ideals of gender on Indigenous populations.[34] Many cultures were eradicated through genocide; others buried their traditional ways of life away from the watchful eye of the imperial soldier or the missionary. The systematic erasure of trans and cultural identities has had a ripple effect that still lasts today. Among them is a persistent and wrong belief in two fixed genders, a belief that contradicts significant bodies of biological, psychological, sociological, and anthropological research. TERF discourse, therefore, maps neatly to neofascist discourse in that it is not only exclusionary, but stands in contradiction to the entire body of evidence built by scholars in multiple fields for decades.

Fascist philosophies have historically involved the rejection of science and scientific evidence when it contradicts their visions of the future, in some cases destroying the research entirely. In the spring of 1933, shortly after the Nationalsozialistische Deutsche Arbeiterpartei—the original Nazi Party—took power in Germany, a group of young fascist students from the Deutsche Studentenschaft (DSt) raided libraries and archives at universities in 34 different German cities. *Die Aktion wider den undeutschen Geist*, or "the action against un-German Spirit," targeted works by leftist, democratic, and Jewish thinkers deemed to be "immoral." Among the archives raided in this action was the research archive of the Institut für Sexualwissenschaft at Humboldt University in Berlin. Led by Magnus Hirschfeld, a Jewish sexologist, the institute held some of the earliest detailed quantitative and qualitative studies on what we would now recognize as queer culture.

The DSt removed almost 25,000 books and piled them in Opernplatz, the square before the opera house. Nazi Joseph Goebbels gave a fiery speech to an estimated 40,000 onlookers, declaring "no to decadence and moral corruption!" as the flames reduced the works to ash.[35]

It is, of course, necessary to identify that the DSt raids targeted Jewish intellectualism, and any analysis of the Nazi Party's raids on queer studies and queer culture cannot be separated from the genocidal antisemitism of the party. But there is room to explore why queer identities were leveraged so effectively by the Nazis to expand populist hatred against Jews, and one must recognize that, when modern-day TERFs begin to question the connections between Jews and transgender people, they are treading on ground already covered with the blood of a genocide. Likewise, when TERFs or Nazis insist that there are only two genders, they enforce the cultural genocide wrought on Indigenous cultures by European colonizers all across the world. There is no significant difference therefore between the trans antagonism brought forth by neo-Nazis and that brought forth by more mainstream, self-described feminist movements, which implies that trans-supporting antifascism must be willing to target elements outside of what we otherwise might consider the "far right."

Empowering Comparative Analyses

Throughout this chapter, I have tread into the occasionally difficult waters of comparative analysis in an attempt to explain why the eradication of trans antagonism must necessarily be antifascist in its core. Comparative analysis runs a risk of treading too far—certainly, we want to be sure not to detract, cheapen, or appropriate the horrors of the oppressions brought on Black Americans during Jim Crow, or on Jewish people during the Holocaust. There are also Black transgender people, Jewish transgender people, and Black Jewish transgender people who can claim ownership over these legacies. In recognizing histories, we have to be careful on which spaces we tread.

We cannot expect the burden of fighting and contextualizing fascism to fall only on those who inherit all possible identity intersections. It is possible to tread carefully while acknowledging the modalities of fascism, and it is of critical importance to do so. Rather than comparing oppressions as if they were battle scars, a proper comparative analysis keeps the lens focused purely on fascists and fascist behavior. We must recognize that the arguments fascists use today to justify denying bathroom access to trans women share the same roots as the arguments they used during the civil rights era to justify segregation. This is, emphatically, not a comparison of modern-day trans folks to the lives and experiences of Jim Crow–era Black folks, but rather a recognition that the mythologies used by fascists to spread their hate have remained unchanged. To wit, consider how bathroom arguments then and now relied on perceptions of vulnerability, purity, and innocence of white women; falsehoods about aggression and predatory natures of the "other"; and lies about rampant, unchecked attacks in progressive, tolerant cities.

Combatting fascism requires us to understand the ways fascists craft arguments, prey on marks, and recruit supporters to their cause. It requires us to understand how these arguments are sanitized and brought forward by mainstream politicians and elected officials. It requires us to know our history and to understand that, although history repeats, it rarely does so in exactly the same ways. To be actively against fascism means one must understand and undermine the weapons fascists use, including their propaganda. Comparative analysis is a powerful tool to defeat the threats of the present using the hard-fought victories of the past.

More than just looking at the past, however, we can explore contemporary issues to understand how fascism evolves, moves, obscures itself, and expands. Kimberlé Crenshaw, who coined the term "intersectionality," describes it as "a lens through which you can see where power comes and collides, where it interlocks and intersects."[36] Intersectionality requires us to consider the experiences and oppressions of people who inherit multiple identities, but it does not require us to restrict it only to that lens. Intersectionality is a tool of power analysis and is therefore a highly effective tool with which to combat fascism—a philosophy principally founded on the concept of consolidating power. When hatred of trans people is used to justify policies that judge women based on appearances, for instance, one can recognize this as a grievous harm to both transgender and cisgender women alike, even if cisgender women are not harmed in exactly the same way. These threats cannot be the sole responsibility of transgender people to resist, but likewise we cannot resist these threats in the absence of transgender voices. As long as fascism is targeting transgender lives, fascism cannot be fought without transgender people sharing a leading role.

Antifascism as (Trans) Self-Defense

It is with hope that I have brought the reader here able to recognize a certain geometry to this chapter: a symmetry with which we descend from the modern context to the historical context and back again while gradually shifting the focus from the ways in which trans antagonism is formulated to the ways in which trans antagonism is fought. For the remainder of this chapter, I'll explore ways that trans people can be and have been at the forefront of fighting 21st-century fascism, including a discussion of what cisgender allies can do to support their trans peers. If the previous sections of this chapter have been any success, it should be easy to sell the reader on the idea that fighting fascism as a trans person is not a matter of political activism or even moral necessity, but rather a necessary action undertaken in self-defense. We use the language of self-defense because fascism, whether it comes from extremist groups, the state, or culture, directly attacks and debases the rights of transgender people to exist as freely as cisgender people in society.

When discussing fascism and white supremacy, one must understand that this analysis must include many contexts that require differing analyses, tactics, and approaches. The struggle against trans antagonism happens on three fronts. First, fringe extremist groups that advocate for violence against and exclusion of trans people continue to pose an emerging threat, particularly of mass murder and terrorism. Second, state repression targets transgender individuals and singles us out for violence, either through direct means via the police or through indirect means via policy. Third, culture at large continues to permit and propagate violence against trans people by reinforcing gender binaries, representing trans people through stereotypes, and leveraging lack of legal and social protections of trans people to create hostile and unsafe environments. To be antifascist in support of trans people means being able to navigate the struggle on these fronts and adapt one's approach as necessary.

Antifascist activism takes many forms, from political and legal advocacy, interpersonal mentorship, street activism, digital activism, communications, media representation, and more. When antifascism is described in the language of self-defense, this often conjures images of street activism and protest. But this is not the complete picture. Trans people must be persistent self-advocates for transgender rights as they are persistent advocates in the struggle against fascism. This activism is full of code-switching. What may be acceptable in fighting a neo-Nazi organization on the streets may not be acceptable in dealing with trans antagonism in the workplace. At the same time, there are many opportunities to muster the energy that trans people and their allies bring to the fight on one front and bring it to bear in the struggle on another front.

For example, the degree to which we see people mobilize to protest neo-Nazis and the police in the street is rarely brought to bear when standing up against TERFs who are organizing to oppress trans kids in schools. Likewise, the legal resources used to defend trans people who are suing workplaces or schools are rarely brought to support trans people who are arrested at demonstrations. The fight against fascism and the fight for trans rights are the same.

Transgender people are intimately aware of the ways that trans antagonism presents itself in everyday life, the so-called microfascisms present in every interaction. Navigating these aggressions—both micro and macro—has created a sort of trans culture of shared experience. Many transgender folks know firsthand the kinds of stares they receive when walking down the street, the clumsiness with which strangers interact in a passing social interaction, or the difficulty (or impossibility) of obtaining appropriate medical care. For many transgender people, particularly white transgender women who transition in adulthood, some of these aggressions are the most blatant and blunt experiences with oppression they have ever faced. It is not uncommon that transgender women first engage in liberatory politics after transition. This is not intended as an affront—I admit that this allegation describes my own political journey well.

Transgender women who are starting to engage with antifascist, social justice, or liberatory movements should remember that trans antagonism is only one way that white supremacy reaches its tendrils into mainstream culture, and that the fight for equality is one that is centuries long. It is important that we appropriately align the fight for transgender rights by claiming the appropriate space alongside of, and not before, other struggles for social justice while paying particular attention to the unique issues faced by transgender people of other races, sexual orientations, genders, religions, citizenship statuses, and so forth.

It is important to recognize that, among wealthy, industrialized nations, transgender culture does not exist in the way that Black culture or Indigenous culture exists, by way of example. Although there are trans ancestors and there is a long history of oppression against transgender people, trans culture does not enjoy the same sort of familial lineage that other identities have. A consequence of this is that trans people must exist in and among a culture that is dominantly cisgender, with few organic refuges for trans people to seek shelter in. The result is that most trans spaces are intentionally created as places of safety, the experience of which is not analogous to the kind that Black folks have growing up in a Black neighborhood caused by redlining policies, for instance.

None of this is to say that transgender people don't have a role in the fight against fascism, but that it must be done with the realization that liberation must be a shared objective. Much like the fight for queer equality does not end with the legalization of gay marriage, the fight for trans equality cannot be over until all trans people are free from all oppression.

Trans folks engaging in antifascist work should therefore challenge themselves and their preconceptions about other axes of oppression and endeavor to become as informed in the political and social movements therein. Antifascist activism requires a breadth of expertise on a wide array of issues, if for no other reason than to understand that fascists have many ways in which they distract and shift narratives to divide their opponents and have them fight among each other.

This tactic is a favored approach by the state. During the 2020 protests in the US following the murder of Floyd, "Astroturf" protest movements grew and attempted to divide more radical elements of the protest movement from more mainstream ones, often arguing along racial boundaries. Trans people are not immune to this divide-and-conquer technique and must be savvy to it, resisting the urge to conflate a trend in legal civil rights victories in LGBT-related cases with true liberation. At the same time, trans folks who find their politics on the more radical side of the spectrum must be aware that radical direct action often carries consequences that are borne by Black, brown, and immigrant communities.

Risk assessment is the core of any form of activism, and trans folks have unique risks. In street activism, a trans person facing arrest may be jailed in a wrongly gendered facility, depending on whether their gender has been legally changed on their documents or their medical or surgical history. For trans folks who have not legally changed their name, arrest risks exposing their deadname in public. Moreover, prominent far-right figures have made it a habit to use their platforms to draw attention to arrests, even for minor misdemeanor charges, leading to harassment, both online and in physical space. Transgender people who have undergone medical interventions (e.g., surgery or hormone therapy) may find themselves unable to access adequate medical care if they are incarcerated.

In addition to risk from the state, trans people who become politically active also risk harassment and other violence. Transgender identity is a focal point for hate, and transgender people may be targeted disproportionately to cisgender people who they are fighting alongside. One particularly insipid form of harassment is when people contact family or employers with intentions of outing the trans person. This can and has led to trans people losing their jobs, homes, or other sources of income and stability. However, this cultural exile is not uniquely the result of transgender activism; many trans people have lost friends, family members, jobs, and social connections simply by virtue of transition itself—no loudmouthed activism necessary. A cisgender reader may begin to understand why trans self-advocacy and antifascist activism are so entangled; the act of gender transition can involve losing or casting off so much of one's old life that there is no longer a substantive difference between the neo-Nazi calling for murder, the politician voting against equal rights, or the coworker who refuses to use correct pronouns.

All available data suggest that transgender people total a little less than 1% of the population. Barring an unthinkable calamity, transgender people will never hold a democratic majority. If transgender liberation could be reduced to this one single-axis issue, then trans people would be forever bound by the tyranny of the majority. Much of the struggle against fascism is an act of convincing the majority that their silence on matters of oppression reflects a tacit approval of that oppression. Within this framework, cisgender people naturally have a role both in the fight against fascism and the struggle for transgender equality. But to do so, cisgender people must acknowledge the ways that fascism and trans antagonism are coupled, and they must be willing to defer leadership roles in transgender matters to transgender people. Trans people, for our parts, will always be found on the front lines of any social movement, so this guidance offers little challenge.

Nevertheless, the unfortunate reality is that even leftist or liberatory spaces are too frequently trans antagonistic and patriarchal. To be an effective antifascist movement, it is necessary to interrogate the biases and behaviors of the group in matters of identity-based oppression. In this regard, it is not enough just to elevate a trans person to a visible role of "leadership." It is too easy to find a trans person whose politics fail to significantly challenge one's own and then coronate them as an outspoken trans social justice champion.

Instead, cisgender people must attempt to understand the dynamics of oppression of trans people. They must understand the many and varied reasons so many trans people are sex workers. They must understand how institutions deny transgender people equal rights. For instance, transgender people (myself included) are sometimes denied name changes without medical or psychological approval, even when this is not required by law. In some legal jurisdictions, it is not lawful for trans people to change birth certificates, passports, official identification cards, university transcripts, or any other assortment of paperwork necessary to buy a house, move to a different country, find a job, and so on. Cisgender people, of course, have to go through no such hurdles to have their legal documentation match their gender. When empowered institutions and states impose legal restrictions on trans people that deny them equal station in our society, this is a form of fascism.

Therefore, to be a cisgender ally to trans people, one must be actively antifascist. It is easy to throw support behind the NGOs and nonprofits, but trans people will tell you this is not enough. The glacial pace of change has a measurable cost in trans lives. If antifascism is self-defense, then trans people require cis people to be willing to act in defense of trans people, and that means assuming the risks inherent in doing so.

To Believe That We Can Win

Antifascism is fundamentally a politics of hope. Antifascism is by its nature a struggle against institutional and exclusionary power; there is no antifascism that is not an uphill battle. It is a battle given to frequent despair, a despair that is too familiar for trans people. Studies show that trans people have a high prevalence of suicidality, largely brought on by unfair and discriminatory treatment in society and loss of social support. There are times when the fight for equality seems overwhelmingly impossible.

In Charlottesville, when neo-Nazis marched with tiki torches through the University of Virginia on the eve of "Unite the Right" in 2017, there was no significant counterdemonstration, no black bloc, no police lines, except for a small group of students and community members who symbolically linked arms around a statue and chanted "Black Lives Matter" while the fascist mob surrounded and beat them. Livestreaming the lead-up to that moment, I turned my phone to myself and asked, to no one in particular, "Where the fuck are you?!" There is no darker feeling than that of being left nearly alone to face a violent, fascist, torch-bearing mob.

That night, August 11th, 2017, was the neo-Nazis' high-water mark. As they gassed us, beat us, and doused us with torch fuel, they rode a wave of nearly sexual energy at the violence and dominance they showed against a crowd of young university students they outnumbered 10-to-1. Driven in part by the dramatic images of that night, images of torch flames searing a spirit of resistance in the soul of the community, the next day would mark the moment that "antifa" became a household word. Hundreds of antifascists of all political stripes came to oppose the thousand-strong neo-Nazi "Unite the Right" rally. The neo-Nazis started with violence, attacking clergy, press, and peaceful community members. As the day unfolded, the world was delivered shocking images of open combat on the normally calm streets of Charlottesville. Six men beat a young Black man, DeAndre Harris, with poles and sticks as he lay on the ground, nearly killing him.[37] The dramatic photographs awakened a nation to the realization that the civil rights movement of the 1960s never ended. And the day would end in tragedy when a neo-Nazi committed a terror attack by driving his car into a celebratory and peaceful crowd walking on a closed street in Charlottesville's pedestrian Downtown Mall, killing Heather Heyer.

When President Trump failed to offer any sincere opposition to the white supremacists and their violence, blaming instead "both sides," antifascist resistance moved from the fringes into the mainstream. Slowly, but steadily, the world began to wake up to a realization that the US had become a fascist state. Battle lines had been drawn.

The division caused by the Trump administration's support for neo-Nazi violence only escalated as it enacted ever more exclusionary policies. Images of migrant children sleeping on cold concrete floors on the southern US border polarized the American people. Police murders of Black people contributed to increasing rage against the unaccountability of law enforcement. And antitransgender policies were implemented, ranging from denial of health care rights to a prohibition on transgender troops in the US military.

Sensing the desperation of the moment, antifascism didn't give in, even as the president threatened to declare antifa a domestic terror organization.[38] (Antifa is not an organization and there is no basis in law for such a declaration, let alone via executive action). Instead, antifascists fought back. Most of the neo-Nazi groups that marched in Charlottesville disbanded or rebranded. Dozens of neo-Nazis were sent to prison for their violence. Antifascists de-anonymized dozens more, awakening communities throughout the country to the extremist threat in their midst. Lawsuits followed. Social media companies finally took action, deplatforming them and denying them necessary avenues for fundraising, recruitment, and legitimacy. Trans people were at the center of this fight, as always. And the fight for trans equality saw victories as well. The US Supreme Court affirmed that Title VII protects transgender individuals, invalidating many of the attempts to block legislative efforts to ensure equality. And more people have awakened to the toxicity of TERFism, successfully marginalizing many of its loudest and most famous proponents.

Internationally, too, resistance is growing against fascism even as oppression has gotten stronger. Transgender activists in Hungary and Romania continue to speak out against the legislative restrictions against gender recognition. International awareness about the treatment of migrants at the European Union border is growing. In Bangkok, Thailand, students raised an LGBT flag during prodemocracy protests, a daring move in a military-led monarchy where *lèse-majesté* laws have been applied broadly to impose heavy sentences on those who publicly dissent. It is too early to declare victory against fascism, or even that the tides are turning in the fight against oppression, but there is inspiration to be found in the small and growing victories.

For my part, my antifascism has always been linked to my transgender identity. I met many of the Charlottesville activists I worked with at a vigil for Sage Smith, a young Black trans woman who went missing in Charlottesville in 2012. Despite the many threats I have faced, the trauma, and the sleepless nights, I have had personal connections to the ongoing unraveling of the neo-Nazi movements in the aftermath of "Unite the Right." Wilson, who screamed at me and assaulted me at the tiki torch rally on August 11th, 2017, went on to commit a failed terror attack against an Amtrak train later that year and was sentenced to 14 years in prison.[39] Fears, the man who claimed he was being silenced for being a cisgender, white male was arrested hours after making that statement for being an accessory to the attempted murder of an antifascist counterdemonstrator. He was sentenced to five years in prison.[40]

Five years later, the dust has not settled from what happened in Charlottesville. But the world moves on and, as protests erupted following the murder of George Floyd, I found myself attending a 15,000-strong vigil in Berlin's Alexanderplatz, a spirit of resistance growing in a city full of reminders of what can happen if antifascists lose the fight. I walk through the grounds of Humboldt University, where the DSt raided the archives of Jewish intellectuals, to the square before the Opera House, now called Bebelplatz, a memorial on the site where the Nazis burned the archives of the Institut für Sexualwissenschaft, knowing that trans people like me have always been part of the story and part of the resistance. The dome of St. Hedwig's Cathedral evokes the image of the University of Virginia's Rotunda, and I think of the many ways history repeats itself as I connect my soul to those whose stories were turned to ash. I look around, knowing that although they may have momentarily lost the struggle then, that my presence there now—a free transgender woman, an antifascist activist, a queer woman, a mixed-race woman, an immigrant—breathing free air is proof that we won. And I believe we will win again.

In memoriam Sage Smith, Amelia Perry, and all the transgender heroes who watch the struggle now from above.

Five Hundred Years of Fascism

Mike Bento

There was no Nazi atrocity—concentration camps, wholesale maiming and murder, defilement of women or ghastly blasphemy of child—which the Christian civilization of Europe had not long been practicing against colored folk in all parts of the world in the name of and for the defense of a Superior Race born to rule the world.[1]

—W. E. B. Du Bois

My mother was 10 years of age when Granddaddy took her to the town of his birth. On the way to the small shack his family was raised in, he stopped in front of an old burnt-out house. He pointed and said the Ku Klux Klan (KKK, or simply "Klan") bombed that house. The family (a husband, wife, and two children) burned to death inside. He said when people pass at night, they can still hear the children screaming inside.

He never explained to her why he did that. But the implication was clear. There was a moral to this grim ghost story. On that day in 1964, on a road in Midway, Alabama, my 10-year-old mother learned that "this is the kind of people you are dealing with. White folk will kill you."

Midway is a small town of fewer than five hundred people on the eastern edge of Bullock County. The county was the site of three documented lynchings during the Jim Crow period: Toby McGrady in 1895, Will Scott in 1907, and Abberdine Johnson in 1911.[2] Johnson was accused of committing "a fiendish crime" upon a white lady. The sheriff sent his deputies to dinner while the mob of Union Springs white folks dragged Johnson from the cell and hanged him.[3]

Midway doesn't seem to be midway between much of anything these days except two of Alabama's medium-security prisons: Ventress Correctional Facility to the south and Bullock Correctional Facility to the north. Bullock lies just outside of Union Springs, where Johnson was lynched.

The Equal Justice Initiative does not list the family of four who burned in that house as victims of lynching.[4] Then again, firebombing doesn't exactly fit their definition of lynching even though it has much the same effect of inflicting terror upon the entire Black community, and even though bombing has been a classic method of Klan violence since its inception.

The KKK, the Original Brown Shirts

Before the Civil War, Southern militias organized regular slave patrols to guard against revolt. These police bodies were charged with enforcing the slave codes, which generally meant disarming Black folks and checking passes for enslaved people found on the road or off their owner's plantations.[5] The plantations were our concentration camps. Because of their financial value, instances of enslaved people being murdered during discipline, however common, were infrequent[6]; but, in panics of fear of insurrection such as those that passed through the state of Mississippi in the 1830s, mass murder of Black people might ensue, generally taking the form of lynchings.[7]

Once the western territories were stolen from México, the burgeoning slave empire of the South sought to expand slavery to every corner of the union and beyond. Slave owners and enthusiastic white supremacists attempted to invade several territories throughout the hemisphere and conquer them to bring them into the Union as slave states. Emboldened by the example of the Alamo, where slave owners invaded and occupied Texas and successfully brought it into the Union as part of the South, similar adventures were attempted in Baja California, Cuba, and Colombia.[8]

In 1856, William Walker and a contingent of white supremacists invaded and conquered Nicaragua. Declaring himself dictator, Walker ruled for over a year until he began to implement his plan to legalize slavery (Nicaragua had already abolished slavery as part of its independence movement in 1824, almost a decade before slavery was abolished in New York state) and encourage immigration of US Southerners to form an army of settler colonizers who could then begin to take over the whole region. Fearing invasion, neighboring countries united and ousted Walker in 1857. When he returned in 1860, he was captured and executed by the Honduran government.[9]

By that time, the South's version of *Lebensraum* had already come into conflict with the immigration of European workers to the growing industrial base of the northeast who were looking forward to owning land in the western territories. These settlers wanted the territories to remain free states so that the land could be divided among the whites instead of monopolized by slave-owning planters who would bring discord to the land by introducing African "savages" to the population. Their vision could be summed up in the founding of the state of Oregon,[10] which was touted as a "white utopia" where Black people were barred from taking up residence by the state's constitution.[11]

These two sides erupted in guerrilla warfare over the territory of Kansas. After the compromise of 1854, which allowed the fate of the territory to be determined by vote of the settlers within it, Northern free soilers and Southern slavers flocked to the territory to have it enter on their side. The two sides led campaigns to chase the other out by setting fire to settlements and killing those who refused to leave. By the time Abraham Lincoln won the presidency as leader of the free soil movement in 1860, the South realized the only way it could achieve its slave empire was through secession.

Since the creation of the word "fascism" in Italy one hundred years ago, the term has been applied to several similar movements in Western Europe during the interwar period. As with the term "genocide," this overbearing focus on the European context of these movements has led to a litany of diffuse, Eurocentric, and profoundly racist uses and definitions.[12]

Fascism and genocide are either defined so narrowly by the European experience that they can never be applied anywhere else in any other historical period, or they are so broad as to leave one searching for the essence of these paramount and dangerous phenomena. If Adolf Hitler's removal and extermination of the Jewish people was a genocide by a fascist regime, then what was the total warfare and removal of Indigenous peoples east of the Mississippi under the Andrew Jackson administration? What was the Atlantic trade of enslaved people and the two million Africans thrown to the sea as rotted cargo?

The truth is these definitions belie the self-serving function of creating an exception to the otherwise shining example of civilization that Europe represents in the minds of its white progeny. It is no surprise then that it was the revolutionary critics of European society who formulated the most profound and enduring definition of fascism. The communist antifascist Georgi Dimitrov put forth this definition as leader of the Communist International in 1935: "Fascism is the open terrorist dictatorship of the most reactionary, most chauvinistic and most imperialist elements of finance capital."[13]

Not only does this definition decouple the possibility of fascist regimes from the European context by linking it to the economic development of finance capital and imperialism, but it also gives an essential description of the form of rule unique to fascism, which is "open terrorist dictatorship." This last piece gives us the key to understanding fascist regimes throughout the world.

Colonization is essential to the development of financial capital. Every phase of expanding financial wealth was linked to an expansion of colonial enterprise. And the form of rule in the colonies of European capital has always been an "open terrorist dictatorship," with the use of police and prisons to terrorize their subjects and political participation of the colonial subject either marginalized to the point of mere symbolism or absolutely denied outright. Of course, the enslaved African in the US were granted three-fifths representation only for the benefit of their masters. All colonized peoples lived under fascist rule.

But when the colonizing power is no longer able to satisfy its financial base by squeezing the colonized, it simply brings the rule of the colony home. And therein lies the profound racism of how the term is generally used. We tend to see as fascist policies applied to Europeans that we see as normal or even heroic when applied to Black and brown people.

The Confederate States of America was probably the first embodiment of a modern fascist state. As the vice president of the Confederacy, Alexander Stephens, declared in a speech during its formation: "Our new government is founded upon . . . the great truth that the negro is not equal to the white man; that slavery—subordination to the superior race—is his natural and moral condition."[14] Despite losing the Civil War, the neo-Confederacy of the former slave states was able to realize the subordination of Black people with the compromise of 1877 and the subsequent formation of the Jim Crow regime. Many of the voting restrictions that disenfranchised Black people also disenfranchised a large portion of the white population, leaving voting to the planter class and a privileged few. Black people were held in place by the terror of the spectacle lynching, which also united poor whites with their despotic ruling class. The result was over a half century of single-party rule in the South.

As the editorial board of the Charleston newspaper *The Charleston News and Courier* declared in 1938: "In South Carolina, the Democratic party has been, so far as the Negro vote is concerned, a *Fascist* party, and that is why the *News and Courier* 'cooperates' with it."[15]

To achieve the compromise of 1877, the former Confederacy would drown the South in African blood. The conduct of the Confederate army foreshadowed what was to come in "peacetime" with their policy of murdering Black Union soldiers who surrendered, resulting in over five massacres, including Honey Springs, Saltville, Plymouth, and Fort Pillow. At the close of the war in 1865, freeman's hospitals reported an influx of patients apparently assaulted and ultimately murdered by resentful whites.

A summary list of cases presented by an army hospital in Montgomery, Alabama reads as follows:

> Nancy, colored woman, ears cut off by a man by the name of Ferguson, or Foster, an overseer.
>
> Mary Steel, one side of her head scalped. Died. She was with Nancy. . .
>
> Washington Booth, shot in the back while returning from work by William Harris of Pine Level, without provocation. . . .
>
> Robert, servant of Colonel Hough, was stabbed while at his house by a man wearing in part the garb of a Confederate soldier, died on the 26th of June in this hospital.[16]

By the following year, this sporadic mass murder of Black people became organized. A group of former Confederate soldiers got together in Pulaski, Tennessee to found the first chapter of the KKK. Continuing a long tradition of white settlers, they used an Indian name to disguise their crimes. The name "Ku Klux" likely came from the local Indigenous tribe, the Clocletz, who were often recruited as slave catchers during the antebellum period and whose name was known to strike fear in the Black community.[17] Long before my grandfather would use ghost stories to teach my mother, the local Africans told the legend of Chief Clocletz, whose ghost was said to roam the swamps in search of escaped enslaved people.

Many Confederate veterans had been part of the slave patrols before the war. With the selection of Nathan Bedford Forest as the first "grand wizard" of the Klan, who oversaw the massacre at Fort Pillow, former patrols and Confederate units quickly regrouped and new chapters appeared throughout the South. That same year, Klan activity was already being reported as far away as Georgia. Dispatches from the Freedmen's Bureau that July reported:

> July – Pike, Georgia, an unknown freed boy was murdered by a party of men (disguised). The boy was taken by force from the sheriff of this county and afterward found in the river with his throat cut from ear to ear. Cato Tomlinson was most brutally beaten by parties unknown. Tomlinson was laid on his back and whipped through to his intestines.[18]

Although the racists of the time lacked gas chambers and automatic weapons, Congressman Robert Smalls estimated that some 53,000 Black people had been murdered by 1887.[19] This is certainly a lower estimate, as the US Congress itself documented two thousand Black people killed or wounded by Klan or Klan-like organizations between 1865 and 1872 in the state of Louisiana alone. In her detailed study of the Reconstruction era, Dorothy Sterling cited 20,000 Black people murdered by the Klan in only four years (1868–71).[20] Weary of this unrelenting violence, the US government began to refuse military assistance to states whose Republican politicians were being assassinated and whose Black voters were being brutally murdered. Finally, as a result of the compromise, the Republican president removed the remaining federal troops from the South, leaving no recourse to the Klan's reign of terror. And so it was through this genocide of African Americans that the KKK built its legend.

White Citizens' Councils: Vanguard of the Neo-Confederacy

When my father lined up to step on the school bus and begin his second first day of the third grade, he was excited to see his new school. His old school in the South Bronx, where he had completed the third grade for the first time, had left him still unable to read, so Grammy decided to sign him up for the new bus program with the hope that the white school would teach him. Nearly one hundred years after emancipation, my father, an 8-year-old Black boy, stepped out to face a white supremacy that was still viciously organized to keep him and everyone like him dispossessed:

> Yes, I was left back in the third grade at then P.S. [Public School] 39 in the South Bronx, now called Banana Kelly High. It was a poor school even though under the authority of the New York public school system. I refused to take a test because I couldn't read it and they left me back. I didn't know how poor it was until I was bused to P.S. 8. The city was then starting a busing program I believe in 1960. My mother signed me up and got me approved. The children that came to P.S. 8 on the program were from Spanish Harlem and the South Bronx. Then P.S. 8, located by the Bronx botanical gardens [New York Botanical Garden], was mostly upper-middle-class whites. We had no idea what we were walking into the first day of school.
>
> Excited and full [of] good expectations, we boarded the bus taking us to our new school. Arriving at the school the two buses from different parts of the city, I could see throngs of white parents lining the sidewalks to the entrance of the school. Some had signs and all [were] screaming at the buses. Some spitting on them. I really didn't understand why and couldn't make out what they were saying but it wasn't welcome.

As the door of the bus opened, we lined up to get off and the parents lined both sides of the walkway. As we walked through the shouting and angry parents some of us were spit on and we saw some brought their children with them as well. We made it inside scared and not sure of why we received this reaction. I think this lasted through the first week of school.

The school was definitely an upgrade from P.S. 39. They had [an] in-school dentist, gym, and was much better looking. At P.S. 39, for lunch we got what I called dishwater soup (actually vegetable) but very little vegetables. We got salami sandwiches, carton of milk, hard boil[ed] egg, and Jello. Some variations but never warm food. [The] first day at P.S. 8, our lunch was fried chicken, mashed potatoes with gravy, milk, roll, and ice cream for dessert. Remember, this is the same school system.

I was placed for one hour a day with a special teacher who taught me how to read. The best thing that happened to me at that age. I was no longer a disciplinary problem disrupting the class but I became another problem. We would find the students who stood with their parents screaming at us and would jack them up, which of course would send us to the principal. We formed a group of about 10 of us, both from Harlem and [The] Bronx led by a guy named Mitchell whose father was in the Nation of Islam in Harlem, then led by Malcolm X. He would bring us knowledge, raising our social consciousness. I remember we were rebelling from being called "Negroes" by the white man. I remember Mitchell telling us we had to stop letting the white man define us so the group started calling ourselves "orgroes," lol [laughing out loud]. We just made it up.

Anyway, during my time at PS 8. Whenever we stayed late for after-school activities, necessitating our missing the bus and having to ride the subway (meaning walking through the neighborhood), we either had to run or fight our way to the train stop, which, of course, would bring about retaliation in school and another trip to the principal.

Origins

The reduction of "free" Blacks to a colony of cheap labor was achieved at first through genocide but it was maintained by the constant threat of genocide displayed in the ritual of the spectacle lynching. By the end of the 19th century, lynching had become an established procedure of racial terror. Normally, a male victim was abducted, either from complicit authorities or from their homes. They'd be paraded in front of their white accusers. Sometimes a notice would go out in the local press and an audience of thousands would form to see the torture. Then the victim would be hung from a tree or set on fire and their body mutilated, fanatic whites clipping off fingers or toes or slices of flesh as souvenirs.[21] Especially if the alleged crime was sexual, the genitals were removed while the victim was alive and displayed before forcing the victim to ingest them. After hours of agony, the victim would be allowed to die when someone finally hung them high to choke or dropped them low into the fire. Many times, the corpse would be left some place public and intermittently riddled with bullets by reveling whites as an example to "the niggers."

As one could imagine, this horrific display of sadism served its purpose of suppressing Black resistance. However, one Black woman was not to be deterred. In June 1892, three Black grocery store owners who had been set up by white grocers angered by the new, dark-complexioned competition, were taken out of a Memphis, Tennessee jail and executed. Even though or, perhaps, because the men were extracted in the presence of sheriff's jailers, a sheriff's investigation ruled that they were killed by "parties unknown." One of the men, Tom Moss, said before he was shot in the head with a shotgun: "Tell my people to go west—there is no justice for them here."[22]

The godmother of Moss's daughter was Ida B. Wells. Although she was already a well-known essayist and contributor to national journals, she had only recently begun to focus on the subject of lynchings. She had already proven her ability to approach the subject with a fearless adherence to the truth when she published these words in her Memphis paper, *Free Speech*:

> Nobody in this section believes the old thread-bare lie that Negro men assault white women. If Southern white men are not careful they will over-reach themselves and a conclusion will be reached which will be very damaging to the moral reputation of their Women.[23]

These words earned her and her coeditor the threat of a lynch mob themselves. Luckily, she was in Philadelphia, Pennsylvania when they were published and the mob had to be satisfied with the destruction of her press office. The murder of one of her close friends, in a lynching where there clearly was no criminal motive, set her on her path. She would later say the lynching had been "an excuse to get rid of Negroes who were acquiring wealth and property and thus keep the race terrorized."[24] She began to investigate lynchings in detail, which led to the publication of her famous pamphlet "Southern Horrors: Lynch Law in All Its Phases." In it she detailed, with compelling evidence, how the charge of rape was only levied in a third of lynchings. In his preface to "Southern Horrors," the then-aged and globally respected Frederick Douglass, impressed by her truth telling, exclaimed: "Brave woman!"[25]

Wells would spend the rest of her life in a fierce campaign to end the practice of lynching as one of our greatest and bravest antifascist fighters. Her work would be taken up in the next century by the newly formed National Association for the Advancement of Colored People and other Black organizations. The radical pan-Africanist Civil Rights Congress, which included Du Bois as one of its organizers, would attempt to indict the US at the newly formed United Nations, citing lynching in its paper, "We Charge Genocide." Thanks in large part to Wells's heroic effort, by the time of the 1954 *Brown v. Board of Education* decision, ruling school segregation illegal, lynching had become a liability to the South's image and the public spectacle lynching had been replaced by the underground, clandestine sort; even then, outright murder and political violence could prove more of a liability than a winning strategy.[26]

No more than a year after the *Brown* decision, the first white citizens' council was formed in Indianola, Mississippi. Positioning itself as the "respectable" face of segregation, it eschewed connections to violence and vowed to use "all legal means to secure the southern way of life."[27] Of course, as history has demonstrated, these citizens councils were never more than twice removed from racial terror groups such as the Klan and the American Nazi Party.[28]

The organization's most famous moment came in 1957 when nine Black students were selected to test the state of Arkansas's compliance with desegregation by attempting to enter Little Rock Central High School. A photograph of 15-year-old Black girl Elizabeth Eckford (62 years of age at the time of this writing and still fighting segregation in schools), walking toward the entrance of the school while a mob of angry white women followed her spitting mad and shouting vitriol, became the face of the white citizens' councils worldwide.[29] The council had successfully lobbied Arkansas Governor Orville Faubus to bring in the National Guard to block the Black students from entering the school. Eckford had to escape the mob and return later that month, this time under escort of the 101st Airborne.[30]

Although the official council chapters seem to have been confined to the South, influence spread to the West and up North. Joseph Mitchell, a local politician from upstate New York, became director of councils in Virginia, Maryland, and Washington, DC.[31] Regardless of direct council affiliation, white people across the country, in the North and South, organized local resistance to school desegregation and continue to do so today.

The drama captured in that famous photograph was replicated hundreds of times throughout the period, in locations across the country, in moments never captured except by the memory of those who endured them. One was an 8-year-old Black boy in The Bronx, starting his second first day of the third grade. Perhaps I can be grateful that my father was not lynched because of the brave work of Black antifascists who came before him. It is certain that I can be thankful for my education because he continued that fight, as he was thrust, unwittingly, into this struggle before he would make double digits.

Home Is Where the Hatred Is

Nothing ever worked right in the home I was raised in. Outlets failed without warning, letting out a spark and an alarming popping sound, lights flickered every now and then in a ghostly manner, and starting the oven could be perilous. I remember one day my mom was baking something. Me and my brothers were in the living room, separated from the kitchen by a short path where the stairs ended at a closet door. The stairs were overflow seating when the best spots were taken on the couch, to see the television. And that's where I was sitting when my mother went to check the food in the oven. All of a sudden, a sound like a rush of air and the crackle of fire came from the kitchen and, just as suddenly, my mother came running into the living room with no eyebrows. When me and my brothers finished laughing at the sight of my mother's extreme makeover, we calmly pondered how lucky it was that she was not seriously hurt.

These "defects" were no accident. The place where I grew up, La Jolla, California, was a sundown suburb of San Diego. In the 1960 census, there were over 230 Black people living there. By 1970, that number had fallen to around 60.[32] At some point in the 1960s, the town had expelled most of its already small Black population. Like many places in the West and Northeast, white people found the beautiful beaches of La Jolla the perfect setting for their white utopia. It would become the breeding ground of racist pissants such as Tucker Carlson and the location of opulent second and third homes for vulture capitalists such as Mitt Romney. By the 1980s, it had become one of the wealthiest zip codes in the country.

At that time, my mother was working at a daycare program for the mostly Mexican house servants who worked in the mansions there and typically travelled obscene distances to work for racist snobs who would never countenance allowing such people to live next door. The program was run out of the African Methodist and Episcopal Church, which was a remnant of the larger Black community that had settled there in the past. The church decided to take advantage of federal funds provided through the Section 8 program and build affordable housing for the people who worked there and the families it served. When the towns' white residents could not stop construction of the new housing complex, the contractors attempted to sabotage the units by putting faulty wiring, plumbing, and gas lines that would not pass federal building codes. Ultimately, the church fought and forced the contractors to bring the buildings up to code. The result was eight two-story townhouses with three rooms each, suitable to raise a large family in, although the infrastructure barely passed code.

When my mother, father, two older brothers, and 6-month-old me moved in, we were an island of color in a violently white neighborhood. My neighbors were Mexican, Vietnamese, African American, and African African (Ugandan American). My Mexican neighbors would later tell me how the police would pick any of the brown kids up after school, especially if they had a pager. They wouldn't charge them with anything. They would just put them in the back of the car and beat them, call them "beaner," and drop them off in the alley behind the library. We learned to fear the police from a young age; luckily for us, though, the police were rarely in the mainly rich and white neighborhood.

One time, when my older brother was in high school, he was riding around with his friends, who were all white. He was in the backseat but, when the police pulled them over, the cop went to the back window and demanded my brother's identification card. Then they asked if the other kids were "OK." When the white kids answered that they were fine, without checking the driver's identification card, the officer let them go on their way.

By the time I got to high school, there were several little cliques of neo-Confederates and neo-Nazis. In history class, we did a re-enactment of the Versailles Treaty process. The white boys in the German delegation decided to make paper armbands emblazoned with swastikas, as part of their costume. Even though this was not historically accurate, the teachers said nothing. In English class, I was asked to confirm stereotypes that my teacher had formed with inspiration from our readings. Apparently, Shakespeare had said something about African people's breath smelling bad: "You know what I mean, right?" I was asked to absolve Joseph Conrad of his racism, my 10th-grade career being a valid counterpoint to Nobel

Prize-winning author Chinua Achebe's critique of *The Heart of Darkness*: "You don't think it's racist, do you?"

These more trivial microaggressions signified more sinister undercurrents. When a friend, who was also Black, and I were walking by the beach, a car full of white boys drove by shouting, "Go home, niggers." We chased them but they drove off. The lunch tables where the Black students ate were vandalized with epithets and swastikas. Years later, while working for the "No on Eight" campaign outside my local polling station, a white man in a black Suburban yelled, "Go home, you faggot nigger!" That same night, the first Black president was elected. By that time, one of the little racist cliques, the La Jolla surf rats as they called themselves, had killed a man in a bar fight.

The sickness that infused the little suburb I grew up in, with beautiful beaches and ugly people, was transmitted directly from the neo-Confederate movement. The segregationists were absorbed into the broader conservative movement and met success in the election of Ronald Reagan as California's governor. Along with legal attacks on queer folk and those living with mental illness, Reagan pioneered color-blind segregation with his attack on the then–tuition-free university system.[33] These efforts would culminate, several years later, in Proposition 13, which drastically reduced funding to public schools by limiting property taxes. This left areas with high property values and the money to fund their own school initiatives with all the resources while Black and poor schools scraped by with the bare minimum.[34]

One of my neighbors and best friends growing up ended up moving southeast, to San Diego's Black belt along Imperial Avenue. The high school he went to, which was the same one my mother graduated from, didn't have books or a library. Students read from "study packets" that consisted of photocopies of textbooks made by the teachers themselves. Meanwhile, not only did La Jolla High School have a library, there was a newly built Nike turf field for the football team and a multimillion-dollar aquatic complex under construction with funds raised from parents and local businesses.

The schools were not the only difference. One day when I was giving my girlfriend at the time a ride back to her house, which was also in the Black belt, we were stopped by the police. With some irony, I recall War's "Why Can't We Be Friends" playing on the radio just before looking over and seeing a police cruiser stopped at the light beside us. What had been a moment of jovial singing and levity quickly transformed into a somber terror as I began to drive with the green light and noticed the cop stayed at the line and then pulled up behind me. He flashed his lights and briefly whooped his siren. When I pulled over, the cop used his floodlight to blind my rear view. He then issued commands from the loudspeaker mounted on his car: "Take your keys out of the ignition and put them on the dashboard and put your hands on the steering wheel where I can see them."

As I nervously tried to follow all his commands, an officer approached my window with his gun aimed at my head. The officer on the loudspeaker yelled again, "Keep your hands on the wheel!" Once the other officer arrived at my window, he ordered me to open the door slowly. I was too afraid even to look in the direction of my girlfriend. I don't know how she was at that moment, but I remember wanting to know so bad. With all my restraint I never looked, imagining that one strange move could put my teenage brains all over the windshield.

Once outside the car and against the wall, while other officers searched my car, I worked up enough courage to ask the officer patting me down why they had stopped us. He informed me that we "fit the description" of a Black male and Black female in a blue car.

With budget cuts to everything from welfare programs to schools, the police and prisons were some of the few well-resourced institutions the Black community was able to have. Although crumbling schools and poverty pushed many students in the Black belt to drop out, those same kids became easy prey for criminalization by the police who would capture them and put them in the burgeoning ranks of the mass incarceration system. By the time I reached high school, the state of California had built 10 new prisons in the past decade but only 2 new universities.[35] The twin "color-blind" policies stemming from the neo-Confederate movement—tuition fees and school defunding—would serve to dispossess a generation of San Diego's Black belt of its youth.

The Face of Fascism

While working on Barack Obama's first campaign in a poor area of Poway, a white suburb of San Diego, several residents threatened to shoot me and my team. People started to come out their houses screaming about private property and one woman, at least, brandishing a gun. I gathered my team as quickly as I could and got us out of there. We later learned Poway was home to the grand wizard of San Diego's KKK. In La Mesa, another mostly white suburb of San Diego, I was talking with a supporter in his backyard when his neighbor opened fire with what appeared to be a .22 caliber rifle, the bullets softly whizzing through leaves and past our heads. When the person I was talking to screamed, the neighbor shouted, "Sorry, I was aiming at the birds." We didn't see any birds around. That same day, the police came to check on my activities on two separate occasions, saying they received calls from concerned residents.

I didn't connect these things to fascism until I moved to London, England, and joined the coalition Unite Against Fascism (UAF). I remember being shocked that, in the 21st century, there was still a fascist movement in Europe and that it was growing. In fact, despite overtures about the spread of democracy in Europe with the US's North Atlantic alliance with Western European countries, many of those countries remained under fascist rule well into the 20th century. Charles De Gaulle of France's collaborationist government only fell in 1968, whereas Portugal's fascist government lasted until the 1970s, and Francisco Franco's party in Spain maintained power until 1999. The US did not fight a war against fascism but against Germany, and allied itself with fascist governments to advance its own imperial interests.

The main fascist movement on the rise at the time was the English Defence League (EDL), a knothead gang of white Brits who would terrorize leftists and Muslims. The main target of its ire was Whitechapel in East London, which was home to the East London Mosque, the UK's largest mosque situated in the heart of London's Bangladeshi community. It was also where I lived. Everything I loved about living there—the sea of brown bodies speaking aggressive Bengali, selling samosas, and operating vegetable stands, bathed five times a day in the beautiful incantations of the mosque's call to prayer—represented everything the dickheads of the EDL despised.

In my first action with UAF, we went to Luton, England, where the EDL held an annual rally in celebration of their founding in that town. Our strategy was to show up early and block the train station so that their supporters from across the country could not disembark. We formed a human barricade around the station gates and the police lined up and began snatching people off the line for arrest. We held strong and when a police officer would try to grab one of our comrades, we grabbed them and pulled them back into the line. Union train conductors hearing about our actions refused to stop the trains and let people out in the next town instead, delaying and preventing their members from even stepping foot in the town.

Later that day, as those fascists who came on buses attempted to march, we charged through police lines to block them. The police were punching antifascists and beating them as we charged, but were overwhelmed by our numbers. The fascists had to be content with a rally in the town square. I learned that to confront fascism required absolute solidarity and trust in the comrade standing next to you. It also became clear that the police were on the side of the fascists and, if they were not members themselves, their very job required that they protect them.

UAF was everywhere the EDL tried to march. UAF had built a strong coalition with mosque leaders and leaders in the Bangladeshi community, and the EDL was never able to march in Whitechapel. We carried on the antifascist tradition of the battle of Cable Street, which took place in that same area when the Hitler-aligned Blackshirts attempted to march on the then-majority Jewish neighborhood in the 1930s. In that battle, residents threw furniture out of the windows onto the police who were trying to escort the Blackshirts down Cable Street. Militants manned barricades and, through fists and blows, were able to turn back the police and the Blackshirts.

Unable to set foot in Whitechapel, the EDL decided to try to march on the large Bangladeshi community in the outer borough of Walthamstow. The UAF and Walthamstow United prepared the community for confrontation for weeks before the march. Having already built strong ties with the Bangladeshi and broader Asian community there, antifascists were able to mobilize the whole community, including the youth, which would prove pivotal on the day of the march. The police used public buses and barricades to keep us from getting near the fascists. We organized our own countermarch with an official route. At the critical moment, the Bangladeshi youth led a splinter march in a direct route to the fascist starting point; using local knowledge of the roads, we were able to out-maneuver the police and crash the EDL's rallying point. As police quickly mobilized to protect the small contingent of fascists who had arrived early, we overwhelmed the space with hundreds of militant youth. The EDL members were forced to flee.

In the months following this decisive defeat, the EDL would dis-integrate in a cycle of infighting. By mobilizing as broad a swath of the community as possible and engaging in concerted action by militant anti-fascists to take away space from the fascists and deny them a platform, the UAF was able to defeat rising fascist organizations in the street.

As I came face to face with self-proclaimed fascists in the streets, I began to recognize these people in the white boys who would yell "nigger" at me from their car where I grew up, in the angry George W. Bush sup-porters who threatened me with guns, in the police who violently enforced the policies these boys' parents helped create. We obscure the homegrown fascist of the US by using the simple label "racists." We can't see the con-nections of the neo-Confederates and neo-Nazis as part of the same fascist movement because we never really took stock of our own history. Neo-Confederates celebrate Jefferson Davis, just as the neo-Nazis celebrate

Hitler. The only difference is Black kids are forced to go to schools that still bear Davis's name whereas the name of Hitler was struck from public spaces in Germany just as it disappeared from birth certificates. The difference is the US has no shame in its fascism.

Fascism Comes to Power

By the time I came back to New York, Trayvon Martin had been dead for two years, killed by the same kind of vigilantes who shot at me with rifles and called the police on me for walking the street. Killed by fascists. More recently, killed by the same jackboots with badges, were Michael Brown and Eric Garner. I joined the Black Lives Matter movement with the understanding that these murders were not the results of a system gone wrong or of individual prejudice, but the concerted effort of a movement to violently dispossess Black people. This analysis found its expression in the group NYC Shut It Down.

After months of battling the police and dozens of arrests, we became police abolitionists and developed the demand, in coalition with other groups, to defund the New York Police Department (NYPD) and redirect those resources to the Black and brown communities that had borne the brunt of their fascist police tactics. We recognized that, while the Black community was engulfed in a wave of violence through the 1980s and 1990s, the community's demands for more resources were only answered with more policing. And that the same dynamic that neo-Confederates had engineered in California had come to pass in New York as well. These policies, meant to control and dispossess the Black population, were merely a continuation of the colonial practices the Spanish had begun when they first brought enslaved Africans to the New World over five hundred years ago. Mass incarceration was a policy of neocolonization.

It should have come as no surprise to those who endeavored to study the history of the US that, in a time of monumental challenge to this neo-colonial regime, the conservative movement would put forward a fascist candidate. Donald Trump, whose father had been a member of the KKK in New York and probably most known to Black New Yorkers for his lynch mob–like crusade to execute the Central Park Five, announced his candidacy with a racist tirade against Mexican immigrants.

At the same time, we began meeting with groups in our abolitionist coalition to develop ways to counter his campaign, recognizing that not only was he the police candidate but that his campaign represented an openly fascist attack on Black and brown people. When we got wind of a fundraiser he intended to hold at the Hyatt Hotel at Grand Central Station, we reached out to other activist groups, labor unions, and immigrant justice organizers to build as broad a coalition as possible. We pushed to unite these groups around three points of unity:

1. Trump's campaign represented an ascendant fascism in the US.

2. We would operate under the principles of "No Platform" and work to deny the Trump campaign any space in New York City (NYC).

3. The strategy for the day of the fundraiser would be maximum disruption with the dual tactics of a rally and several smaller and independently organized direct actions.

In addition to logistics for the rally, which included thousands of union workers who were set to join after a separate march planned for the same day, we spearheaded organization of a direct action. Using an internal code of signaling and flags for directing mass movement, our plan was to lead a three-pronged attack on the hotel, with the goal of entering the fundraiser and shutting it down.

The fascists had also planned for disruption. One operative, one-time actor and gun store owner Angelo Bosignor, who had appeared in the past to inform on and disrupt leftist events, entered our rally with a Make America Great Again (MAGA) hat early in the day. He was obviously a provocateur. The police had already threatened to arrest some of our comrades who had approached the miniscule Trump rally that had formed at the entrance to the hotel. But they looked the other way when this belligerent white man, who was obviously a Trump supporter, approached our rally.

He approached the first Black woman he saw and started pushing her and yelling in her face. When I put my body in between them and told him to back away, I knew he was attempting to provoke a violent response. Knowing that I could not be arrested before the planned direct action, I was determined not to throw the first punch. Instead, I stood there with my hands raised in the air. Frustrated that I was not moving, he pulled back and punched me in the mouth. Comrades then grabbed him from behind and, as he turned around to swing at them, I locked his arm in a hold around the back of his head. Bleeding from a gash in my lip and with a mouth full of blood, I pulled him out of our rally and threw him toward the cops, who had turned a blind eye to his violence. They promptly escorted him to the Trump rally, without questioning him or asking if I was OK, if I wanted to press charges, nothing. He was clearly one of theirs.

Although the incident had resulted in my first and only viral moment, it was only an inconvenience aside from the work to be done that day. The goal was to deny Trump a platform and it would take discipline in the face of violent opposition to have a chance of achieving it. After a speech, the signal was given that Trump would soon arrive, and I led the first contingent to attempt to enter the hotel. The entire front entrance was guarded by two rows of about 50 NYPD officers and presumably some Secret Service agents. The Strategic Response Group (SRG) and Critical Response Command, paramilitary wings of the NYPD, flanked the officers with riot gear and assault rifles. Of course, the front entrance was not an option.

However, we had obtained detailed layouts of the entrances from Grand Central Station and put together a strategy to enter the ones that seemed most insecure. The first march was supposed to be a distraction to pull police from their posts and later provide reinforcements to the second and third prongs. I led about 150–200 people on a long route away from the obvious entrances to the hotel. Sure enough, a large contingent of police with zip ties and riot gear followed us. Receiving the signal that the second prong had begun to mobilize, we began our approach from the rear road ramp under the MetLife building.

The police were able to form a small roadblock, which deterred our less-militant marchers and, in a decisive moment of hesitation, allowed for police to block the road with reinforcements. Undaunted, we circled the police back on themselves and, in the traffic jam, were able to secure an opening to the ramp that service vehicles used to access the service entrances of the hotel. We charged the ramp with about 60 marchers and were able to see the service doors being closed by frightened workers who had not been brought into the planning process. Faced with a phalanx of riot police further up the ramp, we turned back and regrouped with the rest of the march.

At this point, the other prongs had also been turned back and we all regrouped on the floor of Grand Central Station. The police seemed frightened and confused at the large and coordinated effort to enter the hotel. Smaller groups had used their white privilege to walk into the lobby, passing as guests, where they staged a sit in at the entrance to the event. They were promptly arrested and held in a brigade of paddy wagons that had been deployed for the event. In the main concourse, another couple hundred or so antifascists assembled as we coordinated our next push.

The plan was to take three different routes to the valet parking center located on the second floor of Grand Central Station, which was connected by an elevated road to the valet entrance of the hotel. Once police realized what we were doing, they attempted to get the rental car center workers to lock the doors. But in their half-hearted effort, we were able to overrun the entrances; the workers smiled at us while we poured past them through the door. With about 50 people, we rushed the elevated driveway toward the valet entrance. At that moment, a hundred or so police brandishing batons poured out of the valet entrance and formed a phalanx. As people turned back to attempt to make a circle around the road, which provided a different approach, SRG officers started snatching everybody, putting them in handcuffs and throwing them against the walls and parked cars.

One of my comrades, an older white woman, was thrown down by the police. When I went over to help her, they grabbed me. As they put me in handcuffs, I looked down at her and said, "Are you OK?" Although her leg was hurt, upon seeing me she smiled. A journalist who had some-how made it up there in the chaos tried to ask me a few questions, but the police dragged us away. We were led to the bridge that crosses 42nd Street, overlooking the crowd of around a thousand still assembled at the rally. As they shackled us and put us into windowless vans, we could hear the crowd chanting the lyrics to Kendrick Lamar's "Alright." At that moment, I smiled, knowing that, even though fascism had won that day, I was still proud to take my place among my ancestors who have been resisting fascism for five hundred years.

Antiracist Skinheads and the Birth of Anti-Racist Action:
An Interview with Mic Crenshaw

Shane Burley

The militant antifascist movement that has exploded in the US since 2015 has its roots in an earlier tradition that traces back to the 1980s. As young kids were trying to deal with the arrival of neo-Nazi and Ku Klux Klan–connected gangs in cities such as Minneapolis, Minnesota, Chicago, Illinois, and Portland, Oregon, many of them pulled from the earlier British scene of multiracial, antiracist skinhead crews, a working-class subculture that bonded around music such as Reggae, Ska, and, eventually, punk and hardcore. Early crews such as the Baldies and Skinheads Against Racial Prejudice (SHARP) pushed Nazis out of neighborhoods, bars, and venues where they were trying to make inroads, creating a fighting force that started the "where they go, we go" strategy of intervention.

Where I live in Portland, that was especially incendiary because of the absolute density of neo-Nazis patrolling the streets of the city in the 1980s and 1990s: You could barely head to a park, music venue, or bar without seeing boots and braces. Many of those young people fighting back against neo-Nazi violence looked similar, shaved heads and Doc Martens, and were organizing groups to stop the advance of racist groups into neighborhoods where the rest of us lived.[1]

These antiracist skinhead groups started forming networks across the country, first as a confederation called the Syndicate, and eventually what would become Anti-Racist Action (ARA) in the 1990s, the precursor to antifa groups today. One of the earliest founders of the Baldies, one of the first antiracist skinhead crews, and ARA was Mic Crenshaw, a Black teenaged skinhead who started pulling together a group of friends to fight back against racist gangs such as the White Knights.

I talked to Crenshaw, who continues to be a radical organizer, educator, and musician, about those early days, how they formed a movement that would steamroll over the decades, and what lessons we can take from his experiences.

Shane Burley: How did you first get involved in the skinhead scene? What attracted you to it?

Mic Crenshaw: I was a teenage kid in high school. I had a lot of identity stuff going on, you know. We had moved from the South Side of Chicago, mostly Black areas, moving around a lot in the white suburban areas, the semirural areas, by the time I moved to Minnesota in junior high. I didn't really know how to fit in. So I kind of was drawn to misfits, kids who were smoking weed and listening to alternative music.

I was getting exposed to the scene and I was going to shows that were alternative in the way people dressed, the way people behaved and interacted with each other. It didn't look anything like what I was used to in the mainstream.

I ended up with a problem with drugs, so I wound up going to treatment. When I was in treatment, they were like, you need a new group of friends. You can't hang out with your old user friends. So when I got out of treatment, I started going to Uptown, which is the neighborhood where all the hardcore punks and skins hung out.

I would show up by myself, fascinated by people's dress styles and really curious about how I could maybe be part of this. And in that environment, I met a couple guys who were these straight edge skinheads. And we started hanging together. We really just had a lot of chemistry.

For me, it was a lifesaver. I found some guys who can have fun, who can skateboard, who can be ourselves. But they're not getting high and drunk. And we were having just as much fun without the drugs and alcohol and whatnot—that small clique of guys is what started the Baldies.

SB: A lot of the SHARPs I talk to here in Portland have a similar story: that in their punk scene people started getting into hard drugs and they were looking for a better community.

MC: The straight edge culture wasn't like an overt political thing. They weren't going around proselytizing about the power of sobriety or anything like that. We got together with about three or four other guys. And we would just trip around the city, doing stuff. And we had heard rumors about skinhead culture, and we were curious.

We talked a lot about movies like *The Wanderers* and *The Warriors* and the bald-headed gangs that were in those movies. And we're wondering, are those guys supposed to be skinheads? Around that time, we got hold of this book called *Skinhead* by Nick Knight. And that was a really important point of reference for us because it was almost like a bible in terms of the fashion and the history of the skinhead subculture.

We passed that book around, and we all started emulating what we saw in the book. For me, as a Black kid in a mostly white scene, it was really important that there were Black skinheads in that book. And it was really important that I found out that the roots of the skinhead subculture actually came from Jamaican immigrants. And so there was something for me to identify with in there.

And that was the beginning of it. There were seven of us. And I think we had maybe one summer of being kind of innocent—not innocent like ignorant, but just kids, you know? And right after that first summer or maybe even before that first summer was over, we heard about the White Knights.[2]

SB: Was that the first time you came in contact with a white supremacist group?

MC: We were starting to see these guys on TV. They're coming on the talk shows and being Nazi skinheads. And I think that was what fueled the rise of wannabe boneheads and what allowed the White Knights to actually pop up in our community and be a real presence.

So when we confronted them, we all looked at each other like, "Hell no, we're not gonna stand for this." And so we found them and confronted them. And that was my first encounter with an organized white supremacist group.

SB: How did you first encounter them? Like did you see them on the street? They were out in public and that kind of thing, and then you decided to go confront them?

MC: Now, Minneapolis at that time, South Minneapolis, there was a neighborhood called Uptown. It's real, real different today. But back then, it was where the punk scene was central. If you weren't at shows and record stores, you were Uptown. It was just about six square blocks.

And everybody, the punk kids, the goth kids, all the different cliques hung out up there. So these guys were guys that were part of our scene too. They had organized themselves, or had been organized by this Klansman who was also part of the scene, into a group. And they weren't hard to find.

I think I remember the first night we heard that they were in the area. I think they might have been coming from a party or something. Because we found them in the parking lot behind an apartment building. And they were all together. And somebody came and told us where they were. We grouped up, and we went and then we faced off. It was like a circle. We were on one side of the circle. We had our first conversation: "Hey, are you guys white power?"

They said yes, maybe even told us straight out that they were White Knights. We told them that you need to figure out how to denounce that shit. And if you can't denounce it, the next time we see you, there's gonna be a problem. We're gonna basically fuck you up.

And so that was the beginning of the conflict between us and them. A couple of them flipped immediately and started hanging with us and never looked back. There were a couple fence-sitters who tried to go back and forth and be cool with everybody. And then there was definitely a core group of those guys that stayed in the white power scene.

SB: Did you think of yourselves as activists?

MC: I didn't at that point. That's what's always kind of like interesting whenever we talk about this stuff—I think there's certain journalists and academics who, from their perspective, it's a lot clearer of a trajectory or a connection between what we did and what looks like antifascist activism today. But to me, there was something way more organic in that we were just friends who identified that there was a group of problematic individuals in our scene.

And so as friends, we said we're gonna confront these guys. And we all had each other's backs. That was the beginning of what became activism. And it was the beginning of us being politicized. But I think in the beginning we didn't think of it as activism. We just thought of it as, like, we gotta do this shit.

SB: How'd you start moving from just confronting them to actually pushing them out of the city?

MC: It was the natural progression. "The next time we see you guys, if you're still claiming white power, there's gonna be a problem." So that was a commitment to violence, right? We knew that's what that meant for us and what it meant for them was that we were gonna fight. And once it became clear that we were gonna fight them, fights started to happen.

After a handful of fights, it became clear that the white power guys were not just going to disappear and we had to organize to protect our friends and community. And I think that's when we started asking these critical questions about who our allies were going to be.

The scene got divided. There were people who were gonna ride with them. And there were people who were gonna ride with us. There was a question about how we build support for what we were trying to do here. I think that's when we realized we were actually becoming a political force.

There was a spectrum of people who would align with us. There were these gang members that we knew that were either distant family or cousins or friends of ours from the community or high school or whatever and didn't so much have a political consciousness but were like, fuck racism. And then there were these cats who were radical anarchists that were definitely reading theory and more intellectual about their politicized approach to activism. And building allegiances with those groups was the beginning of what ultimately became ARA.

334

SB: How did you first start getting in contact with other skinhead groups, other antiracist skinhead groups?

MC: I think it was through the Scene Reports in *Maximum Rocknroll* and through people who were traveling. It was pretty common for somebody to jump in a van with one of the touring bands. A couple carloads of people would go to Chicago or one of the nearest big cities to see one of our favorite hardcore bands, like Agnostic Front.

And it was during that kind of interscene activity, usually centered around music, that you would meet people. You would party with people. And you would learn about what was happening in their cities. And there was a strong connection to Chicago because I was always going back and forth to Chicago, being as that's where I was originally from.

When I would go to Chicago to visit my family, I would find the scene and go hang out. So I was hearing, listening, the word on the street was that there were Black skinheads in Chicago. There were some notorious Black skinheads. So I sought those guys out.

And I found them. I met them. And I made a point of connecting our crews and staying in touch with them. And those relationships expanded and grew. And we became really close with SHOC, which was Skinheads of Chicago.

Kieran Knutson, another founder of the Baldies and ARA, did a lot of work and he established connections with these guys in Lawrence, Kansas. There was a crew out of Milwaukee [Wisconsin]. There were guys in Madison [Wisconsin], Indianapolis [Indiana]. So all these Midwestern cities came to Minneapolis for this syndicate meeting in like—shit, it was like 1987, 1988, I think. And it was the wintertime.

And that was the hardcore fighting force. Like they were all hardcore antiracist skinheads. Everybody touched down boots, had fight jackets, Doc Martens. And so, to me, there's an important aspect of the skinhead culture that was at the core about violent confrontation and organized mutual aid. From that core, we built relationships with other people who weren't necessarily skinheads.

SB: The Syndicate was a sort of federation of different skinhead crews coming together. How did they coordinate with you? Are they how you first landed in Portland?

MC: There was a trip that was taken to Portland that was part of that outreach and mutual aid culture. It came to our attention that there was a really bad Nazi problem in Portland. A carload of three Baldies went out to Portland and helped fight Nazis over a number of days.

And while they were out here, they met up with another Black skinhead from SHOC, Malachi aka Mickey. And they really put in work. And that work was done to support the Portland SHARPs. From that moment on, we were like blood brothers.

When I then came to Portland later, in 1990, I knew exactly who I was looking for. And they welcomed me with open arms. And so those relationships persist to this day because it was through those relationships that I knew I had family here.

SB: What were the gender dynamics like in the crew? How was sexism addressed?

MC: We had such a male-dominated culture. Somebody was asking me the other day about why I don't hang out in the crew scene anymore. And for many years now, I've distanced myself from that kind of activity. There's a lot of reasons for it, but one of them is that, honestly, there's too many fucking dudes around all the time. It's not a good balance. I don't want to be in an environment where 90% of the people there are dudes. I like women, I like having relationships with women, platonic as well as romantic, and there's always this tension when there's only like 4 or 5 women around and there's 30 dudes. There's a lot of patriarchal possessive shit in the treatment of them. Is that someone's girlfriend? Will I get in a fight if I talk to her?

Some of the strongest women I know to this day were part of our scene. That scene forced them to be strong. Because they were surrounded by all this patriarchy all the time.

But I think there were just a lot of limitations ultimately to being in such a male-dominated scene that I wanted to kind of move beyond. When we talk about patriarchy in our own crew, the women who were down with us, we loved each other, and they wanted to fight with us. Early on, the men were trying to go fight the fights and tell the women to not come along. And they were like—they put their foot down. They were like, fuck that. We're going with you. Don't be sexist.

And so they started rolling with us, and we would all fight together. That's the most concrete example of what the dynamic was that we just thought was normal but realized was problematic and then how that dynamic changed because the women put their foot down.

SB: Once you formed the Syndicate, how did y'all start coordinating? Were people trying figure out where the largest concentrations of white supremacist groups were to get people out to those cities?

MC: People started talking on the phone, figuring out what was what by getting reports from others. Planned activities; a lot of shit revolved around shows. We would go to shows in other cities. I remember going to Agnostic Front. I think it was 1988, they were doing a big tour for their *Live at CBGB's* album.

When you travel from scene to scene like that, you meet people. And it's a pretty tight bond you establish because you're sharing this subculture that only so many people understand and commit to. And you're finding out the comradery that's available in the subculture is one where people will fight with you and stand by your side. And really tight bonds are formed then. So it's almost like an extended family network that just kind of organically emerges from people interacting with each other.

SB: So you moved out to Portland in the early 1990s. Had you already formed ARA by the time you got out here?

MC: ARA had been in existence for a couple years before I left Minneapolis.

SB: How did ARA first start when you were organizing in Minneapolis?

MC: Coming off the Syndicate meetings and building allegiances with people who weren't just hardcore antiracist skinheads, it became apparent that there was a network that was bigger than the Baldies and that that network even extended beyond what the Syndicate, which was all hardcore skinhead crews—it exceeded the capacity of the Syndicate. We were trying to think of a name for that network. And I think Kieran suggested Anti-Racist Action.

I remember the—I vaguely remember the discussion of us deciding, yeah, Anti-Racist Action is the name because we're—we believe in direct action. And we're not just gonna talk. We're gonna take action. And so that was coined by the Minneapolis Baldies.

And that name started to circulate. And then, you know, different kinds of branding and imagery started. You started to see that associated with different crews in different cities and states and stuff.

SB: How was ARA gonna be different from the crews before?

MC: It encompassed activists from a broader spectrum of subcultures and even academics and people who might not even have been part of the hardcore scene but who wanted to do something. Somehow, they got word about organizing direct action against fascists and wanted to do something about fascism and racism in their cities. And so those were the kind of people that were attracted to ARA in Minneapolis and other cities, in Portland too and wherever ARA was springing up. There were people who were traveling.

Kieran did a lot of traveling. And so Detroit, Michigan, Chicago, Toronto, Canada, to my understanding all those places were kind of seeded by some of the work he was doing and the roots he was putting down there.

SB: What were the first kind of campaigns that y'all started doing as ARA?

MC: So my work with ARA back in Minneapolis, it was about trying to find Nazis. Say we get word that they were having a show. A lot of the Nazis, their home, their base of operation, was across the river in St. Paul, [Minnesota] a part of a white, working-class neighborhood in St. Paul.

So we would find out about their activity, and we would go over there and confront them. We'd shut down their shows. Carloads of us would go to one of their shows or where they were gonna have an event. And we'd shut it down and be ready to fight.

And they'd come to our shows, too. It was violence. Periodically, there would be times where there were just words exchanged, like, you guys need to get the fuck out of here, and that would be enough for them to go.

The messy thing that started to happen in that scene, though, was that there were guys who organized themselves into a rival crew called Minneapolis Oi Boys. Minneapolis Oi Boys became our—the enemy that was in closest proximity to us in that we wound up actually fighting more than we fought the White Knights. Because, eventually, the White Knights stopped coming around because it was too much violence.

But some people started to persecute and hate the Baldies because they said we were fascist; because we took a principled, violent stance against racists, we also went hard against people who hung out with the racists. So there were these guys who would drink beer—young men, young women—with them. They'd drink and party with the Nazis.

But they'd be like, "We're not Nazis. We just drink and party with who we want. And you can't control that. And if you guys try to pressure us, then you guys are fascists too." And so they formed themselves into a crew, and we started fighting them.

That level of violence and with that crew, the skinheads who were hanging with Nazis, being closer to us so we had to see them literally like every day, was part of what shaped my experiences. Things that started to emerge later, like people organizing to go to demonstrations and people doxing Nazis and that level of growth within ARA's tactics, that started to emerge around the time I started trying to figure out how to distance myself from the street fighting and the violence.

SB: How central was the violence? Was it the center of the work, of how you thought about it?

MC: For me, it was the core. It was about relationships, my friendships, and the violence. And the violence was an extension of us trying to protect each other, protecting ourselves.

And that defined my daily life for a number of years. That level of commitment and lived experience is different than a lot of what antiracist organizing looks like today. It was less heady, more blood and guts.

And it's also more reactive. You're responding to physical threats in your space and on a daily basis, and you're walking around with a certain degree of PTSD [post-traumatic stress disorder] and situational awareness that's constant. It burned me out; it fucked me up.

I see the Proud Boys and all that shit today, I'm very aware of what it feels like to have a violent confrontation with people. And it's not something I'm actually interested in. Because, for me, even though I'm antiracist, and I'm an activist, and my work is still centered around anti-racist activism, the violence that defined my life in this culture was based on me defending my best friends, my best friends defending me. If they were coming down the street, I knew—based on their swagger and how they walked and their silhouettes, I knew who each one of those people were. So you could have a clearer picture of what you were getting yourself into and why you were doing it. And so to deal with an environment in which you're dealing with assholes like the Proud Boys who—I don't know where these guys are coming from, but I know they're looking for a fight.

There's way more surveillance and criminalization and state support for whatever they're doing today than there was when we were young. That's just too many red flags. I gotta be able to work in a way where I'm influencing people's consciousness. Because unless those dudes come up to me and threaten my life, I'm actually gonna stay the fuck away from that shit.

SB: What was your impression of the lay of the land in Portland when you got out here?

MC: The Nazis had retreated to a degree by the time I got here. It was so bad that my friends told me that basically anyone you saw that was a skinhead in a public space was a Nazi; they were everywhere. So when I got out here, the SHARPs had become dominant and the Nazis seemed to have retreated. And to the degree that there were Nazis in the scene, they weren't stepping to me and making it apparent who they were.

And I imagine some of that shit also had to do with the Mulugeta Seraw trial. The time I moved here was synonymous with that whole trial going on. There had been a series of ARA conferences and, at the same time, there was the lawsuit that bankrupted Tom Metzger and White Aryan Resistance.

For a lot in the white power scene, that was a loss that caused them to figure out ways to be even more underground. That would eventually re-emerge as the violent skinhead gang Volksfront, and other formations.

SB: How did the cops treat the skinhead crews, the antiracist skinhead crews?

MC: So that's when I understood that we were a gang, not so much because—there was always a philosophical rift between those of us who wanted to present more gangster-like and those of us who wanted to present more activist-like. There was even a subtle undercurrent of racism, where like gangs were seen as something that Blacks and Latinos did, but we were somehow better than them.

And when the Gang Task Force started to really surveil us and follow us around and show up every time there were more than two of us, that's when I understood that we had been criminalized as such; regardless of what we wanted, our public image had been decided by the police. And I knew it had to do more with our political activity. Because we were able to observe that, even though there were gangs out here that were involved in the drug trade as their central operating principle, and we were just activists, but they were fucking with us way harder than they were fucking with them. And then you start to see that that's how we're characterized in the media as well and in the law enforcement briefings and so forth.

When I moved to Portland, one of the first nights I went out drinking with the SHARPs, the Gang Task Force rolled up on us. And they had this routine. They took pictures of us. They said, "Anybody got any new tattoos?" It was almost like there was this comradery. They were super cool with us and took pictures of new tattoos. And they let us keep our beer. And they left us the fuck alone.

And many years later, I got pulled over for basically breathing while Black. And there was a young, white cop who did not know what to do because he took my ID and ran it and then came back. He was like, "It says here you're a skinhead gang member." And I just laughed inside because he doesn't know what to do with that information. It makes no—it makes no sense to him.

SB: Were you at any of those ARA conferences, those early ones?

MC: Yeah, I was at a 1990 one held at Portland State University. It was great because I got to see some of the homies from Chicago that were out here from SHOC. I got to meet some other guys from the Bay Area [California].

The conference was regionally focused, mostly West Coast. You had all these guys from California up here. And then there were guys from Seattle [Washington]. So I'm thinking that the regional networks were being strengthened. And the relationships in those networks were being strengthened.

But like a lot of us, I didn't go to a lot of the conference in terms of the sessions, info sessions or workshops, symposiums, and all that. I was just kind of down there kicking it, catching up with people. So when I go to conferences, there's like a couple of approaches. One is to sign up and be in every scheduled activity. And one is just kind of loosely flow with it and see who you bump into. So that was my level of participation in that.

And I had some conflicts because I knew I wanted to make some shifts in my life, particularly away from violence. So I had put up a level of distance.

SB: How did you start changing? How did you kind of shift your involvement when you got out here?

MC: I kept my involvement to social activity with the SHARPs. I would hang out at the houses and party with them. But I wasn't trying to go out looking for Nazis with anybody. You know, a couple times I wound up in situations where we jumped out on people.

I was really explicit about that with those guys. I'm trying to do something different. But it was heavy at the time. Somebody got killed out here. Jon Bair, another Baldies member, took that dude from neo-Nazi band Bound for Glory's life. And I knew Bound for Glory. I was familiar with them because they used to be in a band called Mass Destruction in my time in Minneapolis. And so we used to fight those guys.

So I knew that there were just too many intersections where I could've been central. And I was just trying to stay out of the way. And, eventually, I got into music and activism and education in a different way. Because my consciousness still needed to be engaged with social activity. But just not centered on fighting like it had been back in Minneapolis.

SB: How were things changing for you? How did your consciousness on how you wanted to approach organizing change?

MC: Eventually, I got back in the classroom. That was an important part of my development because it—the reason I started teaching—we all—a handful of Baldies went to an alternative high school. And there were some teachers that were pretty radical there.

And they saw what we were doing on the streets, and they tried to intervene. And two of those teachers actually offered me a teaching job when I was a junior in high school. And they taught me how to create a curriculum that really examined the root causes of systems of oppression. And so, while I was fighting on the streets with the Baldies at night, I was coming into the high school and teaching during the day.

That was like part of the internal shift inside of me. I was meeting these older people from social justice movements, you know, these old revolutionaries. And they were like really giving me the types of props that I didn't get anywhere else.

They were like, "Yeah, it's cool to go fight Nazis. How's that going for you? You're gonna be dead or in jail. But you gotta understand that these systems of oppression have root causes that are bigger than what the symptoms are that you're trying to engage on the streets."

And so I started to get this type of recognition and validation in those circles that made me wanna study, that made me wanna read, and not just be reactive. And so when I came out to Portland, that was kind of simmering inside of me. And so I got back into the classroom.

I was trying to figure out how I can make political education part of the work that I do in the schools. And eventually, that's when I met people who asked me to participate in some of this counterrecruitment work in high schools and meet people in different social justice activist circles out here. And so that's how I got pulled back into the movement.

The American Friends Service Committee and Veterans for Peace were two of the lead organizations that I recall working together to do counterrecruitment, to let high school students know that they could opt out of having military recruiters have access to their test scores and their economic status, like whether they had single-parent families or not. So the recruiters would be targeting these marginalized kids, working-class kids, kids of color. And so we were going into these high schools and organizing and letting them know they didn't—that they could fill out something to opt out of that, recruiters having access to their information.

And during those times in the late 1990s is when I started to hear about Rose City Antifa. And my relationships are still good with Portland SHARP. And so I knew about shit that was going on, but didn't want to be involved in the way I had been back in Minneapolis.

SB: How do you all deal with the violence that you did deal with back then? How long did it stay with you? Does it still stay with you?

MC: That shit is still with me right now, man. I'm so glad that I have the street awareness that comes from that because I feel like it's saved me in many situations. I think I'm able to carry myself with an air of like, don't fuck with me, that prevents people from looking at me like a target. That comes from all that shit. And I wouldn't trade that for anything.

It marks you, though. I still have a visceral gut feeling when I see what's happening in the streets.

During the hundred days of protests that were happening in Portland in 2020, I would go down there. But I'm keeping a certain amount of distance and a certain amount of awareness when I'm in those spaces. I ended up being involved in housing and eviction defense work, and that comes from my experiences then too.

SB: What do you wish young antifascist organizers would learn from your experience?

MC: I don't know if I could impart what I learned through experience. I remember older people trying to tell me, dude, they're gonna—you're gonna fuck up your life. You're gonna be dead or in prison.

But me just being young and full of heart and thinking I'm gonna do this because y'all ain't doing shit, and this is the only thing that's gonna make a difference. So I respect that drive that people have. And I would never shit on that or tell them they're wrong for doing that because it takes that level of commitment for the enemy to think twice about what they're doing.

And we need people to be there making the enemy think twice. Because, otherwise, the enemy would be hurting and killing more people. If there weren't people taking a militant stance. I'm happy that people are militant and courageous and standing in the way and being organized. I just want people to be mindful. And I think people are smart. It doesn't take much to pay attention.

I want people to be mindful about how dangerous it is, you know, and the way that, if you get hurt or if you get killed, and you're part of this militant, antifascist, antiracist organizing culture, there's not gonna be any sympathy in the public or by the police. You're not gonna be presented in a good light. And there's not gonna be justice.

Unless it's done in such a flagrant way that they just have to prosecute somebody, you could die out here, and that would just be the end of it. We live in an environment where the hate and the ignorance and the racist shit is further emboldened by economic conditions and by the demagogue [Donald Trump] who just lost the election. That whole culture is something that's really deeply rooted in this country.

The threat the far right represents is more profound than ever before. And I want people to understand that, when we stand up and get in the way, we're fighting for our lives. And we might fucking die.

We see what happened to that guy who was calling himself antifa, Michael Reinoehl. He was killed by a federal task force in Washington. So I think we're gonna see more of that in the years to come. And we just gotta be diligent. Pay attention to your surroundings and know that there's consequences for how we present in public right now.

In the wake of the killing of George Floyd, there's almost a passive-aggressive retaliatory thing from the police and how they do their jobs, where they're gonna look the other way because they figure that the left wants to fuck over their livelihoods with that abolitionist talk. So they don't care what happens to us. And where they might turn a blind eye to people assaulting us, they're gonna overcriminalize us as well. They're gonna overprosecute us anytime we get caught doing shit on camera.

SB: What was the relationship between, I guess, like SHARPs, Baldies, and like—I don't know—like the Trojan skinhead crews, RCBB [Rose City Bovver Boys], and the kind of left political folks?

MC: Yeah. There was tension. I think when I first came out here the Baldies were on a pedestal because of what had happened where some of

343

these guys got support, material support. Baldies came out, put in work, established themselves as super hardcore street fighters who were fearless and effective.

And so when I came to town, people were like, you're a god. You know? You're a fucking Minneapolis Baldie. You're a Black skinhead. You're Mic Crenshaw. And they kind of rolled out the red carpet.

But because of that, there was . . . immediately, there were a handful of guys who wanted to be Baldies instead of Portland SHARPs. And I think that there are people who felt that they were more like alpha males [laughing] who struggled with that. Because they were like, wait a minute. You know? Don't go be—don't go being something that was invented in Minneapolis. Be proud of being Portland.

And so there was a split where some guys decided they wanted to start Portland United Baldies. And I remember that was tough for me because they were asking me. They were like, Mic, will you give us permission? And I didn't want anything to do with it. I was like, I love y'all, but I'm not trying to be at the center of this shit.

So I gave them contacts to old Minneapolis heads, and I said, talk to them. So they got permission. Those guys are my best friends, you know? And they started the Portland United Baldies. But some of the Portland SHARPs were like, fuck that. How are you guys gonna do that? And they started Rose City Bovver Boys.

And now everybody's cool. But for a while there, those guys were beefing with each other, you know? And it wasn't cool. And I tried to stay out of that. I tried to be like, you guys are all my friends. I love you all. And I'ma stay out the way. You know?

SB: You know, one of the—I think the biggest discussion I hear now between like antifascist folks is what they think is most effective: these really big mass actions, these big kind of coalition things, versus these kind of tight-knit, small groups. I guess a skinhead crew would be one version of it. Rose City Antifa might be another version of it. Everyone knows each other, vetted to get in, takes a while to do work. Whenever you're looking back, not only do you have that time, but you have like 30 years of experience on top of that. Like, what do you think is most effective for confronting these far-right groups?

There's a lot of debates about what type of organizing approach is best for confronting the far right: small, tight-knit groups or large mass movements. What do you think are the most effective approaches?

MC: At this point, my values change. You change a lot, having kids, having a mortgage, waking up early in the morning Monday through Friday. But in the end, this organizing is about relationships; if you can see each other as family, that is stronger than flimsy relationships. But one of the things that pulled me out of some parts of the left was seeing people being destructive, tearing each other down and policing each other based on who could be more politically correct or identity-based orientations. A lot of people, especially among a lot of white people, definitely needed to work on the destructive ideas about things like gender that were showing up in left spaces. But these disagreements were happening more and more among people who didn't actually bleed in the streets together, who had less investment in each other. A lot of this felt really white because the people wrapped up in these internal fights on the left were not Black folks, were not people of color. So you can't have the level of response that we used to have if you are not connected to people personally, more than just ideas.

And those bonds are like through thick and thin. And if you're one of my people, I'm gonna ride for you, and you're gonna ride for me.

And that is what—after all the years of activism and work, that's the shit that's still there. And that's not something you can just sell to somebody. That comes from commitment and struggle and time and love.

Gringos and Fascism

Mirna Wabi-Sabi

grin·go / griNGgō/ [masculine noun]
grin·ga / griNGga/ [feminine noun]
A person, especially an American, who is not Hispanic or Latino(a).

Part I: The Anti-[Blank] Manual

The Antiracist Manual by Djamila Ribeiro came out in Brazil the same month as the Portuguese translation of *Antifa: The Anti-Fascist Handbook* (*ANTIFA - O Manual Antifascista*) by Mark Bray.[1] The difference between these two manuals is not just the subjects they address (fascism and racism), it is who is speaking in each book and to whom. One is written by a Black Brazilian woman about the racism she experienced, aimed at a white audience. The other is written and translated by white-passing men, aimed at a broad audience. Considering Brazil's unique colonial history, evaluating the relationship between racism and fascism, and the resistance movements against them, may be more effective than only adopting Western antifascist tactics.

The first words of Ribeiro's book are, "As a child, I was taught that Black people used to be slaves, and that's it." Bray's book starts with, "I wish there were no need for this book."[2] He has his own marginalized identity, as a person of Jewish descent with ancestors who survived the Holocaust, although he also talks about other marginalized identities. Ribeiro, in contrast, speaks immediately, and only, from her experience as a Black woman, and this contrast between them is the microcosm of a global trend in dissemination of political theory. It is the reason American intellectual production is widely consumed in Brazil (e.g., Bray's book) whereas Brazilian intellectual production is seldom consumed in the US (e.g., hers).

This disparity in flow of knowledge is representative of imperialism, but, more importantly, of how the antifascist movement, along its aesthetic and ideological framework, could, in some cases, can be an extension of racist imperialism by reproducing Western cultural hegemony in Brazil. In other words, when he speaks, he represents all those who fall victim to fascism whereas, when she speaks, she represents only herself.

Beneath the aesthetics of these writers, we see a person describing a painful childhood memory and another stating the relevance of their work. This is worth pointing out because those of us with inescapable and visually dissident bodies are seldom given the chance to speak for all, whereas certain bodies seen as representative of human (Western) civilization are socialized to speak as such. Moreover, some people in Brazil who are fighting against what some would call fascism, and others racism, are not interested in hearing white men continue to make sweeping statements about humanity. There is little trust that these men understand the reality of Black Brazilians well enough to make such claims. And this applies to statements about destroying racist structures—a system white people are least likely to be held back by.

There is knowledge you cannot get from a book. In Brazil, we call that *lugar de fala* (place of discourse). This idea was explained to me by members of a pan-Africanist organization years ago, about my own participation as I offered to help out at their autonomous school: "You can participate, but you cannot raise your hand at a meeting to make suggestions about how we should fight anti-Black racism. White people love to come here and teach us how to do things." In other words, I must acknowledge the political context in which the dialogue is happening, and the reality of my own experience as someone who is not Black, if I want to engage with an Afrocentric movement. Afrocentrism succeeds in undermining anti-Black sentiments when it demands this from whiteness (not the person, but the whiteness in them):

> In a white, patriarchal supremacist society, can white women, black women, black men, transgender people, lesbians, gays talk in the same way as heterosexual cis white men? Is there the same space and legitimacy? When there is some space to speak, for example, for *a black travesti*, is she allowed to talk about Economics, Astrophysics, or is she only allowed to talk about issues related to being *a black travesti?* ...
>
> One of the most recurring misconceptions we see happening is the confusion between place of discourse and *representation. A black travesti may not feel represented by a white cis man, but that white cis man can theorize about the reality of trans and travesti people from* the place he occupies. ...
> In other words, it is increasingly necessary that cis white men study whiteness, cis-ness, masculinity."[3]

The lack of white representation in Afrocentric spaces is threatening only to those who seek to retain the power this representation guarantees to the already established racist structures. Meanwhile, Black representation is only a means to an end—the end of white supremacy. Ribeiro has made way for Black womanhood in academia, but she did not become the "representative" of Black Brazilian women. There is as much diversity in perspectives within the Black Brazilian population as there is everywhere else.

Letícia Parks, a Black Marxist, criticized Ribeiro for overlooking the issue of class when accepting sponsorship from a corporation that exploits workers. Ribeiro's response was to point out that it is easier for Parks to adopt a European ideology (Marxism) and center her activism on class rather than on race because she has much lighter skin and benefits from hierarchies based on skin color (colorism). Indeed, Ribeiro does not concern herself with anticapitalism as much as she does with antiracism. Nevertheless, colorism exists in Brazil and influences people's place of discourse.

No other country experienced the colonial enterprise exactly the way Brazil has—as the epicenter of the trade of enslaved people. The total number of enslaved people who died en route to Brazil was triple the total that went to the US.[4] Such carnage was enough to change the eating habits of sharks in the Atlantic Ocean,[5] who added an unprecedented layer of the macabre to the racialized abuse taking place as they followed ships.

Alongside racialized violence exists a gendered and sexualized one perpetrated against non-European women. A recent study shows that 70% of the Brazilian population are the descendants of Black and Indigenous women and European men[6]: "Such was the sexual mystique enshrouding the colored woman that infidelity and promiscuity on her part were regarded as almost inevitable," as described by a racist Welsh historian in 1977.[7] In truth, colonizers were predominantly male and shielded the few (if any) European women from the brutality of the colonial world—its sexual and political milieu—while exploiting and abusing women of color and having mixed-race children. "Memoirs, diaries, or chronicles written by females in Portuguese America have not survived the ravages of time if they existed at all,"[8] said A. J. R. Russell-Wood, all the while the enslaved population skyrocketed as much as the Indigenous population plummeted.[9]

Both the alarming decrease in the Indigenous population and the massive increase of people of African descent can be seen as genocidal. Not only because of the sheer numbers of deaths en route, but also the forced reproduction under subhuman conditions. When working conditions were not subhuman, they involved the erasure of the African (and Indigenous) identity, of any sense of belonging to a place or community, and a psychic torture that has lasted hundreds of years.

Today, despite (or due to) the history of genocide through assimilation and miscegenation, the whiter the skin, the greater the sense of belonging to the nation. It is referred to as the *complexo de vira-lata*—the "mongrel complex"—well fitting the widespread notion that we are not of pure race. So entrenched it is in our psyche that the Disney Pocahontas story of being rescued by a white "prince" is romanticized, whereas the reality of sexual assault and genocide during the colonial era is boxed away, hidden deep in our subconsciousness.[10]

A movement of Black Brazilian women has resisted this popular tendency toward self-deprecation by pioneering extraordinary spiritual and political mechanisms to reconstruct a cultural identity of the African diaspora. Carla Akotirene, a researcher from Bahia, exemplifies how there is no need to become a Marxist to address the issue of capitalism within an antiracist framework. She does this by approaching intersectionality through a spiritual African diasporic lens, tackling Western dominance with *ancestralidade* ("ancestrality"), which is unlike "ancestry" in the sense that it concerns culture more than genetic lineage. Investing in "this ancestral grammar for analytical meanings about intersectionality" is revolutionary in rescuing non-Western epistemologies from annihilation.[11]

> The initiation process—when the person recognizes and merges with the Orixá—opens the channel for a non-fascist way of life. This is because, in the long walk of reunion with African ancestral roots, we also come to understand its foundations and meanings, making it possible to incorporate a new habitus, different from the habitus created by the Western subjectivity.[12]

In my view, Africana womanism has been the most effective antifascist strategy Brazil has seen, tackling all realms of oppression from self-esteem to material conditions, infrastructure, community development, and, most importantly, survival. Unlike Western patriarchy, which feeds competition, individualism, and authoritarianism through the use of violence or force, the "matricommunity" guarantees all the basic spiritual and practical needs that a fascist government not only fails to provide,[13] but systematically deprives to marginalize and exterminate an unwanted contingent of the population.

Models of matriarchal and community societies embarked on the memories of the youth of enslaved black women and existential baggage deposited on their bodies endured all the massacre and the pain and restored strength so as to guarantee the commitment to reorganize the civilization trail of the dispersed black people, outside Africa.... [R]ecreating links with communities, the vast majority of whom are black, a population that is shattered by colonialist and Judeo-Christian logic.[14]

Candomblé and Umbanda are uniquely Brazilian religions resulting from the African diaspora, and spiritual practices many, in Brazil, describe as being of the "African Matrix." As unique expressions of this matriarchal "ancestrality," they lay out how women and natural forces can (and should also) be Deities. To reject "God" for its association with a (Christian) state is similar to the rejection of an ethnic identity for its association with racism. There are many other Deities, and to reject all is to give way to a similarly pervasive secular Westernness. Moreover, these religions of the African diaspora show how Black culture *is* Brazilian culture, no matter how hard Brazilian "fascists" try to shun it. That is the heart of the matter when speaking of what fascism looks like in this country. There are white-passing Brazilians who do not want people who are Black, Indigenous, and poor to exist.

In the Brazilian context, where miscegenation existed in place of segregation, the concepts of "white passing" and "colorism" are present in everyone's lives, whether acknowledged or not. Passing for white relates to colorism in that, although Brazilians are not broadly considered "white," this society has a structure that rewards the ability to assimilate into whiteness. In this case, assimilation means entering a room and not having Blackness make someone stand out. There are several ways to tone down Blackness, whether through changing one's hair, clothes, behavior, or even body and facial features. The effectiveness of these attempts, and the extent to which each person is able or willing to go, informs a person's level of passability and privilege:

Colorism means, in a simplified way, that discrimination also depends on a person's skin tone and pigmentation. Even among black people or people of African descent, there are differences in treatment, experiences and opportunities, depending on how dark your skin is.[15]

The differences in treatment and opportunities that Bianca Santana describes in this passage can be seen as an aspect of privilege. Having a chance to dial a racial identity up or down, depending on not only convenience but often survival, is an advantage. And when it involves a survival mechanism in the face of white supremacy, it is not quite the same as dialing up a nonexistent marginalized racial identity as entertainment—as is the case of cultural appropriation. Therefore, this issue is not binary—Black or white, privileged or not-privileged. We can simply acknowledge there is a wide range of experiences, approaches toward identity, and personal choices. The choice to access African *ancestralidade* spiritually, through Brazilian religions of the African diaspora, is to undermine the societal structure that marginally rewards those who bow to white supremacist values:

> Umbanda, like Candomblé, is a religion of African origin. And, considering the assumption of the black race and racism, it is the target, or rather, the enemy of fascism. Any work that seeks to value ancestrality can be of great importance for strengthening the fight against fascism insofar as it does not induce the hierarchy of cultural values over the other. Self-respecting work must denounce the historical processes in which there was an attempt to eliminate or discriminate against the other in their cultural existence.[16]

Part II: Capitalism, Fascism, and White Supremacy

A nation that commits genocide within the rhetoric of a superior race and national identity is fascist. Such a state not only seeks to exterminate a specific contingent of its own population, but it also seeks to expand its borders through the extermination of others. This is clear when analyzing Nazi Germany's fascist approach toward German Jews (in Germany). The same can be said about Benito Mussolini's later approach toward Italian Jews (in Italy) and any Slavic peoples between Italy and Austria (Yugoslavia, and the several Slavic identities within it). Fascism is an operation that aims to consume the whole world and to irreversibly alter the course of humanity:

> Fascism is the bourgeoisie in its most savage form. . . . The anti-capitalist struggle hurts the central point of fascism and the bourgeoisie, which is to blind the population to its own class condition, while pointing to the differences that exist within a single people, with countless ethnic and religious groups who do not need to live with the idea of a "uniform mass" which fascism preaches.[17]

Capitalism is not fascism because it often needs people alive to work. In other words, exploitation for profit is not fascism. That in no way is a measure of cruelty, just of terminology. What they have in common is that both use white supremacy and nationalism as tools. And these tools are effective because they can provide justification for both exploitation and mass murder.

Fascism is further away from the Brazilian milieu than capitalism. It was created and developed within a specific European landscape, in a particular period in time. Capitalism, in contrast, as it "developed" from colonialism, is not only thriving in this landscape, it has historically relied on countries like Brazil (colonized) to establish itself as a global ideology. Many people believe the need to re-contextualize fascism to make it fit in the Brazilian context points to how the concept has been mischaracterized, which distracts from issues that apply uniquely to us. Meanwhile, others find it necessary to frame the evolution of colonial violence in Brazil as such to convey in universal terms the scope of the violence we endure:

> Fascism is an authoritarian political movement created in the 1920s that is based on the prevalence of ideas of race and nation over individual freedoms. In Brazil, it is an anachronistic reinterpretation of a historical event that manifests itself in every fundamentally violent and authoritarian attitude that seeks to eliminate any and all manifestations of existence other than hegemonic ones. Radical religious movements, xenophobia, racism and misogyny that carry this preponderant violence against the other, for example, can be read as descendants of a fascist ethos.[18]

Applying the concept of fascism to the Brazilian context is described as anachronism because the violence it refers to comes from much before the rise of fascism in Europe. Overall, Brazilian fascism is not directed at Jews, Slavs, and so on, although there have been movements directly inspired by Mussolini—such as the 1930s Integralista party:

> In Brazil, fascism has an explicit heritage and legacy that connects it to the Integralista movement of the 1930s. However, its survival and forms of reinvention cross personalities (from the controversial Getúlio Vargas to Filinto Muller and Brilhante Ustra) and institutions (especially religious, police and military) that reconnect it to the radical youth subcultures and gerontocratic male fraternities.[19]

Integralistas centered their politics on antisemitism and anticommunism but disappeared that same decade after unsuccessfully attempting a coup against the Vargas dictatorship, which, as Cassio Brancaleone points out, existed ideologically in parallel rather than in opposition to fascism. Moreover, Brazilian fascism does not focus much on land disputes with other countries. Does that mean it is not, then, actual fascism?

For half a millennium, the Western occupation of this territory has led to the genocide of Indigenous peoples. Even after all these years, the occupation of the Amazon Rainforest is still a priority over moving on to other countries due to its sheer size. The annihilation of Indigenous peoples in Brazil has been happening for so long, across such a massive area, that new methods are constantly being tested—a cruel game of looking for the most effortless way to exterminate Indigenous people.

A modern and effective tool for genocide has been, for instance, to sell land to an industry that poisons river waters or drastically affects the fauna of a certain area. Once capitalist expansion makes it impossible for a certain Indigenous community to continue living off the land, its members are forced to enter the urban workforce to survive. Entering the workforce means going to school, using cellphones, and so on, which will likely entice a white-passing Brazilian somewhere to say, "You can't be Indigenous if you have a phone." Unfortunately, this method of erasure works, and we call it *epistemicídio* (epistemic genocide).

Epistemicídio is the genocide of identities (ancestral knowledge, culture, language, and so on) through forced assimilation into white Western society. Forced assimilation has become so rooted in the Brazilian psyche that we come to fantasize about not only assimilation but also miscegenation. Assimilating can mean the ability to marry someone whiter, and to have mixed-race children who not only will assimilate more easily but will also contribute to making the Brazilian "race" a little "purer."

The Brazilian re-contextualization of fascism within the sociological landscape of assimilation, miscegenation, and *epistemicídio* is where many people give up on staying attached to the European concept. We are supposedly given a chance to survive extermination, which introduces fascist white nationalism to the capitalist myth of meritocratic racial democracy. In other words, if we abandon our "past" selves and accept the West into our hearts, we may, perhaps, be spared a life of damnation.

The concept of racial democracy was birthed in Brazil as a response to a sociological comparison with race relations of the early 20th-century US. We did not have formal segregation, which was perceived as racially discriminatory, leading to the false conclusion that we do not have racial discrimination. Being mixed race does not stop anyone from attempting to adopt the white aesthetic—which includes language and demeanor. In fact, it is encouraged, especially within a social framework in which the terms "racial democracy" and "mongrel complex" are a thing.

Meritocracy powered by the illusion of escaping racism through the embracing of a white aesthetic is particularly cruel. Successfully assimilating and entering the workforce depend on bankrupt public resources, such as education, health, and general infrastructure. Most importantly, there is no interest in investing in these resources because, to the capitalist system, Brazil has an excess of people. This means that a large part of the population is not needed as a workforce, making them subject to, once again, extermination. And, as discussed earlier, the section of the Brazilian population least likely to assimilate and most likely to remain poor as a result is Black.

Part III: The White Aesthetic

Was it unfair to apolitical "amateur historians" when Nazi paraphernalia was banned on eBay?[20] One thing fascism and antifascism have in common is that they are often approached through symbolism and aesthetics. We debate whether white people should be allowed to have dreads, do "black face," wear Indigenous costumes, or own swastika pendants and coins. Meanwhile, we stock up on antifa pins, patches, and hoodies to be as easily identifiable to our allies as we hope our enemies to be to antifascists.

In June 2020, a "flag generator"[21] made it possible for people to personalize the antifa logo and share it online; all sorts of people made it their profile picture. In an instant, criticism came from all sides and debate erupted on Brazilian social media. Some thought it trivialized the antifa movement because it should mean more than just an online identity. Others felt the opposite, that it boosted an already trivial thing. Certainly, there is a paradox between the desire to expose an antifa "affiliation" online, symbolic as it may be, and the fact that some of the most useful aspects of the movement's work relies on true identities being kept secret.

Nevertheless, an online form of protest made sense as a response to the list of antifascists circulating on WhatsApp and threatening doxing and exposure that same week. It's unknown by whom and to what end this list was made, but it did coincide with a wave of protests in the US. On May 31st, *Reuters* reported that President Donald Trump responded to the rise of Black Lives Matter protests by designating "Antifa as [a] terrorist organization."[22] The next day, the Brazilian Chamber of Deputies was presented with a request to amend the "Antiterrorism Law No. 13,260, of March 16, 2016, in order to classify "antifa" (antifascist) groups as terrorist organizations."[23]

A trusted comrade forwarded me the 999-page portable document format (PDF) document on WhatsApp. This PDF included addresses, document numbers, shops, bars, football teams, photos, and detailed descriptions of where various antifascists worked and hung out.[24] The individuals were exposed mostly because of their online presence—"[This person] follows several Antifascist [Facebook] pages", is mentioned as an observation more than 750 times. But aesthetic features on their profiles were also used as evidence, such as "tattoos, piercings, etc."[25]

In São Paulo, Brazil, which was mentioned at least once on each page of this document, aesthetics can be a matter of life and death. If you are a skinhead wearing suspenders and Doc Martens, anarcopunks are not going to spend one second giving you the benefit of the doubt. The weight this symbolism has in Brazilian antifascist movements can be seen as hypocritical: They adhere to the standards of white antifascists in northern countries.

The visual artist Lanussi Pasquali runs an open studio in Salvador, Brazil that, among other things, offers risograph printing at cost to antiracist, antifascist, and intersectional anarchist groups. She describes the politics of imagery as such:

> Art is the exercise of freedom, so it is always political and antifascist. Or it is not art. I try to be like this. . . . Ethics and aesthetics. . . .
>
> [An] industry cannot produce art . . . it produces consumers. Art is a place, a state, a way of life that does not seek consumers; Art is never close to fascism, because it produces freedoms, multiplicities. Even if fascists try to use it, its purpose will not be achieved! Otherwise, it's not art, it's entertainment.

Are we enthralled by the antifascist movement? Or are we trying to come to terms with our own traumas and to ensure our children are not massacred the same way our ancestors were? As Lanussi would ask—is the militancy entertainment, or is it art?

Part IV: Conclusion

When I discuss aspects of Brazilian identity with *gringos* (specifically, Western Europeans and non-Mexican North Americans), it often happens that I am asked for academic sources that back my statements. There are many. Some of these are disturbing theories and myths, such as those from the sociologist Gilberto Freyre, a thinker commonly associated with the idea of racial democracy. Others are marvelous Indigenous-centric fiction and political theory, such as Ailton Krenak. And most are neither marvelous nor disturbing, just academic, such as the Portuguese professor Boaventura de Souza Santos, who coined the term *epistemicídio*. But as I said before, there is knowledge you cannot get from books.

Long before I found the words to describe these ideas about Brazilian history, identity, and racism, I saw and felt them everywhere: in my family, my home, at school, on the streets. Growing up light skinned and middle class in São Paulo, for instance, inevitably exposed me to glaring class disparities. One moment I was at a playdate with a blue-eyed girl who lived in a mansion with a tennis court and a swimming pool. Later, I was going home by bus, seeing Black children sleeping on flat cardboard boxes on the sidewalk. If I did not feel anguish knowing there was no excuse for letting families live homeless and in hunger while others luxuriate, I would not have searched for literature, papers, and thinkers that discuss these ideas: capitalism, fascism, and white supremacy. But this research presents a paradox. Must I delve into Western theory to overcome forced Westernization? Perhaps there is a Western solution to the Western problem. Perhaps not. But one thing is for sure: The extermination of human beings must end once and for all, alongside whichever malicious methods may be employed for this purpose.

In the end, it doesn't matter if the issue of fascism is being addressed by self-proclaimed antifa or not. What *gringos* can offer Brazilians through the antifascist movement depends heavily on the approach each one has toward the political conditions at hand, and its complexity and uniqueness. Is the resistance just another extension of Western dominance through its monopoly on behavior, discourse, and aesthetics—entertainment? Or is it a source of information, inspiration, and solidarity—art?

Antisemitism and the Origins of Totalitarianism

Benjamin S. Case

If you know yourself but not the enemy, for every victory gained you will also suffer a defeat. If you know neither the enemy nor yourself, you will succumb in every battle.

—Sun Tzu, *The Art of War*

Many still consider it an accident that Nazi ideology centered around anti-semitism and that Nazi policy, consistently and uncompromisingly, aimed at the persecution and finally the extermination of the Jews.

—Hannah Arendt, *The Origins of Totalitarianism*

During the 2016 election cycle, the political weathervanes turned toward fascism. During Donald Trump's presidency, we witnessed the disintegration of the body politic and learned just how vulnerable our society is to an authoritarian executive fueled by far-right propaganda. As the Joe Biden administration inevitably fails to deliver on most of its promises and a radicalized right regroups, it is worth now thinking back to 2016. The morning after the November election was surreal; the hatred that Trump's campaign kicked up had been frightening enough, but few of us really believed Trump could be president. On the eve of the election, just about every poll had Hillary Clinton comfortably ahead. That next morning, my then-partner and I left our Pittsburgh, Pennsylvania apartment and stepped out onto the street just as a city bus was passing by. The digital panel on the side of the bus ominously read: "*CHANGES COMING.*" After a moment's discussion, we realized it was a Port Authority message about changing service lines, but the sight had still stopped us wide-eyed in our tracks. Changes *were* coming. Following Trump's election, hate crimes skyrocketed, reality seemed to unravel in the mass media, and white identity politics congealed into a potent mainstream force. As civil society watched in horror and disbelief, pundits, public figures, and talking heads turned to political philosopher Hannah Arendt's 1951 book, *The Origins of Totalitarianism*, to understand and interpret what was happening.

For a time, it seemed like everyone was talking about that book: the public explosion of doublethink, the irrational adoration of a demagogue, the use of democracy to destroy democratic institutions, the startling gullibility and cynicism. What otherwise might have appeared to be facets of celebrity culture or the effects of the internet or late capitalism is revealed in *Origins* to have alarmingly close parallels in early 20th-century Europe—perhaps offering us a window into what was to come and what we could do to fight it. The book flew off the shelves; barely a week after Trump's inauguration, Amazon had sold out.

However, despite the surge in attention, few public references to *Origins* mentioned antisemitism. This is especially noteworthy considering the first 117 pages of the book are dedicated exclusively to the history of antisemitism and how it relates to the rise of fascism in Europe. The opening section of the book is titled "Antisemitism," and the following two sections, titled "Imperialism" and "Totalitarianism," build on the first, so even if a reader skipped over the first section altogether (I suspect many skipped to the third), the issue of political antisemitism is a recurring theme and a foundational concept running through the entire work. To Arendt, the role that antisemitism played is no accident of history but was integral to the social processes that led to fascism and totalitarianism.

As a tool of the far right, antisemitism plays on confusion and paradox. It is not surprising that this content in *Origins* seemed to go unmentioned in our time; antisemitism is a difficult subject, and one many on the left prefer to ignore, at least in polite company. The left has little institutional memory of serious engagement with antisemitism, and what we have is mired in misperception and contradiction. A thorough understanding of its history, dynamics, and political functions inoculates and equips antifascist forces for ideological battle.

In this chapter, I introduce Arendt's work and explore the role of antisemitism in fascist politics, drawing primarily from *Origins*. I will then discuss some of the left's weaknesses in analysis around antisemitism and anti-Zionism and how they leave us vulnerable. Finally, I will bring lessons of Arendt's work to bear on the threat of fascism we face today. This is by no means an exhaustive discussion of any of these topics, but *Origins* is an excellent starting point to discuss the importance of understanding antisemitism for the fight against fascism.

Arendt and Antifascist Thinking

Arendt is a useful thinker to turn to in our political moment. Perhaps her greatest strength is her ability to assess political developments with rigor and without dogma. When the reality unfolding before our eyes seems unbelievable, Arendt reminds us just how dangerous it is to force what we see to fit our preconceived theories.

As the Nazis rose to power, the social upheaval in Germany and Europe more broadly confronted leftists with conditions that made no sense when looking through the political lenses many took for granted. Marxist analysis was the standard, and, accordingly, the belief in the fundamental opposition of working people to the capitalist class. The masses were rallying around ideological leaders from the ruling class, but in classical Marxist logic this should have been impossible. That impossibility led political thinkers to misread what was happening in front of their eyes. As Arendt put it:

> In Marxist terms the new phenomenon of an alliance between mob and capital seemed so unnatural, so obviously in conflict with the doctrine of class struggle, that the actual dangers of the imperialist attempt—to divide mankind into master races and slave races, into higher and lower breeds, into colored peoples and white men, all of which are attempts to unify the people on the basis of the mob—were completely overlooked.[1]

The left committed a fatal error, Arendt tells us, when they refused to accept what they were witnessing and instead tried to fit reality to their analytic system. Following the war, and the accompanying discovery of the full scope of the Holocaust, analysts fell into the same trap of ignoring that which seemed to make no sense.

Arendt begins her book, published in 1951, with, "Many still consider it an accident that Nazi ideology centered around antisemitism and that Nazi policy, consistently and uncompromisingly, aimed at the persecution and finally the extermination of the Jews." For Arendt, one of the biggest mistakes historians and social scientists were making in trying to understand Nazi Germany was dismissing the structural role that antisemitism had played in the rise of fascism, preferring to see the Jewish Holocaust as a bizarre and horrifying coincidence and passing the perpetrators off as simply crazy. This view, combined with the creation of the State of Israel, enabled subsequent observers to evade the uncomfortable and fraught "Jewish question," which has hamstrung the left's ability to understand a crucial part of fascism.

Arendt's thinking is nuanced, and this is precisely what we need. Fascism demands purity in thinking, which is another way of saying it requires a lack of thinking, so a strong antifascism therefore demands critical thinking. The left's incapacity to speak the truth and incorporate what they were seeing into their analyses in the early 20th century had disastrous consequences for their ability to counter fascist forces. We can do better, if we learn from their mistakes.

Arendt's nuance can perhaps go too far at times, bending her analyses toward political moderation. It is also important to keep in mind that her thinking, like her context, is Eurocentric and she comes from a school of philosophy that pushes a thinker to come up with universal juridical theories for everything.[2] She also tends toward excessive nitpicking; for example, distinguishing between fascism, National Socialism (Nazism), and totalitarianism based on theoretical technicalities. But Arendt is at her best when she uses her keen eye for social-political dynamics and her prodigious command of language in service of unabashed truth telling. Her analysis of the rise of fascism and her identification of the mistakes the left made in trying to oppose it are razor sharp in part because she resists the shortcuts and assumptions that are built into ideological frameworks. Arendt's own politics are difficult to label because she thinks for herself and is allergic to schools of thought that she sees as stopping people from thinking. Most importantly, one does not have to accept Arendt's politics to incorporate her analysis into our own political thinking—a use of her work I believe she would encourage.

A Jew from Eastern Prussia, Arendt understood antisemitism personally as well as intellectually. In her early academic career, she faced rising discrimination and was eventually jailed, first in Germany and then in France. After escaping internment in occupied France, Arendt immigrated to the US, where she taught at a variety of universities. She became a controversial figure after her reporting and analysis of the Adolf Eichmann trial in Jerusalem, Israel, the source of her famous adage, "the banality of evil," in which her nuanced thinking and commitment to telling the truth led her to publish unpopular conclusions.[3]

Firsthand experience clearly deepens Arendt's analysis of antisemitism, but her identity was not the sole explanation for her attention to this subject. Arendt came from a school of thought committed to objective analytical rigor, and she took this commitment seriously throughout her life, sometimes to the detriment of her career. For all the flaws in the universalist approach to history, Arendt was a clear-eyed and balanced thinker.

It is worth quoting a passage of hers at length, about the "Jewish problem." The Jewish problem, also called the "Jewish question," relates to the problem that Jews posed for the 19th-century organization of Europe into states and populations into nations based on those states. Jews spanned all the borders.[4] As a group, Jews were resisting assimilation, but also had no home state they could be deported to. In other words, Jews were a puzzle piece that did not fit the nationalist *zeitgeist*, and the "Jewish question" was what to do about it. The Nazis thus termed their extermination policies the "Final Solution to the Jewish Question." In other words, the ultimate far-right solution to the unwanted people was to kill them all. But the left too has long struggled with the Jewish problem,[5] as it gets at the crux of contradictions between political rights, nation, place, and state:

> The notion that statelessness is primarily a Jewish problem was a pretext used by all governments who tried to settle the problem by ignoring it. None of the statesmen was aware that Hitler's solution of the Jewish problem, first to reduce German Jews to a nonrecognized minority in Germany, then to drive them as a stateless people across the borders, and finally to gather them back from everywhere in order to ship to extermination camps, was an eloquent demonstration to the rest of the world how to "liquidate" all problems concerning minorities and stateless. After the war it turned out that the Jewish question, which was considered the only insoluble one, was indeed solved—namely by means of a colonized and then conquered territory—but this solved neither the problem of the minorities nor the stateless. On the contrary, like virtually all other events of our century, the solution of the Jewish question merely produced a new category of refugees, the Arabs, thereby increasing the number of stateless and rightless by another 700,000 to 800,000 people. And what happened in Palestine within the smallest territory and in terms of hundreds of thousands was then repeated in India on a large scale involving many millions of people.[6]

Here, Arendt explains how the Jewish question in Europe was not only used as a domestic political tool, but as a blueprint for fascist policies toward undesirable minorities and vulnerable populations. In the same breath, she reminds us that these policies can be applied everywhere, including in Israel in the attempt to solve the Jewish question through statehood. To Arendt, problems must be addressed at their source and based on principle, not particularity. The Jewish problem was based on the particular condition of the Jews, but that did not mean the components of that problem—displacement, statelessness, xenophobia, racism—were particular to Jews. Therefore, solving the Jewish problem for the Jews in their particularity through Political Zionism did not solve its oppressive components, but merely transferred the problem to different people. Furthermore, not only has Zionism failed to liberate the Jews from any of our problems except statelessness—and in doing so created a moral crisis for Jewishness around the occupation of Palestine—but it has been fully incorporated into antisemitic discourse.

Arendt was not focusing on antisemitism or the Jewish problem merely because she was Jewish, she was focusing on these subjects because she understood them to be central to the political developments that led to the rise of fascism in the 20th century. Confronting these issues in Arendt's time can help us fight fascism in ours.

Systemic Antisemitism and Fascism

Antisemitism refers to racism targeting Jews. Today, there is a common perception on the left that, although antisemitism is a problem, it is an individual form of bigotry, distinct from the systemic oppression of racism. For a prominent example, in an interview promoting the 2017 book, *On Antisemitism: Solidarity and the Struggle for Justice*, edited by the organization Jewish Voice for Peace, former chair of the Women's March Linda Sarsour says: "But again, I want to make the distinction that while antisemitism is something that impacts Jewish Americans, it's different than anti-Black racism or Islamophobia because *it's not systemic*."[7] To be clear, by using this example, I do not mean to demonize Sarsour, who has been on the receiving end of a seemingly endless barrage of shameful accusations of antisemitism for her social justice activism.[8] I bring up her comments precisely because she is an ally, and one many on the left look to, as the misunderstanding of antisemitism she voices reflects a widespread view.[9]

Arendt's thorough historical and social analyses demonstrate how antisemitism is not only systemic—meaning it involves long-term patterns of social views and differential treatment that disadvantage some groups to benefit those in power—but was woven into the political and social processes that led toward totalitarianism. At the same time, the sentiment behind Sarsour's remark is not wrong; Jews are indeed not racially oppressed in the ways that many other racialized groups are, such as Black people in the US. Antisemitism is not anti-Black racism but directed toward Jews; it is based on a distinct history with its own dynamics and political implications.[10]

From antiquity to the Middle Ages, religious-based animosity against Jews had been referred to in various languages simply as "Jew-hatred."

Beginning in 15th-century Spain, persecution of Jews started to become racialized, which is to say, based on Jews' blood, attached to their physical bodies instead of their beliefs. As Arendt put it, "Jews had been able to escape from Judaism into conversion; from Jewishness there was no escape."[11] In the 19th century, the term *antisemitism* was introduced in Germany by antisemites to make Jew-hatred appear scientific.[12] Antisemitism was a driving political force in Europe and, with the addition of race science, soon became a linchpin of white supremacist ideology.[13]

In the first section of her book, Arendt traces a long and detailed history of how Jews, as a diasporic people with no home state, established international networks of trade and eventually capital, which enabled wealthy Jews to play a unique role in the development of banking. In this role and others, such as the elite hiring Jews to be tax collectors, distributors of goods, moneylenders, innkeepers, and other middle administrative positions, Jews in feudal Europe were expected to provide services to monarchs and the elite in exchange for the ability to settle in any territory. As foreigners collectively working for their keep, Jews were highly precarious and vulnerable to political and economic conditions. Crucially, as a class, the elite never really trusted their Jewish residents, as the Jews were ultimately foreigners who seemed to have more in common with ordinary people than with them; additionally, the common people resented the Jews because, through their special jobs, they were often the visible face of the ruling class. When Jews were deemed useful, the ruling class would protect them against attack by their neighbors, furthering the association of Jews as being special to the elite. But when rulers were embattled, expelling Jews or allowing citizens to attack Jewish neighborhoods placated angry populations and provided a pressure release valve for popular frustrations.[14]

In German race science, Jews were categorized as an Eastern race living in the West. Antisemites spent a great deal of energy trying to concoct methods for identifying Jews by sight because centuries of dwelling in Europe had allowed many Jews to pass for white.[15] This covert nature made them especially dangerous, as they were seen as being able to corrupt white society from within, both physically and culturally. In the antisemitic worldview, Jews represent a shadow ruling class comprised of a lower race, manipulating society from behind the scenes via their secret international networks. Because of the clandestine, conspiratorial, and totalizing nature of this view, any systemic problem could ultimately be traced back to the Jews.

The most illustrative source material for modern antisemitic theory is *The Protocols of the Elders of Zion*, a fabricated document from Russia first published around the turn of the 20th century, which claims to reveal the Jewish plot for global domination. Combining a variety of antisemitic myths and beliefs into a unified theory, *Protocols* purported to be leaked minutes from a meeting of powerful Jewish conspirators, outlining their plans to rule the world through control of currency, the media, and politics. Perhaps most importantly, *Protocols* tells readers that the Jews are behind both the capitalist banks and the communist ranks, playing both sides against society for their own benefit. This assertion would allow fascists to smoothly commandeer leftist rhetoric directed against capitalist exploitation while simultaneously attacking the left as illegitimate bearers of their own politics.

Antisemitism is a metanarrative; its universal logic transcends specific context, enabling it to fit any political position. In the antisemitic worldview, Jews have characteristics of a lower and a higher caste simultaneously, so Jews can be the targets of classic xenophobic and racist narratives about filth, sickness, perversion, and weakness at the very same time as Jews are ascribed characteristics such as intelligence, cunning, and ruthlessness as part of a class-based resentment against those in control. These combined notions create a unique form of racism with specific characteristics that made it an effective political tool in 19th- and 20th-century Europe, where it became the ideological basis for the Nazi movement. Since the Nazis' failure, and the Jewish Holocaust associated with it, the overt use of antisemitism has taken on a particular stigma—ironically making the accusation of antisemitism an effective political tool in its own right—but antisemitism remains an ideological foundation for contemporary fascists.[16] Here I will focus on three crucial elements of antisemitism in fascist politics.

1. The Master Race, Oppressed

Fascists appeal to regular people with the fantasy of a return to greatness. This requires a mythic past, which the fascists promise to bring back in all its glory with a might-makes-right philosophy of power. But there is an inherent contradiction—if this past was so great and so powerful, why has it fallen? When white supremacy is added to the mix, the problem becomes even more pronounced. White supremacist rhetoric says that white people are supposed to be superior, and yet the average white person who the fascists seek to recruit feels exploited and powerless—the very frustrations that make them susceptible to the allure of racial power. If Black and brown people are supposed to be inferior, what explains members of those groups competing with white people for jobs, intermarrying with whites, and becoming increasingly represented in popular culture? A powerful, behind-the-scenes manipulator is required to hold these views together into one cohesive worldview.

In white supremacist ideology, Jews are essentially secret people of color, but with all the intellect and resourcefulness of white people and more, operating covertly to destroy Western civilization from within. In this view, Jews were always of the East, but have imbedded themselves in the West as part of their "long con" strategy to conquer the world.[17] Robert Bowers attacked the Tree of Life synagogue in Pittsburgh in part because of that congregation's work with the Hebrew Immigrant Aid Society, a Jewish nonprofit that provides assistance to refugees. For Bowers, this was a front in the Jewish conspiracy to flood white America with brown people. His attack on the synagogue, and his words while he opened fire—"all Jews must die!"—represented for him a blow to this conspiracy against Western culture. Antisemitism gives fascists a story for why they, the master race, are inherently superior and yet downtrodden, exploited, and aggrieved.

2. The Socialism of Fools

Antisemitism allows fascists to smuggle their narratives into otherwise left-leaning politics and common-sense class frustrations through the mechanism of the Jewish global conspiracy. This maneuver enables the elite to establish bonds of solidarity with those they oppress and exploit on the grounds of a common enemy. In this light, non-Jewish industry, finance, and government leaders are fighting the good fight in the halls of power on the behalf of good citizens, whereas the material conditions resulting from capitalist exploitation, alienation, and authoritarian government can be blamed on the Jews. This is what white supremacists heard when Trump said he would "drain the swamp" in Washington.

As *Protocols* tells its readers, communism might sound appealing to you as a worker, but it is really just the Jews trying to turn you against the successful members of your own people. All the socialist logic about class struggle remains more or less the same, except the true ruling class is relocated to the Jews. Antisemitism thus allows the right to outflank the left to its left by parroting leftist rhetoric as though it was consistent with their own. They can then claim to be calling for the overthrow of the system or the redistribution of wealth, only from "the real" oppressors and exploiters, making it seem as though the left is a counterfeit of itself for failing to name the Jews as the true class enemy.

In Arendt's time, the left mistook the apparent rise in ostensible class consciousness that came with antisemitism as a boon to their own politics. Antisemitism was so popular in some places and its logic so closely resembled class consciousness that it was often easier to avoid confronting people on Jew-hatred in favor of winning them over to socialist politics. The move backfired, making antisemitism seem to transcend political views, deepening its apparent common sense, and fascism emerged as a more appealing articulation of radical politics. Leftist workers ended up being more susceptible to the idea that Jews were the real enemy because Jewish greed and control could be overlaid on capitalist and imperialist forces and the Jews could be dressed up as the racial embodiment of everything socialists opposed.

Antisemitism allows the far right to appeal to everyday people with seemingly leftist principles; that is, appearing to champion working people against the powers that be and injecting plausible doubt into any political theory that doesn't involve fighting the Jews as the true enemy of the people. This is why, in the late 19th century, the German left began referring to antisemitism as "the socialism of fools."[18]

3. Internationalist Nationalism

Antisemitism provides fascists with the rationale and the model for world conquest. This is another important point for our times, and one that many seem to insist on getting wrong. The term "nationalism," whether attached to "white" or not, is wholly inaccurate for fascist or protofascist forces. Fascists often use the rhetoric of nationalism, but their ideology is necessarily internationalist.[19] Fascists from different nations can ally with one another or at least view each other's successes as boons to their own position while simultaneously attacking the integrity of the nation in which they organize.

In the 1920s, the nationalist rhetoric of the Nazis led many observers to mistake "Nazism for German nationalism, thereby helping underestimate the tremendous international appeal of [Adolf] Hitler's propaganda."[20] By now it is obvious that Hitler's goal was not merely to control Germany, but to conquer the world. The rhetoric of nationalism, initially dressing up as patriotism, is a crucial stepping-stone for fascists. The Jewish global conspiracy, which the fascists hold up as the ultimate enemy, eventually justifies their international aspirations under the guise of what is best for the nation. To combat the international Jewish menace, antisemitic parties would be able to justify their own need to organize internationally without having to sacrifice their claim to nationalism in each state in which they operated.

At the same time, as Arendt tells us, protofascist parties could engage in hypernationalist talk as they planned to destroy the body politic of their own nations by using Jews as the reason for both. By targeting the Jews, fascists could openly attack the state or civil society, as Jews were framed as the ones controlling all these institutions from behind the scenes. The global nature of the antisemitic narrative enabled fascists to establish a supranational network of forces manipulating their local political interests. The fascists would, in a "fight fire with fire" approach, build precisely that which they claimed the Jews were imposing to preserve society—global political domination.

At its psychological core, antisemitism is a form of envy.[21] Maybe this is true for all forms of racism. But Jews in a specific way, with their diasporic character, tenacious maintenance of cultural tradition, and insular social structure absent formal institutions, represent to antisemites how race and nation could transcend the state. As Arendt describes it, the Nazis were trying to create for themselves what they imagined the Jews already had—an international brotherhood, forged over centuries, bonded by eternal nationhood and a belief in their "chosenness"—of course without recognizing that the entire condition of Jewish diaspora had come from forcible expulsion, and that the robust traditions and insular social structure were survival mechanisms as much as anything else.

Anti-Zionism

Zionism is one of the most politically and emotionally charged terms; depending on who you talk to, it can mean very different things. Although a full examination of Zionism is well beyond the capacity of a single chapter, it is crucial to tackle here because, paradoxically, anti-Zionism is a touchstone for both the far right and the far left.

Zionism emerged in the late 19th century as a Jewish nationalist response to European nationalism and anti-Jewish violence. Named for Zion, the biblical City of David in what is now Jerusalem, Zionism took a variety of forms and positions, initially all relating to Jewish liberation, autonomy, and cultural renaissance. Up until the mid-20th century, there were a number of distinct Zionisms that differed on and debated the needs and path of Jewish peoplehood.[22] The version known as Political Zionism emerged as dominant under the leadership of Theodore Herzl, advocating a sovereign state in what was then Ottoman and later British Palestine, to be colonized by Jews from the diaspora, primarily European Jews. Since the victory of Political Zionism with the foundation of the State of Israel in 1948, Zionism has primarily come to mean Israeli nationalism, although there are still variations. However, that isn't how either the far right or far left sees it. When the far right says "Zionism," they usually mean Jewish global domination; when the left says "Zionism," they tend to mean colonialism. Yet when we are not careful, left rhetoric can closely resemble that of the far right, providing fascists with a convenient tool to fracture or recruit from leftist milieus.

In 1978, the founder of the white supremacist National Alliance, William L. Pierce, published a novel entitled *The Turner Diaries* under the pen name Andrew Macdonald. It has been described as the modern "bible of the racist right," and a number of US domestic terrorists have cited it as their inspiration.[23] The book describes a Jewish plot to destroy Western civilization by flooding it with Black and brown people, telling the story of a white revolution that rises to stop it. The modern far right has coined this Jewish conspiracy the "Zionist Occupation Government," or "ZOG," an abbreviation that now serves as shorthand for fascists to refer to Jewish control over media, banks, and government.[24] The Anti-Zionist League is a neofascist "Aryan organization" hosting a website that essentially repackages *Protocols*.[25] The website antizionism.org informs viewers that Zionists are behind the "antiwhite agenda" and therefore must be destroyed. Since the 1980s, "Zio" has become neofascist shorthand for Jew, popularized by Ku Klux Klan (KKK) leader David Duke, and is widely regarded as an antisemitic slur.[26]

The term "Zio" was tweeted by the Chicago Dyke March in 2017 during the fallout from their decision to eject participants holding a rainbow flag with a Star of David, which to some resembled an Israeli flag.[27] That entire episode is an excruciating example of how lack of knowledge about antisemitism on the left splinters and demobilizes movements, and provides the right with easy ammunition to accuse the left of bigotry. Although this incident was highly publicized, sadly it is far from an isolated incident.

That same year, I remember holding part of a float behind the stage at the NYC Women's Strike rally, hearing National Lawyers Guild attorney and human rights activist Lamis Deek on stage saying that Zionist ideology was "*the* colonial center and global exporter of oppression" in the world, and that "where there is oppression and where there is dispossession, you will find Zionism and you will find Israel."[28] Deek framed Zionists not simply as oppressors, but as the center of all oppression worldwide. This move ascribes Jews-as-Zionists an exaggerated and wholly negative role in world politics, a view that directly connects to antisemitic logic. White supremacists see "biologically" white people as superior, but they view Jews as the powerful caste above them, their oppressor class. Antiracists view the socially constructed category of white as the oppressor class, but where Zionists are portrayed in the way Deek did, Jews are essentially placed *above* the category of white, the power behind all oppression—just as white supremacists see it.[29] The crowd erupted in applause to Deek's words. It was an experience I've had too frequently throughout my two decades in leftist organizing, where there is a version of what is being said that I might agree with but where the phrasing and the fervor feel uncomfortably close to political Jew-hatred. In their (mostly) virtuous enthusiasm to answer the rhetorical "which side are you on" question correctly, leftists can stray into far-right rhetoric around Zionism, which, if we are not careful, opens a frightening trapdoor from social justice to fascist politics.

Here is the problem: By at least one definition, most Jews in the US *are* Zionists, in the sense that most believe the State of Israel is vital for the survival of the Jewish people.[30] Most US Jews also oppose the occupation of the West Bank and Gaza.[31] But to many Jewish communities, Zionism just means that Jews have a right to be safe. To some, it means that Jews have a historical and cultural right to at least some of the geographic territory that is currently Israel/Palestine, but regardless most do not intentionally mean colonialism or racism. Inspiring movements of younger Jewish generations have mobilized over the past several years to challenge our own communities and institutions to reckon with the realities of Israeli occupation, withdraw Jewish institutional support, and hasten a just solution. And the left has taken strides in its incorporation of anti-antisemitic positions, but there remains a chasm between the way the left applies the term Zionism and the way most Jews understand it, which means it is not so simple as the common left refrain that "anti-Zionism is not antisemitism."[32]

When it comes to the subject of fascism, Jews are still an iconic historical victim, and their resistance fighters against the Nazis are among the most heralded. When it comes to Palestine—perhaps the most famous and respected struggle for national liberation in our time—Jewish Israelis represent the oppressors. The antifascist left celebrates the partisans of the Warsaw Ghetto Uprising almost as enthusiastically as it derides Zionist oppressors in Israel. Most never engage with the reality that many of the Warsaw Ghetto guerrillas were Zionists and some survivors fought in Jewish militias in Palestine during Israel's founding. To the left, Warsaw Ghetto fighters and Israeli soldiers exist in different ontological universes. The gap in understanding between these histories leaves comrades vulnerable to fascist propaganda, which in contrast to this confusion appears unafraid to tell the truth regarding the Jewish role in world politics.

The far right openly uses anti-Zionist propaganda to recruit from the left and to appear legitimate alongside the left's otherwise sincere attempts to push pro-Palestinian views into the mainstream. In

Pittsburgh, where I live, a recent fascist "Rock against Zionism" concert could have easily been mistaken for a leftist event—if the bands playing had not been known to local antifascists. Only weeks prior, prominent right-wing figures attempted to co-opt a Pittsburgh antiwar rally protesting US escalation with Iran using anti-Zionist rhetoric—they tipped their hand with an overtly antisemitic sign and were unceremoniously ejected from the rally. Reponses to these and other provocations were thanks to the presence of astute comrades, and was probably not unrelated to the robust organizing radical Jews have done in Pittsburgh in recent years. Still, these are just two recent anecdotal examples of uses of anti-Zionism as a combination dog whistle and recruitment tool for the far right.

Certainly, the State of Israel is connected to all kinds of odious things inside and outside of its borders even aside from the heinous occupation in the West Bank and blockade of Gaza—assassinations and spying, arms deals with oppressive regimes, international military and police training, and more. But so are lots of governments. Fighting Israel's occupation and repressive role in world politics does not require claiming that Zionists are behind all oppression in the world, just as fighting to support Kurdish liberation and autonomy does not require claiming that Turkish nationalism is responsible for all oppression in the world. Hyperbole is part of political rhetoric but, in this case, leftist hyperbole happens to be indistinguishable from a particularly potent right-wing politics. A good metric when it comes to discussing Zionism is: If it would sound outlandish or racist to say about Turkish nationalist occupation of Kurdish land, or Chinese nationalist ethnic cleansing in Xinjiang, or Moroccan nationalist occupation of Western Sahara, then it is worth reassessing. This is not to reduce in any way the struggle against Israeli occupation of Palestine, but to avoid engaging in antisemitic politics that are designed to break liberatory movements and establish the most dangerous sort of common ground with the far right.

It is not just white supremacists who are motivated by antisemitic logic. The same view that Jews were behind the destruction of society that drove Bowers, a white supremacist, to attack the Tree of Life synagogue in Pittsburgh also drove David Anderson and Francine Graham, who were Black nationalists, to attack the JC Kosher Supermarket in Jersey City, New Jersey. In the former case, the attack was justified by the attacker on the basis that Jews were behind nonwhite immigration and the destruction of white society; in the latter, the attack was justified on the basis that Jews were behind white gentrification of Black and brown neighborhoods and accompanying racist police violence.[33] Incidentally, growing up in New Jersey not far from JC Kosher, I was asked about *Protocols* on more than a few occasions at school and in my neighborhood, not at all in jest. Anderson and Graham would have hated Bowers and *vice versa*, but all three understood Jews to be the source of their people's problems. On the left, we disagree with Bowers's view that immigration is a problem while we agree with Anderson and Graham that gentrification, systemic racism, and police violence are problems. The key is to understand how antisemitism can drive all these positions simultaneously—and convince both that the solution is to attack Jewish people. Because antisemitism paints Jews as the ruling class, it can appear to fit with leftism as easily as it can with fascism, able to distort politics of liberation into politics of hate. When the left's anticolonial version of anti-Zionism is presented sloppily, it makes it difficult to distinguish between that and classic antisemitism, especially within historically oppressed communities.

It is not for nothing that Palestine has become an international symbol of resistance. The Palestinian struggle for liberation and self-determination is righteous, and solidarity work is crucial. Beyond this, Israel's policies of control and domination in the Palestinian Territories and the export of those technologies give the Palestinian resistance an antifascist character in itself. The Israeli right and their allies in the US use accusations of antisemitism as a political weapon to silence Palestine solidarity work, and domestic politicians use them as a handy excuse to silence protest in general. But the solution to these challenges is not to downplay the historical significance or systemic nature of antisemitism. Antisemitism is not only a systemic racism with its own history and logic, but also a historical lynchpin of far-right ideology. If left unchecked, it functions as a major asset for fascist aspirations to power.

Understanding Antisemitism and Fighting Fascism Today

Just as the ominous text on that city bus had foreshadowed, changes have come since 2016. There has been unchecked privatization across sectors, rapid erosion of civil rights, further unleashing of racist police violence, the fast approach of an ultimate tipping point for the global ecosystem, and the continued separation of political language from reality. Trump's term exposed liberal institutions of the US political system to be much closer to a house of cards than even the left had thought. Learning the correct lessons from the fascist resurgence in our time is necessary if we are to overcome it.

Trump's defeat in the 2020 election was not a victory for antifascist forces; it just bought us time. With the Democrats seeming to have learned nothing from Trump's populist surge, their failure to secure tangible improvements in the lives of working people and to capture imaginations around a positive vision of the future would set the stage for a more organized and coherent far-right run at the executive branch. We now face a fascist movement that is better positioned than at any time since the Nazis made their bid for world dominance. We know that history does not literally repeat itself, but different eras do produce cultural-theoretical artifacts that have resonance across generations. Lessons from the 1920s and 1930s are important for us now, and yet we must be clear-eyed about the specific conditions in which we apply them today.

As a popular demagogue who has become the champion of the right, Trump remains a threat. But it is easy to overemphasize the role of that individual. Trump has long openly traded in white supremacist race theory, but he has neither the ideology nor the political vision of a Hitler.[34] Trump is not Viktor Orbán, who knows exactly what he is doing when he deploys antisemitism in Hungary; nor is he Narendra Modi, who cut his teeth in a political organization inspired by the Nazis; nor is he Rodrigo Duterte, who has likened himself to Hitler in his brutal campaign to eradicate drug users.[35] Furthermore, despite the strongman image, Trump proved himself to be remarkably weak. He certainly has a will to authoritarianism, but lacks the courage for it. When the moment came for him to risk it all for unchecked power in a coup—and he had several bites at the apple—he faltered and retreated, hoping others would do it for him. Not only does he lack the fortitude, he appears to have no political vision beyond gaining his next round of applause. Trump's political genius is that of an internet troll; it is his innate ability to read a room and give the mob what it wants, plus his own latent but undeveloped racism, that leads Trump to racist political rhetoric. When he was president, Trump parroted Fox News at least as much as the other way around. Trump absolutely caused an enormous amount of pain, but his deepest threat was always and remains that he unleashed a fascist movement that could easily outgrow him.

Trump's most worrying consequence has always been the space he opens for those with fascist ideology to implement their plans. Steve Bannon failed to maintain his position in the chaotic Trump administration, which was subject to Trump's nonideological and nonsensical narcissistic whims, but in Biden's term Bannon has re-emerged as a Republican strategist with a plan for US domination. The modern Republican Party has for years been composed of a hodgepodge of political, religious, and economic conservatives, capitalists, and crackpots, all vying for their own interests and political survival. Now a truly fascist contingent among them is gaining legitimacy under the Make America Great Again (MAGA) banner. The deepest material and political threat remains the serious fascists on the ground—including law enforcement, border patrol, and local governments, which are shot through with white supremacists—who were empowered by Trump's words and informed by the disorganization that he brings to the liberal status quo. The linking of boots on the ground with the political elite, which Trump had very nearly formalized with his "stand back and stand by" order to the Proud Boys during a 2020 presidential debate, would be the final lynchpin. That moment came too late during Trump's term, but the next right-wing regime would begin where the last one left off.

In Arendt's time, the left made a crucial error in failing to recognize antisemitism for the political tool it is. The 21st-century US is not 20th-century Europe, but once again antisemitism plays a significant role in the far right's ideology and strategy, and once again the left is at risk of dismissing it. In the US today, Jews are a small minority and are not the main material target of fascists. The structural violence that the US was built upon is colonization and chattel slavery, and to this day the majority of systemic racial violence both from the state and far-right vigilantes is focused on Black people, Indigenous people, Latinos, and nonwhite immigrants. Nevertheless, fascists today remain obsessed with the Jews. Nostalgia might play a role in this, but antisemitism also continues to be an efficacious political tool for them, radicalizing and making sense of the world for frustrated and angry working people, continuing to facilitate international alliances of fascists. This makes it all the more worrisome that so many people who turned to Arendt's work to help them understand the rise of fascism in our time seemed to entirely miss her analysis of antisemitism.

The metanarrative of political antisemitism is extremely durable and malleable; as it turns out, the idea that there is a secret cabal of internal foreigners manipulating things for their own benefit can be a politically mobilizing force in any country or context. This ideology has retained all its potency despite seven decades of the State of Israel (which in and of itself speaks volumes about the futility of the Political Zionist project to eliminate antisemitism by making Jews a state-people "like everyone else"). That right-wing Israeli political figures now not only shake hands with overt antisemites but echo their antisemitic theories (e.g., regarding the influence of George Soros) presents an even clearer window into the insidious political effectiveness of antisemitism.[36]

After the Holocaust, the accusation of antisemitism has become a cutting political tool, and so antisemitism is no longer as easily voiced in its most open and pure form. Its themes must now be publicly trafficked in code. But the appeal of antisemitic logic has also grown amid an increasingly interconnected yet chaotic world. The skeleton of the antisemitic worldview has been more or less stripped of its overt antisemitism and found a massive following in the form of conspiracy theories. The idea of global control by secret cabals like the Illuminati or the Bilderberg Group—and of course, the Rothschilds, where the influence of antisemitism is least hidden—as well as more colorful versions involving aliens or shape-shifting reptilians have become widespread. The antisemitic framework is especially effective when it appears unrelated to Jews at first glance and so can maintain plausible deniability, such as with the QAnon movement, and the internet territories that traffic in such theories are fertile recruitment areas for fascists.[37]

In the broadest sense, countering the appeals of fascism requires honest reckoning with the full historical picture. Understanding the political dynamics of antisemitism is therefore an essential component to effective antifascist struggle. The left's discomfort with the Jewish question, and thus with antisemitism, has undermined our collective power in the face of fascism that thrives in the discomfort and confusion antisemitism and its weaponization foster. There are many dynamics that have led to rise of the far right, but this is one crucial area in which simply increasing our understanding can bolster our defenses.

The left—including, and sometimes especially, the Jewish left—has struggled to incorporate Jewishness into its radical frameworks. Jewishness as a racialized and classed group that is itself multiracial and cross-class, as a diasporic, multiethnic ethnicity with a culture that revolves around religious cultural practices, has not yet been incorporated into class-, race-, or place-based leftist politics of liberation. Especially when antisemitism is a touchstone for fascist politics, it is impossible to engage in holistic struggles for liberation without this work and, slowly but surely, this work is happening. Trump's 2016 election hit Jewish communities hard, as has the sharp rise in antisemitic incidents since. The liberal Jewish group Bend the Arc has pivoted toward the fight against white nationalism, alongside the newer group, Jews Against White Nationalism.

A lot of the positive work I see in Pittsburgh is directly related to the development of a conscious and robust Jewish left in this city, beginning in the years before the Tree of Life shooting with the Pittsburgh chapter of IfNotNow, a Jewish Palestine solidarity group that made the fight against antisemitism central to its fight against the Occupation. That local project has more recently disaffiliated from IfNotNow and seeded a number of local Jewish community and political projects, including Jews Organizing for Liberation and Transformation, Rebellious Anarchist Young Jews, Ratzon: Center for Healing and Resistance, and a host of radical and queer social, study, and youth groups. These groups and individuals led the Safety in Solidarity response to the 2018 Tree of Life shooting, in which we gathered to publicly mourn and take action against the co-optation and use of the attack to push right-wing politics, bolster support for the police, and serve as an excuse for Israeli militarism. Alongside others, these movements are building Pittsburgh into a hub of leftist, in many cases anarchist, and explicitly antifascist Jewish organizing.[38]

By organizing as leftist Jews and engaging in radical community and in solidarity work, we can help shape local radical and antifascist politics. A great deal of work remains, but much has been learned in the past few years. Antisemitism is only an effective political tool amid ignorance of its history and dynamics. This is one area in which knowledge alone really helps. One of the most successful elements of our local organizing has been training sessions and teach-ins on antisemitism and its intersections with white supremacy. Even in areas without radical Jewish groups, thorough knowledge of the history and dynamics of antisemitism is accessible in publications like this one.[39] And connections with radical Jewish groups in other areas can help antifascists avoid traps of the past and better read political terrain. It can help us better identify metaphorical and literal flags of other groups, as well as to send the correct signals with our own practice and rhetoric.

In the midst of turmoil and uncertainty, fascism attempts to offer people connection and meaning. Arendt quotes Mikhail Bakunin in capturing the deepest of human social needs: "I do not want to be *I*, I want to be *we*."[40] Movements of the left and right tap into the same social need to be together, to be *we*. It is noteworthy that Arendt choses Bakunin as a source to mark the commonality between radical left and right thought. Bakunin was a canonical anarchist thinker and an outright antisemite. Furthermore, Bakunin's antisemitism was baked into his class theory—something many anarchists have preferred to ignore.[41] In this quote, Bakunin hits on a central human need that underlies both a politics of commonality and a politics of oppression; beyond the quote's pithiness, Arendt perhaps selects the source to reinforce the complex and sometimes intertwined beliefs and impulses that can lead to the left and right. The will to a *we* connects the left and right, but it is a different *we*. "We" can be inclusive or exclusive; it can mean *we all*, or it can mean *we* here versus *you* there. In the broadest sense, this difference in meaning marks the fundamental opposition of the left and right.

The right's version to *we* is a shortcut, but an effective one for many. It validates people's basest fears of the "other," arms the dominant group with a belief in their innate superiority, and justifies cathartic violence against more vulnerable people. In a society undergoing tectonic transformation, full of confused, lonely, and angry people, the connection fascism offers can be hypnotic.

The Jews are presented as the visage of a powerful ethereal enemy, against whose agenda a *we* can be forged. In the past, antisemitism has not only functioned as a basis for founding a fascist political body, it has also been one of the most effective flanking maneuvers fascists have used to defeat their adversaries on the left. By understanding and incorporating the fight against antisemitism, antifascist forces have an opportunity to take away one of our enemy's most time-tested weapons and, in doing so, build a powerful and holistic politics of solidarity.

"Kops and Klan Go Hand in Hand":
An Interview with Kelly Hayes

Shane Burley

This chant was shouted in street gatherings across the country during the 2020 uprising against white supremacy and police violence. The historic connection of white nationalist vigilante violence and the police became glaringly obvious in the disparity between the treatment of the Proud Boys and that of antiracist protesters, where police often refused to intervene while the far-right gangs leveled attacks on left-wing demonstrators.[1]

Antifascism is built on the notion that these insurrectionary fascist groups, such as the alt-right or the Proud Boys, are extraordinary and distinct from the larger liberal order, yet it's not that simple. Instead, the role of the police as an institution of social control in racial capitalism and settler-colonialism has always had some relationship to the insurgent white supremacist groups that are looking to reinstitute racial hierarchies. This apparently symbiotic relationship forces antifascists to reckon with the similarities and differences between white nationalist groups and the police as they build strategies to deal with both.

I interviewed abolitionist organizer and author Kelly Hayes about her experiences confronting these interlocking systems of oppression, how she became an organizer, how she approaches this relationship between antagonistic forces, and how we can build up an abolitionist antifascism that goes further than only defeating fringe neo-Nazi groups.

Shane Burley: How did you get involved in radical organizing in the first place? What experiences led you on this path?

Kelly Hayes: I would say I became an organizer about a decade ago. I was very politically minded prior to the Occupy [Wall Street] movement. I had been to protests, helped plan protests, but I had never done the kind of relationship work that community-based organizing demands. Occupy is what set me on the path of doing that kind of work, not because Occupy was grounded in these strategies, but because it thrust me into environments where this work was being done.

I was really devoted to photography and building community as an artist when I got caught up in the Occupy movement in Chicago [Illinois]. I was really busy, and a friend kept nagging me to check it out. I saw online that bankers threw a bunch of McDonalds applications out the window at Occupy protesters, holding a sign that read, "We are the 1%." I was so angry that I headed downtown to support the protesters.

In the years leading up to Occupy, there had been a big focus on permitted marches and symbolic protest tactics that were ostensibly legally sanctioned. That practice of politics was not appealing to a lot of people who were incredibly angry about what was happening in society and coming to grips with the ways we have been fucked by the system, learning the system wasn't what we were taught to believe. Their country wasn't what they had been told it was; the futures they had prepared for weren't going to materialize. Occupy created the space to understand that and take on organizing strategies.

SB: What do you think you learned most from the Occupy movement?

KH: There are critiques to be made, but many of the critiques of Occupy do not come from a knowledgeable place of movement history. People show up in messy ways, and newly activated people bring that messiness into a new place where a lot of hope is being grafted onto them, which can breed arrogance. People can feel like they are inventing something rather than figuring out their place within a longer arc of history.

Those flaws were clearly observable on social media because Occupy was the first US movement to really catapult itself into relevance via social media. It was really powerful and important, but that constant gaze also meant that the things that weren't so great were always on display as well—including all the beefs people had. Movements are made of people, and people don't show up embodying everything that we would always want to embody because we are raised in the same society we want to change.

Movements are struggles, not sanctuaries, but we all need sanctuaries as well. I realized I needed a political home, where I could take shelter from all the bullshit. So I cobuilt that home, but when I venture away from it, I know I'm walking into a mess because a lot of activists are not living in a shared reality. There may be common points of understanding, and we can build from there, but now more than ever we are far removed from each other, and building shared space is essential for movement building.

In those early days of Occupy, in Chicago, a lot of what we were doing was expressive rather than instrumental. Because there was suddenly this political vehicle for our anger, and that vehicle had crashed into the mainstream. So just inhabiting it, and yelling about how fucked up things were and connecting with other humans in a way that wasn't commercial—just sort of moving through that moment of mass activation, was really important (and messy). Without an encampment to focus on, we focused on building grassroots connections with community groups and unions. If Rahm Emanuel had let us obsess over a physical, symbolic space, and continue to burn arrests around defending it, and grapple with the cold and dwindling numbers, he would have been way better off.

SB: How did Occupy launch you into your larger organizing work?

KH: I was part of a contingent of folks in Occupy who were pretty militant about showing up for union struggles and fights against austerity. I built relationships with people I never would have met, and I collaborated with folks who were deep in struggle, defending mental health clinics and schools, and fighting for their unions. I shared what skills I had and I learned as much as I could. And when Occupy was done, I was still doing education, health care, and antiausterity work with that group of people. I had a knack for crafting and direct actions, so I've often found myself in niche groups who focus on that. Those community relationships, formed during Occupy, with people I would never otherwise have worked with, or talked to, helped me reach beyond just my core group. Once I was doing that, I was challenged by people I met (and I challenged them as well).

Once prison abolition really clicked for me, a new era of my life and my work took off. My imagination was let loose in ways that weren't compatible with capitalism because I had lost my sense of the permanence of the system, of cops, and prisons. I went from being someone who wanted to tear down everything I knew was rotten to being someone who felt challenged to imagine what the world should look like, modeling a way to take action, what abolition is all about. Ruth Wilson Gilmore says that abolition is about making things, and this life of making things and building bonds and emptying cages made sense to me like nothing ever had.

SB: How did this pathway get you all the way to confronting the carceral state and begin to approach police abolition? What role does the concept of abolitionism hold in your larger political vision, and as a foundation for radical interventions?

KH: It was not the experience of violence, at the hands of police, that led me to abolition, which I think is worth noting. I had experienced violence at the hands of police and lived in fear of police long before the idea of abolishing the police and prisons felt real to me. I think it's really natural for people, even people who don't trust the system or who get beaten down by the system, to still want to hope that the police can be cajoled into doing "what they're supposed to do" and offer us some protection. They want to believe that this system can operate in a way that it never has, and they cling to stories of individual cops or police procedurals. They want to believe that this violent apparatus can be made good, or at least useful, in some cases. Experiencing violence doesn't necessarily give us an analysis of that violence, or a sense of strategy for confronting that violence. Experience can be valuable when forming an analysis, but if trauma, by itself, gave us the political calculus that we needed to get free, we would have gotten free generations ago.

Police preservationism is a knee-jerk response that should be expected in oppressed communities, and it's something to overcome. People feel like they have so little, and so few defenses, and they hear about abolition, and to some people, it just sounds like people want to take away what little they have because all they're hearing is the subtraction part. I hear people ask things like, "If I'm assaulted, who am I going to call?" Having something you know you can do, and theoretically, it becomes someone's job to do something about it—that feels better than nothing.

A lot of people tend to cling to the idea of the panic button because they are not imagining a world where their needs are met or conflicts are de-escalated. They aren't envisioning the construction of a world where people wouldn't perceive state violence as being necessary. When you really get into talking to people about what it would mean to have a healthy community, where people could experience safety and be free, you dig into what people really desire for themselves, for their communities, and what they wish was possible, other than simply avoiding worst-case scenarios, you hear them talk about all the same things abolitionists want. They want health care. They want a society where people's needs are met, and where conditions that generate violence are addressed and de-escalated. The challenge of imagining that world brought me to abolition.

By the time I was an organizer, I had already experienced criminalization, so I already thought of myself as a criminal, in a pretty morally neutral way, and I was accustomed to assessing the police as a threat to my immediate freedom and well-being, and I think that was useful. A lot of people, even people who are at high risk of experiencing police violence, have just never seen or assessed the police that way.

In the first round of arrests at Occupy Chicago, for example, when we were trying to seize a space, and mass arrest was clearly on the table, there were organizers insisting that everyone should show up in their best clothes to counteract notions that we were a bunch of dirty hippies. I, of course, made noise about that because I thought it was so confused. To me, the easiest dismissal of Occupy wasn't that we were hippies, but that folks were mostly white college students who could be characterized as just "not getting it." I don't think being well-dressed countered that idea at all. And given how orderly and polite the arrests were, it all wound up feeling very [public relations] PR-friendly for the city.

Some people thought that police were "part of the 99%" who we could win over. It's a harmful liberal fantasy, but it was a learning process. A lot of white people who eventually got the shit kicked out of them during Occupy became more open to understanding that police are the maintenance workers of oppression. No matter what cause you're fighting for, if you are making enough noise to potentially alter the situation, the police are the force that's going to fall down on you to maintain the current order of things. And if you have the nerve, as a movement, to say that your safety or the means of your survival are now the cost of order, the police are going to show up for war.

As an organizer, I have grappled with contradictions that I didn't have to deal with when I was just an activist. As an activist, you can be very task focused, and that was me. I was a doer. If you needed someone to show up to help construct a scene, or ruin some politician's event, or make someone miserable, I was good for that. But as my work expanded, and I stepped into leadership more and felt the demands of building something and developing relationships.

In abolition, I found a creative political dance where I can grapple with contradictions while opposing human disposal and the extractions killing our world. It's really telling that abolition is a banner that has brought together a lot of anarchists, socialists, communists, and unaffiliated people.

The whole framing around prison slavery, and prison as slavery, and police as slave catchers, was getting a lot of traction as I was becoming an abolitionist. But as Ruthie, and imprisoned organizers such as Stevie Wilson, have pointed out, prisons don't exist to extract labor. There are states like mine where prisoners are not allowed to work at all, and that hasn't led to decarceration because the extraction of labor wasn't its prime function.[2] Instead, it's time that is extracted: days, months, years. Neoliberalism, the destruction of the social safety net, the evisceration of unions, what's led us to this GoFundMe gig-economy nightmare, has created a lot of surplus people who no longer fit. When people's labor isn't wanted, or they lose the ability to offer it, they become a sort of social mess that needs to be swept up.

SB: What organizations have you been a part of that do this work and what are the strategies that you have worked with?

KH: I was a cofounder of the Chicago Light Brigade in Chicago, which played a visual role in a lot of struggles. The first Light Brigade, which was called Overpass Light Brigade, formed in Wisconsin during the mass protests against Scott Walker when people occupied the capitol rotunda.

They used corrugated plastic and battery-powered LED lights to create an alphabet of boards that could be shuffled to spell out political messages in public places, making banners out of light in a way that has become a popular tactic in the last few years.

I appreciated the value of this sort of entry-level tactic that people found fun and beautiful, and that was usually pretty low risk. I knew we were in an era of activation and radicalization, and I wanted to create pathways into direct action for people. When we were still Occupy Rogers Park, we started running nonviolent direct action trainings for local youth. A lot of times, you'll see people hit up a few marches or direct actions, and then declare they've been "educated in the streets." And I'm not saying people don't learn a lot that way, but creating intentional spaces for learning and exploration is important.

My time with Chicago Light Brigade overlapped with my work with We Charge Genocide, a project that existed for a couple of years. We Charge Genocide was the first organization I organized with that dealt exclusively with police violence and we did a lot of political education work. That was a huge time of growth for me and a time of walking fine lines because a lot of us who were abolitionists, or becoming abolitionists, marched with people who wanted to send killer cops to jail. I helped people stage protests where they leveled those demands, even as I became increasingly convinced that those demands availed us nothing. Every time a cop was acquitted, or got a throwaway sentence, people felt defeated, and, on the rare occasion that one got convicted and faced some kind of penalty, the system claimed redemption. I learned that sometimes we have to support people who are raging against the system, even if we don't share their demands. It's a matter of figuring out our boundaries, and we influence each other through this struggle. And I think that's how we influence each other's ideas, through struggle. A lot of people became more radicalized, moving from demands for punishment to demanding abolition.

Part of this shift is that people are starting to understand systems of disposal. The pandemic got a lot of people to consider their own proximity to disposability. Project NIA, Critical Resistance, and other abolitionist organizations have gone a long way toward facilitating those realizations. I have worked with Project NIA a lot over the years, and with the Chicago Freedom School. In 2015, I cofounded the Lifted Voices collective, which is a direct action–oriented collective of Black and Indigenous organizers. We also do a lot of movement education and mutual aid work. Lifted Voices is a small group and I consider it my political home. We have trained thousands of people in nonviolent direct action, gotten a lot of people out of jail, and prepped people for more actions than I can count.

SB: How does police abolition work connect to antifascism?

KH: Police, who are themselves fascistic, are the entry point to incarceration. There's nothing more fascistic in the US than our prison system. If fascism escalates, it already has a mass disposal system for human beings and a populace that has been conditioned to ignore what happens in those places. We already know that people suffer and die horribly in those places, and we know people allow it. People participate in mythologies about the purpose and function of it all. These facilities manufacture conditions that bring about premature death and they extract time, as Ruth Wilson Gilmore has explained. The prison-industrial complex and its many tentacles are the beast the fascists would feed us to.

It's important to remember that fighting fascism means fighting the erosion of human empathy. It means fighting the further normalization of mass suffering and death. That makes the prison-industrial complex ground zero.

SB: What role do the police have in the growth of the far right?

KH: The police are a natural home for right-wing militants and it's important not to think of far-right forces and police as distinct. The membership overlap between police and white supremacist organizations is quite telling.

But I think people also sort of limit themselves sometimes in how they perceive that overlap. Most racist people don't join racist organizations. We need to understand the police as a white supremacist organization that has formalized power. It's entrenched in the government, and maintains state interests, and has a whole mythology of "upholding decency" around it. Policing, as an idea, appeals to a lot of people who aren't down with the [Ku Klux] Klan. Since police can be well paid in an economy that generally screws over Black and brown communities, we see a lot of nonwhite cops, and that demographic diversity helps legitimize police violence.

People have a narrow image of what white supremacy and the far right looks like because we are conditioned to see state violence as inherently legitimate. Police don't just have legal immunity, for the most part, they also have social immunity, and their actions are not scrutinized in the ways that everyday people are. If they were, people would have no trouble recognizing, based on simple inventories of events, that the police are a force for white supremacy.

A lot of vigilante violence that helped impose order under Jim Crow became institutionalized as the police became more professionalized, and more heavily armed. Lynchings where no one was charged gave way to shootings and beatings and other violence that was dealt out from a place of police legitimacy.

It's not surprising to see collaboration between police and right-wing vigilantes because they're natural allies and grown out of the same cultural formation. We rarely see them clash, and, when they do, they often do it with kid gloves. You cannot effectively pit these forces against one another because they are too entwined and have too many shared values and purposes.

SB: We saw these two forces, the police and the far right, even more explicitly collapse into each other over the past few years. How do you think we can build social movements capable of taking on both forces simultaneously?

KH: We have to understand that there is no alternative to taking on both the police and the far right simultaneously. The police are the most powerful right-wing gang in the country.

When strategizing against them, it must be understood that they are in collaboration with other white supremacist organizations. When countering white supremacist organizations, it must be understood that police are either actively entrenched in those organizations, or could come to their aid at any time, because they're on the same side.

SB: What role does mutual aid have in sustaining these offensive and defensive social movements? What role do coalitions and different types of organizations, such as environmental groups or unions, have in fighting white supremacist policing?

KH: There simply is no future of resistance without mutual aid, and anyone who doesn't understand that is in denial about the state of the world. These aren't stable times, we are living in disastrous times, and the idea that people are disposable will drive widespread tolerance of mass death unless we build an opposition.

Mutual aid is practical because we need to survive some rough shit, and our movements will require sustenance and care in order to thrive. Mutual aid is also strategic because building a culture of care is essential to combatting individualism. We can't just hand people a set of politics and say it's the truth and expect them to bite if we aren't really invested in what happens to those people.

To overcome individualism, a movement has to value life and it has to encourage people to act as though preserving life matters, and it has to be something that people want to be a part of.

SB: How should we think about street confrontation? Is this a useful strategy, or should antifascists be thinking of something new? What kind of strategies are most effective in pushing back on the far right and police in the coming years?

KH: Street confrontation is complicated. I am not averse to it on any moral level, but I have concerns around effectiveness, and the risks involved, given that fascism is a trenchant threat. I believe in social consequences for fascists and I believe it makes sense to stomp some threats out, and never allow them to get any traction or territory in our communities. Once they do, only bad things can happen. I believe that about fascism.

I also believe that stage of the fight has passed, to some extent. I want to be careful here because I am not speaking with any certainty about where violence falls within the environmental and economic collapse we are living through.

Historically, people have always had to size up their own situation and what their community is up against when choosing tactics. I don't think we are in a place where showing up to fight the fascists necessarily always helps because we're past the period where those confrontations have the utility folks want. I think the fascists kind of want us there, to be honest. They want those fights, and for the most part, they are much more inclined and prepared to commit violence than us. So what does it look like to counter them, rather than just let them have the run of a city?

I think we have seen some really creative ideas, some of which involve absurdity. I think that self-defense is really important right now, and I think it would be wise to funnel some of our confrontational energy into organized efforts around community defense and preparedness. I don't think we have nearly enough organized infrastructure around safety planning, safe houses, and the defense of vulnerable individuals. My collective, Lifted Voices, has done a lot of self-defense trainings over the years, and a lot of them have been organized by request, for marginalized people and groups who were concerned about being targeted for particular reasons. I think we need a lot more of that.

V.

RETHINKING THE WORLD OF RESISTANCE

A Partial Typology of Empathy for Enemies: Collaborationist to Strategic

Joan Braune

In work against fascism, appeals for empathy, love, compassion, friendship, inclusion, dialogue, forgiveness, and kindness toward fascists often pose unexpected difficulties. Often, such appeals are made by people who are naïve about the true danger posed by fascist movements, or who underestimate how entrenched fascists are in their belief system and who thus erroneously believe that divisions can be easily overcome through mutual understanding. Acting in good faith, researchers, journalists, activists, and community leaders may call for compassion and love in ways that lead to blurred boundaries and problematic alliances. At other times, appeals for compassion are made in bad faith, including by law enforcement initiatives to shut down antifascist protest or by grifters seeking publicity, or, very often, by fascists themselves, fascist-adjacent members of the far right, and other sympathizers with fascism who seek to widen the "Overton window" of acceptable political opinion and to increase space for extremists to their right. Whatever the motivations, problematic or poorly framed appeals to compassion for fascists can often dangerously erode necessary boundaries that can keep individuals and communities safe, can normalize fascism, and can contribute to victim-blaming of fascism's targets. For these reasons and others, the left is rightly nervous about discourses of compassionate outreach toward fascists and can be impatient toward such talk.

However, the left also need not cede the rhetoric or praxis of love to its reductionist or collaborationist defenders. For the left, love retains a deep radicality and is crucial for dismantling capitalism, white supremacy, cisheteropatriarchy, and other interlocking systems of oppressive violence. The rhetoric of love must be critiqued when it is deployed in ways that do harm, but genuine love and empathy can also play radical and liberationist functions, both as practical tools within certain contexts and as part of a wider programmatic restructuring of a contemporary society based on greed, oppression, and violence.

To explore both the dangers and potentials of love and empathy regarding antifascist praxis, I begin by exploring writer and academic Benjamin Teitelbaum's deeply problematic "friendship model" of research on fascists. Using Teitelbaum as a starting point, I then examine a series of damaging forms of empathy toward fascists that can render activists and targeted communities less safe. I discuss seven problematic uses of empathy toward fascists, ranging from outright collaboration with fascists, to simply being emotionally harmed by them to the point of "fash fatigue" through a lack of necessary boundaries.

Following this negative typology of empathy for fascists, I discuss some ways in which "strategic empathy" (empathy thoughtfully directed toward the dismantling of fascism) and love do remain relevant to radical left theory and practice. Strategic empathy and love contribute to an understanding of social conditions, as well as to a project of social transformation aimed at liberation and at overcoming the threat of fascism. I suggest, for example, that the impressive and courageous protests of the United Front Against Fascism (UFAF) against the Aryan Nations compound in the 1980s and 1990s in the Pacific Northwest might have been even stronger if the organizers had not been so wary of the rhetoric of love. I then discuss the role of love in broader left antifascist strategy, including the place of mutual aid and building "dual power," and specifically the need for acts of direct service in a spirit of solidarity, to combat fascists' strategies and tactics.

Friends with Fascists: Teitelbaum's "Immoral Anthropology"

Teitelbaum's article "Collaborating with the Radical Right: Scholar-Informant Solidarity and the Case for an Immoral Anthropology" in *Current Anthropology* has caused some controversy due to its highly unusual defense of forming "friendships" with fascists as part of anthropological research. An assistant professor of ethnomusicology at University of Colorado Boulder, Teitelbaum earlier wrote a book on the Scandinavian white power music scene and has more recently published a book on Steve Bannon's ideology and some other far-right figures titled *War for Eternity: Inside Bannon's Far Right Circle of Global Power Brokers*. Teitelbaum's work has sometimes been seen as curiously "neutral" in its study of fascist and far-right research subjects. *War for Eternity* has caused some concern, in that Teitelbaum appears perhaps overly friendly with

Bannon and some other far-right or fascist figures in the course of the book. Teitelbaum's work runs the risk, in my view, of helping popularize certain far-right ideologies or helping normalize fascism, and he also appears to be encouraging academics to bond with fascists as a research method.

Teitelbaum's defense of a friendship with fascists leading to "collaboration" with them is troubling, and his research model is in some way unethical, although how and why it is unethical is an interesting question that is fruitful to explore. Teitelbaum notes in the *Current Anthropology* article that his anthropological research on far-right racists in the Nordic countries stands in tension with prevailing anthropological methods and ethical standards in the field of anthropology for researching right-wing extremism. Teitelbaum points out that earlier standards of anthropological research, which became the norm in the 1970s, emphasized that anthropologists should *always* prioritize the interests of their research subjects, stand in solidarity with them and advocate for them, and possibly even commit to developing "friendship" with them. As understanding later developed that anthropological research involved researching those who wield power to oppress others, ethical standards of the field were amended to show that solidarity with and advocacy for one's research subjects was not always required.

Objecting to the implied insistence that research on such subject matter as organized racists implies that one should *not* engage in friendship, advocacy, and solidarity with one's research subjects, Teitelbaum outlines the ways in which his research involved such activities. Perhaps for shock value but with apparent honesty, Teitelbaum opens his article by listing white nationalist Magnus Söderman, "white power singer" Saga, cofounder of fascist publishing house Arktos John Morgan, and other prominent white nationalists as among his "friends."[1] He proceeds to describe agreeing to be interviewed for an antisemitic newspaper in exchange for a research subject's participation, offering editorial advice on a racist novel by Söderman (after its publication, as feedback for future novels), and writing numerous op-eds "advocating" for his research subjects by defending them from inaccurate media portrayals or by condemning violence against them. Teitelbaum writes that he did not engage in any of these activities to signal political agreement with his research subjects. However, his thickly layered defenses of his actions suggest that he may be partial to some of their views.

Teitelbaum writes that, by consciously choosing to engage in a "friendship model" of research, one may obtain additional information, but that working closely with research subjects naturally gives rise anyway to "empathy," "affection," a "yearning for closeness," and an "impulse to collaboration" with one's research subjects.[2] Rather than initially setting out to befriend his research subjects, Teitelbaum professes to have begun his work with a hostility to the idea of the necessity of love in research and an insistence on objectivity: "It even crossed my mind that my work might someday serve as a small protest against ethical dogmas that appeared to me premised on a loathsome obligation to love."[3] However, as time went on, "personal solidarity and empathy grew as frequent interviewees and I became interested in each other as people"; "my work grew more penetrating, informed, and sinister in the process."[4]

Teitelbaum's "collaboration with the radical right" (as his article is titled) does not occur simply in exchange for information. For example, he agrees to offer editorial advice on a racist novel even though he does not believe it will grant him further access to the research subject, but simply because refusing the request seemed like it might be "paranoid and insulting."[5] His "advocacy" for white nationalists, in the form of op-eds defending them from alleged misunderstandings or from violence, similarly does not seem to have been undertaken in exchange for information. Rather, Teitelbaum insists that these defenses of white nationalists—incidentally, he insists throughout the article on calling them simply "nationalists" rather than white nationalists, fascists, racists, or extremists—occurred in part because he wanted to correct misunderstandings. "Inaccurate or misleading characterizations of them now anger me," he writes, and he notes that, "Never have I felt the urge to make a public statement condemning nationalists or their politics."[6]

There is a tension within Teitelbaum's professions of ethical or moral commitment.[7] On the one hand, he presents his research method and public advocacy as a kind of defense of the basic human dignity of his research subjects—that is, an ethical/moral argument. He strives to, he says, "find and communicate what is good about [his research subjects]."[8] However, Teitelbaum also admits that his model "prioritizes research efficacy over moral integrity."[9] His initial impulse in beginning his research—to stand up against "ethical dogmas" and against "a loathsome obligation to love"[10]—appears to be retained in his new friendship model of "immoral anthropological" research. That is, from beginning with a skepticism about received ethical views and perhaps about his field's sense of ethical duty to serve the common good, Teitelbaum proceeds to a research method that holds close "friendships" with those promoting an amoral, power-driven, bullying political program.

Although I believe there are deep problems with Teitelbaum's approach to research ethics, I do not believe that the problem is his empathy for fascists or his professed desire to tell the truth about them. Knowledge of fascism is needed to fight fascism effectively, and this includes knowledge of fascism as a social movement seeking power and knowledge of fascism as being composed of individuals with certain motivations for their choice of participation in the fascist movement. In seeking to understand motivating factors that lead individuals to join fascism, researchers may benefit from an empathic curiosity about their research subjects. This is quite different, though, from a "friendship" with fascists that includes questionable "collaboration" with them, as in the case of Teitelbaum.

What Strategic Empathy is Not

To understand what proper strategic empathy is not, we must consider several ways that a commitment to empathy can lead to failures to establish or maintain necessary boundaries. Therapist and activist Cristien Storm highlights the need for boundaries in work against fascism in her book, *Empowered Boundaries: Speaking Truth, Setting Boundaries, and Inspiring Social Change.*[11] After the murder of Mia Zapata of the Seattle, Washington band The Gits in the early 1990s, Storm cofounded a self-defense training program called Home Alive, which emphasized self-defense as empowerment rather than preventing vulnerability. Today, she works as a therapist and offers workshops and interactive displays on countering white nationalism. Storm writes in the introduction to her book:

> Our boundaries are political whether we want them to be or not. . . . When we do not respond to a sexist comment, for example, the space becomes one in which sexism can expand, which in turn creates conditions where escalating sexist behaviors are more possible. However, if we can assert a clear boundary in the face of a sexist comment, we demark that space as one where sexism is not tolerated. Boundaries then, are not just individual and interpersonal but social as well.[12]

But the necessary assertion of boundaries goes beyond responding to particular individuals' statements or behaviors. White nationalism, she continues, is a social movement, and clear boundaries with this movement are necessary. Storm writes that her own experience with the Bay Area, California punk scene as a young adult taught her early on about such boundaries: There was a general consensus that white nationalists were not allowed in the music scene.[13] She continues to see such boundaries as essential.

> If someone was trying to organize in our community by promoting white supremacy, no matter what the language ("We just want our own space too, it's just a different opinion. It's not hateful to be proud of being white" or, "Reverse racism is real and hurts white people . . ."), the boundary needed to clearly and in no uncertain terms identify our space as anti-racist. If someone was open to conversation and committed to nurturing and supporting vibrant anti-racist spaces, they were welcome.[14]

Iron-clad boundaries of this sort—for example, "White supremacists are not welcome at our concerts"—are often the only way to deal with a threatening situation and to keep people safe, especially in situations in which law enforcement turns a blind eye to violent white supremacist activity. Furthermore, these boundaries make it more difficult for fascists to organize and recruit, as well as to bully and antagonize. Contested spaces (physical and virtual) are on the rise under "global Trumpism,"[15] as fascists are more than ever supported by political power and funding sources alongside the global rise of far-right authoritarian movements. Of course, each situation calls for particular discernment based upon its unique context and by the individuals impacted, but it is essential that communities be able to set these sorts of boundaries without being shamed by would-be allies and supporters.

When such boundaries are asserted, others often object that such boundaries may "radicalize" fascists further. After all, they argue, there is some evidence to suggest that social isolation may increase fascists' tendencies toward terroristic violence.[16] However, it is possible that the degree to which social isolation drives right-wing radicalization is exaggerated, and there have been cases as well in which individuals who were driven into isolation by their right-wing extremist views were thereby challenged to leave behind the movements in which they were engaged. For example, former white supremacist Derek Black (son of prominent white supremacist Don Black) left the white supremacist movement after being socially ostracized in college. Although Derek Black did form friendships with Jewish students that enabled him to break away from his ideology, these friendships are often highlighted to the exclusion of what preceded it: Derek Black's expulsion from almost all the campus's social life as a result of antifascist organizing.[17] There does not seem to be conclusive evidence one way or another as to whether ostracism and exclusion are more or less beneficial in disengaging convinced fascists from their movements, but it is clear that ostracism and exclusion can provide forms of protection for potential targets and can make it more difficult for fascists to organize and recruit.

From an ethical standpoint, telling communities or individuals not to set protective boundaries with fascists because it might lead those fascists to "radicalize" further seems to me to be clearly problematic, even if it turns out that it is true that expelling fascists radicalizes them. Telling communities or individuals that their protective boundaries radicalize fascists actually instrumentalizes vulnerable people, treating their current safety as secondary to the prevention of predicted possible later events. Additionally, it contributes to victim-blaming: Even if acts of exclusion might sometimes prolong some individuals' involvement in fascist movements by making it more difficult for them to find a way out by forging social connections outside the movement, vulnerable communities cannot be blamed for keeping themselves safe in the interim. And, in fact, many acts of exclusion and boundary setting are courageous acts that help stop a dangerous movement from spreading and recruiting. To burden activists or marginalized communities with the task of keeping the door open at their own risk in the name of the potential "deradicalization" of racist extremists fosters victim-blaming. When activists and vulnerable communities do not engage in "inclusive" or "compassionate" behavior toward their enemies and are subsequently victimized by them, their prior fierce opposition may be condemned by naïve liberals or politically ambiguous "deradicalization" experts (e.g., some former fascists or government-funded "countering violent extremism" groups) as simply another kind of "extremism," and activists and vulnerable communities may end up being blamed for their own victimization. Thus, whatever role empathy for fascists might play in strategic work against fascism, it cannot ever take the form of undermining healthy boundaries or shaming people for setting them.

Although certain boundaries with fascists should be relatively obvious—don't date them, for example—others can be less clear. Appeals to the power of empathy and compassion, as well as the confused affectionate ties that individuals can develop toward fascists by working in close proximity to them, can easily weaken and erode necessary and healthy boundaries. Although I argue at the end of this chapter that empathy, even for fascists, can have practical uses in work against fascism, for empathy to be used strategically and ethically, it must be tempered by clear boundaries. In particular, it should be noted that strategic empathy is *not*, among other things:

1. preaching empathy for oppressors to members of marginalized groups;

2. platforming the enemy to have a "dialogue";

3. collaborating with the enemy;

4. passively participating in the enemy's activities to gain "objective" information about the enemy;

5. forgetting to critique the enemy;

6. being swayed by the enemy's views; or

7. being emotionally destroyed by the enemy.

My use of the word "enemy" here is quite deliberate. Fascists are enemies, and pretending that they are not is dangerous. Although some may feel called spiritually or ethically to love for enemies, pretending one does not have any is another matter entirely. I will illustrate these issues with some brief examples:

1. Not Preaching Empathy for Oppressors to Members of Marginalized Groups

Proper strategic empathy is not *preaching empathy for oppressors to members of marginalized groups* (i.e., to members of groups targeted by fascists). Pressure on others to show compassion or forgiveness toward haters can do harm. Activists and members of marginalized groups often have already taken on extremely high levels of responsibility for the protection or improvement of their communities, environment, or world, and may also face additional pressure from family, community, or social norms to take on yet more emotional labor. Women have often been socialized to view their self-sacrificial love as transformative for others (especially men). People of color, immigrants, members of the lesbian-gay-bisexual-transgender-queer-plus (LGBTQ+) community, and members of other groups may feel the need to both positively represent their group to others in the dominant social group while serving as mentors, protectors, and allies to many or countless individuals in their own social group. Black people face particular pressure from white Americans and white American society to forgive racist acts immediately,[18] to always be willing to patiently explain racism to white people in a gentle and non-"threatening" manner,[19] and to semimagically "heal the racial divide" through the power of their love and forgiveness.[20] American Muslims, to consider another (and sometimes intersecting) group, also face particular pressures, such as pressure to represent Islam at all times and to prove their nonviolence and patriotism; a recent study suggests very high levels of vicarious traumatization occurring in the American Muslim community due to the constant pressure imposed by stereotypes, profiling, and hate acts.[21]

Contemporary Jewish life and practice, deeply impacted by the legacy of the Holocaust, has been influenced by such questions as those presented in Simon Wiesenthal's book *The Sunflower: On the Possibilities and Limits of Forgiveness*, which tells the famous story of Wiesenthal's conflicted refusal to forgive a dying Nazi Schutzstaffel officer while Wiesenthal was a prisoner at Auschwitz. The book includes short responses to Wiesenthal's decision from writers of various backgrounds, many of whom roundly reject the idea of forgiving those who engaged in Nazi atrocities and many of whom also caution against individuals offering forgiveness on behalf of a group (e.g., all Jews). (Sidenote: I do not know which books former fascists who are now active in work dismantling hate groups tend to read, but Wiesenthal's should be considered mandatory to ward off the naturally occurring temptation to burden individuals or communities with pleas for forgiveness.)

The problems with demanding that members of marginalized groups offer empathy, compassion, forgiveness, et cetera to those who wish them harm are often overlooked in the midst of naïve appeals to the power of love to ostensibly heal and transform haters. Burdening fascism's targets with "saving" fascists underlies many detrimental forms of empathy for enemies, and many problematic forms of empathy for enemies could be prevented by increased solidarity with fascism's targets, including by prioritizing supporting the efforts of Black, Indigenous, and people of color activists at the grassroots level.

2. Not Platforming the Enemy to Have a "Dialogue"

Proper strategic empathy is not *platforming the enemy to have a "dialogue."* This phenomenon is so widespread that it is difficult to know where to begin. In the past several years, numerous controversies have swirled as members of the far right have been interviewed in the media and invited to speak in public spaces such as university campuses, often with the defense that providing them a hearing might make them or their followers feel less aggrieved and might lead them to moderate their views. In reality, such platforming usually simply provides a larger audience to propagandists, whose cause benefits from the publicity and attention and who rarely enter into dialogue or debate as honest actors. For individuals like Richard Spencer or Milo Yiannopoulos, who thrive on attention, entering into a public conversation is a tactic and not an attempt to be open-minded or even to feel included. The attempt to "include" fascists or fascist-adjacent members of the far right by platforming them and thus to allegedly "deradicalize" them or their followers is an excellent example of the wider problem of the inability to set needed boundaries, and how this in turn plays into victim-blaming. Those who drive far-right speakers from internet platforms, campuses, and other spaces are then often unreasonably blamed for the growth and violent intensification of far-right movements based on an unproven thesis that fascists are more ardent or violent because they are excluded.

3. Not Collaborating with the Enemy

Proper strategic empathy is not *collaborating with the enemy*. Some academics and researchers have arguably crossed ethical boundaries in the process of attempting to understand fascist research subjects. Teitelbaum's "immoral anthropology," discussed earlier, seems to be an example of this. To return briefly to Teitelbaum specifically, I would suggest that some of his actions, such as providing editorial advice on Söderman's racist novel, showed a lack of appropriate boundaries not because such actions violate a professional standard, but because such boundaries are necessary even in friendship. Leaving aside the question of whether Teitelbaum should become friends with fascists (probably not), his notion of friendship strikes me as immature. Not only did Teitelbaum agree to something he appears conflicted about having agreed to (in a mature friendship, one would be able to say no to a request to participate in something that violates one's personal values without worrying about seeming "paranoid"), he is also failing to protect his friend. Teitelbaum's notion of friendship seems to include a fair bit of what those who study addiction might term "enabling." Whether it is ethical for Teitelbaum and Söderman to be friends, there is no need to assume that *this* is what friendship is. It is a junior high notion of friendship, a fascism-tinged friendship in which one's friendship is shaped by an "us" (white nationalists and the "open-minded" researchers who hang out with them) and a "them" (antiracist activists), such that one defends one's friend (in *The New York Times*, say) from outsiders, but does not feel under any obligation to oppose one's friend's harm to others. This is a "help your friends and harm your enemies," "let's see what we can get away with" kind of friendship. However, there have always been other notions of friendship that see friendship as grounded in each friend seeking the good of the other, and that see the good as expansive, impacting the good of others beyond the friendship. Although Teitelbaum is willing to sacrifice his personal reputation among others because of loyalty to his friends—his solidarity with racists no doubt tarnishes his reputation—he is not willing to stand up to his "friends" when their behavior is wrong, or even to resist their requests when they pose a conflict with his own values. In short, based on what he has shared in his article, I believe that Teitelbaum is not truly a good friend to Söderman. Instead, he is a hanger-on who feels some warmth ("affection") for him and desires some measure of acceptance from him.

Another way in which misapplied claims of empathy can bleed over into collaboration with the enemy might appear to be found in the activities of the increasingly controversial "deradicalization" organization Light Upon Light (LUL). LUL was cofounded by former pro–al-Qaeda propagandist Jesse Morton and former director of intelligence analysis for the New York City Police Department Mitch Silber.[22] In 2019, one of LUL's representatives at the time began working closely with the Clarion Project, which the Southern Poverty Law Center (SPLC) designated an anti-Muslim hate group.[23] Meanwhile, Morton has associated with and praised fascist-adjacent "journalist" Andy Ngo, whose doxing of journalists and left activists is widely believed to have assisted in landing many of them on the "kill list" of the accelerationist fascist terrorist group the Atomwaffen Division. LUL also picked up and promoted Jeff Schoep, who led the neo-Nazi National Socialist Movement (NSM) for over two decades and very quickly emerged as a spokesman for LUL when he had been out of the NSM for less than a year and while still facing a lawsuit connected to his involvement in the Charlottesville, Virginia, "Unite the Right" hate march. In 2020, LUL recruited former Traditionalist Worker Party leader Matthew Heimbach and presented him as reformed, even after Heimbach publicly commented that he considered Romanian fascist leader Corneliu Codreanu a "saint," praised Holocaust denier David Irving, and endorsed "degeneracy" laws that threw LGBTQ+ people in prison.[24]

No doubt it is necessary for any organization that is attempting to pull people out of hate groups to communicate with people who are in hate groups, but promoting and even defending active members of hate groups online or getting into alliance with hate groups such as the Clarion Project is deeply problematic. LUL claims to be getting people out of hate groups through its message of empathy and understanding and through rejecting polarization, but seems to be collaborating with bigots more than challenging them.

4. Not Passively Participating in the Enemy's Activities to Gain "Objective" Information about the Enemy

Proper strategic empathy is not *passively participating in the enemy's activities to gain "objective" information about the enemy.* "Participant observation" research on fascists can involve helping fascist movements and can endanger others in the researcher's social circle. This is made clear from the work of Italian sociologist Alessandro Orsini, who formally joined an Italian fascist militia to write a book about the group and participated significantly in their activities during the course of his research.[25] Through his involvement with the group, which he calls "Sacrifice" (probably Italian fascist organization CasaPound), Orsini distributed fascist leaflets and propagandized members of the public, and offered to help with actions such as a banner drop or driving fascists to an event in a carpool. Orsini also deliberately and without warning brought nonfascists into contact with fascists at a dinner party he hosted and at a bar during the course of his research project.

Orsini's attempt to understand the world of fringe fascist violence by joining a fascist group did not necessarily lead him to a more accurate understanding. In fact, it is clear from Orsini's research that such participation can lead to inaccurate information and biases more easily avoided by an outside researcher. At times, he appears to underestimate the degree to which "Sacrifice" engaged in violence, not merely self-defense; he sees the antifascists and fascists as mutually reinforcing parties, with each creating a "parallel world" that makes the other possible, and does not seem to see fascism as necessarily more violent in its ideology or praxis than antifascism. He also contrasts "Sacrifice" a bit too blithely, it seems to me, with American-style skinheads of the 1980s and 1990s, seeing it as less violent than US skinhead movements.[26] Although Orsini resists a demand to submit his manuscript early for approval by the leaders of "Sacrifice" before publication and thus is expelled from membership in the group, his book is so "objective" toward "Sacrifice" that it sometimes reads as though he did in fact receive organizational approval from "Sacrifice." Orsini closes his book with a reflection on his own experiences with violence, and it is clear that he comes from a place of both fascination with and opposition to ideologically motivated violence. In the process of his attempts to understand—possibly even to process some past trauma as a victim of fascist violence alluded to in his book's conclusion—he brings others into close proximity with fascist movements without their informed consent. His research project appears to have endangered some of those around him, and he seems peculiarly dismissive of the fears of those impacted by his research, including his alarmed mother and a girlfriend who broke up with him to avoid the fascists he had surrounded himself with.

5. Not Forgetting to Critique the Enemy

Proper strategic empathy is not *forgetting to critique the enemy*. Even researchers and journalists very ardently opposed to fascism have sometimes felt their boundaries weakening while spending significant time embedded in far-right movements. In his excellent book, *Everything You Love Will Burn: Inside the Rebirth of White Nationalism in America*, journalist Vegas Tenold opens up about being uncomfortably surprised to realize that he had avoided asking the fascist Heimbach about his views on the Holocaust: "I realized that a part of me had begun to enjoy Matthew's [Heimbach] company, and perhaps subconsciously I knew that asking about the Holocaust—a subject about which I was fairly certain I knew what Matthew thought—would mean shattering the illusion that perhaps he was different from the others."[27] In the end, Tenold produced a book that was both illuminating and insightful, but in the process he had to examine his own feelings and assumptions to produce an honest work that did not recapitulate the fascists' own self-understanding. Tenold's self-reflection enabled him to remain critical, and his own self-observation helps the reader reflect upon the necessity of not allowing empathy for fascists to lead us to accept their propaganda at face value or overlook the scope of their ideological hate.

6. Not Being Swayed by the Enemy's Views

Proper strategic empathy is not *being swayed by the enemy's views*. Without careful self-reflection and a plan to protect one's own emotional vulnerabilities, one may end up being swayed by far-right ideologues, regardless of one's prior political commitments. The journalist James Pogue embedded with the armed occupation of the Oregon Malheur Wildlife Refuge led by Ammon Bundy; Pogue felt himself being sucked in by Bundy's charisma, eventually visiting Bundy in jail and painfully rejecting his movement.[28] (This example differs from the others slightly in that Bundy was not ideologically fascist but rather a conspiracy-minded far-right leader, but that difference is not highly relevant here.) One can sympathize with Pogue deeply. First, he rightly saw that the concerns of some of the working-class people involved in the Bundy standoff were being dismissed in reductionist and condescending ways by the media and that their demands were misunderstood by the public. Second, he is candid about going through something personally at the time (coping with a loss, losing track of his surroundings while taking drugs, etc.).

However, Pogue's feelings of affinity for Bundy and his final conflicted break from him at the end of the book leave us much to ponder. (His book is very worth reading for reflecting upon these issues.) Unlike Orsini or Teitelbaum, Pogue empathizes with his research subjects from a position clearly grounded in progressive or left politics. However, going alone into a far-right encampment at a time when he was emotionally vulnerable and searching made him susceptible to Bundy's charisma (even if it also led him to some interesting reflections on America and class along the way). Ultimately, Pogue's struggles may show his need in this situation for both a community of solidarity with other leftists and a more rigorous analysis, which would have enabled him to more easily separate the legitimate grievances of some of the Bundy movement's participants from the twisted answers offered to those grievances by a charismatic leader such as Bundy.

7. Not Being Emotionally Destroyed by the Enemy

Proper strategic empathy is not *being emotionally destroyed by the enemy*. Finally, it should be noted that empathy that fails to maintain adequate emotional distance can be psychologically damaging to the individual. Those involved in research and activism against fascism can be prone to compassion fatigue, a phenomenon so widespread in the field of research on fascism that it now has its own name, coined by researcher Samantha Kutner: "fash fatigue."[29] A Proud Boy apparently warned Kutner that he planned to systematically desensitize her to violence and hate through their interactions and proceeded to subject her to a wide range of hateful content, until this along with other pressures of her research threw her into a deep depression.[30]

One does not even need to engage directly with members of hate groups to suffer fash fatigue, however—this fatigue is well known to even the best researchers in the field. It is not an ethical violation, unlike some of the other misunderstandings or misuses of empathy discussed here, but rather shows the ways in which even activists and researchers with the best intent and solid research methods can be harmed by the content with which they engage. There are ways to protect oneself from this emotional toll, and there are ways for activists and researchers to support one another in their struggles to make the toll easier to bear.[31]

Researchers on hate and supremacist violence bear particular psychological burdens, taking on emotional labor that is often socially isolating and bears certain risks and dangers.[32] Researchers have described a range of effects including feelings of numbness, desensitization to violent or racist content, panic attacks, nightmares, and hypervigilance.[33] These are risks that many researchers and activists are aware of and remain willing to take on, but there are few structural supports for these individuals, and those new to the field may struggle to identify the emotional toll of the research early on and to form the necessary boundaries and the self-care and community-care practices they need to sustain their work.[34] Due to increasing awareness of the trauma and other effects suffered by online content moderators for social media platforms such as Facebook, there is also increasing awareness that *mere exposure* to white supremacist content—let alone contact with white supremacists, activism, or focused research—comes with certain health risks.[35]

The monitoring of online hate often falls not only to paid professionals specializing in that work, but to community activists, including members of targeted groups, who sometimes must protect themselves against threats and must attempt to anticipate possible dangers by watching for threatening activity online by those who wish them harm. Sikh activist lawyer and hate crime researcher Arjun Sethi and Jewish antifascist Talia Lavin have both recently addressed the particular toll of researching those who hate and stereotype your group, and Sethi comments in particular on the difficulty of not knowing where to turn for support.[36] More public discussion of the health risks facing researchers, the formation of strong communities and networks of support for researchers and activists, and mentorship of those new to the work could go a long way toward reducing the emotional toll.

———

The seven misunderstandings or misapplications of empathy toward fascists discussed here all revolve in some way around the question of healthy boundaries, a concept that needs to be further fleshed out and explained (not merely mentioned) in public discourse on these topics. As Storm points out, boundaries are both individual and social. Setting good boundaries is essential both for communities and individuals to preserve their physical and emotional well-being as well as to curtail the ability of fascists to organize and take over broader sections of society. None of this is to say, however, that empathy for fascists is always reactionary (right wing) or collaborationist. Such values as empathy, compassion, and love are not mere liberal claptrap. In fact, I believe that love remains an essential left value. In the final sections of this chapter, I address some of the ways love and empathy remain relevant to antifascist theory and practice.

Understanding Fascism is Not Sympathizing with Fascism

Although it is wise to be on the alert against dangerous appeals to empathy for fascists, antifascism also needs to steer clear of a kind of anti-intellectualism that fears that any psychological understanding of fascists might be a kind of ideological sympathizing. There is a long intellectual tradition of critical exploration of fascist psychology, including significant work in critical theory and psychoanalysis. I agree with critical theorist and psychoanalyst Erich Fromm's deceptively simple claim in the opening to one of his most famous books on fascism, *Escape from Freedom* (1941): "If we want to fight Fascism we must understand it"[37]; and I agree with Mark Bray, who makes a similar point in *Antifa: The Anti-Fascist Handbook* (2017), pointing out the necessity of "a clear and precise understanding of fascism" for antifascist praxis.[38] Self-defense and moral outrage have their place, but neither substitutes for an analysis that can enable fascism's ultimate defeat; we must collectively understand what we are fighting, including the factors that spur recruitment into fascist movements.

The apparent truism that fighting fascism requires understanding it requires deeper exploration. Why and by what means is fascism to be understood? Surely, it is possible to study and explain fascism without lending it any legitimacy as an ideological or political option. However, attempts to study and explain fascism can lend it legitimacy when such attempts are not made in a theoretically rigorous and practically ethical way, and the work must be undertaken in solidarity with fascism's targets and with emancipatory intent. The left is rightly wary about the motives of those studying fascism, wanting to know if such study seeks to legitimate it or not. Some who are engaged in opposing fascism from less overtly activist angles, such as some teachers, counselors, and social workers seeking to disengage students or clients from the far right, may also be hesitant to seek to understand fascism as an ideology or its function as a social movement with connections to power, viewing fascism solely as a response to individual unmet psychological needs and reducing it to a kind of clinical condition akin to addiction. This purely psychological standpoint also gives rise to its own kind of anti-intellectualism due to its desire to abstract fascism from its political context.

Understanding fascism to fight it requires examining its two dimensions: societal and personal. At the level of society, fascism is a social movement seeking power, and is always already connected to sources of power (media outlets, politicians, think tanks, funding sources, some members of law enforcement and the military, etc.).[39] Simultaneously, fascism is a product of the unethical choices of individuals who may join the fascist movement to satiate their personal cravings for meaning, identity, belonging, pride, attention, glory, and an outlet for sadism and rage. Too often, the two aspects of fascism—social movement seeking power, product of individual choices—are treated in isolation from one another, and failing strategies are constructed based on a single one of the two aspects. Perhaps this bifurcation stems to some degree from a warranted nervousness that studying or understanding fascism can lead too easily to collaboration with it, but it is possible to undertake such research from a position of solidarity with fascism's targets.

Case Study: United Front Against Fascism in the Pacific Northwest

Another aspect of potential anti-intellectualism, tied to fear of exploring fascists' psychology and motives, would be a fear of exploring the concepts of "love" and "hate." The hesitancy about exploring these concepts on the left often emerges as a way of pushing back against naïve, apolitical ways of talking about fascism that ignore the ways in which structures of oppression, including structural white supremacy, give rise to fascism as a possibility. Appeals to "love" as the way to combat "hate" can even involve victim-blaming, as noted previously, which tasks fascism's targets with "saving" fascists. Crystal M. Fleming rightly points out that the solution to oppression is not love and we will not "end white supremacy by 'hugging it out.'"[40] She adds: "No one who has even semi-seriously studied the matter would conclude that the history of racial oppression boils down to people of color having a love deficit. And yet, the fact remains that minorities who stand up against racism are routinely accused of being 'the real racists' and not 'loving enough.'"[41] She continues:

> Clearly, racism and all forms of oppression are the very opposite of love. To dominate another person—or an entire group of persons—is to deprive them of their power, to deny their inherent value, and to subject them to forms of abuse and exploitation. If love involves an active commitment to our mutual growth and fulfillment, then interracial love cannot be about mere sentimentality; it has to involve both recognizing and radically resisting the weaponry of terror that maintains white supremacy at the expense of racialized "others." What we need, quite desperately, is the willingness to cultivate revolutionary love, grounded in knowledge, compassion, courage, and collective action.
>
> What we don't need is more kumbaya, postracial bullshit.[42]

I wholly agree—in fact, love in the context of antifascist struggle should be "revolutionary love, grounded in knowledge," not sentimentality that ignores structural oppression and seeks a peace that is merely the absence of overt conflict. When we hear that fascism is flourishing merely because of a lack of "love," or when we see well-intentioned lawn signs announcing, "Hate has no home here" (I always want to ask, "Are you *sure* it doesn't?"), we absolutely should push back against this narrative, demanding an analysis that takes into account power relations and histories of struggle against oppression.

Talk of love and hate isn't always pablum. In fact, there is a kind of anti-intellectualism that fears talk of love and hate as counterrevolutionary, and that takes concerns about sentimentalizing too far, needlessly alienating potential allies and ignoring certain theoretical questions that might prove to be important to understanding fascism and how to overcome it.

For example, I see this hesitancy about the language of love and hate in the history of an important historic protest movement in my region of the US. Considering current struggles internationally, nationally, and locally in the Pacific Northwest, a region that right-wing racists have claimed for the "Northwest Territorial Imperative" and the "Great American Redoubt," I have returned to the literature of the UFAF, based in Seattle in the 1990s. The coalition combined socialists from groups including the Freedom Socialist Party and Communist Party, anarchists, organized labor, and members of the LGBTQ+ community in Seattle, which was being targeted violently by hate groups. At a time when many counseled ignoring fascists or dialoguing with them, UFAF protested face to face with its enemies and was unafraid to name them. UFAF even, in the face of considerable opposition from liberals and police, mobilized a brave and controversial protest at Whidbey Island. UFAF's courage made other kinds of protests more possible by widening the window of acceptable public action against fascist movements. It also, for better or for worse, butted heads with perhaps more respectable, mainstream organizations against hate, including the Kootenai County Task Force on Human Relations, which focused more on achieving prosecutions for hate crimes and keeping fascists at arm's length. (Eventually, this task force in collaboration with the SPLC participated in a successful lawsuit that forced the Aryan Nations compound to close.)

The UFAF should be studied and commended for its anticapitalist politics, its daring head-to-head protests against fascist groups, and its practice of naming its enemy. Furthermore, the coalition's belief that mass marches play a significant role in making communities safe from fascist attack continues to be borne out today—consider the 40,000 people who marched in Boston, Massachusetts following the violent fascist rally in Charlottesville. What are two-dozen Proud Boys against 40,000 marchers?[43] The far-right ralliers ended up, predictably, huddled in a small pagoda in a park, surrounded by teaming masses of protesters against racism. Or consider, in my own current home of Spokane, Washington, how a rally of seven hundred people in 1938 helped defeat the fascist Silver Legion of America. The "Silver Shirts" in Spokane collapsed soon after this mass protest, at which eleven Spokane protesters affiliated with labor and Communist Party unemployed councils were arrested blocking a sidewalk to shut down an event promoting William Dudley Pelley's presidential campaign.[44] (The Spokane newspaper, *Spokesman-Review*, reported the 1938 protest as "Spokane's first anti-fascist demonstration.")

Where UFAF suffered, however, was in its belief, manifested in its rhetoric and perception of potential allies, that fascism needs to be fought solely as a faceless, amorphous mass representing the interests of capital. Psychology is not relevant, in this view—it is only a distraction from economic forces. The view seems to have been that only naïve liberals are interested in loving their enemies or understanding the psychological mechanisms of hate. Here is a typical summation of UFAF's outlook from a 2009 speech; looking back on her involvement with the UFAF in the 1990s, Guerry Hoddersen writes:

> The lesson we learned is that the white supremacists who espouse a fascist/conspiratorial ideology are not a police problem; they are a social and political problem. They are our problem as working [people]. And as radicals, we have a particular responsibility to stand together—whatever our differences are—to defend our class: anarchists, socialists, communists, Trotskyists, Stalinists—it doesn't matter. We need to work together because many liberals don't see fascists as the same danger. *They don't recognize them as a natural by-product of capitalist economic depressions, but rather as a by-product of an unhealthy emotion—hate—which can be overcome with love.* [italics mine][45]

Hoddersen's article, "The High Price of Ignoring Teenage Fascists," is also worth checking out; in that article, she analyzes the Columbine High School shooting with the context of fascism, racism, and far-right militias while making the same claim about the limitations of psychological exploration and of theories of hate and love.

Hoddersen is right that fascism is not a problem that can be solved solely by law enforcement or the ballot box (by electing a different capitalist political party). I also agree with her that fascism is linked to crises of capitalism. However, I disagree on the question of love and hate. One might begin by noting some practical considerations. At the simplest level, dismissing talk of love and hate as liberal claptrap just isn't good praxis and needlessly alienates potential allies. For example, it makes it difficult to work with faith communities; some liberal or left pastors will tolerate a fair degree of militancy from coalition partners, but polemicizing against love won't win over people of faith. (For example, one of the major leaders of the opposition to the Aryan Nations compound in north Idaho was a Catholic priest, Father Bill Wassmuth, whose house was bombed by the Aryan Nations, but UFAF and Wassmuth, from what I have heard, did not work together much.) Love may be an important value to people of many backgrounds and identities, and, I suspect, it fuels the activism of campaigns such as the UFAF, whether the word "love" itself is promoted or shunned.

As seen in the case of the UFAF's rhetoric, those who rightly wish to emphasize class conflict, systemic oppression, and state power as structural forces underlying fascism can sometimes be too dismissive of those who seek to understand the mechanism of hate in relation to love. There is a temptation to see all talk of "love" as evidence of a liberal banality that ignores social structures. There is also a prudent concern about not letting talk of love fall into "both sidesism" that gives cover to fascism by equating fascism with antifascism. Fascism and antifascism are opposites, but some wrongly claim that antifascism is inspired by "hate" because of the diversity of tactics it uses to defend against fascist threats. Talk of love, empathy, compassion, forgiveness, and so on, in the context of debates about fascism, *does* often stem from a reductive understanding or from false equivalencies, but this is not always the case. Dismissing philosophical inquiry into human needs for connection, in the name of a more "radical" analysis, can in fact lead to overlooking some of the root causes of fascist remobilization and can weaken both antifascist theory and practice in the process. Perhaps most crucially, discarding the question of love and hate can elide the examination of the pursuit of meaning that is being undertaken by those mistakenly seeking fulfillment on the far right. Understanding this fanatical pursuit of meaning through ideology and power not only assists with the development of a program for counter-recruitment and disengagement from the far right, but, if done properly, leads us to a critique of capitalism and to a deeper understanding of fascism's causes and its possible ultimate defeat. In the following and final section of this chapter, I address how "strategic empathy" can assist antifascist strategy, particularly regarding the importance of mutual aid and dual power.

Strategic Empathy

What I am calling "strategic empathy" plays a role in the attempt to understand and defeat fascism. Strategic empathy in antifascism is directed to understanding the factors that lead individuals to join or voluntarily leave fascist ideology, and developing countermeasures to not only respond to particular situations but to begin constructing a society that makes fascism less possible in the long term. This does not mean that it is ever anyone's obligation to conjure up caring emotions toward fascists, and it is especially not the obligation of fascism's targets.

I would add the word "solidarity" to any discussion of empathy, and I would define solidarity as *love mobilized for justice*, and justice, in the words of Cornel West, as "what love looks like in public." It is this solidarity that the journalist Pogue, discussed earlier, attempts and somewhat fails to capture in his book on the Bundy standoff. Pogue correctly notes that not everyone involved in far-right militia movements is a hardened ideologue. We might add that the long-time work of projects such as the Highlander Research and Education Center, as well as experiments such as those of the Young Patriots in the 1960s and, more recently, Redneck Revolt, made inroads in right-wing rural movements, although much more work in this area remains to be done. A grandmother at the Oregon wildlife refuge occupation told Pogue that she got involved in the Bundy ranchers' movement because right-wing militia members in her hometown were building a playground for kids and fighting wildfires, which suggests the need for leftists to be engaged in projects of mutual aid and building dual power, a topic I will return to momentarily.[46] Pogue is right to empathize with her, but perhaps because Pogue lacks a community with whom he is undertaking this project of solidarity, he gets dragged down by the forces of Bundy's charisma and the Bundy movement's cohesiveness and paranoia. He is thus unable to succeed in the arena of praxis (although his book is still a useful contribution to understanding the Bundy movement).

To ask about the nature of love in the context of antifascism is to ask about the relationship between theory and practice, a classic question of socialist and left thought. Theory and practice are dynamically, dialectically related, and each informs the other. To fight fascism, as I have stated, we must seek to understand it. And unlike Teitelbaum, we must seek to understand it precisely with the intention of fighting it. Seeking understanding with the intent of liberating humanity does not bias the researcher in a way that leads to diminished knowledge, but rather opens up new vistas of understanding. Marxist philosopher Georg Lukács stressed that achieving the "standpoint of totality" (being able to see the direction in which humanity may be able to move toward liberation) requires a simultaneous shift in theoretical perspective and a practical commitment to solidarity. One understands the revolution by joining it, that is; and one joins by understanding.[47]

The work of the critical theorist Fromm, mentioned earlier, has been influential on my own thinking about theory and practice, and his analysis suggests the necessity of a kind of radical hope that rejects catastrophe. Fromm's antifascist theory and praxis, alongside his defense of "social-ist humanism," were motivated by a defense of what he called "prophetic messianism."[48] Prophetic messianism was a spirit of radical hope that he believed had almost been defeated with World War I and the 1919 assassi-nations of socialist leader Rosa Luxemburg and anarchist leader Gustav Landauer, both Jewish revolutionaries who stood up to nationalism and stood for working-class solidarity.[49] Both Luxemburg and Landauer, according to Fromm, were "prophets" in the sense of recognizing the nature of the moment facing them, and of calling upon people to under-stand the crucial juncture at which history was standing and to make the correct choice. Prophets present the public with "alternatives," demon-strating possible courses of action and warning about the consequences of choosing wrongly. Luxemburg's theory of the "mass strike" reflected a deep understanding that history is made not through transcendent interventions, but through the somewhat unpredictable emergence of uprisings that occur when the people are ready to move. Landauer's vision of anarchist revolution similarly rests on his understanding that, when revolutionary transformation occurs, it is not so much a bolt of lightning from above but something that grows up from within the present, through the construction of new structures. "Appealing to the people" is insuf-ficient, Landauer writes; instead, we must "show others and ourselves what socialism means *in action*. We must realize as much of socialism as possible *right here and right now*."[50] Echoing Landauer's commitment to "building it now," Fromm insists in his best-selling *The Art of Loving* that love is possible under capitalism. Although "the *principle* underlying capi-talistic society and the *principle* of love are incompatible . . . 'capitalism' is in itself a complex and constantly changing structure which still permits a good deal of non-conformity and of personal latitude. In saying this how-ever, I do not wish to imply that we can expect the present social system to continue indefinitely, and at the same time to hope for the realization of the ideal of love" [italics in original].[51]

Traditions of radical love and hope form the spiritual backbone of socialist and anarchist revolutionary praxis. Far from being utopian in a negative sense (abstract, unmoored from reality), such commitments form the glue between our theory and practice and remind us to begin dismantling oppression and violence within our own circles, and to begin constructing within the present the society we hope to see in the future. Rather than making us mere liberals or sluggish reformists, such a commitment to love and hope distinguishes us from accelerationists, catastrophists, Blanquists—pick your term; Fromm called them "catastrophic messianists." Catastrophic messianists believe that history is regulated according to predetermined cycles or mysterious laws and that it is only by making conditions worse and heightening catastrophic suffering that history can magically reset itself. In contrast to the catastrophic messianist, the "prophet's" work is an essentially pedagogical (i.e., educational) activity, and pedagogy requires brave love to achieve effectiveness. (We might look to the importance of love in the work of radical education theorists such as Paulo Freire and bell hooks, for example, both of whom were influenced by Fromm.[52])

Going forward, the work of "building it now" as part of strategic empathy challenges us to the work of dual power and mutual aid, realizing the increased urgency created by the attempts of fascists and the far right to co-opt these practices. Appropriating tactics from the left of mutual aid and building alternative structures (dual power),[53] and drawing from the ideas of leftist thinkers such as Antonio Gramsci, the European far right has engaged in a number of ambiguous "service" projects. Fascist group CasaPound in Italy has been particularly active in this regard, operating a medical clinic and hostel for white Italians.[54] The European "Identitarian" movement takes similar actions, such as deliberately distributing pork soup to the needy in a predominantly Muslim neighborhood, where Muslims would be unable to eat the soup because of their religion.[55]

Fascist groups in the US have taken on similar work, such as occasionally distributing clothes (Traditionalist Worker Party), cleaning up highways (Ku Klux Klan and neo-Nazi groups), and conducting food drives (American Blackshirts Party). In my current city of Spokane, a city with a massive housing crisis due to "no cause" eviction policies and a lack of rent control, the fascist group Identity Evropa (later renamed American Identity Movement) engaged in a showy racist charity action for local homeless people, distributing "ham hash" (i.e., pork, presumably in an attempt to exclude Jews and Muslims, echoing the European Identitarian movement). On Twitter, Identity Evropa claimed to be helping "Americans neglected by our globalist ruling class." This language is deliberately obscurantist. A local progressive activist on Facebook seemed a bit confused: Yes, they are racists, but isn't it good that they see there's a problem with the ruling class? *No*—I had to explain—*"globalist" is an antisemitic dog whistle, and they don't mean "American" the way you do. They just mean they believe they are protecting white people from a purported Jewish conspiracy.*

Such antics of deliberately exclusionary "service," of compassion mixed with cruelty as a propagandistic display, remind the left to reflect on the role of service and solidarity in our own praxis. If this is a direction in which some fascist groups are moving, even though they are mostly still very bad at it, the left must be careful not to cede ground. The activities of Democratic Socialists of America in providing a "free brake light clinic," or Food Not Bombs distributing food to the hungry or unhoused, or the organized mutual aid projects in many communities responding to the coronavirus disease 2019 pandemic are neither mere charity nor mere propaganda (nor, as in the case of many fascist service projects, mere "optics"). Over the past couple of decades, numerous projects in the US have brought together radical politics with direct aid, from responses to Hurricane Katrina, to Occupy movement participants assisting after Hurricane Sandy, to, most recently, antifascists assisting in response to wildfires in the Pacific Northwest.[56] Many of these projects included collaboration with churches, as well. There are long-running radical traditions of aid on the left in the work of the Industrial Workers of the World, Communist Party unemployed councils, the Black Panther Party's free breakfast for children program, and Grace Lee Boggs's community building in Detroit, Michigan, among others. We do not really need to invent anything out of whole cloth but continue to carry on a tradition.

Such efforts are, although not in isolation or exclusion, revolutionary and antifascist activities. Racism and other forms of hate are not fueled solely by economic deprivation, but, if people do not find a coherent narrative that speaks to their suffering or alienation, and do not know where to find community in diversity, their desperation and alienation may incline them to the far right. The left should never attempt to be inclusive of fascists, nor cede an inch on our demands to appear less "extreme." Rather, we can prevent people from moving to the far right if we provide clear sources of community, aid, and coherent understanding of social realities. The grandmother Pogue describes, for example, perhaps might have been helping out with a local socialist free clinic, if there had been one, rather than helping out the Bundys, but a right-wing militia got to her first.

As we have seen, leftists need to be wary of calls for empathy, compassion, forgiveness, inclusion, and so on toward fascists. Such calls often undermine necessary boundaries, normalize fascism, or foster victim-blaming, and can make individuals and communities less safe. It is necessary to continue to explore the possible harms of such rhetoric and to push back when it is deployed in harmful ways. Simultaneously, justified concern about forms of rhetoric of empathy does not imply that love is irrelevant to antifascism. In fact, radical love remains at the root of left praxis and theory broadly, and it may only be in part through the understanding provided by strategic empathy, and the mutual aid or dual power structures made possible through radical love, that we can begin to permanently dismantle the fascist threat by abolishing the capitalist system under which fascism arises and tearing down structures of racism and oppression that maintain the worldview of fascism. These are deep questions from the standpoint of theory and practice that cannot be solved by a single chapter, but rather are the subject of a long historical discussion within the left that continues to play out, as we seek to understand the roles love plays in the relationship between the present and the future and between theory and practice. We must continue to engage this theme in a way that understands that, although radical love animates our work, naïve appeals to love in the absence of boundaries and safety can do real harm and can undermine the project of the more loving, solidaristic society we seek to construct.

The Meme Alibi

Margaret Rex

Even at the close of the 2020 election, it was clear right-wing authoritarianism had grown rather than receded. We are now collectively turning our attention to stifling these ideologies, both socially and individually. Questions remain about governing, and about how families can cope with the loss of loved ones to QAnon, Proud Boys, militia groups, and other far-right movements. Because they ignored the alarm bells raised by activists for 30 years, Americans are now confronting the real possibility of increased violence and seeing in real-time the way the Overton window has shifted so far to the right that the basic tenets of democracy hang in the balance. But right-wing radicalization is not a new phenomenon, and despite years of warnings, we remain paralyzed about how to address it, as a country and within our own lives.

On August 13th, 2017, mourners in the small upstate city of Rochester, New York gathered for a vigil for Heather Heyer, an antifascist activist murdered during the "Unite the Right" rally in Charlottesville, Virginia. Heyer was killed, and 19 others injured, when a 20-year-old neo-Nazi rammed into a crowd of counterprotesters with his car.[1] In the days following her murder, conspiracy theories swirled and damage control measures were discussed throughout the far right's online circles. What emerged was a contention that the driver of the car that hit Heyer had been attacked by antifascists and fled into the crowd,[2] or that the car was driven by a Central Intelligence Agency operative,[3] despite no evidence that supported those claims and ample evidence to the contrary. Unbeknownst to many of his friends and loved ones, on the evening of the vigil, "Kurt Kadaver" had already decided to run with this narrative and was discussing whether he and his fellow Proud Boys should go down and harass the mourners.[4]

"You going to stop down and say hi to them?" one asked.

"I just might. Depends on how I feel." Kurt answered. He added, "Might be best to just leave them alone. Having one of your own get so

413

sick of your shit that they use a car as a weapon makes for an emotionally challenging time."

Kurt was a 40-something white tattoo artist and former punk and goth scene staple. He, like many others, had undergone an ideological shift in 2014–15, and Heyer's alleged "antifa murderer" wasn't the only right-wing conspiracy theory that he embraced. He was an active member of the far-right street gang the Proud Boys—helping found a local chapter, including initiating new members—and was a constant online presence, trolling anyone who questioned his increasingly right-wing beliefs. His involvement with the Proud Boys was, at the time of the "Unite the Right" rally, just becoming known publicly, and his friends struggled deeply with whether they could or should maintain ties with him. I interviewed five of his friends in the fall of 2019 to try to understand what the process of watching a friend undergoing right-wing radicalization was like.

The experiences of Kurt's friends are instructive. The "lone wolf" archetype that has dominated common understandings of right-wing violence has unraveled.[5] Many of those who radicalized under Donald Trump have been socially connected, not isolated. The shocking, full-throated fascism that undergirds Trumpism grew in part due to the success of the "alt-light" in cultivating paths toward radicalization that even invested loved ones could not undo.[6] Years later, many of us know people who have turned sharply to the right. And neither time nor Trump's departure have enlightened those asking why. Many parents, cousins, and friends who were silent when children were ripped from their parent's arms and then simply vanished within the US detention system still defend those policies.[7] Comments about shooting or running over protesters are no longer solely the purview of militia members or neo-Nazis. They are found in the comments section of nearly every local newspaper reporting on Black Lives Matter (BLM) rallies.[8] They are happening over dinner. Loved ones tell us, straight-faced, about Democrats farming children to rape and drink their blood. Understanding how to respond to this will preoccupy us as a community for years. Platitudes about reaching out to Trump supporters abound on social media, and are met with forceful rejections. Calls to shun and shame those who have embraced the authoritarian nightmare are commonplace. No one seems to know what to do.

And the advice that pervades often feels made from and, more importantly, made for the internet. In many ways, it is entirely antithetical to the bonds of love that we have for the people in our lives. It is much easier to walk away from strangers online than people we have known for decades or longer. The conversations that consumed Kurt's friends between 2012 and 2016 were early precursors to the conversations that we are currently having about how to bring our friends and families back from the brink. Some of his people reached out to him, some ignored him, and some pushed back. Most seemed to feel that he was slipping away but had no idea what their role was in bringing him back. And their assessments, plans, worries, and strategies were complicated by perhaps the most insidious element of the alt-light: the meme alibi. Within the alt-light, every post, threat, or comment could be burgeoning fascism or a bad joke. This meme alibi is a method of offering extremist views in a way that is serious in its effect while claiming that taking it seriously is the height of oversensitivity. It is paralyzing. And it is wielded with intent.

In February 2017, Kurt tweeted a meme with a picture of an open gas canister. "Dark humor is like Zyklon-B. It's a real gas."

Is He Serious?

The people who I spoke to are not Proud Boys. In fact, they all identify as liberal, leftists, or progressives. Sarah, Kurt's closest friend, has a hard science doctor of philosophy degree and teaches at a local charter school. She is active in the state's progressive Democratic Party and has volunteered extensively with nonprofits providing resettlement aid to refugees and Black queer organizers. John, Kurt's former roommate, worked for a local, progressive nonprofit. Kieran, who had at one point been Kurt's best friend, worked for a nongovernmental organization that runs literacy programs for kids. Amy and Helen both identified as feminists. Each of them expressed real disgust about the Proud Boys and their ideology, and made clear the values Kurt espoused were not ones that they shared.[9]

Kurt was described by his friends as an argumentative attention junkie, so at first the shifts in his online behavior seemed fairly in line with the person they had known, some for 20 years or more. "He was always rabidly antiestablishment," Amy told me. Sarah described him as "antigovernment, anti–New World Order." But mostly his friends described him as a contrarian. "He'd play devil's advocate on whether this puppy is cute or not," said Sarah. Kieran described Kurt as a constant antagonist, "who was almost malevolent about it" and that this wasn't a new development. "You could put him anywhere on the political spectrum and that's who he was, but he ended up on the far right."

His early trolling in 2013 and 2014 seemed to his friends to be in line with the parts of his personality that had made him a lovable asshole for most of his life. But in 2016, as the alt-right and alt-light exploded in influence, Kurt's positions changed and his demeanor online became more extreme. His Twitter feed and multiple Facebook accounts transformed into a stream of misogynistic jokes, links to conspiracy theory videos, and crude and incendiary memes about everything from antifa and Islam to BLM and the Holocaust. His Twitter feed was openly supportive of the Proud Boys whereas his Facebook accounts were not.

Kurt's emerging radicalization was painful and confusing to his friends. It had come as a particular shock to his friend John. The two had lived together briefly in the late 1990s. John is white, in his late 30s, and actually looks a little like a lumberjack as opposed to a hipster trying to look like a lumberjack. He has a steady, calm presence and spoke about his relationship with Kurt as though he had been having this conversation with himself for a very long time. John described himself as a "leftie." He worked part-time for Fair Fight, a local, progressive nonprofit that had been active since the 1960s. John and Kurt were not particularly close by 2016, but they were still friends on Facebook, and John was baffled by the changes he was seeing in Kurt. John told me: "He was always larger than life. His personality always had to be the biggest in the room. And social media is a big room, so that act made sense in that regard. [Kurt thought,] 'If I play along with the dialogue of the left, I'm blending into the crowd. But if I'm all of a sudden this big douchebag personality, that's gonna set me apart and everyone's gonna pay attention to me.' And I thought, 'This is really dumb humor to be so right-wing about it, but it kinda felt like he's gonna have a big reveal eventually.'"

"So it felt like a shtick?" I ask.

"Yeah. It felt performative," John replied.

Even much newer friends had trouble pinning down what was real and what wasn't. Helen met Kurt in 2015. Helen is white and in her early 30s. She does construction and works nights at a bar. By then, Kurt's online behavior was firmly established. "It was the height of all the shit," she told me. "When I first met him, I didn't realize that he was a total jerk on social media. Shortly after we became friends on Facebook, I stopped following him." They never talked about his political beliefs in person. "And after being Facebook friends with him I had no desire to talk to him about it in person," she told me. "I almost saw it as a twisted hobby, like . . . fucking with people." When I asked her how this compared with his online behavior, she said, "Because I saw so little of that in his face-to-face experiences, that it seemed like a joke." But the line between performance and reality was blurred.

The lack of clarity about what was a performance and what was not was common to everyone I spoke to. I asked John, "Did it ever stop feeling like a shtick and start feeling like this is what he actually thinks?"

"I got very concerned when he started parroting Proud Boys stuff," John said. "But there was always, in the back of my mind, like some sort of end to the means that I just wasn't picking up on. Like some sort of final result that he wanted out of all of this rather than just getting laughs."

The Proud Boys and other groups in the so-called alt-light represent the most successful rebranding and mainstreaming of white supremacy in the last decade. The Proud Boys, specifically, argue that they are not white supremacist or white nationalists but "Western chauvinists."[10] This shift in image worked. They have been largely embraced by the Republican establishment. Their methods for recruiting members borrow some strategies from old-school white power gangs, but the Proud Boys cannot be understood outside of an online context.[11] The particular tactics, actions, and online recruiting practices of the Proud Boys—using memes, trolling, and humor to buttress a particularly potent mix of misogyny, mythologized machismo, and racism—represents a significant departure from past extremist organizations. We are poorly equipped to deal with them at every level. And this is due at least in part to the way that the meme alibi allows limitless deflection, redirection, and avoidance of responsibility while being an incredibly effective way to spread fascist ideologies.

Sarah recalls that Kurt's language eventually became more militant and deliberately provocative. Sarah is white and in her early 40s. She describes herself as a liberal. She volunteers with the local Working Families Party. When she met Kurt, she was 15 years of age and homeless, and Kurt offered her and her boyfriend a place to stay. He lived in a trailer park in a small rural town in central New York with his grandmother and was in his early 20s. She remembered his youthful politics as being "big time anti-Nazi, antiskinhead." Sarah described their entire crew as, "rabidly antiestablishment. . . . This was around 9/11 and we all believed it was an inside job so the US could take Iraqi oil." But she also remembers Kurt as, "a guy who was always trying to make sure that the people around him felt included. To the point that the older punks would tease him about it." Kurt's later identity was about the exact opposite. It was about drawing lines between who got protection—white people, nonimmigrants, non-Muslims, and friends who agreed with him—and everyone else. "9/11 Truth" conspiracies attracted many people across the political spectrum, and became a sort of gateway to the far right for many people on the left whose politics were based on distrust of systems.[12] Callous and ideologically unmoored antiestablishment sentiment can lead to support for truly heinous acts and actors, such as supporting authoritarian dictatorships in the name of anti-imperialism or supporting Trump in the name of antielitism.

Memelord

"This character, Kurt Kadaver," Sarah said, "emerged, initially as an artist name for tattooing, but it grew online into a virulent troll identity." Sarah saw Kurt's anger about "globalism" and North American Free Trade Agreement (NAFTA) "start to turn into this deeper resentment about elites . . . during the end of the second [Barack] Obama term." She felt that his resentment, "combined with a true endorphin rush of pissing people off," changed him. "When he was younger, he was never provocative to be mean, he never did it to hurt people," Sarah said. But that all changed.

"As time went on," Sarah told me, "reality happened" and she got pregnant. Kurt helped her get an apartment in 2002. He stepped up and helped with childcare. They eventually stopped seeing each other much, but kept texting. In 2006, Sarah started dating Kieran, who was Kurt's best friend. Kieran later told me, in great detail, about how his friendship with Kurt started several years before he dated Sarah: "I met him approximately five minutes after he slept with my girlfriend. I forgot my keys so I pounded on the door, and Kurt answered, mohawk all flopping over . . . and I walked past him and went to bed. We ended up being best friends. And I think that's sort of germane to this conversation because, like, this is a person that I was compelled to look past many things that other people might have been like, 'What the fuck?' And many of them did."

Eventually, Sarah told me, "He was being the ultimate asshole and in his mind by doing that he was making some grand statement." Sarah said that, although she understood that her friend was sliding into fascism, she believed that he could still be helped. She, John, and Kieran all offered commonly understood correlates of extremism—depression, economic struggles, and wounded, toxic masculinity—as a way to explain what may have driven Kurt into the alt-light. "No happy person behaves that way," said John. And they may be right. But there is another possibility, which seemed much harder for his people to face: that their friend had actually changed because his beliefs had changed, and that he was acting the way he did because he liked to. Sarah edged close to admitting this several times in our conversation: "It was like he put on this costume and then actually liked wearing it. . . . [H]e started becoming the character that he'd been playing."

Kurt's friends saw him as many things in his youth, but the mainstay of his personality was contrarianism. For contrarians, and people whose entire identity is about being in opposition to social norms and perceived authority, maybe it does seem normal to pivot away from anticapitalism and antifascism as the world at large pivoted toward those things. When the commonly accepted views in their cultures get better, they have to regress. As racism, sexism, xenophobia, and homophobia have become less openly acceptable, there have been whole swaths of people more willing to embrace fascism than to see themselves as "normies." Gavin McInnes capitalized on this impulse, placing it at the heart of the alt-light with the assertion that conservatism is the "new punk."[13]

Denying White Supremacy

When I talked to Kieran, he was nervous. Like John and Sarah, it seemed as though it was a conversation he had been waiting to have, or having in his head, for a long time. Thinking about Kurt and his radicalization seemed to be part of how his friends had coped. They seemed to think that if they could have just figured him out, they could have fixed him.

Kieran told me, "to be witness to" Kurt's behavior was really difficult for him. He thought that his friend "was looking for his new tribe, and he found the Proud Boys." Kieran suspects that Kurt was attracted to the Proud Boys because of a need for "extreme things." He admits that Kurt was:

> Definitely sexist. Definitely into men's rights. But he wasn't a racist. But . . . he did have racist ideas. Like, "Why don't they just get themselves out of the ghetto?" That kind of bootstrap libertarian thing that's blind to socioeconomic racism and sexism. He was what you could think of as a postfeminist. "Oh, we don't need to worry about these issues anymore. Sexism is done, racism is done. If people think that stuff is happening, they're lying to themselves." Which we all know is a pretty racist idea but, in his mind, wasn't.

Trying to make some sense out of what he's saying, I ask, "So he wasn't overt? He didn't have a specific racial animus but he had racist ideas?"

"Exactly!" Kieran says. "That's why these conversations need to be nuanced. There are levels to these things. And in order to get someone who has racist ideas to adjust them, you need to understand the difference between the vitriol of racism, the willingness to use violence for its own sake, to use the 'N-word' . . . and simply having misplaced ideas about how we got to where we are in this country." Kieran is smart. He understands social justice and social change; as he spoke, he struggled to muster that knowledge to insulate Kurt from an obvious truth: that he embraced white supremacist ideas. I flash to Kurt's racist Twitter feed: "#n*****navy: Today we naming these couple a boats. USS 'no henny noremy' and the USS 'fried hard all flats.'"

In 2017, Yahoo Finance tweeted about Trump's request for a bigger Navy, but misspelled "Bigger" as "Ni—er" in the headline. Black Twitter jumped on it, making jokes about the #ni—ernavy, and it started trending.[14] Black scholars and activists have talked about how these moments of levity are about taking terms and moments that used to have to be swallowed in silence and turning them on their heads.[15] The right wing has used them to cry foul, saying that Black folks using words that whites can't is "reverse racism." The result of this line of reasoning is white people who insist that they are not racist also insisting on their right to use the most offensive racial slur in American history and then crying foul when their actions are called out.

This is the issue with contrarianism as a political position. It is inherently empty. It has no actual, objective content, and thus no objective limits. It's not about a desire to say or do any specific thing. It is defined entirely by the compulsion to do what one perceives themselves as being told they can't. It is a tendency held by people who think of themselves as ruggedly individual and fiercely independent, and yet it is completely externally determined.

Kieran saw his friend as someone who wouldn't say the N-word out of a sense of racial animus, or the desire to use violence for the sake of racist ideals. In Kieran's mind, and in the minds of many people, "real" racism is serious. Racists believe in the superiority of the white race and the inferiority of people of color, and speak out hatefully and earnestly about those beliefs. Kieran saw Kurt as having a different level of racism. What he misunderstood was that Kurt's commitment was less to an old-school Ku Klux Klan (KKK)–style racial hatred and more to a ruthless contrarianism that made shockingly racist statements acceptable, as long as they were ostensibly tongue-in-cheek. The entire approach of the trolls of the far right is to simultaneously posture as pseudointellectuals while denying the relatively straightforward and noncontroversial reality that context matters: Two people using the same words can have very different meanings depending on who those people are. When people of color on Twitter make jokes about racial stereotypes, they do so to make fun of racism. Whether motivated by real vitriol or not, trolls like Kurt use racism as a way to position themselves as provocateurs, and in doing so assume racism as part of their identity, but in ways in which they pick up and down at will.

This strategy makes pinning down his actual positions on race and racism difficult for Kurt's friends, many of whom see themselves not just as *not* racist, but as *anti*racist. This was just one example of the ways that the particular path to radicalization that Kurt and many folks in the alt-light took that was deeply confusing. And this confusion has consequences because those who stayed friends with him were often accused of being racist themselves. Kieran clung to a notion of "levels of racism" and a need for nuance because he seemed unable to acknowledge that, although Kurt may not have been a fully formed white nationalist, he was certainly a white supremacist. He may not have been advocating for a white ethno-state, but his racist and sexist biases were rampant and justifying them was the basis of his identity. Failing to recognize and take this seriously made many people see Kurt's friends as complicit.

Kieran recalled Kurt approaching him about setting up a tattooing website designed specifically to appeal to bikers and Trump-supporting conservatives. Kurt had moved back to a city after living rurally for a few years and was trying to entice his clientele to follow him. Kieran saw this as evidence that his extremism was primarily motivated by his finances, not his beliefs.

"So you feel like his online persona was all strategic?" I ask.

"At first, yes, but it gets gray," says Kieran.

Turning Gray to Gold

This gray area is like fog, enveloping most meaningful conversations around right-wing radicalization, especially via the alt-light. In his book, *Anti-Social: Online Extremists, Techno-Utopians, and the Hijacking of the American Conversation*, Andrew Marantz conducts interviews with several prominent alt-light content creators. Each of them describes the process by which they have used right-wing rhetoric as a career. Each recognized that extremist content gets attention, and that attention is the real currency in terms of being professional trolls. These men all built followings by pushing racism, sexism, nationalism, xenophobia, and conspiracy theories. But many, like Kurt, maintained that their online behavior was more about upsetting liberals than anything else. They remained deliberately opaque about what their ideas actually are, and have used the meme alibi to avoid any responsibility for the movements and ideas they propel.

Marantz spends a great deal of time talking to Mike Cernovich, an alt-right content creator. He has 700,000 Twitter followers and has said, "Conflict is attention and attention is influence." Cernovich began by writing about masculinity and hookup culture, but learned that trolling celebrities about politics got the most pushback, and that, the more pushback he got, the more followers he also got. These strategies are being emulated by other would-be right-wing demicelebrities, and they incentivize online abuse.

But the particular form that they take is labyrinthine. The vilest statements made by far-right provocateurs are often as memes or tweets. Social media companies benefit financially from trolls whose provocations keep people scrolling, and these companies have little to no incentive to rein them in.[16] Policymakers and companies who try to address these actions are accused of infringing upon the free speech of conservatives.[17]

Eventually, inside the circle of Kurt's friends, many people just walked away. They were disgusted by his abusive behavior, they were being criticized for not speaking out, and they found the content Kurt was sharing to be no laughing matter. Kieran declined to help build Kurt's tattoo website, but there was increasing pressure on those closest to him to speak out, publicly. But no one that I spoke to did. They all described themselves as peacemakers, as fixers, and had a history of shared trauma. They all seemed unable to pull apart what was real and what was simply a performance.

Maintaining a friendship with Kurt "cost me a perception of allyship from many people that I love," said Sarah. Her Black, Latinx, and lesbian-gay-bisexual-transgender-queer (LGBTQ) friends stopped talking to her or said outright that her defense of him was wrong. "And at first," she told me, "I was like, 'I've known him for 20 years and this isn't who he is, I promise.'" But eventually, she had to stop making that promise because she herself wasn't sure anymore. Instead, she would just say, "I'm sorry that I'm hurting you."

A Shadow Over the Moon

Although she stopped professing that this was all an act by Kurt, I ask her if she ever stopped believing that herself. Her gift for metaphor reveals itself as she says, "It's like an eclipse. You have the moon, and you have the shadow passing over it. And, in my mind, the moon was always the same. But the shadow got bigger and bigger and bigger. Until, like, in ancient times, they didn't know if the moon was coming back." She sniffed back tears.

"You really felt like you could save Kurt?" I ask.

"Yeah. For better or for worse, I genuinely believe I could," she said.

The majority of resources available to those concerned about the right-wing radicalization of a loved one in 2017 failed to capture the experiences of Kurt's friends in several ways. First, the majority of those resources assumed the radicalization of young people, and were therefore aimed at families, usually of teenagers[18]. There were fewer resources for friends, and especially for friends of adults radicalizing in their 30s and 40s.

In the wake of the January 6th, 2021, Capitol riot and general proliferation of QAnon, this has improved significantly, as the vulnerability of adults to right-wing radicalization became undeniable. Second, the majority of these resources talked about stark personal transitions in loved ones.[19] They describe people who change their appearance, who abandon family and friends for a new extremist social circle, or who isolate completely. They describe the radicalizing individual as "becoming a different person."[20] This remains true today. And third, these resources are all predicated on a fundamental but rarely discussed assumption: that the radicalizing individual is always serious about what they are saying; that they are earnest and zealous and that there is no question that they fervently ascribe to their new beliefs.

These resources are poorly equipped at helping friends and families of adults radicalizing into the alt-light, where the path to radicalization sometimes begins as bad jokes and edgy memes, not with a white power recruiter waiting outside of a high school with a zine. Kurt's friends were adults trying to help another adult, not parents with the ability to regulate the online behavior of a child. And they had 20 years of cherished history clashing with 1 to 2 years of alarming extremism.

They also didn't see a stark transition. Each described Kurt as a contrarian, and an attention junkie. The changes in his behavior and professed beliefs seemed, at first, very much in line with those traits. Each drew on that history and on the things that seemed continuous to deny or downplay the obvious changes.

Every one of Kurt's friends revealed that their single biggest struggle in dealing with his rightward slide was figuring out whether he was even serious. This is perhaps the greatest rhetorical and strategic strength of the alt-light. When people tried to call Kurt on his behavior, or on the content he was sharing, the response was often that this behavior was a persona and that his posts and goading were jokes. He argued that, although he was being intentionally provocative, it was the fault of the humorless leftie for taking the bait and being so easily offended. The meme alibi blocked Kurt's friends almost completely. But as they discussed, agonized, unfollowed, and ignored, his rhetoric moved offline and into real life.

In the last year of his life, it was an open secret that Kurt bankrolled the Punks' Picnic, a yearly concert and gathering for their generation. Kieran describes how Kurt showed up in a Make America Great Again (MAGA) hat with a jar to raise money for activists fighting the Dakota Access Pipeline. The spectacle added to the confusion and unease people felt about Kurt's politics, and to the social capital that discouraged some people from speaking up. But Kieran described the contradictory and deliberately incendiary act not as something new, but as "quintessential Kurt." While funding the Punk's Picnic, Kurt helped start a Proud Boys chapter in upstate New York that is still active today. He initiated members and patrolled neighborhoods, posting flyers and stickers encouraging "action" against antifascists; he menaced local antifascist activists.

"I felt really scared for him," Sarah told me, unaware of the irony this presented. "And I felt really angry at the scene as everybody was like, 'Fuck him and fuck anybody that talks to him.'" But she acknowledges that, as time went on, these supposed differences between Kurt online and Kurt "in real life" began to break down. "He was still worse online. But in person he just . . . he lost his smile. He lost his ability to joke around. He became angrier," she said.

Kieran told me, "It was extreme, even for him. He was already trolling, and soon after [asking to set up a tattoo website] was the first time he blocked me. At the time . . . I was devastated." This was when Kieran realized that something really had changed. "Early trolling, he would eventually apologize. He was still kind of a human being. . . . It made me realize that shit is going off the rails in America. It was like one of these moments in a novel where the small thing makes you think of the big thing." Dealing with it made Kieran feel very alone. Kurt was relatively unique in this way: He didn't reserve his ire for strangers. He trolled his friends, too.

Unfollow

Amy also saw the divisions Kurt was creating in their scene as emblematic of the broader tribalization of America under Trump. She tells me that she found Kurt's behavior and the response to it fascinating because, "The specific push-and-pull reactions . . . it's sort of like a storyline that's reflective of our country. And if things are going to shift in our favor in this country, then looking at this is important." But she drew something very different from that observation. Amy is white and in her late 40s. She grew up in upstate New York and had been in the same scene as Kurt, Sarah, John, and Kieran. But unlike the others I spoke to, Amy became closer to Kurt as his public persona became more incendiary. She explains this in part by saying that she saw Kurt not as a right-wing troll but as an "intellectually bored agitator." She disagreed with the things that he said online, but in person found him to be "a good listener" who "wanted dialogue." When people began to cut ties with him, it made her feel bad for him. It made her want to move closer.

"I remember when several of his oldest, closest male friends all cut him off in the same week. . . . I could tell that it hurt him," she said. She goes on to tell me, "I feel like I questioned [his beliefs] less than everyone else, honestly. I'm very liberal leaning. I don't really subscribe to partisan or identity politics, and I want to keep a very, very open mind with people. My favorite people are those with whom I fiercely disagree. I was more interested in why he had the opinions that he did, and I really felt like understanding why was the only thing that was going to keep everybody together."

Amy's description of herself in this way was ironic because the idea that being open to every idea, no matter how heinous, is a sign of maturity or equity is a talking point directly out of right-wing social media. It is used regularly to suggest that leftists are closed-minded censors who won't engage in debate and discourse. This strategy of engaging people in debate around settled and formerly unspeakable positions, such as biological racism or open fascism/Western chauvinism, is how the Overton window shifts right. The problematic justifications created implications for her as well: By relegating racist or oppressive behavior to the realm of "disagreement," she aided in the plausible deniability that Kurt used as a cover for his actions. This is part of what allowed him to function within his old social circles, by creating a strategic bond with people who would otherwise disagree. Allowing this to go on, embracing Kurt's framework and resorting to liberal justifications, was how Kurt found unintentional allies.

Amy didn't necessarily see Kurt as radicalizing, and consistently minimized or downplayed his behavior. When I pushed back at her suggestion that Kurt was seeking dialogue, she blamed Facebook and the online format. She said, "I definitely saw him share things that would be offensive . . . [but] I didn't see personal attacks."

When I ask her if there were things he was doing that bothered her, she admits that she disagreed with his "anti-immigration points of view, feminism points of view, and offensive memes." But unlike his other friends, these posts were something that she cleanly separated in her mind from the "real" Kurt. She seemed to struggle less because she didn't take his political beliefs seriously and therefore wasn't particularly bothered by them.

Helen had also struggled less with maintaining ties with Kurt, although she concedes that most of his social media was "pretty heinous." I asked her how she dealt with seeing his online behavior and she told me simply, "I unfollowed it. I stopped seeing it. Facebook is pretty good about that. I didn't even have to unfriend him."

In many ways, Amy and Helen exemplified the alt-light's suggested approach to its own misbehavior: Don't be so easily offended. Stop taking us so seriously. Just don't follow me if what I say bothers you. But it is a bad idea to take the advice of fascists on how to deal with fascists.

This approach is not a strategy for bridge building. If people just "stopped being offended," it will not heal the divides that are spreading. And it will do nothing to make those targeted by far-right groups safer. Although social media has undoubtedly changed the ways that we engage in political struggle, at the personal and national level, it isn't helpful to use these mediums as a way to absolve groups such as the Proud Boys of their actions, or ourselves of our responses. History has shown, in so many cases, that ignoring the spread of fascism does not deprive it of oxygen,[21] and features such as simply unfollowing someone on social media represent an insidious temptation: to remove ourselves from the discomfort and potential conflict inherent in witnessing the radicalization of our loved ones. Social media companies have systematized denial.

Violence Is Deadly Serious

The alt-light proudly proclaims that they used social media to "meme Trump to the White House."[22] In many ways, they are right. Not only did the switch from earnestly making a case for fascism to making it tongue-in-cheek work on a national level, Amy exemplifies the ways that it also works on an interpersonal one. Very few people are comfortable seeing themselves as bigots. But people are very comfortable with edgy humor; the line between the two has become blurred. This is used intentionally by those on the alt-light to avoid accountability. The meme alibi is a powerful one, and none use it better than the Proud Boys.

In a 2020 CNN interview, Russell Shultz, a former Proud Boy from Oregon, talks about his history of violence in exactly this way. He admits that a desire to "be in a gang"—to be able to commit violence with the backup of others—is the main motivator for men joining the Proud Boys. But he also argues that the most egregious of his behaviors—attacking antifascists and making direct threats to kill and maim people—were just trolling; that it was about making people upset.[23] He claims it wasn't serious, except when it was.

The interviewer said of Shultz, "It's harder for someone to be held accountable for what he believes if it's not clear what, exactly, he believes. And it allows him to try on a persona with the safety valve of being able to say later it was all fake." This same sentiment was expressed by Kurt's friends. When Shultz threatened to murder antifascist activists, he claimed that it was because they were planning on bringing potentially deadly AIDS-tainted feces to throw at right-wing protesters. These kinds of claims are so unhinged that it is genuinely difficult to know how to react. When asked for comment on Shultz's allegations, the local anti-fascist organization in Portland, Oregon told CNN, "No one from our organization threatened to throw poop. . . . Rose City Antifa has never put AIDS in poop. Nor am I certain how one would do so."

The options about how to respond to these types of allegations are all bad. On the one hand, when people take this behavior seriously, the response is that this is obviously only trolling. And it is tempting to simply laugh it off. But Shultz's threats were very real. Ignoring them puts people in real danger. Prior to a 2018 rally, he posted, "At the last rally I nearly ran over you [antifascists] with a car and I didn't feel bad about it one bit. You're lucky I didn't kill you because I wouldn't feel any remorse. . . . I am going to shoot you. And here's where the best part of the odds is [sic], I still have a chance to fight for my freedom in court. You don't have a chance to fight for your freedom cause you're f**king dead. See I'm going to shoot you in the chest or your head."[24] Regarding the odds, Shultz is right.

In October 2020, after years of ignoring the fascist creep, the Department of Homeland Security, in its annual assessment of violent threats to the US, declared that of white supremacists to be significant. Within days, militia group members were arrested for plotting to kidnap and kill Michigan Governor Gretchen Witmer.[25] The recruiting and organizing of these groups has been ramping up since 2015, and culminated in the US Capitol riot in 2021. But the report also showed that the more localized these issues are, the more difficult they can be to address. Although federal law enforcement has been largely remiss in dealing with groups such as the Proud Boys, local law enforcement has been even worse. The Proud Boys, along with many militia groups, cling to a twisted nationalism to paint themselves as super-Americans and everyone who falls outside of their circles as non-Americans, and therefore not entitled to rights or protections.[26] It is a mindset that appeals to many Americans and justifies almost anything. Activists report that police often ignore or even support fascist violence. This occurs because these groups have strategically and successfully infiltrated local law enforcement agencies, but also because they share ideological common ground, and perhaps even have acquaintances with many officers.

Laws have been passed in several states making it easier to murder left-wing protesters, both with vehicles and with guns.[27] An antifascist activist who killed right-wing protesters in what many say was an act of self-defense was extrajudicially murdered by law enforcement, whereas right-wing protesters who have killed antifascists have received overwhelming political and monetary support, including donations from law enforcement personnel.[28]

Shultz was eventually kicked out of the Proud Boys, but not for hurting people. He was rejected for having a sloppy social media presence. In other words, by posting videos of himself hurting people and threatening to hurt others—both sanctioned behaviors—he was hurting the image of the organization. He displayed consistency between words and actions, and his consistency hurt the Proud Boys' ability to say one thing but do another. He gave up the meme alibi, which was bad for their brand. He was doxed by antifascists, kicked out of the Proud Boys, and banned from Twitter and Instagram.

Instructively, the goal of those doxing Shultz wasn't to change his mind or deradicalize him. The activists who doxed him didn't accept the meme alibi. They took Shultz seriously and took action to warn the people in their community of who he was, what he believed, and what he was capable of. This raises an important question: When we know a radicalized person, who is our ultimate responsibility to? Is it our job to try to help that particular person, to stay a voice of reason in their lives, even as they harass and harm others? Or is our responsibility to those they harm or could harm?

The Trolley Problem

Pushing back against fascism delivered as jokes is complicated. Sarah tried to parse out what was genuine and what wasn't, but never seemed able to. When she disagreed with Kurt, "He would say, 'It's just a character. I just do this to get a rise out of people.' But . . . he would select the most defensible piece of his terrible opinions," she says, "and he would redirect me every single time into a discussion of this point." So she would try to talk him through that one point, sometimes for hours. I ask her what was harder, watching what was going on with Kurt or the pressure to walk away from him?

"The worst thing was my own internal dialogue because I could hate myself from any direction," she said. "It was horrible to watch what happened to him. It was horrible to see how he hurt other people. And it was horrible to be in this constant tug of war inside of myself about my fundamental tenets as a human. *What do you do, what do I do*, in this situation? It's the trolley problem!"

She's yelling and I have no clue what she's talking about. She grabs a pen and a scrap of paper. She's a teacher, after all. The trolley problem, she tells me, is a famous ethics exercise where you have a trolley headed toward a junction in the tracks. On one possible route for the trolley, one person is tried to the tracks. On the other side, five people are tied to the tracks. You are in charge of the switch that determines where the trolley will go. "The utilitarian view is that you kill one to save many. And then the question is, What if the one person is your mother? What if it's your child?"

What if it's your best friend of 20 years, who gave you a place to stay when you were a homeless 15-year-old addicted to heroin? "It was the ultimate trolley problem because, when I tried to save Kurt, I hurt all of these people, and if I pleased all of these people, I hurt Kurt. And there was no middle ground," Sarah explains.

The trolley problem became less abstract as Kurt's behaviors moved off the internet and the threat he posed to people in the community became more tangible. Kieran and Kurt eventually found themselves literally on separate sides: Kieran was part of a BLM march that ended in protesters doing a sit-in whereas Kurt showed up to be a right-wing shock jock, livestreaming himself heckling protesters and complaining about them blocking access to bars. "And that was his whole perspective," Kieran said, "that the disruptive nature of their protests was really only harming small businesses. . . . At the end, it became very clear that I was here, and he was there. If I felt strong enough to be there, and he felt strong enough to go down and yell about it, then that was really that."

I ask if he ever tried to push back, in person or through text, and in a moment of incredible honesty he says, "I was afraid to. I'll be honest. And it's a big regret of mine. And I'll never, ever be afraid to talk to someone about that stuff again." "What were you afraid of?" I ask. "I was afraid of shattering my image of him. I was afraid that it was all true. That he would turn his directionless ire on me. And he did," he replied.

Their relationship finally ended when Kurt threatened to kill Kieran online. "He screen captured everyone he had blocked on Facebook and he posted it online and said, 'Sometimes I fantasize that all these people are dead.' And I was third from the top of the list. A friend of mine sent me screenshots. And I wept. Cognitively, I knew he wasn't serious. But I couldn't get past the fact that someone I once called my best friend just, online, wished that I was dead." Several months later, Kurt died. He went to bed and didn't wake up. His family never revealed a cause of death.

Speak Honestly of the Dead

Kurt's friends largely put aside their critiques to mourn him. Eulogies filled Facebook and someone printed up "I♥Kurt Kadaver" stickers. They were on light poles and bathroom bars in many parts of the city.

The friends who hadn't known about his actual membership in the Proud Boys could no longer deny it when they posted a tribute to him on their Facebook accounts and showed up to the memorial that Sarah organized. But the overwhelming majority of his friends looked past that. They celebrated and mourned in the ways that people do.

Local antifascists, and others who had been victims of Kurt's abuse, in contrast, celebrated his death. They found the fact that so many people who had been critical of Kurt were suddenly lionizing him to be heinous. They felt safer with him gone, and objectively it's likely they were. Kurt had always been divisive, and was perhaps never quite as divisive as he was in death. People battled online over the "right" way to react to his death. It was complicated and deeply hurtful for his friends. They perceived themselves to be under attack for mourning, and reacted by holding their experience up as evidence of equivalence between the extremes of the far left and the far right.

"As I saw it," Helen told me, "a lot of people who didn't really know him, who knew him from Facebook where he was an asshole, were really thrilled that he died. One person actually said that anyone who was grieving his death was also just as bad as he was. And wasn't that y'all's whole problem with him? That he didn't recognize your humanity?"

Kieran said something very similar. "Honestly, it felt just as blind and ignorant as anything a fascist would say. That's why groups like antifa make me nervous. It doesn't matter that I agree with them politically. I don't agree with the methodology, . . . What's the point of cancel culture if there's no path to redemption?" This sentiment was echoed by John, Sarah, and Amy as well. People's reactions made them suspicious and resentful of what felt like extremism from the left. Kieran felt like these judgments made him re-evaluate some of his own perspectives. He felt like he had been part of what he identifies as "cancel culture" and that he moved away from the kinds of harsh judgments he used to make. He asked me, "Are we just going to end up with two Americas that canceled each other out?" "That's the antithesis of everything I believe. Which means that redemption has to be on the table," he continued.

The embrace of a manufactured parity between the far left and the far right is a consistent problem for antifascist activists. The portrayal of the American left as equally violent and dangerous as the American right has been debunked many times.[29] But it is repeated again and again. Kurt's friends found solace in this lie because, at that moment, they had their own trolley problem. Their pain ran in direct conflict with the reality that other people were targeted, harassed, and endangered by someone they loved. It reminded them that, although redemption is possible for anyone, Kurt was not redeemed. He was a Proud Boy, working to expand their power and influence when he died. They addressed this disconnect by believing that it was somehow an act of extremism to insist that Kurt's actions not be sanitized in his death.

But ignoring the radicalization of loved ones, even in death, doesn't decrease the chances of real political violence. The Proud Boys chapter that Kurt founded didn't die with him. And, again, it leaves pretty terrible options for leftist activists. Allowing the pain and fear Kurt caused to be washed away because he had died was an act of abandonment and additional victimization to those who he had harmed. They saw people celebrating a person who had threatened to rape and beat them, who had stalked them, and who had organized others to systemically violate their rights. But criticizing his friends as they mourned was not without cost. In their eyes, an insistence upon accountability was framed as equally "intolerant" and "extreme" as the rhetoric of the Proud Boys. It pushed each of them further right. In some ways, this is the trolley problem of antifascist activism. To whom are we responsible in this situation? Our obvious first responsibility is to communities and individuals who are the most vulnerable to the Proud Boys' fascist violence: people of color, immigrants, women, and leftists. But Kurt was dead. Effective organizing begins with meeting people where they are, and where they were at was a funeral. At that moment, should his friends have been allowed to mourn him?

Those strategic and ethical questions aside, what was obvious was that the meme alibi didn't lose potency when Kurt died. In fact, the dichotomy between the "real Kurt" and who he was online seemed to sharpen in the minds of his loved ones, with the judgment of his "persona" shed to make room to grieve for him "as a human being."

Lost Loved Ones

Dealing with the radicalization of friends and family members isn't easy. Figuring out what role one can play in their lives has always been complicated. In this moment, right-wing radicalism is becoming mainstream. But the path our childhood friends or uncles or cousins take in becoming full-on QAnon acolytes, militia members, or Proud Boys often begins subtly. There is a temptation to ignore conspiracy theories such as 9/11 Truth, antifeminist Tik Toks, and edgy memes. They may be ridiculous, but they are working. And we have to stop letting them immobilize us.

The meme alibi allows the alt-light to avoid accountability by making it possible to pick up and put down fascist ideology at will. When no one is challenging these ideas, they become serious attempts to express one's beliefs. When people do call them out, these posts are explained as only jokes meant to provoke the humorless and "fragile Libs" (liberals). This strategy works by stopping both governments and social media companies from regulating violent and far-right speech. They simply equivocate over whether something qualifies as unacceptable content, accumulating more time on their platforms as we argue it out.

The interviews with Kurt's friends demonstrate that the meme alibi also works at the interpersonal level. When Kurt's friends didn't know whether he was actually serious about his right-wing beliefs, they coped by rationalizing, ignoring, minimizing, or compartmentalizing them. They talked about his contrarianism and libertarianism, and about the ways these may have explained his trolling and white supremacist beliefs. Each of them drew distinctions between Kurt's online behavior—his persona—and the "real" Kurt. These strategies were less about deradicalization than about relieving tension that was felt observing changes they weren't sure how to counteract. They were attempting to understand, not intervene. And it may be that the tension was not just about the changes they were seeing in their friend, but also about what it meant about them to have a Proud Boy in their circle.

There is also a historical component. All the interviewees were in their mid-30s to mid-40s. For older Millennials, Gen-Xers, and other cohorts who are not "digital natives," the temptation to compartmentalize may be particularly potent. There may be more of a tendency to see our real lives and our online lives as genuinely separate; to rationalize that one ought not be fully accountable for online behavior. What has come to be referred to as "cancel culture" may represent a rejection of this position: the idea instead that we are fully accountable in real life for things we do online. This tenet is met with deep hostility by Kurt's friends, exemplified when Kieran said that we may become two Americas who "cancel each other out." The meme alibi is much less effective in a media and social environment in which emphasis has shifted from one's intent to the impact their behavior has on others; the standard is that what we post should be taken seriously, and fascist content cannot be accepted as a joke.

Much of the funding to combat domestic terrorism and extremism has been guided by a conservative obsession with radical Islam. These resources are less useful for families and friends countering the messages from the alt-light. The resources on radicalism also assume that the groups and behaviors people are seeing now are somehow out of step with the mainstream. This translates poorly to understanding the grandmothers who stormed the Capitol on January 6th to overturn a legitimate election, or the churchgoers in their 50s and 60s who became QAnon adherents. And it translates poorly to the alt-light, where extremist content and influencers hide behind the meme alibi.

Right-wing radicalization is not extraordinary anymore, it doesn't happen when an otherwise placid individual is manipulated by extreme "outsider" content like that of a neo-Nazi band. It is instead embedded into the everyday discourse of millions of people. The main failure of existing resources, even good ones, is that the advice they offer assumes that people we love are serious about what they think and say. They advise us to listen earnestly, to empathize, not to challenge our loved ones' extremist beliefs. They assert that staying available and showing love is the key to helping our friends and loved ones escape right-wing extremism.

This advice assumes that the person is already fully entrenched in their ideology, and that active pushback will reinforce a sense of being judged and ostracized. It does not provide context for the process we see here: someone may not be fully serious at the start, or may be doing things for shock value, yet whose beliefs radicalize nonetheless as they act out these behaviors more and more. And it does not deal with the fact that racist content and behavior has the same effect whether serious or as some kind of elaborate performance art piece meant to provoke the allegedly sensitive ears of the rest of the world.

Kurt's friends seemed to instinctively approach Kurt's behavior by assuming that they had to reason with him, that challenging him would further alienate him, thus entrenching his violent behavior and views. But each found it complex to do so when they weren't sure what he actually believed. They found their attempts to reach out complicated by the reaction that there was nothing to reach out about: His behavior was just an act, and so there was nothing to "deradicalize." Kurt's path to extremism was characterized by continuities, not stark changes. He was a troll before trolling was a thing. When being a contrarian is part of someone's identity, how do their friends know when saying outrageous things stops being a joke?

If there is a time to try to actively intervene, it is before our friends and families become entrenched in far-right ideas. It is when these are ideas that they are still exploring, not firm parts of their identity. Kurt's friends struggled to see where he was in this progression. The meme alibi defies good-faith efforts at deradicalization by obscuring that line. It creates a shape-shifting neofascism that even those closest to the person struggle to see clearly.

Antifascism is defense, and those close to someone radicalizing and causing harm have a responsibility to intervene. To not do this, to stay silent because of confusion, can be a form of complicity, and may allow that person more cover. To not intervene pushes the burden onto the marginalized communities they threaten and onto the antifascist community groups that have to reckon with the consequences of their rightward slide.

The Overton window has moved, and swaths of the Republican Party base openly support extremist positions. But antifascist ideology has risen in turn, answering these tendencies with a groundswell of activism as huge numbers dedicate themselves to addressing these threats. We will all do so imperfectly, and in myriad ways.

If we want to address the power and influence of the Proud Boys and other factions of the alt-light, we have to stop accepting the meme alibi, within our personal circles and as a culture. We have the ability to separate the message from the medium, and to critique the former without being drawn into arguments about the latter. We can refuse to accept engineered distinctions between what people do and "who they are." Activists must practice messaging around this problem and offer what we have learned to those struggling with their friends and loved ones. In some cases, trolling people back and showing the ridiculousness of their behavior may be best. In other cases, we may need to talk about these things head-on or engage in community defense, as protecting communities from far-right violence and harm is the priority. And we have to have those hard conversations before the people we love are so entrenched in their ideologies that doing so would only drive them further right. We can also support those struggling with these relationships in ways that recognize their confusion and heartache but without letting them off the hook if they are enabling terrible behavior. It is possible to find a balance between accountability, strategic precision, levity, and human compassion, within our relationships and larger movements. It is imperative that we do so. This is not a question simply of morality; it is not about who we leave behind or who we fight. This is about what it takes to win in the struggle against the far right. Because the train is coming.

Make Journalism Antifa Again

Abner Häuge

So here's how you make an antifascist news outlet:

1. Be an Antifascist

If you don't consider your main job to be stopping the existential crisis of fascism, you should get a new job and stop being a journalist. When you get another job, please make sure it's one where there's no possible way for you to interact with the conflict between fascism and humanity. Journalists who choose to cover the rise of fascism do so at the perpetual risk of giving fascists credibility, spreading far-right propaganda, and bringing undue attention and subsequent harm to the victims of white nationalist violence. If you are an antifascist before you are a journalist, you are doing the journalistic equivalent of waving around a loaded weapon with your finger on the trigger.

To responsibly cover fascists requires you to recognize that they have two primary obsessions: normalizing their genocidal and authoritarian ideas and committing acts of violence against all perceived enemies. Fascists care first and foremost about controlling the narrative about what they do. Back in the day, it might have been, "Oh no, we're not white nationalists, we're identitarians! Oh no, we're not identitarians, we're alt-right! Oh no, we're not alt-right, we're dissident Right!" Every time you let them change their label, you allow them to weasel further into a broader milieu of the political right. Every time you let them change their label, you enable them to recruit from larger audiences who may have previously only flirted with the milder forms of these hateful ideas. When you fail to report on Proud Boys as fascists while they are participating in mainstream Republican events, you make the participation of these violent fascists appear as though it is a normal, and allowable, occurrence. Every time you fail to clearly say that fascists showed up to an event with the intention to hurt people, and subsequently tried to hurt people, you give them cover to enact even worse violence in the future.

435

What this means is that fascists always lie. Fascists always try to game reporters into repeating and broadcasting their own talking points. Therefore, the conventional rules of journalism do not apply. In a normal journalistic investigation, for example, you might see some fascist group in an online forum plotting violence at an upcoming rally. If you're a normal journalist working for, say, Channel 2 News or the local paper, you email one of the public-facing organizers of the event and give these fascists a chance to explain themselves. I can tell you what they'll do when they respond to your inquiry: They will lie, they probably won't tell you anything useful, and they'll do everything in their power to obfuscate and downplay the violent plans and vitriol you uncovered in their private chats. If you print their response, you're helping cover up their violence by allowing their plausible deniability to be a key part of the story. If you don't print their response, you're breaking an old journalism ethics norm around letting people respond to accusations against them. Reaching out to them for comment is also a surefire way to get you noticed by people who sometimes physically attack journalists on sight. It puts reporters in danger. If I absolutely have to do it, I try to paint the target on myself by reaching out for comment as the editor and spare my writers the danger. But, in general, Left Coast Right Watch's policy is that we rarely reach out for comment and instead we use what fascists say to each other in private and their actions in public to paint a picture of who they are and what they do. Truth, as my First Amendment law professor said, is an absolute defense against a libel suit. The solution is simple: Make sure you have the receipts for your claims. This brings us to another problem with traditional journalism. In journalism—or at least how they taught me at the University of California at Berkeley—you have to talk broadly to everyone you can in a story and try to get every possible perspective represented. In doing so, you're supposed to give equal weight to what everyone says. This is often colloquially called "both-sidesing." There are two main reasons not to do this. First, there is not two sides in genocide. Second, fascists will game a reporter's obligation to get quotes from them. They will try to spread their message and, if their victims are going to be interviewed, they'll try to further target said victims both in the article and after it's published.

This is especially true if you try to coerce someone to go on the record with their legal names. Traditional journalism says you have to get someone to go on the record with their first and last name. It's a preinternet rule that supposes that you're less likely to lie if you tie what you're saying to your legal name. In an age of cyberstalking and mass online harassment, especially in a field like reporting on right-wing radicalism, insisting on this rule is malicious malpractice. You have to take the security concerns of everyone you interview into account. You have to let people choose aliases if they need to and sometimes even obscure details that open-source intelligence analysts could use to track them. In essence, you have to prioritize the victims of fascists—and I don't mean the people who get suckered into fascist movements. I mean the people who fascists call their enemies and target and harass and hurt and kill: typically, trans people, the unhoused, Indigenous people, immigrants, and all the "others" who fascists set their sights on. Doing anything less enables hate and violence.

So, in essence, you can't be a journalist first and an antifascist second. An abstract commitment to some Platonic ideal of "the truth" or "objectivity" will not help you cover fascists accurately or effectively. If you use the old conventions of journalism to cover fascists, they will exploit you. If you don't start off day one as an antifascist, you're not only doing a disservice to their victims, but your reporting will not be as accurate as well.

2. Push the Overton Window

So why should one frame antifascist research as journalism? You might ask yourself why you should bother with journalism at all. Why shouldn't you only publish doxes, after-action reports, and other types of antifascist intelligence briefs?[1] Although there's a lot of overlap between what antifascist researchers and journalists do, there are things that one of these roles can do that the other cannot.

Here's what antifascists can do that journalists can't or are mostly reluctant to do. If you're an antifascist, you can dox people without hesitation because you're often anonymous when you do the work. Doxes, including using public information, can be a legal gray area, especially if a fascist is particularly litigious. Most fascists, if they're identified at all, risk losing jobs and relationships and all sorts of social standing. It is well within the purview of journalism to "out" people as members of fascist groups. Fascists themselves have a very loose definition of what a dox is. To a fascist, saying anything about them except repeating their propaganda is often considered doxing. Anything they don't like is doxing. Some antifascists distinguish "IDing" (identifying), as in naming someone involved with fascist organizing, from "doxing," as in publishing their addresses, where they work, and other identifying details. Journalists, as far as I know, won't publish addresses because that's commonly seen as an incitement to go over to a fascist's house and do something about them. Journalists do regularly identify fascists, however, and often expose what jobs they're working at because that is in the scope of the journalist's job to reveal news that is in the public interest.

Antifascists also can put out calls to action, whereas journalists usually cannot. Generally, journalists aren't activists. They don't tell people what to do; they just give the public information. Myself and some other journalists will announce and boost calls to actions, but usually only ones like, "get this actual Nazi off of Twitter" or, "help us fundraise for this person or that cause."[2] If you're positioned as an independent journalist, or simply are not afraid of speaking your mind, most people in the journalism industry aren't going to hassle you for the kind of calls to action that are relatively benign.

There is a somewhat good old-school reasoning behind journalists' reluctance to engage in activist work. Journalists assume they aren't supposed to intervene in what they're reporting on. This is, to a certain extent, impossible. Being at an event and observing it changes the event. Recording video certainly does—sometimes for better and sometimes for worse, but that's another discussion entirely.[3] This is the idea of a "conflict of interest." In the strictest journalistic approaches, you aren't supposed to meaningfully participate in activism around the subject you're covering. If you aren't a blank slate, you're considered biased and therefore your coverage is allegedly tainted, so the old thinking goes. This is, of course, bullshit.

If you're a journalist, your job is to figure out what happened and tell an honest story about it for the benefit of the community, be it local or national. There are obvious moral calculations one makes in choosing what and how to report. Journalism is, therefore, a kind of activism in its own right, albeit one with strict guidelines.

Conflicts of interest aren't always a reason to completely remove a reporter from covering a story in traditional journalism. If, say, a reporter owned stock in a company and sold it six months ago and is now reporting on said company, it's usually fine—the reporter just has to acknowledge they used to own stock in the company and be transparent. Parallel calculations may apply to antifascist journalism. Say you used to be in some activist organization and there was a fascist infiltrator about a year after you left. You should be honest and say you used to work with that organization when you report on it unless there's a good reason not to. I'm personally not above omitting one's involvement with an organization if you have personal safety or privacy reasons not to, or if it just doesn't have very much to do with the story.

One thing antifascist activists, researchers, and journalists have in common is they're not supposed to make themselves the center of attention, although these groups traditionally have very different reasons for this. In old-school journalism, you're usually supposed to erase yourself from the picture. Journalism is traditionally supposed to maintain authoritative veneer of objective reality. When you erase yourself from the story completely, you are pretending to be an impartial arbiter of the truth instead of a flawed, limited observer of reality, as we all are. Coupled with old-school journalism's constant reliance on "official sources" such as governments and police to declare what's true and what isn't, erasing the reporter is also a way of erasing every person who the reporter (or their editor) doesn't give a shit about hearing from.

Antifascists have always had more noble reasons for self-effacement. For one, they don't want to get identified and murdered by fascists. Two, they tend to recognize that their work isn't about getting accolades for themselves, it's about stopping fascists. If you're an antifascist journalist either writing under a pseudonym or with your real name, your intentions should obviously align with the latter. Frame your activism, or should I say your journalism, in antifascist terms and the rest tends to follow.

In the realm of journalism at this specific moment in history, there's a lot to be gained by being an antifascist journalist. Although journalism, outside of a few countries, isn't something you get a license to do, you do have credentials and that opens up a lot of doors in liberal societies. If you're operating as a journalist, you have an excuse to ask anything you want of anyone. It's expected that even the most powerful people (or at least their press agents) are supposed to respond to you. Building your legitimacy as a journalist does indeed give you access to information and places and people you might not otherwise be able to get access to.

To give a personal example, I was able to film behind Los Angeles Police Department lines after the Lakers won and was allowed to walk through police barricades others couldn't because I had a press badge. People are also more likely to give me valuable information when I email them because I've got a website with articles to back me up. I'm also able to apply for grants, get travel funded, et cetera. Playing the game does yield rewards that are strategically advantageous to antifascism as a cause. Not everyone in your antifascist organization needs to play by these rules, but it is a good idea to get a point person to deal with the normies.

But more importantly, if you're practicing antifascist ethics in journalism, you're raising the bar for every other journalist. Changing the culture around how reporting is done so that it lessens the grip of fascists and their terror should be one of your primary goals.

The "Overton window" is a term for the spectrum of what's considered acceptable discourse. Fascists in the alt-right movement considered it their project to push the Overton window to the right and make racist beliefs, and therefore racist policies, increasingly normalized. They have largely succeeded in this mission. There are more people out in the streets and online radicalized to their messages now than before the alt-right's heyday in 2015–17. Remember that people such as the white nationalist Patrick Buchanan were on the fringes of the Republican Party when he ran for president in the early 1990s, building on the campaign of Ku Klux Klan leader David Duke. When Donald Trump ran with basically the same talking points, he won.

Your goal as an antifascist journalist is to normalize practices and attitudes in journalism that do not tolerate fascism. In other words, you need to push the Overton window firmly out of the reach of fascism. You need to pay attention to mainstream, liberal scholarship and reporting on fascism and see how far they're willing to go. Then it's your job to push them further. You always go harder on fascist groups and provide ample evidence of why you're calling them white supremacists or fascists. You want to make it so that every journalist who writes about these fascists and doesn't do the five minutes of research to figure out how bad they are looks bad. You want to boldly say that your sources, the ones using aliases so law enforcement and fascists won't attack them, are just as credible as anyone else's sources. You want to make every dated and harmful practice in journalism invalidated by doing such good reporting while using anti-fascist practices that journalism as a whole has to acknowledge.

And they will acknowledge you. They will come to you as an authoritative source, and when they do, you can leverage it to say important shit about antifascist work and bring the whole enterprise more credibility in mainstream liberal circles. In essence, you should look for opportunities to make antifascism look good.

3. Train Antifascist Researchers and Reporters

You absolutely can do this work alone. I did for a while. Some people are better tempered to work alone, and that's fine. But if you can work with others, you should. And if you can start training others to do this kind of work and give them an outlet to do so, you absolutely should do that as well.

Antifascism requires many different types of skills. You have to have people who are good at writing and people who are good at digging into public records and other kinds of open-source research. You have to have people who know how to conduct interviews. You need photographers, videographers, and good copyeditors. You need people who know how to do on-the-ground surveillance. You need data analysts, coders, cybersecurity experts, and web developers. You need infiltrators to spy on fascists' secret chats. You need artists to make good propaganda. You need people who know hand-to-hand combat and have firearms expertise for self-defense and analysis of the paramilitary side of fascist organizing. There's a lot of jobs to do to publish antifascist research. Work together. Share skills. Check each other's work.

I've given writers for Left Coast Right Watch, the investigative reporting outlet I run, the option of either going by their real name or using an alias. I'm the public-facing person in the organization, so all the legal trouble goes to me no matter what. Some of my writers use aliases. Those who do generally have two reasons. The first is to mitigate the harm of being doxed. The second reason writers choose aliases while working for me is to give them the freedom to write the way they want to without losing credibility with more mainstream news outlets. Mainstream outlets are still, as of this writing, reluctant to let you call a fascist a fascist, and they're uncomfortable with writers who do.

One thing I like doing is working with student journalists in community college and undergraduate programs. These are usually people who just learned the rules and understand the ways in which the conventional rules of the journalism industry are bigoted and uphold patriarchy and white supremacy. The city council meetings and puff pieces about businesses student journalists often have to do are usually mundane and unsatisfying. Having them do antifascist reporting can give them a new field to work in and extra sets of investigative and on-the-ground skills journalism school doesn't really teach. Plus, it's really fucking fun. The obvious word of caution here is make sure your collaborators know what kind of security risks they face in person and online, and have them bulk up their digital and in-person security as they're able.

So there you have it. If you want to make journalism antifa again, you have to be a fucking antifascist, push journalism toward antifascism, and teach others to do the same. Because if we don't, the fascists are going to fucking win again. And I'll be damned if that happens on my watch.

Nazis Don't Get Nice Things

Margaret Killjoy

When the Nazis come to town, you know who your friends are. Or your comrades. Or whatever descriptor you prefer. When the Nazis came to Olympia, Washington while I lived there, a friend of mine, a comrade of mine, got in her pickup truck and drove around the city the entire night. She tracked the fascists, yes, and she was ready to fight if need be, but she wasn't there for them. She was there to offer a ride to safety to anyone who needed it. This meant anyone, antifascist or bystander, who felt threatened by the Nazi presence.

A few weeks earlier, I'd driven with her to Seattle, Washington so she could get a huge tattoo of Mjolnir, Thor's hammer, across her belly. My friend listens to black metal, writes in runes, is misanthropic as hell, and finds solace in the Old Gods. Which is to say, she spends a lot of her time in a contested cultural terrain. The world needs more people like her.

———

The far right wants to lay claim to a lot of cultural terrain, and we shouldn't let them have any of it. We shouldn't let them have paganism, we shouldn't let them have metal. We shouldn't let them have Christianity, either, or Islam, or Hinduism. They don't get punk rock. They don't get neofolk. They don't get atheism.

Nazis don't get to have nice things.

———

There's a war happening right now. A cold war in some places, and a hot war in others. It's a class war, but it's also more than a class war. It's a war between the "haves" and the "have nots," but it's more than that too. It's a war between at least two ideologies, and it can be roughly understood as a war between the left and the right. Between tolerance and intolerance.

As the climate crisis deepens, so will this conflict. There are two ways to respond to a neighbor in crisis: help them or shun them. There are two ways to respond to the global climate crisis: We can overcome our differences and come together, removing barriers like borders and dismantling the oligarchy that hoards the world's wealth, or we can scream, "I've got mine, fuck you" to the people suffering, who are dying and trying to flee a crisis they didn't cause.

The latter ideology is the ideology of the far right. It's also an ideology that would see the entire world burn.

It behooves us to win this war.

There are two primary fronts to this particular war: There's the cultural front and the political front.

The cultural front is fought in the terrain of ideas and aesthetics. It's a war of art. The political front, in contrast, is fought in terms of actual material power; it's fought over what will actually happen. A cultural battle, for example, might be fought over whether walls ought to be erected between nations. The political battle would be over whether those walls themselves will be built. Political power in this context isn't just about existing governmental systems, but about the control of physical territory and infrastructure.

If this were a game—and it's not—the cultural front would be the setup phase, when you position your pieces on the map. The political front is when you start rolling dice to see who wins.

Because this isn't a game, the setup phase is ongoing. The cultural war continues at the same time as the political war is waged.

Nazis have been consciously waging a cultural war ever since they had to step off the world's political stage. They've intentionally produced art that is "apolitical," that doesn't make use of the swastika. They've been producing music that aims to promote certain values: patriotism, glory, the traditional family, the rejection of modernity, and the like. They do this consciously to make people more willing to accept far-right political indoctrination.

The thing is, though, us antifascists are actually better at cultural warfare than fascists. We're better artists. We're more imaginative writers and musicians. We make better television shows and movies. Our ideas are also, frankly, better. Our ideas are ideas of liberation and equality.

It's this framework that helps me understand the current political crisis in the US (and potentially elsewhere, but I cannot speak to that). Ideas that were wildly radical 20 years ago, only held by anarchists and people from other fringe ideologies and cultures, are mainstream today. Sexual consent. Gender liberation. Lesbian-gay-bisexual-transgender-queer-plus

(LGBTQ+) acceptance. The acknowledgement of and attempt to disempower white supremacy. Even anticapitalism and socialism are entering the mainstream political conversation. Ideas such as decolonization, which challenge the very existence of the US, have started to become buzzwords from talking heads. Although it's terrible to see radical ideas watered down and turned into talking points, it shows that we are making advances into the public conversation.

Overall, we (in the broadest possible understanding of "we") have been winning the cultural war.

The far right fights too, of course, but it's not the field of battle in which they are strong. Realizing they were losing the cultural war, they fought back by playing to their strength: political power. Their most powerful tool they can leverage for political power? Racism.

Before Donald Trump's election, I had incorrectly assumed that the next rise of the far right would adopt "progressive" identity politics to do it. I had assumed fascism would say, "We don't care what color you are or who you sleep with, as long as you're an American citizen. Everyone else can get fucked." I was wrong. New fascism looks a lot like the old fascism. It's blatant xenophobia. It's trans exclusion. It's rolling back the bodily autonomy of people with wombs. It's wild ableism, it's stripping people of citizenship, it's forcing everyone back into the closet.

———

It's easy for artists and writers to overstate the importance of the cultural war. It's easy to be defensive when it's implied that the skill you're best at isn't "what the revolution really needs," so it's easy to exaggerate about how crucial protest music is, how important it is to speak truth to power.

Sowing seeds is not the same action as harvesting the fruits of the field. There is a time for sowing and a time for reaping. Again, because analogies are garbage and inherently limited, it's worth realizing that it's always time to sow. But sometimes, reaping is more important, and they can be necessary simultaneously.

The revolution needs you, and it needs you to focus on contributing what you're best at, be it mediation or music, street fighting or graphic design, hacking or gardening. But it also might need you to do other things, too. It might even need you in the streets. Just the same as a whole community who comes together to raise a barn or bring in the harvest, it's going to take all of us to tear down this system and replace it with something that won't kill us all.

If you're looking at our global cultural conflict like a board game (which I too often am), one can see different territories that can be controlled or contested by various players. If a player controls a territory, uncontested, they are able to recruit additional forces from that territory. In the 1970s and 1980s, punk was contested terrain. Antifascists fought both culturally and politically—with zines and music and fists and knives—and, for years, they've largely been able to control punk rock and keep out the fascists. Punk, as a result, became a recruiting ground for anarchists and leftists who have gone on to participate in struggle outside of their subculture while becoming inhospitable to the far right's recruitment efforts.

The American rural working class is contested terrain that used to be held largely by the left and is now held primarily by the right. Therefore, the right has been able to recruit from this terrain.

Romanticism is contested terrain. The far right romanticizes the simple life and struggle, just as many on the left do. This isn't to say we engage with these concepts in the same way they do: Whereas the far right might romanticize the "glory" of war, we focus on the beauty of struggle against impossible odds. We try not to sanitize war of its horrors, yet we find value in bravery, in breathtaking acts of solidarity. We romanticize these things. And we cannot let them have them.

The absolute wrong response to that dynamic is to cede that cultural terrain to our enemies. It's wrong strategically. It's also wrong ethically. I live at the end of a dirt road in the mountains and, although there are more Confederate flags than rainbow flags around here, we love and care about a lot of our neighbors. We cannot abandon the rural working class to the enemy, just as we can't abandon any subculture or community to the fascists.

Metal is also culturally contested terrain, and the aesthetics of that culture (particularly black metal) are aesthetics that the far right has been trying to claim for decades. To be fair, Nazis have been involved since the early days of black metal, but so have leftists and just regular old not-fucking-Nazi misanthropic people who like swords and cloaks as much as I do. If we give the Nazis black metal, we're giving them a powerful recruitment tool and we're abandoning an awful lot of people like me.

It's even worse when this gets into religion. I've met antifascists who won't trust anyone with runic tattoos, but when the neo-Confederates tried to rally in my small Southern town, one of the most vocal—and ready to throw down—antifascist contingents held signs like "heathens against hate." They were fucking mad that fascists are trying so hard to co-opt their spirituality. Norse Paganism is a living religion practiced over much of the world, and its practitioners—many of whom are queer or nonwhite—cannot cede that territory. We should help them hold on to it.

———

In this framework, all political subcultures are also aesthetic subcultures in that they have aesthetic ideas embedded in them. All aesthetic subcultures are political subcultures as well: Ideas about how to organize society and how to live as people are themselves embedded in art, music, and the ways in which people gather.

Protest movements are essentially subcultural spaces as well. Their participants collectively develop an aesthetic and then propagate that aesthetic, often across generations.

The fact that protest movements develop into subcultures is inherently limiting. Not everyone will be attracted to certain aesthetics or political ideas, and any particular movement has an inherent cap on the number of people it will attract and the amount of power it can actually exert. People aware of that limitation have resorted to two different solutions.

Some people have attempted to fight against the subculturalization of their movements. They've attempted to strip away all aesthetics from protest, to join an unmarked "mainstream" culture. I disagree with the efficacy of this method. Making our movements blander is no way to attract people or gain real power. It ignores how important aesthetic ideas are to our sense of self and, furthermore, it ignores how subcultures fulfill one of the most basic human needs, the need for a sense of belonging and community.

The other method, which I find far more viable and worthwhile, is to accept that our movements will wind up subcultural. Instead of attempting to create one great mass movement, which would need to be more or less unified in its aesthetics as well as its politics, it's better to learn to interweave various movements. Most of the most powerful demonstrations I've participated in have involved people from all walks of life; not crushed into a meaningless homogeny, but walking side by side, proudly diverse.

Punk should be a recruiting ground for antifascists. Metal should be a recruiting ground for antifascists. Hip-hop, country, goth. Hell, model train collecting could be a recruiting ground for antifascists, if the participants in that subculture wanted it to be.

When I think about how to reach the world I want to live in, I'd prefer one with no government or capitalism, but, honestly, I'd probably settle for one that just isn't being destroyed by fire and floods and Nazis. The only way that seems realistic is to see a movement of movements. A federation of equals, with our own needs and tactics and strategies and ideas and aesthetics, learning to work together, not in unity but in diversity.

I want that. The only way I can have that is if I refuse to let the fascists have anything. They can't have Jesus, they can't have Odin, they can't have science. And for fuck's sake, they can't have metal.

Surreal Antifascism, 1921–45

Alexander Reid Ross

{The author would like to thank Ali Neff, Caroline Harrison, Adrian Cox, and Kristian Williams for their important contributions to the development of this piece.}

In a world ravaged by a pandemic and the effects of war, the art movement of Surrealism filled the void caused by despair with joy and solicitude. Their bold efforts were often met by violence and police and state crackdowns as they overturned social relations by transforming the way people interact with their world. Of course, liberating all social relations, which the Surrealists aimed to accomplish, doesn't attract the praise and support of the far right, so they faced constant harassment from fascist and monarchist forces—particularly the reactionary group Action Française. An eye to Surrealism's antifascism of hope against despair and misery offers useful creative potential today considering the similar problems we share during our crisis of democracy.

From the avant-garde of the 19th century, the Surrealists inherited revolutionary aspirations and sweeping criticisms of everyday life. In this tradition, they vented their rage against colonialism and capitalism, but also all institutions of incarceration and even work itself.[1] With these conditions guiding their uncompromising politics, Surrealists tended to alienate, and be alienated by, large swathes of the French republic. Their unflinching commitment to human freedom also set the Surrealists at odds with the Communist Party, despite the Surrealists' sincere efforts to mount a revolution against nationalism and capitalism by uniting with the Communists. Their struggle against authoritarianism exhibited courage and, at times, folly, all too susceptible to clichéd sensationalism.

Yet, Surrealism's allure remains undeniable. Their intelligence and honest commitment to the marvelous can inspire anyone, which is why they refused to distort their message through realism, despite the complaints of anti-intellectuals. Their tacit contradictions produced disciplined, scientific writing exploring theoretical subjects as ineffable and unfalsifiable as the spirit and the unconscious. Indeed, the tableau of creatives attracted to the Surrealist group never spoke in one unified voice, nor did they intend to, and their discourses provided interesting intellectual fodder, even if internal disagreements became wrathful.

It should come as no surprise, then, that the Surrealists openly and avidly opposed fascism as a group from the beginning, yet some of them slipped into the fascist temptation individually. The far right's tactical appropriation of left-wing tropes toward national solidarity promised to invigorate the mythopoesis that Surrealists sought to produce, even if Surrealism shared different myths. The Martiniquais poet Pierre Yoyotte observed this in his 1934 essay, "Antifascist Significance of Surrealism," declaring, "[T]he essential originality of fascism is its utilization of the *irrational* as autonomous and important factors in the political domain," adding that "surrealists immediately addressed themselves to the defense of desire, to individual inspiration, to solutions that were diametrically opposed to the Mussolinian or racist militarization."[2] If the Surrealists opposed fascism in spirit, thought, and deed, many of its members also fought—quite literally—against the far right from their first moments together until the end of the war.

The Eternal Importance of Surrealism

How does a movement situated between the two World Wars relate to today's antifascist struggle, Black Lives Matter (BLM), and movements to "Defund the Police"? Engagement with Surrealism requires the rejection of a binary between "Western" and other arts (and between art and life), particularly during the modern period, not by denying the influence of imperialism on "Western" art but by exposing its aesthetic emptiness. Surrealism takes sides; it seeks to interrogate the canon, sorting imperial from universal, and embracing internationalism. Reflecting on the North African Maghreb region, Egyptian poet Habib Tengour observed, "It was, after all, in Maghrebian Sufism that surrealist subversion asserts itself: pure psychic automatism, mad love, revolt, unanticipated encounters."[3] Surrealists purposefully flipped the position of the intellectual from the leader of the coming socialist world to a subject of decolonial uprising, prioritizing the struggle against imperialism as, fundamentally, the struggle for the liberation of the universal human spirit.

Corroborating Tengour's theory, Senegalese poet Cheikh Tidiane Sylla reflected that, "In Africa, that is, the *living experience of surreality* has since prehistoric times enjoyed supremacy over its theoretical justification.... Surrealism and black African art show that History's last step—the step *beyond* History—coincides with a return to first principles." For Sylla, this involves "nothing less than the systematic and *definitive liberation* of the whole of human society and of Nature itself."[4] It was perhaps the most essential goal of Surrealism to repudiate modernity as a limit and to recreate another way of living—to repurpose life.

Of course, the Surrealist groups in Paris, Spain, England, the Czech Republic, Japan, Martinique, Yugoslavia, Egypt, Cuba, México, Belgium, and Haiti developed Surrealism together largely as a collective, iconoclastic form of mythmaking, but their obsession with shared experience (informed by traditional art around the world) relied less on bourgeois eclecticism than reciprocal fascination with cultural development counterposed against modern features. It is a mere bromide to state that some of Surrealism's most famous protagonists—Aimé Césaire and Octavio Paz—were anti-imperialists borne outside Europe. Deeper still, Surreal cosmopolitanism produced a truly transnational movement. Martiniquais Surrealists moved to France and participated in the Paris, France group in the 1930s; a Cuban Surrealist married an English woman and fought fascists in Spain; Surrealists fleeing the Nazis turned to Martinique and México, and so on.

Attempting to delimit the movement to a clear list of Parisian intellects is a simplistic and boring way to speak of a group that, in their more ludic moments, fantasized about a bloody revolution that would end work and communally reform every facet of everyday life—fantasies that, for many, bent back toward disillusionment with the rise of Stalinism.[5] Yet Surrealism did not spring fully formed from the head of Zeus so much as it emerged from the hothouse of France's radical literary tradition.

The Small Origins of Surrealism, 1871–1918

Surrealists in France were true, and acknowledged, inheritors of the ideas of pre-Marxist utopian socialists such as Charles Fourier and the convergence of anarchism and symbolism associated with France's *Belle Epoque* of the late-Romantic end of the 19th century, which found unity through opposing antisemitism. Surrealists were influenced by Franco-Uruguayan poet Comte de Lautréamont, whose nihilistic egoism sought to transcend humanity's repression of fantasy. Although his work is tainted with misogyny, Lautréamont's contribution to the avant-garde and its historical context should be elaborated briefly.

Dying in obscurity during an epidemic while France lay under siege from the German military at the end of the Franco-Prussian War in 1871, Lautréamont's posthumous celebrity among the literary vanguard marked the beginning of an era of radical writing tied to anarchism and anti-authoritarianism.[6] As the war ended, the citizens of Paris rose up and established a short-lived commune dedicated to direct democracy and supported by such artists as Gustave Corbet and another of Surrealism's influences, the poet Arthur Rimbaud.[7] A diverse literary and aesthetic vanguard assembled in the aftermath of the brutally suppressed commune both within and against the Republic (or even politics, itself), clinging to self-imposed marginality while rising to a significant role in cultural life—especially during the Dreyfus Affair, a hellacious scandal that roiled France for over a decade.[8]

A Jewish captain in the French army named Alfred Dreyfus stood accused of aiding the Germans and betraying the Republic, leading to widespread antisemitic outbursts, rioting, and targeted attacks on his defenders by chauvinist leagues and journals such as the Action Française, along with their fighting section, the Camelots du Roi.[9] Among Dreyfus's literary sympathizers, who rejected the accusations (later proven completely false), the Polish-Belarusian poet Guillaume Appolinaire and the bawdy French playwright Alfred Jarry enraptured the later Surrealists.[10] The basis for Surrealist ideas relied on Appolinaire's imaginative commitment to the truth (even, or particularly, in the discovery of the unknown) and Jarry's notion of "pataphysics," which he viewed as an epiphenomenon of metaphysics produced through junctures and interconnections rather than discrete units of things.[11]

Yet, as the Romantic epoch wound to a close in the early 20th century, most important symbolist literary reviews folded and celebrities such as André Gide gained control of a more aristocratic aesthetic movement committed to neoclassicism. Politically tumultuous and filled with shifting political groups, France before World War I saw some Dreyfusard symbolists such as Henry de Bruchard swing to ultranationalism, and even Jarry and Appolinaire appear to have drifted toward chauvinism during the end of their respective lives.[12] A dismal cloud of misogyny blanketed much of the literary world at the time, leaving very few free from its miasma.

When World War I finally broke out, very few resisted the pull of patriotism, feeding the trenches their flesh and blood until much of Europe had been exsanguinated. In the desiccated, etiolated space of pyrrhic victory over Germany, the avant-garde revolted—first with Dada and then with Surrealism—against a return to normal, against neoclassicism and nationalism, against chauvinism and the re-establishment of the same order that brought about such devastation and lifelessness. In jazz, so-called primitive art, the rejection of modernity, and exuberant acts of spontaneity, they found the basis for the reassertion of avant-garde revolutionary politics.

Surrealism and the "Sovereignty of Thought"

On July 23rd, 1918, a Franco-Romanian poet named Tristan Tzara climbed onto the stage at the Zunfthaus zur Meisen guild house in Zurich and delivered a wild Dadaist manifesto. As the iconoclastic and aggressive rant rounded toward its conclusion, Tzara shouted: "Freedom: DADA DADA DADA, howling of tense colors, interweaving of opposites and all contradictions, grotesques of inconsistencies: LIFE."[13] To a generation of artists and intellectuals, Dada represented the wildness of invention at the core of the desire to destroy the limitations of human potential. But already, a movement within Dada was churning and threatening its own existence.

The year before Tzara's speech, Appolinaire had coined the term "Surreal" to describe something like his friend Jarry's pataphysics—not merely the overcoming of reality but the exaltation of a better, realer reality conceivable through analogies that destroy old presuppositions and open new, surprising ways of thinking and understanding.[14] Obsolete by design, Dada gave rise to a new, creative movement born of some of its leading figures—Surrealism.

Surrealism's break with Dada was a slow process provoked by serious differences between Tzara and André Breton, as well as two important deaths coming in 1919: that of Appolinaire and Jacques Vaché, a close friend of the early Surrealist Breton. A force of nature and brilliant poet, Appolinaire bridged the symbolist milieu with the young avant-garde emerging after the war, in which he had fought. Thus, his name, when applied to a journal or magazine, provoked powerful sentiments, and his death from the 1918 influenza pandemic, was a deeply felt tragedy.[15] Similarly, Vaché had served with Breton in a psychiatric hospital for soldiers during the war, and his death from an overdose of opium stunned his close associates.[16] Surrealism took form, in part, to pay tribute to these two figures and their philosophy of life while reckoning with the existence of death.

Surrealism departed from Dada by rejecting progress while embracing constructive liberation.[17] Surrealism would be most plainly described as the effort to render an external representation of the internal reality, thus issuing a truer, if more surprising, expression, often by combining secondary and/or tertiary allegories.[18] Surrealism asserts the irrational development of an asymptotically closer comprehension of truth through the exploration of the psyche in relation to empirical reality. Surrealism, therefore, manifests efforts to explore and articulate the unknown and ineffable qualities of consciousness in all its complexity and uncertainty. In its efforts to overcome the knowable, Surrealism, would *replace* progress.

In his essential text, *Communicating Vessels*, Breton notes, "I hope [Surrealism] will be considered as having tried nothing better than to cast a *conduction wire* between the far too distant worlds of waking and sleep, exterior and interior reality, reason and madness, the assurance of knowledge and of love, of life for life and the revolution."[19] It would not be unfair to say that Surrealism has more to do with mediums, séances, and the occult than with the world of clinics, hospitals, and laboratories, but the form plays in the interstices between the utterly fantastical, the uncanny, and the scientifically normal to "prune life" and encourage the marvelous into being.[20]

These are the depths the Surrealists believed—at least in the early years—they could navigate with psychic automatism, a mode of thought process through which the thinker or thinkers release themselves (sometimes through intoxication, sleep, and somnambulance, or hypnosis) from normal reality, comprising a "ridiculous web" of interlinked symbols and associated meanings, to recreate by chance a spontaneous group of associations that reproduce meaning in different ways.[21] This recreation of meaning, according to Surrealists, would lead to extraordinary opportunities for the release of social tensions originating in repressed desires. The alienation from reality encouraged by the Surrealists promised an indifferent gaze through which the "seers"—a term commandeered from the poet Rimbaud—might even obtain insight into the future, arcane secrets of the past, and perhaps the unity of the two.[22] In short, free association of the mind became, through Surrealism, part of the free association of workers who, in solidarity, would liberate the world from the very reality of work, toward internationalist socialism.[23]

And for Surrealists, desire sat at the throne of socialism—the passions of the universe expressed in near-mystical fashion as both natural and mad, as pure autonomism that both evoked and destroyed the modern ideal of the machine. Automatism for Surrealists did not merely amount to machinic relations. Instead, automatism rang out in the madcap laugh or exuberant dance, the clairvoyant's magic, and the expressions of precolonial, uncolonized, and colonized people persisting in spite of oppression.[24] The secret of automatism manifested in desire above all else.

By refining a specific mode of everyday life, modernism repressed as inferior, abnormal, or pathological those discursive and aesthetic forms that stem from processes outside of normative, industrial lifestyles. Instead, Surrealists sought, even more than the revolutionary "sovereignty of the people," the "sovereignty of thought," in which they saw infinite possibility.[25]

Surrealism split into two irreconcilable camps—one, led by that poet Breton, that called for a diversity of the furthest possible dialectical syntheses of human experience on the way to the marvelous, and the other, led by Georges Bataille, that rejected "universal cultural translatability."[26]

Bretonian Surrealism understood the marvelous as immanent and achievable through a process not unlike a form of spiritual ecstasy that comprehends contradictions in reality. The dissidents who ultimately rebuked Breton utterly opposed the sublime potential of compassion as a universal human bond, insisting on a "base materialism" particularly attracted to sensory responses of pain and revulsion.[27] In Bataille's words, there was space for "too many fucking idealists" in Breton's Surrealism.[28]

Together, however, Surrealists recognized the disastrous implications of understanding human civilization as replicating some form of natural law. In fact, they embraced the absurdity of denatured human existence as part of rebelling against it through "cruel automatism," producing "an ideal world similar to those in a childhood neurosis."[29] For instance, when Breton called Marcel Duchamp's work, *The Large Glass*, a "mechanistic, cynical interpretation of love," he was not repudiating it but engaging with the complexities of love within and outside of normative heteropatriarchal desire.[30] Surrealism's fellow traveler, Walter Benjamin, wrote, "The uncovering of the mechanical aspects of the organism is a persistent tendency of the sadist," and the Surrealists were attempting to uncover the unconscious! "One can say that the sadist is bent on replacing the human organism with the image of machinery," Benjamin continued. "Sade is the offspring of an age that was enraptured by automatons."[31]

If automatism compelled Surrealists to dismantle the mind to understand its inner workings, like engineers of the soul, it was the excessive desire to "break" that machine—or, deeper, the terror at the notion of its state of being broken already—that brought them back to the Marquis de Sade's writings as a feature of human desire.[32] Surrealists invited erotic play, which of course experimented with sadomasochism, as well as gender bending and the idea of love as the ultimate liberating power. They pushed erotic pleasure and virtue together as functions of human potentiality but united in the urgency of human freedom and integrity, using Sade as a point of departure from which the Other is imagined in its worst, but altogether human, forms.[33]

Yet the most important part of the automatic within Surrealism lay in the human spirit that develops art and invention as reflected in the production itself, transmitting the form of ritual into the substance of myth with not only the laws of motion and matter but the rules and the content of play. The presence of chance and probability at play within the process of ritual emerges doubly within art, creations both aesthetic and technological (because the two so often function together), such that the automatic response to art is locked into the spirit of its creation. Play becomes a kind of alchemy that enchants the world, opens a magical potential within the constraints of the real, and smuggles dreams into everyday life.[34] All these things—the often-problematic interplay of themes drawing from a deep, oneiric well of exoticism, the occult, and the erotic—fostered the Surrealists' fervent antifascism.

The Formative Years, 1921–25

The group that would become Surrealists saw Dada as a continuation of the Jacobin Terror that marked the worst excesses of the French Revolution, and even developed a vigilant Tribunal of Dada Safety to maintain internal purity.[35] Comprised mostly of anarchist-leaning leftist revolutionaries, the Surrealist group hoped to undermine all social and political hierarchies, although they were, themselves, mostly from middle-class backgrounds, some with medical and psychological training. Their principled love of freedom drove them to a form of artistic liberation that often exceeded the broader working-class public in its ecstatic extremities, which remained more accessible to students and educated society. Nevertheless, their antics caused chaos that gripped headlines and inspired revolutionary thought in new ways that opposed the right with uncanny prescience.

We must acknowledge that the anthology in which this work appears, edited by Shane Burley, arrives at the one hundredth anniversary of one of the most important milestones in the Dadaist avant-garde as it congealed into the Surrealist movement: the spiritual trial of Maurice Barrès. A celebrated young poet and novelist who turned toward ultranationalism and antisemitism during the Dreyfus Affair to become one of the leading patriots clamoring for war in 1914, Barrès had an intimate relationship with the French avant-garde—he was known and feared. For this reason, in May 1921, the Surrealists tried Barrès *in absentia* for crimes against the spirit and "an attack on the security of the mind."

The trial's motivating force came from the poets Breton and Louis Aragon, who read and admired Barrès's individualist work prior to his conversion to ultranationalism.[36] Breton would insist the trial hoped "to determine the extent to which a man could be held accountable if his will to power led him to champion conformist values that diametrically opposed the ideas of his youth."[37] For Breton, the implications of this experiment in justice laid bare intrinsic problems of the ego, which could flip from subversion to conformism by the force of its own myopia. Yet Aragon, while bitterly breaking from Barrès, remained more ambivalent and would himself flip from anti-Bolshevik individualism to vulgar Stalinism just 10 years later.

A gravely serious Breton sought the death penalty for Barrès, symbolized by a mannequin and defended by Aragon. Witnesses came forward to testify to Barrès's misdeeds. Despite Tzara dissenting based on "absolutely no confidence in justice even if that justice is enacted by Dada," the tribunal found Barrès guilty.[38] One of the participants, a poet and friend of Breton and Aragon named Pierre Drieu la Rochelle, was a minor literary figure at the time attracted to powerful symbols and especially myths, insisting on emphasizing more violent spectacles of ritual. It is neither difficult to see how these notions may have found acceptance among the Surrealists nor to imagine how they might have drawn Drieu la Rochelle to fascism 15 years later. He would become, after the Nazi invasion, one of the most prominent fascists of the French literary world while retaining the ghosts of his admiration for Aragon and the others.

Through the controversy surrounding the *"Procès Barrès,"* the Surrealists gained momentum and the attention of Gide, himself, who deigned to write to Aragon, "How can you fail to understand that it is not from scandal you will perish, but from boredom?"[39] From Dada, Surrealism took shape through séances, somnambulant experiments, and automatic writing.

The poet Robert Desnos became a central figure, known for his expertise in falling asleep and susceptibility to hypnosis. The bizarre sessions mounted in intensity, including threats and acts of violence and humiliation. The stories are manifold. At one point, Desnos chased fellow poet Paul Éluard around his own house and garden with penknife in hand after the latter woke him up with a jug of water.[40] At another, a sleeping Desnos locked his audience into a room and only came out of his trance when one of the captives, the famous painter Francis Picabia, began dismantling the lock from inside.[41] Another haunting scene portrays Breton breaking in on several participants preparing to hang themselves at the word of writer René Crevel.

This was the last straw, and the "Time of Slumbers" ended amid serious news of the far right. Following a far-right putsch attempt against Germany's Social Democratic government, a massive workers' uprising took place in 1920 in the industrial Ruhr Valley, which was repressed by military and paramilitary forces. Responding to the German military's presence in the Ruhr in defiance of the Versailles Treaty, the French military occupied the Ruhr—a move reviled by the left. In retaliation against the French nationalist leagues that called for the occupation, on January 23rd, 1923, an anarchist woman named Germaine Berton assassinated a leader of the Action Française named Marius Plateau. Later that year, Berton's intended target, Action Française's leader Léon Daudet, faced another serious tragedy when his 14-year-old son Philippe Daudet fled home and ultimately committed suicide. Philippe Daudet's suicide letter professed a passionate love for Berton, who attempted to kill herself as well shortly thereafter.[42]

The Surrealists applauded both Berton and the young Phillipe Daudet as righteous heroes. During her trial, they circulated a letter declaring, "[W]e are of one heart with Germaine Berton and Philippe Daudet, we appreciate the value of all true acts of revolt."[43] Although the letter recognized the tragedy of Philippe Daudet's death, it also put on display the vexing excesses of their scathing political critique. A month after Berton attempted suicide, the Surrealists dedicated a full page of the first issue of the journal, *La Révolution surréaliste*, to a rogues' gallery featuring their own mugshots ordered around Berton's and including the question of suicide.

Regarding her "admirable act," Aragon would extoll Berton's "greatest defiance of slavery, the most beautiful protest before world opinion against the hideous lie of happiness."[44] In his book, *Libertinage*, published later that year, Aragon announced, "If it were up to me, everything which is opposed to love would be abolished. That's roughly what I mean when I claim to be an anarchist."[45] Aragon had written fawningly of anarchist criminality and the illegalists of the Bonnot Gang during the Dada days, but he quixotically added that he would participate in the gang only to inform the gendarme in an ultimate ploy to subvert all sides.[46]

Surrealism's commitment to scandal would culminate in the final split between Dadaism and Surrealism during an especially dramatic evening at the Théâtre Michel. After an opening round of modern music, a group of Dadaists and their associates gave poetry readings. But Éluard and Philippe Soupault scorned association with some of the poets, especially Jean Cocteau, and the scene grew restive. A Tzara ally named Pierre de

Massot took the stage to announce that Gide, Pablo Picasso, and Picabia were killed in action. And Duchamp? Vaporized! Breaking onto the stage, Desnos and Éluard restrained de Massot while Breton brutally assaulted him with his cane, breaking his arm. Police removed Breton and Desnos, but Éluard eluded them, later charging the stage again during Tzara's play. Police returned but were fought off by other Surrealists while Éluard rained punches on Tzara and others.[47] Tzara was later shamed for calling the police.[48]

Other events unfolded with similar results. A ruthless public denunciation at the Saint-Pol-Roux banquet by Aragon of the left-wing author Anatole France upon the latter's death in 1924 became so boisterous and vulgar that the police were called.[49] The following year, a protest by 18 Surrealists against 3 other Surrealists who collaborated with the capitalist Ballets Russes involved showering the haute audience from above with leaflets while other members shouted and brayed at the performers from the stands. In her communiqué about the event, Surrealist writer Nancy Cunard wrote, "Pandemonium soon followed, but everything went on at the same time—the snowfall, the whistling, the counter-manifestation, threats and blows—the dancers courageously footing it, one hand up to their ears to catch any musical indications still audible."[50] It can be said with no hint of irony that the far right was only one of Surrealism's many targets—a list that often included one another. Of the Surrealists, one bemused columnist wrote, "They are hysterically explosive against their age."[51]

But the top of their list of enemies was colonialism. During 1925, the French government intervened on the side of the colonial powers in the protracted Spanish counterinsurgency war against the Riffian Berber tribes in the mountains of Morocco. For the Surrealists, this crime could only be met with scorn, and they retaliated by cosigning an incendiary letter from the fledgling French Communist Party addressed to soldiers and sailors, declaring, "You are being sent to die in Morocco to allow the bankers to get their hands on the natural resources of the Rif Republic to line the pockets of a few capitalists" and instructing them to "fraternize with the Riffians."[52] This incident marked an early turn of the Surrealists from searing hatred of the Communists to an open collaboration cemented two years later by core members joining the party and lasting until the rise of Adolf Hitler in Germany.

The Communist Years, 1925–33

In their 1925 Declaration, Surrealists rejected the notion that their movement contained novelty, insisting, "We are specialists in Revolt." Directing themselves to "the Western world in particular," the group calling itself the "Bureau of Surrealist Research" declared, "SURREALISM is not a poetic form. It is a cry of the mind as it turns back towards itself and is determined to smash its fetters, if necessary with material hammers."[53] They viewed the avant-garde as how the working class could liberate themselves from ordinary misery and embrace the commune as a revolution against a rationalism that justifies labor and incarceration.

Many Communists found their Romanticism shockingly out of line, but the Surrealists worked toward a synthesis of stagnant Soviet aesthetics and the avant-garde to develop art explicitly for the working class.[54] The result of such efforts was a new review called *Clarté*, which included Upton Sinclair, Thomas Hardy, and H. G. Wells on its international steering committee. The Surrealists abandoned their "sentimental, individualist, subjective, or anarchist conceptions of the revolution . . . for a political conception."[55]

This shift did not cause a break with the Surrealists' tactics, however. At another Saint-Pol-Roux banquet, the Surrealists built on an earlier rejection of "all that is French" by disrupting other speeches with antinationalist interjections leading to another brawl.[56] Their old nemeses at Action Française issued demands for their exclusion from the press and expulsion from the country.[57]

Whereas the Communist Party pushed away from the Surrealist collaborations, the Surrealists stuck to the anticolonial position ever more prominently with Breton penning the important 1926 text, *Légitime défense*, which aligned Surrealist revolution with the colonized and Indigenous.[58] For Breton, anticolonialism was not a matter of economy to be fixed under state control; it was a reunion of the creative mind and the "realm of facts" that defied modernity and made an "appeal to the marvelous."[59] Additionally, Surrealism was beginning to gain an international following, with journals springing up as far away as Japan opposing the rise of the ultranationalism that was laying the groundwork for fascism in East Asia.[60]

Whereas Breton agreed to effectively suppress *Légitime défense* upon entry into the Communist Party along with Aragon, Éluard, Benjamin Péret, and other Surrealists the following year, the Surrealists' commitment to the Communist Party was not set in stone. Regardless, the group itself cracked in several places, recriminations flew in every direction, and a new course was set. With the Time of Slumbers finished and Desnos's disturbing essay about French Jewry read as antisemitic, Desnos's individualism made him an obvious object of the Surrealists' purge. The following year, the dramatist Antonin Artaud and the poet Soupault also fell by the wayside as the distance between absurdism and automatism grew wider. Joining the Communist Party set the Surrealists' core at odds with some of its founding assumptions, and more fell out, including painter André Masson, anthropologist Michel Leiris, and sociologist Pierre Neville. The renegade Surrealists banded together behind Bataille and denounced Breton in incisive terms, whereas Breton penned a new Second Surrealist Manifesto filled with flamboyant accusations in 1930.[61]

While the Paris group shed members bitterly, new groups emerged elsewhere. In Martinique, a group called Légitime Défense with a journal by that name grew under the leadership of poet Etienne Léro, announcing, "For want of a black proletariat to whom international capitalism has not given the means to understand us, we speak to the children of the black bourgeoisie; we speak to those who are not already killed established fucked-up academic successful decorated decayed endowed decorative prudish decided opportunist; we speak to those who can still accept life with some appearance of truthfulness."[62] The staunchly Marxist group called for a revolt against bourgeois values and a commitment to dialectical materialism.

A new figure loomed large in the Paris group. Long-time friends of the poet Federico García Lorca, the artist Luis Buñuel, and the artist Salvador Dalí joined the Surrealist orbit with their new film, screened the same year as the combative second manifesto, called *Chien Andalou* (Andalusian Dog), which assembled semirandom images into a deliberately incoherent stream.

Regardless of its closer proximity to something like a normal film, Action Française's combat wing, Camelots du Roi, broke up the screening of *Chien Andalou*'s follow-up, *Age d'Or*, slashing the Surrealist art on the walls. The authorities banned the film, revealing their complicity with the far right. The Surrealists responded with a manifesto:

The day will come soon when we realize that, in spite of the wear and tear of life that bites like acid into our flesh, the very cornerstone of that violent liberation which reaches out for a cleaner life in the heart of the technological age that corrupts our cities is LOVE.[63]

Dalí was certainly no Marxist, but his theories fascinated the Surrealists. In "Rotting Donkey," appearing in 1929, Dalí proclaimed "a thought process of a paranoiac and active character" that would "systematize confusion and thereby contribute to a total discrediting of the world of reality."[64] Of course, Surrealism contained multitudes, but Dalí's shocking and sharp break with reality manifested something inconsistent with its differentiation from Dadaism and in some respects reflected another stage in the movement's transformation.

Dalí's theories on Surrealist objects were put to the test in a new collaborative enterprise with the Anti-Imperialist League (a group related to the Communist Party that included associates from *Clarté* and such international delegates as Jawaharlal Nehru) in protest of the 1931 Colonial Exposition in Paris. The five thousand or so visitors to the Surrealist exhibit, "The Truth About the Colonies," were treated to an array of objects created by colonized peoples throughout the world; however, unlike the Colonial Exposition, which did the same thing in efforts to glorify *la plus grande France*, the Surrealists intermixed objects from modern France. The effect was to powerfully expose the hidden meanings of both—the material reliance of French objects on foreign materials but also the similar spiritual qualities taken on by both. "The Surrealists critiqued 'whiteness' even when no explicit racial rhetoric or image was present," observes Donald Lacoss.[65]

The exhibition seemed consistent with Dalí's "critical paranoia"—"a spontaneous method of irrational knowledge based on the critical and systematic objectification of delirious associations and interpretations"—but still remained within the mainstream of Surrealist thought as Surrealism continued to be pulled in different directions at once.[66] After a visit to Moscow, Aragon returned absolutely committed to the Communist Party and Stalinist aesthetics, which insulted his colleagues. Regardless, Aragon's latest poem, "Front Rouge," with its injunction to "kill the cops," brought an apoplectic state to charge the poet with "provocation to murder" and censor the poem.[67]

The state repression did not quell Surrealist radicalism. In one of his last acts with the group, Aragon joined the Surrealists in recommitting themselves to the cause of Spanish revolutionaries in 1931, penning a letter in support of a massive anticlerical upheaval that saw churches burn across the country. "Bringing the great materialist illumination of torched churches to oppose the bonfires once erected by the Spanish Church, the masses will be able to find enough gold in the coffers of these churches to arm themselves, join battle, and transform the bourgeois revolution into a proletarian revolution," they declared with a feverish tone in one of their most radical texts.[68]

For all its scandalous implications, the Aragon Affair did motivate French Communists to abandon their hostility toward other leftists and form a "united front" that included a group called the *Association des Écrivains et des artistes révolutionnaires* (AEAR), which would protect authors from state crackdowns while building solidarity toward revolutionary goals. After joining the AEAR, the Surrealists went into action, taking part in antifascist committees and organizing a conference called "Fascism Against Culture." When the Surrealists continued to publish tracts against the Stalinist purges of the Russian avant-garde, however, a prominent Russian communist named Ilya Ehrenburg accused them of trading in political activism for "onanism, pederasty, fetishism, exhibitionism, and even bestiality."[69] The AEAR ostracized the Surrealists, and the Surrealists ceased publication of *Le Surréalisme au service de la Révolution*, starting a new review named, simply, *Minotaure*.

As they broke with the Communist Party, the group continued toward more theoretical analyses of the object and Surrealism's approach to objectivity in discourses that often featured Dalí prominently. However, the rise of Hitler in Germany provoked horror among the Surrealists, and Dalí shocked them more by refusing to condemn the antisemitic despot. More unsettling still, Dalí claimed to fantasize about Hitler. "Whenever I started to paint the leather strap that crossed from his belt to his shoulder, the softness of that Hitler flesh packed under his military tunic transported me into a sustaining and Wagnerian ecstasy that set my heart pounding," he would later recall, "an extremely rare state of excitement that I did not even experience during the act of love."[70] The eccentric painter faced expulsion from the Surrealist group as a Nazi sympathizer in 1933 (although he would continue to promote himself as Surrealism's leading light).[71] Breton would later call Dalí "the Neo-Falangist bedside-table" and Aragon "the raving false witness."[72]

Facing the Rise of Fascism, 1934–40

With Hitler gaining power in 1933, the European far right received a massive boost. In France, the emboldened activists of the Camelots du Roi and the fascist group Jeunesses Patriotes seized on a scandal involving a con artist named Alexandre Stavisky and his connections to high-level politicians in the center-left government. Organizing a riot on February 6th, 1934, the chauvinist leagues descended on the Place de Concorde and fought with police, who killed 15 in turn. Fearing a putsch, the Surrealists hurried to Breton's apartment that night and produced an *appeal à la lutte* (call to struggle). Gaining some 90 signatures from famous cultural figures, the piece repudiated the Stalinist attacks on "social traitors" among the Social Democrats rather than fascists, and not one member of the Communist Party signed it.[73] Antifascist leagues emerged, drawing on the days of the left-wing alliance of pro-Dreyfus groups that opposed the rise of antisemitism during the *Belle Epoque* when everything seemed in flux, resulting in the Comité de Vigilance des Intellectuels Antifacsistes, which the Surrealists promptly joined.[74]

The Surrealists joined workers' mobilizations in the streets during that year and worked within the avant-garde to promote antifascist unity. With a group of intellectuals including André Malraux, the Surrealists attempted to develop a "Survey on the Unity of Action," asking labor leaders and working-class politicos about the conditions necessary for antifascist solidarity, but few responded.[75] The government had fallen and was replaced by the right wing, but the fascists and monarchists remained largely outside of power.

Catastrophe mitigated, the Surrealists returned to confront the Communist Party as an antagonist. In a series of declarations and tracts issuing their position, the Surrealists took up Leon Trotsky's cause against Joseph Stalin and unleashed violent criticism against the Communists. When the AEAR convened an International Congress of Writers for the Defense of Culture in Paris, Surrealists demanded the inclusion of the right of artists to pursue "new means of expression."[76] Crevel, a committed Surrealist since the Time of Slumbers, lobbied strenuously for their inclusion, which was finally granted, but it would not take place without tragedy.

During the evening prior to the Congress, Breton ran into Ehrenburg, who had accused the Surrealists of, among other things, bestiality and pedophilia. Breton slapped Ehrenburg repeatedly, and the latter complained to the AEAR, which promptly struck Breton's speech from the Congress program. Crevel committed suicide in protest, and the AEAR decided to allow Éluard to read Breton's speech at the Congress (slotted for after midnight). "It is not by stereotyped declarations against fascism and war that we will manage to liberate either the mind or man from the ancient chains that bind him and the new chains that threaten him," Éluard orated to the dwindling Congress, "it is by the affirmation of our unshakeable fidelity to the powers of emancipation of the mind and of man that we have recognized one by one and that we will fight to cause to be recognized as such. 'Transform the world,' [Karl] Marx said; 'Change life,' Rimbaud said. These two watchwords are one for us."[77]

Now exhausted and enraged by the Communist Party and shaken by Crevel's death, the Surrealists astonishingly reunited with the Bataille group under a new name—Contre-Attaque—and aimed both against the fascists and the Stalinists. However, in short order, the group fell apart, with former members accusing Bataille and others of latent fascist tendencies.[78] In his ensuing piece, *The Political Position of Surrealism*,

Breton lambasted Stalinists and those too afraid or timid to criticize the Communist Party, cautioning against "a whole host of political nonentities—who are also flirting seriously with fascism."[79] He further attacked a cultural gravitation toward fascism that sought to draw Surrealists into its reactionary orbit: "rightist circles are remarkably cordial, particularly friendly in this respect. Monsieur Léon Daudet, the editor of the royalist journal *L'Action Française*, is pleased to repeat that Picasso is the greatest living painter; a large daily paper a few days ago reported in a three-column article that with the patronage of [Benito] Mussolini primitives, classical painters, and Surrealists were soon going to occupy the Grand Palais simultaneously in a huge exhibition of Italian art."[80]

There is no denying the allure of fascism to the avant-garde. Upon attending the 1934 *Mostra della rivoluzione fascista* in Rome, an exhibition dedicated to fascism's rise, Bataille remarked "the effect is very strong."[81] Raymond Roussel, a globetrotting dandy beloved by the Surrealists in their early years, also developed an eerie fascination with fascism, writing letters personally to Mussolini himself.[82] The reality was that the radical philosophy favored a great clash between the "old elite" and the "New Man," delighting in vitality and exuberance more than the staid methodologies of liberal institutions and their associated bureaucracies. The forces of the right could just as easily charge into this breach against the liberal Republic, and deliberately promoted cultural trends that opposed the Republic from a position attempting to join left and right.[83] Breton fought against such tendencies, insisting, "It is up to us to unite in opposing [Hitler] through the invincible force of that which *must be*, of *human becoming*."[84]

At the same time, Surrealism's break with the authoritarian left inspired new adherents. A group of Black poets in Paris assembled under the auspices of breaking with petty differences to produce a journal titled *L'Etudiant noir*. Their names—Aimé Césaire, future president of Senegal Leopold Senghor, and Léon-Gontran Damas—would loom large over the 20th century. Theirs was precisely the form of "human becoming" that Breton had in mind.

The following year, civil war broke out in Spain with the colonial general, Francisco Franco, invading the country from Morocco to thwart the democratic election of the left-wing Popular Front. The war tore the country apart. Luis Buñuel spied for the Republican side and organized clandestine support from Paris, even flying into Spain on missions, but he also helped give the fascists the location of a bandit and known rapist who called himself a "socialist" and was subsequently hanged in the Canary Islands. Luis's brother Alfonso Buñuel and fellow Spanish Surrealist Adriano del Valle joined the ranks of the Falangists and Franquistas, without reservation. Luis Buñuel's later reflections on the war evoke a complex sense of despair over the civil war, whose early embers his Surrealist friends had so eagerly stoked in 1931: "As they burned churches and convents and massacred priests, any doubts anyone may have had about hereditary enemies vanished completely.... And in the cocoon of my timid nihilism, I tell myself that all the wealth and culture on the Falangist side ought to have limited the horror. Yet the worst excesses came from them; which is why, alone with my dry martini, I have my doubts about the benefits of money and culture."[85]

Péret expressed less doubt. Disappointed with the Stalinist interventions and infighting among Marxists, he took part in the initial anarchist militia's armed response to Franco's invasion. Soon, Péret joined the Iron Column and fought at the Battle of Teruel, a sanguinary effort on the Aragon Front that ended in defeat.[86] He fell in love with Remedios Varo, a Spanish militant and brilliant painter, and the two fled Spain together to Paris as the war drew to its terrible conclusion.

Cunard, who had recorded the Surrealist disruption at the Ballets Russes during the early days, also went to Spain as a journalist for the Associated Negro Press of the US and *The Guardian*. Another Surrealist volunteer in Spain, a Yugoslav communist named Koča Popović, went on to make a name for himself as a partisan fighting Hitler's forces in the Balkans. Additionally, poet Valentine Penrose joined the Spanish workers' militia.[87]

English Surrealist Mary Low joined her partner and fellow avant-gardist, Cuban poet Juan Breá, to enter the conflict on the side of the Partido Obrero de Unificacion Marxista, the Trotskyist militia, and further edited their English-language paper, *Spanish Revolution*. While organizing the women's militia, Low wrote about their efforts to combat the corrosive force of patriarchy on the left and the women's commitment to the cause. "We sang the 'Internationale' very loudly and tried to convince [the men] that our uniform was as serious as their own.... We drilled for four hours without stopping, in every weather.... Some of [the women's] bodies were stiff and awkward, out of corsets for the first time. Yet they bore it all, and returned for more."[88] In his introduction to Low and Breá's 1937 book on the conflict, *Red Notebook*, Trinidadian Marxist C. L. R. James wrote, "The flame has been lit and Fascism can pour on it the blood of thousands of workers, can stamp upon it, and even stifle it for a time. But it will burn underground, is imperishable, and will blaze again."[89]

In a tract published by a group of Surrealists in Paris the following year titled "NEITHER YOUR WAR NOR YOUR PEACE!" the authors denounced "the pseudo-democratic powers" for allowing "Italy to annihilate Ethiopia notably because any successful resistance against the *white* invader would have encouraged colonial peoples to free themselves from the imperialist grip." They further attacked "the scandalous complicity of the Second and Third Internationals" and insisted that the efforts to respond to fascism by peacefully returning to the interwar period were as bad as efforts to ignite another world war. Instead, they called for recreating "Europe from top to bottom through the proletarian revolution."[90]

At this dire time, some hope came out of Egypt, where a new Surrealist group called Art et Liberté grew from an antinationalist manifesto in which they pronounced: "The individual against State Tyranny. Imagination against the routine of dialectical materialism. Freedom against terror in all its forms."[91] A statement by Anwar Kamel published in the left-wing journal *Al-Tattawor* read: "We roar in the face of those who call for a reactionary order and exploitation. . . . [I]f liberating people from bondage and slavery is corrupt, then from hereon our mission and message in life is: to corrupt the minds of men. We desire, and we know what we desire."[92]

Disaster followed disaster in successive years, with Franco defeating the Popular Front's forces in 1939 and the Soviets entering a nonaggression pact with Germany. As a result, Hitler invaded Poland and carved up the new *Lebensraum* with Stalin. The French government declared war on the Nazi state, and the French Communists immediately became functionally allies of the enemy through alignment with Stalin. The Communist Party was banned, and Communists had to choose between fidelity to the party and antifascism.[93] Before long, it would cease mattering.

Interlude By Way of the "Phony War"

The Germans invaded Belgium, and French troops began to mobilize in a kind of lackluster effort to gain positional strength known as "the phony war." Léro and Yoyotte, from Légitime défense, were called up early and both tragically died from wounds sustained in operations. Aragon was also sent to the hazy front, where he often found his way fighting back from behind enemy lines. Finally, surrounded at Dunkerque, France, he managed to escape to England with his sleeping bag and uncorrected proofs of his novel. After only one night in Plymouth, England, his unit returned to fight on the Seine at the rear-guard of the retreating army. But the Nazis caught up with them and Aragon found himself in a prisoner of war (POW) camp, which he escaped along with 30 other men and 6 automobiles.[94]

Awkwardly, a completely destroyed French government gave its formidable enemy, Aragon, a collection of high military decorations for his efforts forestalling the fascist advance that eventually seized power. Yet by dint of that same military record (among other past achievements), he found himself unpublishable under the Vichy regime until his poem, "The Lilacs and the Roses," appeared in the center-right publication *Le Figaro* (according to one report, against his wishes).[95] Although removed from his Surrealist work, the poem also exceeds the doggerel of "Front Rouge," standing today as a marvel of French poetry that rivals Appolinaire's disorienting war poetry.

The poem deserves some attention for its powerful description of the war's rapid escalation and strange ambiguity.[96] It begins in May, when Aragon is summoned to Belgium, and drifts to the solstice, which Hitler selected for the actual invasion of France: "O months of blossoming, months of transfigurations / May without a cloud and June stabbed to the heart / I shall not ever forget the lilacs or the roses / Nor those the Spring has kept folded away apart." And then, the second stanza perpetrates a sleight of hand in the grips of the moment's confusion, passing from triumph to fear to the harbinger of retreat—"the sorry rig of refugees." In the third, a general appears at "a Norman villa where the forest stops. . . . And Paris has surrendered, so we have just heard— / I shall never forget the lilacs nor the roses / Nor those two loves whose loss we have incurred." The two loves, "bouquets of the first day, lilacs," and "Bouquets of the Retreat, delicate roses," frame a liminally quiet and empty space of loss—the space of a threshold in which the French surrender and defeat come as a surprise impossible to accept.

A comparison with Appolinaire's poem, "Simultaneities," written during World War I, suggests that Aragon had indeed abandoned much of his Stalinist style for a return to the symbolist works he so admired in his youth.[97] Now Appolinaire: "In his hands he holds his helmet / To salute the memory / Of lilies roses jasmine / That bloom in France's gardens / And behind his hooded mask / Imagines darkest hair / But who waits for him on the quay / O vast sea of mauve shadows." Appolinaire's tone, as suggested by the pacing, is less lachrymose and more confident, with the flowers of French gardens revealing longing rather than framing a traumatic loss. The gravity of the poems, their nostalgic longing for love and its symbols, and the way repetition and change evoke a wistful sense of despair for the future.

With the capture of Paris, many Surrealists were forced to flee. A painter associated with Surrealism, Marc Chagall, was stripped of his citizenship and arrested with his wife and other Jews. The US journalist

Varian Fry pressed for the Chagall's release and organized the extraction of some two thousand artists. The Surrealist Max Ernst was arrested by the Gestapo and similarly released after a few weeks. The Bretons waited in Marseille with Cuban poet Wilfredo Lam, who helped develop a Surrealist tarot game called the Marseille Game, and joined the couple on a ship to Martinique, where they met up with the Césaires and others as exiles.[98] Other Surrealists chose to remain and resist. A number of them paid with their lives.

Surreal Antifascism in Resistance, 1941–45

Aragon and Éluard remained public figures in Vichy France following the armistice with the Nazis, assisting the Resistance in whatever ways they could. They helped ease political repression of various artists and worked to protect Resistance members. They also contributed to the clandestine press, working tirelessly at writing and even, in Aragon's case, participating in the reception of an air drop from the Allies. However, the Vichy and Nazi authorities were ruthless, murdering and raping innocent villagers assumed to support the Resistance, so everything had to be handled carefully.[99]

In 1941, Nazi authorities discovered a Resistance cell associated with the Surrealists at the Musée de l'Homme in Paris. Created by the French Popular Front government in 1937 as a successor to the Musée d'Ethnographie du Trocadéro, where Surrealists organized the first exhibition of pre-Columbian art, the Musée de l'Homme was run by Paul Rivet, a key member of the Comité de Vigilance des Intellectuels Antifacsistes born of the 1934 crisis and a friend of the Surrealists. The Musée network consisted of nuclei, which helped POWs and stranded airmen and officers escape France through Toulouse. An additional nucleus run by anthropologist Germaine Tillion sought to extract and aid Black and brown colonial troops being slaughtered by the Nazis in North Africa. The network also planned a journal called *Résistance*, but was betrayed by an informant before they could publish. Rivet and some others escaped to the Free Zone but 10 members of the Musée network met their deaths at the hands of Nazi executioners in the fort at Mont Valérien.[100]

A less-tragic story of Resistance came with Surrealist poet, René Char, who had signed tracts such as "Murderous Humanitarianism" and "BURN THEM DOWN." Going underground immediately with the *nom de guerre* "Capitaine Alexandre" to cover his clandestine activities in the French Alps, Char led a rural *maquis* unit in Provence-Alpes-Côte d'Azur along the Durance tributary to the Rhône river. Char was responsible for maintaining a crucial supply drop zone that was also a landing area for British planes. Unlike Aragon and Éluard, he refused to publish poetry even in Resistance journals; however, once finally published in 1946, the poems he wrote from 1943–44 gained widespread acclaim. For his work, the French government gave him a *Croix de Guerre* and named him to the National Order of the Legion of Honor.[101]

Char's Resistance poems take on the quality of epigrams mixed with journal entries about powerful experiences fighting Nazis and defending French villages. "Resistance is nothing but hope," he writes, observing with incredible clarity the responsibility of resisting Nazis and the lack of character exhibited by collaborators.[102] In another section, he writes, "Between reality and the account you give of it, there is your own life, which magnifies reality, and this Nazi abjection which ruins that account."[103] Char's Surrealism remains intact—the account of reality magnifies it, thus creating the Surreal. Nazism, for Char, represents the destruction of this honest accounting, thus creating the need to fight back in the simplest ways possible.

Char recalls how, from the window of a safe house, he watched Nazi interrogators viciously beat a mason in a village street, recounting with elation how villagers—women, children, and old men whom he had trained—swarmed the Nazis, forcing them to abandon the scene.[104] With more somber notes, he remembers his unit witnessing a Nazi execution that he could not stop without alerting the fascists to their location and putting the nearby villagers in danger.[105]

Meanwhile, Péret worked to mobilize more martial opposition to the Nazi occupation and Vichy government. In 1940, Péret faced arrest with Varo, another Surrealist named Leo Malet, and two leftists, Béno Stenberg and Jean-François Chabrun, for reconstituting a dissolved league. Freed, they moved to Paris, where they led early meetings of a new project called La Main à Plume (taken from a line from Rimbaud, "The hand that holds the pen is as good as the one that holds the plow"). Stemming from a neo-Dadaist group called Les Réverbères organized in part by Chabrun, La Main à Plume believed the fascist occupation made Surrealism more urgent.[106]

In a letter to Breton, the group's members wrote:

At the start of 1941 a few of us came together who, while in general being too young to have participated in the surrealist movement before 1939, were nevertheless not old enough to be resigned to detaching ourselves through intellectual fatigue, opportunism or through fear of displeasing the conquerors who were bringing us, with organized stupefaction, a hatred of "degenerate" art or of any intellectual activity capable of provoking in the most diverse spheres the slightest reaction other than strict obedience and resignation to stupidity and force.[107]

The young Surrealists lamented the state of Surrealism in Paris: "From the old group there remained just a few scattered and inactive individuals; others sometimes returned from captivity or else from the free zone, bringing back ever more alarming news about the mystical-cretinising nature of the intellectual activities on display down there, channeled through sub-prefecture magazines or pre-war no-hopers taking a revenge only defeat could offer them."[108] In particular, they singled out Bataille, going as far as to pen a stinging rebuke of him in a letter identifying him as a *curé* and oppressive priest. It should, however, be noted that Bataille worked on the journal *Messages* with Jean Lescure, a member of the armed group, Ceux de la Résistance (Those of the Resistance).

What is clear is that La Main à Plume had militant intentions, which they expressed to Breton, perhaps unwisely, in their letter: "There is a time to prepare arms, and a time to use them," they stated bluntly. "We do not intend to arrive on the day of the battle with rusty or, worse still, blunt weapons. This is why we have decided to continue action, even if it is by taking advantage of this period of 'calm' to devote ourselves in some way to a veritable poetic training destined to maintain our discipline and our contact with reality."[109]

Breton did not reply for obvious reasons but, unable to join the war effort in exile, he joined the US Office of War Information. Along with the Frankfurt School émigrés Herbert Marcuse and Franz Neumann, as well as the Dadaist Walter Mehring and the leftist author Leo Lania, Breton collaborated with the US's clandestine efforts to aid the Allies in psychological warfare. Here, he was again awkwardly working alongside Stalinists in an effort made even more awkward by their joint collaboration with a state they viewed as imperialist.[110]

It was true that a new generation of Resistance Surrealists was blossoming in jazz clubs such as the Hot Club de France, famous haunt of Django Reinhardt and Stefan Grappelli. The first issue of *La Main à Plume* featured poetry by the Hot Club's cofounder, Jacques Bureau, who himself joined the Prosper-PHYSICIAN network and worked on radio communications before his arrest by Nazi intelligence.[111] An early La Main à Plume member, Robert Rius, joined several different maquis from 1943 to 1944, when he was denounced and incarcerated at Fontainebleau. Under torture, he kept silent, and his captors executed him in the plains of Chanfroy with 2 of his fellow Surrealist maquis, Charles-Jean Simonpoli and Marco Ménégoz, and 17 other Resistance fighters.[112] Other members of the rebel Surrealists met similar fates: Edith Hirschová was sent to a concentration camp; Jean-Pierre Mulotte was shot on the Pont d'Austerlitz; Jean-Claude Diamant-Berger parachuted into France and was killed in Normandy; Hans Schoenhoff was imprisoned in Cherche-Midi and sent to Auschwitz, where he and so many others would perish.[113]

A Resistance member charged with forging documents, Desnos was arrested in 1944 and sent to Auschwitz, then Buchenwald, then Flossenberg, and finally Terezín. Although he survived through liberation, he died in Terezín of typhus a month later.[114] Nazi concentration camps served as the final destination for other Surrealists—communist militant Fanny Beznos, Surrealist dancer Hélène Vanel, and dancer and model Sonia Mossé.[115] Some other Surrealists found themselves confined to mental institutions—for instance, Artaud, who, despite significant depravations and the deaths of his dearest friends, Desnos and Mossé, began to express antisemitic sentiments and affinity with fascism.[116]

Surrealists also died at the hands of Axis powers elsewhere in Europe and in Japan. Fernand Dumont, a key Belgian Surrealist, continued his work with the underground Groupe Surréaliste en Hainaut Belgium despite Nazi occupation. The Gestapo arrested him in 1942 and he died three years later of dysentery in Bergen-Belsen.[117] Hendrik Cramer, Dutch Surrealist and member of the group Le Grand Jeu, faced arrest for smuggling Resistance gasoline in Marseille and died in a concentration camp.[118] Forming a subversive Surrealist group in the Prague, Czech Republic neighborhood of Spořilov, Czechoslovak poet Rudolf Altschul was arrested in 1943 and killed at the end of the war. In Yugoslavia, Surrealist Đorđe Jovanović fought with the partisans and lost his life in the People's Liberation Struggle. Japanese Surrealists Kiyotaka Asahara, Seiichi Fujiwara, Koji Otsuka, and Hironobu Yasaki also died at the hands of ultranationalists.[119]

Toward the Marvelous

Those who survived the Nazi years went on to profoundly influence the development of postwar France both in the mainstream and in continued resistance. Aragon became a national hero even as he continued his support for the Communist Party. Éluard was dubbed the "poet of the Resistance." Popović became foreign minister of Yugoslavia under Josip Broz "Tito." A cofounder of Les Réverbères and partisan of La Main à

Plume, Noël Arnaud went on to edit the *Situationist Times* and became a major figure in the Oulipo poetry movement. Malet, who faced incarceration in Rennes prison and Stalag X-B, took to writing famous crime novels after liberation, although, unlike Arnaud, he became a recalcitrant reactionary.

As for Breton, he returned to France and continued to offer motivating energy with Péret to the Surrealist group for the ensuing two decades. Surrealism opposed the Soviet attack on the Hungarian Revolution, the war in Vietnam, and other imperial misadventures. In their retaliation against the Soviets for the invasion of Hungary, the Surrealists screamed, "THE FASCISTS ARE THOSE WHO TURN THEIR GUNS AGAINST THE PEOPLE!"[120] The Surrealist group in Hungary was suppressed by the Soviets, as was the Czech group in turn. Despite Communist repression, a letter produced by the Surrealists and signed by a host of intellectuals was credited with contributing to the French abandonment of colonialism in Algeria.[121] Meanwhile, in Egypt, the Surrealists found themselves suppressed by the Gamal Nasser regime.

Breton's group lost much of the ideological radicalism of the interwar days, moving further into a kind of erotic-spiritualist tendency that incorporated elements of Traditionalism. In one of his final works, largely written by his occultist companion, Breton responded to Julius Evola, an intellectual leader of the fascist movement who had also contributed to the early review, *Dada*, in 1920. On the one hand, Breton strongly criticized mystical tendencies that would contribute to the modern New Age movement. On the other, his own assessment of "Magic Art" opened a critical gateway for Traditionalism with incredibly destructive tendencies in the name of transgression.[122]

After Breton's death, the Surrealist group disbanded, showing his profound influence. It had not succeeded in its ambitious mission to overthrow capitalism with the sovereignty of thought. But its boldness influenced antifascist freedom fighters around the world, from Amílcar Cabral to Senghor to so many others—many of whom obtained independence from colonial powers still backed by parafascists such as António de Oliveira Salazar.[123] Surrealism would continue to inform the imagination of rebels and revolutionaries from the COBRA group, its spinoff the Letterists, and, subsequently, the Situationists. Additionally, between the art of Anselm Kiefer and Joseph Beuy, Surrealism became a crucial influence in rendering and representing the Holocaust in postwar art.[124]

During the 1970s, the militant, antifascist Autonomist journals of Italy were riddled with references to Jarry, Dadaism, and the Surrealists.[125] At the same time, the concepts and methods of Surrealists continue to inspire artists in the US, from Ted Joans and the Beat Generation to the Chicago Surrealist School, which helped promote the marvelous within rebellious activist groups that developed at the end of the Cold War, including Earth First![126] In a republication of a 1945 piece by Breton, initially translated by the Chicago Surrealists in 1966, the anarchist and antifascist CrimethInc. ex-Workers' Collective offered their support to the surreal notion that, "Liberty does not consent to caress this earth except in taking into account those who have known, or have at least, partly known, how to live because they have loved her to a point of madness."[127]

In the Donald Trump era, Surrealist artists, particularly women and people of color, used the confrontation with reality to wage aesthetic warfare against the disintegration of truth and fact.[128] Amid a plethora of popular movies, albums, art, and poetry with clear Surrealist influences, *The Guardian*'s Lanre Bakare declared a "new age of Afro-surrealism" in 2019, noting, "it's no wonder our pop cultural landscape is turning Afro-surreal at a time when society is wrestling with racial violence, bias and inequality."[129] Drawing on the influence of the Black Surrealist experience from *Légitime défense* to *Négritude* to Joans and the Beats to modern writers such as Toni Morrison, artists such as Kevin Jerome Everson and directors such as Jenn Nkiru navigate the Surreal within the divided and embattled human condition. In the words of scholar Terri Francis, Afro-surrealists' "work is very realistic in representing the absurdity of black life. [In America] the ideals are there and you're aware of what should be going on . . . but that's not the reality."[130]

One of the lessons of Surrealism is that art thrives during hard times. The Iranian painter Arghavan Khosravi, whose work personalizes intercultural and temporal contradictions, suffered under the travel ban, blocked from leaving the US during Trump's time in office.[131] Under Trump, the art of Allison Sommers continued to challenge ideals of beauty from an antifascist perspective whereas Maria Fragoso contextualized her own innovative art with reference to the BLM movement and opposition to Trump.[132] Among artists experiencing breakout moments following the Trump period, the Weird Records founder and visual artist Pieter Schoolwerth promotes countercultural resistance to the far right, and Dominique Fung uses Surrealism to critique Orientalism in Western society.[133] Beyond the art world, generations of antifascists continue to fill zines traded at punk shows and book fairs with images, concepts, and ideas that would have delighted the original group.

Postscript

The first thing that Surrealism's legacy revealed was the transnationality of political phenomena. Some of Surrealism's greatest influences derived from international figures such as the Franco-Ecuadorian Lautréamont and the Polish-Belarusian poet Appolinaire. They were heavily impacted by international political engagements, such as the occupation of the Ruhr and subsequent assassination of Plateau. Yet their greatest emphasis was on anti-imperial politics, which engaged in adventurous anthropologies and artistic experimentation to challenge not just the architecture of capitalism but the social conditions that foster it.

And this was the ultimate outcome of Surrealism's most uncompromising radicalism. They attacked the modern world at the point of norms and practices deemed the very source of sanity and safety. In doing so, they revealed pathological tendencies within modernity that appeared so necessary, so fundamental, that civilization could hardly withstand the challenge.

The far right hated Surrealism not because of their outlandish stunts or the brawls they started (the right was more than happy to oblige in the latter). The monarchists and fascists loathed Surrealists because the latter set up camp in the dangerous territory of the unknown, which presented the great weakness of the civilized world to the free thinker. Fascism, it would turn out, compensated for the disruptive force of Surrealism by integrating aspects of the avant-garde that the old reactionaries could not, thus offering cultural inroads from the revolutionary left to the far right. And the allure of fascism drew some Surrealists and their associates, such as Drieu la Rochelle and Alfonso Buñuel, as well as Dalí, into the darkest side of politics. Surrealism's antifascist promise led the younger generation of artists and poets into violent resistance against the Vichy authorities and Nazis.

Yet the uncompromising radicalism of the Surrealists tended to lead into unlikely alliances. Because they opposed colonialism, they submitted to a partnership with the Stalinists, whom they regarded as cultural authoritarians. When the Stalinists began to compromise with imperialist powers, the Surrealists broke fiercely with them, only to end up allying with the French Republic they so loathed in the effort to stave off fascist invasion. Under occupation, Surrealists worked with the England-supported Resistance and the US anti-Axis forces, not just because they prioritized the destruction of fascism more than the uncompromising total liberation of the human spirit but because they viewed fascism as the ultimate apotheosis of repressive force.

At every stage, one can point out a compromise and dole out denunciations. Indeed, Surrealists themselves did. Compromising with the Communists against capitalism brought denunciations. Compromising with the Republic against the fascists cut back against their earlier denunciations, bringing still more. And then those who continued to write under the occupation, such as Bataille and Éluard, were harshly censured by the younger Surrealists. It becomes tempting to criticize Surrealism for these compromises while failing to realize that the artists lived through this difficult and painful process to protect what meant the most to them: life and the uncompromising freedom that it holds. Perhaps activists will continue to recognize this apparent paradox as one of Surrealism's most important legacies—the Surrealist struggle against fascism was and remains a revolutionary struggle for liberation in pursuit of the marvelous.

The author would like to add that suicide is not a necessary conclusion, and that alternatives exist. If you or someone you know is contemplating suicide, you are not alone. Reach out and get help through the National Suicide Prevention Hotline, (800) 273-8255, or a mental health support network in your area.

Perspectives for Antifascists

David Renton

The chapters in this book were written during, or in the immediate after-math of, Donald Trump's presidency. There was a reciprocal relationship between Trump and his followers while he was in power. To keep them interested in him, he had to some extent adopted their worldview, espe-cially in the weeks leading up to the 2020 elections, telling the press that a street army of antifascists was on the verge of seizing power and that only Trump could stop the rise of "people that you've never heard of. People that are in the dark shadows. People that are controlling the streets . . . thugs wearing these dark uniforms, black uniforms with gear."[1] Antifascists ("antifa") were blamed by Trump's followers for forest fires, for causing police violence, even for the January 6th attempted coup.

Trump, however, lost the presidential election in November 2020, and whether he ever believed he could use a street army to overturn the vote, that attempt failed. The immediate prospect facing hundreds of his supporters is now of lengthy trials and perhaps (for some of them) short periods of imprisonment.

As long ago as February 2017, the novelist Ursula K. Le Guin com-plained of the effect that Trump was having on his opponents. She called herself "appalled" at "the constant, obsessive attention paid to Trump." She warned that his opponents were giving him their attention and allow-ing him to dominate their own lives. "Every witty parody, hateful gibe, clever take-off," she insisted, "merely plays his game."[2]

Five years later, his Twitter account has been taken away, severing one of the loudest parts of his bully pulpit. How antifascists organize in this new period will be shaped by our assessment of whether we see Trump's reverse as temporary or permanent. In the liberal press, the assumption is the latter. Democrats will hold on to the institutions of the US state, reverse the Republican majority on the US Supreme Court, take back the state legislatures, et cetera so that, on a short timescale, the US will once again be a thriving democracy. Even if that hope was correct, it remains true that the far right has been able to build up infrastructure in these past six years and has the benefit of its recent success: funds, habits of networking, an audience. Even if Trump himself was to disappear, the far right's successful organizing has left a legacy. For years to come, in the cities where we live, antifascists will be facing an emboldened enemy.

The other problem is that, ever since 2008, politics worldwide have taken a common form. Perhaps once electorates were willing to cast their vote for an inoffensive, middle-of-the-road politician, believing that if they did what the system expected of them, their own life chances would improve from generation to generation. If that belief was held then, it is no longer. Rather, the trillions spent on bailing out the banks left a subtle but indelible message—that the politicians will only promote the interests of the rich, that none of the old "rules" apply.

Because the left in most countries has failed to learn those lessons, the right is winning elections. We face a new populist right willing to ally with fascists, and to mimic their language on immigration, culture wars, et cetera. The states that are building their global influence—Russia, Israel, India—sponsor authoritarians. Why should we expect a return to democratic innocence when more countries are abandoning democracy than joining it? Why should we expect liberalism to prosper in the US when it is dying in Italy, in Britain, and in France?

Should Trump regain power in November 2024, or even if something less dramatic happens and we see an echo of Trump—a member of his family, or Tucker Carlson, or whoever else it turns out to be—standing on a platform that is recognizably Trump 2.0, then the political crisis of 2016–20 will recur save with higher stakes. Imagine a movement leadership that shared Trump's dark fantasies of building walls and imprisoning his opponents but, next time, combined that malice with the competence Trump lacked and a new resolution to turn authoritarian plans into actuality. Or think of the Trump movement, invigorated by stories of liberal betrayal, and determined to secure revenge for the January 6th martyrs.

There are few examples of antifascists in history prospering following their rival's defeat. After 1945, antifascists failed to impose their politics on postwar Germany, dominated as that country was by the politics of the occupying powers—the US, Britain, France, and the Union of Soviet Socialist Republics. In consequence, of the 150,000 Germans identified as having carried out war crimes, just one in five were prosecuted. West German intelligence agent Klaus Barbie had tortured prisoners in Lyon, France. Heinrich Lübke, the designer of concentration camps, served for 10 years as president of West Germany.[3]

After the defeat of fascism in Italy, millions of people hoped that a new society would be born, characterized by workers' control of industry. Instead, under the influence of the Partito Comunista Italiano (PCI [Italian Communist Party]), workers were told to disarm, and an amnesty was offered to virtually all war criminals. In July 1948, the leader of the PCI, Palmiro Togliatti, was shot and nearly killed. There followed a general strike, placing workers in control of the cities—and again the PCI demobilized the movement. Seven thousand people were arrested, five million rounds of ammunition impounded. Never again would that country's radical opposition get close to taking power.[4]

One possible way to think of antifascism after the temporary eclipse of our opponents is to take seriously Max Horkheimer's famous saying that "whoever is not willing to talk about capitalism should also keep quiet about fascism." Writing in 1939, the Frankfurt theorist's point was that fascism is the product of capitalism and cannot be defeated so long as the latter thrives. Several chapters of this book have shown that this relationship remains in place. Fascism is the successor, developed in some of the richest countries of the world, to the inequality and violence that were commonplace under colonialism. Fascism thrives on racism, sexism, and even transphobia, which recur in multiple forms under capitalism.

The insight that fascism is a recurring antagonist suggests that there can be no permanent victory over it except through the defeat of capitalism. All we can do on the far left is build our own forces, innovate where we can, and, by capturing the politics of the moment better than our opponents, extend the periods of relative quiet. That is the best that history offers us.

Knowing that our enemy's defeat is temporary, we can allow ourselves a short period of relaxation. Then, as the cycle begins again—we prepare for the battles to come.

Notes

Introduction / Shane Burley

1. Moe Bowstern, Mic Crenshaw, Alec Dunn, Celina Flores, Julie Perini, and Erin Yanke, eds., *It Did Happen Here: An Antifascist Peoples' History* (Oakland, CA: PM Press, forthcoming).

2. My chapter, "Antiracist Skinheads and the Birth of Anti-Racist Action: An Interview with Mic Crenshaw," talks about this issue.

3. Shane Burley, *Fascism Today: What It Is and How to End It* (Chico, CA: AK Press, 2017), 196–203.

4. Shane Burley, "The End of Violence: 100 Days of Protest in Portland," *Verso* (blog), *Verso Books*, September 28, 2020, https://www.versobooks.com/blogs /4862-the-end-of-violence-100-days-of-protest-in-portland.

5. Katie Shepherd, "Portland Police Stand by as Proud Boys and Far Right Militias Flash Guns and Brawl with Antifa Counter Protesters," *The Washington Post*, August 22, 2020, https://www.washingtonpost.com/nation/2020/08/22/ portland-police-far-right-protest.

6. Neil MacFarquhar, "Drivers Are Hitting Protesters as Memes of Car Attacks Spread," *The New York Times*, July 7, 2020, https://www.nytimes.com/2020/07/07/us/ bloomington-car-attack-protesters.html; Lexi McMenamin, "How Cars Became a Deadly Anti-protest Weapon," *Mic*, December 30, 2020, https://www.mic.com/ impact/how-cars-became-a-deadly-anti-protest-weapon-53291831.

7. Shane Burley and Alexander Reid Ross, "Conspiracy Theories by Cops Fuel Far Right Attacks Against Antiracist Protesters," *Truthout*, September 18, 2020, https://truthout.org/articles/conspiracy-theories-by-cops-fuel-far-right-attacks -against-antiracist-protesters.

8. Chris Faraone, "The Crowds in Boston Shouted Themselves Hoarse. Did Anyone Really Hear Them?," *The New Republic*, August 21, 2017, https://newrepublic.com/ article/144428/crowds-boston-shouted-hoarse-anyone-really-hear-them.

9. Shane Burley, "The Capitol Rioters and Punitive State Power," *Protean Magazine*, January 6, 2022, https://proteanmag.com/2022/01/06/the-capitol-rioters-and-punitive -state-power.

10. The best example of this was "A resolution calling for the designation of Antifa as a domestic terrorist organization," S. Res. 279, 116th Cong. (2019), introduced by Senators Ted Cruz and Bill Cassidy, https://www.govtrack.us/congress/bills/116/ sres279/text.

11. Shane Burley, "Anti-Mask Bills Targeting Leftists Ignore the Real Perpetrators of Violence," *Truthout*, March 7, 2020, https://truthout.org/articles/anti -mask-bills-targeting-leftists-ignore-the-real-perpetrators-of-violence.

12. Jason Wilson, "Armed Civilian Roadblocks in Oregon Town Fuel Fears Over Vigilantism," *The Guardian*, September 16, 2020, https://www.theguardian.com/ us-news/2020/sep/16/oregon-fires-armed-civilian-roadblocks-police; EJ Dickson, "How the Right Spread a False Rumor About Antifa and Wildfires," *Rolling Stone*,

481

September 11, 2020, https://www.rollingstone.com/culture/culture-news/oregon-wildfire-antifa-false-rumors-1058252.

13. The most complete version of this was Andy Ngo, who created a gothic fantasy about antifa by tracing lines on a chalk board between the political left and acts of violence by people with, possibly, lukewarm nonconservative politics. For more, see Shane Burley, "Andy Ngo's *Unmasked*: The Next Phase of the Grift," March 3, 2021, *Protean Magazine*, https://proteanmag.com/2021/03/03/andy-ngos-antifa-unmasked-the-next-phase-of-the-grift.

14. Lois Beckett, "Anti-Fascists Linked to Zero Murders in the US for 25 Years," *The Guardian*, July 27, 2020, https://www.theguardian.com/world/2020/jul/27/us-rightwing-extremists-attacks-deaths-database-leftwing-antifa.

15. Two chapters in this book carry on this tradition. Jeanelle K. Hope's "The Black Antifascist Tradition: A Primer" and Mike Bento's "Five Hundred Years of Fascism" are wonderful introductions to this important analysis.

16. Burley, *Fascism Today*, 47–55. For more on the "New Consensus" approach, read Roger Griffin, "The Primacy of Culture: The Current Growth (Or Manufacture) of Consensus within Fascist Studies," *Journal of Contemporary History* 37, no. 1 (January 2002): 21–43; Roger Griffin, "Studying Fascism in a Postfascist Age. From New Consensus to New Wave?," *Journal of Comparative Fascist Studies* 1, no. 1 (2012): 1–17; Roger Griffin, *Fascism: An Introduction to Comparative Fascist Studies* (Cambridge, UK: Polity Press, 2018), 49–58.

17. I have discussed this concept further in relationship to the idea of an interdisciplinary "Antifascist Studies": Shane Burley, "Introduction to Antifascist Studies" (panel presentation, American Studies Association Conference, Atlanta, November 9, 2018, https://burlesshanae.medium.com/an-introduction-to-antifascist-studies-6aad5edf5obe).

18. Nigel Copsey, "Preface: Towards a New Anti-Fascist 'Minimum'?," in Nigel Copsey and Andrzej Olechnowicz, eds., *Varieties of Anti-Fascism: Britain in the Inter-War Period* (New York: Palgrave Macmillan, 2010), xiv–xxi.

19. Devin Zane Shaw, *Philosophy of Antifascism: Punching Nazis and Fighting White Supremacy* (London: Rowman & Littlefield International, 2020), 5.

20. I also use the term "militant antifascism" slightly differently than Shaw does. I designate "militant antifascism" as the antifascism that necessarily hinges its tactical specificity on the use of direct confrontation rather than primarily focusing on other tactics. This would be movements correctly called "antifa" or earlier groups such as ARA. Groups could include a mix of tactics, engaging in "militant antifascism" one day and other tactics other days, but this would not make them "liberal antifascism" in Shaw's characterization unless they channel their vision of antifascism through some type of state intervention or electoralism.

21. Moishe Postone, "History and Helplessness: Mass Mobilization and Contemporary Forms of Anticapitalism," *Public Culture* 18, no. 1 (2006): 93–110.

22. David Renton, *No Free Speech for Fascists: Exploring "No Platform" in History, Law and Politics* (Abingdon, UK: Routledge, 2021), 150–62.

23. Peter Beinart, "The Rise of the Violent Left," *The Atlantic*, September 2017, https://www.theatlantic.com/magazine/archive/2017/09/the-rise-of-the-violent-left/534192.

24. Stanislav Vysotsky, *American Antifa: The Tactics, Culture, and Practice of Militant Antifascism* (London: Routledge, 2021), 155.

25. Shane Burley, "Amid the Coronavirus Crisis, Mutual Aid Networks Erupt Across the Country," *Waging Nonviolence*, March 27, 2020, https://wagingnonviolence.org/2020/03/coronavirus-mutual-aid-networks-erupt-across-country.

26. Shane Burley, "Life and Times at the Capitol Hill Autonomous Zone," *ROAR Magazine*, June 16, 2020, https://roarmag.org/essays/life-and-times-at -the-capitol-hill-autonomous-zone.

27. Author interview with Kelly Hayes, January 13, 2021. Also see the chapter in this book titled "'Kops and Klan Go Hand in Hand': An Interview with Kelly Hayes."

28. Shane Burley, *Why We Fight: Essays on Fascism, Resistance, and Surviving the Apocalypse* (Chico, CA: AK Press, 2021), 21–26.

29. Author interview with William Tull, January 7, 2021.

30. Shane Burley, "Community Bonds and Mutual Aid Sustain Anti-Fascists Targeted by the State," *Truthout*, January 4, 2022, https://truthout.org/articles/ community-bonds-and-mutual-aid-sustain-anti-fascists-targeted-by-the-state.

31. Author interview with Andrew Dial, November 30, 2021.

32. Jeff Burlew, "Daniel Baker Sentenced to Federal Prison in Florida Capitol Threat Case," *Tallahassee Democrat*, October 12, 2021, https://www.tallahassee.com/story/ news/local/fbi/2021/10/12/daniel-baker-sentenced-federal-prison-florida-capitol -threat-case/8424086002.

33. Alex Riggins, "Experts Say San Diego Case Likely First to Use Conspiracy Charges against Antifa," *San Diego Tribune*, December 11, 2021, https://www .sandiegouniontribune.com/news/courts/story/2021-12-11/experts-say-san-diego -case-likely-first-to-use-conspiracy-charges-against-antifa.

34. Author interview with Eric K. Ward, December 16, 2021.

35. See Abner Häuge's chapter in this book, "Make Journalism Antifa Again."

36. This book has a number of great chapters on antifascist history, including "Surreal Antifascism, 1921–45" by Alexander Reid Ross and "Lessons from a Lifetime of Anti-racist and Antifascist Struggle: A Memoir and Analysis" by Michael Novick. For more on antifascist tactics, see the chapter in this book titled "It Takes a Network to Defeat a Network: (Anti)Fascism and the Future of Complex Warfare" by Emmi Bevensee and Frank Miroslav.

37. Author interview with Lara Messersmith-Glavin, January 6, 2022.

38. Shane Burley and Alexander Reid Ross, "A Popular Mobilization Is Forming in Portland to Stop the Growth of Hate Groups," *Truthout*, August 1, 2018, https://truthout .org/articles/popular-mobilization-forming-in-portland-to-stop-growth-of-hate -groups.

39. Author interview with Raven, January 11, 2021.

40. Bridging Divides Initiative. "BDI Issue Brief: Unaffiliated Armed and Unidentified Militia Actors at Demonstrations, January 2020 – June 2021," 2021, https://bridging divides.princeton.edu/sites/g/files/toruqf246/files/documents/BDI%20Issue%20 Brief%20-%20Unaffiliated%20Armed%20and%20Unidentified%20Militia%20 Actors%20at%20Demonstrations%2C%20January%202020%20-%20June%202021 .docx.pdf.

41. Sam Levin, "Revealed: How California Police Chased a Nonexistent 'Antifa Bus,'" *The Guardian*, August 23, 2021, https://www.theguardian.com/us-news/2021/aug/23/ revealed-california-police-antifa-misinformation; Aleszu Bajak and Javier Zarracina, "How the Antifa Conspiracy Theory Traveled from the Fringe to the Floor of Congress," *USA Today*, January 13, 2021, https://www.usatoday.com/in-depth/news/2021/01/12/ how-antifa-conspiracy-theory-traveled-fringe-floor-congress/6620908002.

42. Robert Pape, "Why We Cannot Afford to Ignore the American Insurrectionist Movement," *American Political Violence* (blog), *Chicago Project on Security & Threats, University of Chicago*, https://cpost.uchicago.edu/research/domestic_extremism/why_we _cannot_afford_to_ignore_the_american_insurrectionist_movement.

43. "Written Testimony of Heidi L. Beirich, Ph.D., Co-Founder/Executive Vice President/Global Project Against Hate and Extremism, Before the Congress of the United States House of Representatives Committee on Homeland Security Intelligence and Counterterrorism Subcommittee, Regarding 'Assessing the Threat from Accelerationists and Far Right Militia Extremists,'" July 16, 2020, https://homeland.house.gov/imo/media/doc/Testimony%20-%20Beirich.pdf.

44. Shane Burley and Alexander Reid Ross, "How the Denver Shooter's Digital Trail Exposes the Violent Fantasies of the 'Manosphere,'" *Bellingcat*, January 6, 2022, https://www.bellingcat.com/news/americas/2022/01/06/how-the-denver-shooters-digital-trail-exposes-the-violent-fantasies-of-the-manosphere.

45. Seth G. Jones, Catrina Doxsee, and Nicholas Harrington, "The Escalating Terrorism Problem in the United States," *Center for Strategic and International Studies*, June 17, 2020, https://www.csis.org/analysis/escalating-terrorism-problem-united-states.

46. David Graeber, *Fragments of an Anarchist Anthropology* (Chicago: Prickly Paradigm Press, 2004), 92.

47. David Graeber and David Wengrow, *The Dawn of Everything: A New History of Humanity* (New York: Farrar, Straus and Giroux, 2021), 524.

48. Author interview with Daryle Lamont Jenkins, January 7, 2022. See Jenkins's contribution to this book, "Some Names Have Been Changed."

Three Way Fight Politics and the US Far Right / Matthew N. Lyons

1. Large sections of this chapter are excerpted, condensed, or adapted from: Matthew N. Lyons, *Insurgent Supremacists: The U.S. Far Right's Challenge to State and Empire* (Oakland, CA: PM Press, 2018); Matthew N. Lyons, "Ctrl-Alt-Delete: The Origins and Ideology of the Alternative Right," *Political Research Associates*, January 20, 2017, https://www.politicalresearch.org/2017/01/20/ctrl-alt-delete-report-on-the-alternative-right; and Matthew N. Lyons, "Ctrl-Alt-Delete: The Origins and Ideology of the Alternative Right," in Kersplebedeb, ed., *Ctrl-Alt-Delete* (Montréal: Kersplebedeb, 2017).

2. See Lyons, *Insurgent Supremacists*, 228–29.

3. Anti-Fascist Forum, ed., *My Enemy's Enemy: Essays on Globalization, Fascism and the Struggle against Capitalism*, 3rd ed. (Montréal: Kersplebedeb, 2003); Don Hamerquist, J. Sakai, Anti-Racist Action Chicago, Mark Salotte, *Confronting Fascism: Discussion Documents for a Militant Movement*, 2nd ed. (Montréal: Kersplebedeb, 2017); *Three Way Fight* (blog), https://threewayfight.blogspot.com.

4. "About Three Way Fight," *Three Way Fight* (blog), https://threewayfight.blogspot.com/p/about.html.

5. Natasha Lennard, "Even the FBI Thinks Police Have Links to White Supremacists—but Don't Tell the *New York Times*," *The Intercept*, November 5, 2018, https://theintercept.com/2018/11/05/new-york-times-police-white-supremacy.

6. For more on my approach to the concept of fascism, see Matthew Lyons, "Two Ways of Looking at Fascism," *Socialism and Democracy* 22, no. 2 (July 2008): 121–56. On Trump and fascism, see Lyons, *Insurgent Supremacists*, chapter 11, especially 196–99.

7. See Chip Berlet and Matthew N. Lyons, *Right-Wing Populism in America* (New York: Guilford Press, 2000), chapters 3 and 7.

8. Eric K. Ward, "Skin in the Game: How Antisemitism Animates White Nationalism," *Political Research Associates*, June 29, 2017, https://www.politicalresearch.org/2017/06/29/skin-in-the-game-how-antisemitism-animates-white-nationalism.

Notes

9. Leonard Zeskind, *Blood and Politics: The History of the White Nationalist Movement from the Margins to the Mainstream* (New York: Farrar, Straus and Giroux, 2009), 34–35, 37–41, 40–45, 87–93; Martin Durham, *White Rage: The Extreme Right and American Politics* (New York: Routledge, 2007), 39–42; James Ridgeway, *Blood in the Face: The Ku Klux Klan, Aryan Nations, Nazi Skinheads, and the Rise of a New White Culture* (New York: Thunder's Mouth Press, 1990), 85–88.

10. Anti-Defamation League, *Tattered Robes: The State of the Ku Klux Klan in the United States*, 2016, *Anti-Defamation League*, https://www.adl.org/education/resources/reports/state-of-the-kkk.

11. Ridgeway, *Blood in the Face*, 109–29; Thomas Murphy, with Steve Vetzner, "The Posse Comitatus in Wisconsin," *Public Eye* 3, nos. 1 and 2 (1981): 17–24 [Political Research Associates].

12. Ken Lawrence, "The Ku Klux Klan and Fascism" (speech to the National Anti-Klan Network Conference, Atlanta, 19 June 1982), *Urgent Tasks*, no. 14 (Fall/Winter 1982).

13. William L. Pierce [Andrew Macdonald, pseud.], *The Turner Diaries* (Arlington, VA: National Vanguard Books, 1978), 63.

14. Sara Diamond, *Roads to Dominion: Right-Wing Movements and Political Power in the United States* (New York: Guilford Press, 1995), 262–65, 270–73; Durham, *White Rage*, 44–45, 121–22.

15. Durham, *White Rage*, 30–31, 94–95; Ridgeway, *Blood in the Face*, 169–76; Zeskind, *Blood and Politics*, 215–16; Spencer Sunshine, "Nazi Skinhead Economics," *Souciant*, August 7, 2014, http://souciant.com/2014/08/nazi-skinhead-economics.

16. Zeskind, *Blood and Politics*, 91.

17. Durham, *White Rage*, 28.

18. Zeskind, *Blood and Politics*, 91–93.

19. Zeskind, *Blood and Politics*, 97–99; Durham, *White Rage*, 101–02; Ridgeway, *Blood in the Face*, 89–100. On the neo-Nazi underground in the 1980s, see Kathleen Belew, *Bring the War Home: The White Power Movement and Paramilitary America* (Cambridge, MA: Harvard University Press, 2018); Matthew N. Lyons, "Book Review: *Bring the War Home* by Kathleen Belew," *Three Way Fight* (blog), May 25, 2019, https://threeway fight.blogspot.com/2019/05/book-review-bring-war-home-by-kathleen.html.

20. David Cunningham, *There's Something Happening Here: The New Left, the Klan, and FBI Counterintelligence* (Berkeley, CA: University of California Press, 2004); John Drabble, "From White Supremacy to White Power: The FBI, COINTELPRO-WHITE HATE, and the Nazification of the Ku Klux Klan in the 1970s," *American Studies* 48, no. 3 (Fall 2007): 49–74; and Lyons, *Insurgent Supremacists*, 166–69.

21. Ward Churchill and Jim Vander Wall, *Agents of Repression: The FBI's Secret War Against the Black Panther Party and the American Indian Movement* (Boston: South End Press, 1988), 182; Everett R. Holles, "A.C.L.U. Says F.B.I. Funded 'Army' to Terrorize Antiwar Protesters," *The New York Times*, June 27, 1975; Noam Chomsky, "Domestic Terrorism: Notes on the State System of Oppression," *New Political Science* 21, no. 3 (September 1999): 303–24.

22. Frank Donner, *Protectors of Privilege: Red Squads and Police Repression in Urban America* (Berkeley, CA: University of California Press, 1990), 146–50.

23. Michael Newton, *The FBI and the KKK: A Critical History* (Jefferson, NC: MacFarland & Company, Inc., 2005), 170.

24. William Karl Ziegenhorn, "'No Rest for the Wicked': The FBI Investigations of White Supremacist Groups, 1983–1988" (master's thesis, San Jose State University, 1995), 16, 65–76, https://scholarworks.sjsu.edu/cgi/viewcontent.cgi?article=2041&context =etd_theses; Zeskind, *Blood and Politics*, 146–47, 158–69.

25. Dennis King, *Lyndon LaRouche and the New American Fascism* (New York: Doubleday, 1989), xiv, 377.

26. Zeskind, *Blood and Politics*, 148.

27. Intelligence Project of the Southern Poverty Law Project, "Terror From the Right: Plots, Conspiracies and Racist Rampages Since Oklahoma City," 2012, https://www .splcenter.org/sites/default/files/d6_legacy_files/downloads/publication/terror_ from_the_right_2012_web_0.pdf; Zeskind, *Blood and Politics*, 406, 414.

28. Zeskind, *Blood and Politics*, 279.

29. Louis Beam, "Leaderless Resistance" [1983 and 1992], *Army of God*, http://armyofgod .com/LeaderlessResistance.html.

30. Matthew N. Lyons, "Fragmented Nationalism: Right-Wing Responses to September 11 in Historical Context," *Pennsylvania Magazine of History and Biography* 127, no. 4 (December 2003): 398–401.

31. Patrick J. Buchanan, "Why I Am Running for President," *Human Events*, December 28, 1991, 11.

32. Southern Poverty Law Center, "The Second Wave: Return of the Militias," *Southern Poverty Law Center*, August 1, 2009, https://www.splcenter.org/20090731/second -wave-return-militias; Alexander Zaitchick, "'Patriot' Paranoia: A Look at the Top Ten Conspiracy Theories," *Intelligence Report*, August 1, 2010, https://www.splcenter .org/fighting-hate/intelligence-report/2010/patriot-paranoia-look-top-ten-conspiracy -theories; Berlet and Lyons, *Right-Wing Populism in America*, 258–60.

33. Robert H. Churchill, *To Shake Their Guns in the Tyrant's Face: Libertarian Political Violence and the Origins of the Militia Movement* (Ann Arbor: University of Michigan Press, 2009), 188–95; Berlet and Lyons, *Right-Wing Populism in America*, 290–92.

34. For a recent example of the former view, see Belew, *Bring the War Home*, 190–91; for the latter, see Churchill, *To Shake Their Guns in the Tyrant's Face*, 7–13. For an example of leftists seeing the militia movement as potential allies, see James Murray, "Chiapas & Montana: Tierra y Libertad," *Race Traitor*, no. 8 (Winter 1998), https://libcom .org/book/export/html/63630.

35. Zeskind, *Blood and Politics*, 359–60.

36. James Scaminaci III, *The Christian Right's Fourth Generation Warfare in America*, book 2, chapter 15: "The Christian Right and the Formation of the Patriot Militia," *Academia.edu*, 15–16, 23, https://www.academia.edu/19364671/CHAPTER_15_THE_ CHRISTIAN_RIGHT_AND_THE_FORMATION_OF_THE_PATRIOT_MILITIA; Mark Rupert, "Articulating Neoliberalism and Far-Right Conspiracism: The Case of the American 'Gun Rights' Culture" (lecture, International Studies Association, New Orleans, LA, February 2015); Churchill, *To Shake Their Guns in the Tyrant's Face*, 213–15; Ryan Lenz and Mark Potok, "War in the West: The Bundy Ranch Standoff and the American Radical Right," *Southern Poverty Law Center*, July 9, 2014, https:// www.splcenter.org/20140709/war-west-bundy-ranch-standoff-and-american-radical -right; William Kevin Burke, "The Wise Use Movement: Right-Wing Anti-Environmentalism," in Chip Berlet, ed., *Eyes Right! Challenging the Right Wing Backlash* (Boston: South End Press, 1995), 135–45.

37. Churchill, *To Shake Their Guns in the Tyrant's Face*, 201, 203–206, 224, 243; J. J. Johnson, "A Heartfelt Invitation to Black Americans," *The Buffalo Soldiers*, https:// www.zianet.com/web/blackman.htm; Southern Poverty Law Center, "False Patriots," *Intelligence Report*, May 8, 2001, https://www.splcenter.org/fighting-hate/ intelligence-report/2001/false-patriots.

38. Churchill, *To Shake Their Guns in the Tyrant's Face*, 180, 230, 265–66.

39. See Zeskind, *Blood and Politics*, 400, 456. In *Bring the War Home* (p. 215), Belew claims

that McVeigh served as security guard to Mark Koernke, one of the leaders of the militia movement's "millennial" wing. However, former Southern Poverty Law Center Senior Fellow Mark Potok counters that most experts see this claim as discredited. See Potok, "Book Review: 'Bring the War Home' by Kathleen Belew," *Center for Analysis of the Radical Right*, May 18, 2018, https://www.radicalrightanalysis.com/2018/05/18/book-review-bring-the-war-home-by-kathleen-belew.

40. On common law courts, see Mark Pitcavage, "Common Law and the Uncommon Courts: An Overview of the Common Law Court Movement," *Militia Watchdog*, July, 25 1997 [archived at *Anti-Defamation League* website].

41. See Vladmir I. Lenin, "The Dual Power," *Pravda*, no. 28, April 9, 1917, https://www.marxists.org/archive/lenin/works/1917/apr/09.htm; Black Rose Anarchist Federation, "Active Revolution: Organizing, Base Building and Dual Power," *Black Rose Anarchist Federation*, March 29, 2018, https://blackrosefed.org/base-building-dual-power; DSA Libertarian Socialist Caucus, "Dual Power: A Strategy to Build Socialism in Our Time," *DSA Libertarian Socialist Caucus*, December 31, 2018, https://dsa-lsc.org/2018/12/31/dual-power-a-strategy-to-build-socialism-in-our-time.

42. Zeskind, *Blood and Politics*, 365; Southern Poverty Law Center, "The 'Patriot' Movement Timeline," *Intelligence Report*, https://www.splcenter.org/fighting-hate/intelligence-report/2015/patriot-movement-timeline.

43. J. M. Berger, "PATCON Revealed: An Exclusive Look Inside The FBI's Secret War with the Militia Movement," *IntelWire*, October 8, 2007, http://news.intelwire.com/2007/10/patcon-revealed-exclusive-look-inside.html; "The Neo-Militia News Archive: January–June 1996: Militia Leader Revealed to have FBI Connections," *The Militia Watchdog*, June 19, 1996 [archived at *Anti-Defamation League* website]; Bill Swindell, "Militia Coordinator On Federal Payroll," *Tulsa World*, April 7, 1996.

44. Lincoln Caplan, "The Destruction of Defendants' Rights," *The New Yorker*, June 21, 2015, https://www.newyorker.com/news/news-desk/the-destruction-of-defendants-rights; Elaine Cassel, "Anti-Terrorism," *CounterPunch*, October 19, 2002, https://www.counterpunch.org/2002/10/19/anti-terrorism-2.

45. See Lyons, "Ctrl-Alt-Delete" or *Insurgent Supremacists*, chapter 4.

46. See Richard Spencer, "The Conservative Write," *Taki's Magazine*, August 6, 2008, https://www.takimag.com/article/the_conservative_write; Kevin DeAnna, "The Alternative Right," *Taki's Magazine*, July 26, 2009, https://www.takimag.com/article/the_alternative_right; and Jack Hunter, "Whither the Alternative Right?" *Taki's Magazine*, November 3, 2009, https://staging.takimag.com/article/whither_the_alternative_right.

47. Matthew N. Lyons, "AlternativeRight.com: Paleoconservatism for the 21st Century," *Three Way Fight* (blog), September 10, 2010, https://threewayfight.blogspot.com/2010/09/alternativerightcom-paleoconservatism.html.

48. Lyons, "AlternativeRight.com"; Berlet and Lyons, *Right-Wing Populism in America*, 283–84.

49. Roger Griffin, "*Plus ça change!* The Fascist Pedigree of the Nouvelle Droite," in Edward Arnold, ed., *The Development of the Radical Right in France 1890–1995* (London: Routledge, 2000) [available on *ResearchGate* (website)]; Anton Shekhovtsov, "Aleksandr Dugin's Neo-Eurasianism: The New Right a la Russe," *Religion Compass* 3, no. 4 (2009): 697–716; Alain de Benoist and Charles Champetier, "The French New Right in the Year 2000," *Telos*, no. 115 (Spring 1999): 117–44.

50. On *Counter-Currents Publishing*, see Greg Johnson, "Theory & Practice," *Counter-Currents Publishing*, September 30, 2010, https://counter-currents.com/2010/09/theory-practice.

51. See Lyons, *Insurgent Supremacists*, 70–76.

52. Dylan Matthews, "Why the Alt-Right Loves Single Payer Health Care," *Vox*, April 4, 2017, https://www.vox.com/policy-and-politics/2017/4/4/15164598/alt-right-single-payer-health-care-trump; Ahab, "Environmentalism and the Alt Right," *AltRight.com*, June 6, 2017.

53. Antifascist Front, "Alternative Internet Racism: Alt Right and the New Fascist Branding," *Anti-Fascist News*, December 18, 2015, https://antifascistnews.net/2015/12/18/alternative-internet-racism-alt-right-and-the-new-fascist-branding; George Hawley, *Making Sense of the Alt-Right* (New York: Columbia University Press, 2017), chapter 3.

54. See Lyons, *Insurgent Supremacists*, 66–69, 115–20; Matthew N. Lyons, "Alt-Right: More Misogynistic Than Many Neonazis," *Three Way Fight* (blog), December 3, 2016, https://threewayfight.blogspot.com/2016/12/alt-right-more-misogynistic-than-many.html.

55. Matthew N. Lyons, "The Alt-Right Hates Women as Much as It Hates People of Colour," *The Guardian*, May 2, 2017, https://www.theguardian.com/commentisfree/2017/may/02/alt-right-hates-women-non-white-trump-christian-right-abortion.

56. Lyons, *Insurgent Supremacists*, 65–66, 120–22; Ben Lorber, "Understanding Alt-Right Antisemitism," *Doikayt*, March 24, 2017, https://doikayt.com/2017/03/24/understanding-alt-right-antisemitism.

57. Hawley, *Making Sense of the Alt-Right*, 18–19, 25–26, 81–85, 94–96; Lyons, *Insurgent Supremacists*, 79–80.

58. Lyons, *Insurgent Supremacists*, 76–77.

59. Ted Sallis, "Democratic Multiculturalism: Strategy & Tactics," *Counter-Currents Publishing*, November 19, 2014, https://counter-currents.com/2014/11/democratic-multiculturalism.

60. See Matthew N. Lyons, "Trump: 'Anti-Political' or Right Wing?," *Three Way Fight* (blog), March 13, 2016, https://threewayfight.blogspot.com/2016/03/trump-anti-political-or-right-wing.html.

61. Lyons, *Insurgent Supremacists*, 78–79; Lyons, "Trump's Impact: A Fascist Upsurge Is Just One of the Dangers," *Three Way Fight* (blog), December 22, 2015, https://threewayfight.blogspot.com/2015/12/trumps-impact-fascist-upsurge-is-just.html.

62. On the alt-right's #DraftOurDaughters meme campaign, see Don Caldwell, "#DraftOurDaughters," *Know Your Meme*, October 28, 2016, https://knowyourmeme.com/memes/draftourdaughters; Lyons, *Insurgent Supremacists*, 80.

63. Lyons, *Insurgent Supremacists*, 80–82; Antifascist Front, "Going Full Fash: Breitbart Mainstreams the 'Alt Right,'" *Anti-Fascist News*, April 5, 2016, https://antifascistnews.net/2016/04/05/going-full-fash-breitbart-mainstreams-the-alt-right; Antifascist Front, "Meet the Alt Lite, the People Mainstreaming the Alt Right's White Nationalism," *Anti-Fascist News*, November 3, 2016, https://antifascistnews.net/2016/11/03/meet-the-alt-lite-the-people-mainstreaming-the-alt-rights-white-nationalism; Hawley, *Making Sense of the Alt-Right*, chapter 6.

64. Richard Spencer, "We the Vanguard Now," *Radix Journal*, November 9, 2016, https://radixjournal.com/2016/11/2016-11-9-we-the-vanguard-now; Matt Parrott, "Trump Apocalypse Now," *Traditionalist Worker Party*, November 10, 2016.

65. Antifascist Front, "The Alt Right Has Taken the Public Step Towards Violence," *Anti-Fascist News*, April 28, 2017, https://antifascistnews.net/2017/04/28/the-alt-right-has-taken-the-public-step-towards-violence; Emma Grey Ellis, "Don't Look Now, but Extremists' Meme Armies Are Turning Into Militias," *Wired*, April 20, 2017, https://www.wired.com/2017/04/meme-army-now-militia; "Gavin McInnes' 'Alt-Right' Fan Club Drifts Toward Neo-Nazi Violence," *IdaVox*, May 18, 2017, https://

idavox.com/index.php/2017/05/18/gavin-mcinnes-alt-right-fan-club-drifts-towards -neo-nazi-violence; Northern California Anti-Racist Action, "How 'Based Stickman' & Proud Boys are Working with Neo-Nazis in So-Cal," *It's Going Down*, July 8, 2017, https://itsgoingdown.org/based-stickman-proud-boys-working-neo-nazis-cal.

66. Spencer Sunshine, "I Almost Died in Charlottesville," *Colorlines*, August 15, 2017, https://www.colorlines.com/articles/i-almost-died-charlottesville; Jason Wilson, "Charlottesville Reveals an Emboldened Far Right That Can No Longer Be Ignored," *The Guardian*, August 14, 2017, https://www.theguardian.com/world/2017/aug/14/ charlottesville-far-right-neo-nazis-violence.

67. Michael Edison Hayden, "Is the Alt-Right Dying? White Supremacist Leaders Report Infighting and Defection," *Newsweek*, March 5, 2018, https://www .newsweek.com/alt-right-white-supremacist-movement-roiled-infighting-defection -and-arrests-831491; Shane Burley, "The Fall of the Alt-Right Came from Anti-Fascism," *Truthout*, April 7, 2018, https://truthout.org/articles/the-fall-of-the-alt -right-came-from-anti-fascism.

68. Lyons, *Insurgent Supremacists*, 206–8; Matthew N. Lyons, "'Racial Dissidents Have Lost the Ability to Organize Openly': Alt-Rightists on Trump, ICE, and What Is to Be Done," *Insurgent Notes*, August 4, 2018, http://insurgentnotes.com/2018/08/ racial-dissidents-have-lost-the-ability-to-organize-openly-alt-rightists-on-trump-ice-and-what-is-to-be-done. The quotation beginning with, "We were promised" is from Marcus Cicero, "President Trump Pulls Off Excellent Peace Talks With North Korea," *Occidental Dissent* (blog), *Occidental Dissent*, June 12, 2018, https://occidentaldissent.com/2018/06/12/president-trump -pulls-off-excellent-peace-talks-with-north-korea.

69. George Monbiot, "Neoliberalism—the Ideology at the Root of All Our Problems," *The Guardian*, April 15, 2016, https://www.theguardian.com/books/2016/apr/15/ neoliberalism-ideology-problem-george-monbiot; Arun Gupta, "How the Democrats Became the Party of Neoliberalism," *teleSUR*, October 31, 2014, https://www .telesurenglish.net/opinion/How-the-Democrats-Became-The-Party-of-Neoliberalism -20141031-0002.html; Thomas Ferguson, Paul Jorgensen, and Jie Chen, "Party Competition and Industrial Structure in the 2012 Elections," *International Journal of Political Economy* 42, no. 2 (Summer 2013): 3–41; Jeremy Scahill and Anthony Arnove, "Rebranding War and Occupation," *Socialist Worker*, https://socialistworker .org/2009/06/17/rebranding-war-and-occupation.

70. Henry Giroux, "Neoliberal Fascism and the Echoes of History," *TruthDig*, August 2, 2018, https://www.truthdig.com/articles/neoliberal-fascism-and-the-echoes -of-history; see also Anthony DiMaggio, "The Shutdown as Fascist Creep: Profiling Right-Wing Extremism in America," *CounterPunch*, January 4, 2019, https:// www.counterpunch.org/2019/01/04/the-shutdown-as-fascist-creep-profiling-right -wing-extremism-in-america.

71. On right-wing politics' complex relationship with neoliberalism and global capitalism in the current period, see Unity and Struggle, "Morbid Symptoms: The Rise of Trump," *Unity and Struggle*, November 15, 2016, http://www.unityandstruggle .org/2016/11/morbid-symptoms-the-rise-of-trump; Unity and Struggle, "Morbid Symptoms: The Downward Spiral," *Unity and Struggle*, December 19, 2016, http://www.unity andstruggle.org/2016/12/morbid-symptoms-the-downward-spiral; Bromma, "Notes on Trump (Dec. 2016 – Revised Jan. 2017)," *Kersplebedeb* (blog), December 17, 2016, https://kersplebedeb.com/posts/notes-on-trump.

72. See Butch Lee and Red Rover, *Night Vision: Illuminating War & Class on the Neo-Colonial Terrain* (New York: Vagabond Press, 1993); Bromma, "Exodus and Reconstruction:

Working-Class Women at the Heart of Globalization," *Kersplebedeb* (blog), September 11, 2012, https://kersplebedeb.com/posts/exodus.

73. Leo Ribuffo, *The Old Christian Right: The Protestant Far Right from the Great Depression to the Cold War* (Philadelphia: Temple University Press, 1983), 183, 193–211; David Caute, *The Great Fear: The Anti-Communist Purge Under Truman and Eisenhower* (New York: Simon and Schuster, 1978), 178.

Building Communities for a Fascist-Free Future / Shane Burley

1. Shane Burley, "Building Communities for a Fascist-Free Future," *ROAR Magazine*, Autumn 2021, https://roarmag.org/magazine/antifascism-building-communities.

2. Shane Burley, "Portland Anti-Fascist Coalition Shows Us How We Can Defeat the Far Right," *Truthout*, August 20, 2019, https://truthout.org/articles/portland-anti-fascist-coalition-shows-us-how-we-can-defeat-the-far-right.

3. Learn more about Pop Mob at popmobpdx.com.

4. Shane Burley, "Trump Losing the 2020 Election Has Only Increased the Chance of Right-Wing Violence," *NBC News*, August 14, 2021, https://www.nbcnews.com/think/opinion/trump-losing-2020-election-has-only-increased-chance-right-wing-ncna1276707.

5. Shane Burley, "A History of Violence," *Commune*, December 23, 2018, https://communemag.com/a-history-of-violence.

6. Shane Burley, "Deaths at the Capitol, a Pro-Trump, Far-Right Mob — and Months of Red Flags," *NBC News*, January 7, 2021, https://www.nbcnews.com/think/opinion/deaths-capitol-pro-trump-far-right-mob-months-red-flags-ncna1253205; David Neiwart, *Red Pill, Blue Pill: How to Counteract the Conspiracy Theories That Are Killing Us* (Lanham, MD: Prometheus Books, 2020).

7. David Renton, *No Free Speech for Fascists: Exploring "No Platform" in History, Law and Politics* (Abingdon, UK: Routledge, 2021).

8. Sam Levin, "White Supremacists and Militias Have Infiltrated Police Across US, Report Says," *The Guardian*, August 27, 2020, https://theguardian.com/us-news/2020/aug/27/white-supremacists-militias-infiltrate-us-police-report.

9. Shane Burley, "The Great 2020 Antifa Scare," *Political Research Associates*, July 13, 2021, https://www.politicalresearch.org/2021/07/13/great-2020-antifa-scare.

10. Shane Burley, "'A Huge Difference': Volunteers Mobilise in Oregon Fire Aftermath," *Al Jazeera*, September 25, 2020 https://www.aljazeera.com/news/2020/9/25/a-huge-difference-activists-mobilise-in-oregon-fire-aftermath.

11. Renton, *No Free Speech for Fascists*.

12. Learn more about Left Coast Right Watch at leftcoastrightwatch.org.

13. Sara Morrison, "How Feds Used a YouTube Livestream to Arrest a Portland Protester," *Vox*, July 21, 2020, https://vox.com/recode/2020/7/21/21332653/portland-oregon-protests-feds-dhs-youtube-livestream.

"We Can Do More Together" / Hilary A. Moore

1. "*OstDeutschland*" translates to "East Germany" or "Eastern Germany." This term refers to the region formerly known as the German Democratic Republic, a communist state that existed between 1949 and 1990.

2. Hilary Moore, "Nothing is Untouched: The Aftermath of Chemnitz," *Political*

Research Associates, June 11, 2020, https://www.politicalresearch.org/2020/06/11/ nothing-untouched.

3. For more information on far-right labels, brands, and tournaments, as well as analysis of responses from state structures, visit the organization No Hand Shake with Nazis at https://runtervondermatte.noblogs.org.

4. Ali Winston and A. C. Thompson, "American Hate Group Looks to Make Allies in Europe," *ProPublica*, July 5, 2018, https://www.propublica.org/article/ robert-rundo-denis-nikitin-hooligans-europe-hate-group.

5. United States Department of Justice, US Attorney's Office, Western District of Virginia, "Three Members of California-Based White Supremacist Group Sentenced on Riots Charges Related to August 2017 'Unite the Right' Rally in Charlottesville," news release, July 19, 2019, https://www.justice.gov/usao-wdva/pr/three-members-california-based-white-supremacist-group-sentenced-riots-charges -related.

6. Przemysław Witkowski, "Polish Pipe Fitters, Treatment of Gays and the 'Spirit of the Slavs,' That Is, the Extreme Right, Infiltrates Martial Arts [*Polscy fajterzy, leczenie gejów i „Duch Słowian", czyli skrajna prawica infiltruje sporty walki*]," *KrytykaPolityczna*, March 12, 2020, https://krytykapolityczna.pl/kraj/mma-skrajna -prawica-przemyslaw-witkowski.

7. Witkowski, "Polish Pipe Fitters."

8. Dominique Soguel and Monika Rębała, "When the Right Wing Is Still 'Too Socialist': Poland's Far Right Unites," *The Christian Science Monitor*, October 9, 2019, https:// www.csmonitor.com/World/Europe/2019/1009/When-the-right-wing-is-still-too -socialist-Poland-s-far-right-unites.

9. Marc Santora, "Poland's Populists Pick a New Top Enemy: Gay People," *The New York Times*, April 7, 2019, https://www.nytimes.com/2019/04/07/world/europe/poland -gay-rights.html.

10. Monika Sieradzka, "Poland Shocked by Documentary Exposing Church Pedophilia," *Deutsche Welle*, May 27, 2020, https://www.dw.com/en/pedophilia-shocks -polish-church/a-53590830.

11. Jan Cienski, "Poland's PiS in Bed with Catholic Church, Backs Abortion Ban," *Politico*, April 5, 2016, https://www.politico.eu/article/polands-church-state-alliance -to-ban-abortion.

12. Santora, "Poland's Populists Pick A New Top Enemy."

13. Claudia Ciobanu, "A Third of Poland Declared 'LGBT-Free Zone,'" *Balkaninsight*, February 25, 2020, https://balkaninsight.com/2020/02/25/a-third-of-poland -declared-lgbt-free-zone.

14. James Frater and Lianne Kolirin, "EU Blocks Funding for Six Towns That Declared Themselves 'LGBT-Free Zones,'" *CNN*, July 31, 2020, https://edition.cnn .com/2020/07/31/europe/poland-lgbt-eu-funding-intl/index.html.

15. Witkowski, "Polish Pipe Fitters."

16. Claudia Ciobanu, "Polish Far Right Emboldened By Ruling Party Propaganda," *Balkaninsight*, July 31, 2019, https://balkaninsight.com/2019/07/31/polish -far-right-emboldened.

17. Witkowski, "Polish Pipe Fitters."

18. Raphael Thelen, "How Germany's Citizens Arm," *Stern*, January 13, 2016, https:// www.stern.de/politik/deutschland/fluechtlinge-und-deutsche-angst--deutschlands -buerger-ruesten-auf-6644480.html.

19. Global Database on Violence Against Women, "Concluding Observations of the Committee on the Elimination of Discrimination against Women," January 19, 2009,

https://evaw-global-database.unwomen.org/en/countries/europe/germanyhttps://evaw-global-database.unwomen.org/en/countries/europe/germany.

20. Thelen, "How Germany's Citizens Arm."

21. Marcel Leubecher, "Martial Arts of the Antifa Causes Concern for the Protection of the Constitution," *Welt*, August 23, 2020, https://www.welt.de/politik/deutschland/article 214068746/Linksextremismus-Kampfsport-der-Antifa-bereitet-Verfassungsschutz -Sorge.html.

The Black Antifascist Tradition / Jeanelle K. Hope

1. Langston Hughes, "Too Much of Race," *The Crisis*, September 1937, 272.

2. Since the 2016 election of President Trump, the antifascist movement in the US has gained resurgence, largely in response to the Trump administration's regressive and fascist politics. In turn, the administration continually vilified "antifa," short for anti-fascism, going as far as to deem the ideology and movement participants domestic terrorists, anarchists, and fascists.

3. Jeanelle Hope, "Black Antifa AF: The Enduring Legacies of Black Anti-Fascism," *Essence*, June 20, 2020, https://www.essence.com/feature/fascism-black -antifa-rallies.

4. See Robin D. G. Kelley, *Freedom Dreams: The Black Radical Imagination* (Boston: Beacon Press, 2003); Gaye Theresa Johnson and Alex Lubin, eds., *Futures of Black Radicalism* (Brooklyn: Verso, 2017); George Lipsitz, *How Racism Takes Place* (Philadelphia: Temple University Press, 2011).

5. As mentioned in Mark Bray, *Antifa: The Anti-Fascist Handbook* (Brooklyn: Melville House, 2017), xvii; Aimé Césaire, *Discourse on Colonialism* (New York: Monthly Review Press, 2000), 36.

6. Leon Trotsky, *Fascism: What It Is and How to Fight It* (Atlanta: Pathfinder Press, 1996), https://www.marxists.org/archive/trotsky/works/1944/1944-fas.htm#p2.

7. Robert Wistrich, "Leon Trotsky's Theory of Fascism," *Journal of Contemporary History* 11, no. 4 (October 1976): 158.

8. Trotsky, *Fascism*.

9. Keith Crawford, *East Central European Politics Today: From Chaos to Stability?* (Manchester, UK: Manchester University Press, 1996), 44.

10. Crawford, *East Central European Politics Today*, 44.

11. Bill Mullen and Christopher Vials, eds., *The U.S. Anti-fascism Reader* (New York: Verso Books, 2020), 5.

12. For more on King Leopold II, see Adam Hochschild, *King Leopold's Ghost: A Story of Greed, Terror, and Heroism in Colonial Africa* (Boston: First Mariner Books, 1999).

13. Lisa Lowe, *The Intimacies of Four Continents* (Durham, NC: Duke University Press, 2015), 3.

14. Carol Boyce Davies, *Left of Karl Marx: The Political Life of Black Communist Claudia Jones* (Durham, NC: Duke University Press, 2008), 87.

15. Davies, *Left of Karl Marx*, 43.

16. Davies, *Left of Karl Marx*, 197.

17. As an internationally renowned artist and activist of the time, Robeson frequently traveled and performed. As the Cold War era intensified, Robeson's supportive comments about the Union of Soviet Socialist Republics and trips to the region were heavily scrutinized. These acts, as well as his refusal to sign a "loyalty oath," led to Robeson being stripped of his passport.

18. American Social History Project/Center for Media and Learning (Graduate Center, CUNY) and Roy Rosenzweig Center for History and New Media (George Mason University), "'You Are the Un-Americans, and You Ought to be Ashamed of Yourselves': Paul Robeson Appears Before HUAC," http://historymatters.gmu.edu/d/6440.

19. American Social History Project/Center for Media and Learning and Roy Rosenzweig Center for History and New Media, "'You Are the Un-Americans.'"

20. Johnetta Richards, "Fundamentally Determined: James E. Jackson and Esther Cooper Jackson and the Southern Negro Youth Congress, 1937–1946," *American Communist History* 7, no. 2 (2008): 200.

21. C. Alvin Hughes, "We Demand Our Rights: The Southern Negro Youth Congress, 1937–1949," *Phylon* 48, no. 1 (1987): 38.

22. Richards, "Fundamentally Determined," 202.

23. SNCC Digital Gateway, "Southern Negro Youth Congress Organizes March of Veterans Demanding the Vote in Birmingham," *SNCC Digital Gateway*, https://snccdigital.org/events/snyc-organizes-march-of-veterans-demanding-the-vote-in-birmingham.

24. Becci Robbins, *History Denied: Recovering South Carolina's Stolen Past* (Columbia, SC: South Carolina Progressive Network Education Fund and the Modjeska Simkins School for Human Rights, 2018), 3.

25. Richards, "Fundamentally Determined," 202.

26. Robbins, *History Denied*, 8.

27. Robbins, *History Denied*, 15.

28. Robbins, *History Denied*, 9.

29. Robbins, *History Denied*, 10.

30. Robbins, *History Denied*, 11.

31. *The Lighthouse and Informer* was an African-American newspaper based in Charleston, South Carolina that ran from 1941–54 and was edited by John Henry McCray.

32. Noah Berlatsky, "At the United Nations, Chicago Activists Protest Police Brutality," *The Atlantic*, November 17, 2014, https://www.theatlantic.com/national/archive/2014/11/we-charge-genocide-movement-chicago-un/382843.

33. United Nations, "History of the United Nations," *United Nations*, https://www.un.org/en/sections/history/history-united-nations/index.html.

34. William L. Patterson, ed., *We Charge Genocide: The Crime of the Government Against the Negro People* (New York: International Publishers, 2017), xxv–xxvi.

35. Ida B. Wells-Barnett, "Southern Horrors: Lynch Law and All Its Phases," 1892, https://www.gutenberg.org/files/14975/14975-h/14975-h.htm.

36. Wells-Barnett, "Southern Horrors."

37. Charles Martin, "Internationalizing 'The American Dilemma': The Civil Rights Congress and the 1951 Genocide Petition to the United Nations," *Journal of American Ethnic History* 16, no. 4 (1997): 37.

38. Martin, "Internationalizing 'The American Dilemma,'" 38.

39. Martin, "Internationalizing 'The American Dilemma,'" 39.

40. Martin, "Internationalizing 'The American Dilemma,'" 40.

41. United Nations, "The Genocide Convention," *United Nations Office on Genocide Prevention and the Responsibility to Protect*, https://www.un.org/en/genocideprevention/genocide-convention.shtml.

42. Martin, "Internationalizing 'The American Dilemma,'" 43.

43. Gerald Horne, *Black Revolutionary: William Patterson and the Globalization of the African American Freedom Struggle* (Champaign, IL: University of Illinois Press, 2013).

44. Horne, *Black Revolutionary*, 27.

45. Horne, *Black Revolutionary*, 29.

46. William L. Patterson, *The Man Who Cried Genocide: An Autobiography* (New York: International Publishers, 2017), 156.

47. Patterson, *The Man Who Cried Genocide*, 157.

48. Martin, "Internationalizing 'The American Dilemma,'" 44.

49. Martin, "Internationalizing 'The American Dilemma,'" 46.

50. Patterson, *We Charge Genocide*, 23–24.

51. Patterson, *We Charge Genocide*, 81.

52. Patterson, *We Charge Genocide*, 153.

53. Martin, "Internationalizing 'The American Dilemma,'" 49.

54. For more on the BPP and state repression, see Joshua Bloom and Waldo E. Martin, Jr., *Black Against Empire: The History of the Black Panther Party* (Oakland, CA: University of California Press, 2013); It's About Time Black Panther Party Digital Archive, "Sacramento Chapter of the Black Panther Party," *It's About Time Black Panther Party Legacy & Alumni*, http://www.itsabouttimebpp.com/chapter_history/pdf/sacramento/sacramento_chapter_of_the_black_panther.pdf.

55. Bigman, "Fascist California Grape Growers Use Mass Media to Combat a Living Wage," *The Black Panther*, July 26, 1969, 18.

56. John E. Moore, "People of the Community VS the Slumlords and Fascist Pigs of Winston-Salem," *The Black Panther*, March 1970, 2.

57. Moore, "People of the Community," 2.

58. See Robyn Spencer, *The Revolution Has Come: Black Power, Gender, and the Black Panther Party in Oakland* (Durham, NC: Duke University Press, 2016); Bloom and Martin, Jr., *Black Against Empire*; Aaron Dixon, *My People Are Rising: Memoir of a Black Panther Party Captain* (Chicago: Haymarket Books, 2012); Alondra Nelson, *Body and Soul: The Black Panther Party and the Fight Against Medical Racism* (Minneapolis: University of Minnesota Press, 2011); Donna Jean Murch, *Living for the City: Migration, Education, and the Rise of the Black Panther Party in Oakland, California* (Chapel Hill, NC: University of North Carolina Press, 2010); Charles E. Jones, ed., *The Black Panther Party Reconsidered* (Baltimore: Black Classic Press, 1998).

59. Aside from Spencer's essay, "The Black Panther Party and Black Anti-Fascism in the United States," very few scholarly works exist on the topic. Robyn C. Spencer, "The Black Panther Party and Black Anti-Fascism in the United States," *Duke University Press* (blog), January 26, 2017, https://dukeupress.wordpress.com/2017/01/26/the-black-panther-party-and-black-anti-fascism-in-the-united-states.

60. Jeanelle K. Hope, "Black, Yellow, and Shades of Purple: Radical Afro-Asian Collective Activism in the San Francisco Bay Area from the Perspectives of Women in the Struggle, 1966–1972" (master's thesis, Syracuse University, 2014), 96.

61. Bobby Seale, "What is the United Front Against Fascism?," *The Black Panther*, June 1969, 19.

62. Spencer, "The Black Panther Party."

63. Hope, "Black, Yellow, and Shades of Purple," 97.

64. The Black Panther Party, the International Liberation School, and the National Committees to Combat Fascism, "Poster for the National Conference for a United Front Against Fascism," *Student Digital Gallery*, http://digitalgallery.bgsu.edu/student/items/show/6582.

65. Roberta Alexander, "Black Panther Tells IT Like it Is: U.F.A.F Women's Panel: Roberta Alexander at Conference," *The Black Panther*, August 1969, 7.

66. Penny Nakatsu, "Penny Nakatsu, speech at the United Front Against Fascism Conference, July 1969," in Bill Mullen and Christopher Vials, eds., *The U.S. Anti-fascism Reader* (New York: Verso Books, 2020), 270–71.

Notes

67. Author interview with Gayle, Sacramento, California, 2013.
68. It's About Time Black Panther Party Digital Archive, "The Intercommunal Committee to Combat Fascism (ICCF)," *It's About Time Black Panther Party Legacy & Alumni*, http://www.itsabouttimebpp.com/Our_Stories/Chapter1/The_iccf.html.
69. It's About Time, "The Intercommunal Committee to Combat Fascism (ICCF)."
70. Huey P. Newton and Vladmir I. Lenin, *Revolutionary Intercommunialism and the Right of Nations to Self-Determination*, ed. Amy Gdala (Wales, UK: Superscript, 2004), 31.
71. Newton and Lenin, *Revolutionary Intercommunialism*, 32.
72. Delio Vasquez, "Intercommunalism: The Late Theorizations of Huey P. Newton, 'Chief Theoretician' of the Black Panther Party," *Viewpoint Magazine*, June 11, 2018, https://www.viewpointmag.com/2018/06/11/intercommunalism-the-late-theorizations-of-huey-p-newton-chief-theoretician-of-the-black-panther-party.
73. Although MOVE mostly operated as an anarchist collective, John Africa served as a leader, thus creating some sense of a loose hierarchical structure.
74. Dana Williams, "Black Panther Radical Factionalization and the Development of Black Anarchism," *Journal of Black Studies* 46, no. 7 (October 2015): 686.
75. Williams, "Black Panther Radical Factionalization," 686.
76. Assata Shakur, *Assata: An Autobiography* (Chicago: Lawrence Hill Books, 2001).
77. Ashanti Alston, "The Panthers, the Black Liberation Army and the Struggle to Free all Political Prisoners and Prisoners of War" (speech, Law and Disorder Conference, Portland, OR, April 2010, https://theanarchistlibrary.org/library/ashanti-omowali-alston-the-panthers-the-black-liberation-army-and-the-struggle-to-free-all-poli).
78. Alston, "The Panthers, the Black Liberation Army."
79. Ashanti was also charged with burglary; however, he maintains that this was a political act because he was stealing to fund the BLA.
80. Alston, "The Panthers, the Black Liberation Army."
81. Alston, "The Panthers, the Black Liberation Army."
82. Cathy Cohen, "Punks, Bulldaggers, and Welfare Queens: The Radical Potential of Queer Politics?," *GLQ: A Journal of Lesbian & Gay Studies* 3 (1997): 439.
83. Cohen, "Punks, Bulldaggers, and Welfare Queens," 439.
84. Street Transvestite Action Revolutionaries, *Street Transvestite Action Revolutionaries: Survival, Revolt, and Queer Antagonist Struggle*, https://untorellipress.noblogs.org/files/2011/12/STAR.pdf.
85. New York Public Library, "Street Transvestites Action Revolutionaries," *1969 The Year of Gay Liberation*, http://web-static.nypl.org/exhibitions/1969/revolutionaries.html.
86. Marsha P. Johnson, "Rapping with a Street Transvestite Revolutionary: An Interview with Marsha P. Johnson," in Street Transvestite Action Revolutionaries, *Street Transvestite Action Revolutionaries*.
87. Arthur Bell, "STAR trek," *The Village Voice* (New York), July 1971, 1.
88. Critical Resistance, "About," *Critical Resistance*, http://criticalresistance.org/about.
89. In 2012, CeCe McDonald, a Black transwoman, was sentenced to serve 41 months for second-degree manslaughter. McDonald and a group of her friends were verbally and physically attacked while passing by a bar in June 2011. As an act of self-defense, McDonald fatally stabbed her assailant in the chest with a pair of scissors or sharp object. Throughout the pretrial proceedings, McDonald argued that she feared for her life and that the assailant had spouted several transphobic and racist epithets during the altercation. However, the judge dismissed most of McDonald's evidence of self-defense, including a toxicology report that proved her assailant had methamphetamine in his system and a report that he had a swastika tattoo on his chest,

among other pieces of key information. After realizing that she would not fare well during trial given the dismissal of key evidence, McDonald chose to accept a plea bargain. Throughout her incarceration, she was forced to reside in two men's facilities and was denied hormone treatment. After serving 19 months, McDonald was released in January 2014.

90. CeCe McDonald, "Foreword," in Eric A. Stanley and Nat Smith, eds., *Captive Genders: Trans Embodiment and the Prison Industrial Complex*, 2nd ed. (Chico, CA: AK Press, 2015), 2.

91. See Barbara Ransby, *Making All Black Lives Matter: Reimagining Freedom in the Twenty-First Century* (Oakland, CA: University of California Press, 2018); Keeanga-Yamahtta Taylor, *From #BlackLivesMatter to Black Liberation* (Chicago: Haymarket Books, 2016).

92. Avery Gordon, "Some Thoughts on Haunting and Futurity," *borderlands* 10, no. 2 (2011): 8.

93. Gordon, "Some Thoughts on Haunting and Futurity," 8.

The Campus Antifascist Network / Maximilian Alvarez

1. See the complete CAN syllabus at http://campusantifascistnetwork.com/resources.

2. Mullen illustrates this well in his primary-source anthology: Bill Mullen and Christopher Vials, eds., *The U.S. Anti-fascism Reader* (New York: Verso Books, 2020).

3. See Clayton J. Plake and Edna Bonhomme, "Opposing Far-Right and Openly Fascist Groups on Campus," *University World News*, September 15, 2017, universityworldnews .com/post.php?story=20170912130021905.

Lessons from a Lifetime of Antiracist and Antifascist Struggle / Michael Novick

1. I am a veteran and cofounder of the JBAKC, PART in Los Angeles (LA), the ARA Network, the Torch Network, and White People for Black Lives, the SURJ affiliate in LA.

2. Brooklyn College is now 50% larger than when I attended; is now 70% people of color, predominantly low-income and including immigrants and refugees from all over the world, as well as many Black and brown Brooklynites; still has a sterling academic reputation; and reports that 40% of their graduates were the first in their family to earn a college degree.

3. This had grown out of the network that came together to reprint and distribute the book *Prairie Fire*, produced clandestinely by the WUO.

4. This same error gripped many somewhat more proletarianized New Left organizations in the same period, as an alphabet soup of new communist parties declared themselves and tried to subsume various Black, Asian, Puerto Rican, and Chicano/Mexicano organizations into "multiracial" but often white-dominated Maoist (or sometimes Trotskyist) formations.

5. Also known as Estado Libre Asociado (ELA).

6. "Bonehead" is a term used to describe neo-Nazi skinheads because the term "skinhead" itself is contested space, used also by antiracist and traditionalist skinheads. The argument goes that, by calling them boneheads, the neo-Nazi skinheads no longer are able to claim themselves to be the legitimate inheritors of the skinhead tradition.

7. As George Jackson said, "Settle your quarrels, come together, understand the reality

of our situation, understand that fascism is already here, that people are dying who could be saved, that generations more will die or live poor butchered half-lives if you fail to act." See George L. Jackson, *Blood in My Eye* (Baltimore, MD; Black Classic Press, 1996).

8. See Jeanelle K. Hope's chapter, "The Black Antifascist Tradition: A Primer" and Mike Bento's chapter, "Five Hundred Years of Fascism."

9. See Kim Kelly's chapter, "Antifascism Is Not a Crime: An Interview with David Campbell."

10. I invite discussion of these ideas, which continue to appear in the pages of *Turning the Tide: Journal of Inter-communal Solidarity*, available from Anti-Racist Action Los Angeles/People Against Racist Terror (ARA-LA/PART), PO Box 1055, Culver City CA 90232 or online at https://www.antiracist.org, where you can also subscribe to a periodic ARA e-newsletter that we produce and distribute via email.

It Takes a Network to Defeat a Network / Emmi Bevensee and Frank Miroslav

1. Kim Kelly, "The 3D-Printed Gun Isn't Coming. It's Already Here," *GEN*, August 13, 2020, https://gen.medium.com/the-3d-printed-gun-isnt-coming-it-s-already-here -6855fd394a47.

2. Emmi Bevensee, "The Decentralized Web of Hate," *Rebellious Data*, October 29, 2020, https://rebelliousdata.com/p2p.

3. David Hambling, "Mexican Drug Cartel Carries Out 'Drone Strikes' In Gang War," *Forbes*, August 24, 2020, https://www.forbes.com/sites/davidhambling/2020/08/24/ mexican-drug-cartel-carries-out-drone-strikes-in-gang-war/#31507bbb9432.

4. This definition is drawn from complex systems theorist Yaneer Bar-Yam's paper "Complexity Rising: From Human Beings to Human Civilization." See Yaneer Bar-Yam, "Complexity Rising: From Human Beings to Human Civilization, a Complexity Profile," in *Encyclopedia of Life Support Systems (EOLSS)*, developed under the Auspices of the UNESCO (Oxford: EOLSS Publishers, 2002), https://necsi.edu/ complexity-rising-from-human-beings-to-human-civilization-a-complexity-profile.

5. Martin Gurri's *The Revolt of the Public: And The Crisis of Authority in the New Millennium* (San Francisco; Stripe Press, 2018) is a good, albeit conservative, overview of how the elite were caught off guard by the public having increased access to information in such a short amount of time.

6. Susannah George, "The Taliban and the Afghan Government Are Finally Talking Peace: What They're Negotiating and What to Expect," *The Washington Post*, September 13, 2020, washingtonpost.com/world/asia_pacific/afghan-talks-faq/2020/ 09/13/68675d94-f4f8-11ea-8025-5d3489768ac8_story.html.

7. Gabriel Emile Hine, Jeremiah Onaolapo, Emiliano De Cristofaro, Nicolas Kourtellis, Ilias Leontiadis, Riginos Samaras, Gianluca Stringhini, and Jeremy Blackburn, "Kek, Cucks, and God Emperor Trump: A Measurement Study of 4chan's Politically Incorrect Forum and Its Effects on the Web," *arXiv*, October 1, 2017, https://arxiv .org/abs/1610.03452.

8. Siddharth Venkataramakrishnan, "Defying Crackdowns, QAnon Continues Its Relentless Global Spread," *Financial Times*, 2020, https://www.ft.com/content /2b51118a-5162-4189-8817-56a43ce69416.

9. Center for Strategic and International Studies, "The Age of Mass Protests: Understanding an Escalating Global Trend," March 2, 2020, https://www.csis.org/analysis/ age-mass-protests-understanding-escalating-global-trend.

10. The Soufan Center, "The Atomwaffen Division: The Evolution of the White Supremacist Threat," *The Soufan Center*, August 2020, https://thesoufancenter.org/wp-content/uploads/2020/08/The-Atomwaffen-Division-The-Evolution-of-the-White-Supremacy-Threat-August-2020-.pdf.

11. "13-year-old Found To Be Leader of International Neo Nazi Group, Marcy Oster, *Jewish Journal*, April 12, 2020, https://jewishjournal.com/news/314051/13-year-old-found-to-be-leader-of-international-neo-nazi-group.

12. Jason Wilson, "Prepping for a Race War: Documents Reveal Inner Workings Of Neo-Nazi Group, *The Guardian*, January 25, 2020, https://www.theguardian.com/world/2020/jan/25/inside-the-base-neo-nazi-terror-group. Ben Makuch and Mack Lamoureux, "Neo-Nazi Terror Leader Said to Have Worked With U.S. Special Forces," *Vice*, September 24, 2020, https://www.vice.com/en_us/article/k7qdzv/neo-nazi-terror-leader-said-to-have-worked-with-us-special-forces.

13. Eugene Antifa, "Feuerkrieg Division Exposed: International Neo-Nazi Terrorist Network," *Eugene Antifa*, February 24, 2020, https://eugeneantifa.noblogs.org/post/2020/02/24/feuerkrieg-division.

14. J. M. Berger, "The Strategy of Violent White Supremacy Is Evolving," *The Atlantic*, August 7, 2019, https://www.theatlantic.com/ideas/archive/2019/08/the-new-strategy-of-violent-white-supremacy/595648.

15. Kelly Weill, "Neo-Nazi Group Implodes Over Love Triangle Turned Trailer Brawl," *The Daily Beast*, May 14, 2018, www.thedailybeast.com/matthew-heimbachs-traditional-workers-party-implodes-over-love-triangle-turned-trailer-brawl.

16. Emmi Bevensee, "You Are Not Alone!: Stigmergic Parity and Revolt," *Center for a Stateless Society*, January 4, 2019, https://c4ss.org/content/51553. Ali Fisher, "Swarmcast: How Jihadist Networks Maintain a Persistent Online Presence," *Perspectives on Terrorism* 9, no. 3 (2015): 3–20.

17. The classic text on this form of organizing is Clay Shirky, *Here Comes Everybody: The Power of Organizing Without Organizations* (New York: Penguin Books, 2008).

18. David Wengrow, "A History of True Civilisation is Not One of Monuments," *Aeon*, October 2, 2018, https://aeon.co/ideas/a-history-of-true-civilisation-is-not-one-of-monuments.

19. See Chet Richard, *Certain to Win: The Strategy of John Boyd, Applied to Business* (self-pub., Xlibris Corporation, 2004).

20. John Arquilla, "It Takes a Network," *LA Times*, August 25, 2002, https://www.latimes.com/archives/la-xpm-2002-aug-25-op-arquilla25-story.html.

21. Quoted in Michael Miklaucic, "An Interview with Stanley McChrystal," *PRISM*, December 7, 2016, https://cco.ndu.edu/PRISM-6-3/Article/1020271/an-interview-with-stanley-mcchrystal.

22. Such attempts at control are likely to come with massive consequences and unforeseen trade-offs beyond just being literally 1984. The classic text on the subject is James C. Scott, *Seeing Like a State: How Certain Schemes to Improve the Human Condition Have Failed* (New Haven, CT: Yale University Press, 1998). For a more recent take that incorporates developments in artificial intelligence (AI), see Henry Farrell, "Seeing Like a Finite State Machine," *Crooked Timber*, November 25, 2019, https://crookedtimber.org/2019/11/25/seeing-like-a-finite-state-machine.

23. Jared Holt, "Richard Spencer: The Alt-Right Is Not Pro-Free Speech," *Right Wing Watch*, May 23, 2018, https://www.rightwingwatch.org/post/richard-spencer-the-alt-right-is-not-pro-free-speech.

24. Prior to the internet and cheap information technology, media access was restricted by how expensive broadcast and recording technology was. When it comes to

political competition, outsiders are restricted by ballot access laws, a winner-take-all voting structure, and lack of access to debates (in America, anyway).

25. Jason Wilson, "The Weakening of the 'Alt-Right': How Infighting and Doxxing Are Taking a Toll, January 25, 2017, *The Guardian*, https://www.theguardian.com/world/2017/jan/25/alt-right-movement-doxxing-richard-spencer-interview.

26. This problem is known as the "Ontological Update Problem in AI." The classic paper on this is Peter de Blanc, "Ontological Crises in Artificial Agents' Value Systems," *Machine Intelligence Research Institute*, May 2019, http://intelligence.org/files/OntologicalCrises.pdf.

27. Christopher Boehm, Harold B. Barclay, Robert Knox Dentan, Marie-Claude Dupre, Jonathan D. Hill, Susan Kent, Bruce M. Knauft, Keith F. Otterbein, and Steve Rayner, "Egalitarian Behavior and Reverse Dominance Hierarchy," *Current Anthropology* 43, no. 3 (1993), https://www.journals.uchicago.edu/doi/epdfplus/10.1086/204166.

28. Kate Starbird, "Information Wars: A Window into the Alternative Media Ecosystem," *Design, Use, Build*, March 15, 2017, https://medium.com/hci-design-at-uw/information-wars-a-window-into-the-alternative-media-ecosystem-a1347f32fd8f; Emmi Bevensee, "How COVID and Syria Conspiracy Theories Introduce Fascism to the Left Part 3: The Red-Brown Media Spectrum," *Centre for Analysis of the Radical Right*, September 25, 2020, http://www.radicalrightanalysis.com/2020/09/25/1-6-2.

29. Large corporations also do this; see, for example, the infamous Amazon ambassador program on Twitter: Ken Klippenstein, "Amazon's Twitter Army Was Handpicked for 'Great Sense of Humor,' Leaked Document Reveals," *The Intercept*, March 31, 2021, https://theintercept.com/2021/03/30/amazon-twitter-ambassadors-jeff-bezos-bernie-sanders.

30. For an overview of the concept, see Christopher Paul and Miriam Matthews, "The Russian 'Firehose of Falsehood' Propaganda Model: Why It Might Work and Options to Counter It," *RAND Corporation*, 2016, https://www.rand.org/pubs/perspectives/PE198.html.

31. Sarin, *Bodyhammer: Tactics and Self-Defense for the Modern Protester, Sprout Distro*, 2012, https://www.sproutdistro.com/catalog/zines/direct-action/bodyhammer.

32. Agency: An Anarchist PR Project, https://www.anarchistagency.com.

33. One of the most important guides for this is "Exposing the Invisible – The Kit," available at https://kit.exposingtheinvisible.org/en.

34. Internet Archive, https://archive.org/index.php. Archive.Today, https://archive.ph

35. The Social Media Analysis Toolkit (SMAT) is an important resource for this work: https://www.smat-app.com.

36. Kashmir Hill, "Activists Turn Facial Recognition Tools Against the Police," *The New York Times*, October 21, 2020, https://www.nytimes.com/2020/10/21/technology/facial-recognition-police.html.

37. Allan Hoffman, "The Vulnerable Society," *Lapsed Physicist* (blog), July 19, 2017, http://www.lapsedphysicist.org/2017/07/19/the-vulnerable-society.

38. Shodan, https://www.shodan.io.

39. Brian Eckhouse, "Solar and Wind Cheapest Sources of Power in Most of the World, *Bloomberg News*, April 28, 2020, https://www.bloomberg.com/news/articles/2020-04-28/solar-and-wind-cheapest-sources-of-power-in-most-of-the-world.

40. G. Hays and Ivan T. with N.R. Jenzen-Jones, "ARES Research Report No. 8 Desktop Firearms: Emergent Small Craft Production Technologies," *Armament Research Services*, March 30, 2020, https://armamentresearch.com/wp-content/uploads/2020/03/ARES-Research-Report-8-Desktop-Firearms.pdf.

41. See FarmBot, https://farm.bot.

42. Gufi.net is the largest mesh network in the world, spanning over 60,000 kilometers in Spain.

43. Four Thieves Vinergar, https://fourthievesvinegar.org.

44. David L. Chandler, "Simple, Solar-Powered Water Desalination," *MIT News*, February 6, 2020, https://news.mit.edu/2020/passive-solar-powered-water-desalination-0207.

45. WikiHouse, https://www.wikihouse.cc.

46. Open Source Ecology, https://www.opensourceecology.org.

47. Catherine Tubb and Tony Seb, "Rethinking Food and Agriculture 2020–2030: The Second Domestication of Plants and Animals, the Disruption of the Cow, and the Collapse of Industrial Livestock Farming," *RethinkX*, 2019, https://www.rethinkx.com/food-and-agriculture.

48. An example of such a call for autarky can be found in Curtis Yarvin, "RIP Globalism, Dead of Coronavirus," *The American Mind*, February 1, 2020, https://americanmind.org/essays/rip-globalism-dead-of-coronavirus.

49. See Ronald F. Ingelhart, "Changing Values among Western Publics from 1970 to 2006," *West European Politics* 31, no. 1–2 (2008): 130–46.

50. Bevensee, "The Decentralized Web of Hate."

51. Scuttlebutt Social Network, https://www.scuttlebutt.nz.

52. Alexander Cobleigh, "TrustNet," *cblgh*, June 29, 2020, https://cblgh.org/trustnet.

53. Emmi Bevensee, "Reputation Markets: Reality, Dangers, and Possibility," *Center for a Stateless Society*, June 18, 2019, https://c4ss.org/content/52196.

54. LibreMesh, https://libremesh.org.

55. @luandro, "Connecting peoples of the Earth," Scuttlebutt, https://viewer.scuttlebot.io/%25hMC%2FIx%2FmnDvkoKYGcvXGo%2FKt8UuegWYz6vB91RyhIKQ%3D.sha256.

56. CryptoParty, https://www.cryptoparty.in.

57. Electronic Frontier Foundation, "Surveillance Self-Defense: Tips, Tools and How-tos for Safer Online Communications," *Electronic Frontier Foundation*, https://ssd.eff.org; DeepMay, https://www.deepmay.io.

58. For a quick summary, see Kevin Carson, "The Iron Fist Behind the Invisible Hand: Corporate Capitalism As a State-Guaranteed System of Privilege," *Mutualist.Org*, 2001, http://www.mutualist.org/id4.html.

59. Cory Doctorow, "Coase's Specter," *Crooked Timber*, May 10, 2017, https://crookedtimber.org/2017/05/10/coases-spectre.

Subcultural Antifascism / Ryan Smith

1. Carolyn Holland, "Centering Frontline Communities," *Ecotrust*, May 20, 2017, https://ecotrust.org/centering-frontline-communities.

2. CrimethInc. ex-Workers' Collective, "How Antifascists Won the Battles of Berkeley." *It's Going Down*, January 3, 2018, https://itsgoingdown.org/antifascists-won-battles-berkeley.

3. Arun Gupta, "Riotlandia: Why Portland Has Become the Epicenter of Far-Right Violence," *The Intercept*, August 16, 2019, https://theintercept.com/2019/08/16/portland-far-right-rally.

4. Jason Wilson, "Portland Police and Far Right Leader Had Friendly Relationship, Texts Reveal," *The Guardian*, February 15, 2019, https://www.theguardian.com/world/2019/feb/15/joey-gibson-portland-police-relationship-cooperation-text-messages.

5. Jamie Mann and Billy Briggs, "Right-Wing Hatemongers Flee Glasgow Pub After

Anti-fascist Group Arrive to Confront Them," *Daily Record*, August 21, 2017, https://www.dailyrecord.co.uk/news/scottish-news/right-wing-nerds-flee-glasgow-11023129; "Glasgow ANTI-fascists Mobilise to See Off Far Right Rally," *Freedom News*, July 20, 2018, https://freedomnews.org.uk/glasgow-antifascists-mobilise-to-see-off-Far Right-rally.

6. Wee Ginger Dug, "End the Annual Shame of Orange Order Marches," *The National*, July 11, 2018, https://www.thenational.scot/politics/16345692.end-the-annual-shame -of-orange-order-marches; "Glasgow Marches to Go Ahead in Fear of Flute Band Reprisal," *STV News*, September 19, 2019, https://stv.tv/news/west-central /1440900-glasgow-marches-to-go-ahead-in-fear-of-flute-band-s-reprisal.

7. Antonio Gramsci, *Selections from the Prison Notebooks*, (London: Lawrence and Wisehart, 2003), 8–11.

8. Tyler Dupont, "From Core to Consumer: The Informal Hierarchy of the Skateboard Scene," *Journal of Contemporary Ethnography* 43, no. 5 (2014): 564.

9. Dupont, "From Core to Consumer," 560–61.

10. Kim Kelly, "Riding the New Wave of Anti-fascist Black Metal," *Vice*, August 23, 2018, https://www.vice.com/en_uk/article/ywkj8y/riding-the-new-wave-of-antifascist -black-metal.

11. *Innengard* means something akin to "in group," and *utengard* means something like "out group." These are concepts embedded into Heathen philosophy, yet are misinterpreted by white nationalists to be about ethnic inclusion and exclusion.

12. Two Viking Age kings of Norway whose regimes were especially despotic. Harald's byname Hard-Ruler was a direct reference to his tyrannical reign and Erik Bloodaxe was driven from the throne by a popular revolt. Both are glamorized in pop culture surrounding the period as fearsome Viking warriors in ways that gloss over how widely hated they actually were.

13. Some Heathens refer to fellow practitioners who are part of the same local group, known alternatively as kindreds, fellowships, or *blotlags* (blot-teams), as kinsmen, kinswomen, and kinfolk. There is also a divide within inclusive Heathen practice between more centrist elements, who often self-identify as liberals, and actively antiracist elements, who often self-identify as radicals.

14. A joint declaration released in September 2016 by 189 Norse Pagan organizations from around the world titled "Declaration 127" denounced and disavowed the Asatru Folk Assembly, the largest and most well-known promoter of fascism in Heathenry. See http://declaration127.com.

15. Hank Shteamer, "Brooklyn Anti-Fascist Metal Fest Was a Beacon for a Troubled Scene," *Rolling Stone*, January 28, 2019, https://www.rollingstone.com/music/music -live-reviews/black-flags-over-brooklyn-kim-kelly-anti-fascist-metal-fest-785088; Vince Bellino, "Bindrune Releases 'Overgrow to Overthrow' Compilation," *Decibel Magazine*, July 3, 2020, https://www.decibelmagazine.com/2020/07/03/bindrune -releases-overgrow-to-overthrow-compilation.

16. Declaration 127, http://www.declaration127.com; Between the Veils, "About BTV," *Between the Veils*, https://www.betweentheveils.org/about.

Why Does the US Far Right Love Bashar al-Assad? / Leila al-Shami and Shon Meckfessel

1. "Bashar al-Assad's White Supremacist Fans in Charlottesville," *The New Arab*, August 13, 2017, https://english.alaraby.co.uk/english/blog/2017/8/13/bashar-al -assads-white-supremacist-fans-in-charlottesville.

2. Yaakov Lappin, "White Supremacist Holds Rally in Syria," *Ynet News*, November 27, 2005, https://www.ynetnews.com/articles/0,7340,L-3175767,00.html.

3. Richard B. Spencer (@RichardBSpencer), "#StandWithAssad," Twitter, April 7, 2017, 12:47 a.m., https://twitter.com/RichardBSpencer/status/850208440899182592.

4. Richard B. Spencer (@RichardBSpencer), "The #AltRight is against a war in Syria," Twitter, April 6, 2017, 4:30 p.m., https://twitter.com/richardbspencer/status/850083186713513985.

5. *VDARE* (@vdare), "The #AltRight is now totally independent of Trump," Twitter, April 6, 2017, 11:05 p.m., https://twitter.com/vdare/status/850182790616408065.

6. Chris Menahan, "Ann Coulter: 'I Don't Care If It Was Assad Who Used Chemical Weapons, I'm Tired of Regime Change,'" *Information Liberation*, April 13, 2017, https://www.informationliberation.com/?id=56583.

7. Cited in Eyes on the Right, "#NoMoreJewishWars: The Alt Right turns on Trump over Syria Bombing," *Angry White Men: Tracking White Supremacy*, April 6, 2017, https://angrywhitemen.org/2017/04/06/nomorejewishwars-the-alt-right-turns-on-trump-over-syrian-bombing.

8. "Based" is popular alt-right slang for "cool." Cited in "#general (Discord ID: 274262571367006208) in Vibrant Diversity, page 240," "Discord Leaks," *Unicorn Riot*, April 7, 2017, https://discordleaks.unicornriot.ninja/discord/channel/165?per_page=250&page=240#message-695879.

9. Author of *World Fascism: A Historical Encyclopedia* (Santa Barbara: ABC-CLIO, 2006).

10. Cited in "#tradworker (Discord ID: 421518143937052672) in tradworker, page 5," "Discord Leaks," *Unicorn Riot*, March 9, 2018, https://discordleaks.unicornriot.ninja/discord/channel/118?per_page=250&page=5#message-296634.

11. For background on the establishment of the Ba'ath Party, see Raymond Hinnebusch, *Syria: Revolution from Above* (London: Routledge, 2002) and Robin Yassin-Kassab and Leila Al-Shami, *Burning Country: Syrians in Revolution and War*, 2nd ed. (London: Pluto Press, 2018).

12. Michel Aflaq, *On the Way of Resurrection* [in Arabic: Fi-Sabil al-Ba'th] (1943).

13. For in-depth discussion of Assad's state building and crackdown on opposition, see Sam Dagher, *Assad or We Burn the Country: How One Family's Lust for Power Destroyed Syria* (New York: Little, Brown and Company, 2019) and Hinnebusch, *Syria*.

14. Lisa Wedeen, *Ambiguities of Domination: Politics, Rhetoric, and Symbols in Contemporary Syria* (Chicago: University of Chicago Press, 2015).

15. Rahaf Aldoughli, "Belonging to a Militarized Syria as a Woman," *Syria Untold*, January 5, 2018, https://syriauntold.com/2018/01/05/belonging-to-a-militarized-syria-as-a-woman.

16. "Nazi War Criminal Alois Brunner 'Died in Syrian Squalor,'" *BBC News*, January 11, 2017, www.bbc.co.uk/news/world-europe-38586945.

17. Yassin-Kassab and Al-Shami, *Burning Country* and Dagher, *Assad or We Burn the Country*.

18. UN Human Rights Council, "Out of Sight, Out of Mind: Deaths in Detention in the Syrian Arab Republic," *Office of the United Nations High Commissioner for Human Rights*, February 3, 2016, https://www.ohchr.org/Documents/HRBodies/HRCouncil/CoISyria/A-HRC-31-CRP1_en.pdf.

19. John Hudson, "U.N. Envoy Revises Syria Death Toll to 400,000," *Foreign Policy*, April 22, 2016 https://foreignpolicy.com/2016/04/22/u-n-envoy-revises-syria-death-toll-to-400000. For a discussion of the difficulty of accurate casualty counts, see Megan Specia, "How Syria's Death Toll Is Lost in the Fog of War," *The New York Times*, April 13, 2018, https://www.nytimes.com/2018/04/13/world/middleeast/syria-death-toll.html.

20. Robert Paxton, *The Anatomy of Fascism* (New York: Vintage, 2005), 84–85.

21. Syrian Network for Human Rights, "The Six Main Parties that Kill Civilians in Syria and the Death Toll Percentage Distribution among them," *SNHR*, November 14, 2016, https://www.sn4hr.org/blog/2016/11/14/29132. The SNHR is generally recognized by journalists working in the area as holding to the highest evidentiary standards in collecting data, such as by counting only casualties verified by multiple independent eyewitnesses.

22. Yasser Munif, *The Syrian Revolution: Between the Politics of Life and the Geopolitics of Death* (London: Pluto Press, 2020), chapter 1.

23. Munif, *The Syrian Revolution*, 25.

24. Munif, *The Syrian Revolution*, 32.

25. David Duke (@DrDavidDuke), "(((VERY FAKE NEWS)))," Twitter, March 13, 2017, https://twitter.com/DrDavidDuke/status/841131794942566400 (since suspended).

26. ChristianSyrian, "About Syria," forum, *Stormfront*, July 3, 2011, https://www.storm front.org/forum/t813567.

27. Raniah Salloum, "Former Prisoners Fight in Syrian Insurgency," *Spiegel International*, October 10, 2013, https://www.spiegel.de/international/world/former-prisoners -fight-in-syrian-insurgency-a-927158.html.

28. Yassin Al-Haj Saleh, "Terror, Genocide, and the 'Genocratic' Turn," *Al-Jumhuriya*, September 19, 2019, https://www.aljumhuriya.net/en/content/terror-genocide-and -%E2%80%9Cgenocratic%E2%80%9D-turn.

29. Flaxxer, "#tradworker (Discord ID: 274535531927568384) in tradworker, page 370," *Unicorn Riot*, December 24, 2017, https://discordleaks.unicornriot.ninja/discord/ channel/139?per_page=250&page=370#message-394859.

30. Rose Troup Buchanan, "The Alt Right Is in Love with a Brutal Arab Dictator," *BuzzFeed News*, September 22, 2017, https://www.buzzfeednews.com/article/rosebuchanan /the-Alt Right-is-in-love-with-a-brutal-muslim-dictator.

31. Jules Etjim, "Notes on Syria and the Coming Global Thanatocracy," *Paths and Bridges* (blog), July 11, 2018, https://pathsandbridges.wordpress.com/2018/07/11/ notes-on-syria-and-the-coming-global-thanatocracy.

32. Munif, *The Syrian Revolution*, 33.

33. Munif, *The Syrian Revolution*, 28.

34. Munif, *The Syrian Revolution*, 29.

35. The term "bonehead" refers to neo-Nazi skinheads. As the origins of the skinhead movement were in multiracial working-class unity, and as there remains today a heavy proportion of antiracist skinheads, the term "bonehead" is meant as an epithet to distinguish neo-Nazis without allowing the erasure of antiracists by making the term "skinhead" synonymous with "Nazi."

36. Southern Poverty Law Center, "Freed From Prison, David Duke Mounts a Comeback," *Intelligence Report*, July 20, 2004, https://www.splcenter.org/fighting-hate/ intelligence-report/2004/freed-prison-david-duke-mounts-comeback.

37. The "Overton window" refers to the range of political discourse that is seen as being acceptable to the mainstream.

38. Yassin Al-Haj Saleh, "Syria, Iran, ISIS and the Future of Social Justice: In Dialogue with Yassin al-Haj Saleh," *Radio Zamaneh*, May 29, 2015; quoted in Yassin-Kassab and Al-Shami, *Burning Country*, x.

39. Buchanan, "The Alt Right Is in Love."

40. Jason Stanley, *How Fascism Works: The Politics of Us and Them* (New York: Random House, 2018), 58.

41. The original article has been taken down from the *Al-Masdar News* site but was

re-posted elsewhere. Paul Antonopoulos, "Jumping to Conclusions; Something is Not Adding Up in Idlib Chemical Weapons Attack," *Global Research*, April 5, 2017, https://www.globalresearch.ca/jumping-to-conclusions-something-is-not-adding-up-in-idlib-chemical-weapons-attack/5583500.

42. The term "alt-light" refers to a far-right movement that, while sharing some rhetorical and organizational style with the alt-right, falls short of open white nationalism or fascism and tends to focus on nativism, "civic nationalism," and extreme cultural conservatism, usually presenting an antagonistic form of politics yet reviving the right flank of the Republican Party on paper.

43. George Monbiot, "A Lesson from Syria: It's Crucial Not to Fuel Far-Right Conspiracy Theories," *The Guardian*, November 15, 2017, https://www.theguardian.com/commentisfree/2017/nov/15/lesson-from-syria-chemical-weapons-conspiracy-theories-alt-right.

44. Southern Poverty Law Center, "Dubious Broadcast 'Experts' Seen on Many Networks,"*Intelligence Report*, November 21, 2014, https://www.splcenter.org/fighting-hate/intelligence-report/2014/dubious-broadcast-'experts'-seen-many-networks.

45. For more information, see Monbiot "A Lesson from Syria."

46. See Eliot Higgins, "Khan Sheikhoun, or How Seymour Hersh 'Learned Just to Write What I Know, And Move On,'" *Bellingcat*, July 28, 2017, https://www.bellingcat.com/news/mena/2017/07/28/khan-sheikhoun-seymour-hersh-learned-just-write-know-move; "Syria Forces Behind Khan Sheikhoun Gas Attack: UN Probe," *Al Jazeera*, September 6, 2017, https://www.aljazeera.com/news/2017/09/syria-forces-khan-sheikhoun-gas-attack-probe-170906115601017.html.

47. Jason Wilson, "Why Is the Far Right So Against US Intervention in Syria?," *The Guardian*, April 13, 2018, https://www.theguardian.com/us-news/2018/apr/13/syria-intervention-conservative-rightwing-opposition-trump.

48. Tucker Carlson Tonight, "Tucker: Would War against Assad Make US Safer?," *Fox News*, video, 07:18, April 10, 2018, https://video.foxnews.com/v/5767243543001#sp=show-clips.

49. Quoted in Wilson, "Why is the Far Right So Against."

50. Embassy of Russia in the USA, "СООБЩЕНИЕ ДЛЯ СМИ МИД РОССИИ," Facebook, April 8, 2018, https://www.facebook.com/RusEmbUSA/photos/a.493759737501088/769473706596355/?type=1&theater.

51. See Charles Lyons, "White Helmets and Not So White Lies," *Altright.com*, April 11, 2018, https://altright.com/2018/04/11/white-helmets-and-not-so-white-lies; LaRouche Political Action Committee, "British Escalate with a Hoax in Syria; This Propaganda Could Lead to World War," *LaRouche PAC*, April 9, 2018, https://larouchepac.com/20180409/british-escalate-hoax-syria-propaganda-could-lead-world-war; David Icke, "Organ Theft & Staged Attacks – White Helmets Criminal Activities Ignored by the Media," *YouTube*, video, January 23, 2019, https://www.youtube.com/watch?v=p5HI0ZQCYn8 (since removed).

52. Max Blumenthal, "How the White Helmets Became International Heroes While Pushing US Military Intervention and Regime Change in Syria," *The Grayzone*, October 2, 2016, https://thegrayzone.com/2016/10/02/white-helmets-us-military-intervention-regime-change-syria.

53. The Syria Campaign, "Killing the Truth: How Russia Is Fuelling a Disinformation Campaign to Cover Up War Crimes in Syria," *The Syria Campaign*, 2017, http://thesyriacampaign.org/wp-content/uploads/2017/12/KillingtheTruth.pdf.

54. Olivia Solon, "How Syria's White Helmets Became Victims of an Online Propaganda

Machine," *The Guardian*, December 18, 2017, https://www.theguardian.com/world/2017/dec/18/syria-white-helmets-conspiracy-theories.

55. Hisham Al Ashqar, "A Reading Into the New Wave of the European Far-Right and the Reasons Behind Its Support for the Syrian Regime," *Al Manshour*, January 27, 2014 [Arabic], https://tahriricn.wordpress.com/2014/04/24/syria-a-reading-into-the-new-wave-of-european-far-right-and-the-reasons-behind-its-support-for-the-syrian-regime.

56. The KKK has of course been considerably larger than America First, and historically has had much overlap with US fascist movements. However, the KKK is generally not regarded as a fascist organization due to its distance from and at times opposition to specifically European nationalist movements, as well as its purported conservativism. The Klan and Nazi groups have grown closer in recent decades, but the Klan's numbers in this time have come nowhere near its pre–World War II numbers.

57. Charles Lindbergh, "Aviation, Geography, and Race," *Reader's Digest*, November 1939, 64–67; quoted in Stanley, *How Fascism Works*, xi.

58. Charles Lindbergh, "Des Moines Speech: Delivered in Des Moines, Iowa, on September 11, 1941, This Speech Was Met with Outrage in Many Quarters," *Charles Lindberg: An American Aviator*, http://www.charleslindbergh.com/americanfirst/speech.asp.

59. Matthew N. Lyons, *Insurgent Supremacists: The U.S. Far Right's Challenge to State and Empire* (Oakland, CA: PM Press, 2018), 123.

60. David Roberts; quoted in Lyons, *Insurgent Supremacists*, 126.

61. Vladmir I. Lenin, "The Socialist Revolution and the Right of Nations to Self-Determination," *Marxists.org*, https://www.marxists.org/archive/lenin/works/1916/jan/x01.htm.

62. Lyons, *Insurgent Supremacists*, 127.

63. Lyons, *Insurgent Supremacists*, 129.

64. George Hawley, *Right-Wing Critics of American Conservativism* (Lawrence, KS: University Press of Kansas, 2017), 207–42.

65. Arktos Media, "Beyond Human Rights," *Arktos Media*, https://arktos.com/product/beyond-human-rights-hardback.

66. Lyons, *Insurgent Supremacists*, 130.

67. Lyons, *Insurgent Supremacists*, 132.

68. ML Today, "World Trade Union Solidarity with Syrian Workers," *Marxism-Leninism Today*, September 17, 2019, https://mltoday.com/world-trade-union-solidarity-with-syrian-workers.

69. Charles Lyons, "Bashar Al Assad Never Called Me Goyim," *Altright.com*, September 9, 2017, https://altright.com/2017/09/09/bashar-al-assad-never-called-me-goyim.

70. "TWP [Traditionalist Worker Party] leader Matthew Heimbach has called Putin 'the leader, really, of the anti-globalist forces around the world.' . . . Richard Spencer has even praised Russia as 'the sole white power in the world,'" (Lyons, *Insurgent Supremacists*, 140).

71. Russia Today, "'Thugs, Islamists chaos' Welcome to New Libya," *RT*, video, 04:38, July 12, 2012, https://youtu.be/3uUUmGG2r_w; "Gregory Hood of *Counter-Currents Publishing* wrote that he wouldn't want to live in Chávez's Venezuela . . . but praised the 'powerful nationalist and even traditionalist overtones' of his policies, his efforts to imbue his people with 'a sense of mission and national pride that transcended class,' and his break with neoliberal orthodoxy. Hood argued that 'White Nationalists and Hugo Chávez share common interests and a common enemy: global capitalism.'" (Lyons, *Insurgent Supremacists*, 141).

72. Lyons, *Insurgent Supremacists*, 141.

73. Gregory Hood, "Standing with Syria," *Counter-Currents Publishing*, quoted in Lyons, *Insurgent Supremacists*, 141–42.

74. Stanley, *How Fascism Works*, 19–23.

The Other Aryan Supremacy / Maia Ramnath

1. Alliance for Justice and Accountability, "Indian Americans: The Time to Stand Up to Hindu Fascism Is Now," *Medium.com*, September 10, 2018, https://medium.com/@stophindutva/indian-americans-the-time-to-stand-up-to-hindu-fascism-is-now-ce879b4b5f53.

2. The Campaign to Stop Funding Hate, "Rashtriya Swayamsevak Sangh: A Primer," http://www.stopfundinghate.org/resources/rssprimer.htm.

3. Among the texts central to the brahminical worldview were the Dharmashastras, especially the Manusmriti, which laid out brutal rules for enforcing caste; the Vedas, aspects of the Upanishads (roots of Vedanta philosophy); and certain episodes of the classical epics, the Ramayana and Mahabharata, including the Bhagavad Gita.

4. The Dravidian language group native to southern India and Sri Lanka includes Tamil, Telugu, Kannada, Malayalam, and many other dialects.

5. The speed and degree of violence of this encounter are still debated—that is, whether it was a rapid aggressive invasion or a long slow intermingling. Furthermore, the question of genetics and origins of South Asian population groups has become highly politicized. Genetic researchers have posited two major population groups (Ancestral North Indian and Ancestral South Indian) traced to a mixture of the Indus Valley civilization with Iranian and central Asian steppe populations, and the Indus Valley civilization with Iranian and Adivasi hunter-gatherer populations, respectively. See Tony Joseph, "How We the Indians Came to Be." *The Quint*, February 4, 2018, https://www.thequint.com/voices/opinion/genomic-study-vedic-aryan-migration-dravidian-languages-sanskrit; Rohan Venkataramakrishnan, "Aryan Migration: Everything You Need to Know about the New Study on Indian Genetics," *Scroll.in*, April 2, 2018, https://scroll.in/article/874102/aryan-migration-everything-you-need-to-know-about-the-new-study-on-indian-genetics.

6. Tayyab Mahmud, "Colonialism and Modern Constructions of Race: A Preliminary Inquiry," *U of Miami Law Review* 53 (1999): 1228.

7. Mahmud, "Colonialism and Modern Constructions of Race," 1228.

8. It might also be noted in light of recent events that the words "looting" and "thug" both originate from Anglicized Hindustani terms, adapted from 19th-century British colonial counterinsurgency discourse to demonize enemy natives.

9. Heather Pringle, *The Master Plan: Himmler's Scholars and the Holocaust* (New York: Hyperion, 2006), 33.

10. Nicholas Goodrick-Clarke, *Hitler's Priestess: Savitri Devi, the Hindu-Aryan Myth, and Neo-nazism* (New York: New York University Press, 1998), 37.

11. Goodrick-Clarke, *Hitler's Priestess*, 37.

12. Christophe Jaffrelot, *The Hindu Nationalist Movement in India* (New York: Columbia University Press, 1996), 20.

13. Jaffrelot, *The Hindu Nationalist Movement in India*, 76–77.

14. Jaffrelot, *The Hindu Nationalist Movement in India*, 18–19. Regional Hindu Sabhas then consolidated into an all-India Mahasabha in 1915.

15. Mahmud, "Colonialism and Modern Constructions of Race," 1244.

16. Quoted in Mahmud, "Colonialism and Modern Constructions of Race," 1245, and The

Campaign to Stop Funding Hate, "The Rashtriya Swayamsevak Sangh."

17. Quoted in Jaffrelot, *The Hindu Nationalist Movement in India*, 28, and The Campaign to Stop Funding Hate, "The Rashtriya Swayamsevak Sangh."

18. Marzia Casolari, "Hindutva's Fascist Heritage," *Sabrang/Communalism Combat*, March 2000, excerpted from Marzia Casolari, "Hindutva's Foreign Tie-up in the 1930s: Archival Evidence," *Economic and Political Weekly* 34, no. 4 (2000): 218–28.

19. M. S. Golwalkar, *We, Or, Our Nationhood Defined* (Bharat Publications, 1939), 37.

20. Golwalkar, *We, Or, Our Nationhood Defined*, 47–48.

21. Jaffrelot, *The Hindu Nationalist Movement in India*, 68; A. G. Noorani, *The RSS: A Menace to India* (New Delhi: LeftWord Books, 2019), loc. 1254.

22. Noorani, *The RSS*, loc. 10150. See also Jaffrelot, *The Hindu Nationalist Movement in India*, 37.

23. Readers may wonder why I have not mentioned Gandhi here. Not all these national leaders agreed on everything, but they did converge around the basic consensus values of the secular democratic republic ideal. Gandhi was obviously a major political figure and popular hero whose role in the Indian independence movement goes without saying. However, precisely the spiritual/moral tenor of his politics that made him a universally renowned figure brought him criticism within India, particularly on the secular left, who feared that his framing of politics in terms of Hindu values, however benevolent and attentive to Muslim and "Harijan" interests, left the door dangerously open to the Hindu nationalist element. More recently, important critiques have been raised about Gandhi's anti-Black racial attitudes, questionable sexual practices, and reformist versus abolitionist approach to caste. These critiques should be applied generally and systemically to all the Indian independence leaders of the time.

24. Alexandra Minna Stern, *Proud Boys and the White Ethnostate* (Boston: Beacon Press, 2019), 27–28.

25. Jaffrelot, *The Hindu Nationalist Movement in India*, 126.

26. The Campaign to Stop Funding Hate, "The Rashtriya Swayamsevak Sangh."

27. Hinduism was never a monolithic religion but a collection of many sects and paths, a vast body of texts and practices that include a full range of multiple orthodoxies and heterodoxies, spawning a vigorous proliferation of sometimes diverging and sometimes recombining branches. In Hindutva, what we're really talking about is the brahminical worldview, whose attempts to assert itself as the dominant, monolithic religion can be traced to the eighth-century Shankara (reformer and founder of Vedanta philosophy) to promote orthodoxy and counter the challenge from Buddhism by rivaling the latter's organized structures, monasteries, and textual authority.

28. Scholars of yoga's history note that the classical yoga sutras contain little mention of the physical postures familiar today; instead, the physical postures popularized in modern ashtanga yoga have been linked to a gymnastic training program developed by Danish fitness enthusiast Niels Bukh (who later became a Nazi sympathizer), and popularized in British India via the YMCA in the early 20th century. On this history, see Meera Nanda, Robert Worth, Mark Singleton, et al.

29. Alliance for Justice and Accountability, "Indian Americans."

30. Noorani, *The RSS*, loc. 8458.

31. The Campaign to Stop Funding Hate, "The Rashtriya Swayamsevak Sangh."

32. Thomas Blom Hansen, *The Saffron Wave: Democracy and Hindu Nationalism in Modern India* (Princeton, NJ: Princeton University Press, 1995), 84–85; Noorani, *The RSS*, loc. 4538, 4550.

33. Not just in government, but on the ground too: between 1977 and 1982, shakhas tripled from 6,000 to 19,000, with over 70,000 dedicated swayamsevaks (Noorani, *The RSS*, loc. 4741).

34. Jaffrelot, *The Hindu Nationalist Movement in India*, 128.

35. These events have been extensively covered in Indian and international media. For a few thorough accounts, see Human Rights Watch, "'WE HAVE NO ORDERS TO SAVE YOU': State Participation and Complicity in Communal Violence in Gujarat," *Human Rights Watch*, April 2002, https://www.hrw.org/reports/2002/india/gujarat; Rana Ayyub, *Gujarat Files: Anatomy of a Cover Up* (self-published, CreateSpace Independent Publishing Platform, 2016); and Rakesh Sharma, director, *Final Solution*, India 2004, http://www.rakeshfilm.com/finalsolution.htm.

36. The Shiv Sena is a Maharashtrian right-wing chauvinist group that shares many political stances with the RSS. Although it originated as a regionally specific nativist group hostile to migrants coming to Mumbai from elsewhere in the country, it has expanded into a more generally pan-Indian Hindu nationalism.

37. After declining slightly in the 2000s, the number of shakhas ballooned in the 2010s: by 2015, reports Noorani, "51,335 shakhas held daily sessions across India." By the end of the decade, 10–15,000 recruits were joining each month in cities and villages all over the country, with a couple of notable exceptions: Assam and Kashmir (Noorani, *The RSS*, loc. 7747, 7759).

38. Spoken at a rally he addressed in Azamgarh on April 10, 2008. Sharat Pradhan, "Yogi Adityanath Marks BJP's Return to Aggressive Hindutva Line," *Rediff.com*, September 3, 2014, http://www.rediff.com/news/report/yogi-adityanath-marks-bjps-return-to-aggressive-hindutva-line/20140903.htm. See also TR Vivek, "With Yogi Adityanath as CM of India's Largest State, the BJP Has Launched Project Polarisation 2.0," March 20, 2017, *Scroll.in*, https://scroll.in/article/832222/with-yogi-adityanath-as-cm-of-indias-largest-state-the-bjp-has-launched-project-polarisation-2-0.

39. Nilanjana Bhowmik, "Meet the Militant Monk Spreading Islamophobia in India," *The Washington Post*, March 24, 2017, https://www.washingtonpost.com/news/global-opinions/wp/2017/03/24/meet-the-militant-monk-spreading-islamophobia-in-india.

40. The court ruling grants alternate land elsewhere to build a mosque; previously, an agreement had been in effect for the use of both Hindu and Muslim worship areas within the site.

41. Noorani, *The RSS*, loc. 4765.

42. Walter K. Anderson and Shridhar D. Damle, *The RSS: A View to the Inside* (New York: Penguin Random House, 2018).

43. See The Campaign to Stop Funding Hate, "The Rashtriya Swayamsevak Sangh."

44. The Campaign to Stop Funding Hate, "The Rashtriya Swayamsevak Sangh."

45. The Campaign to Stop Funding Hate, "The Rashtriya Swayamsevak Sangh."

46. The Campaign to Stop Funding Hate, "The Rashtriya Swayamsevak Sangh."

47. This is why projects such as Youth Solidarity Summer and Bay Area Solidarity Summer have been so important in giving second-generation desi diasporic youth an alternative way to connect to their heritage: through a lens of progressive/left values and history, understanding their nonwhite immigrant positionality in connection to the intersecting struggles for racial justice in the US as well as struggles against oppression in South Asia. See the illuminating work of Simmy Makhijani or Sunaina Maira.

48. The Campaign to Stop Funding Hate, "The Rashtriya Swayamsevak Sangh."

49. See Sangay K. Mishra, *Desis Divided: The Political Lives of South Asian Americans*

(Minneapolis: University of Minnesota Press, 2016); Vivek Bald, Miabi Chatterji, Sujani Reddy, and Manu Vimalassery, eds., *The Sun Never Sets: South Asian Migrants in an Age of U.S. Power* (New York: New York University Press, 2013).

50. For the early stages of the race for the 2020 Democratic presidential nominee, two of the candidates were Kamala Harris, a California state prosecutor whose parents were of Indian and Jamaican origin, and Gabbard. Although both dropped out of the race, the "Hindu-American" take on these candidates was revealing. Their preferences explicitly weighted ideological Hindutva over ethnic Indian-ness while betraying their anti-Blackness in suggesting that Harris was more in tune with the African-American side of her ancestry than the South Asian side, implying disapproval that she seemed more interested in serving the interests of the former community than the latter, and was failing to perform proper appreciation for Indians (she had never been seen in public wearing a sari, had she?). See Bhargavi Kulkarni, "Tulsi or Kamala: Indian-Americans Are Conflicted about Potential Choice in Democratic Primary," *India Abroad*, January 15, 2019, https://www.indiaabroad .com/us_affairs/tulsi-or-kamala-indian-americans-are-conflicted-about-potential -choice-in-democratic-primary/article_d8acc3b0-1925-11e9-a80c-4f129574a284.html. This is ironic, given the skepticism with which much of the African-American voting public viewed Harris due to her harsh record on law enforcement—an irony compounded even further by her Tamilian immigrant mother's involvement in the 1960s civil rights movement.

51. Rashmee Kumar, "The Network of Hindu Nationalists Behind Modi's 'Diaspora Diplomacy' in the US." *The Intercept*, 25 September 2019. Kadirgamar, Skanda. "Activists Plan Boycott of US Companies Backing India's Anti-Muslim Policies." *Truthout*, 25 January 2020.

52. Kumar, "The Network of Hindu Nationalists."

53. Pallabi Munsi, "Could Modi's Break with Diplomatic Tradition Help Trump?" *OZY*, February 20, 2020, https://www.ozy.com/news-and-politics/will-modis -break-with-diplomatic-tradition-help-trump-in-november/278750

54. Krishna Kumar, "Hindu-Americans Withdraw Their Unconditional Support for the Democratic Party," *India Post*, February 13, 2020, https://www.indiapost.com/ hindu-americans-withdraw-their-unconditional-support-for-the-democratic-party.

55. Kumar, "Hindu-Americans Withdraw."

56. Kumar, "Hindu-Americans Withdraw."

57. These two are despised "for trying to buttress their progressive credentials" by knowingly taking "positions antithetical to Hindu-Americans." Islamophobic as Hindutva supporters are, they hate Jayapal's allies Ilhan Omar and Rashida Tlaib, and they hate Jayapal for allying with them. Just as bad from their perspective, Khanna issued them a "proverbial slap in the face" by joining the Congressional Pakistan Caucus, thereby "raising the stature of a country" they define as their existential nemesis, fomenter of terrorism, and serial wartime enemy; and Jayapal had dared to "actively [promote] anti-India legislation" by sponsoring a resolution condemning Modi's actions in Kashmir since August 2019. They implored the Democratic Party to "silence, ostracize or expel" her; Indian foreign minister S. Jaishankar cancelled a meeting scheduled with a US congressional delegation for their refusal to exclude Jayapal. Rashmee Kumar and Akela Lacy, "India Lobbies to Stifle Criticism, Control Messaging in U.S. Congress Amid Rising Anti-Muslim Violence," *The Intercept*, March 16, 2020, https://theintercept.com/2020/03/16/india-lobbying-us-congress.

58. Kumar, "Hindu-Americans Withdraw."

59. Kumar, "Hindu-Americans Withdraw."

60. This attitude in the US directly echoes savarna resentment of reservations (analogous to Affirmative Action) in India, which require them to cede a quota of positions to which they feel entitled to members of so-called Scheduled Castes. Protests against the recommendations of the Mandal commission report released in the 1990s, which revealed statistics on the deep inequities that made reservations necessary, was yet another catalyst for RSS/BJP ascendancy.

61. See Equality Labs, "Facebook India: Towards a Tipping Point of Violence: Caste and Religious Hate Speech," Equality Labs, 2019, https://static1.squarespace.com/static/58347d04bebafbb1e66df84c/t/5d0074f67458550001c56af1/1560311033798/Facebook_India_Report_Equality_Labs.pdf. India Spend (https://www.indiaspend.com) formerly operated a Hate Crimes Tracker but it was pulled down along with other such data tracking sites. See Harsh Mander, "New Hate Crime Tracker in India Finds Victims Are Predominantly Muslims, Perpetrators Hindus," *Scroll.in*, November 13, 2018, https://scroll.in/article/901206/new-hate-crime-tracker-in-india-finds-victims-are-predominantly-muslims-perpetrators-hindus; Ayush Tiwari, "FactChecker Shuts Down Hate Crime Watch, Samar Halarnkar's Stint with India Spend Ends," *Newslaundry*, September 11, 2019, https://www.newslaundry.com/2019/09/12/FACT-CHECKER-SHUTS-DOWN-HATE-CRIME-WATCH-SAMAR-HALARNKARS-STINT-WITH-INDIA-SPEND-ENDS.

62. Rashmee Kumar, "The Network of Hindu Nationalists Behind Modi's 'Diaspora Diplomacy' in the U.S.," *The Intercept*, September 25, 2019, https://theintercept.com/2019/09/25/howdy-modi-trump-hindu-nationalism.

63. Press Trust of India, "Indian-American Manga Anantatmula to Run for US Congress from Virginia," *Business Standard*, February 8, 2020, https://www.business-standard.com/article/pti-stories/indian-american-woman-to-run-for-us-congress-from-virginia-120020800357_1.html.

64. Namely, a politically opportunistic lawsuit using the claim that Asians are discriminated against in admissions to Ivy League schools (and using Asian students as tools) to further an anti–Affirmative Action agenda. (*Students for Fair Admissions v. Harvard Corp.*, 397 F. Supp. 3d 126 (D. Mass. 2019).)

65. Press Trust of India, "Indian-American Manga Anantatmula."

66. M. K. Bhadrakumar, "Shallow Shalom," *The Week*, January 28, 2018, https://www.theweek.in/columns/mk-bhadrakumar/israel-pm-netanyahus-visit.html?fb_comment_id=2122238734469748_2415745671785718.

67. Noorani, *The RSS*, loc. 5479.

68. Christophe Jaffrelot, "A *De Facto* Ethnic Democracy?: Obliterating and Targeting the Other, Hindu Vigilantes, and the Ethno-State," in Angana P. Chatterji, Thomas Blom Hansen, and Christophe Jaffrelot, eds., *Majoritarian State: How Hindu Nationalism is Changing India* (Oxford: Oxford University Press, 2019), 41–68.

69. Abdulla Moaswes, "What's Happening in Kashmir Looks a Lot Like Israel's Rule of Palestine," *+972 Magazine*, August 12, 2019, https://www.972mag.com/kashmir-india-israel-palestine-occupation. As it happens, here too the influences are reciprocal: Israel had used India's Evacuee Property Law, applied after the mass ethnic transfer of the 1947 Partition, as the model for its Absentee Property Law to expropriate the homes of Palestinian refugees in 1948.

70. Ipsita Chakravarty, "Parleying with Palestine: After Decades of Warmth, Delhi and Ramallah Maintain a Fragile Equilibrium," *Scroll.in*, January 7, 2018, https://scroll.in/article/863732/parleying-with-palestine-after-decades-of-warmth-delhi-and-ramallah-maintain-a-fragile-equilibrium.

71. Azad Essa, "India Consul General in United States Calls for 'Israeli Model' in

Kashmir," *Middle East Eye*, November 26, 2019, https://www.middleeasteye.net/news/india-consul-general-united-states-calls-israeli-solution-kashmir.

72. Vijay Prashad quotes a member of the AJC: "We shared with [USINPAC] the Jewish approach to political activism. We want to give them the tools to further their political agenda" (Vijay Prashad, *Uncle Swami: South Asians in America Today* [New York: The New Press, 2012], 69, 75).

73. Rama Lakshmi, "India Wants to Turn 25 Million in the Diaspora into Global Ambassadors," *The Washington Post*, February 18, 2015, https://www.washingtonpost.com/world/asia_pacific/india-wants-to-turn-25-million-in-the-diaspora-into-global-ambassadors/2015/02/17/908ee6ff-a650-42bc-ac58-0a2c91530a26_story.html.

74. Goodrick-Clarke, *Hitler's Priestess*, 39.

75. Goodrick-Clarke, *Hitler's Priestess*, 66.

76. Pringle, *The Master Plan*, 117.

77. Pringle, *The Master Plan*, 80.

78. Shrenik Rao, "Hitler's Hindus: The Rise and Rise of India's Nazi-Loving Nationalists," *Haaretz*, December 14, 2017, https://www.haaretz.com/opinion/hitlers-hindus-indias-nazi-lovingnationalists-on-the-rise-1.5628532.

79. A 2019 anti-Modi slogan in Mumbai reads, "*Jo Hitler ki chaal chalega, vo Hitler ki maut marega*" ("He who makes moves that Hitler made, shall also die Hitler's death"). Noopur Tiwari uses Hannah Arendt's *The Origins of Totalitarianism* (New York: Harcourt, Brace and Co., 1951) as a key to decoding Modi's rhetorical moves in the time of the anti-CAA protests, including eliminating the reliability of truth and facts; scrambling the difference between truth and lies so that people don't mind hearing lies and instead choose what they want to believe, unmoved by the proving of the lie; Indian communalists' version of "patriotism" echoing the form of German antisemitism of the 1930s, and the message that what's "right is what's good for the German people"; defining citizenship and laws that are explicitly not to be equally applied to all people, with the exemptions designating statelessness. Noopur Tiwari, "Gaslighting, Deception and Lies: A 10-Point Guide to Narendra Modi's Speech at Ramlila Maidan," *Newslaundry*, December 23, 2019, https://www.newslaundry.com/2019/12/23/deception-lies-modi-speech-ramlila-maidan-citizenship.

80. Vidhi Doshi, "A Look Inside the School Professionalizing India's Hindu Nationalists," *The Atlantic*, May 5, 2019, https://www.theatlantic.com/international/archive/2019/05/india-school-hindu-nationalists/588127.

81. Vidhi Doshi, "A Look Inside".

82. Doshi, "A Look Inside."

83. Arun Anand, "RSS Roadmap for 21st Century India—Rewrite History, 'Indianise' Education, Museum Revamp," *The Print*, September 30, 2019, https://theprint.in/politics/rss-roadmap-india-rewrite-history-indianise-education-museum-revamp/298828.

84. Pringle, *The Master Plan*, 81.

85. Anand, "RSS Roadmap for 21st Century India."

86. Noorani, *The RSS*; drawing upon Alex Traub, "India's Dangerous New Curriculum," *The New York Review*, December 6, 2018, https://www.nybooks.com/articles/2018/12/06/indias-dangerous-new-curriculum.

87. The Campaign to Stop Funding Hate, "Rashtriya Swayamsevak Sangh."

88. The Campaign to Stop Funding Hate, "Rashtriya Swayamsevak Sangh." (HAF sought an injunction to override the decision but failed.)

89. Noorani, *The RSS*.

90. Robert F. Worth, "The Billionaire Yogi Behind Modi's Rise," *The New York Times*, July 26, 2018, https://www.nytimes.com/2018/07/26/magazine/the-billionaire-yogi-behind -modis-rise.html.

91. Alliance for Justice and Accountability, "Indian Americans."

92. Varghese K. George, "World Hindu Congress Ends with Calls for Hindu Unity, Resolves to Fight 'Fake News,'" *The Hindu*, September 11, 2018, https://www.the hindu.com/news/international/world-hindu-congress-ends-with-calls-for-hindu -unity-resolves-to-fight-fake-news/article24918501.ece.

93. George, "World Hindu Congress."

94. Romila Thapar, A. G. Noorani, and Sadanand Menon, *On Nationalism* (New Delhi: Aleph Book Company, 2016), 26.

95. A. G. Noorani, "India's Fascist Challenge," *Frontline*, July 19, 2019, https://frontline .thehindu.com/the-nation/fascist-challenge/article28259898.ece#!.

96. One of the latest caravans, he said, was Islam, which had flowed into the culture's other culture's currents like the converging waters of the Ganga and Yamuna, and, now, a thousand years later, had as much a claim to Indian soil as any other. Noorani, *The RSS*, loc. 1617.

97. It strikes me that the modern Mexican ideal of *mestizaje* as national cultural-political identity is parallel in certain ways.

98. The two are not unconnected: Narayan Subramaniam, a contributor to the text of the 2015 Paris Climate Accords, "tied Hindu philosophy to *other* indig-enous ways of life" (emphasis mine) that "center on loving and preserving the earth." Murali Balaji, "Hindu Climate Activists Take Lead on Combating Cli-mate Change," *YaleNews*, February 15, 2019, https://news.yale.edu/2019/02/15/ hindu-climate-activists-take-lead-combating-climate-change.

99. Balaji, "Hindu Climate Activists"

100. Noorani, *The RSS*, loc. 3485.

101. Thomas Blom Hansen, "Democracy Against the Law: Reflections on India's Illiberal Democracy," in Chatterji, Hansen, and Jaffrelot, eds., *Majoritarian State*, 19.

102. Meghna Rao, "The American Diaspora Protests CAA," *The Juggernaut*, January 21, 2020, https://www.thejuggernaut.com/american-diaspora-protests-caa.

103. Simi Kadirgamar, "Activists Plan Boycott of US Companies Backing India's Anti-Muslim Policies," *Truthout*, January 25, 2020, https://truthout.org/articles/ activists-plan-boycott-of-us-companies-backing-indias-anti-muslim-policies.

104. Abdulla Moaswes, "Hindu Nationalists Are Transforming India into an Israel-style Ethnostate," *+972 Magazine*, January 8, 2020, https://www.972mag.com/caa-hindu -nationalism-zionism.

105. Alliance for Justice and Accountability, "Indian Americans."

106. On this, see Arendt, *The Origins of Totalitarianism*.

107. Liza Featherstone, "Joe Biden's Fascist Friends Should Worry Us More Than Tulsi's," *Jacobin Magazine*, November 5, 2019, https://jacobinmag.com/2019/11/ joe-biden-narendra-modi-tulsi-gabbard-amit-jani-bjp.

How Far-Right Fantasies About Refugees Became Mainstream in Greece / P. Strickland

1. Marion MacGregor, "Clashes on Greek Islands Over New Migrant Camps," *Info-Migrants*, February 25, 2020, https://www.infomigrants.net/en/post/22986/clashes -on-greek-islands-over-new-migrant-camps.

2. Apostolis Fotiadis, "Greece's Refugee Plan Is Inhumane and Doomed to Fail. The

EU Must Step In," *The Guardian*, February 16, 2020, https://www.theguardian.com/commentisfree/2020/feb/16/greece-refugee-plan-eu-detention-centres-refugees.

3. Niki Kitsantonis. "Riot Police Pulled from Greek Islands After Clashes Over New Camps," *The New York Times*, February 27, 2020, https://www.nytimes.com/2020/02/27/world/europe/lesbos-chios-riot-police.html.

4. Patrick Strickland, "Anger and 'Fatigue' on Greek Islands Over Migration Limbo," *Politico EU*, February 25, 2020, https://www.politico.eu/article/anger-and-fatigue-on-greek-islands-over-migration-limbo.

5. Patrick Strickland, "Greece Mourns Slain Anti-Fascist Rapper Pavlos Fyssas," *Al Jazeera*, September 15, 2017, https://www.aljazeera.com/features/2017/9/15/greece-mourns-slain-anti-fascist-rapper-pavlos-fyssas.

6. "Greek Anarchists Attack and Destroy Fascists' Offices," *LibCom*, March 18, 2012, http://libcom.org/blog/greek-anarchists-attack-destroy-fascist%E2%80%99s-offices-18032012.

7. Patrick Strickland, "What the Fight against Far-Right Violence in Greece Tells Us," *OpenCanada*, June 12, 2019, https://opencanada.org/what-fight-against-far-right-violence-greece-tells-us.

8. Patrick Strickland, "When Prosecuting Far-Right Violence Fails," *The New Republic*, October 30, 2018, https://newrepublic.com/article/151947/prosecuting-far-right-violence-fails.

9. "Greece Opens Detention Camp for Immigrants as Election Looms," *Reuters*, April 29, 2012, https://www.reuters.com/article/us-greece-camp/greece-opens-detention-camp-for-immigrants-as-election-looms-idUSBRE83S0GB20120429.

10. "Greece Confirms First Coronavirus Case, a Woman Back from Milan," *Reuters*, February 26, 2020, https://www.reuters.com/article/us-china-health-greece-idUSKCN20K1IA.

11. "Thousands of Migrants Gather on Turkey-Greece Border Amid Erdogan Threat," *France 24*, February 29, 2020, https://www.france24.com/en/20200229-greece-stops-4-000-migrants-at-turkey-border.

12. Patrick Kingsley and Matina Stevis-Gridneff, "Turkey, Pressing E.U. for Help in Syria, Threatens to Open Borders to Refugees," *The New York Times*, February 28, 2020, https://www.nytimes.com/2020/02/28/world/europe/turkey-refugees-Geece-erdogan.html.

13. Justin Higginbottom, "'It's a Powder Keg Ready to Explode': In Greek Village, Tensions Simmer between Refugees and Locals," *CNBC*, March 1, 2020, https://www.cnbc.com/2020/03/01/refugee-crisis-in-greece-tensions-soar-between-migrants-and-locals.html.

14. Patrick Strickland, "A Journey through the Refugee Crisis on the Greece-Turkey Border," *Al Jazeera*, March 18, 2020, https://www.aljazeera.com/features/2020/3/18/a-journey-through-the-refugee-crisis-on-the-greece-turkey-border.

15. "Anti-refugee Protesters Attack Journalists in Greece," *Committee to Protect Journalists*, March 3, 2020, https://cpj.org/2020/03/anti-refugee-protesters-attack-journalists-in-gree.

16. "Greece Says Nightclubs, Gyms, Cinemas Shut for 2 Weeks as Virus Precaution," *Reuters*, March 12, 2020, https://www.reuters.com/article/health-coronavirus-greece-gatherings-idUKA8N29K01B.

17. Human Rights Watch, "Greece: Move Asylum Seekers, Migrants to Safety," *Human Rights Watch*, March 24, 2020, https://www.hrw.org/news/2020/03/24/greece-move-asylum-seekers-migrants-safety#.

18. Fahrinisa Campana and Patrick Strickland, "The Looming Refugee Coronavirus Dis-

aster," *Slate*, March 23, 2020, https://slate.com/news-and-politics/2020/03/refugees -coronavirus-greece.html.

19. Strickland, "What the Fight against Far-Right Violence."

20. Joanna Kakissis, "Greece Records First Coronavirus Cases Among Refugees, Imposes Quarantine on Camp," *NPR*, April 2, 2020, https://www.npr.org/sections/ coronavirus-live-updates/2020/04/02/825981261/greece-records-first-coronavirus -cases-among-refugees-imposes-quarantine-on-camp.

21. "150 People Test Positive for Covid-19 at Kranidi Refugee Facility," *Ekathimerini*, April 21, 2020, https://www.ekathimerini.com/news/251872/150-people-test -positive-for-covid-19-at-kranidi-refugee-facility.

22. Anthee Carassava, "Greece Sidelines Thousands of Asylum-Seekers in National Inoculation Drive," *Voice of America*, March 7, 2021, https://www.voanews.com/a/covid -19-pandemic_greece-sidelines-thousands-asylum-seekers-national-inoculation -drive/6202996.html.

23. Notara 26, "Athens: Themistokleus Refugee Squat Evicted," *[Squat!net]*, May 19, 2020, https://en.squat.net/2020/05/19/athens-themistokleus-refugee-squat-evicted.

24. Cara Hoffman, "The Anarchist Neighborhood of Athens," *The Daily Beast*, August 23, 2020, https://www.thedailybeast.com/exarchia-the-anarchist-athens-neighborhood -where-no-government-is-good-government.

25. Katy Fallon, "Greece Ready to Welcome Tourists as Refugees Stay Locked Down in Lesbos," *The Guardian*, May 27, 2020, https://www.theguardian.com/global-development /2020/may/27/greece-ready-to-welcome-tourists-as-refugees-stay-locked-down-in -lesbos-coronavirus.

26. "Greece Opens Two More Holding Centers for Migrants on Islands," *Reuters*, November 27, 2021, https://www.reuters.com/markets/commodities/greece-opens-two -more-holding-centres-migrants-islands-2021-11-27.

27. Katy Fallon and Stavros Malichudis, "Greece Says Migration Crisis Over; Refugees Beg to Differ," *The New Humanitarian*, October 5, 2021, https://www.thenew humanitarian.org/news-feature/2021/10/5/Greece-says-migration-crisis-over -refugees-beg-to-differ.

28. Helena Smith, "Greece Accused of 'Biggest Pushback in Years' of Stricken Refugee Ship," *The Guardian*, November 5, 2021, https://www.theguardian.com/global -development/2021/nov/05/greece-accused-of-biggest-pushback-in-years-of-stricken -refugee-ship.

29. Amnesty International. "Greece: Authorities Abusing Power to Trample on Right to Protest," *Amnesty International*, July 14, 2021, https://www.amnesty.org/en/latest/ news/2021/07/greece-authorities-abusing-power-to-trample-on-right-to-protest.

Global Neoliberalism, Fascism, and Resistance / Geo Maher

1. This is the title of chapter 28 of Karl Marx, *Capital: A Critique of Political Economy, Vol. I* (New York: Penguin, 1982).

2. Marx, *Capital*, 926.

3. Marx, *Capital*, 925.

4. David Harvey, *A Brief History of Neoliberalism* (Oxford: Oxford University Press, 2005), 19.

5. Harvey, *A Brief History of Neoliberalism*, 203.

6. Despite his blind spots regarding questions of the state and power in Venezuela and Bolivia in particular, Raúl Zibechi has made this point forcefully. See Raúl Zibechi,

Territories in Resistance: A Cartography of Latin American Social Movements (Chico, CA: AK Press, 2012).

7. On the relationship between war of position and war of maneuver, see Antonio Gramsci, *Selections from the Prison Notebooks* (New York: International Publishers, 1971), especially 237–38. "Whip of the counter-revolution" is Leon Trotsky's fuzzy paraphrasing, in his *The History of the Russian Revolution*, of Marx's own words about 1848. See Leon Trotsky, *The History of the Russian Revolution, Vol. Two: The Attempted Counter-Revolution, Marxists.org*, https://www.marxists.org/archive/trotsky/1930/hrr/ch35.htm.

8. For a balanced assessment of the limitations, contradictions, and above all the erroneous pragmatism of some Pink Tide governments, see Steve Ellner, ed., *Latin America's Pink Tide: Breakthroughs and Shortcomings* (Lanham, MD: Rowman & Littlefield, 2020).

9. Gramsci, *Prison Notebooks*, 260.

10. Gramsci, *Prison Notebooks*, 245.

11. Mike Davis, "The Great God Trump and the White Working Class," *Jacobin*, February 2017, https://jacobinmag.com/2017/02/the-great-god-trump-and-the-white-working-class.

12. Joseph Bernstein, "Here's How Breitbart and Milo Smuggled White Nationalism into the Mainstream," *BuzzFeed News*, October 5, 2017, https://www.buzzfeednews.com/article/josephbernstein/heres-how-breitbart-and-milo-smuggled-white-nationalism.

13. Founded in 2017, CAN seeks to fulfill the nationwide need for a unified clearinghouse to resist far-right media outrage campaigns against faculty and students by providing an alternative counter-script and by confronting fascism on individual campuses through a combination of "mass counter-mobilizations and broad-based coalitions." Endorsed by high-profile celebrities such as Tom Morello and Junot Díaz, CAN has more than a dozen campus chapters. For CAN's mission statement and organizing resources, see https://campusantifascistnetwork.com.

14. For those interested, the key section of the *Phenomenology of Mind/Spirit* is available at: https://www.marxists.org/reference/archive/hegel/works/ph/phba.htm.

15. Or, as Tariq Ali is reputed to have once said: "If joining the National Front means broken bones then its support will be lost." See also Natasha Lennard, "Is Antifa Counterproductive? White Nationalist Richard Spencer Would Beg to Differ," *The Intercept*, March 17, 2018, https://theintercept.com/2018/03/17/richard-spencer-college-tour-antifa-alt-right.

16. We could mention Lee Fang's persistent downplaying of the threat of the far right, or within the far left itself, the absurdity of Marianne Garneau's claim that "antifa is liberalism," which has been thoroughly dismantled by A. M. Gittlitz; see A. M. Gittlitz, "Anti-Anti-Antifa," *Commune*, December 6, 2018, https://communemag.com/anti-anti-antifa.

17. See Kathleen Belew, *Bring the War Home: The White Power Movement and Paramilitary America* (Cambridge, MA: Harvard University Press, 2018).

18. In January 2020, several members of The Base were arrested after being infiltrated by the FBI. A month later, several more members of the Atomwaffen Division were arrested.

19. In 2017, Wax argued that "not all cultures are created equal," going further to suggest that European cultures are "superior." Dan Spinelli, "'Not All Cultures Are Created Equal' Says Penn Law Professor in Op-ed," *The Daily Pennsylvanian*, August 10, 2017, https://www.thedp.com/article/2017/08/amy-wax-penn-law-cultural-values. A month later, she suggested—incorrectly—that her own Black law students rarely graduated in the top quarter or even top half of their class. Glenn Loury and Amy

Wax, "The Downside to Social Uplift," *The Glenn Show*, video, 1:00:34, September 11, 2017, https://www.youtube.com/watch?v=cb9Ey-SsNsg.

20. Lili Loofbourow, "Chile's People Have Had Enough," *Slate*, October 26, 2019, https://slate.com/news-and-politics/2019/10/chile-protests-against-president-pinera-and-deep-inequality.html.

21. This mistranslation was popularized by Slavoj Žižek in "A Permanent Economic Emergency," *New Left Review* 64, no. 1 (2010):85–95, possibly based on the French edition of *Prison Notebooks*.

Some Names Have Been Changed / Daryle Lamont Jenkins

1. Traditional Skinheads follow the style, music, and crew orientations that go back to the 1960s, when multiracial dockworkers bonded over Jamaican music and celebrated their blue-collar roots. Although these crews were not always intentionally political, they stood up against racism and celebrated their class backgrounds.

2. In a fight between skinheads, a "boot party" is when a group uses their Doc Martens to kick an opponent in unison.

3. Don Black, "re: Richard Barrett, head of the Nationalists Movement, found dead, murdered (2010 thread)," forum, *Stormfront*, April 25, 2010, https://www.stormfront.org/forum/t702173-13/#post8045773.

Antifascism through the Lens of Transgender Identity / Emily Gorcenski

1. Jessica Schulberg, Christopher Mathias, and Luke O'Brien, "These Are the Three Richard Spencer Fans Arrested for Attempted Homicide in Gainesville," *HuffPost*, October 20, 2017, https://www.huffpost.com/entry/attempted-homicide-richard-spencer-speech-gainesville-florida_n_59ea766ae4b0958c468228ff.

2. United States Department of Justice, "Attorney General Loretta E. Lynch Delivers Remarks at Press Conference Announcing Complaint Against the State of North Carolina to Stop Discrimination Against Transgender Individuals," news release, May 9, 2016, https://www.justice.gov/opa/speech/attorney-general-loretta-e-lynch-delivers-remarks-press-conference-announcing-complaint.

3. Katy Steinmetz, "The Transgender Tipping Point," *Time*, May 29, 2014, https://time.com/135480/transgender-tipping-point.

4. George Hawley, *Making Sense of the Alt-Right* (New York: Columbia University Press, 2017).

5. Matt Lees, "What Gamergate Should Have Taught Us about the 'Alt-Right,'" *The Guardian*, December 1, 2016, https://www.theguardian.com/technology/2016/dec/01/gamergate-alt-right-hate-trump.

6. Noah Michelson, "Here's a Fact-Check on Milo Yiannopoulos' Incendiary Claims about Trans People," *HuffPost*, February 18, 2017, https://www.huffpost.com/entry/milo-yiannopoulos-transgender-people-truth_n_58a84dcae4b07602ad551487.

7. Brittney McNamara, "Milo Yiannopoulos Harassed a Transgender Student at Her School," *Teen Vogue*, December 16, 2016, https://www.teenvogue.com/story/milo-yiannopoulos-harassed-a-transgender-student-at-her-school.

8. ACLU Washington, "Timeline of the Muslim Ban," *ACLU Washington*, https://www.aclu-wa.org/pages/timeline-muslim-ban.

9. Dakin Andone, "These states Have Introduced Bills to Protect Drivers Who Run Over

Protesters," *CNN*, August 19, 2017, https://edition.cnn.com/2017/08/18/us/legislation-protects-drivers-injure-protesters/index.html.

10. German Lopez, "HB2, North Carolina's Sweeping Anti-LGBTQ Law, Explained," *Vox*, May 30, 2017, https://www.vox.com/2016/2/23/11100552/charlotte-north-carolina-lgbtq-pat-mccrory.

11. Stephanie Sprague Sobkowiak, "Texas District Court Preliminarily Enjoins Partial Enforcement of Section 1557," *The National Law Review*, January 5, 2017, https://www.natlawreview.com/article/texas-district-court-preliminarily-enjoins-partial-enforcement-section-1557.

12. Lauren Kent and Samantha Tapfumaneyi, "Hungary's PM Bans Gender Study at Colleges Saying 'People Are Born Either Male or Female,'" *CNN*, October 19, 2018, https://edition.cnn.com/2018/10/19/europe/hungary-bans-gender-study-at-colleges-trnd/index.html.

13. "Calls for Romania's President to Reject Gender Studies Ban," *Associated Press*, June 18, 2020, https://apnews.com/article/50be6902fbef23bfb2e2d7a796d2267d.

14. "Romanian Top Court Overturns Ban on Gender Identity Studies," *Reuters*, December 16, 2020, https://www.reuters.com/article/us-romania-lgbt-rights-idUSKBN28Q2NF.

15. Emma Reynolds, "'Living in Fear,'" *CNN*, June 2020, https://edition.cnn.com/interactive/2020/06/world/hungary-transgender-portraits-cnnphotos.

16. "Polish Election: Andrzej Duda Says LGBT 'Ideology' Worse than Communism," *BBC News*, June 14, 2020, https://www.bbc.com/news/world-europe-53039864.

17. Miriam Elder, "Russia Passes Law Banning Gay 'Propaganda,'" *The Guardian*, June 11, 2013, https://www.theguardian.com/world/2013/jun/11/russia-law-banning-gay-propaganda.

18. Kareem Fahim and Antonia Noori Farzan, "Turkish Police Break Up Pride Parade with Tear Gas," *The Washington Post*, June 26, 2021, https://www.washingtonpost.com/world/2021/06/26/istanbul-pride.

19. Oscar Lopez, "Reported Murders, Suicides of Trans People Soar in Brazil," *Reuters*, September 8, 2020, https://www.reuters.com/article/us-brazil-lgbt-murders-trfn-idUSKBN25Z3I0.

20. J. K. Rowling, "J.K. Rowling Writes about Her Reasons for Speaking Out on Sex and Gender Issues," *In My Own Words* (blog), *jkrowling.com*, June 10, 2020, https://www.jkrowling.com/opinions/j-k-rowling-writes-about-her-reasons-for-speaking-out-on-sex-and-gender-issues.

21. Thea De Gallier, "David Davies 'Welcomes' Big Lottery Fund's 'Review' of Grant to Transgender Charity," *TalkRadio*, December 17, 2018, https://web.archive.org/web/20190602203550/https://talkradio.co.uk/news/david-davies-welcomes-big-lottery-funds-review-grant-transgender-charity-18121729229.

22. In the same way that I do not accept the sanitization of white supremacists by conceding the term "identitarian" or "alt-right," I do not sanitize the movement in this piece by using "gender critical," which is neither accurate nor true.

23. Lois Beckett, "White Supremacists or Anti-Police Libertarians? What We Know about the 'Boogaloo,'" *The Guardian*, July 8, 2020https://www.theguardian.com/world/2020/jul/08/boogaloo-boys-movement-who-are-they-what-do-they-believe.

24. Ben Lorber and Heron Greenesmith, "Antisemitism Meets Transphobia," *The Progressive Magazine*, April 28, 2021, https://progressive.org/magazine/antisemitism-meets-transphobia-greenesmith-lorber.

25. Heron Greenesmith, "Racism in Anti-Trans 'Feminist' Activism," *Political Research Associates*, February 20, 2019, http://politicalresearch.org/2019/02/20/racism-in-anti-trans-feminist-activism.

26. German Lopez, "Myth #8: Transgender People Are Mentally Ill," *Vox*, November 14, 2018, https://www.vox.com/identities/2016/5/13/17938120/transgender-people-mental-illness-health-care.

27. Stephen T. Russell, Amanda M. Pollitt, Gu Li, and Arnold H. Grossman, "Chosen Name Use Is Linked to Reduced Depressive Symptoms, Suicidal Ideation, and Suicidal Behavior Among Transgender Youth," *Adolescent Health Brief* 63, no. 4 (2018): 503–05.

28. Kristina R. Olson, Lily Durwood, Madeleine DeMeules, and Katie A. McLaughlin, "Mental Health of Transgender Children Who Are Supported in Their Identities," *Pediatrics* 137, no. 3 (2016):e20153223.

29. Tim Fitzsimons, "Conservative Group Hosts Anti-Transgender Panel of Feminists 'from the Left,'" *NBC News*, January 29, 2019, https://www.nbcnews.com/feature/nbc-out/conservative-group-hosts-anti-transgender-panel-feminists-left-n964246.

30. Anti-Defamation League, "The Antisemitism Lurking Behind George Soros Conspiracy Theories," *ADL Blog* (blog), October 11, 2018, https://www.adl.org/blog/the-antisemitism-lurking-behind-george-soros-conspiracy-theories.

31. Helen Joyce, *Trans: When Ideology Meets Reality* (London: Oneworld Publications, 2021).

32. Human Rights Watch, "George Soros to Give $100 million to Human Rights Watch," *Human Rights Watch*, September 7, 2010, https://www.hrw.org/news/2010/09/07/george-soros-give-100-million-human-rights-watch.

33. Judith Butler, "Why Is the Idea of 'Gender' Provoking Backlash the World Over?," *The Guardian*, October 23, 2021, https://www.theguardian.com/us-news/commentisfree/2021/oct/23/judith-butler-gender-ideology-backlash.

34. Qwo-Li Driskill, *Asegi Stories: Cherokee Queer and Two-Spirit Memory* (Tucson, AZ: The University of Arizona Press, 2016).

35. Tamara Tischendorf, "Sexualwissenschaft und die Bücherverbrennung," *Deutschlandfunk*, May 7, 2008, https://www.deutschlandfunk.de/sexualwissenschaft-und-die-buecherverbrennung.691.de.html?dram:article_id=51607.

36. Columbia Law School, "Kimberlé Crenshaw on Intersectionality, More than Two Decades Later," *Columbia Law School*, June 8, 2017, https://www.law.columbia.edu/news/archive/kimberle-crenshaw-intersectionality-more-two-decades-later.

37. Ian Shapira, "The Parking Garage Beating Lasted 10 Seconds. Deandre Harris Still Lives with the Damage," *The Washington Post*, September 16, 2019, https://www.washingtonpost.com/local/the-parking-garage-beating-lasted-10-seconds-deandre-harris-still-lives-with-the-damage/2019/09/16/ca6daa48-cfbf-11e9-87fa-8501a456c003_story.html.

38. Nicholas Bogel-Burroughs and Sandra E. Garcia, "What Is Antifa, the Movement Trump Wants to Declare a Terror Group?," *The New York Times*, September 28, 2020, https://www.nytimes.com/article/what-antifa-trump.html.

39. Ryan J. Reilly, "Neo-Nazi Sentenced to 14 Years on Federal Terrorism Charges for Amtrak Attack," *HuffPost*, October 5, 2018, https://www.huffpost.com/entry/neo-nazi-domestic-terrorism-taylor-michael-wilson_n_5bb7931be4b01470d051338a.

40. Raven Hodges, "Colton Fears Sentenced to Five Years in Prison," *Hatewatch*, March 20, 2019, https://www.splcenter.org/hatewatch/2019/03/20/colton-fears-sentenced-five-years-prison.

Notes

Five Hundred Years of Fascism / Mike Bento

1. W. E. B. Du Bois, *The World and Africa and Color and Democracy* (Oxford: Oxford University Press, 2007).
2. William Thornton, "More than 300 African-Americans Lynched in Alabama in 66 years," *Al.com*, March 6, 2019, https://www.al.com/news/2018/04/alabamas_racial_lynching_victi.html.
3. "Supreme Court Decides Bullock Sheriff's Case," *The Elba Clipper*, May 26, 1911, 1.
4. Equal Justice in America, "Lynching in America: Confronting the Legacy of Racial Terror," *Equal Justice in America*, https://lynchinginamerica.eji.org.
5. Salley E. Hadden, *Slave Patrols: Law and Violence in Virginia and the Carolinas* (Cambridge, MA: Harvard University Press, 2003).
6. Susanna Delfino, Michele Gillespie, and Louis M. Kyriakoudes, eds., *Southern Society and Its Transformations, 1790–1860* (Columbia, MO: University of Missouri Press, 2011), 46–47.
7. Philip Dray, *At the Hands of Persons Unknown: The Lynching of Black America* (New York: The Modern Library, 2003), 22.
8. Christopher Minster, "Biography of William Walker, Ultimate Yankee Imperialist," *ThoughtCo*, July 30, 2019. https://www.thoughtco.com/the-biography-of-william-walker-2136342.
9. John E. Norvell, "How Tennessee Adventurer William Walker became Dictator of Nicaragua in 1857: The Norvell Family Origins of The Grey Eyed Man of Destiny," *Middle Tennessee Journal of Genealogy & History* XXV, no. 4 (2012), http://www.thenashvillecitycemetery.org/william_walker_article.pdf.
10. Cheri Brooks, "Race, Politics, and Denial: Why Oregon Forgot to Ratify the Fourteenth Amendment," *Oregon Law Review* 83, no. 2 (2004): 731–62.
11. Matt Novak, "Oregon Was Founded As a Racist Utopia," *Gizmodo*, January 21, 2015, https://gizmodo.com/oregon-was-founded-as-a-racist-utopia-1539567040.
12. Robert Paxton's five stages of fascism literally use the term in the definition, stating that stage one is "the initial creation of fascist movements," thus begging the question: What is a fascist movement? Of course, the Nazis never called themselves "fascist," so how do we know the movement was? These stages assume so much of the European context that they forget to even define what it is that is being staged. Of course, the response is assumed and the definition is simply a teleology leading back to "the Third Reich" or "Mussolini" or "Franco's Spain," so that it loses all usefulness in describing future and past regimes—and the crimes of Europe can remain strictly off limits for such terms, for how could any of this be applied to the Belgian Congo or Germany in Namibia?
13. Georgi Dimitrov, *Georgi Dimitrov: Selected Works in Three Volumes*, vol. 2, (Sofia Press, 1972).
14. James W, Loewen and Edward H. Sebesta, eds., *The Confederate and Neo-Confederate Reader: The "Great Truth" about the "Lost Cause"* (Jackson, MS: University Press of Mississippi, 2010), 377–85, Kindle.
15. Harry Haywood, *Negro Liberation* (New York: International Publishers, 1948), 81.
16. Dray, *At the Hands of Persons Unknown*, 36.
17. Dray, *At the Hands of Persons Unknown*, 40.
18. Dray, *At the Hands of Persons Unknown*, 43.
19. Douglas R. Egerton, *The Wars of Reconstruction: The Brief, Violent History of America's Most Progressive Era*, (New York: Bloomsbury Publishing, 2014).
20. Dray, *At the Hands of Persons Unknown*, 49–50.

21. In some parts of the South, Brazil nuts are known as "nigger toes" for their resemblance to the shriveled remnants of these souvenirs.

22. Dray, *At the Hands of Persons Unknown*, 62–65.

23. Dray, *At the Hands of Persons Unknown*, 66.

24. Dray, *At the Hands of Persons Unknown*, 64.

25. Dray, *At the Hands of Persons Unknown*, 69.

26. Paula J. Giddings, *Ida: A Sword Among Lions* (HarperCollins e-books, 2009), Kindle.

27. Michael Newton, *The Ku Klux Klan in Mississippi: A History* (Jefferson, NC: McFarland & Company, Inc., 2010), 117.

28. Newton, *The Ku Klux Klan in Mississippi*, 110–15. Citizens' councils members would later be implicated in the assassination of Medgar Evers and several council leaders also served as "grand wizards" of local Klan chapters.

29. Erin Blakemore, "The Story Behind the Famous Little Rock Nine 'Scream Image,'" *History*, June 9, 2020, https://www.history.com/news/the-story-behind-the-famous-little-rock-nine-scream-image.

30. Neil R. McMillen, "The White Citizens' Council and Resistance to School Desegregation in Arkansas," *The Arkansas Historical Quarterly* LXVI, no. 2 (2007): 125–44.

31. "CITIZENS COUNCILS SPREAD TO NORTH; Segregationist Groups Also Seek Members in West," *The New York Times*, August 5, 1964, https://www.nytimes.com/1964/08/05/archives/citizens-councils-spread-to-north-segregationist-groups-also-seek.html.

32. Social Explorer, "1960 U.S. Census, Total Black Population Census Tract T0082000, San Diego, Ca.," *Social Explorer*, https://www.socialexplorer.com/a9676d974c/explore.

33. Oakland Museum of California, "The New Right Elects Ronald Reagan Governor," in Oakland Museum of California, "Unforgettable Change: 1960s," *Picture This: California Perspectives on American History*, http://picturethis.museumca.org/timeline/unforgettable-change-1960s/new-right-elects-ronald-reagan-governor/info.

34. Manuel Pastor, "After Tax Cuts Derailed the "California Dream," Is the State Getting Back on Track?," *The Conversation*, November 1, 2017, https://theconversation.com/after-tax-cuts-derailed-the-california-dream-is-the-state-getting-back-on-track-77919.

35. Saki Knafo, "Prison-Industrial Complex? Maybe It's Time for a Schools-Industrial Complex," *HuffPost*, August 30, 2013, https://www.huffpost.com/entry/california-prisons-schools_n_3839190.

Antiracist Skinheads and the Birth of Antiracist Action / Shane Burley

1. An especially good, and recent, look at this history in Portland, Oregon in the 1980s and 1990s came from the podcast "It Did Happen Here." This podcast is being turned into a book: Moe Bowstern, Mic Crenshaw, Alec Dunn, Celina Flores, Julie Perini, and Erin Yanke, eds., *It Did Happen Here: An Antifascist Peoples' History* (Oakland, CA: PM Press, forthcoming).

2. The White Knights were a Klan-related white supremacist gang that terrorized Minneapolis, Minnesota in the 1980s.

Gringos and Fascism / Mirna Wabi-Sabi

1. Djamila Ribeiro, *Pequeno Manual Antirracista* (Rio de Janeiro: Companhia das Letras, 2019). Mark Bray, *Antifa - O Manual Antifascista* (São Paulo: Autonomia Literária, 2019)

Notes

2. Ribeiro, *Pequeno Manual Antirracista*; Mark Bray, *Antifa: The Anti-Fascist Handbook* (Brooklyn: Melville House, 2017).

3. Djamila Ribeiro, *O que É Lugar de Fala* (Belo Horizonte: Letramento, 2017). Note that the word *"travesti"* is used instead of "transgender." The term refers to the Latin American word for a concept of feminine expressions outside the cis paradigm that is regarded by some as a third gender. Historically, it also exists in a framework of class and access to medical/material resources.

4. SlaveVoyages, "Tráfico Transatlântico de Escravos," *SlaveVoyages*, https://www.slavevoyages.org/assessment/estimates.

5. Marcus Rediker, "History from Below the Water Line: Sharks and the Atlantic Slave Trade," *Atlantic Studies* 5, no. 2 (August 2008): 285–97.

6. Gabriel Alves, "Estudo com 1.200 Genomas Mapeia Diversidade da População Brasileira," *Folha de S. Paulo*, September 23, 2020, https://www1.folha.uol.com.br.

7. A. J. R. Russell-Wood, "Women and Society in Colonial Brazil," *Journal of Latin American Studies* 9, no. 1 (May 1977): 1–34.

8. Russell-Wood, "Women and Society in Colonial Brazil," 2.

9. Justin R. Bucciferro, "A Forced Hand: Natives, Africans, and the Population of Brazil, 1545–1850," *Journal of Iberian and Latin American Economic History* 31, no. 2 (May 2013): 285–317.

10. Janice Cristine Thiél, *Pele Silenciosa, Pele Sonora: A Construção Da Identidade Indígena Brasileira E Norte-americana Na Literatura* (Curitiba: Universidade Federal do Paraná, 2006).

11. Carla Akotirene, *Interseccionalidade* (São Paulo: Pólen, 2019).

12. Rafael Almeida, a black man of Candomblé, and an anarchist from Sergipe living in Bahia.

13. Marcel Heusinger, "Practical Challenges of Sustainable Human Development: Community-Driven Development as Response" (paper, Human Development and Capability Association's Annual International Conference: "Human Development: Vulnerability, Inclusion and Wellbeing," Managua, Nicaragua, September 9–12, 2013).

14. Katiúscia Ribeiro, "Mulheres Negras e a Força Matricomunitária," *Revista Cult* 254 (February 2020), 38–40.

15. Bianca Santana, "Quem é Mulher Negra No Brasil? Colorismo e o Mito da Democracia Racial," *Revista Cult*, May 8, 2018, https://revistacult.uol.com.br/home/colorismo-e-o-mito-da-democracia-racial. Santana is also the author of the book *Quando Me Descobri Negra* [*When I Discovered Myself as Black*] (São Paulo: SESI-SP Editora, 2016), Ebook.

16. Karina Ramos, head chef and doctoral student of history, specialist in Angolan food.

17. Ana Botner, political theorist, member of Plataforma9 and Enemy of the Queen.

18. Author interview with Ramos.

19. Cassio Brancaleone, professor of sociology at Universidade Federal Fronteira Sul and researcher at the Research Group on Anticapitalisms and Emerging Sociabilities.

20. Lisa Guernsey, "Ban on Nazi Items Upsets Collectors," *The New York Times*, May 10, 2001, https://archive.nytimes.com/www.nytimes.com/learning/teachers/featured_articles/20010510thursday.html.

21. "Gerador De Bandeira Antifascista" ["Antifa-Flag Generator"], https://felipealencar.github.io/antifascismo/gerador-bandeira.

22. "Amid Protests, Trump Says He Will Designate Antifa as Terrorist Organization," *Reuters*, May 31, 2020, https://www.reuters.com/article/uk-minneapolis-police-trump-antifa-idUKKBN2370LP.

23. "PL 3019/2020 Projeto de Lei," *Câmara dos Deputados*, January 6, 2020, https://www
.camara.leg.br/proposicoesWeb/fichadetramitacao?idProposicao=2254171.

24. One of the women mentioned on this list is currently in a legal battle against a Brazilian politician. She believes he knows who made the list and had plans to send it to
authorities in the US (under the Trump administration).

25. Giovana Fleck, "So-Called Anti-Fascist Files in Brazil Expose the Personal Information of Hundreds of People," *GlobalVoices*, July 14, 2020, https://globalvoices
.org/2020/07/14/so-called-anti-fascist-files-in-brazil-expose-the-personal-information
-of-hundreds-of-people.

Antisemitism and the Origins of Totalitarianism / Benjamin S. Case

1. Hannah Arendt, *The Origins of Totalitarianism* (New York: Harcourt, Brace and Co.,
1951), 152.

2. Arendt is razor sharp on the politics and cultures she herself experienced, amid historical conditions she saw, heard, and felt. However, she was unable to step outside
her European perspective when discussing Africa, specifically the colonial conditions of South Africa, to which she devotes some pages in Section II of *Origins*.
Arendt is not a political radical and in fact is suspicious of all ideologies. For this
and other things, such as her belief in democracy, she has been accused by some
(primarily Marxists) of being a liberal, or even a reactionary. In *Origins*, some read
her as equating fascism with communism, although to me this is a clear misreading.
What she does is describe elements of Stalinist totalitarianism that are particular to
that case, such as the mentality of subverting oneself to the party, as in show trials in which party members would confess to crimes they knew were fabrications
and declare their loyalty to Joseph Stalin as they were being executed. In any case,
anti-Arendt positions among some radicals smack of a discomfort the left has with
real self-criticism; she sees and says things some of us would prefer not to talk about.

3. See Hannah Arendt, *Eichmann in Jerusalem: A Report on the Banality of Evil* (New York:
Viking, 1963).

4. The Roma are also transnational and they too were targeted for extermination by the
Nazis and are to this day demonized by governments across Europe. But members
of the Roma people did not have access to the capital that members of the Jewish
people did, which elevated the visibility and political status of the Jews.

5. See Marx's 1844 essay, "On the Jewish Question."

6. Arendt, *Origins*, 290.

7. Jewish Voice for Peace, "Linda Sarsour on antisemitism," Facebook Video, February
28th, 2017, https://www.facebook.com/watch/?v=10156056191824992.

8. To be even clearer, Sarsour's commitment to speak out against antisemitism as a Palestinian woman, whose people continue to suffer under the tyranny of a state that
grew from Jewish aspirations to their own self-determination, is honorable.

9. When I was coming up as an organizer in the early 2000s, the only times antisemitism would be discussed were in reference to the Nazis or the ways that accusations
of antisemitism are used to defend Israel. Many Jews, my younger self included,
lean all the way into the role of assuring non-Jewish comrades that their critiques
of Israel are not antisemitic. The Jewish Voice for Peace book, *On Antisemitism: Solidarity and the Struggle for Justice* (Chicago: Haymarket Books, 2017), that Sarsour's
comments above were promoting is an example; it is a book published by a Jewish
organization that in fact is about what antisemitism is not. There is precious little in

the book regarding what antisemitism is, and even less about why we need to take it seriously. A more recent example can be found in the 2021 *Jewish Currents* editorial column, "How Not to Fight Antisemitism" (Jewish Currents, "How Not to Fight Antisemitism," *Jewish Currents*, April 5, 2021, https://jewishcurrents.org/how-not-to-fight-antisemitism.) In the role of allies, highlighting the ways antisemitism can be used as a political weapon is certainly crucial. Accusations of antisemitism are levied at Palestinians and solidarity activists, as well as at Movement for Black Lives activists and just about anyone else on the left for a host of disingenuous reasons. This use of antisemitism from all sides to sow confusion, mistrust, and infighting on the left is, as we will see, consistent with the initial purpose of the most pernicious antisemitic texts. This is precisely why systemic analysis and holistic strategy to fight antisemitism are crucial.

10. See Benjamin Steinhardt Case, "Decolonizing Jewishness: On Jewish Liberation in the 21st Century," *Tikkun*, April 23, 2018, https://www.tikkun.org/decolonizing-jewishness-on-jewish-liberation-in-the-21st-century-2.

11. Arendt, *Origins*, 86. This is based on a useful distinction we can make between Judaism (Jewish religion and spiritual belief), Jewishness (Jewish ethnicity, tradition, and cultural practice), and Jewry (Jewish peoplehood). See Albert Memmi, *Dominated Man: Notes Toward a Portrait* (Boston: Beacon Press, 1968), 27–31.

12. Technically, a German Jew coined the term "*antisemitisch*" to refer to antisemites before antisemites popularized the term "*antisemitismus*" ("antisemitism"). Either way, it was a singular term referring to Jew-haters/hatred, which is why the spelling "anti-Semitism" that many insist on using is incorrect, as is the ignorant argument that "anti-Semitism" should refer to the hatred of other "Semitic" peoples such as Arabs. Anti-Arab racism and Islamophobia are phenomena of their own; the term "antisemitism" was created specifically to refer to racialized Jew-hatred.

13. Otto Dov Kulka and Eberhard Jackel, *The Jews in the Secret Nazi Reports on Popular Opinion in Germany, 1933–1945* (New Haven, CT: Yale University Press, 2010). See also Hitler's manifesto, *Mein Kampf*. On antisemitism and contemporary white supremacists, see Eric K. Ward, "Skin in the Game: How Antisemitism Animates White Nationalism," *Political Research Associates*, June 29, 2017, https://www.politicalresearch.org/2017/06/29/skin-in-the-game-how-antisemitism-animates-white-nationalism.

14. On this dynamic, see also Michael Lerner, *The Socialism of Fools: Anti-Semitism on the Left* (United States: Tikkun, 1992) and April Rosenblum, "The Past Didn't Go Anywhere: Making Resistance to Antisemitism Part of All of Our Movements," 2007, https://www.aprilrosenblum.com/thepast.

15. See Sander Gilman, *The Jew's Body* (New York: Routledge, 1991).

16. See Ward, "Skin in the Game."

17. Accusing Jews of being traitors to nation, which is usually code for accusing them of being traitors to race, has perpetuated systemic antisemitism for centuries. Prominent historical examples include the Dreyfus Affair in France and the Rosenberg Trial in the US. Reflections of this dynamic appeared more recently in the Republican discourse around Adam Schiff and Alexander Vindman during Trump's first impeachment trial.

18. This phrase is often attributed to German socialist August Bebel, although it almost certainly originated before his usage, and the phrase was widely used in late 19th-century Germany. It is also the title of a 1971 article in *The New York Times* by Seymour Martin Lipset, a 1992 book by Michael Lerner, and a 2019 article by Shane Burley in *Journal of Social Justice*, all of which are worth reading. See Seymour Martin Lipset, "The Socialism of Fools," *The New York Times*, January 3, 1971; Michael Lerner,

The Socialism of Fools: Anti-Semitism on the Left; Shane Burley, "The Socialism of Fools," *Journal of Social Justice* 9 (2019), http://transformativestudies.org/wp-content/uploads/Socialism-of-Fools.pdf.

19. Arendt, *Origins*, 165.

20. Arendt, *Origins*, 165.

21. Arendt, *Origins*, 241.

22. In Noam Chomsky's words, "Zionism meant something different in the pre-state and poststate period. From 1948 on, Zionism meant the ideology of the state. A state religion. Like Americanism, or the magnificence of France. In fact even in this period the notion has changed . . . in 1967, which was a sea change in the way many Israelis saw themselves and what the state was like. Fundamentally, in the pre-state period, it was not a state religion. For example, in the mid-1940s I was a Zionist youth leader, but strongly opposed to a Jewish state. I was in favor of Jewish-Arab working-class cooperation to build a socialist Palestine. . . . You go back a bit further, my father, his generation they were Zionists, but they were Ahad Ha'amists [Cultural Zionists]. They wanted a cultural center as a place where the diaspora could find a new way to live together with the Palestinians" (Noam Chomsky and Ilan Pappé, *On Palestine*, Frank Barat, ed., [Chicago: Haymarket Books, 2015], 51–52). Arendt too was a Zionist in her youth who had argued strenuously against the creation of an exclusive Jewish state in Palestine, and was sharply critical of nationalist and chauvinist Israeli politics following the state's founding.

23. See Camille Jackson, "*The Turner Diaries*, Other Racist Novels, Inspire Extremist Violence," *Intelligence Report*, October 4, 2004, https://www.splcenter.org/fighting-hate/intelligence-report/2004/turner-diaries-other-racist-novels-inspire-extremist-violence.

24. The creation of this term is credited to white supremacist Eric Thompson in a 1976 article, which he updates at: Eric Thompson, "Welcome to Zog-World," *First Amendment Exercise Machine*, http://www.faem.com/eric/2000/et047.htm.

25. See https://antizionistleague.com.

26. Ben Samuels, "'Violent History' of 'Zio': How Chicago's Dyke March Adopted an Anti-Semitic Slur Dear to White Supremacists," *Haaretz*, July 18, 2017, https://www.haaretz.com/us-news/.premium-how-chicago-s-dyke-march-adopted-an-anti-semitic-slur-dear-to-far-rights-1.5494579.

27. The Chicago Dyke March tweeted, "Zio tears replenish my electrolytes!" with pictures of Beyoncé, in response to the reporter who originally reported on the march being fired. See Samuels, "'Violent History' of 'Zio'"; Yael Horowitz and Rae Gaines, "We Don't Have to Choose Between Dyke and Jewish Identities," *Washington Blade*, June 6, 2019, https://www.washingtonblade.com/2019/06/06/we-dont-have-to-choose-between-dyke-and-jewish-identities; Dahlia St. Knives, "As a Black Jewish Trans Woman, the Chicago Dyke March Does Not Include Me," *Hey Alma*, June 14, 2018, https://www.heyalma.com/as-a-black-jewish-trans-woman-the-chicago-dyke-march-does-not-include-me. On the controversy, see also Horowitz and Gaines, "We Don't Have to Choose."

28. See Yoko Liriano, "Lamis Deek speaks at the International Women's Strike - NYC - 8 March 2017," *Samidoun Network*, video, 5:51, https://www.youtube.com/watch?v=FLh2ipm4GMs.

29. This view has material consequences. Describing attacks against Jews by Black people in Brooklyn in 2018, Mark Winston Griffith, the director of the Black Movement Center, explained that many Black people see Jewishness as "a form of almost hyper-whiteness" (quoted in Ari Feldman, "Is a String of Attacks Against Brooklyn

Jews Really About Anti-Semitism?" *Forward*, December 5, 2018, https://forward.com/news/national/415385/is-a-string-of-attacks-against-brooklyn-jews-really-about-anti-semitism). See also David Schraub, "White Jews: An Intersectional Approach," *AJS Review* 43, no. 2 (2019): 379–407.

30. See American Jewish Committee, "AJC 2019 Survey of American Jewish Opinion," *American Jewish Committee*, June 2, 2019, https://www.ajc.org/news/survey2019.

31. American Jewish Committee, "AJC 2019 Survey of American Jewish Opinion."

32. The Union of Soviet Socialist Republics contributed to this confusion on the left with its propaganda beginning with Stalin, who deployed antisemitism in Russia in many of the same ways the Tsars had. Following his death, the Soviet government converted much of this same rhetoric to anti-Zionism when they backed Israel's neighbors in the regional wars of the 1960s and 1970s. Zionism, the party line went, was aligned with Nazism in the belief that Jews were a distinct, non-European people. "Turning a traditional antisemitic argument on its head," the Soviets claimed the cultural productions of Jews as those of Soviet Russians, Poles, et cetera, and that Jews who lay claim to a Jewish identity beyond this were inherently anti-Communist. The Jewish global plot simply became the Zionist global plot, recycling all the same themes, only claiming to distinguish antisemitism (narrowly defined as individual hatred of Jews) from anti-Zionism (a radical political position). See Richard Levy, ed., *Antisemitism in the Modern World: An Anthology of Texts* (Lexington, MA: D. C. Heath and Company, 1991), 259–61. Reflections of this position are visible today in the common perception on the left that antisemitism is an individual form of bigotry separate from systemic racism, as discussed earlier in this chapter.

33. See Brandy Zadrozny and Ben Collins, "Online Posts Tied to Suspected New Jersey Deli Shooter Pushed Anti-Semitic Conspiracies," *NBC News*, December 11, 2019, https://www.nbcnews.com/tech/social-media/online-posts-tied-suspected-new-jersey-deli-shooter-pushed-anti-n1100136.

34. Tim Dickinson, "Trump Preached White Supremacy in Minnesote, America Barely Noticed," *Rolling Stone*, September 22, 2020, https://www.rollingstone.com/politics/politics-news/trump-white-supremacy-racehorse-theory-1064928.

35. See Ira Forman, "Viktor Orbán is Exploiting Anti-Semitism," *The Atlantic*, December 14, 2018, https://www.theatlantic.com/ideas/archive/2018/12/viktor-orban-and-anti-semitic-figyelo-cover/578158; Shrenik Rao, "Hitler's Hindus: The Rise and Rise of India's Nazi-Loving Nationalists," *Haaretz*, December 14, 2017, https://www.haaretz.com/opinion/hitlers-hindus-indias-nazi-loving-nationalists-on-the-rise-1.5628532; Karen Lema and Manuel Mogato, "Philippines' Duterte Likens Himself to Hitler, Wants to Kill Millions of Drug Users," *Reuters*, September 29, 2016, https://www.reuters.com/article/us-philippines-duterte-hitler/philippines-duterte-likens-himself-to-hitler-wants-to-kill-millions-of-drug-users-idUSKCN1200B9.

36. See Zeev Sternhell, "Why Benjamin Netanyahu Loves the European Far-Right," *Foreign Policy*, February 24, 2019, https://foreignpolicy.com/2019/02/24/why-benjamin-netanyahu-loves-the-european-far-right-orban-kaczynski-pis-fidesz-visegrad-likud-antisemitism-hungary-poland-illiberalism.

37. See Julia Carrie Wong, "QAnon Explained: The Antisemitic Conspiracy Theory Gaining Traction Around the World," *The Guardian*, August 25, 2020, https://www.theguardian.com/us-news/2020/aug/25/qanon-conspiracy-theory-explained-trump-what-is.

38. See Cindy Milstein, ed., *There Is Nothing So Whole as a Broken Heart: Mending the World as Jewish Anarchists* (Chico, CA: AK Press, 2021).

39. Some excellent sources on Jewish positionality and antisemitism are: Hannah Arendt, *The Jew as Pariah: Jewish Identity and Politics in the Modern Age* (New York:

Grove Press, 1978); the 1965 preface to Albert Memmi, *The Colonizer and the Colonized* (Boston: Beacon Press, 1991); Ella Shohat's postscript to the Hebrew translation of Frantz Fanon's *The Wretched of the Earth*, titled "Black, Jew, Arab," available in English in Ella Shohat, *Taboo Memories, Diasporic Voices* (Durham, NC: Duke University Press, 2006); Rosenblum, "The Past Didn't Go Anywhere"; Jews for Racial & Economic Justice, "Understanding Antisemitism: An Offering to Our Movement," *Jews for Racial & Economic Justice*, 2017, https://www.jfrej.org/assets/uploads/JFREJ-Understanding -Antisemitism-November-2017-v1-3-2.pdf; Milstein, ed., *There Is Nothing So Whole as a Broken Heart*; Aurora Levins-Morales, "Latin@s, Israel, and Palestine: Understanding Anti-Semitism," *Aurora Levins-Morales* (blog), *Aurora Levins-Morales*, http://www.aurora levinsmorales.com/blog/latins-israel-and-palestine-understanding-anti-semitism; Yotam Marom, "Toward the Next Jewish Rebellion: Facing Antisemitism and Assimilation in our Movement," *Medium.com*, August 9, 2016, https://medium.com/@Yotam Marom/toward-the-next-jewish-rebellion-bed5082c52fc; Ami Weintraub, "Silent Rage," *Tikkun*, September 16, 2019, https://www.tikkun.org/silent-rage; and Case, "Decolonizing Jewishness."

40. Arendt, *Origins*, 330.
41. See María Castro and Javier Sethness Castro, "'Dangerous Minds': Wagner and Bakunin's Social Imaginaries – Nationalist or Anarchist?," *Anarchist Studies*, October 6, 2019, https://anarchiststudies.org/dangerous-mindswagner-and-bakunins -social-imaginaries-nationalist-or-anarchist.

"Kops and Klan Go Hand in Hand" / Shane Burley

1. Shane Burley and Alexander Reid Ross, "Conspiracy Theories by Cops Fuel Far Right Attacks Against Antiracist Protesters," *Truthout*, September 18, 2020, https://truthout.org/articles/conspiracy-theories-by-cops-fuel-far-right-attacks-against -antiracist-protesters.
2. That's not to say that slave patrols aren't part of the lineage of policing because of course they are, just like the control of colonized peoples in occupied territories and the suppression of labor unrest are part of how policing took shape.

A Partial Typology of Empathy for Enemies / Joan Braune

1. Benjamin Teitelbaum, "Collaborating with the Radical Right: Scholar-Informant Solidarity and the Case for an Immoral Anthropology," *Current Anthropology* 60, no. 3 (2019): 414.
2. Teitelbaum, "Collaborating with the Radical Right," 418.
3. Teitelbaum, "Collaborating with the Radical Right," 419.
4. Teitelbaum, "Collaborating with the Radical Right," 419.
5. Teitelbaum, "Collaborating with the Radical Right," 420.
6. Teitelbaum, "Collaborating with the Radical Right," 421.
7. Teitelbaum, "Collaborating with the Radical Right," 416.
8. Teitelbaum, "Collaborating with the Radical Right," 421.
9. Teitelbaum, "Collaborating with the Radical Right," 422.
10. Teitelbaum, "Collaborating with the Radical Right," 419.
11. Cristien Storm, *Empowered Boundaries: Speaking Truth, Setting Boundaries, and Inspiring Social Change* (Berkeley, CA: North Atlantic Books, 2018).

12. Storm, *Empowered Boundaries*, xii–xiii.

13. Storm, *Empowered Boundaries*, xii–xiii.

14. Storm, *Empowered Boundaries*, xiii.

15. Mark Blyth, "Global Trumpism: Why Trump's Victory Was 30 Years in the Making and Why It Won't Stop Here," *Foreign Affairs*, November 15, 2016, https://www.foreign affairs.com/articles/2016-11-15/global-trumpism.

16. Michaela Pfundmair, "Ostracism Promotes a Terroristic Mindset," *Behavioral Sciences of Terrorism & Political Aggression* 11, no. 2 (2019): 134–48.

17. Eli Saslow, *Rising Out of Hatred: The Awakening of a Former White Nationalist* (New York: Doubleday, 2018).

18. Nadine V. Wedderburn and Robert E. Carey, "Forgiveness in the Face of Hate," in Ana-Maria Pascal, ed., *Multiculturalism and the Convergence of Faith and Practical Wisdom in Modern Society* (Hershey, PA: IGI Global, 2017), 322; Andre E. Johnson and Earle J. Fisher, "'But, I Forgive You?': Mother Emanuel, Black Pain, and the Rhetoric of Forgiveness," *Journal of Communication & Religion* 42, no. 1 (2019): 5–19.

19. Robin DiAngelo, *White Fragility: Why It's So Hard for White People to Talk About Racism* (Boston: Beacon Press, 2018), 64, 123–24.

20. Crystal M. Fleming, *How to Be Less Stupid About Race: On Racism, White Supremacy, and the Racial Divide* (Boston: Beacon Press, 2018), 156–58.

21. Anjabeen Ashraf and Sylvia Nasser, "American Muslims and Vicarious Trauma: An Explanatory Concurrent Mixed-Methods Study," *American Journal of Orthopsychiatry* 88, no. 5 (2018): 516–28.

22. Tiffany Stanley, "Only Human: How an American Ex-Jihadi Struggled to Rebuild His Life in the Country He'd Once Vowed to Destroy," *The New Republic*, November 15, 2017, https://newrepublic.com/article/145433/only-human-american-ex-jihadi -rebuild-life-country-once-vowed-destroy.

23. Southern Poverty Law Center, "Anti-Muslim," *Southern Poverty Law Center*, https://www.splcenter.org/fighting-hate/extremist-files/ideology/anti-muslim. Clarion Project, "Former Extremists Frank Meeink and Tanya Joya: The Way Back," *Clarion Project*, https://clarionproject.org/former-extremists-frank -meeink-and-tanya-joya-the-way-back.

24. Light Upon Light, "Ctrl+Alt+Del-Hate; The Future of the Far-Right and Combating Reciprocal Radicalization," *Parallel Networks*, video, 1:30:56, July 30, 2020, https:// www.youtube.com/watch?v=fEOXvwkoW10 (typed comments section).

25. Alessandro Orsini, *Sacrifice: My Life in a Fascist Militia*, trans. Sarah Jane Nodes (Ithaca, NY: Cornell University Press, 2017).

26. Orsini, *Sacrifice*, 155.

27. Vegas Tenold, *Everything You Love Will Burn: Inside the Rebirth of White Nationalism in America* (New York: Nation Books, 2018), 204.

28. James Pogue, *Chosen Country: A Rebellion in the West* (New York: Henry Holt and Company, 2018).

29. DJ Cashmere, "Deradicalization in the Deep South: How a Former Neo-Nazi Makes Amends," *Yes!*, November 12, 2019, https://www.yesmagazine.org/issue/ building-bridges/2019/11/12/deradicalization-in-the-deep-south; Samantha Kutner, "Introducing the Fash Fatigue Chronicles," *Medium.com*, March 29, 2019, https:// medium.com/@ashkenaz89/introducing-the-fash-fatigue-chronicles-34b80c 679698.

30. Kutner, "Introducing the Fash Fatigue Chronicles."

31. I particularly suggest studying Laura Van Dernoot Lipsky's book *Trauma Stewardship*, for numerous strategies, as well as watching her Ted Talk for a short introduction.

Laura van Dernoot Lipsky, *Trauma Stewardship: An Everyday Guide to Caring for Self While Caring for Others* (San Francisco: Berrett-Koehler, 2009); Laura Van Dernoot Lipsky, "Beyond the Cliff," *TEDx Talks*, video, 19:23, April 23, 2015, https://www.youtube.com/watch?v=uOzDGrcvmus.

32. Paris Martineau, "The Existential Crisis Plaguing Extremism Researchers," *Wired*, May 2, 2019, https://www.wired.com/story/existential-crisis-plaguing-online-extremism-researchers; Hannah Allem, "'It Gets to You.' Extremism Researchers Confront the Unseen Toll of Their Work," *NPR*, September 20, 2019, https://knpr.org/npr/2019-09/it-gets-you-extremism-researchers-confront-unseen-toll-their-work; Tina Askanius, "Studying the Nordic Resistance Movement: Three Urgent Questions for Researchers of Contemporary Neo-Nazis and Their Media Practices," *Media, Culture & Society* 41, no. 6 (2019): 878–88; Michael Kroner, "Vicarious Trauma from Online Extremism Research—A Call to Action," *Global Network on Extremism & Technology*, March 27, 2020, https://gnet-research.org/2020/03/27/vicarious-trauma-from-online-extremism-research-a-call-to-action.

33. Kathleen Blee, "Studying the Enemy," in Barry Glassner and Rosanna Hertz, eds., *Our Studies, Ourselves: Sociologists' Lives and Work* (New York: Oxford University Press, 2003), 13–23, 18, 20.

34. Askanius, "Studying the Nordic Resistance Movement," 884, 886.

35. Casey Newton, "The Trauma Floor: The Secret Lives of Facebook Moderators in America," *The Verge*, February 19, 2019, https://www.theverge.com/2019/2/25/18229714/cognizant-facebook-content-moderator-interviews-trauma-working-conditions-arizona.

36. Talia Lavin, *Culture Warlords: My Journey into the Dark Web of White Supremacy* (New York: Hachette Books, 2020), 237–40. Arjun Sethi, *American Hate: Survivors Speak Out* (New York: The New Press, 2018), 161.

37. Erich Fromm, *Escape from Freedom* (New York: Avon Books, 1969), 20.

38. Mark Bray, *Antifa: The Anti-Fascist Handbook* (Brooklyn: Melville House, 2017), 135.

39. I am indebted for this very important phrase and formulation to Cristien Storm.

40. Fleming, *How to Be Less Stupid About Race*, 156.

41. Fleming, *How to Be Less Stupid About Race*, 158.

42. Fleming, *How to Be Less Stupid About Race*, 160.

43. Alexander Reid Ross and Shane Burley, "Alexander Reid Ross & Shane Burley: Fascism Today," *KODX Seattle*, video, 1:37:00, February 4, 2018, https://www.youtube.com/watch?v=mR4eLFo1lEU&t=3020s.

44. David Neiwert, *In God's Country: The Patriot Movement and the Pacific Northwest* (Pullman, WA: Washington State University Press, 1999), 47–48.

45. Guerry Hodderson, "Standing Up to Fascist Creeps" (lecture, Seattle Radical Women meeting, Seattle, WA, July 14, 2009).

46. Pogue, *Chosen Country*, 102.

47. Georg Lukács, *History and Class Consciousness: Studies in Marxist Dialectics*, trans. R. Livingstone (Cambridge, MA: MIT Press, 1971).

48. Joan Braune, *Erich Fromm's Revolutionary Hope: Prophetic Messianism as a Critical Theory of the Future* (Rotterdam: Sense Publishers, 2014).

49. Erich Fromm, *The Sane Society* (New York: Henry Holt and Company, 1955), 239.

50. Gustav Landauer, "A Free Workers' Council," In Gustave Landauer, *Revolution and Other Writings: A Political Reader*, ed. and trans. Gabriel Kuhn (Oakland, CA: PM Press, 2010), 218–21.

51. Erich Fromm, *The Art of Loving* (New York: Harper Perennial, 2006), 120–22.

52. Paulo Freire, *Pedagogy of the Oppressed*, trans. Myla Bergman Ramos (New York:

Bloomsbury Publishing, 2006). bell hooks, *All About Love: New Visions* (New York: Harper Perennial, 2001)

53. Fascism is constantly appropriating from the Left; for more insight on this topic, see Alexander Reid Ross *Against the Fascist Creep* (Chico, CA: AK Press, 2017).

54. "Fascism in Italy: The Hipster Fascists Trying to Bring Mussolini Back Into the Mainstream," *Channel 4 News*, video, 10:18, March 2, 2018, https://www.youtube.com/watch?v=I3×-ge4w46E.

55. Hélène Barthélemy, "How to Write History Like an Identitarian," *Hatewatch*, February 14, 2018, https://www.splcenter.org/hatewatch/2018/02/14/how-write-history-identitarian.

56. Alejandra Molina, "In Oregon, Churches and Anti-Fascists Unite to Provide Mutual Aid to Fire Evacuees and Others in Need," *Religion News Service*, September 22, 2020, https://religionnews.com/2020/09/22/in-oregon-churches-and-anti-fascists-unite-to-provide-mutual-aid-to-fire-evacuees-and-others-in-need/?fbclid=IwAR3H-bBi8kA39TUdzqNiaWovnRrKOOMU8Pu4328XtlIM09Nmg9qNlmU77yc.

The Meme Alibi / Margaret Rex

1. Michael Mark Cohen, "Charlottesville 2017: The Legacy of Race and Inequity/Summer of Hate: Charlottesville, USA," *The Journal of Southern History* 85, no. 4 (2019), 974–976.

2. Brett Barrouquere, "How the 'Unite the Right' Murder Trial Helped Debunk Alt-Right Myths," *Hatewatch*, December 11, 2018, https://www.splcenter.org/hatewatch/2018/12/10/how-unite-right-murder-trial-helped-debunk-alt-right-myths.

3. Brennan Gilmore, "Two Years After Charlottesville, I'm Fighting the Conspiracy Theory Industrial Complex," *USA Today*, August 11, 2019, https://www.usatoday.com/story/opinion/voices/2019/08/11/charlottesville-anniversary-alex-jones-conspiracy-theorists-column/1955910001.

4. The subject's name is known to the author but changed for this work.

5. Kathleen Belew, *Bring the War Home: The White Power Movement and Paramilitary America* (Cambridge, MA: Harvard University Press, 2018).

6. The "alt-light" is a term used for a loose confederation of mostly online figures who use much of the style and argumentation from the alt-right, such as around immigration and reactionary cultural issues, but do not stray into explicit white nationalism.

7. Eric O. Silva and Matthew B. Flynn, "Liminal Stigma and Disaligning Activity: Online Comments about Trump's Family Separation Policy," *Symbolic Interaction* 43, no. 1 (2020), 126–55.

8. Lexi McMenamin, "How Cars Became a Deadly Anti-Protest Weapon," *Mic*, December 30, 2020, https://www.mic.com/impact/how-cars-became-a-deadly-anti-protest-weapon-53291831.

9. Five interviews were conducted between October and November 2019. Interviewees were given pseudonyms, and interview quotes will be used throughout, with attributions made in-text rather than endnoted.

10. Talia Lavin, *Culture Warlords: My Journey into the Dark Web of White Supremacy* (New York: Hachette Books, 2020).

11. Shannon E. Reid and Matthew Valasik, *Alt-Right Gangs: A Hazy Shade of White* (Oakland, CA: University of California Press, 2020).

12. Francesco Farinelli, "Conspiracy Theories and Right-Wing Extremism – Insights

and Recommendations for P/CVE," European Commission Radicalization Awareness Network, 2021, https://ec.europa.eu/home-affairs/system/files/2021-04/ran _conspiracy_theories_and_right-wing_2021_en.pdf.

13. Gavin McInnes, "Gavin McInnes: I'm Not a Conservative," *Rebel News*, video, 4:52, May 1, 2015, https://www.youtube.com/watch?v=9rrtttOCtq8.

14. Tamerra Griffin, "Black Twitter Roasted Yahoo Finance After the 'Nigger Navy' Typo Tweet," *BuzzFeed News*, January 6, 2017, https://www.buzzfeednews.com/article/ tamerragriffin/yahoo-finance-nigger-navy-typo.

15. Claudia Bianchi, "Slurs and Appropriation: An Echoic Account," *Journal of Pragmatics* 66 (2014), 35–44.

16. Andrew Marantz, *Anti-Social: Online Extremists, Techno-Utopians, and the Hijacking of the American Conversation* (New York: Viking, 2019).

17. William Davies, "The Free Speech Panic: How the Right Concocted a Crisis," *The Guardian*, July 26, 2018, https://www.theguardian.com/news/2018/jul/26/the-free -speech-panic-censorship-how-the-right-concocted-a-crisis.

18. Parents 4 Peace, "Are You Concerned?," *Parents 4 Peace*, June 2019, https://www .parents4peace.org/wp-content/uploads/2019/06/Radicalization-toolkit.pdf.

19. Pete Simi, Steven Windisch, and Karyn Sporer, "Recruitment and Radicalization among US Far-Right Terrorists: Report to the Office of University Programs, Science and Technology Directorate, U.S. Department of Homeland Security," *National Consortium for the Study of Terrorism and Responses to Terrorism*, November 2016, https:// www.start.umd.edu/pubs/START_RecruitmentRadicalizationAmongUSFarRight Terrorists_Nov2016.pdf.

20. Inkblot Project, "Be the Solution," Inkblot Project, 2021, https://www.inkblotproject .com/toolkit-1.

21. Mark Bray, *Antifa: The Anti-Fascist Handbook* (Brooklyn: Melville House, 2017)

22. Whitney Phillips, "The Oxygen of Amplification: Better Practices for Reporting on Extremists, Antagonists, and Manipulators," *Data & Society*, May 22, 2018, https:// datasociety.net/library/oxygen-of-amplification.

23. Elle Reeve, "He's an Ex-Proud Boy. Here's What He Says Happens Within the Group's Ranks, *CNN*, October 11, 2021, https://www.cnn.com/2020/11/25/us/ex-proud-boys- member/index.html.

24. Reeve, "He's an Ex-Proud Boy."

25. Ed Pilkington, "'It Is Serious and Intense': White Supremacist Domestic Terror Threat Looms Large in US," *The Guardian*, October 11, 2021, https://www.theguardian.com/ us-news/2020/oct/19/white-supremacist-domestic-terror-threat-looms-large-in-us.

26. Amy B. Cooter, "Americanness, Masculinity, and Whiteness: How Michigan Militia Men Navigate Evolving Social Norms" (doctoral dissertation, The University of Michigan, 2013).

27. Cameron Peters, "State-Level Republicans Are Making It Easier to Run Over Protesters," *Vox*, April 25, 2021, https://www.vox.com/2021/4/25/22367019/gop-laws -oklahoma-iowa-florida-floyd-blm-protests-police. Greg Allen, "Florida Enacts Nation's Toughest Restrictions on Protest," *NPR*, April 19, 2021, https://www.npr .org/2021/04/19/988791175/florida-adopts-nations-toughest-restrictions-on-protests. The Florida law, HB1, was blocked by a US district judge in September 2021. Governor Ron DeSantis is expected to appeal to the 11th Circuit Court of appeals

28. Evan Hill, Mike Baker, Derek Knowles, and Stella Cooper, "'Straight to Gunshots': How a U.S. Task Force Killed an Antifa Activist," *The New York Times*, December 4, 2020, https://www.nytimes.com/2020/10/13/us/michael-reinoehl-antifa-portland -shooting.html. Aila Slisco, "Marjorie Taylor Greene Urges Supporters to 'Remember

Kyle Rittenhouse', Shares Fundraising Page," *Newsweek*, October 8, 2021, https://www.newsweek.com/marjorie-taylor-greene-urges-supporters-remember-kyle-rittenhouse-shares-fundraising-page-1637265. Jemima McEvoy, "Kyle Rittenhouse Defense Fund Raising Hundreds Of Thousands Of Dollars Ahead Of His November Murder Trial, *Forbes*, June 21, 2021, https://www.forbes.com/sites/jemimamcevoy/2021/06/21/kyle-rittenhouse-defense-fund-raising-hundreds-of-thousands-of-dollars-ahead-of-his-november-murder-trial. Jason Wilson, "US Police and Public Officials Donated to Kyle Rittenhouse, Data Breach Reveals," *The Guardian*, April 16, 2021, https://www.theguardian.com/us-news/2021/apr/16/us-police-officers-public-officials-crowdfunding-website-data-breach.

29. As noted by Ryan Cooper: "[S]ince 9/11 some 114 people have been killed by far-right extremists, as compared to 107 by jihadists, and one (1) by a leftist. The Center for Strategic and International Studies has numbers going back to 1994, and finds 335 deaths from right-wing extremists against 22 from left-wing ones. And while 9/11 was the deadliest terrorist attack in American history, before that, the record was held by the far right. Timothy McVeigh, the main perpetrator of the Oklahoma City bombing, was an antigovernment extremist with ties to the militia movement who used to drive around to gun shows selling copies of *The Turner Diaries* [by William L. Pierce] (an explicitly genocidal white supremacist tract)." Ryan Cooper, "Political Violence Is Coming from One Direction in This Country: The Far Right," *The Week*, October 2, 2020, https://theweek.com/articles/941014/political-violence-coming-from-direction-country-far-right.

Make Journalism Antifa Again / Abner Häuge

1. "Doxing" means the revelation of personal information of a far-right person as part of a pressure campaign.
2. This means that we will announce activist events, such as public protests, marches, rallies, pressure campaigns, et cetera. The "call to action" is an invitation for people outside of the core circle of organizers and journalists to participate in the larger campaign in some way.
3. There is a long debate about the complicated use of video. On the one hand, it can be the best way to reveal the behavior of fascists and the police. On the other, it can reveal the identities of antifascists and leave them vulnerable to fascist retaliation or state repression. Proceed with caution.

Surreal Antifascism, 1921–45 / Alexander Reid Ross

1. Gavin Grindon, "Surrealism, Dada, and the Refusal of Work: Autonomy, Activism, and Social Participation in the Radical Avant-Garde," *Oxford Art Journal* 34, no. 1 (March 2011), 79–96.
2. Pierre Yoyotte, "Antifascist Significance of Surrealism," in Franklin Rosemont and Robin D. G. Kelley, eds., *Black, Brown, and Beige: Surrealist Writings from Africa and the Diaspora* (Austin: University of Texas Press, 2009), 43–44.
3. Habib Tengour, "Maghrebian Surrealism," in Rosemont and Kelley, eds., *Black, Brown, and Beige*, 179.
4. Cheikh Tidiane Sylla, "Surrealism and Black African Art," in Rosemont and Kelley, eds., *Black, Brown, and Beige*, 180.

5. See the manifesto, "THE REVOLUTION FIRST AND ALWAYS!," in Michael Richardson and Krysztof Fijaòkowski, eds., *Surrealism Against the Current: Tracts and Declarations* (London: Pluto Press, 2001), 96. "We are the revolt of the spirit; we consider bloody revolution to be the unavoidable revenge of a spirit humiliated by your works. We are not utopians: we conceive this Revolution only in social form."

6. See Henry-Alexander Grubbs, "L'Influence d'Isidore Ducasse sur les débuts littéraires d'Alfred Jarry," *Revue d'Histoire littéraire de la France* 42, no. 3 (1935), 437–40.

7. For a glimpse at some proto-Surrealist attributes of the Paris Commune, see Kristin Ross, *Emergence of Social Space: Rimbaud and the Paris Commune* (Minneapolis: University of Minnesota Press, 1988).

8. Christophe Charle, *Birth of the Intellectuals: 1880–1900*, trans. David Fernbach and G. M. Goshgarian (Cambridge, UK: Polity, 2015).

9. Michel Winock, *Nationalism, Antisemitism, and Fascism in France*, trans. Jane Marie Todd (Stanford, CA: Stanford University Press, 1998).

10. For more on Jarry and the Dreyfus Affair, see J. A. Cutshall, "'Celui Qui Dreyfuse': Alfred Jarry and the Dreyfus Case," *Symposium: A Quarterly Journal in Modern Literatures* 43, no. 1 (Spring 1989): 20; for Appolinaire's influence, see Willard Bohn, "Surrealism to Surrealism: Apollinaire and Breton," *The Journal of Aesthetics and Art Criticism* 36, no. 2 (Winter 1977), 197–210.

11. For more on Appolinaire, see Walter L. Adamson, "Apollinaire's Politics: Modernism, Nationalism, and the Public Sphere in Avant-garde Paris," *Modernism/modernity* 6, no. 3 (September 1999): 33–56.

12. Although some of Jarry's drift is debatable, antisemitic tendencies are laced throughout his final, unfinished play, and Appolinaire began favoring Action Française toward the end of his life. Jarry was irrational and tubercular, whereas Appolinaire had been hit with a shell fragment during the end of the war, leaving him partially paralyzed and perhaps affecting his thinking. See Alastair Brotchie, *Alfred Jarry: A Pataphysical Life* (Cambridge, MA: MIT Press, 2015); and Adamson, "Apollinaire's Politics."

13. Dada 3, *andrebreton.fr*, https://www.andrebreton.fr/en/work/56600101000418?back_rql=DISTINCT%20Any%20M%2CST%2CD%20ORDERBY%20ST%20WHERE%20M%20in_series%20X%2C%20M%20title%20MT%2C%20M%20sorttitle%20ST%2C%20M%20short_description%20D%2C%20X%20eid%206507&back_url=https%3A%2F%2Fwww.andrebreton.fr%2Fen%2Fseries%2F128%3Fvid%3Dprimary.

14. Bohn, "Surrealism to Surrealism."

15. Willard Bohn, *The Rise of Surrealism: Cubism, Dada, and the Pursuit of the Marvelous* (New York: SUNY Press, 2002), 132.

16. Franklin Rosemont, *Jacques Vaché and the Roots of Surrealism: Including Vaché's War Letters & Other Writings* (Chicago: Charles H. Kerr, 2007).

17. Dadaism was viewed as a "negation for the sake of negation," whereas Surrealists affirmed the dialectical method. See "LET'S GET TO THE POINT," in Richardson and Fijaòkowski, eds., *Surrealism Against the Current*, 56. "It is revolutionary to know how to retain what needs retaining and to renew what needs renewing. The motto "Something new! Something new!" is a Dada motto, a reactionary one," wrote a group of young, clandestine Surrealists to Breton during the Occupation. See "LETTER TO ANDRÉ BRETON," in Richardson and Fijaòkowski, eds., *Surrealism Against the Current* (London: Pluto, 2001), 31.

18. Bohn, "Surrealism to Surrealism."

19. André Breton, *Communicating Vessels*, trans. Mary Ann Caws and Geoffrey T. Harris (Lincoln, NE: Bison Books), 86.

20. J. A. Boiffard, P. Éluard, and R. Vitrac, "Introduction, La Révolution surréaliste (1), 1924," in Richardson and Fijaòkowski, eds., *Surrealism Against the Current*, 23.

21. André Breton, *Manifestoes of Surrealism*, trans. Richard Seaver and Helen R. Lane (Ann Arbor, MI: University of Michigan Press, 1972), 286. From the introduction to the first issue of *La Révolution surrealiste*: "Surrealism is the crossroads of the enchantments of sleep, alcohol, tobacco, ether, opium, cocaine, and morphine. But it is also the breaker of chains: we do not sleep, we do not drink, we do not smoke, we do not inhale, we do not inject ourselves but we dream, and the speed of the lamps' needles introduces into our brains the marvelous deflowered sponge of gold." See "Introduction, La Révolution surréaliste," in Richardson and Fijaòkowski, eds., *Surrealism Against the Current*, 22.

22. Breton, "Surrealist Situation of the Object," in *Manifestoes of Surrealism*, 274.

23. Alastair Hemmens, *The Critique of Work in Modern French Thought From Charles Fourier to Guy Debord* (Cham, CH: Palgrave Macmillan, 2019), 106–9.

24. Although the Parisian Surrealists certainly indulged in Romantic idealizations and assumptions about the "savages" and the "primitives"—a problem whose implications cannot be underplayed and to which we will return—their primitivism and exoticism did far more to advance anthropological studies toward more cautious and inclusionary models than to cast European thought back toward colonial ideas, and Surrealists from Martinique, Egypt, Cuba, and elsewhere overthrew colonial prejudices. For instance, Michel Leiris joined Surrealism and anthropology in ways that seriously challenged his academic field by repudiating the notion of an objective, outside scientist neutrally observing their surroundings, and adopting instead an almost impressionistic approach to recording field notes and reporting the findings of his expeditions. See Louise Tythacott, *Surrealism and the Exotic* (London: Routledge, 2003), 201–02.

25. Breton, "Second Manifesto of Surrealism," in *Manifestoes of Surrealism*, 154.

26. See Tythacott, *Surrealism and the Exotic*, 191.

27. Tythacott, *Surrealism and the Exotic*, 215–16.

28. Rory Dufficy, "Dream-work: Surrealism and Revolutionary Subjectivity in André Breton and Georges Bataille," *Australia and New Zealand Journal of European Studies* 9, no. 3 (2017), 44.

29. Thomas Mical, *Surrealism and Architecture* (London: Routledge, 2004), 4.

30. Neil Cox, "Desire Bound: Violence, Body, Machine," in David Hopkins, ed., *A Companion to Dada and Surrealism* (Oxford: John Wiley & Sons, 2016), 345.

31. Cox, "Desire Bound," 345.

32. Alyce Mahon, *The Marquis de Sade and the Avant-Garde* (Princeton, NJ: Princeton University Press, 2020).

33. Mahon, *The Marquis de Sade*, 111.

34. See Susan Laxton, *Surrealism at Play* (Durham, NC: Duke University Press, 2019), 699–712, Kindle.

35. Elizabeth Legge, "Nothing, Ventured: Paris Dada into Surrealism," in Hopkins, ed., *A Companion to Dada and Surrealism* (Oxford: John Wiley & Sons, 2016), 94.

36. Aragon played the defense attorney for Barrès, which might have reflected his own continued, although somewhat secret, appreciation of the author's prose. See Emilien Carassus, "De quelques surréalistes et du «Procès Barrès» Lettres inédites de Louis Aragon et de Pierre Drieu la Rochelle à Maurice Barrès," *Littératures* 13, no. 1 (1985): 151–68.

37. Avi Feldman, "Performing Justice–From Dada's Trial to Yael Bartana's JRMiP Congress," *Curating Degree Zero Archive: Curatorial Research*, Issue 26, October 2015,

https://www.on-curating.org/issue-26-reader/the-curator-and-her-double-the-cruelty-of-the-avatar-copy-183.html.

38. Feldman, "Performing Justice," 70–85.

39. André Breton, "Artificial Hells. Inauguration of the '1921 Dada Season,'" trans. Matthew S. Witkovsky, *OCTOBER* 105 (Summer 2003), 137–144.

40. Katharine Conley, *Robert Desnos, Surrealism, and the Marvelous in Everyday Life* (Lincoln: University of Nebraska Press, 2003), 23.

41. Conley, *Robert Desnos*, 23.

42. Jonathan Paul Eburne, *Surrealism and the Art of Crime* (Ithaca, NY: Cornell University Press, 2008), 81.

43. Richard David Sonn, *Sex, Violence, and the Avant-garde: Anarchism in Interwar France* (University Park, PA: Pennsylvania State University, 2010), 76–77.

44. David Bate, *Photography and Surrealism: Sexuality, Colonialism and Social Dissent* (New York: Routledge, 2020), 47.

45. Cox, "Desire Bound," 544.

46. Legge, "Nothing, Ventured," 94.

47. Colin Roust, *Georges Auric: A Life in Music and Politics* (Oxford: Oxford University Press, 2020), 75.

48. See Breton, "Second Manifesto of Surrealism."

49. As a result, Aragon lost his stipend from the fashion designer Jacques Doucet, and Drieu la Rochelle intervened on Aragon's behalf, saying, "Wise kings have always sheltered mad monks." Drieu la Rochelle and Aragon fell out the following year. See Frederick Brown, *The Embrace of Unreason: France, 1914–1940* (New York: Random House, 2014), 169.

50. Nancy Cunard, "Surrealist Manifestation at the Diaghilev Ballet," in Penelope Rosemont, ed., *Surrealist Women: An International Anthology* (Austin: The University of Texas Press, 1998), 23.

51. Eugene Jolas, *Eugene Jolas: Critical Writings, 1924–1951*, eds. Klaus H. Kiefer and Rainer Rumold (Evanston, IN: Northwestern University Press, 2009), 103.

52. "To the Soldiers and Sailors," in Richardson and Fijaòkowski, eds., *Surrealism Against the Current*, 181.

53. "Declaration of January 27, 1925," in Richardson and Fijaòkowski, eds., *Surrealism Against the Current*, 24

54. Breton, "Speech to the Congress of Writers," in *Manifestoes of Surrealism*, 235–36.

55. David Drake, "The PCF, the Surrealists, Clarté and the Rif War," *French Cultural Studies* 17, no. 2 (2006): 173–88.

56. Raymond Spiteri, "Surrealism and the Question of Politics," in David Hopkins, ed., *A Companion to Dada and Surrealism* (Oxford: John Wiley & Sons, 2016), 112.

57. Spiteri, "Surrealism and the Question of Politics," 112.

58. Spiteri, "Surrealism and the Question of Politics," 113.

59. Tythacott, *Surrealism and the Exotic*, 30–31.

60. See Majella Munro, "Dada and Surrealism in Japan," in Hopkins, ed., *A Companion to Dada and Surrealism*, 144.

61. See Breton, *Manifestoes of Surrealism*.

62. "Légitime Défense," in Rosemont and Kelley, eds., *Black, Brown, and Beige*, 37.

63. Cristina Chimisso, *Gaston Bachelard: Critic of Science and the Imagination* (New York: Taylor & Francis, 2001), 197.

64. Chimisso, *Gaston Bachelard*, 265–66.

65. Donald Lacoss, *Surrealism, Politics and Culture* (New York: Taylor & Francis, 2020)

66. Breton, "Surrealist Situation of the Object."

67. Spiteri, "Surrealism and the Question of Politics," 122.

68. "BURN THEM DOWN!," in Richardson and Fijaòkowski, eds., *Surrealism Against the Current*, 97.

69. Spiteri, "Surrealism and the Question of Politics," in Hopkins, ed., *A Companion to Dada and Surrealism*, 123.

70. Barbara McCloskey, *Artists of World War II* (Westport, CT: Greenwood Publishing Group, 2005), 162.

71. Tim McNeese, *Salvador Dalí* (New York: Infobase, 2006), 92

72. Breton, "Prolegomena to a Third Surrealist Manifesto," in *Manifestoes of Surrealism*, 282.

73. Gérard Durozoi, *History of the Surrealist Movement*, trans. Alison Anderson (Chicago: University of Chicago Press, 2002), 257.

74. The position of the Surrealists and the Committee was somewhat fraught. They argued that "telling the German people that Hitler (and only he among all capitalist and fascist governments!) wants war is not a good way to persuade them." In a significant stretch of the imagination, apparently to ensure opposition to capitalism on the same footing as opposition to fascism, the Committee called for an international negotiation for disarmament and peace that included Germany. The obvious problem that went unmentioned was that Hitler's expansionism had gone unchallenged by Western powers through appeasement. Breton, "Speech to the Congress of Writers," in *Manifestoes of Surrealism*, 238.

75. Durozoi, *History of the Surrealist Movement*, 257.

76. Breton, "On the Time When the Surrealists Were Right," in *Manifestoes of Surrealism*, 243.

77. Breton, "Speech to the Congress of Writers," 240–41.

78. Clifford Browder, *André Breton, Arbiter of Surrealism* (Geneva: Droz, 1967), 34–35.

79. Breton, "Political Position of the Surrealists," in *Manifestoes of Surrealism*, 210.

80. Breton, "Political Position of the Surrealists," 215.

81. Claudio Fogu, "Fascismo-Style and the Posthistorical Imaginary," in Angelica Fenner and Eric D. Weitz, eds., *Fascism and Neofascism: Critical Writings on the Radical Right in Europe* (New York: Palgrave Macmillan, 2016), 67.

82. Mark Ford, *Raymond Roussel and the Republic of Dreams* (Ithaca, NY: Cornell University Press, 2000), 170–71, 213–14.

83. No lesser poet than T. S. Eliot would become enraptured by the Vitalist teachings of Henri Bergson only to find himself under the spell of Action Française.

84. Breton, "Political Position of the Surrealists," 233.

85. Luis Buñuel, *My Last Sigh: The Autobiography of Luis Bunuel* (New York: Vintage Books, 2013), 170.

86. Esther Rowlands, *Redefining Resistance: The Poetic Wartime Discourses of Francis Ponge, Benjamin Peret, Henri Michaux and Antonin Artaud* (Leiden, Netherlands: Rodopi, 2004), 11.

87. Breton, "Political Position of the Surrealists," 210.

88. Mary Low, "Women and the Spanish Revolution," in Rosemont, ed., *Surrealist Women*, 98.

89. C. L. R. James, "Introduction to Red Spanish Notebook," in Rosemont and Kelley, eds., *Black, Brown, and Beige*, 60.

90. "NEITHER YOUR WAR NOR YOUR PEACE," in Richardson and Fijaòkowski, eds., *Surrealism Against the Current*, 121.

91. Georges Henein, Hassan el Telmisany, Adel Amiu, Kamel Zehery, Fouad Kamel, and Ramses Younane, "Manifesto," trans. P. Wood, in Rosemont and Kelley, eds., *Black, Brown, and Beige*, 151.

92. Anwar Kamel, "The Propagandists of Reaction and Us," trans. Judy Cumberbatch, in Rosemont and Kelley, eds., *Black, Brown, and Beige*, 160.

93. See W. D. Redfern and Paul Nizan, *Committed Literature in a Conspiratorial World* (Princeton, NJ: Princeton University Press, 1972).

94. Malcolm Cowley, "Poet of This War," in Hannah Josephson and Malcolm Cowley, eds., *Aragon: Poet of the French Resistance* (New York: Duell, Sloan and Pearce, 1945), 9–10.

95. Josephson and Cowley, eds., *Aragon*, 11–12, 81.

96. Relying on Louis MacNeice's famous translation of "The Lilacs and The Roses" in Josephson and Cowley, eds., *Aragon*, 34.

97. From "Calligrams," found in Guillaume Appolinaire, *Selected Poems with Parallel French Text*, trans. Martin Sorrell (Oxford: Oxford University Press, 2015), 185.

98. For a brief description of the game, see Alyce Mahon, "The Search for a New Dimension: Surrealism and Magic," in Amy Wygant, ed., *The Meanings of Magic: From the Bible to Buffalo Bill* (New York: Berghahn Books, 2006) 228–29.

99. Josephson and Cowley, eds., *Aragon*, 81, 104.

100. Robert Gildea, *Fighters in the Shadows: A New History of the French Resistance* (Cambridge, MA: Belknap Press, 2015), 66–69; Josephson and Cowley, eds., *Aragon*, 91.

101. Don Skemer, "René Char and the French Resistance," *Princeton University Libraries Manuscripts News*, April 12, 2018, https://blogs.princeton.edu/manuscripts/2018/04/12/rene-char-and-the-french-resistance.

102. René Char, *Hypnos*, trans. Mark Hutchinson (London: Seagull Books, 2021). 46.

103. Char, *Hypnos*, 34.

104. Char, *Hypnos*, 35–36.

105. Char, *Hypnos*, 38–39.

106. Keith Aspley, *Historical Dictionary of Surrealism* (Plymouth, UK: Scarecrow Press, 2010), 311.

107. "LETTER TO ANDRÉ BRETON," 30.

108. "LETTER TO ANDRÉ BRETON," 30.

109. "LETTER TO ANDRÉ BRETON," 32.

110. Anthony Heilbut, *Exiled in Paradise: German Refugee Artists and Intellectuals in America from the 1930s to the Present* (Lexington, MA: Plunkett Lake Press, 2019).

111. Melissa Jones, "The Hot Club of France," *Hot Club New York*, March 2020, https://www.hotclubny.com/history; Daisy Fancourt, "Double Vie Du Jazz Français," *Music and the Holocaust*, https://holocaustmusic.ort.org/fr/resistance-and-exile/french-resistance/double-life-of-french-jazz.

112. Louis Armand, "Realism's Antipodes: Max Ernst, Bella Li, China Miéville," *Journal of the European Association for Studies of Australia* 9, no. 1 (2018): 65–75.

113. Rosemont, ed., *Surrealist Women*, 154; René Passeron, *Surrealism* (Paris: Terrail, 2007), 150; Steven Harris, "The Surrealist Movement since the 1940s," in David Hopkins, ed., *A Companion to Surrealism and Dada* (West Sussex, UK: Wiley Blackwell, 2016), 389–90; Jonathan Eburne, *Outsider Theory: Intellectual Histories of Unorthodox Ideas* (Minneapolis: University of Minnesota Press, 2018).

114. Conley, *Robert Desnos*, 198–203.

115. Rosemont, ed., *Surrealist Women*, 30–31, 112, 119.

116. Daniel Meyer-Dinkgräfe, *Ethical Encounters: Boundaries of Theatre, Performance and Philosophy* (Newcastle-upon-Tyne, UK: Cambridge Scholars Publishing, 2020), 100.

117. Kim Connell, ed., *The Belgian School of the Bizarre: An Anthology of Short Stories* (Vancouver: Fairleigh Dickinson University Press, 1998), 216.

118. Guido Snel, "Three Forsaken Poets: Significant Absences in Balkan Modernism," *Slavonica* 21, no. 1–2 (2016), 6.

119. Harris, "The Surrealist Movement," in Hopkins, ed., *A Companion to Surrealism and Dada*, 390.

120. "HUNGARY, RISING SUN," in Richardson and Fijaòkowski, eds., *Surrealism Against the Current*, 125.

121. "DECLARATION OF THE 121," in Richardson and Fijaòkowski, eds., *Surrealism Against the Current*, 195.

122. Although Evola contributed to early Dada, Breton is also purported to have crossed paths with him at a conference of Maria de Naglowska, a member of Evola's Ur Group who created the quasi-Satanist sex cult Brotherhood of the Golden Arrow. See William Traxler, "The Reconciliation of the Light and Dark Forces," in Maria de Naglowska, *The Light of Sex: Initiation, Magic, and Sacrament*, trans. Donald Traxler (Rochester, VT: Inner Traditions, 2011), 4–8. Although it is not necessarily disputed, if this anecdote is credible, it may only establish fleeting intersections within occult spaces. For Evola and Breton's exchange in the 1950s, see Julius Evola, "Mot d'Accompagnement d'un Ancien Dada, Peintre à la Réponse à l'Enquête," *andrebreton.fr*, https://www.andre breton.fr/en/series/85. For Breton's critiques of New Age, see "RUN IF YOU MUST," in Richardson and Fijaòkowski, eds., *Surrealism Against the Current*, 168–71.

123. The Portuguese Surrealist group was closely tied to African revolutionaries through Antonio Domingues, who spent much time living with, conversing with, and drawing the great minds of his generation. For his part, Cabral professed his admiration for Césaire and Senghor in particular. See Rosemont and Kelley, eds., *Black, Brown, and Beige*, 186–87.

124. Robyn Anderson, "Dwall: Between Awake and Asleep" (doctoral dissertation, University of Saskatchewan, 2015).

125. Donato Tagliapietra, *Gli Autonomi: L'Autonomia Operaia Vicentina: Dalla Rivolta di Valdagno alla Repression di Thiene* (Rome: Derive Approdi, 2019), 146.

126. Penelope Rosemont, *Dreams & Everyday Life: André Breton, Surrealism, Rebel Worker, SDS and the Seven Cities of Cibola* (Chicago: Charles H. Kerr, 2008).

127. André Breton, "The Colors of Freedom," *Arcane17*, Paris, 1945, in "The Rebel Worker #7," December 1966, found in CrimethInc. ex-Workers Collective, "Every Flag Is Black in a Fire The Black Flag—Emblem of Rebellion, Negation, and Hope," *CrimethInc.*, June 14, 2021, https://crimethinc.com/2021/06/14/every-flag-is-black-in-a-fire-featuring-louise-michel-andre-breton-and-jean-genet.

128. Artspace Editors, "The New Surrealism: Contemporary Women Artists Against Alternative Facts," *Artspace.com*, February 23, 2019, https://www.artspace.com/magazine/interviews_features/in_depth/the-new-surrealism-contemporary-women-artists-against-alternative-facts-55944.

129. Lanre Bakare, "From Beyoncé to Sorry to Bother You: the New Age of Afro-Surrealism," *The Guardian*, December 6, 2019, https://www.theguardian.com/tv-and-radio/2018/dec/06/afro-surrealism-black-artists-racist-society.

130. Bakare, "From Beyoncé to Sorry to Bother You."

131. Caitlin Thompson, "The Journey to Addressing Suppression and Censorship," *Art & Business Council*, July 14, 2021, https://artsandbusinesscouncil.org/the-journey-to-addressing-suppression-and-censorship.

132. Deianira Tolema, "Allison Sommers: What Passing Bells," *Juxtapoz*, January 23, 2016, https://www.juxtapoz.com/news/painting/allison-sommers-what-passing-bells; María Fragoso, "A Very Anxious Feeling: Voices of Unrest in the American Experience: 20 Years of the Beth Rudin DeWoody Collection," *Taubman Museum of Art*, 2020, https://static1.squarespace.com/static/57068a4c2fe13140b89958ea/t/603922a7 b6a994783119b3df/1614357159374/Taubman_Essay_Maria.pdf.

133. Benjamin Sutton, "8 Artists Who Had Breakout Moments at March Auctions," *Artsy.com*, April 5, 2021, https://www.artsy.net/article/artsy-editorial-8-artists-breakout-moments-march-auctions; Brian Boucher, "Five Years Ago, Dominique Fung Was Painting in a Basement Below a Toronto Nail Salon. Now, She's the Toast of the Art World," *Artnet News*, August 25, 2021, https://news.artnet.com/art-world/dominique-fung-2002197.

Afterword / David Renton

1. David Smith, "Donald Trump Makes Baseless Claim that 'Dark Shadows' Are Controlling Joe Biden," *The Guardian*, September 1, 2020, https://www.theguardian.com/us-news/2020/sep/01/donald-trump-makes-baseless-claim-that-dark-shadows-are-controlling-joe-biden.

2. Ursula K. Leguin, "Constructing the Golem," *The Wonder Reflect*, January 24, 2018, https://thewonderreflex.blogspot.com/2018/01/ursula-k-le-guin-on-trump.html.

3. John R. Bradley, "The Myth of Leader and the Sheep," *Independent*, May 4, 1996, https://www.independent.co.uk/arts-entertainment/the-myth-of-leader-and-the-sheep-1345823.html.

4. Tom Behan, "A Spontaneous General Strike Gripped Italy," *Socialist Review* 243 (July/August 2000), http://pubs.socialistreviewindex.org.uk/sr243/behan.htm.

Index

11th Circuit Court of Appeals, 530
14 words, 28, 113
14th Amendment, 31, 519
1st Amendment, 278
2nd Amendment, 31
4chan, 35, 143, 497
5th Amendment, 112
8chan, 35, 143, 145

ableism, 15, 294, 297, 444
abortion, 28–29, 35, 131, 289, 295, 488, 491
academia, 90, 93–94, 108, 111, 119, 169, 202, 211, 213, 229, 245–49, 256, 277–79, 293, 334, 337, 348, 356, 360, 389–90, 397, 460, 496, 533. *See also* Campus Antifascist Network (CAN)
accelerationism, 398, 410; defined 16
Achebe, Chinua, 323
ACT UP, 176
Action Française, 448, 451, 457, 459–60, 464, 532, 535
Adams, Haley, 6
Adivasis, 214, 245, 250–51, 506
affinities, 116–17, 129, 167, 218, 235–37, 242, 401, 471
Affordable Care Act Section 1557, 292, 298
Afghanistan, 119, 132, 134, 138, 249, 265, 497
Aflaq, Michel, 194–95, 502
Africa, 64, 68, 70, 127–28, 136, 229, 256, 449, 492, 518, 522, 531. *See also* diasporas, African; Egypt; Libya; Morocco; South Africa
African Blood Brotherhood, 135–36
Africana womanism, 349
Afrocentrism, 347–48
agency, 47, 52, 143, 151–52

Agnostic Front, 335–36
Agricultural Adjustment Act, 70
Akhil Bharatiya Vidyarthi Parishad (ABVP), 223, 226, 229, 245
Akotirene, Carla, 349, 521
Al-Arsuzi, Zaki, 194
al-Assad, Bashar, 192–209, 502, 505
al-Assad, Hafez, 194
Al-Bitar, Salah Al-Din, 194
al-Qaeda, 138, 203, 398
Al-Tattawor, 466
Alabama, 69–70, 114, 312, 316, 518
Alberto Torres, Carlos, 112
Albizu Campos, Don Pedro, 111
Alexander, Roberta, 78–79, 495
algorithms, 155, 160, 163, 204
alienation, 186, 230, 244, 293, 365, 411, 448, 453; from the left 47; of potential allies 405, 407
All of Us or None, 118
All-Polish Youth club, 57–58, 495
Allende, Salvador, 271, 279
Alliance for Justice and Accountability (AJA), 211, 221, 246, 248, 256–57, 313, 483
Alston, Ashanti, 82–83, 495
alt-light, 37–38, 202, 414–15, 417–21, 423, 425–26, 431–34, 504; defined, 529
alt-right, 6, 11, 15, 22, 33–39, 42, 45, 88, 93, 133, 143, 145, 148, 152, 158, 168, 179, 192, 201, 207, 222, 242–44, 249, 275–76, 292–93, 295–96, 370, 377, 415, 421, 435, 439–40, 488–89, 499, 502, 504, 516–17, 529; defined, 36
Altschul, Rudolf, 471
Ambedkar, B. R., 212, 221–22, 254
Ambekar, Sunil, 245
America Israel Public Affairs Committee (AIPAC), 238
American Blackshirts Party, 410

American Civil Liberties Union (ACLU), 116, 516
American Federation of Labor (AFL), 107
American Friends Service Committee, 342
American Guard, 13
American Identity Movement: *see* Identity Evropa
American Indian Movement (AIM), 120, 485
American Nazi Party, 320
American Renaissance, 34, 36, 289
American Vanguard, 92
Amin, Dilip, 249
Amygdaleza detention center, 263–66
Anand, Mulk Raj, 253
Anantatmula, Manga, 236, 510
anarchism, 17, 32, 35, 52, 57, 64, 66, 81–84, 100, 102, 113, 118, 120, 125–26, 130, 142, 145, 157, 171, 181, 187, 265, 269, 334, 355, 375, 381, 405–6, 409, 443, 445, 450–51, 457, 459, 465, 473, 484, 487, 492, 495, 499, 513, 521, 525–26, 533. *See* Anarchist Agency, manarchism
Anarchist Agency, 157
ancestralidade ("ancestrality"), 349–51
Anderson, David, 370–71
Anglin, Andrew, 35
anthropometry, 213–14
Anti-Defamation League (ADL), 301, 485, 487, 518
anti-imperialism, 10, 25, 110, 113, 118, 129, 131, 140, 205, 207, 255–57, 417, 450, 461, 474
Anti-Imperialist League, 461
anti-interventionism, 30–31, 136, 204–5, 207, 504–5
anti-masking laws, 8, 481
Anti-Racist Action (ARA), 5, 45, 114, 284, 331–45, 484, 489, 497
Anti-Racist Action Los Angeles/People Against Racist Terror (ARA-LA/PART), 114, 116–19, 121, 125, 497
anti-Zionism, 93, 358, 367–71, 524–25
antiauthoritarianism, 118, 141–42, 144, 151, 165, 178
anticapitalism, 25, 119, 120, 125–26, 129, 131, 164, 348, 351, 405, 418, 444, 482, 521
anticolonialism, 14, 110–11, 117, 119, 211–12, 221, 249–50, 253–56, 371, 459

anticommunism, 29, 46, 71, 74, 108, 125, 221, 490, 524
Antifa International collective, 52
Antifascistische Aktion, 1
antifascists: Black 65–87; everyday 47, 101; Jewish 375, 402; political diversity of 81–82, 116; security of movement 56, 94, 96, 117, 155, 159, 176, 182, 189, 437, 441; self-definition 9, 116; student 88–96; transgender 306; white 140, 355; women 69, 78–79, 84–85, 110, 117, 121, 244, 336, 349, 465, 469. *See also* media, coverage of antifascism
antiglobalization movement, 116–18, 137
antiracism, 5, 11, 14, 25, 34, 50, 60–61, 88–89, 93, 106–9, 111, 113–19, 121–23, 125, 127, 129, 131, 133, 135–37, 139, 174–77, 183, 188, 206, 211, 244, 255, 257, 275, 331, 333, 335, 337–39, 341, 343, 345–46, 348–49, 368, 377, 420, 481, 496–97, 503, 526. *See also* Anti-Racist Action, Skinheads Against Racial Prejudice (SHARP)
antisemitism, 24–25, 30, 34, 120, 208, 215, 237, 238–39, 243, 275, 294, 297, 300–301, 303, 357–76, 390, 450–51, 455, 459, 462–63, 471, 484–85, 488, 511, 517–18, 522–25, 531–32; and myth of Jewish media control 205. *See also* conspiracy theories, antisemitic; dog whistles
Antiterrorism and Effective Death Penalty Act, 33
Antiterrorism Law No. 13, 260 of March 16, 2016, 355
antiwar movements, 14, 27, 107, 114, 137–38, 192–93, 207, 370. *See* peace movements, Youth Against War and Fascism
Antonopoulous, Paul, 202
apocalypticism, 32, 410
Appolinaire, Guillaume, 451–52, 467, 474, 531–32, 535
Arab Spring, 143, 165
Aragon, Louis, 456–59, 461–62, 465–69, 471, 533–36
Arbery, Ahmaud, 86
Arendt, Hannah, 357–63, 365–67, 373, 375, 511–12, 521–26
Argentina, 134, 272
Arizona, 26
Arkansas, 320, 520

Arktos John Morgan, 390, 505
Arnaud, Noël, 472
Art et Liberté, 466
art, antifascist, 2, 355–56, 448–76
Artaud, Antonin, 460, 471, 535
Arya Samaj, 216–17
Aryan Invasion theory, 213–14, 247, 250
Aryan Resistance Movement, 26
Aryan supremacism, 210, 217, 241, 247, 249, 254
Asatru Folk Assembly (AFA), 187, 501
Ashraf, Ajaz, 221
Asian American movement, 77–78
Asian American Political Alliance, 78
assimilation, 218–20, 232, 349, 350, 353–54, 361, 525
Association des Écrivains et des artistes révolutionnaires (AEAR), 461–63
atheism, 442
Athens, 262–63, 268–69, 514. *See also* Exarcheia
Atlanta Antifascists, 6
Atlanta Justice Alliance, 15
Atomwaffen Division (AWD), 144, 277, 398, 498, 515
Australia, 129, 202–3, 270
Austria, 60, 262, 351
autarky, 162, 500
authoritarianism, 22, 34–35, 40–41, 63, 67–68, 89, 131, 145, 151–52, 154, 156, 178, 197, 208, 224, 257, 349, 352, 357, 365, 393, 414, 417, 448, 464, 478
Autonomists, 472, 537
autonomy, bodily, 444
Ayodhya riot, 225–26, 228
Ayoub, Serge, 204

Ba'ath Party, 193–95
Ba'athism, 193–95, 206
Bahujan people, 242, 256. *See also* caste system (varna)
Bair, Jon, 341
Bajrang Dal, 193–95, 222–23, 206, 225, 230
Bakare, Lanre, 473, 537
Baked Alaska, 192
Baker, Daniel, 13, 483
Bakunin, Mikhail, 375, 526
Baldies, 5, 331–32, 335, 337–38, 341, 343–44
Bannon, Steve, 38, 233, 245, 275, 372, 389–90
Barbie, Klaus, 478

Barrès, Maurice, 455–56, 533
Barrett, Richard, 288–89
base-building strategy, 45, 140, 211, 487
Bataille, Georges, 454, 460, 463–64, 470, 475, 533
Bayrakdar, Faraj, 196
Beam, Louis, 26–28, 145, 486
Beat Generation, 473
Bebel, August, 523
Beinart, Peter, 11, 482
Beirich, Heidi L., 16, 484
Belarus, 56, 143, 451, 474
Belgium, 68, 450, 466–67, 471, 519
Bellingcat, 158, 203, 484, 504
Bend the Arc, 374
Benjamin, Walter, 454
Berg, Alan, 27
Bergson, Henri, 535
Berkeley, 7, 79–80, 294, 436, 485, 500
Berlin, 55, 302, 311
Berrigan, Daniel, 138
Berrigan, Phillip, 138
Berton, Germaine, 457
Beznos, Fanny, 471
Bhagavad Gita, 233, 241, 506
Bharatiya Jana Sangh (BJS), *see* Bharatiya Janata Party (BJP)
Bharatiya Janata Party (BJP), 223–26, 228, 233, 237–38, 244–46, 256, 508, 510, 512. *See also* Rashtriya Swayamsevak Sangh (RSS)
Biden administration, 134, 357
Biden, Joseph, 132, 274, 372, 512, 537
Biko, Stephen, 123
biopolitics, 253
Birmingham, 69, 114, 493
black blocs, 14, 42, 44, 47–48, 309
Black Liberation Army (BLA), 66, 82–83, 495
Black Lives Matter (BLM), 12, 15–16, 42–43, 89, 122–23, 138, 143, 187, 296, 299, 309, 327, 354, 414, 416, 429, 449, 473, 496
black metal: *see* heavy metal
Black Panther Party (BPP), 9, 66, 77–78, 81–82, 89, 91, 102, 119, 120, 411, 485, 494–95
Black Panther, The, 77
Black people, 27, 31, 63–87, 109, 115, 130, 138, 243, 312–30, 340, 346–51, 353–54, 356, 362, 364, 368, 370, 373, 382–83, 395–96, 410–11, 414–15, 420, 422, 449–50, 460, 464, 468, 473,

485–86, 492–97, 509, 515, 519–20, 524–26, 529, 531, 534–37. *See also* Black, Indigenous, and People of Color (BIPOC); intersectionality; nationalism, Black

Black Power movement, 66, 76–77, 82, 85, 494

Black Riders Liberation Party (BRLP), 120

Black Student Union, 78, 107

Black Youth Project 100 (BYP100), 65, 72, 77

Black, Derek, 393

Black, Don, 288, 393, 516

Black, Indigenous, and People of Color (BIPOC), 92, 110, 176. *See also* Black people, Desis, Indigenous people, Mexican people, Mexican-American people

Blanquism, 410

Blood and Honor, 57

Blumenthal, Max, 504

Bluntschli, Johann Kasper, 217

Boggs, Grace Lee, 411

Bolivia, 272, 514

Bolsonaro, Jair, 63, 143, 257, 272, 298

bombings, 24, 26–29, 32–33, 41, 64, 82, 127, 237, 284, 312–13, 502, 530. *See also* massacres, Tulsa; Oklahoma City bombing

"bonehead" subculture, 52, 113–14, 201, 284–87, 333, 496–97, 503

Bonnot Gang, 457

Boogaloo Bois 299, 517

both sidesism, 310, 407

Bound for Glory, 341

Bowers, Robert, 365, 370–71

Boycott, Divestment, and Sanctions campaign (BDS), 89, 255

Boyd, John, 147, 152–53, 498

Bradley, Tom, 116

Brahmins, 210, 212–14, 216–18, 221, 223, 239–40, 242, 248, 252–54, 257, 506–7. *See also* caste system (varna)

Brancaleone, Cassio, 353, 521

Branch Davidian cult, 30

branding and rebranding, 144, 157–58, 270, 299, 337, 417, 488–89

Bray, Mark, 346, 403, 492, 520, 528, 530

Braz, Rose, 85

Brazil, 63, 163, 272, 298, 346–56, 517, 520

Brazilian Chamber of Deputies, 354–55

Breá, Juan, 465

Breitbart News Network, 38, 46, 275, 294–95, 488, 515

Breton, André, 452–54, 456, 458–60, 462–64, 468–70, 472, 532–37

Bridging Divides Initiative, 483

Britain, 25, 51, 63, 68, 126–28, 194, 206, 213–15, 217–18, 222, 239, 243, 250–51, 253–54, 270, 299, 331, 367, 469, 478, 482, 504, 507

Brooklyn College, 107, 109, 496

Brotherhood of the Golden Arrow, 536

Brown Berets, 78, 121, 325, 496

Brown, Michael, 86, 327

Brunner, Alois, 196, 502

Buchanan, Patrick, 28, 30, 37, 284, 440, 486

Buckley, William F., 108

Bundy, Ammon, 400–401, 408, 411, 486

Buñuel, Alfonso, 464

Buñuel, Luis, 460, 464–65, 474, 525

Bureau of Alcohol, Tobacco, and Firearms (BATF), 27

Burger, Justin, 193–94

Butler, Judith, 301, 518

Cable Street, Battle of, 14, 326

Cabral, Amílcar, 472, 537

California, 7, 16, 55, 77–79, 85, 89, 110, 112, 114, 118–19, 121, 132, 157, 168, 204, 247, 255, 270, 288, 294, 321, 323–24, 327, 340, 392, 436, 483, 489, 491, 494, 509, 520

Camelots du Roi, 451, 460, 462

Campaign to Stop Funding Hate, 230, 506–9, 511

Campbell, David, 13

Campus Antifascist Network (CAN), 88–96

Canada, 87, 91, 119, 129, 230, 337

Candomblé, 349–51, 521

capitalism, 21, 40–41, 66–68, 71, 83, 90, 92, 124, 126, 128–30, 136, 139, 162, 164, 178, 182, 195–97, 205–6, 270–71, 273–74, 321, 349, 352–53, 356, 359, 364–66, 372, 379, 388, 406–7, 409, 412, 447–48, 458, 472, 474–75, 479, 500, 534; American, 77, 81; critiques of, 407; global, 19, 225, 244, 271, 460; late 242, 358; monopoly, 25, 67, 71; neoliberal, 225, 236, 274; racial, 46, 64, 76, 122–23, 377. *See also*: anticapitalism, class

Capitol Hill Autonomous Zone/Capitol Hill Organized Protest (CHAZ/CHOP), 12, 481
Capitol insurrection of January 6, 2021, 7, 9, 16, 132, 423, 427, 432, 490
Caplan, Lincoln, 33, 487
car-ramming attacks, 7, 192, 310, 413, 481
Carlson, Tucker, 203, 321, 478, 504
Carto, Willis, 25–26
CasaPound, 55, 399, 410
caste system (varna), 211–16, 221, 227, 232, 234, 239, 241–42, 247–49, 254–56, 506–7, 510; abolition of, 221. *See also* Brahmins, Dalit people
catastrophism, 410
Catholics, 24, 58, 108, 138, 171, 183, 407, 491
Center for Strategic and International Studies, 16, 484, 498
Central America, 25, 134. *See also* Honduras, Mexico, Nicaragua
Central Intelligence Agency (CIA), 107, 116, 413
Central Park Five, 327
Cernovich, Mike, 421
Césaire, Aimé, 64, 68, 253, 450, 464, 468, 492, 537
Chabrun, Jean-François, 469
Chagall, Marc, 467–68
Chaney, James, 112
Char, René, 468–69, 536
Charleston News and Courier, The, 315
Charlottesville, Virginia: *see* Unite the Right
Chávez, Hugo, 208, 505–6
Chicago, 12, 49, 65, 69, 72, 74, 77, 110, 114, 117, 136, 248, 331–32, 335, 337, 340, 378, 380, 484, 493. *See also* Chicago Dyke March, Chicago Freedom School, Chicago Light Brigade, Chicago Police Department, Chicago Southside ARA, Chicago Surrealist School, Skinheads of Chicago (SHOC), University of Chicago
Chicago Dyke March, 524
Chicago Freedom School, 382
Chicago Light Brigade, 381–82
Chicago Police Department, 27, 72
Chicago Southside ARA, 6
Chicago Surrealist School, 6, 473
Chicano movement, 77–79, 110–11, 120, 121, 122, 139, 496

Chile, 134, 143, 157, 270–71, 273, 277, 279, 515
China, 63, 134, 370, 513
Chios, 258–61, 512
Chomsky, Noam, 203, 485, 523–24
Christian Reconstructionists, 31
Christian supremacy, 297
Christopher Commission, 116
Churchill, Robert H., 31, 486–87
cisheteronormativity, 297
Citizenship Amendment Act (CAA), 228, 234, 249, 252, 255, 511–12
City University of New York (CUNY), 108–9
Civil Rights Congress (CRC), 74–77, 493
Civil Rights movement, 23, 26, 31, 42, 65, 69–70, 73–74, 76, 77, 112, 232, 284, 297, 304, 309–10, 320, 371, 509
Clarion Project, 398, 527
class, 125–27, 129, 195, 205, 232, 244, 348, 351, 356, 359, 364–65, 374–75, 401, 520; antisemitic concepts of, 363–65, 368, 371, 375, 410–11; Black proletarian, 460; bourgeois, 126–29, 131, 133, 197, 351, 359, 450, 460–61; consciousness, 366, 528; crony-capitalist, 196; cross-class identification, 124–25, 505–6; elite as, 363; fascist theory of, 205–6; formation of, 124; lower-middle, 103, 108, 125, 356; metropolitan working, 133; middle, 103, 108, 232, 317, 455; peasantry, 129; petty bourgeois, 66–67, 124; planter, 315; political, 299; "proletarian nation" theory of, 207; ruling 21–22, 39, 124, 126, 129, 132, 205, 271, 315, 359, 363; rural working, 400, 445; struggle, 129, 178–79, 195, 206, 359, 365, 406–7, 442; upper-middle, 317; "white working," 515; working, 45, 66, 89, 103, 106, 108, 124–25, 127, 129, 133, 232, 263, 331, 337–38, 342, 400, 409, 442, 445, 455, 459, 461, 463, 466, 490, 496, 503, 515–16, 523; working women, 490. *See also* capitalism, caste system (varna), intersectionality, Marxism
Cleaver, Eldridge, 78, 82
climate change, 44, 123, 252–53, 443, 512
Clinton administration, 33, 114–15
Clinton, Bill, 273
Clinton, Hillary, 37–38, 274–75, 296, 357

Coalition Against Genocide, 223, 230, 247

Coalition Against Police Abuse, 116

Cocteau, Jean, 457

Codreanu, Corneliu, 398

Cohen, Cathy, 83, 495

Colombia, 272, 313

colonialism, 9, 11, 45, 49, 64, 67–68, 111, 124, 129, 136, 182, 205–6, 211–12, 249–50, 253–57, 295, 297, 302, 350, 352, 369, 377, 448, 458–59, 472, 474, 479, 492, 506–7, 533. *See also* anticolonialism, empire, fascism, imperialism, Zionism

Colorado, 16, 112, 389

colorism, 249, 256, 348, 350, 521

Columbine High School shooting, 406

Columbus, 114–15, 117

Comité de Vigilance des Intellectuels Antifacsistes, 463, 468

communalism, 221, 256, 511

communism, 25, 69, 73–75, 80–82, 88, 111–13, 118, 125, 130, 136, 139, 194, 196–97, 206, 222–23, 271, 274, 365, 381, 405–6, 492, 496, 517, 522. *See also* anarchism; conspiracy theories, antisemitic; Communist Party of the United States (CPUSA); Communist International; Communist Workers' Party; French Communist Party (Parti Communiste Français, PCF); Italian Communist Party (Partito Comunista Italiano, PCI); Marxism; Maoism; Trotskyism

Communist International, 78, 314

Communist Party of the United States of America (CPUSA), 41, 69–71, 85, 108, 111, 405–6, 411

Communist Workers' Party, 112

complexity, 141–42, 145–46, 156, 164, 166, 497

Compromise of 1877, 315

Confederate States of America, 315

Congress of Industrial Organizations (CIO), 107

Conrad, Joseph, 322

conspiracy theories, 5, 7–8, 29–30, 44, 46, 48, 120, 156, 172, 185, 198, 400, 406, 413, 416, 421, 486, 490, 529, 535; about antifa, 8, 16, 414, 483; about Muslims, 226; about Syria, 499, 504–5; among police, 481, 526;

antielite, 30; antisemitic, 10, 21, 23, 26, 31, 41, 301, 363–66, 368, 374, 411, 524–25; element of truth in, 300; laundering of, 202–4; marketing of, 156; "9/11 Truth," 417, 431; QAnon, 16, 143, 525. *See also* disinformation; infiltration; false-flag operations; Soros, George

Constitutional articles 370 and 35A, revocation of, 227

Contras, 116

Contre-Attaque, 463

Cop Watch, 118, 136

Copsey, Nigel, 9, 482

Corradini, Enrico, 205, 207

Coulter, Ann, 193, 203, 502

Counter Intelligence Program (COINTELPRO), 113, 120, 136, 139, 485

Counter-Currents Publishing, 34, 208, 488, 505–6

"countering violent extremism" groups, 394

Courbet, Gustave, 451

COVID-19 pandemic, 44, 46, 48–49, 57, 63, 91, 101, 123, 136, 143, 266–69, 298, 499, 514

Cox, Laverne, 292

Crack the CIA Coalition, 116

Cramer, Hendrik, 471

Crawford, Keith, 67, 492

Crenshaw, Kimberlé, 304, 518

Crevel, René, 457, 463

CrimethInc ex-Workers' Collective, 158, 473, 500, 537

Criminal Tribes Act of 1871, 215

Critical Resistance, 85–86, 382, 495

CryptoParty, 163, 500

Cuba, 74, 80, 139, 236, 313, 450, 465, 468, 533

culture, 34, 36, 58–59, 77, 80, 118, 124, 146, 214, 220, 222, 247, 251, 302, 305, 353, 418–19, 434, 439, 443, 463, 465, 482, 515, 521, 534; Adivasi, 251; African antiracist, 119, 137, 339, 343; and fascism, 219, 462, 465; antifa, 482; Arab, 194; Aryan, 240; as area of contestation, 442, 445, 496–97; Bharatiya, 212; Black, 306, 349–50; callout, 184; cancel, 430, 432; celebrity, 358; gay, 36; "gun rights," 486; nation as, 217; of care, 384; hookup, 421; of racism, 343; Hindu,

218–19; Islamic, 512; Jewishness
as, 374; Kashmiriyat, 227–28; mainstream, 283, 293, 306, 443, 446;
male-dominated, 336; offense, 172,
293; pluralistic, 212; political, 109;
popular, 245, 364–65, 501; queer,
302–3, security, 117, 189; skinhead,
332, 335; straight edge, 332; trans,
306; Vedic, 237; wars, 294–97, 478;
white, 485; youth, 25. *See also* Indigenous people; genocide, cultural;
subcultures
Cunard, Nancy, 458, 465, 534
Curry, Tommy, 275
Czech Republic, 450, 471, 472

D'Souza, Dinesh, 90
da Silva, Luiz Inácio Lula, 272
Dadaism, 451–52, 455–57, 461, 469–70,
472, 531–34, 536–37
Daily Stormer, The, 35
Dalí, Salvador, 460–62, 474, 534; fanta-
sies about Hitler, 462
Dalit people, 211, 227, 242–43, 250,
252, 255–56. *See also* caste system
(varna)
Daudet, Léon, 457, 464
Daudet, Philippe, 457
Davis, Angela, 70, 74, 85
Davis, Jefferson, 326–27
Davis, Mike, 274, 515
Davis, Sallye, 70
de Benoist, Alain, 206, 487
de Gaulle, Charles, 325
de Naglowska, Maria, 536
de Souza Santos, Boaventura, 356
decentralization, 2, 149–50, 153, 164; in
Sarvodaya, 224; of Black Liberation
Army (BLA), 82; of far right, 26, 28,
143–44, 497, 500; of infrastructure,
154–58, 161–63; of warfare, 146–47,
152
"Declaration 127," 184–85, 187; explained
501
decolonization, 110, 147, 194, 244, 249,
252, 444, 449, 522, 525
Deek, Lamis, 368–69, 524
Deep May project, 164
Deepstate Dogs, 8
del Valle, Adriano, 464
democracy, 28, 75, 81, 196, 198, 198, 310,
325, 358, 413, 508, 518, 522; crisis
of, 448; direct, 451; ethnic, 237, 510;

illiberal, 512; liberal, 11, 20, 115, 128,
138, 273, 477–78; racial, 353–54, 356;
secular, 234; social, 67, 164, 212, 457,
462
Democracy Now!, 203
Democratic Party, 16, 113, 120, 133, 137,
152, 234–35, 274–76, 315, 371–72,
414–15, 477, 489
Democratic Socialists of America
(DSA), 93, 487
Denver, 16, 27, 484
deplatforming, 3, 13, 48, 175–76, 230,
179, 294, 310, 326, 328–29, 396–97,
482, 490
depression, 186, 300, 401, 517; economic
69–70, 406, 418, 490
deradicalization, 104, 394, 397–98, 428,
432–33, 527
desegregation, 320–21, 520
Desis, 231–32, 255, 508–9
Desnos, Robert, 456, 458–59, 471, 533,
536
Detroit, 337, 411
Deutsche Studentenschaft (DSt), 302–3,
311
Dharmashastras, 237, 506
Diamant-Berger, Jean-Claude, 471
diasporas: African, 69, 349–51, 531; Jewish, 238, 367, 523–24; South Asian,
210–57, 509–12. *See also* Desis
Die Aktion wider den deutschen Geist,
302
Dimitrov, Georgi, 78, 314, 519
direct action, 11, 56, 64, 66, 77, 113,
117–19, 168, 307, 328, 337, 379, 382;
nonviolent, 382; far right, 132
disinformation, 156, 202, 505
disruption as a tactic, 14, 94, 96, 108, 137,
139, 144, 161, 163, 177, 328, 465
Doctorow, Cory, 165, 500
dog whistles, 88, 236, 243, 296, 370, 411
domestic terrorism, 236, 310, 368, 432,
481, 530; antifa labeled as, 8
Domingues, Antonio, 537
Doniger, Wendy, 248
Donovan, Jack, 34–35
Doshi, Vidhi, 243–44, 511
Douglas, Emory, 77
Douglass, Frederick, 320
Douma chemical weapons attack, 203
doxing, 8, 36, 141, 159, 275, 338, 354, 398,
428, 437, 441, 499; defined, 36, 159;
versus IDing, 437

Dravidian peoples, 214, 216, 248, 250, 506

Dreyfus Affair, 451, 455, 463, 523, 531

Drieu la Rochelle, Pierre, 456, 474, 533–34

Du Bois, W. E. B., 64–65, 70–75, 312, 320, 518

dual power strategy, 45, 389, 407–8, 410, 412, 487; defined 32; appropriation of by far right 32, 410

Duchamp, Marcel, 454, 458

Duda, Andrzej, 298, 517

Dugin, Aleksandr, 207

Duke, David, 24–25, 28, 41, 192, 198, 201, 203, 288, 295, 368, 440, 503

Dumont, Fernand, 471

Dupont, Tyler, 169–70, 501

Duterte, Rodrigo, 63, 171, 372, 525

Eckford, Elizabeth, 320

Ecuador, 270, 474

education, 69, 90–92, 103, 107, 146–47, 166, 180, 232, 234–36, 277, 279, 301, 316–18, 320–23, 341, 354, 403, 410, 415, 428, 455; abolitionist, 86; antifascist, 3, 47–48, 51, 91, 94, 108, 137, 163, 188, 375, 441; as left-wing plot, 24; fascist, 180, 219, 221, 229–30, 245–47, 250, 252, 271, 511; higher, 91–92; nonviolence, 58; political, 79, 83, 86, 342, 379, 382; role in legitimating fascism, 14. See also Freire, Paulo; Highlander Research and Education Center; Hindu Education Foundation (HEF); Hindu Students Council (HSC)

Egypt, 206, 449–50, 466, 472, 533

Ehrenburg, Ilya, 462–63

Eichmann, Adolf, 196, 360, 522

electoralism, 10, 26, 47–48, 482

Electronic Frontier Foundation (EFF), 500

Element, 155

Eliot, T. S., 535

Éluard, Paul, 456–59, 463, 468

empathy, 12, 49, 145, 383; toward fascists, 388–412: collaborationist, 389–95, 397–98, 402, 404; strategic, 389–401, 407–8, 410, 412. See ethics

empire, 68, 80, 113, 126–27, 131–34, 136–37, 204–5, 214, 221, 225, 250, 257, 313–14, 484, 494, 505. See also colonialism, imperialism

Endgame, Kat, 47

English Defence League (EDL), 235, 325, 326

entryism, 12, 167–68, 295 295. See also infiltration

epistemicídio: see genocide, epistemic

Equal Justice Initiative, 312

Erdoğan, Recep Tayyip, 298

Ernst, Max, 468, 536

essentialism, 146, 153, 166, 299

ethics, 428, 431, 445, 536; and aesthetics, 355; antifascist, 11, 18, 57, 156, 166, 188, 394–95; and fascism, 200–201, 252, 391, 403; journalistic, 436, 439; research, 356, 389–92, 397–98, 401–4, 527; versus antifascist values, 153

eugenics, 35, 127, 213, 278–79

Europe, 65, 69, 76, 127, 173, 194, 217, 253–54, 257, 312, 314, 325, 359–61, 363, 466, 519, 535; Central and Eastern 56; Western 314

European New Right (ENR), 34–35, 206–7, 222

Everson, Kevin Jerome, 473

Evola, Julius, 241, 472, 536

Exarcheia, 265, 514

exclusion, 49, 212, 297, 299, 302, 305, 309–10, 410, 444, 501; as antifascist tactic, 393–94, 397; antifascist struggle against, 309; of women and people of color notably from academic freedom, 279

extraction: of labor, 381; of resources, 50, 68, 251–52, 381; of rents, 164

Facebook, 57, 94, 155, 159, 161, 163, 185, 192, 203, 241, 355, 402, 410, 416, 425, 429–30, 504, 510, 522, 527–28

facial recognition, 160, 499

Fair Fight, 416

false-flag operations, 202–3, 226

Fang, Lee, 515

far right, 6–7, 9–10, 12–14, 16, 20–41, 43–47, 49–52, 55, 88–89, 91–92, 155, 157, 167–68, 170–72, 175–76, 180, 186, 189, 191–95, 197–99, 201, 203–5, 207–9, 212, 236, 239, 257, 262, 268, 277, 282–83, 294, 298–99, 301, 303, 343–44, 358, 366–69, 370, 373–74, 383–84, 388–89, 396–97, 403, 407, 410–11, 413, 415, 417, 420, 430, 442–45, 448–49, 457–58, 460, 462,

473-74, 478, 481, 484, 489, 490-91, 501-2, 504-5; as autonomous force, 20-21; as capitalist tool, 20; as contradictory, 22; as "extremist," 20; differentiated from fascism, 22;

Farage, Nigel, 245

Farmer, J. C., 76

fascism, analyses of, 11, 47, 106, 125, 519; as a social movement seeking power and connected to sources of power, 403; as already present, 124, 139, 497; as "extraordinary," 45, 377; as colonialism coming home, 124, 127-28, 133-34; as internalized colonialism, 216, 242, 249, 256; as internationalist nationalism, 257, 366; as imperialism *in extremis*, 129; as irrational, 449; as subset of "far right," 22; as the product of capitalism, 277, 406-7, 479; colonialism as, 9, 11, 64, 67-68, 106, 211, 254, 257, 351-52, 479; in relation to women, 138

Faubus, Orville, 320

Fears, Colton, 518

Featherstone, Dave, 64

Featherstone, Liza, 257, 512

Federal Bureau of Investigation (FBI), 8, 10, 25-28, 32-33, 61, 93, 111, 115, 120-21, 139, 274, 284, 483-85

Federal Reserve System, 25, 29

Female, Lesbian, Intersex, Nonbinary, or Trans people (FLINT), 60. *See also* gender, intersectionality, LGBTQ people, transgender people, women

feminism, 15, 34-35, 37, 60-61, 68, 80, 83, 94, 110, 116, 242, 255, 293-94, 299, 301-3, 415, 419, 431, 517-18

Ferguson, 86, 316, 489

Fesperman, William "Preacherman," 78

Filatov, Fedor, 56

Fleming, Crystal M., 404, 526, 528

Floyd, George, 7, 15, 86, 102, 187, 299, 307, 311, 343, 530

folkism, 125, 180, 184, 186, 241, 251

Food Not Bombs, 411

Foreman, Clark, 70-71

Forrest, Nathan Bedford, 316

Fort Smith trial, 27-28

fourth-generation warfare, 146-49

Fox News, 46, 203, 275, 284, 372, 504

Fragoso, Maria, 473, 537

France, 34, 60, 68, 126, 128, 194, 203-6, 325, 360, 448, 450-51, 455-59, 461-62, 466-72, 474, 478, 487-88, 513, 523, 531-36

France, Anatole, 458

Francis, Terri, 473

Francisco Franco, 1, 128, 273, 325, 464-66, 519

Free Speech (newspaper), 319

free speech, 5, 107, 278-79, 482, 490, 499, 529; as farce, 118; as myth, 278; as right-wing pretext, 38, 88, 91, 152, 172, 278-79, 294, 422, 529. *See also* deplatforming

free trade, 37, 39-40, 273, 418. *See* neoliberalism

Freedmen's Bureau, 316

Freedom Socialist Party, 405

Freire, Paulo, 410, 528

French Communist Party, 458-64, 471

Freyre, Gilberto, 356

Fromm, Erich, 403, 409-10, 528

Fry, Varian, 468

Fuerzas Armadas de Liberación Nacional (FALN), 111-12

Fukuyama, Francis, 16

Fung, Dominique, 473, 537

Fyssas, Pavlos, 262, 513

Gabbard, Tulsi, 233, 509, 512

Gamal Nasser regime, 472

GamerGate, 149, 293-95, 516

Gandhi, Mahatma, 210, 222, 224, 237, 507

Gang Task Force, 340

García Lorca, Federico, 460

Garneau, Marianne, 515

Garner, Eric, 327

Gates, Darryl 115-16

Gautier, Francois, 248, 250

gay liberation movement, 83-85, 495

Gaza, blockade of, 369-70

gender, 22, 34, 49, 58-60, 84, 146, 242, 336, 345, 348, 520; bending, 454; equality, 162; politics of, 77-79, 216, 292-311, 443, 494, 516-18; traditional roles, 138, 177. *See also* Female, Lesbian, Intersex, Nonbinary, or Trans people (FLINT), identity politics, intersectionality, LGBTQ people, masculinities, transgender people, travesti people, women

Geneva, 72

genocide, 1–2, 16–17, 24, 63–65, 67–68, 72–77, 102, 106, 124, 127–28, 135, 198–202, 209, 220, 223, 226, 230, 247, 253; 255, 277, 302–3, 314, 318, 320, 382, 435–36, 493–94, 503, 531; and colonization, 348–49, 351, 353; cultural, 303; epistemic, 353, 356. *See also* We Charge Genocide

Georgia, 7, 15, 73, 193, 316

Germany, 54–55, 59–61, 67, 71–72, 113, 126–29, 172, 182, 205–6, 217, 219, 221, 239–41, 246, 253–54, 262, 302, 322, 325, 327, 351, 359–61, 363, 366, 418, 451, 457–58, 462, 466, 478, 491–92, 511, 516–17, 519, 523, 534–36; Indology in, 210, 212–13, 215. *See also* Nazism, Romanticism

Germenis, Giorgios, 174

Gibson, Joey, 5–6, 501

Gide, André, 451, 456, 458

Gideonse, Harry, 107

Gilman, Sander, 523

Gilmore, Ruth Wilson, 85, 379, 383

Gingrich, Newt, 284

Giroux, Henry, 40, 484–85, 489

Gittlitz, A. M., 515

globalization, 21, 29, 34, 146, 242, 244, 484, 490; as object of far-right conspiracy theory, 37, 192, 208, 236, 410, 418, 500, 505. *See also* antiglobalization movement

Golden Dawn, 174, 262–63, 268

Golwalkar, M. S., 219–22, 224, 237, 252, 507

Goodman, Andrew, 112

Gordon, Avery, 87, 496

goth, 333, 414, 446

Gottfried, Paul, 34

Graeber, David, 17, 484

Graham, Francine, 370–71

Gramsci, Antonio, 169, 272–73, 280, 410, 501, 514

Grappelli, Stefan, 470

"Great American Redoubt," 405

Great Replacement theory, 16, 277

Greece, 55, 174, 258–69, 512–13

Greene, Marjorie Taylor, 530

Ground Game LA, 123

Groupe Surréaliste en Hainaut, 471

Guevara, Ernesto "Che," 122

Gujarat, 234. *See also* massacres, Gujarat

gun control, 25

Haiti, 270, 450

Hale, Matt, 288

Hamburg, 74

Hammerskins, 6

Hampay, Arash, 263

Hampton, Fred, 77

Hansen, Thomas Blom, 224, 254, 508, 510, 512

Hard Times Conference, 110

hardcore, 297, 331–32, 337

Hardy, Thomas, 459

Hare Krishnas (International Society for Krishna Consciousness, ISK-CON), 233

Harris, DeAndre, 309, 518

Harris, Kamala, 509

Harris, Kevin, 39

Harvey, David, 271, 514

Häuge, Abner, 47–48, 483

Hayes, Kelly, 12, 49, 483

heathenry, 241, 253, 445, 501. *See also* heavy metal

Heathens United Against Racism (HUAR), 175, 188

heavy metal, 167–89, 442, 445–47, 501; black 186, 442, 445; antifascist black, 170, 181, 186–87, 501; Nazi, far right, and white supremacist 172–74, 445

Hebrew Immigrant Aid Society (HIAS), 365

Hedgewar, K. B., 217, 219–20, 222

Hegel, Georg Wilhelm Friedrich, 276, 515

hegemony, 186, 212; capitalist, 271, 273; informational, 143; subcultural, 169; Western, 206–7, 246, 252, 347; hegemonic identities, 352

Heimbach, Matthew, 398, 400, 498, 505

Henry de Bruchard, 451

Hersh, Seymour, 203, 504

Heyer, Heather, 192, 310, 413–14

hierarchy, 9, 11, 18, 35, 40, 58, 81–82, 120, 124, 142, 144–45, 147–50, 153–54, 160, 207–9, 214, 242, 238, 253, 256, 348, 351, 377, 455, 495, 499; of caste system, 212–14, 218–19, 248, 253–54; informal, 169, 501. *See* colonialism, colorism, racism, sexism

Highlander Research and Education Center, 408

hijacking: airplanes, 82; emotions, 45; environmentalism, 25, 35, 249,

252–53; ideologies, 224, 249; organizations, 118, 251–52

Himmler, Heinrich, 182, 240, 246, 506

Hindu America Foundation (HAF), 230, 238, 244–45, 247, 249, 253, 511

Hindu Education Foundation (HEF), 247

Hindu Sabha, 217, 507

Hindu Students Council (HSC), 229–30, 244

Hindu Swayamsevak Sangh (HSS), 228–30, 244, 247–48

Hindutva, 210–57, 506–9; defined, 211. *See also* Akhil Bharatiya Vidyarthi Parishad (ABVP), Bharatiya Jana Sangh (BJS), Bharatiya Janata Party (BJP), Hindu America Foundation (HAF), Hindu Education Foundation (HEF), Hindu Sabha, Hindu Students Council (HSC), Hindu Swayamsevak Sangh (HSS), Rashtriya Swayamsevak Sangh (RSS), Sangh Parivar, Vishwa Hindu Parishad (VHP), Vanvasi Kalyan Kendra, Vishwa Hindu Parishad of America (VHPA)

Hironobu Yasaki, 471

Hirschfeld, Magnus, 302

Hirschová, Edith, 471

Hitler, Adolf, 1, 25, 64, 67, 72, 76, 106, 127–28, 138, 183, 197, 314, 326, 327, 361, 366, 372, 458, 462, 464–67, 506, 511, 523, 525, 534–35; adulated by Hindutva adherents, 210, 217, 219, 239–41, 243

Hoddersen, Guerry, 406

Holocaust denial, 203, 398

Home Alive, 392

Honduras, 272, 313

Hong Kong, 157, 165

hooks, bell, 410, 528

Horkheimer, Max, 479

Horne, Gerald, 64, 494

House Committee on Un-American Activities (HUAC), 69, 493

Hughes, Langston, 63–65, 68, 492

Human Earth & Animal Liberation (HEAL) conferences, 114

Hungary, 298, 310, 372, 517, 525, 536; revolution and invasion, 472

hunger strikes, 121–22, 263, 266

Hurricane Katrina, 411

Hurricane Sandy, 411

Icke, David, 504

Idaho, 26, 30, 113, 407

Identity Evropa, 157, 410

identity politics, 83, 103, 295, 444. *See also* intersectionality

ideology, 8, 10, 18, 30, 39–40, 47, 49, 51, 68, 85, 120, 123–26, 229, 231, 236, 297, 358–60, 372, 393, 399, 403, 414, 417, 427, 433–34, 442, 472; alt-right, 34–36, 38; anarchist, 17, 81–83, 130, 145; antifascist, 7, 10, 64–65, 80–82, 117, 347, 399, 434; authoritarian, 151–52, 413; Ba'ath, 194 conservative, 24, 107; far right, 3, 22, 30–32, 59, 242, 299, 371, 373, 389–90, 400, 408, 413, 415, 443; fascist, 9, 22, 34, 45, 124, 129–30, 145, 178, 186, 189, 197, 211–12, 217–24, 230, 246, 248, 250, 253–55, 352–53, 364, 366, 372, 399–400, 403, 406, 408, 417, 431; Nazi, 24–25, 127, 180, 357, 359, 364; white supremacist, 23, 297, 363, 365. *See also* anarchism; antisemitism; militia movement, constitutionalism and millennialism; Hindutva; imperialism; Marxism; misogyny; Trans Exclusionary Radical Feminism (TERFism); Zionism

Idle No More, 165

Idlib, 266, 504

IfNotNow, 374–75

Illinois, 7, 12, 69, 110, 112, 331, 378, 494

immigration, 5, 16, 20, 23, 25, 29, 34, 36–37, 39–42, 44, 46, 58, 60, 63, 87, 89, 95, 100, 106, 115, 127, 132, 138, 211, 228, 230–32, 234–36, 251, 274, 277, 295, 307, 310–11, 313, 327–28, 333, 360, 370–71, 373, 395, 425, 431, 437, 478, 496, 508–9, 513. *See also* Hebrew Immigrant Aid Society (HIAS), refugees

Immigration and Nationality (Hart-Celler) Act, 231

imperialism, 10, 64, 67–69, 80, 123–31, 134–35, 195, 204–7, 239, 251, 302, 314, 325, 346–59, 366, 449, 466, 470, 472, 519. *See also* anti-imperialism

incels, 242

India, 210–57, 361, 506–12

India Development and Relief Fund, 229

India Spend Hate Crimes Tracker, 510

Indian American Muslim Council, 245

Indian Institute for Democratic Leadership (IIDL), 243-44
Indian National Congress (INC), 217, 221
Indiana, 335
Indianapolis, 335
Indigeneity, distortion of discourse of, 249-51
Indigenous people, 9, 17, 67-68, 92, 94, 109-10, 119, 122, 127-29, 135-36, 139, 163, 250-51, 253, 297, 302-3, 306, 314, 316, 348-50, 353-54, 354, 373, 382, 437, 459, 506, 521. *See also* Adivasis; Black, Indigenous, and People of Color identities (BIPOC); Indigeneity, distortion of discourse of; Native American movement; Women, Indigenous
Industrial Workers of the World (IWW), 52, 182, 411
inequality, 11, 15, 17, 22-23, 3, 43, 45, 74, 120, 473, 479
infiltration: of antifascist spaces by the state, 43, 111, 139; of antifascist spaces by fascists, 438; of fascist spaces by antifascists, 2, 137, 155, 159, 161, 275, 440; of fascist spaces by the state, 26, 33, 515; of left discourses by fascists, 204-5; of other spaces by fascists, 5, 51, 56, 59, 91, 93, 173, 276, 491; of police forces by fascists, 21, 427, 490. *See also* entryism, informants, spaces
Infinity Foundation, 248-49
informants: police 33, 112, 468; anthropological 254, 389, 526
Infowars, 202. *See also* Jones, Alex
infrastructures of care, 49-51. *See also* culture of care
Ingram, Rosa Lee, 75
Instagram, 155, 428
Integral Humanism, 224
Integralista party, 352-53
Inter-Klan Newsletter & Survival Alert, 26
Intercommunal Committees to Combat Fascism (ICCFs): *see* National Committees to Combat Fascism (NCCFs)
intercommunalism, 66, 495; as internationalism 135; reactionary 80; revolutionary 80-81. *See also* National Committees to Combat Fascism (NCCFs)

International Labor Defense, 74
International Women's Strike, 29
International Writers Congress, 63
internet, 33, 36 38, 93, 136, 143-44, 150, 156, 158-63, 165, 188, 294, 358, 372, 374, 397, 414, 429, 436, 488. *See also* media, social; networks, social
intersectionality, 10, 14-15, 51, 83, 91, 122, 138, 255, 291, 294, 304, 355, 518
intolerance, 128, 199, 223, 275-76, 283, 384, 392, 440, 442; and repressive tolerance, 107. *See also* multiculturalism, political correctness
irony, right-wing, 35. *See also* memes as alibi for fascism
Irving, David, 398
Islamic State of Iraq and Syria (ISIS), 144, 148, 193, 503
Islamophobia, 38, 46, 89, 185, 199, 232-33, 237, 243, 294, 297, 300, 362, 508-9, 523, 527
Israel, 29, 36-37, 39, 89, 90, 129, 134, 208, 230, 236-39, 256, 359-61, 367-71, 373, 375, 478, 510-12, 522-25. *See also* anti-Zionism, US Campaign for the Academic and Cultural Boycott of Israel (USACBI), Palestinian people, Zionism
It's Going Down, 157-58, 489, 500
Italian Communist Party (Partito Comunista Italiano, PCI), 67, 479
Italy, 25, 55, 66-67, 69, 126-27, 172, 205-6, 219, 314, 351, 410, 464, 472, 478-79, 528

Jackson, Esther Cooper, 69, 493
Jackson, George, 65, 85, 121, 130, 497
Jackson, James, 70, 493
Jackson, Jesse, 113
Jaffrelot, Christopher, 216, 224-25, 237, 506-8, 510
jail support, 12-13, 50, 99-100, 104-5, 121, 125, 137
James, C. L. R., 465, 535
Japan, 72, 129, 450, 459, 471, 534
Jarry, Alfred, 451-52, 531-32
Jayapal, Pramila, 235, 509
JC Kosher Supermarket attack, 370
Jena, 60-61, 215
Jenkins, Daryle Lamont, 18, 51, 484
Jericho Movement, 120, 139
Jesus, 447
Jeunesses Patriotes, 462

Jewish Defense League, 108
Jews, 23–24, 26–27, 35–36, 44, 63, 71, 76,
    95, 106, 108, 128, 131, 180, 203, 219,
    237–39, 241, 289, 300, 302–3, 311,
    314, 326, 346, 351–52, 363, 393, 396,
    402, 409, 467, 511, 522–25; Black
    303. *See also* American Jewish
    Committee (AJC), antisemitism,
    Jewish Defense League, Jews
    Organizing for Liberation and
    Transformation, Ratzon: Center
    for Healing and Resistance, Rebel-
    lious Anarchist Young Jews
Jews Against White Nationalism, 374
Jews Organizing for Liberation and
    Transformation, 375
Jim Crow laws, 23, 74, 243, 303–4, 312,
    315, 383
Jinping, Xi, 63
Joans, Ted, 473
John Brown Anti-Klan Committee
    (JBAKC), 45, 50, 113–14, 125, 496
Johnson, Abberdine, 312
Johnson, Boris, 63
Johnson, Gaye Theresa, 64, 492
Johnson, J. J., 31
Johnson, Marsha P., 84, 495
Jolas, Eugène, 534
Jones, Alex, 203
Jones, Claudia, 65, 68–69, 71, 492
Jones, Jeff, 78
Jones, Leslie, 295
Jones, Sir William, 213, 215
journalism, 3, 7, 30, 33, 48, 58, 107, 136,
    158, 192, 223, 238, 245, 260, 263–64,
    267, 289, 292, 330, 334, 341, 360,
    398, 400, 408, 414, 436–41, 465,
    467–68, 503, 513, 524, 530; antifas-
    cist, 14, 72, 435–41; independent,
    207, 245, 436, 438; student, 441.
    See also Caplan, Lincoln; Cunard,
    Nancy; Doshi, Vidhi; ethics, jour-
    nalistic; media; Pogue, James; Rao,
    Shrenik; Wells, Ida B.
Jovanović, Đorđe, 471
Joyce, Helen, 301, 518
June 28th Union, 110
Jung, Carl, 182

Kaba, Mariame, 72
Kaczynski, Jaroslaw, 58
Kali Yuga, 240–41
Kamel, Anwar, 466, 535

Kansas, 314, 335
karma yoga, 216, 221, 233
Kashmir, 227, 231, 233, 237–38, 242,
    249–50, 255–56, 508–11
Kazakhstan, 143
Kelley, Robin D. G., 64, 492
Kesiqnaeh, Enaemaehkiw Wakecana-
    paew, 253
Khalifeh, Mustafa, 196
Khan Sheikhoun chemical weapons
    attack, 193, 202–3, 504
Khanna, Ro, 235, 509
Khosravi, Arghavan, 473
Kiev, 55–56
Kinnar, 302
Kirk, Charlie, 90
Kiyotaka Asahara, 471
Knutson, Kieran, 335, 337, 415, 418–24,
    429–30, 432
Koernke, Mark, 487
Koji Otsuka, 471
Kootenai County Task Force on Human
    Relations, 405
Ku Klux Klan (KKK), 23–27, 32, 34, 45,
    64, 112–14, 117, 127, 131, 136, 145, 192,
    201, 210, 288, 312–13, 316–17, 320,
    324, 327, 333, 368, 383, 410, 420,
    483, 485, 505, 510–20; Fifth Era, 26;
    Knights of the, 24, 201
Kumar, Krishna, 235, 509
Kumar, Rashmee, 234, 509

La Jolla, 321, 323
La Liga Socialista Puertorriqueña, 111
labor unions, 5, 57, 78, 92, 94–95, 107,
    109, 328, 381, 384, 505
Lacoss, Donald, 461, 534
Lam, Wilfredo, 468
Lane, David, 28
LaRouche, Lyndon, 28, 486, 504
Lautréamont, Comte de, 450–51, 474
Lavin, Talia, 402, 528–29
Law and Justice Party (Prawo i Spraw-
    iedliwość, PiS), 57–58
Lawrence, Ken, 24, 485
Le Surréalisme au service de la Révolution,
    462
leaderless resistance, 26, 28, 144–45,
    486
Lebanon, 270
Left Coast Right Watch, 47, 436, 441, 490
Leipzig, 59–60
Leiris, Michel, 460, 533

Lenin, Vladimir I., 194, 205, 219, 487, 495, 505. *See also* Marxism
Lennard, Natasha, 276, 484, 515
Leonard Peltier's Defense/Offense Committee, 118
Léro, Etienne, 460, 466
Lesbos, 260–61, 267, 512, 514
Leuven Anarchistische Groep, 52
Levins-Morales, Aurora, 525
LGBT-free zones, 59, 491, 517
LGBTQ people, 22, 58, 84–85, 92, 94–95, 138, 174, 206, 292, 298, 307, 310, 395, 398, 405, 422, 444, 516
liberalism, 7–8, 10–11, 14–15, 20, 23, 33–35, 37, 39, 41, 48, 64, 68, 113, 115, 124–25, 162, 165–66, 179, 182, 187, 206, 211, 217, 225, 230, 235, 247, 273–74, 276, 278, 294, 296–97, 371, 373–74, 377, 381, 394, 402, 405–7, 410, 415, 417, 421, 425, 439–40, 464, 477–78, 501, 522. *See also* progressive politics
Libre Mesh, 163
Libya, 127, 206–7, 505
Lifted Voices collective, 382, 385
Light Upon Light (LUL), 398
Lincoln, Abraham, 314
Lindbergh, Charles, 204–5, 505
Linehan, Graham, 299
Lipset, Seymour Martin, 523
Lipsitz, George, 64, 492
Lokteff, Lana, 203
London, 202, 325
London Review of Books, 203
Long Beach, 118
Los Angeles, 113–16, 118–22. *See also* Anti-Racist Action Los Angeles, Los Angeles Community Action Network, Los Angeles Police Department (LAPD)
Los Angeles Community Action Network, 122
Los Angeles Police Department (LAPD), 77
Los Angeles uprising, 115
Los Macheteros, 110–11
Los Siete de la Raza, 78
Louisiana, 25, 201, 317
love, 99, 122, 189, 336, 344–45, 388–89, 391, 395–96, 409, 412–14, 422–23, 426, 430–31, 433–34, 445, 460; as offense 227, 249; as radical 166, 402, 404–10, 412, 449, 453–54, 457, 465, 467, 473, 528; rhetoric of 388. *See* empathy toward fascists
Low, Mary, 465, 535
Lübke, Heinrich, 478
lugar de fala (place of discourse), 347, 520
Lukács, Georg, 408, 528
Luqman, Shahzad, 262
Lynch, Loretta, 292, 516
lynching, 24, 65, 72–75, 226–27, 312–13, 315, 318–21, 327, 373, 383, 493, 518–19
Lyons, Charles, 207, 505

MacNiece, Louis, 535
Macri, Mauricio, 272
Madhav, Ram, 239
Madison, 335
Maghreb region, 449, 531
Mahabharata, 506
Mahmud, Tayyab, 217, 506–7
mainstreaming, 276, 417, 488
Make America Great Again (MAGA) slogan, 155, 243, 328, 423, 373, 423
Makhlouf, Rami, 196
Malet, Léo, 469, 472
Malheur Wildlife Refuge occupation, 400–401, 408, 411
Malhotra, Rajiv, 248, 250, 252
Malloy, Sean L., 80
manarchism, 116. *See also* masculinities, toxic
manosphere, 16, 35–36, 484. *See also* masculinities, toxic
Manusmriti, 252, 506
Maoism, 77, 82, 118, 496. *See also* Revolutionary Communist Party (RCP)
maquis, 468, 470–71
Marantz, Andrew, 421, 529
Marcuse, Herbert, 107, 470
marginalized groups, 171, 184, 188, 232, 255, 315, 342, 346, 351, 385, 394–96
Marie, Bubbles Rose, 84
Marley, Jon, 50
Marom, Yotam, 525
Martin, Trayvon, 86, 90, 199, 327
Martinique, 449–50, 460, 468, 533
Martinsville Seven, the, 75
Marxism, 21, 32, 78, 194–95, 270–71, 359, 465, 514–15, 522; and Surrealism, 450, 460, 463; as colonial, 348; classical, 359; Black, 64, 348; -feminism, 68; -Leninism, 82, 487, 505.

See also Lukács, Georg; Maoism; Partido Obrero de Unificacion Marxista; Trotskyism

Maryland, 107, 320

masculinities: normative, 125, 195, 214, 347, 421, 530; hyper-, 106, 242; rhetoric of, 79; toxic, 59, 117, 124, 417–18. *See also* manarchism

masking: *See* anti-masking laws

Mass Destruction, 341

mass incarceration, 18 40, 85, 274, 324, 324, 327. *See also* prisons

mass shootings, 145, 244, 275. *See also* massacres

massacres: Christchurch, 277; colonial, 350, 355; El Paso, 277; Greensboro, 203; of priests, 465; Khan Sheikhoun, 193, 202–3, 504; Tulsa, 64; Gujarat, 226, 230, 242, 508; of Black Union soldiers, 315–16; under Reconstruction, 73. *See also* mass shootings

Masson, André, 460

Massot, Pierre de, 457–58

master race, myth of the, 210, 240, 253, 359; as "oppressed," 364–65

materialism, 461; base, 454; dialectical, 460, 466

Mathews, Robert Jay, 26–28

Maximum Rocknroll, 335

Mbembe, Achille, 198

McCarthy, Tara, 193

McCarthyism, 69, 71

McChrystal, Stanley, 149, 498

McDonald, CeCe, 86, 495–96

McGee, William, 75

McGrady, Toby, 312

McInnes, Gavin, 419, 489, 529

McKaine, Osceola, 70

McVeigh, Timothy, 28, 32, 487, 530

media: mainstream, 1, 13, 77, 87, 92–93, 132, 136, 143, 164, 230, 245, 248, 403, 432, 499; coverage of antifascism, 48, 185–86, 340; coverage of fascism, 131, 249, 390, 396; social, 3, 8, 13, 36, 38, 55, 60, 93, 104, 136, 155–57, 159–60, 178, 183, 204, 243, 245, 265, 284, 293–95, 310, 354, 378, 402, 414, 422, 425–26, 428, 432; alternative, 156–57, 499; left-wing, 48, 305; right-wing, 38, 46, 203, 245, 275, 284, 294–95, 372, 488, 504, 515; state, 202. *See also* antisemitism

and myth of Jewish media control, Breitbart News Network, Fox News, Left Coast Right Watch, mainstreaming, Social Media Analysis Toolkit (SMAT)

Meghani, Mihir, 230, 233

memes, 193, 245, 295–96; antifascist, 143, 157–58, 184; as alibi for fascism, 415–17, 421–23, 428, 431–34; fascist, 36, 425–26, 481, 488–89

Memmi, Albert, 523, 525

Ménégoz, Marco, 471

Messersmith-Glavin, Lara, 14, 483. *See also* Pop Mob

messianism: catastrophic, 410; prophetic, 409, 528

Metzger, Tom, 6, 254l, 113–14, 145, 339. *See also* White Aryan Resistance (WAR)

Mexican people (personas Mexicanos/ Mexicanas), 111, 120, 122, 136, 139, 321, 496

Mexican-American people (personas Chicanos/Chicanas), 111, 120, 122, 322, 327, 496; hatred of, 132, 327. *See also* women, Chicana

Mexico, 313, 450, 497, 512

microaggressions, 323

microfascisms, 306

Middle East, 25, 39, 193, 511. *See also* Israel, Lebanon, Palestinians, Syria

Miles, Robert, 26–27

militia movement, 8, 22, 29–33, 46, 132, 227, 277, 299, 313, 399, 408, 411, 413–14, 427, 431, 465, 483–84, 486–87, 489–90, 527, 530 constitutionalism, 31–32; millenialism, 32. *See also* Hindu Yuva Vahini

Miller, Stephen, 38

Milwaukee, 335

Minneapolis, 114, 136, 284, 331, 333, 335, 337–38, 341–42, 344

Minneapolis Oi Boys, 338

Minnesota, 114, 121, 136, 284, 331–32, 338, 520

Minotaure, 462

misogyny, 34–35, 78–79, 103, 106, 175, 179, 212, 242, 257, 294, 297, 300, 352, 416–17, 450–51, 488. *See also* manarchism, patriarchy, sexism

Mississippi, 112, 313–14, 320, 519

Missouri, 26

Mobus, Hendrick, 174

"model minority" myth, 231–32
Modi, Narendra, 63, 171, 210, 226–27, 233–36, 238, 246, 255, 257, 372, 509–12
Monbiot, George, 489, 504
Montes, Carlos, 121
Moonje, B. S., 217, 219, 254
Mormons, 31
Morocco, 458, 464
Morrison, Toni, 473
Morton, Jesse, 398
Moscow, 56–57, 74, 461
Moss, Tom, 319
Mossé, Sonia, 471
MOVE, 82, 495
Movement for Black Lives (M4BL), 63, 65, 522. *See also* Black Lives Matter
movement of movements, 447
Movimiento de Liberación Nacional (MLN), 111, 136
Mukherji, Asit Krishna, 240
Mukherji, Savitri Devi (Maximiliani Portas), 240–41, 253
Muller, Filinto, 352
Müller, Max, 215
Mulotte, Jean-Pierre, 471
multiculturalism, 30, 33, 92, 211, 229–30, 235, 247–48, 488, 526
Munif, Yasser, 198, 200, 503
Muslims, 36, 46, 94–95, 129, 131–32, 138, 178, 192, 194, 196, 198–99, 217–23, 226–28, 230–32, 237, 241–43, 245, 247, 249–52, 274, 296, 300, 325, 396, 398, 410, 417, 503, 507–10, 512–16, 526–27. *See also* Indian American Muslim Council; women, Muslim; Islamic State of Iraq and Syria (ISIS); Islamophobia
Mussolini, Benito, 25, 64, 66–67, 69, 127, 183, 194, 205, 210, 219, 351–52, 449, 464, 519, 528
mutual aid, 8, 11–12, 15, 46, 49–51, 136, 335, 382, 384, 389, 408, 410–12, 482–83
Myanmar, 228, 249

Nakatsu, Penny, 78–79, 495
Narayan, Jayaprakash "JP," 224
National Alliance, 26, 368, 368
National Anti-Klan Network, 485
National Association for the Advancement of Colored People (NAACP), 42, 70, 320

National Association for the Advancement of White People, 25
National Committees to Combat Fascism (NCCFs), 66, 79–81
National Federation for Constitutional Liberties, 74
National Lawyers Guild, 368
National Negro Congress (NNC), 69, 73–75
National Population Register (NPR), 228, 234, 252, 255
National Rebirth of Poland, 57
National Register of Citizens (NRC), 228, 234, 249, 252, 255
National Socialist Black Metal (NSBM), 172–73, 181–82, 188
National Socialist Movement (NSM), 298, 398
National Student Association, 107
national-anarchism, 35
nationalism, 10, 39, 44, 125, 175, 177–78, 352, 361, 409, 421, 427, 448, 451, 457, 487, 505, 524, 532; America First, 30–31, 37–38, 204, 505; Arab, 194–95, 206; Black, 77, 82, 370; Chinese, 370; civic, 37, 212, 218, 249, 251, 504; cultural, 224; economic, 37; ethno-, 210–11, 213, 217, 221, 223–37, 251–52, 254, 257; internationalist, 366–67; Mazzinian, 217; racial, 106, 124; Turkish, 370; ultra-, 58; white, 6, 9, 14, 24–27, 30–31, 34, 37, 43–44, 55, 88, 97, 100, 129, 145, 180, 192–93, 203, 208, 242, 251, 276, 288, 353, 374, 377, 390–92, 397, 400, 417, 421, 440, 485, 488, 501, 504, 506, 515, 523, 526–27; Zionism as, 361, 367. *See also* Movimiento de Liberación Nacional (MLN), Nationalist Movement organization, national-anarchism, Puerto Rican Nationalist Party
Nationalist Movement organization, 288
Nationalsozialistische Deutsche Arbeiterpartei (Nazi Party, NSDAP), 113, 127, 206, 303. *See also* American Nazi Party, Nazism
Native American movement, 77, 110
Naval Intelligence, 111
Nazism, 24, 41, 55, 131, 171, 173, 183, 200, 217, 239, 243, 275, 360, 366, 469, 534. *See also* Nationalsozialistische

Deutsche Arbeiterpartei (NSDAP), *see* neo-Nazism

necropolitics, 198, 253

neo-Confederates, 133, 317, 322, 324, 326–27, 445, 519

neo-Nazism, 24, 26, 28, 506

neoconservatives, 29, 203, 208, 293

neofolk, 170–71, 174, 442

neoliberalism, 16, 40, 67, 97, 92, 113, 196, 226, 236, 242, 244, 252, 270–80, 299, 381, 486, 489, 506, 514; as ideology, 489; as recolonization, 129

neoreactionaries (Nrx), 35, 293–94

Netanyahu, Benjamin, 236, 257, 510, 525

networks, 81–82, 86, 112, 135, 138, 141–66, 200, 245, 257, 337, 493, 496; anti-fascist, 52, 54–62, 88–96, 112–14, 116–19, 141–66, 331, 468; carceral, 197; fascist, 32, 148–49, 159, 257, 272, 478, 498, 510; multiracial, 79; mutual aid, 482; of support, 105, 137, 402, 475; patronage, 244; regional, 340; snitch, 139; social, 159, 293; stigmergic, 145; trade, 363; versus pyramids, 28. *See also* Anti-Racist Action (ARA), Black Liberation Army (BLA), Campus Antifascist Network (CAN), Los Angeles Community Action Network, National Anti-Klan Network; National Committees to Combat Fascism (NCCFs), Racist Violence Recording Network, The Syndicate, Syrian Network for Human Rights (SNHR), Torch Network, Traditionalist Youth Network

Neville, Pierre, 460

New Afrikan liberation movement, 125

New Brunswick, 282–89

"New Consensus" model of fascism, 9, 482

New Democracy party, 262–63, 268

New Jersey, 82–83, 233, 255, 370. *See also* New Brunswick

New Left, 78, 129, 485, 496

New Mexico, 112

New Movement in Solidarity with Puerto Rican Independence, 111

New World Order, The, 30

New York, 82–85, 112, 320, 327, 413, 417, 424. *See also* New York City

New York Antifa, 6

New York City, 83, 107, 109, 136, 238, 255, 283, 288, 317, 327–28, 368, 398

New York Police Department (NYPD), 317, 398

New York Times, The, 71m 276, 484, 523

New York University, 85

Newton, Huey P., 66, 74, 80–82, 136, 495

Ngo, Andy, 398, 482

Nicaragua, 116, 313, 419, 521

Nikitin, Dennis, 56, 491

Nkiru, Jenn, 473

No Justice, No Pride campaign, 138

no-platforming: *see* deplatforming

nonstate actors, 1–2, 27, 29, 35, 147, 198. *See also* vigilantes

Noorani, A. G., 246, 251, 507–8, 510–12

"normies," 104, 295, 419, 439

Norse Paganism, 167–70, 175–180, 187–88, 446, 501

North American Free Trade Agreement (NAFTA), 273, 418

North Atlantic Treaty Organization (NATO), 39, 115

North Carolina, 26–27, 77, 298. *See also* North Carolina House Bill 2 (HB2)

North Carolina House Bill 2 (HB2), 298, 516

"Northwest Territorial Imperative," 405

Nuremberg Laws, 76

NYC Shut It Down, 327

Oak Park neighborhood, 77

Oakland, 78, 80–82, 119, 121, 136, 494

Oath Keepers, 132

Obama administration, 120, 418

Obama, Barack, 29, 88, 126, 324

Obergefell v. Hodges, 294, 297

objectivity, 391, 395, 399, 439, 462

observe, orient, decide, act loop (OODA), 147–48, 153

Occidental Quarterly, The, 34

occultism, 177, 182, 241, 453, 455, 472, 536

Occupy movement, 90, 120–21, 377–82, 411. *See also* Occupy Wall Street

Occupy Wall Street, 43, 87, 120, 143, 165

Odin, 177, 182, 447

official sources, reliance on, 439

Ohio, 31, 114–15, 284

Ohio Unorganized Militia, 31

Oklahoma City bombing, 28–29, 32–33, 41, 284, 486, 530

Omvedt, Gail, 248

One People's Project, 51, 282, 289

open-source investigation (OS-Inv), 158–60, 203, 440
Operation Clean Sweep (FBI), 27
Orange County, 132
Orange Order, 168, 501
Orbán, Viktor, 298, 372, 525
Order, The, 26, 113. *See also The Turner, Diaries*
Oregon, 46, 52, 314, 400, 408, 426, 481–82, 490. *See also* Portland
Organicism, 224
organizing, 6, 12–15, 18, 42, 45, 49–50, 52, 56, 70, 78, 86, 88, 96, 110, 118, 122, 138, 182, 252, 256, 279, 310, 328, 369–70, 375, 389, 402, 405, 411, 415, 431, 465, 477, 487, 498, 515, 522, 531; fascist, 221, 366, 390, 393–94, 417, 431, 436–37, 441, 462, 478, 489, 504. *See also* Crenshaw, Mic; Hayes, Kelly; mutual aid; radicalization
Orientalism, 80, 210, 214, 254, 473
Orsini, Alessandro, 399, 401, 527
Oulipo, 472
Overpass Light Brigade, 381
Overseas Friends of the BJP (OFBJP), 228, 233
Overton window, 36, 174, 201, 388, 413, 425, 434, 437, 439–40, 503

P2P technologies, 141, 144, 155, 163, 497
Pacific Northwest, 8, 26, 389, 404–6, 411, 528. *See also* Oregon, Portland, Seattle, Washington
pacifism, 135, 138–39, 188. *See also* nonviolence, self-defense, violence against fascists
paleoconservatives, 29
Paleologos, Nick, 258
Palestinian people, 89, 134, 237–38, 256, 258, 266, 361–62, 367, 369–71, 374, 510, 522–25
Panther 21 trial, 83, 109
Parks, Letícia, 348
Parsons, John, 33
Partido Obrero de Unificacion Marxista (POUM), 465
party politics, 37, 44, 124, 132–33, 315, 325, 406, 491. *See also* electoralism; *see also* American Blackshirts Party, American Nazi Party, Ba'ath Party, Bharatiya Janata Party (BJP), Black Panther Party, Black Riders Liberation Party (BRLP), Communist

Party of the United States of America (CPUSA), Democratic Party, Golden Dawn, Italian Communist Party (PCI), Law and Justice Party (PiS), National Socialist German Workers' Party (NSDAP), Integralista party, New Democracy party, Partido Obrero de Unificacion Marxista (POUM), Populist Party, Progressive Labor Party, Red Guard Party, Republican Party, Revolutionary Communist Party (RCP), Syriza, Traditionalist Worker Party, Workers World Party, Working Families Party, Young Lords Party
Pasquali, Lanussi, 355
patriarchy, 17, 35, 122, 248, 293, 297, 308, 336, 347, 349, 388, 441, 465. *See also* manarchism, misogyny, sexism
Patriot Conspiracy (PATCON), 33, 487
Patriot Prayer, 5–6, 9, 14–15
Patriotic Europeans Against the Islamicisation of the Occident (Patriotische Europäer gegen die Islamisierung des Abendlandes, PEGIDA) 60
Patterson, William L., 65, 72, 74–76, 493–94
Paz, Octavio, 450
peace movements, 114–15. *See also* antiwar movements
Peinovich, Mike "Enoch," 203
Pelican Bay State Prison, 121
Pelley, William Dudley, 406
Pennsylvania, 139, 279. *See also* Philadelphia, Pittsburgh
People Against Racist Terror (PART). *See also* Anti-Racist Action Los Angeles/People Against Racist Terror
people of color, 24, 35, 40, 79, 81, 84, 89, 92, 95, 100, 109, 114, 118, 130, 135–36, 275, 279, 345, 395–96, 404, 420, 431, 473.
Péret, Benjamin, 459, 465, 469, 472
Perry, Amelia, 311
Peterson, Albert, 76
Philadelphia, 6, 112, 114, 282, 319
Philippines, 63, 171, 525
Philly Antifa, 6
Picabia, Francisco, 456, 458
Picasso, Pablo, 458, 464

Pierce, William L., 24–26, 288, 368, 485, 531

Pilger, John, 203

Pink Tide, 272, 515

Pinochet, Augusto, 134, 271–72

Piraeus, 262

Pittsburgh, 275, 277, 357, 365, 369–70, 374–75

Plainfield (New Jersey), 82–83

Płock, 58

Pogue, James, 400–401, 408, 411, 527–28

Poland, 55–59, 61, 106, 298, 466, 491, 517

police, 7–10, 18, 21, 27, 30, 40, 81–82, 84, 96, 102–6, 109, 112–16, 122, 132, 138, 158, 160, 182, 250, 254, 259–61, 263–65, 272, 276, 278, 287–88, 313, 323–30, 339–40, 343, 315, 327, 370, 375, 377, 383–84, 405–6, 439, 448, 458, 462, 483, 526; abolition of, 86, 125, 327, 379, 383, 449; community control of, 78–80, 86, 109, 116; complicity with fascists, 21, 76, 89, 131–32, 168, 226, 309, 326, 328, 383–84, 427, 481, 484, 526; militarization of, 40, 77, 115, 118, 137; preservationism, 379–81; violence, 46, 49, 56, 72, 76–77, 83–84, 88–89, 97, 114–16, 186, 296, 305, 310, 322, 330, 370–71, 377, 379–83, 382–83, 477, 493; *See also* Chicago Police Department, Coalition Against Police Abuse, conspiracy theories among police, Cop Watch, Los Angeles Police Department, Federal Bureau of Investigation (FBI), Sacramento Police Department

police states, 30, 67, 106, 119, 138, 195

political correctness, 172, 293, 345

Pop Mob, 14–15, 47, 50, 490

Popović, Koča, 465, 471

populism, 274–75; right-wing, 9, 25, 37, 39, 57, 195, 223–24, 226, 303, 371–72, 478, 484, 491; left-wing, 274

Populist Party, 25, 57

Portland, 5–7, 12–14, 42, 47, 49–50, 114, 157, 168, 331–32, 335–37, 339–40, 342, 344, 427, 481, 483, 490, 501, 520, 530

Portland State University, 340

Portland United Baldies, 344

Portugal, 325, 537

Posse Comitatus, 24, 31

post-traumatic stress disorder (PTSD), 300, 311, 339, 396, 402, 527–28

postcolonial, 254–55

Postol, Theodore, 203

Postone, Moishe, 482

Poznań, 56–57, 62

Prairie Fire Organizing Committee (PFOC), 110, 113, 496

Pratt, Geronimo, 50

Preston, Keith, 35

Princeton University, 16

prisons, 13, 17, 28, 33, 41, 82, 85–86, 97, 100–101, 103, 113, 118–19, 121–22, 130, 136–37, 145, 166, 178, 196–97, 200–201, 218, 241, 270, 276, 288, 310, 312, 315, 324, 379, 381, 383, 471–72, 477–78, 483, 496, 520; abolition, 85–87, 379. *See also* jail support

Progressive Labor Party (PLP), 108

progressive politics, 21, 42, 47–48, 95, 185, 205, 211, 223, 234–35, 246, 253, 255, 292, 294, 296–99, 304, 401, 410, 415–16, 444, 493, 508–509, 517

Project NIA, 382

propaganda, 57, 94, 206, 221, 230, 233, 235, 238, 241, 244, 246, 249, 255, 300, 304, 357, 366, 369, 397, 399–400, 411, 435, 440, 494, 499, 504, 517, 534, 535; kernel of truth in, 194, 300

Proposition Eight, 323

Proposition Thirteen, 323

protectionism, 29, 37, 39

Protocols of the Elders of Zion, 301

Proud Boys, 38, 42, 92, 210, 276, 339, 377, 406, 413–17, 419, 424, 426–28, 431, 434–35, 481, 489, 507

Puerto Rican Nationalist Party, 111

Puerto Rico, 28, 107–11, 136, 139, 270, 496

Puerto Rico Solidarity Committee (PRSC), 110–111

punk, 113–14, 174, 283, 331–33, 355, 392, 414, 417, 419, 423–24, 442, 445–46, 473, 495. *See also* Punks' Picnic, Skins and Punks Against Racism (SPAR)

Punks' Picnic, 423

QAnon, 16, 143, 374, 413, 423, 431, 433, 498, 525

racism, 2, 5–7, 10, 22, 24, 27, 31, 60, 68, 71–75, 90, 108, 112–16, 120, 125, 129, 131–32, 134, 136, 145, 171, 173–78, 180, 182–88, 199, 202, 209, 215, 232, 243,

256-57, 278-79, 288, 294, 297, 300, 314-16, 321-23, 327, 331, 334, 337-38, 343, 346-48, 350-52, 354, 356, 361-62, 364, 367-70, 372, 383, 390-91, 393-95, 397-98, 404-6, 410-12, 417, 419-21, 425, 433, 444, 449, 479, 486, 488, 492, 494, 496, 507, 509, 516, 523, 524, 526; color-blind, 31, 323-24; as ideology, 68, 101-2, 419, 439; systemic, 65-68, 73, 75, 90, 118, 296, 347-48, 371, 525. *See also* antisemitism, colorism, white privilege, white supremacy, whiteness

Racist Violence Recording Network, 262

radicalization: left wing, 51-52, 74, 108, 114, 120, 158, 165, 382; right wing, 16, 44, 51, 108, 158, 173, 295, 299-300, 357, 373, 393-94, 413-14, 416, 419-23, 425-26, 431, 433, 440, 529-30. *See also* deradicalization, entryism

Raj, 214, 222, 250

Ram Janmabhoomi movement, 115

Ramayana, 225, 506

Rao, Shrenik, 241

Rashtriya Swayamsevak Sangh (RSS), 210-11, 217, 219-30, 237, 242-46, 248, 506-9, 511

Ratzon: Center for Healing and Resistance 375

Reagan Administration, 28-29, 112, 114, 277

Reagan, Ronald, 323, 520

realpolitik, 39

Rebellious Anarchist Young Jews, 375

recruitment: *see* radicalization

Red & Anarchist Skin Heads (RASH), 113

red and anarchist black metal (RABM), 181

Red Guard Party, 78

Red Nation, 136

Reddit, 35

Redneck Revolt, 408

redpilling: *see* radicalization, right wing

refugees, 55, 60, 128, 228, 233, 258-69, 361, 365, 415, 467, 496, 510, 512-14

reggae, 331

Reinhardt, Django, 470

Reinoehl, Michael, 343

Renton, David, 10, 45, 51, 477-79

Republican Hindu Coalition, 233-34

Republican Party, 25, 28, 30, 37, 39, 45, 93, 124, 132-33, 233-35, 276, 284, 292, 372, 417, 434-35, 440, 464, 477, 504, 530; during Reconstruction, 317. *See also* Young Republicans, Republican Hindu Coalition

research, antifascist, 6, 8, 72-73, 76, 114, 169, 176, 213, 223, 300-302, 349, 356, 408; ethics of, 356, 389-92, 397-398, 401-4, 527; open-source (OS-Int), 14, 158-59; relation to journalism, 437-38, 440-41

Resistance, French, 468-71, 474

Revolutionary Communist Party (RCP), 118

Revolutionary Youth Movement (RYM), 108

Ribeiro, Djamila, 346, 348, 520

Riker's Island prison, 100

Rimbaud, Arthur, 451, 453, 469, 531

Riot (platform), 155

Rise Above Movement (RAM), 55-56

risk assessment, 307, 309

Rittenhouse, Kyle, 530

Rius, Robert, 470

Rivera, Sylvia, 84

Rivet, Paul, 468

Robertson, Pat, 30

Robeson, Paul, 64-65, 69-71, 74-75, 492-93

Robinson, Cedric, 64, 74

Rochester, 413, 536

Rock Against Racism (RAR), 114

Rock Against Zionism, 370

Rohingya, 228

Roma, 522

Romania, 298, 310, 398, 452, 517

Romanticism, 178, 194, 212-13, 215, 339, 445, 450-51, 459, 532

Rome, 55, 464

Romero, Ricardo, 112

Romney, Mitt, 321

Roosevelt, Eleanor, 73

Roosevelt, Franklin D., 23, 70, 128

Rose City Antifa, 5-6, 13, 42, 50, 342, 344, 427

Rose City Bovver Boys (RCBB), 343

Ross, Alexander Reid, 6, 481, 483-84, 526, 528-29, 531

Rouse, Wendy L,. 60

Rowling, J. K., 299, 517

Różalski, Marcin "Róźal," 58

Rozbrat squat, 57

Ruby Ridge, 30, 32
Ruhr Valley uprising, 457, 474
Run Against Racism, 50
Russell-Wood, A. J. R., 348, 520–21
Russia, 39, 55–56, 66, 71, 134, 144, 197, 202–4, 206–8, 298, 360, 363, 451, 462, 478, 499, 504–5, 515, 517, 524. *See also* Soviet Union

Sacramento Police Department, 77
Sade, Marquis de, 454–55, 533
Sahasrabuddhe, Vinay, 244–45
Sahay, Raghupati (Firaq Gorakhpuri), 251
Saint-Pol-Roux, 458–59
Sakai, J., 253
Saleh, Yassin Al-Haj, 196, 199, 201, 503–4
same-sex marriage, 131, 292, 297–98, 307
San Diego, 13, 321, 323–24, 483, 520
San Francisco Bay Area, 74, 79, 89, 93, 110, 168, 255, 288, 340, 494, 508
Sangh Parivar, 210–11, 220, 222–30, 235, 241, 243, 247–49, 253, 255
Santana, Bianca, 350, 521
sarvodaya movement, 224
Saudi Arabia, 198, 204
Savarkar, Vinayak Damodar, 211, 217–22, 237
scapegoating, 21, 29, 41, 58, 131, 203, 228, 262, 274, 365, 477
Schelling, Friedrich, 215
Schlegel, Friedrich, 215
Schoenhoff, Hans, 471
Schoep, Jeff, 398
Schoolwerth, Pieter, 473
Schwerner, Michael, 112
science, 155, 246, 213, 231, 246, 302, 415, 447, 453, 533–34; pseudo-, 203, 213, 278, 296, 449; race, 127, 363; social, 245, 359
Scott, James C., 498
Scott, Will, 312
Scottsboro Boys case, 69, 74–75
Seale, Bobby, 78, 80, 494
search engines, 158–60
Seattle, 340, 392, 405, 442, 528
Seattle Radical Women, 528
Second Italo-Ethiopian War, 69, 127, 206, 465–66
Secret Army Organization, 27
Secure-Scuttlebutt, 163
Sedition Hunters, 8

segregation, 23–24, 37, 71, 74, 109, 239, 304, 320–21, 323, 353, 520
Seiichi Fujiwara, 471
self-defense, 13, 45, 59–61, 86, 157, 309, 392, 394, 403, 427, 495–96, 499; community, 94, 96, 114, 137, 304–5, 385; against surveillance, 164, 500
Sen, Amartya, 248
Senegal, 449, 464
Senghor, Léopold, 464, 472, 537
September 11th, 118–19, 232–33, 237–38, 490. *See also* conspiracy theories, "9/11 Truth"
Seraw, Mulugeta, 6, 339
Serrano, Miguel, 241
Sethi, Arjun, 402, 528
Seventh World Congress of the Communist International, 78, 314
Sewa Vibhag, 222, 229
sex workers, 158, 308
sexism, 90, 114, 116–17, 419, 421; among antifascists, 78, 116, 336, 382; combatted by antifascists, 78–79, 117. *See also* manarchism, misogyny, patriarchy
shakhas, 219–20, 229, 508
Shakur, Assata, 82, 102, 495
Shakur, Mutulu, 82
Shiv Sena, 226, 508
Shodan, 161, 499
Shohat, Ella, 525
Showing Up for Racial Justice (SURJ), 119, 496
Shukla, Suhag, 230
Shultz, Russell, 426–28
Signal, 155, 159
Silber, Mitch, 398
Silent Brotherhood (Bruder Schweigen), 26, 113
Silver Legion of America, 406
Silver Shirts, 406
Simkins, Modjeska, 69–70
Simonpoli, Charles-Jean, 471
Sinclair, Upton, 459
ska 283, 285–86, 288, 331
Skid Row, 120, 122
Skinheads Against Racial Prejudice (SHARP), 5, 113, 331–32, 336, 339–44
Skinheads of Chicago (SHOC), 335
Skins and Punks Against Racism (SPAR), 113
Skrewdriver, 113

slavery, 17, 20, 64–65, 67–68, 70–72, 75–76, 86, 106, 124, 128, 130, 135, 198, 313–16, 327, 346, 348, 350, 359, 373, 381, 457, 466, 518, 520

Slavic people, 127, 351–52, 491

Smalls, Robert, 316

Smith Act, 41

Smith, Sage, 311

Social Media Analysis Toolkit (SMAT), 160, 499

social media: *see* media, social

socialism, 5, 27, 52, 67, 74, 81–82, 88, 90–91, 93, 110–11, 123, 125–26, 194–95, 204, 212, 224, 236, 271, 274, 381, 405–406, 408–9, 411, 444, 449–50, 453, 464, 487, 491; of fools 365–66, 523

Söderman, Magnus, 390, 397–98

Sojourner Truth Organization (STO), 24

solidarity, 13, 18, 49–50, 66, 71, 74, 94, 99, 101, 110–11, 113–15, 119, 121–22, 125, 136, 139, 166, 182, 187, 191, 207, 209, 217, 231–32, 255–57, 260, 268–69, 301–2, 356, 365, 371, 374–76, 389–91, 396, 398, 401, 403–4, 408–9, 411, 445, 449, 453, 462–63, 497, 505, 508, 522

Solon, Olivia, 204, 505

Sommers, Allison, 473, 537

Soros, George, 203, 301, 373, 518

Soupault, Philippe, 457, 460

South Africa, 70–71, 123, 256, 522

South Asian Americans Leading Together, 245

South Carolina, 60–71, 315, 493

South Dakota, 33

Southern Christian Leadership Conference (SCLC), 116

Southern Negro Youth Congress (SNYC), 69–71

Southern Poverty Law Center (SPLC), 145, 398, 405, 486–87, 503–4, 527

Soviet Union, 16, 127, 206, 493, 524

spaces, 11, 14–15, 52, 92, 163, 167–70, 177, 179, 248, 266, 272, 279, 287, 299–300, 303, 382, 393, 397; Afrocentric, 348; antifascist, 15, 65, 183, 262, 342; antiracist, 393; digital, 183, 187, 295; fascist, 15, 174–75; LGBT, 85; leftist, 14, 103, 205, 294, 308, 345; public, 61, 298, 327, 339, 396; racist, 393; subcultural, 14, 168–69, 170, 179–80, 187, 446, 536; trans, 306; women's, 299

Spain, 68, 126, 128, 136, 205, 258, 273, 327, 325, 363, 450, 458, 461, 464–65, 500, 519; Civil War, 1, 465, 535

speaking truth to power, 444

Spencer, Richard, 14, 34, 41, 91, 152, 193, 201–3, 208, 276, 292, 294, 397, 487–488, 499, 502, 505, 515–16

Spencer, Robyn, 64, 494

Spokane, 406, 410

Spokeo, 159

St. Paul, 338

Stalin, Josef, 197, 463, 466, 522, 524

Stalinism, 406, 450, 456, 461–465, 467, 470, 474, 522

Standing Rock action, 87

state, the, 7, 9–12, 17, 28–32, 35, 38, 44–45, 56, 67, 70, 81–82, 86, 89–90, 106, 109, 111, 124–30, 132–36, 138, 147, 149, 150, 163, 165, 194–95, 199–200, 204–5, 208, 211–12, 218, 224–25, 229, 236–37, 245, 249–50, 255–56, 272, 279, 339, 350, 361, 366–67, 380, 383, 407, 459, 461, 470, 482, 491, 502, 523; repression 12, 18, 21, 41, 43, 68, 72, 77, 106, 109, 117–19, 138, 146, 195–96, 199, 228, 373, 351, 448, 461, 466, 481, 494, 531; monopoly of legitimate use of force 11, 18, 135. *See also* nonstate actors, Three Way Fight analysis, thanatocracy

Stavisky, Alexandre, 462

Stenberg, Béno, 469

Stephens, Alexander, 315

Sterling, Dorothy, 317

Sternhell, Ze'ev, 525

Stetson, Tom, 31

stigmergy, 145, 154, 166, 498

Stoner, J. B., 114

Stonewall riot, 83–84, 138

Stop LAPD Spying Coalition, 122

Storm, Cristien, 392, 402, 528

Stormfront, 198, 202, 288

Strasser, Gregor and Otto, 206

Street Transvestite Action Revolutionaries (STAR), 66, 84–85, 495

Students for a Democratic Society (SDS), 78, 107–8, 537. *See also* Progressive Labor Party, Revolutionary Youth Movement

subcultural capital, 167, 169–70

subcultures, 10, 14, 29, 35, 52, 85, 113, 167–89, 331–45, 352, 445–47

Sufism, 449

Sun Tzu, 243, 357
sundown towns, 321
Sunshine, Spencer, 485, 489
Surrealism, 448–75; break with Dada-
    ism, 452; relation to Communist
    Party, 448–64, 471; relation to fas-
    cism
surveillance, 163–64, 500; by law
    enforcement, 33, 40, 48, 77, 123, 136,
    139, 150, 215, 237, 339–40; by fas-
    cists, 155; of fascists, 2, 440
Susli, Maram, 203
Swadeshi movement, 217, 219, 221
Swaraj movement, 217
Switzerland, 60, 72
Sylla, Cheikh Tidiane, 449, 531
Syria, 39, 192–204, 207–9, 258, 260–61,
    266, 499, 502–6, 513
Syrian Network for Human Rights
    (SNHR), 197, 503
Syriza, 262

tactics, 2, 7, 10, 13–14, 27, 33, 36, 42–45,
    47–48, 52–53, 57, 90, 94, 104, 110,
    115, 124, 131, 144–45, 148–49, 150–53,
    155–59, 161, 165, 167, 172–73, 180, 182,
    186, 187, 211, 216, 223, 225, 238, 242,
    253, 275–76, 289, 295, 305, 307, 327,
    328, 338, 346, 378, 382, 385, 389,
    397, 407, 410, 447, 449, 459, 482–83,
    488, 499. See also deradicalization,
    doxing/IDing, entryism, exclusion,
    infiltration, infrastructures of
    care, jail support, masking, mutual
    aid, no-platforming, open-source
    investigation, Overpass Light Bri-
    gade, Pop Mob, surveillance
Taliban, 138, 143, 497
Taylor, Breonna, 86
Taylor, Jared, 36
Taylor, Keeanga-Yamahtta, 275, 496
Tea Party movement, 293
Teen Vogue, 276
Teitelbaum, Benjamin, 389–92, 397–98,
    401, 408, 526
Telegram, 155, 157, 161
Tengour, Habib, 449, 531
Tennessee, 316, 319, 519
Tenold, Vegas, 400, 527
terror, 16, 23, 238, 466, 484, 509, 526;
    fascist, 305, 310–11, 439, 486, 498,
    518; Jacobin, 455; racial, 23, 67, 71,
    75, 312–13, 315, 318, 320, 323, 404;

stochastic, 144; war on, 33, 188,
    149, 199, 201, 236–37, 355, 487. See
    also domestic terrorist designa-
    tion, People Against Racist Terror
    (PART), Antiterrorism and Effec-
    tive Death Penalty Act
Texas, 7, 30, 234, 275, 298, 313, 516
Thackeray, Bal, 226, 241
Thailand, 310
thanatocracy, 197–98, 200–201, 503
Thapar, Romila, 248–49
ThatsThem, 159
The Grayzone, 204, 504–5
The Guardian, 204, 301, 465, 473
The Syndicate, 331, 335–37
Thiel, Peter, 90
Thind, Bhagat Singh, 235
Third Positionism, 25, 206–7
Third World Liberation Front, 78
Thompson, Eric, 524
Three Way Fight analysis, 2, 20–41,
    484–88
TikTok, 155
Tilak, Bal Gangadhar, 216–17
Tillion, Germaine, 468
Time, 292–93
Tito (Josip Broz), 471
Togliatti, Palmiro, 479
Torch Network, 6, 121, 284, 496
Toronto, 337, 537
traditionalism, 141, 208–9, 224, 472, 497,
    505. See also Traditionalist Worker
    Party, Traditionalist Youth Net-
    work
Traditionalist Worker Party, 145, 193,
    199, 398, 410, 488, 505
Traditionalist Youth Network, 208
trans antagonism, 294–98, 303, 305–6,
    308. See also trans exclusionary
    radical feminism
trans exclusionary radical feminism
    (TERFism), 299, 301–2
transgender people, 84, 292–311, 347,
    516–18, 520. See also FLINT,
    LGBTQI+ people, trans exclu-
    sionary radical feminism, trans
    antagonism, transphobia
transphobia, 5, 103, 175, 296–97, 299–
    300, 479, 496, 517
travesti people, 347; differentiated from
    transgender people, 520
Tree of Life synagogue, attack on, 275,
    277, 365, 370, 374–75

Trinidad, 231, 465
Trochmann, John, 31
trolling, 144, 149, 158, 372, 415, 417, 418, 420–24, 427–34
Trotskyism, 36, 66–67, 139, 406, 463, 465, 482, 496, 514–15
Truman administration, 75, 111, 490
Trump, Donald, 5–8, 15–16, 22, 30, 34, 36–39, 41, 44–45, 48, 57, 63, 66–67, 85, 88–89, 93, 97, 126, 131–34, 143, 152–53, 158, 168, 184, 193, 233–36, 241, 257, 273–77, 295–96, 298, 310, 327–29, 343, 354, 357–58, 365, 371–74, 414, 417, 421, 424, 426, 440, 444, 473, 477–78, 484, 488–90, 492, 497, 502, 515, 518, 521, 523, 525–26, 529, 537
Trumpism, 100–101, 133, 393, 414, 526
TrustNet, 163, 500
Tulsa massacre, 64
Turkey, 259, 260, 262, 267, 298, 370, 513, 517
Turner Diaries, The, 24–26, 31–32, 368, 485, 524
Turning Point USA (TPUSA), 93
Turning the Tide: Journal of Inter-communal Solidarity, 114, 121, 136
Tuskegee University, 69
Twitter, 155, 159, 193, 199, 203–4, 207, 245, 410, 416, 419–21, 428, 477, 499
Tzara, Tristan, 452, 456–58
Tzu-Chun, Judy, 80

Ukraine, 55, 207
Umbanda, 350–51
Umbrella Revolution, 165
Unicorn Riot, 158, 193, 502–3
Unite Against Fascism (UAF), 325–26
Unite the Right rally, 7–8, 38, 132, 192, 296, 309, 398, 413–14, 491, 529
United Front Against Fascism (UFAF), 66, 78–81, 389, 405–7
United Nations (UN), 29, 64, 71–76, 197, 203, 268, 320, 493, 502, 504; Committee Against Torture, 72; Genocide Convention, 74, 493
United Racist Front, 112
United States India Political Action Committee (USINPAC), 238, 511
United States v. Windsor, 297
Universal Declaration of Human Rights, 119
University of Chicago 16; "Chicago Boys" 271

University of Florida, 91, 292
University of Pennsylvania, 279
University of Virginia, 296, 309, 311
Upadhyaya, Deendayal, 224
Upanishads, 506
US Campaign for the Academic and Cultural Boycott of Israel (USACBI), 90
US Federal government, 8, 21, 23, 25–33, 61, 77, 111–12, 284, 298, 317, 322, 343, 427, 483, 487, 518; see also Federal Bureau of Investigation (FBI)
US Supreme Court, 235, 310, 477, 518
Ustra, Brilhante, 352

Vaché, Jacques, 452, 532
Vaishnav, Gaurang, 233
values: antifascist, 61, 144, 153–54, 156–57, 162, 164, 180, 344, 351, 384, 407, 445, 457, 508; far right, 71, 194, 209, 224, 233, 351, 384, 402, 415; traditional, 58, 216, 230, 278, 443, 456, 457, 460, 507
Vanel, Hélène, 471
Vanvasi Kalyan Kendra, 250
Vargas, Getúlio, 352–53
Varo, Remedios, 465, 469
VDARE, 193, 502
Vedas, 215–16, 223, 237, 240, 506–7
Venezuela, 272, 505, 514
Verfassungsschutz, 61
Veterans Aryan Movement, 33
Veterans for Peace, 342
vice-signaling, 172
Vichy regime, 467–69, 474
vigilantism, 7, 15, 20–21, 27, 132–33, 226, 228, 230, 267–68, 327, 372, 377, 383, 384, 510
violence against fascists, use of, 2, 9, 18, 81, 96, 167, 188, 276, 334–35, 338–39, 342, 385, 391, 434, 474. See also non-violence, self-defense
Vishwa Hindu Parishad (VHP), 223, 225–26, 242, 249
Vishwa Hindu Parishad of America (VHPA), 229–30, 233, 248
Volksfront, 6, 339
von Leers, Johann, 206
Vorrias, Antonis, 258–61
Vysotsky, Stanislav, 11, 482

W. E. B. Du Bois Club, 108
Waco, 30, 32

Wagner, Richard, 462, 526
Walker, Scott, 381
Walker, William, 313, 519
Wallace, George, 37
war: cultural, 294, 296, 443–44, 478; fourth-generation, 146–50; of maneuver vs. war of position, 272, 514; Second Italo-Ethiopian, 69; Vietnam, 80, 107, 256, 472; World War I, 136, 239, 409, 451, 467; World War II, 21, 23, 30, 41, 60, 63–65, 72, 74, 129, 146, 204, 206, 505
Ward, Eric K., 14, 23, 396, 484–85, 523
Ware, Jason, 72
Warsaw Ghetto Uprising, 369
Washington, 340, 343, 392, 406, 442
Washington, D.C., 24, 26, 29, 238, 284, 320,
Wax, Amy, 279, 515
We Charge Genocide, 65, 72, 76–77, 320, 493–94
Weather Underground Organization (WUO), 110, 496
Weaver, Randy, 30
Weeks, Richard "Lord Gaylord," 170, 172–74, 181–82, 184, 188
Wells, H. G., 459
Wells, Ida B., 64, 72–73, 172, 210, 272, 301, 319–20, 493
Wengrow, David, 17, 484, 498
West Bank, occupation of, 202, 237, 369–70
West Papua, 270
"Western chauvinism," 417, 425
Westernization, 356
WhatsApp, 265–66, 354–55
White Aryan Resistance (WAR), 6, 25, 113, 145, 339
White Citizens' Councils, 64, 317, 320, 519
White Helmets, 203–4, 504–5
White Knights, 6, 331, 333, 338, 520
white nationalism: see nationalism, white
White People for Black Lives, 119, 123, 496
white privilege, 119, 130, 329. See also whiteness
White Rex, 55–56, 61
white supremacy, 11, 16, 20–28, 32, 38, 45–46, 68, 76, 86, 88, 92, 94, 102, 109, 113, 122, 124, 127, 131–32, 143–44, 159, 163, 173, 178, 187, 198, 202, 211,
232, 235, 243, 255–56, 275–79, 284, 288, 293–97, 299–301, 305–6, 310, 313, 317, 348, 351–52, 356, 363–65, 368, 370, 372, 375, 377, 383–84, 388, 393, 402, 404, 406, 417, 419, 421, 427, 432, 440–41, 444, 484, 485, 489, 490–91, 498, 502, 517, 520, 524–26, 528–31
White, Walter, 74
whiteness, 67, 119, 237, 235, 295, 297, 347, 350, 461, 524, 530
Whitmer, Gretchen, 427
Williams, Johnny Eric, 275
Wilson, Stevie, 381
Wisconsin, 335, 381, 485
wise use movement, 31, 486
women, 92, 201, 279, 473, 522; Afghan, 119; agency of, 110, 117, 336, 457, 465, 469, 495; Asian-American, 79, 494; bisexual, 300; Brazilian, 346, 348, 520–21; Black, 69, 72, 78–79, 84, 176, 295, 316, 319–20, 328, 346–49, 494–496, 524 ; Chicana, 78–79; cisgender, 293, 299–300, 304–5; Dalit, 242; fascist recruiting of, 6, 25, 34, 125, 138, 201–2, 222, 239, 242, 286, 338; Heathen, 501; Indigenous, 348; lesbian, 22, 58, 60, 84, 92, 138, 174, 206, 300, 311, 347, 395, 443, 495, 524; Muslim, 227, 242, 300; of color, 244, 395, 473; oppression of, 22, 24, 37, 103, 121, 125, 131, 226–27, 247, 260–61, 293, 299–301, 312, 395, 488, 492; represented as oppressors of men, 35; self-defense, 60–61, 465; Surrealist, 534–37; trans 84–86, 92, 138, 244, 293, 298, 299–301, 303–4, 306, 311, 347, 495–96, 524; white, 304, 306, 319–20, 330, 338, 347–48; working-class, 490. See also feminism, FLINT, International Women's Strike, manarchist, manosphere, misogyny, patriarchy, Rashtrasevika Samiti, TERFs, Women's March
Women's March, 43, 362
Workers World Party, 108
Working Families Party, 417
World Hindu Congress (WHC), 210, 248–49, 511–12

X, Malcolm, 65, 72, 76, 318

Yiannopoulos, Milo, 7, 38, 90, 275,
    294–95, 397, 516
Yockey, Francis Parker, 206
Young Americans for Freedom, 108
Young Lords Party, 78
Young Patriots, 78, 408
Young Republicans, 89
Youth Against War and Fascism, 108
YouTube, 9, 155, 179, 185, 192, 490
Yoyotte, Pierre, 449, 466, 531
Yugoslavia, 207, 352, 450, 465, 471

Zapata, Mia, 392
Zeskind, Leonard, 26, 28, 32, 485–87
Zibechi, Raúl, 514
Zimmerman, George, 86, 199
Zinzun, Michael, 115–16
Zionism, 89, 129, 131, 192, 207–8, 236–39,
    361–63, 367–70, 373, 523–25
Zitaway, Nadir, 258
Zurich, 452